SAP PRESS e-books

Print or e-book, Kindle or iPad, workplace or airplane: Choose where and how to read your SAP PRESS books! You can now get all our titles as e-books, too:

- By download and online access
- For all popular devices
- And, of course, DRM-free

Convinced? Then go to www.sap-press.com and get your e-book today.

Inventory Planning and Optimization with SAP° IBP

SAP PRESS

SAP PRESS is a joint initiative of SAP and Rheinwerk Publishing. The know-how offered by SAP specialists combined with the expertise of Rheinwerk Publishing offers the reader expert books in the field. SAP PRESS features first-hand information and expert advice, and provides useful skills for professional decision-making.

SAP PRESS offers a variety of books on technical and business-related topics for the SAP user. For further information, please visit our website: www.sap-press.com.

Sandy Markin, Amit Sinha
SAP Integrated Business Planning: Functionality and Implementation (2nd Edition)
2018, 504 pages, hardcover and e-book
www.sap-press.com/4615

Jandhyala, Kusters, Mane, Sinha
Sales and Operations Planning with SAP IBP
2018, 499 pages, hardcover and e-book
www.sap-press.com/4589

Jawad Akhtar, Martin Murray
Materials Management with SAP S/4HANA: Business Processes and Configuration
2019, 946 pages, hardcover and e-book
www.sap-press.com/4711

Justin Ashlock
Sourcing and Procurement in SAP S/4HANA
2018, 503 pages, hardcover and e-book
www.sap-press.com/4551

Lei Wang, Sanchit Chandna, Jeroen Kusters, Atul Bhandari

Inventory Planning and Optimization with SAP® IBP

Rheinwerk
Publishing

Editor Meagan White
Acquisitions Editor Emily Nicholls
Copyeditor Melinda Rankin
Cover Design Graham Geary
Photo Credit Shutterstock.com/1061659742/© Vera Petrunina
Layout Design Vera Brauner
Production Hannah Lane
Typesetting III-satz, Husby (Germany)
Printed and bound in the United States of America, on paper from sustainable sources

ISBN 978-1-4932-1792-2

© 2019 by Rheinwerk Publishing, Inc., Boston (MA)
1st edition 2019

Library of Congress Cataloging-in-Publication Data
Names: Wang, Lei (Supply chain manager), author.
Title: Inventory planning and optimization with SAP IBP / Lei Wang, Sanchit
   Chandna, Jeroen Kusters, Atul Bhandari.
Description: 1st edition. | Bonn ; Boston : Rheinwerk Publishing, 2019. |
   Includes index.
Identifiers: LCCN 2018061060 (print) | LCCN 2018061337 (ebook) | ISBN
   9781493217939 (ebook) | ISBN 9781493217922 (alk. paper)
Subjects: LCSH: Inventory control--Data processing. | Business
   logistics--Data processing. | SAP IBP.
Classification: LCC TS160 (ebook) | LCC TS160 .W36 2019 (print) | DDC
   658.5--dc23
LC record available at https://lccn.loc.gov/2018061060

All rights reserved. Neither this publication nor any part of it may be copied or reproduced in any form or by any means or translated into another language, without the prior consent of Rheinwerk Publishing, 2 Heritage Drive, Suite 305, Quincy, MA 02171.

Rheinwerk Publishing makes no warranties or representations with respect to the content hereof and specifically disclaims any implied warranties of merchantability or fitness for any particular purpose. Rheinwerk Publishing assumes no responsibility for any errors that may appear in this publication.

"Rheinwerk Publishing" and the Rheinwerk Publishing logo are registered trademarks of Rheinwerk Verlag GmbH, Bonn, Germany. SAP PRESS is an imprint of Rheinwerk Verlag GmbH and Rheinwerk Publishing, Inc.

All of the screenshots and graphics reproduced in this book are subject to copyright © SAP SE, Dietmar-Hopp-Allee 16, 69190 Walldorf, Germany.

SAP, the SAP logo, ABAP, Ariba, ASAP, Concur, Concur ExpenseIt, Concur TripIt, Duet, SAP Adaptive Server Enterprise, SAP Advantage Database Server, SAP Afaria, SAP ArchiveLink, SAP Ariba, SAP Business ByDesign, SAP Business Explorer, SAP BusinessObjects, SAP BusinessObjects Explorer, SAP BusinessObjects Lumira, SAP BusinessObjects Roambi, SAP BusinessObjects Web Intelligence, SAP Business One, SAP Business Workflow, SAP Crystal Reports, SAP EarlyWatch, SAP Exchange Media (SAP XM), SAP Fieldglass, SAP Fiori, SAP Global Trade Services (SAP GTS), SAP GoingLive, SAP HANA, SAP HANA Vora, SAP Hybris, SAP Jam, SAP MaxAttention, SAP MaxDB, SAP NetWeaver, SAP PartnerEdge, SAPPHIRE NOW, SAP PowerBuilder, SAP PowerDesigner, SAP R/2, SAP R/3, SAP Replication Server, SAP S/4HANA, SAP SQL Anywhere, SAP Strategic Enterprise Management (SAP SEM), SAP SuccessFactors, The Best-Run Businesses Run SAP, TwoGo are registered or unregistered trademarks of SAP SE, Walldorf, Germany.

All other products mentioned in this book are registered or unregistered trademarks of their respective companies.

Contents at a Glance

1 Introduction to Inventory Planning and Optimization 21
2 Understanding Inventory Variables 57
3 Configuring SAP IBP for Inventory 105
4 Modeling a Supply Network 157
5 Optimizing Inventory in SAP IBP 185
6 Structuring Inventory 231
7 Designing Your Inventory Planning Process 253
8 Measuring Inventory Performance 275
9 Building Intuition and Conducting What-If Analysis 311
10 Integrating SAP IBP for Inventory 339
11 Planning Your Implementation 369
12 Case Studies 393

Dear Reader,

We intuitively understand the basics of inventory planning.

Every time we stock up at the grocery store, we make inventory calculations. Do I have the space to store paper towels in bulk so I can reduce the price per roll (inventory costs!)? Will my family drink a gallon of orange juice before it expires (demand!)? How much sand and salt will I need to weather snow storms in the next week or the next month (safety stock!)?

For companies with complex supply chains, inventory planning is only the beginning—and inventory optimization is where it starts to get interesting. Inside these pages, you'll get the in-depth information you need to unlock the potential of SAP Integrated Business Planning for inventory: to calculate the ideal safety stock and inventory levels, to perform what-if analysis, to incorporating time-varying demand, and beyond. You'll also find hundreds of screenshots, dozens of detailed inventory formulas, and step-by-step instructions for your system.

What did you think about *Inventory Planning and Optimization with SAP IBP*? Your comments and suggestions are the most useful tools to help us make our books the best they can be. Please feel free to contact me and share any praise or criticism you may have.

Thank you for purchasing a book from SAP PRESS!

Meagan White
Editor, SAP PRESS

meaganw@rheinwerk-publishing.com
www.sap-press.com
Rheinwerk Publishing · Boston, MA

Contents

Preface 15

1 Introduction to Inventory Planning and Optimization   21

1.1	What Is Inventory?	22
	1.1.1 Cost of Inventory	22
	1.1.2 Purposes of Inventory	23
	1.1.3 Types of Inventory	26
1.2	Where Is Inventory Held?	28
	1.2.1 Supply Chain Networks	28
	1.2.2 Extended Supply Chain Networks	29
1.3	Building an Inventory Management Approach	29
	1.3.1 Inventory Control Systems	30
	1.3.2 Inventory Management Approaches	31
1.4	Objectives of Inventory Planning and Optimization	34
1.5	Role of Technology in Inventory Planning and Optimization	36
	1.5.1 Technology in Inventory Control Systems	36
	1.5.2 Technology in Inventory Management	37
	1.5.3 Technology in Inventory Planning and Optimization	38
	1.5.4 Technology Platform Criteria	39
1.6	Introducing SAP Integrated Business Planning	40
	1.6.1 History and Capabilities	40
	1.6.2 Solution Overview	47
	1.6.3 Network Inventory Planning	51
	1.6.4 Demand-Driven MRP	53
1.7	Summary	56

2　Understanding Inventory Variables — 57

2.1	**Primary Factors that Drive Inventory**		57
	2.1.1	Demand Forecast	57
	2.1.2	Lead Time	64
	2.1.3	Order Cycle	68
	2.1.4	Variability	69
	2.1.5	Service Level Target	69
2.2	**Breakdown of Variability Drivers**		75
	2.2.1	Demand Variability	75
	2.2.2	Lead Time Variability	88
	2.2.3	Service Variability	91
2.3	**Additional Factors that Influence Inventory**		92
	2.3.1	Service Level Type	92
	2.3.2	Replenishment Strategy	94
	2.3.3	Stocking Policy	95
	2.3.4	Sourcing Decisions	97
	2.3.5	Bill of Materials	99
	2.3.6	Lot Size and Economic Order Quantities	101
	2.3.7	Inventory Holding Cost	103
2.4	**Summary**		104

3　Configuring SAP IBP for Inventory — 105

3.1	**Architecture**		105
3.2	**Building Blocks**		106
	3.2.1	Attributes	108
	3.2.2	Master Data Type	111
	3.2.3	Time Profiles	116
	3.2.4	Planning Area	118
	3.2.5	Planning Levels	120
	3.2.6	Key Figures	123
	3.2.7	Key Figure Calculation	130

3.3	Planning Area Setup Using Predelivered Content		134
3.4	Versions		139
3.5	Scenarios		142
3.6	Planning Operators		143
3.7	Reason Codes		146
3.8	Data Integration		148
3.9	Planning Views		148
	3.9.1	Connection to SAP IBP System	149
	3.9.2	Creating a New Planning View	150
3.10	Dashboard and Analytics		153
3.11	Summary		156

4   Modeling a Supply Network   157

4.1	Introduction to Supply Networks		157
4.2	Supply Network Complexity		159
	4.2.1	Static Sources	160
	4.2.2	Dynamic Sources	163
4.3	Elements of a Supply Network		164
	4.3.1	Locations	165
	4.3.2	Suppliers	166
	4.3.3	Products	167
	4.3.4	Customers	168
	4.3.5	Source Customer Group	171
	4.3.6	Location Product	171
	4.3.7	Ship-From Location and Ship-To Location	174
	4.3.8	Location Sourcing	175
	4.3.9	Production Sourcing	177
	4.3.10	Production Sourcing Item	180
4.4	Visualizing Supply Networks in SAP IBP		181
4.5	Summary		184

5   Optimizing Inventory in SAP IBP   185

5.1   What Is Network Inventory Optimization in SAP IBP? 185
5.2   Building Blocks for Inventory Calculation 187
   5.2.1   Inventory Replenishment Process Definitions 187
   5.2.2   Impact of Primary Drivers on Inventory Targets 189
   5.2.3   Impact of Time-Varying Demand 200
5.3   Network Multiechelon Inventory Calculation 201
   5.3.1   Constructing the Network Topology 202
   5.3.2   Historical Forecast Accuracy for Customer Demand 204
   5.3.3   Future Demand Forecast and Variability 216
   5.3.4   Demand Forecast Variability Propagation 216
   5.3.5   Estimating Service Variability from Source Location 220
   5.3.6   Finalizing the Inventory Targets 226
5.4   Summary 230

6   Structuring Inventory   231

6.1   Types of Inventory 231
   6.1.1   Flow of Materials and Purpose 232
   6.1.2   Cycle Stock 234
   6.1.3   Pipeline Stock 235
   6.1.4   Safety Stock 235
   6.1.5   Merchandizing Stock 236
   6.1.6   Prebuild Stock 236
6.2   Further Decomposition of Safety Stock 237
   6.2.1   Safety Stock Due to Demand Variability 237
   6.2.2   Safety Stock Due to Supply Variability 238
   6.2.3   Safety Stock Due to Service Variability 239
6.3   Calculating Inventory Components 241
   6.3.1   Operator to Calculate Inventory Components 241
   6.3.2   Inputs to Calculate Inventory Components 243
   6.3.3   Outputs of Inventory Components Calculation 248
6.4   Summary 251

7 Designing Your Inventory Planning Process   253

7.1	Centralized and Decentralized Inventory Planning Teams	253
7.2	Frequency of the Inventory Planning Cycle	255
7.3	From Reactive to Proactive Planner Tasks	257
7.4	Inventory Planning in Sales and Operations Planning	258
7.5	Sequence of Planning Tasks	260
	7.5.1 Step 1: Validate Inputs for Inventory Optimization	262
	7.5.2 Step 2: Running Inventory Optimization	264
	7.5.3 Step 3: Analyze Inventory Optimization Results via Scenario Planning	266
	7.5.4 Step 4: Finalize Inventory Plan	269
7.6	Segmentation	270
7.7	Role of the Inventory Planner	272
7.8	Summary	273

8 Measuring Inventory Performance   275

8.1	Example Supply Chain for Inventory Planning	275
8.2	Key Performance Indicators for Inventory Optimization	279
8.3	Validate Input Quality	281
8.4	Review Inventory Plan	287
8.5	Assess Inventory Drivers	289
8.6	Finalize Inventory Plan	294
8.7	Create Custom Inventory Alerts	299
	8.7.1 Inventory Alerts Key Figures	299
	8.7.2 Inventory Alerts through Custom Alerts Application	304
8.8	Summary	310

9 Building Intuition and Conducting What-If Analysis — 311

9.1	What-If Analysis with Versions and Scenarios	312
9.2	Perform What-If Analysis	313
9.3	Simulating Situations	319
	9.3.1 Service Level	319
	9.3.2 Distribution Lot Size	326
	9.3.3 Periods between Review	328
9.4	Intuition Building	332
9.5	Strategic What-If Analysis	334
9.6	Tactical What-If Analysis	337
9.7	Summary	338

10 Integrating SAP IBP for Inventory — 339

10.1	Data Integration Technologies	339
10.2	Manual Data Integration Using the Web UI	342
	10.2.1 Integration Process	343
	10.2.2 Time Periods	346
	10.2.3 Master Data	347
	10.2.4 Key Figures	349
10.3	Integration using SAP Cloud Platform Integration for Data Services	350
	10.3.1 Architecture	351
	10.3.2 Predefined Content	354
	10.3.3 Creating Your First Integration	355
10.4	With SAP IBP Applications in the Unified Planning Area	361
10.5	With SAP ERP and SAP S/4HANA	362
10.6	With SAP APO	365
10.7	With Non-SAP Systems	366

10.8	Exporting Data Using OData Services	367
10.9	Summary	367

11 Planning Your Implementation — 369

11.1	Cloud Software Considerations	369
	11.1.1 Provisioning	369
	11.1.2 Implementation	370
	11.1.3 Integration	372
	11.1.4 Upgrades	373
11.2	Manual versus Automated Workflow	374
	11.2.1 Job Scheduling	374
	11.2.2 Process Management	380
11.3	Agile versus Waterfall Implementation Methodology	382
	11.3.1 Agile Principles	382
	11.3.2 User Stories	383
	11.3.3 Agile Teams and Roles	386
	11.3.4 Agile Phases	386
11.4	Roles and Responsibilities	389
11.5	Summary	391

12 Case Studies — 393

12.1	Case Study 1: Manufacturing Industry	393
	12.1.1 Company Background	393
	12.1.2 Case for Action	394
	12.1.3 Implementation Scope and Approach	394
	12.1.4 Value Drivers	396
	12.1.5 Lessons Learned	396
12.2	Case Study 2: Consumer Goods	396
	12.2.1 Company Background	397

	12.2.2	Case for Action	397
	12.2.3	Implementation Scope and Approach	397
	12.2.4	Value Drivers	399
	12.2.5	Lessons Learned	399
12.3	**Case Study 3: High-Tech Company**		399
	12.3.1	Company Background	399
	12.3.2	Case for Action	400
	12.3.3	Implementation Scope and Approach	400
	12.3.4	Value Drivers	401
	12.3.5	Lessons Learned	401
12.4	**Case Study 4: Consumer Products**		402
	12.4.1	Company Background	403
	12.4.2	Case for Action	403
	12.4.3	Implementation Scope and Approach	404
	12.4.4	Value Drivers	405
	12.4.5	Lessons Learned	405
12.5	**Summary**		406

The Authors	407
Index	409

Preface

Welcome to our book on SAP Integrated Business Planning for inventory. After the acquisition of SmartOps by SAP in 2013, SmartOps' advanced algorithms have become part of the foundation of the SAP IBP system. This has dramatically increased the appeal of the solution, adding a market-leading inventory optimization capability to the user-friendly sales and operations planning environment which SAP started with.

In this book, we've provided a look under the hood of this advanced multiechelon inventory optimization technology. We've aimed to find a good balance between explaining the science of the algorithms and explaining the practical usage in your day-to-day role as a supply chain planner or inventory analyst.

Who This Book Is For

This book is intended for anyone interested in learning more about the SAP capabilities in the domain of inventory planning and optimization: from customers aspiring to implement a technology-enabling solution in inventory planning to partners and consultants supporting organizations; from business leaders who feel their inventory is spinning out of control to broader supply chain stakeholders.

How This Book Is Organized

We've organized this book by finding a balance between explaining both basic and advanced concepts in theoretical inventory planning, like algorithms and configuration, and very practical concepts, like organizing your process and implementation. The book is structured in such a way that it forms a story from end to end, but it allows you to directly jump to your topic of interest if you'd prefer.

The chapters cover the following content:

- **Chapter 1: Introduction to Inventory Planning and Optimization**
  This chapter starts by explaining some key concepts in inventory, setting the foundation for the remainder of the book. It defines inventory, explains the reasons that inventory is held, and introduces the role of technology in building an

inventory planning and optimization capability. It closes with an overview of SAP Integrated Business Planning (SAP IBP) and how SAP IBP for inventory helps to deliver an end-to-end planning capability.

- **Chapter 2: Understanding Inventory Variables**
  This second chapter goes deeper into the inventory variables, explaining the primary factors that drive inventory, such as order cycles, lead times, demand forecasts and their accuracy, supply chain variability, and service-level targets. It complements these core drivers with concepts that form the foundation of what will turn out to be the parameters to control a technology-enabled inventory optimization capability, such as stocking policies, replenishment strategies, sourcing decisions, lot-sizing approaches, and inventory holding costs. In this chapter, we set you up with all the concepts you need to leverage SAP IBP to drive inventory planning for your environment.

- **Chapter 3: Configuring SAP IBP for Inventory**
  In this chapter, we go deeper into the technical configuration of the SAP IBP for inventory application. We guide you through the end-to-end aspects to set up your own planning area for inventory planning and optimization, including core building blocks such as the time profile, master data types and attributes, planning levels, and key figures. We'll show you how to accelerate your implementation by leveraging the templates SAP provides out of the box, and we'll demonstrate how to further tweak those to your needs. We'll explain most of the concepts core to SAP IBP, such as versions and scenarios, planning operators and subnetworks, and data integration considerations. Finally, we'll demonstrate how to enable planning views and dashboards, which will be used by end users to plan and optimize inventory.

- **Chapter 4: Modeling a Supply Network**
  Once we've explained how to configure the SAP IBP for inventory application, we'll zoom into the supply network definition that forms the foundation of the master data model for the operators to act upon. This chapter focuses on the concept of a supply network, built up out of locations such as manufacturing and distribution centers, customers, and suppliers. It introduces products, their bills of material, and the sourcing rules to perform the multiechelon part of the inventory optimization. This chapter will provide some considerations around the complexity of the supply networks and will close with a section on visualizing the supply networks by leveraging visualization techniques available in SAP IBP for inventory.

- **Chapter 5: Optimizing Inventory in SAP IBP**
  In this chapter, we'll hit on the core of SAP IBP for inventory, explaining the core logic behind inventory optimization in SAP IBP. This chapter will explain the fundamentals the algorithm uses to calculate the inventory targets across the network simultaneously and will teach you how multiechelon inventory calculations really work.

- **Chapter 6: Structuring Inventory**
  This chapter looks beyond calculating safety stock and provides more background on the other components in inventory planning and optimization. Concepts like pipeline stock, cycle stock, and merchandising stock are covered, as well as the way the SAP IBP for inventory application can help identify and optimize them.

- **Chapter 7: Designing your Inventory Planning Process**
  In this chapter, we go a little bit outside of the technical realm to provide some more background for best practices around establishing an inventory planning process. We'll explain the advantages and disadvantages of centralized versus decentralized inventory planning teams, talk about the frequency of running inventory optimization, and discuss the sequence of the steps in inventory planning. We'll also consider the impact of segmentation on inventory planning. Finally, we'll provide a perspective on the role of the inventory planner and how it has evolved over time.

- **Chapter 8: Measuring Inventory Performance**
  This chapter will teach you how to execute the monthly inventory plan you've set up, using screenshots and step-by-step instructions. It describes how to use analytics tools such as Excel templates, analytics charts, and dashboards to evaluate the success of the recurring inventory planning process. It also introduces the key measurements that are critical for tracking the inventory optimization performance.

- **Chapter 9: Building Intuition and Conducting What-If Analysis**
  The objective of this chapter is to bring the inventory planning and optimization controls to life by leveraging the what-if capabilities of the SAP IBP solution. This way you can build intuitions based on the implications and the sensitivity of the controls, allowing you to formulate an inventory strategy and parameterization that achieves the objectives of your organization.

- **Chapter 10: Integrating SAP IBP for Inventory**
  This chapter will provide more background on how to integrate your inventory planning processes with your technology landscape. We'll cover both the internal

integration inside of SAP IBP and integration with external business planning processes. External integration will focus on integration with other planning solutions, such as cases in which SAP Advanced Planning and Optimization (SAP APO) is still available in the technology landscape or integration with systems such as SAP ERP or SAP S/4HANA. Finally, we'll provide a perspective on integration with non-SAP environments.

- **Chapter 11: Planning Your Implementation**
  In this chapter, we'll provide some guidelines and recommendations for how to plan your implementation of SAP IBP for inventory. As a cloud application, SAP IBP follows a slightly different trajectory than most on-premise solution implementations that project teams tend to be familiar with. This chapter guides you through key decisions such as implementation methodology, key tasks and deliverables, and roles and responsibilities.

- **Chapter 12: Case Studies**
  In this final chapter, we'll walk through a couple of examples of companies that have successfully revolutionized their inventory planning and optimization capabilities by implementing SAP Integrated Business Planning for inventory.

Acknowledgements

As mentioned earlier, a book such as this one, which covers all different areas and the latest functional and technical innovations of SAP Integrated Business Planning for inventory, must be a true team effort. We're glad to have collaborated as a team with Deloitte and SAP to put this book together, combining practical knowledge of implementation with the in-depth knowledge of how the solution operates under the hood. Beyond the key authors, this book would not have existed without the support of key people in both organizations. At Deloitte, special thanks goes to Imran Dalwai, Bipin Umarale, Vishvanath Sumant, Ajinkya Thakre, Ashish Singh, Anand Srinivasan, and Amit Sinha.

Thanks also to Meagan White and Emily Nicholls from SAP PRESS for their support, patience, and guidance for keeping us on track. We would also like to thank the SAP product development team, who should be recognized for building SAP IBP for inventory from the ground up. We would like to thank Gerry Perham, Eduardo Lara, Vivek Ghai, Alexis Lozada, Louis Smolenski, Oleg Shigiltchoff and Ajit Wadatkar. Finally we would like to thank our families for their continuous support and motivation.

Conclusion

Reading this book will provide you with a comprehensive overview of SAP IBP for inventory and empower you to engage confidently in any inventory planning and optimization endeavors enabled by SAP IBP. This book fits within a broader series of books focused on SAP IBP, such as *SAP Integrated Business Planning: Functionality and Implementation* (2nd Edition, *www.sap-press.com/4615*) by Amit Sinha and Sandy Markin, and *Sales and Operations Planning with SAP IBP* (*www.sap-press.com/4589*) by Raghav Jandhyala, Jeroen Kusters, Pramod Mane, and Amit Sinha, both from SAP PRESS.

Now let's move to Chapter 1 for an introduction to inventory planning and optimization!

Chapter 1
Introduction to Inventory Planning and Optimization

Delivering the right product to the right place in the right quantity at the right time is key to every organization's success, and balancing demand and supply in this uncertain environment is a challenging task. This balance can be achieved by planning the right inventory, so inventory is of paramount importance for any supply chain, as we'll discuss in this chapter.

Managing the flow of materials in a supply chain network with entities such as suppliers, manufacturers, distributors, retailers, and end customers is the essence of supply chain management. Most of the activities linking these entities involve procurement, transfer, storage, and management of inventory. As such, inventory plays a critical role in the supply chain.

All organizations keep inventory to service customer needs at an acceptable service level. Inventory is required to achieve an organization's strategic and operational objectives. Inventory management has an impact on all of an organization's functions, sales, marketing, operations, procurement, finance, and accounting. Inventory levels can give you a great insight into the performance of the supply chain, along with other logistic activities.

Let's use Apple Inc. as an example. Apple is famous for its innovation, creativity, and design, but the way Apple manages its inventory compared to its competitors is another factor that's led to its success. To remain competitive in today's environment, reducing supply chain costs has become a top priority. Many supply chain professionals focus primarily on reducing inventory-related costs to make an efficient supply chain. Throughout this chapter, we'll come back to key elements that led Apple, and other market-leading companies, to build a world-class inventory management operation.

1 Introduction to Inventory Planning and Optimization

Because managing inventory is a key function of supply chain management, it's necessary to start with the basics. The purpose of this chapter is to provide the key concepts of inventory, inventory management, and control systems and explain why it's important to plan for inventory.

1.1 What Is Inventory?

From a supply chain perspective, *inventory* can be defined as materials held for use in the future, either for sales or in the production process. Inventory can be held in direct relationship to the products being sold or produced, such as finished products inventory, raw materials inventory, or work in progress. Or the relationship with the production or sales process can be more indirect, such as inventory for maintenance, repair, and operations.

Inventory can be found in organizations to support different purposes and comes in various types. Different classifications can be leveraged to describe the various inventories, either with respect to their purpose or with respect to the types of materials kept in inventory. Before going into the details of where inventory can be held in an organization, let's look at the cost of inventory and its various purposes and types, following the APICS classification (APICS OMBOK Framework 5.2).

1.1.1 Cost of Inventory

Holding inventory is often required by companies to ensure good customer service or to enable the core supply chain processes that companies perform to deliver products to their customers. Carrying inventory comes at a cost that is above and beyond the investment in inventory, which should be considered carefully in the context of the purpose of the inventory. Although acquiring products as inventory typically makes up a substantial amount of the cash outflow of a company, the inventory is meant to be used to produce products or sell products or services to clients, hence making up a key element in the cost of goods sold. Looking at the purchasing price isn't the right approach. There are several important elements that contribute to the cost of inventory:

- **Inventory holding cost**
  Every day that inventory is in possession of a company, there's capital tied up in the inventory, which could be used to invest in other initiatives in the organization. Often this tied-up capital is valued at the weighted average cost of capital of the organization, resulting in an inventory holding cost expressed in yearly terms.

- **Inventory scrapping risk**
  Carrying inventory always has an inherent risk of the inventory becoming useless, either because it ages or because it can be damaged or destroyed during the processes it goes through (e.g., transport or storage).
- **Inventory storage cost**
  Storing inventory in a location incurs a cost of maintaining a facility, the headcount to staff the facility, and the utilities to power the facility.
- **Inventory order preparation cost**
  This is the cost associated with the preparation of the inventory replenishment order, typically part of selling, general, and administrative expenses (SG&A).

With these main elements of the costs associated with inventory in mind, let's now look at why companies would keep inventory—that is, the purposes of inventory.

1.1.2 Purposes of Inventory

Inventory can be classified by the purpose for which it's kept. Some purposes will allow a lot of control by an organization, whereas others follow basic laws of the supply chain. For every inventory purpose, we'll describe the decisions that drive the magnitude of this inventory. The following are some common inventory classifications:

- **Pipeline stock**
  Pipeline stock, often referred to as *transit inventory*, is the inventory of materials that are transported between locations in the supply network, or from suppliers and to customers. Transport can often take days, if not weeks or months, and can be performed via various modes of transport. Slower modes of transport are typically more cost-efficient, such as ocean vessels, but require a long lead time and thus lead to high pipeline inventories in the organization. This inventory needs to be considered when making cost decisions based on the means of transport.

  The longer the lead time, the higher the pipeline inventory. When dealing with customers and suppliers, companies can manipulate the impact of inventory ownership via the international commercial terms (Incoterms) governing the ownership of pipeline inventory.

- **Cycle stock**
  Cycle stock is inventory that's present as a result of the economies of scale associated with transportation, procurement, and manufacturing. For example, if order quantities increase, the cycle stock inventory will go up, and so will the cost of

carrying the inventory, but this will also lead to low annual costs for preparing orders. Traditionally, companies try to find an economic balance between stock-holding costs and ordering costs, as reflected in Figure 1.1.

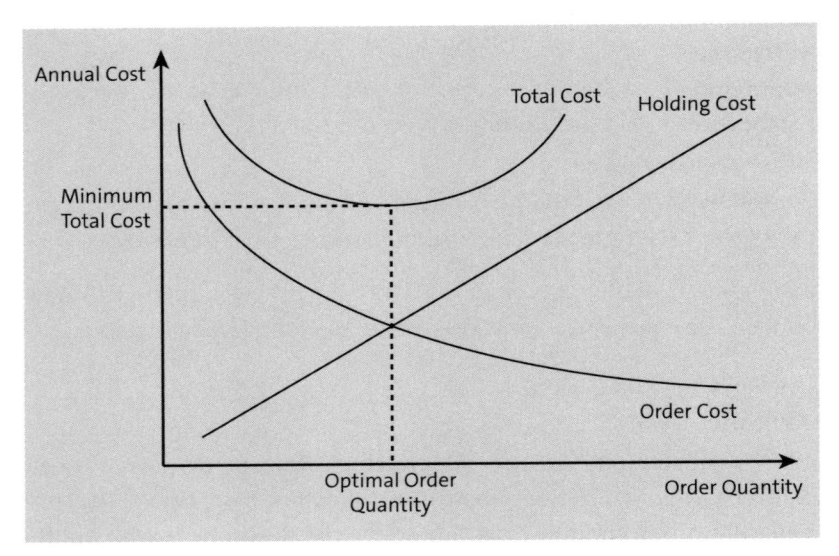

Figure 1.1 Optimal Order Quantity

Looking at it from an annual cost perspective, the ordering cost decreases with the order quantity. Ordering costs include administration, shipping, and other fixed costs that occur per order. The more orders are placed, the lower each order quantity and hence the higher the total ordering cost will be. If the order quantity increases, fewer orders are placed, so lower ordering costs are incurred. On the other hand, the holding costs increase with larger orders because it takes longer to sell the inventory built up by such orders. The optimal order quantity is where the holding cost curve and the order cost curve cross, representing the minimum total cost for ordering and holding inventory.

- **Anticipation inventory**
  Often, companies will hold inventory in anticipation of a future possible event. This could be for a future promotion, a product launch, or a pending supply disruption like a strike or factory shutdown. Anticipation inventory typically results from trying to balance the peaks in demand, ensuring a smooth factory or shipping calendar. For example, it can be used to keep the factory running during periods of lower demand and ensure that no overtime is required during periods of

higher demand. This smoothing typically has a value, which offsets the cost of building up this inventory—for example, the cost of hiring new employees, working overtime, or starting up factories after a shutdown.

- **Safety stock**

  Safety stock, also referred to as *buffer inventory*, is inventory carried to protect companies from uncertainty in demand or supply. Safety stock is the amount of inventory held above and beyond what's needed to meet the known demands, and it's leveraged to ensure customer service or production flow when real-world uncertainties kick in. Safety stock can be held at the finished goods level to maintain customer service levels when demand can be erratic, and on the raw materials and work in process levels to protect the production flow from unexpected delays in the arrival of raw materials (*lead-time variability*).

  Safety stocks will form the foundation of this book as the pivotal inventory to protect in an inventory management and control system.

- **Hedging inventory**

  Hedging inventory, also known as *stockpile inventory*, is leveraged to protect companies from future price or availability fluctuations. Hedging inventory includes inventory procured because the price might go up shortly or because there are future shortages anticipated. In this context, the cost of carrying the inventory can be offset against the cost of procuring the inventory later at a higher cost or with a risk of lower availability.

- **Seasonal inventory**

  Seasonal inventory, also known as *prebuild inventory*, refers to inventory built due to capacity constraints at manufacturing plants during seasonal or peak demands. This option allows inventory to be built during the lean (nonpeak) periods leading up to the season, thereby letting companies meet customer demand without adding additional capital investment.

- **Obsolete inventory**

  As opposed to the inventory types discussed so far, *obsolete inventory* is not so much a type that serves a purpose as it is a consequence. By having inventory stacked up in the organization, there's a risk that a certain amount of it will become obsolete over time. This risk is more prevalent in some industries than others; consider, for example, the high-tech industry. With product lifecycles that are typically short, there is a vast risk of obsolescence of material if too much inventory is maintained. Similarly, in the fresh foods industry, maintaining a high inventory carries a high risk of perished products.

1.1.3 Types of Inventory

The different inventory types summed up in the previous section can be found in different categories of inventory, such as the following:

- **Raw materials**
  Raw materials inventory includes inventory items that are used in the production process to create finished products. Raw materials are typically the lowest level in a bill of materials (BOM) and either can be procured externally or come from another entity in the organization. Figure 1.2 shows a bill of materials example for assembling a bike, in which you can see that most assembly parts are procured, with the exception of the wheel. All the lowest-level materials (spokes, tire, rim, gear, frame, seat, and fork) can be considered raw materials.

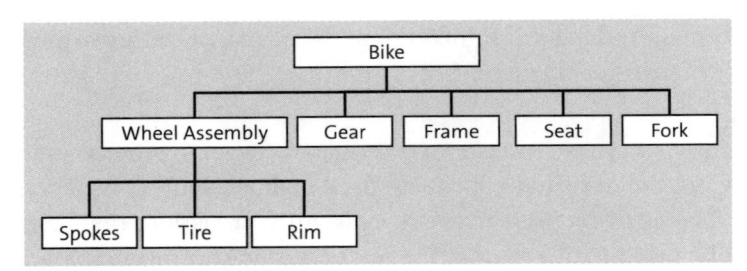

Figure 1.2 Bill of Materials for Bike

Raw material inventory includes all the types are mentioned in the previous section. Raw materials are procured from a supplier, so they'll be in the pipeline inventory during the shipping of materials. It's unlikely they'll be bought on a one-by-one basis for producing bikes, so while depleting the previous order they're available in cycle stock. Because it's never certain that suppliers will be consistent in their supply, some components can be put into safety stock. When anticipating big orders, it might be good to order some extra spokes to ensure the uptick won't cause supply disruptions. If there's an expectation that rubber prices will soon increase, it might be worthwhile to hedge the company against this price increase buying more tires than needed, so long as the cost of carrying the inventory is more than the price increase. Finally, if too much inventory is procured, some of the gear systems used might no longer be aligned with customer expectations and will be obsolete.

- **Work in progress**
  Inventory is designated as work in progress as soon as it enters the production process. In Figure 1.2, the moment the raw materials enter the production process,

they're considered work in progress up to the moment the final bike passes its final inspection and is ready to be sold.

Work in progress inventory might be kept strategically in certain situations, especially when there are decisions to be made. For example, it could be a good idea to produce wheel assemblies if a wheel is always be composed out of the same spokes and rim. Bikes might be assembled based on customer-specific specifications—for example, with respect to the gear system which is put on the bike. This example and more examples of postponement manufacturing strategies will be covered in Section 1.3 on inventory control systems.

- **Finished goods**
  Continuing the example of the bike, as soon as the bike is through its final inspection, it becomes a finished good, available for customers to buy. Finished goods inventory can be stored at the manufacturing location or in the distribution network, closer to the customers. For the example of the bike, this could be the assembly location where the bike is produced, a centralized warehouse through which all bikes pass before being shipped through the dealership channels, or at the dealerships themselves, ready for end customers to buy.

- **Maintenance, repair, and overhaul (MRO)**
  The examples covered so far are materials directly included in the production process. However, to produce finished products, there might be equipment and assets required that have a risk of failure, too. Keeping this equipment or these assets running might require products to service them in maintenance, repair them when broken, or overhaul them completely in specific cases. This might induce an inventory as well, to be kept close to the equipment or assets, called *MRO inventory*. Think, for example, about consumables like oil, filters, or gaskets, or service parts to replace broken elements in the equipment. Although often not as visible, these inventories can be substantial as well, especially in manufacturing-heavy industries.

- **Service parts**
  Service parts can be considered part of MRO when they're leveraged for the equipment and assets used for production. But the products sold by your organization might have service parts also. In our example of the bike, imagine the tires as service parts. Your customer might buy a bike and then blowout the tire. In that case, you have to be able to provide the replacement tire alone. This means that some of the elements in the bill of materials could also induce a demand themselves to be sold as service parts.

In this section, we covered the definition of inventory and how to consider the costs of inventory. We've looked at various purposes of keeping inventory and how they relate to the costs and various types of inventory. In the next section, we'll look at the supply network and where inventory is held.

1.2 Where Is Inventory Held?

Now that we've defined what inventory is and what the purposes and types of inventory are, this section will focus on where inventory is typically held in organizations. We'll start by defining inventory in the supply chain network of an organization before moving to the implications of inventory in the extended supply chain network.

1.2.1 Supply Chain Networks

To explain where inventory can be held in an organization, it's important to define the supply chain network. Figure 1.3 shows the supply network for an organization, which in this case consists of five levels.

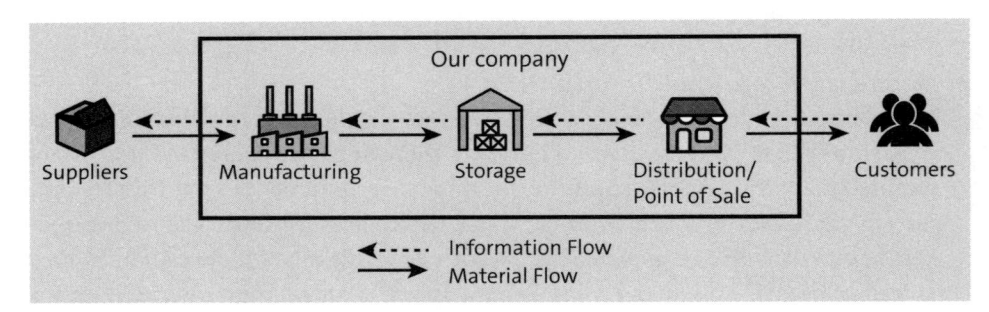

Figure 1.3 Supply Chain Network

Inventory can be kept at every level in the supply network. In this section, we'll focus on inventory inside the walls of our company, but in the next section, we'll expand the assessment to the extended supply chain. Within a company, you have the following sites at which inventory can be held:

- **Manufacturing facilities**
  Inventory kept at manufacturing facilities are typically raw materials, work in progress, and finished goods. At manufacturing facilities, MRO inventory often can be found as well to ensure the production process runs smoothly.

- **Storage facilities**
  Storage facilities often are put in between the manufacturing facilities and the distribution networks to ensure efficient storage of products that aren't immediately

due for sales. Storage facilities can be colocated with manufacturing or with distribution centers or can be completely separate.

- **Distribution/point of sale**
  The distribution channel is the customer-facing part of the supply network. It consists of points of sale or shipment locations that ship directly to customers.

1.2.2 Extended Supply Chain Networks

The examples in the previous section focused on keeping inventory inside of an organization. In a lot of cases, inventory can be held at your organization's suppliers or customers as well. Within the extended supply chain network, you can find inventory in the following places:

- **Inventory at customers**
  In some industries, it's common to keep inventory at customer locations so that customers can have access to the inventory when they need it. Think about the automotive industry or the technology sector, in which the inventory from OEM suppliers often is kept close to or on the customer side. For example, Intel has a lot of inventory facilities, or hubs, close to its customers' locations.

  Going one step further would result in a *consignment inventory location*, in which the inventory is de facto handed over to customers without the customers paying for the inventory up to the moment the inventory is pulled or sold. Examples of this system can be found in the fashion industry, for example, in which retailers consign inventory from fashion brands, but only pay at the moment the inventory is sold.

- **Inventory at suppliers**
  Similarly, companies can force their suppliers to keep inventory for them. It's less common to have this inventory be the property of the company already, but it's possible, especially in cases of very specialized products. For example, in the semiconductor industry, the usage of outsourced assembly and test (OSAT) partners drives the inventory at partners or suppliers.

1.3 Building an Inventory Management Approach

As an inventory manager, you're responsible for establishing an effective inventory management approach that will let you respond effectively to customer demands. To effectively manage and plan for inventory at the right time, in the right place, and for the right price, an understanding of inventory control systems is required, including the information available for building an inventory management approach.

After we discuss inventory control systems, we'll cover inventory management approaches, first distinguishing a pull from a push model, then explaining postponement strategies as a critical element in inventory management.

1.3.1 Inventory Control Systems

Inventory control systems provide the necessary information about inventories to build an inventory management approach. They are typically classified into two main families: period inventory control and perpetual inventory control. Inventory control systems are closely related to the accounting rules for and valuation of the inventory, which we'll cover for both systems in a little more detail.

Periodic Inventory Systems

In a *periodic inventory control system*, updates to the inventory are made on a periodic basis. There's no real effort made to keep the inventory up to date on a daily basis. Inventory is only updated during periodic physical inventory counts. During the inventory count, changes are made to the inventory valuation on the balance sheet, using either a first in, first out (FIFO) or last in, first out (LIFO) inventory accounting technique.

There are some major disadvantages of using periodic inventory systems:

- There's no good inventory information at a given moment in time between inventory counts.
- During inventory counts, operations are typically disrupted, because inventory must be frozen for a certain amount of time to perform the physical inventory counts.
- It's hard to identify why discrepancies arise because there's often a substantial amount of time in between inventory counts.

However, given their simplicity and low labor requirement, periodic inventory systems are still very common, especially in smaller organizations. Needless to say, periodic inventory systems aren't suited for the advanced inventory management, planning, and optimization techniques we'll cover in the remainder of this book.

Perpetual Inventory Systems

When you're using a perpetual inventory system, inventory records are constantly updated based on incoming and outgoing operations information. This allows you to assess the amount of all different inventory types at any time and use that information during inventory planning.

The main disadvantage of perpetual inventory systems is that they require specialized equipment and software to keep track of inventory at any operation. Barcode inventory systems commonly are used to track what inventory leaves the warehouse for specific operations. More recently, the use of radio-frequency identification (RFID) inventory systems have become more popular, allowing companies to track when products enter or leave a facility via little RFID tags. Taking this one step further, in the context of the internet of things (IoT) movement, RFID tags can be replaced by IoT tags that can share real-time locations for specific products. This allows access to continuous factual information on all inventory positions anywhere in the world at any time of day.

Perpetual inventory control systems are substantially more complex to establish, but they've become the standard in all professional supply chains.

Once you have information from the inventory control system about the exact position of inventory in the supply network, you can move on to create an inventory planning approach.

1.3.2 Inventory Management Approaches

The need for inventory is always driven by customer demand. The way in which an organization plays into customer demand can be split into two broad categories: push systems and pull systems. Taking a middle path drives us toward hybrid approaches focused on establishing an effective postponement strategy.

Push Systems

In a *push* inventory management approach, the customer demand is forecasted and companies produce to the forecasted demand. Companies therefore need to predict the anticipated demand and use inventory buffers to protect against inaccuracies when trying to predict customer demand. The key in this environment is to balance the level of inventory against the level of service to the customer.

In many cases, push inventory systems are the only viable option. For example, all retail goods need to be available at the point of sale to be considered for purchase. However, producing to a forecast carries the inherent risk of the forecast being wrong. This will lead to either not being able to fulfill the customer demand, thus impacting customer service, or producing and positioning too much material, risking some of it becoming obsolete.

In the bike example discussed earlier, you could be considering producing bikes to deploy to bike stores across the country. In that case, you'd have to assess up front how many bikes in different configurations should be produced and push them to the retail channels. If the wrong mix of bikes is produced, you'll lose sales on some bikes that have more demand than predicted while being stuck with an inventory of bikes that are less popular than expected.

Pull Systems

In a *pull* inventory management approach, production only starts on receipt of a customer order. The main advantage of this approach is that products are produced the moment there's an order and not before, so the likelihood of obsolescence is very low. However, this approach has considerably longer lead times, making it impossible to operate in certain markets. The key focus of this approach is to get the product requirements and configurations from customers and translate them into capacity terms for the organization.

Consider again the bike example: instead of producing off-the-shelf bikes and making them available in retail stores for customers to try, we could consider producing samples only and letting customers select which components they want. In such a case, the delivery time for the bike would be substantially longer because it will take time to procure the components, assemble the wheels, and then assemble the bike. This model has proven successful both in heavily customized, high-end bike sales and in many other industries.

Hybrid Systems

Combining the advantages from both approaches leads to a hybrid system in which there's a clearly defined postponement strategy. In this model, some levels in the production process follow a push model and thus are procured or assembled based on anticipated requirements, whereas others follow a pull model. In this approach, companies are looking to find the right balance between the risk of inaccurately forecasting products and the time customers are willing to wait for their products.

Returning to our running example, let's simplify the product structure to three key components that go into the bike: wheels, a gear system, and a seat. Imagine there are three sizes of wheels; two gear systems, with either 12 or 18 speeds; and two seats, either comfort or performance. With these three components and limited choices for each, the number of possible bikes already reaches 12, as reflected in Figure 1.4.

If you add the lead times, you can assume the final assembly time in the shop is only one day. The time to procure the components is substantially more, though—in this case, 12 days for gears and seats. Wheels are being produced as subassemblies and take a bit more time, and procuring the components for the wheels would require a substantial amount of time because they might be produced internationally.

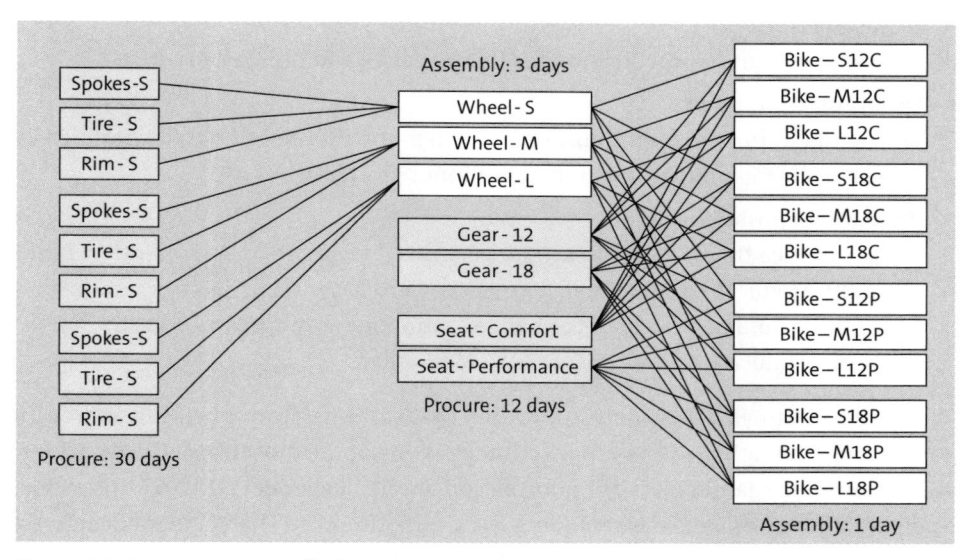

Figure 1.4 Postponement Bill of Materials

In a push model, you'd have to forecast exactly how many of each of the bikes would be sold. There are a lot of bikes, and that number will only grow if you add other components. For example, adding one more dimension, such as having two fork-stiffness levels, would mean that you now have to forecast 24 bikes.

In a pure pull model, it would take 34 days at minimum to fulfill a customer order, which might be a risk to retaining customers. But imagine a customer is open to waiting two weeks for a bike. In that case, your best choice is procuring and assembling the wheels to stock (push model) while waiting to order the other components when a customer places an order. For the wheels, there's no real reason not to assemble them because every wheel is unique in the components it uses (the size of the spokes, tire, and rim need to be aligned). So we can produce the wheels as soon as the components arrive, when time permits, because there's no differentiation point.

From this example, we can derive the characteristics that are relevant to define a postponement strategy, suggesting which elements in the production process to run in a push model and which to run via a pull model:

- **Customer wait time**
  How long a customer is willing to wait for a product is critical to define which steps can be performed for a customer order.

- **Lead times**
  How long it takes to procure or make intermediate and finished products.

- **Differentiation points**
  The points in the production process at which the number of output products is substantially higher than the number of input products.

- **Breakdown possibilities**
  If you produce the wrong product, how hard is it to use the components to build the right product? For example, it could be very easy to change the saddle on a bike, but it could be very hard to change a component in a laptop once the laptop has been produced.

When setting up your organization for a successful inventory planning approach, establishing the right postponement strategy is one of the most impactful decisions. It's important to gather accurate information about all elements driving this choice and perform due diligence when doing so. It's important to challenge preconceived notions about customer wait times, negotiate with suppliers on reliable and accurate lead time information, and consider production lead time carefully.

1.4 Objectives of Inventory Planning and Optimization

After setting up an accurate inventory management approach with the appropriate postponement strategy, we can start looking into inventory planning and optimization. In this section, we'll introduce the key objectives in inventory planning and optimization before moving into the role of technology and the SAP Integrated Business Planning (SAP IBP) solution in this space:

- **Achieving customer service levels**
  The primary objective of planning and optimizing for inventory is meeting customer needs. Inventory can be positioned at the point of sale, such as retail stores carrying products; it also can be stored in distribution centers, fulfilling orders from those retail stores. Inventory can be carried at the production facilities, either in finished goods to distribute to the distribution centers or in raw materials to produce those finished goods. Not all customers require the same service level for

all products all of the time, which requires companies to segment their customers and products.

The optimal location to store inventory is dependent on the definition of good customer service. For some products, good customer service means the product is right there when the customer wants it. This is typically true for most retail items, like shampoo, soda, or customer electronics. If the product isn't available on the shelves when the customer comes for it, it's likely sales will suffer because the customer will either buy an alternate product or decline to buy the product at all. Good customer service means having the product available in abundance when the customer is looking for it.

Other products aren't like that. Consider, for example, heavily customized manufacturing equipment or a computer server. There's a lead time that customers expect when deciding to order such a product. This lead time can range from a couple of days for a computer server to a couple of months for heavily customized manufacturing equipment. Good customer service, in this case, means delivering products aligned with the customer expectations and commitments.

- **Minimizing working capital**
  As we noted earlier in this chapter, inventory comes at a cost. Inventory planning and optimization is the art and science of meeting customer expectations in a cost-effective way. Minimizing working capital, which means as much as minimizing inventory, is, of course, opposed to leveraging inventory to ensure organizations can meet a customer's service expectations. The remainder of this book will unveil the elements that influence and the algorithms that allocate inventory across the entire supply chain to meet customer service levels in such a way as to minimize working capital.

- **Strategic positioning of inventory**
  Bringing the two opposing objectives, meeting customer needs and minimizing working capital, together in inventory planning and optimization leads to the importance of strategic inventory positioning. To meet customer service needs at a minimal cost, the when, where, and how much questions of inventory buffers are really what inventory optimization is all about.

A lot of organizations start their inventory planning and optimization journeys after realizing their inventory is organized in a bimodal fashion, meaning they have too much of the wrong product and not enough of the right product. Figure 1.5 shows what the distribution of inventory looks like in a lot of organizations: a bimodal inventory distribution.

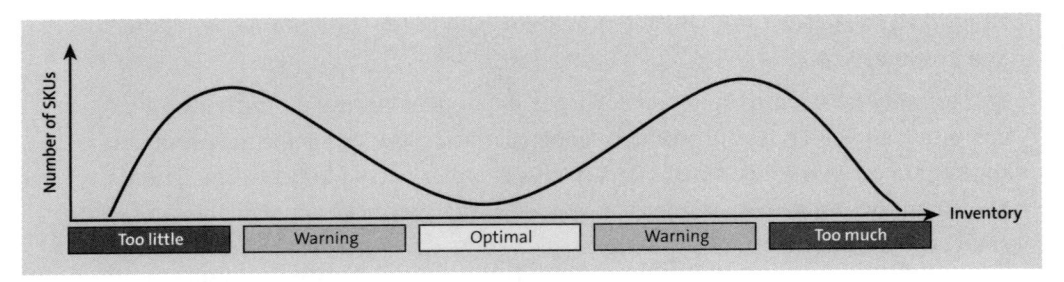

Figure 1.5 Bimodal Inventory Distribution

From the figure, you can see there are a lot of stock keeping units (SKUs) with too little or too much inventory, for which the optimal zone often isn't achieved. The good thing about a bimodal inventory position is that there often are no structural supply chain problems preventing you from resolving it. With the capacity to manufacture or procure the "wrong" products, it's implied that you can build the "right" products from a capacity perspective. The biggest cause of this bimodal inventory position is often the lack of "correct" information or the lack of ability to translate the "correct" information into the right actions. Throughout this book, we'll help you address some key aspects that drive this situation. Technology can help you build the right products, ensuring the right information flow in your organization and having the right processes in place to decide what to build.

1.5 Role of Technology in Inventory Planning and Optimization

Technology plays a key role in establishing a good inventory planning and optimization process. Before introducing the SAP IBP solution, we'll focus more in general on the impact of technology on inventory control, management, and planning processes. Now we'll introduce some core elements a technology platform should exhibit in the competitive market of inventory planning and optimization technology.

1.5.1 Technology in Inventory Control Systems

You can easily imagine a periodic inventory control system working without enabling technology, writing down inventory numbers at the end of every quarter on paper, running advanced inventory management processes would be a challenge. Perpetual inventory control systems that provide continuously updated inventory positions are a much better foundation for inventory management and planning processes, but they're much harder to support manually. To keep track of stock movements for every product, calculating the on-hand inventory requires a certain amount of calculation power. Technology makes it easy to keep track of every movement, however, while continuously updating the inventory position.

Imagine a simple local grocery store. Keeping an inventory of all goods on the shelves up to date is possible by taking a physical inventory at the end of the day or week, for example, to place new orders. But to continuously track what happens, it's impossible to keep track of every product and its real-time inventory in a manual fashion. Technology can help document all product movements and keep a single record of all on-hand inventories for all products. If a simple registry is implemented in which scanning barcodes marks products going out and coming in, then inventory can be assessed in real time by calculating the movements of every product.

The simplest inventory control systems leverage a scanning system, but today we've seen substantially more advanced techniques to keep track of inventories in real time—for example, leveraging RFID chips for every batch. That allows organizations to eliminate the physical act of scanning when products enter or leave the facility; instead, they can measure these movements via the RFID tag. One step further would be to enable the RFID tag with GPS sensors, making it part of the IoT world. This would make it possible to provide visibility into the inventory in real time wherever it is in the world. Consider, for example, the company Brambles, one of the biggest logistics groups in the world. It's been focusing on building IoT devices into its pallets, allowing its customers to track their inventory globally, wherever it is. This, of course, provides a substantial competitive advantage: this information could be key in inventory management, planning, and optimization processes.

1.5.2 Technology in Inventory Management

Once you can track inventory for all products in your facilities or in the broader supply network, you can look at how technology enables functions in the inventory management space. When introducing inventory management approaches, we talked about order-based pull models and inventory-target-based push models. In both cases, technology plays a key role in the calculation of requirements, resulting in purchase or production orders to be generated.

In the case of a push model, companies historically leverage material requirements planning (MRP) systems. This was exactly the context in which the first mainframe computer started supporting supply chain processes. These programs focused on an unconstrained explosion of a manufacturing schedule through all the levels of sometimes very complex bills of materials. Traditionally, the solutions would focus on the explosion of demand through the BOM and render the result, but as integrated inventory management solutions continued to emerge, MRP grew to become a central part of enterprise resource planning (ERP), integrating the planning processes with procurement and shop-floor control.

The same logic applies in a pull or make-to-order environment, in which the complexity can quickly escalate with the number of products and components. As we explained in Section 1.3.2, in most cases companies will adopt a hybrid approach, buying components to stock while building the finished products to order. This requires a strong supporting platform to allow placing orders that define the product, and logic to plan and buffer for inventory of raw materials.

Moving forward, aligned with enabling technology, in today's inventory management environments, we use optimization models in the space of supply planning. Companies can leverage linear programming techniques to build a model that optimizes profit based on the inventory information, demand projections, and supply networks. This approach today forms the foundation of the technology-enabled supply planning solutions, leveraging all information in the supply chain to determine the best way to propagate demand signals for supply requirements.

1.5.3 Technology in Inventory Planning and Optimization

This finally leads us to inventory planning and optimization techniques, which focus on building a model to optimize the inventory components in the supply network.

Historical techniques of inventory planning were composed from rules of thumb—for example, the usage of a coverage profile when calculating supply requirements. Based on experience, planners could suggest they expected two weeks of demand to be available in the grocery store "to be on the safe side." Although the calculation isn't hard, it would be extremely tedious to perform manually. But this calculation can be infused into the technology foundation that runs the MRP, ERP, or supply chain optimization engines.

The rules of thumb, however, quickly showed their limitations as they made the inventory planning functions more of an art than a science, leaving room for more scientific approaches to proliferate. The typical impact companies observed was that they would overuse inventory, exposing themselves to the costs noted in previous sections. It was quickly determined that elements like lead times, demand variability, and supply variability played an important role in inventory planning. Moreover, with the use of simple statistics it was possible to scientifically approach the meaning of customer service and suggest a target customer service level that would fuel inventory optimization approaches. Of course, given the calculation intricacies, with the rise of more advanced calculation capabilities in technology more and more of these techniques would be made available as part of supply chain planning solutions.

1.5.4 Technology Platform Criteria

Embedding advanced algorithms in technology is one key aspect of bringing inventory planning and optimization to clients. However, there are other key aspects that have proven to be critical in building a strong inventory planning and optimization engine. Let's now introduce key concepts behind a good technology platform in inventory planning and optimization:

- **Integration**
  Inventory planning and optimization isn't a standalone function in supply chain planning: it's an integral part of broader processes like demand planning, supply planning (using MRP and ERP), and demand fulfillment. Having technology that's "integrated" with other supply chain planning functions and the supply chain management process in general is critical to the success of an inventory planning and optimization engine.

- **Scenario planning capability**
  Planners have learned that the real world isn't as deterministic as traditional supply chain planning solutions have led them to believe. Rather than counting on singular statistics, planners seem more often to look for the ability to plan out multiple cases, providing various possibilities to their stakeholders. Plans for worst case, baseline, and best cases provide more information about risks to take and the corresponding exposure to risk. Imagine that in a hybrid inventory management approach, you're deciding to buy and assemble wheels for bikes pending a large order with a short cycle time. Imagine a buyer is interested in buying 1,000 extra bikes, provided you can deliver them in three days, implying you'd have to stock up on all the components and start producing wheels immediately. What should you do? You need to calculate the benefit this brings as profit to the company while understanding the exposure to risk in case the order doesn't come through.

- **Speed**
  With the need for scenario planning capabilities comes an implied requirement for speed. If the calculation of the scenario to buy components for the extra order

takes a long time, the opportunity might be lost. Faster calculations mean more ability to do real-time scenario planning when needed, allowing better supply chain decisions. With the rise of in-memory computing, supply chain planning and optimization algorithms—known for their heavy technological demands due to advanced mathematic processes—have become more impactful as they allow for quicker turnaround.

- **Usability**
  With technology maturing, the usability of technology is playing a more and more important role. Traditionally, given the advanced calculations that advanced planning systems could perform, usability was overlooked in the light of added value. Today, however, in a world in which technology is all around us and with many key examples of easy-to-use technology, there has been an increased focus on usability. Usability represents itself from various angles, from maintaining and entering data to overrunning the algorithms and scenarios to reporting in a professional and easy-to-understand fashion.

1.6 Introducing SAP Integrated Business Planning

SAP Integrated Business Planning is the latest generation of advanced planning system from SAP. It covers the whole array of supply chain planning, from demand sensing and demand planning to supply network planning and optimization to response management and operational planning. This section provides an overview of the SAP IBP platform before diving into the key capabilities of SAP IBP for inventory. We'll close this section with some considerations for network inventory planning and a preview of the demand-driven MRP (DDMRP) capability that was recently added.

1.6.1 History and Capabilities

To introduce the SAP IBP solution, we'll first provide a short history of its roots. We'll discuss the revolutionary user experience SAP IBP has brought to planners, and we'll cover some of the key platform capabilities differentiating the solution from its predecessors.

History of SAP IBP

What's known today as SAP Integrated Business Planning saw the light of day in 2012 as a sales and operations planning (S&OP) solution. The history and key highlights from six years of SAP IBP are depicted in Figure 1.6. The original release, called SAP Sales and Operations Planning powered by SAP HANA, was focused on delivering a foundational platform for organizations to enable their S&OP processes. Its key focus was bringing together information from various platforms that contributed to running an efficient S&OP cycle, rendering it in an efficient user-friendly way, and allowing planners to run scenario planning capabilities against it. On the demand side, the solution came with several statistical forecasting techniques. On the supply planning side, the planning model was equipped with a supply planning heuristic, which allowed users to propagate demand plans through the supply network, validate rough-cut capacity assumptions, and plan high-level distributions.

As of version 3, the supply planning capability was expanded to include a time-series-based, linear-programming-based supply optimizer that calculated an optimized constraint supply plan. Providing planners with the ability to create scenarios in a heartbeat and continuously keep various versions of the plan running provided a distinct advantage over the traditional SAP planning environment, called SAP Advanced Planning and Optimization (SAP APO).

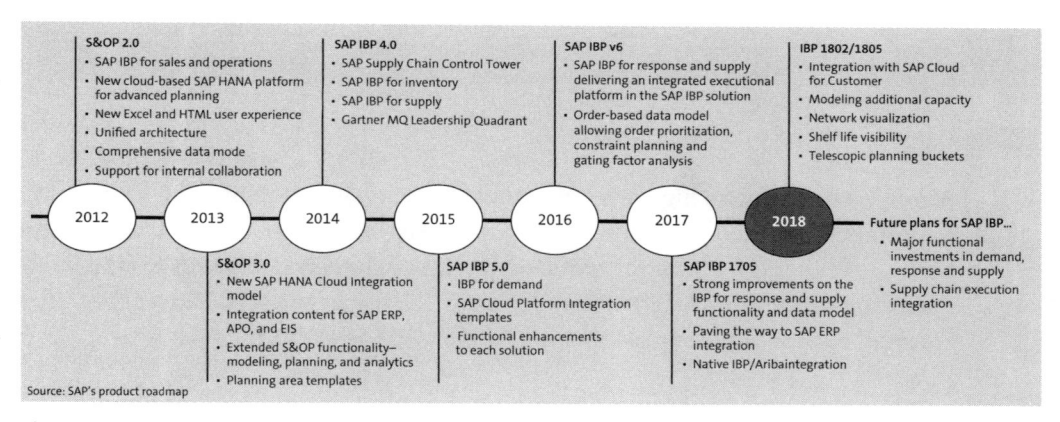

Figure 1.6 History of SAP IBP

In 2014, the solution's name changed from SAP Sales and Operations Planning powered by SAP HANA to SAP Integrated Business Planning (version 4 at the time). This version was the first to differentiate various applications in the solution, with the introduction of SAP IBP for inventory focusing on inventory optimization and the SAP Supply Chain Control Tower providing more advanced data visualization, dashboarding, and management-by-exception capabilities. In 2015, the demand planning capabilities were expanded with the introduction of the SAP IBP for demand application, incorporating demand-sensing capabilities and adding to the originally limited set of statistical forecasting techniques. In 2016, the solution scope was completed by differentiating the SAP IBP for response and supply application from the SAP IBP for sales and operations application and introducing the order-based planning concepts that make up SAP IBP for response and supply.

This deep history of vast scope resulted in the main solution with five applications as we know it today. Figure 1.7 gives an overview of these applications.

Enhanced User Experience
SAP Supply Chain Control Tower End-to-End Visibility, Monitoring, and Alerting
SAP IBP for Sales and Operations Strategic and Tactical Demand/Supply/Operations Alignment Processes

SAP IBP for Demand Demand Sensing and Statistical Forecasting	**SAP IBP for Inventory** Global Multi-Stage Inventory Optimization	**SAP IBP for Response and Supply** Constrained/Unconstrained Supply Planning and Allocations and Order Rescheduling

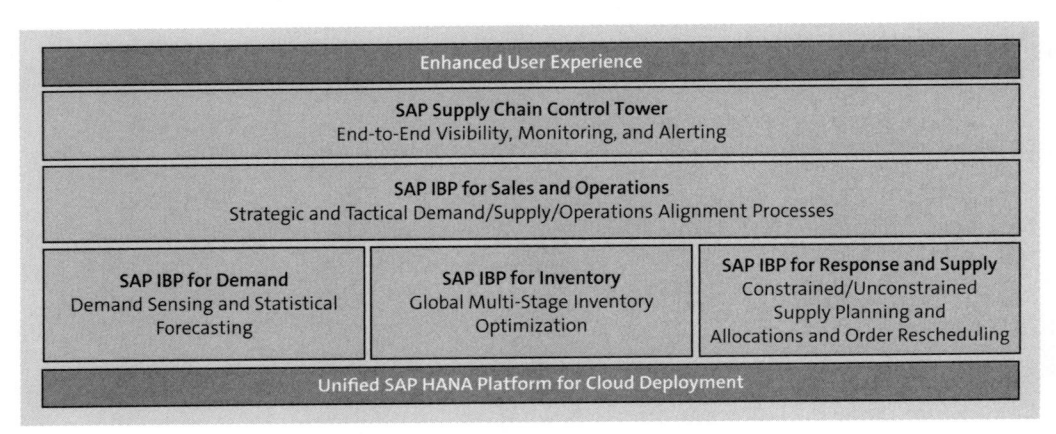

Unified SAP HANA Platform for Cloud Deployment

Figure 1.7 SAP IBP Application Overview

Before we move into a high-level functionality overview of the five applications, it's important that you understand the shift the SAP IBP solution has brought to planners' user experience. After introducing the user experience in SAP IBP, we'll introduce some of the key platform capabilities SAP IBP brings to users. Those capabilities are independent of the applications and come with the platform.

User Experience

Traditional SAP planning solutions have mostly relied on offering solid planning capabilities, often at the cost of the user experience. With the SAP IBP solution, SAP has revolutionized the user interface, marrying the two most preferred ways for planning users to interact with technology: Microsoft Excel and a web browser.

For most day-to-day planning activities, SAP IBP relies on the user interacting with Microsoft Excel. This typically enables planners to leverage years of experience using Excel to perform planning functions that traditional package technology couldn't fulfill in their use of SAP IBP, providing a unique advantage in terms of user adoption. This is achieved by using an Excel add-in users install on their computers, which makes the connection between the local Excel spreadsheets and the cloud-based SAP IBP solution.

1.6 Introducing SAP Integrated Business Planning

Users can create planning views, run planning operators, create scenarios, and change master data all from Excel. Figure 1.8 shows an example of an SAP IBP Excel planning view. It looks like a standard Excel sheet, but there's an extra tab (**IBP**) in the Excel ribbon, enabled by the installed add-in. This tab allows you to interact with the SAP IBP application. Upon connecting to the system, the SAP IBP Excel add-in receives the data from SAP IBP and renders it in a tabular format. From that table, all standard Excel functions can be used. This means the chart shown in Figure 1.8 and the formatting performed leverage all the standard Excel capabilities.

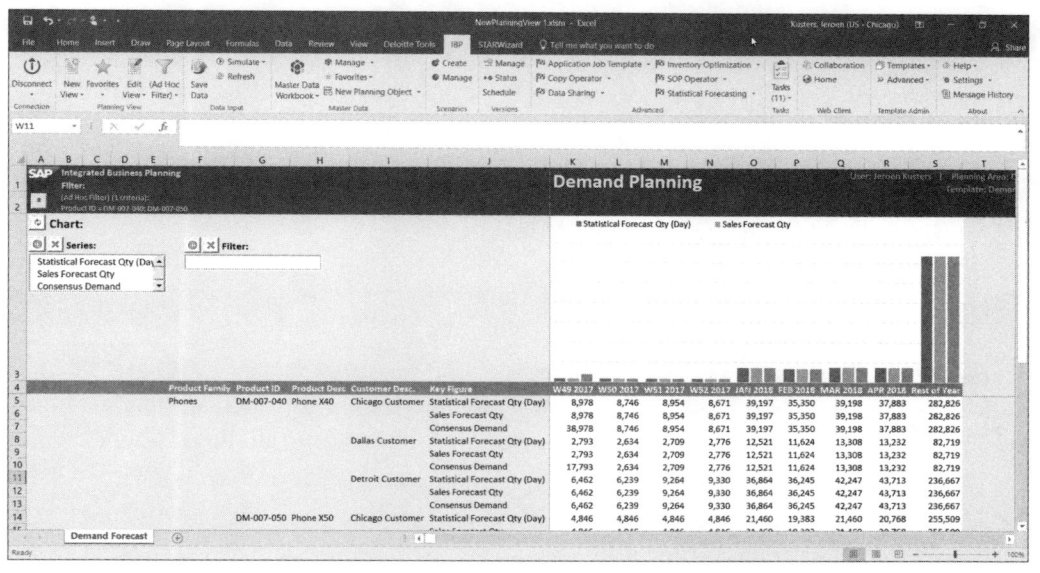

Figure 1.8 SAP IBP Excel Planning View

A lot of planning activities are performed using the SAP IBP Excel planning views, but specific activities are rendered in a web browser leveraging SAP Fiori applications. This makes it possible to access SAP IBP from almost any device via a web browser. Moreover, this approach is consistent with other SAP applications, like SAP S/4HANA, ensuring a consistent user experience for users active on multiple platforms.

SAP Fiori provides a launchpad as the main landing page for users, as shown in Figure 1.9. The SAP Fiori launchpad contains active tiles, which provide information for planners to immediately assess specific key aspects of the planning situation, such as the number of active alerts. For an example of an application, see Figure 1.10, which shows the Dashboard app, one of the key data-visualization applications in the web-based user interface for SAP IBP.

43

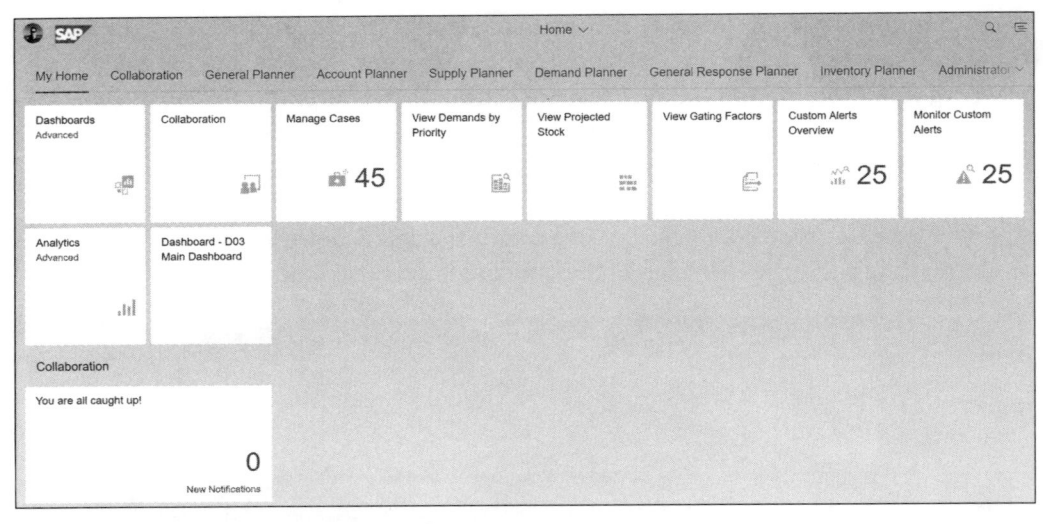

1   Introduction to Inventory Planning and Optimization

Figure 1.9 SAP Fiori Launchpad for SAP IBP

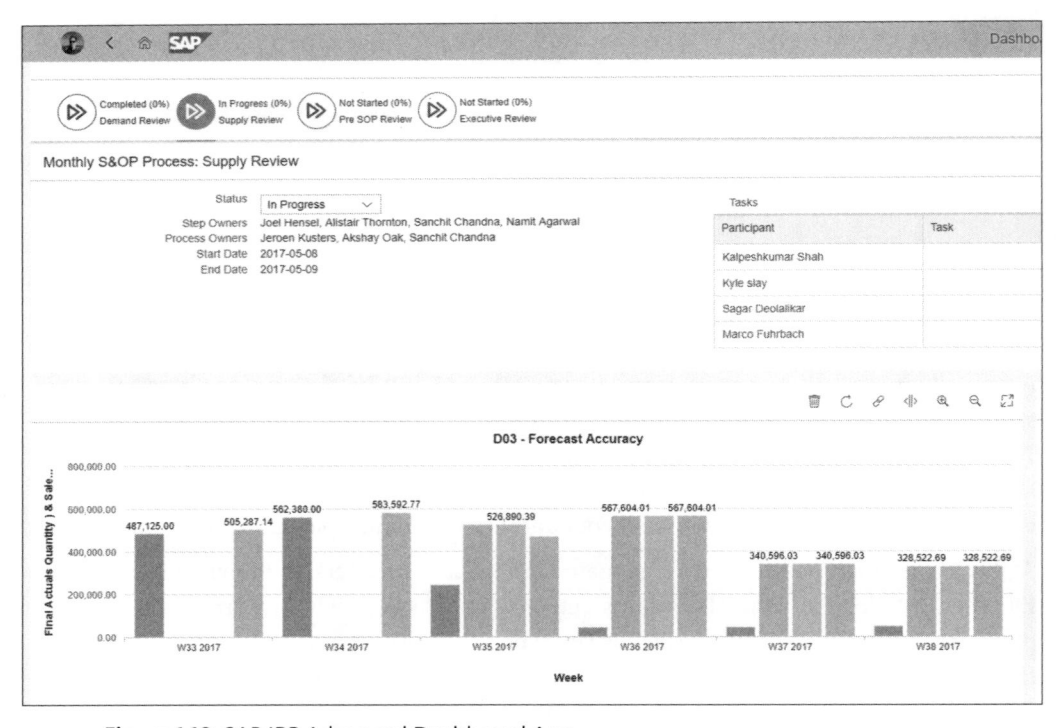

Figure 1.10 SAP IBP Advanced Dashboard App

44

1.6 Introducing SAP Integrated Business Planning

Now that we've introduced the user interface for SAP IBP, let's talk about the key platform capabilities enabled in SAP IBP before diving into more details of the capabilities unlocked by specific SAP IBP applications.

Platform Capabilities

SAP IBP comes with a substantial set of platform capabilities, which are available across applications to support the integrated business planning processes. The following is not meant to be an exhaustive overview of the platform capabilities, but rather a listing of key functions of relevance to planners:

- **Real-time analytics**
  These analytics play a key role in building an integrated business planning environment. Providing dashboards and charts in a user-self-service fashion is a key differentiator of SAP IBP versus traditional SAP APO applications in which data visualization was substantially more challenging.

- **Collaboration**
  Collaboration enabled by SAP Jam brings a performance management platform into the integration business planning process. It allows users to define groups and tasks, post updates, and perform content management as part of a social collaboration platform based on the SAP SuccessFactors solution. Figure 1.11 shows the SAP Jam group-based collaboration platform.

- **Version planning and simulation**
  Version planning and simulation functionality is another key differentiator of the SAP IBP solution, allowing you to perform what-if analysis on various levels of planning activities:

  – **Simulation**
  In the Excel planning view, you can make changes and interactively run operators to see the impact of the changes on the key figures and sheets in the planning view.

  – **Scenarios**
  You can define a scenario on the fly in the Excel-based planning view by editing a key figure and storing the change not in the baseline but in a scenario. These scenarios can be shared with your colleagues, promoted to baseline, or reset to the baseline as needed.

  – **Versions**
  You can define a version if you want to do a more sustainable comparison of different situations. Whereas scenarios are meant to be fast to create and fast to

45

1 Introduction to Inventory Planning and Optimization

accept or reset, versions are established in the configuration of the solution but allow more involved capabilities, such as changing master data for the version alone.

- **Change history**
  This tracking allows you to keep tabs on who changed what when. Upon saving changes to a key figure, you can enter a reason code for the change and a comment. With the Change History application, it's possible to trace back the changes you made, viewing the reason codes and the comments made to ensure the change was justified and can be audited ex post.

- **ABC analysis and classification**
  This provides algorithms to classify planning objects based on the values of one or more key figures. Two options are available:
  - *ABC segmentation*, which allows prioritization of the planning objects based on their relative importance. For example, classification based on revenue.
  - *XYZ segmentation*, which allows classification of planning objects based on their demand volatility. For example, classification based on forecasting error measures such as mean absolute percentage error (MAPE).

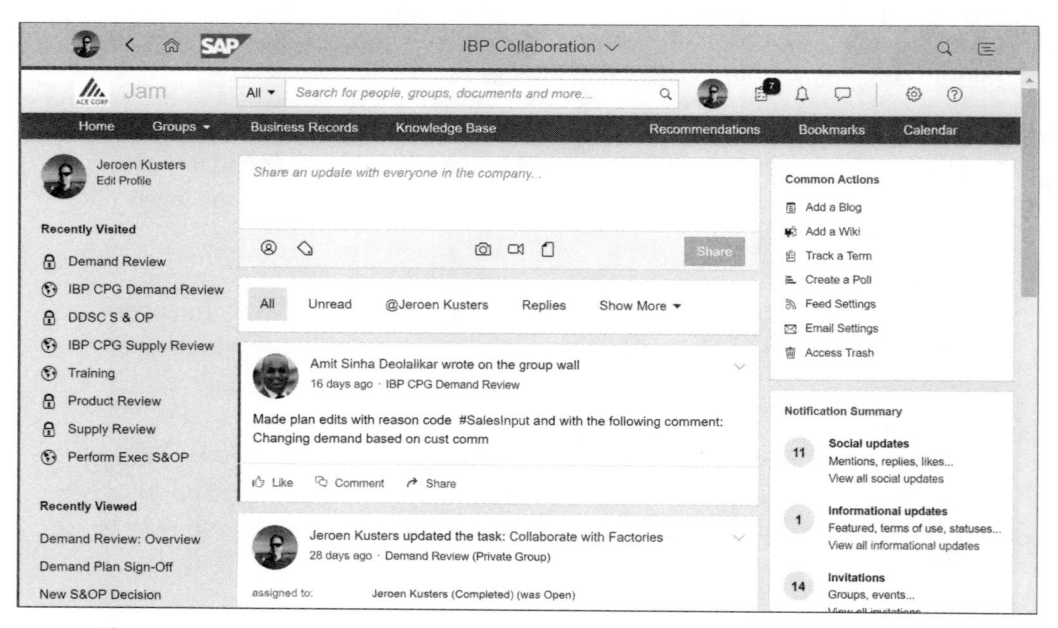

Figure 1.11 SAP Jam

These platform capabilities are available in all the SAP IBP applications we'll describe.

1.6.2 Solution Overview

Beyond the platform capabilities available when leveraging the SAP IBP solution in general, the remainder of the functionality is organized into five applications. In this section, we'll give a short overview of SAP Supply Chain Control Tower and SAP IBP for sales and operations, SAP IBP for demand, and SAP IBP for response and supply. The fifth application, SAP IBP for inventory, will be discussed in the following section.

SAP Supply Chain Control Tower

SAP Supply Chain Control Tower provides end-to-end visibility, monitoring, and management-by-exception capabilities. Real-time analytics have been mentioned as a platform capability, implying that dashboards and charts are available to all applications, but SAP Supply Chain Control Tower enhances this capability with predelivered content. SAP Supply Chain Control Tower includes performance management analytics, using the predefined supply chain operations reference (SCOR) model content and metrics.

SAP Supply Chain Control Tower also enables more advanced management-by-exception capabilities, embedded in the custom alerting and case management applications. Custom alerting allows you to define your own alerts on a user-self-service basis, subscribe to alerts, and visualize the alerts in an easy-to-use alert monitor. These alerts can be prioritized and can take you immediately to the Excel planning view, in which corrective action can be taken if necessary. Figure 1.12 gives an example of the SAP Fiori app Custom Alerts Overview, and Figure 1.13 shows the monitoring of a custom alert, which can be reached by clicking a specific alert.

To manage the work related to alerts and drive a collaborative solution, alerts allow you to create a case via the SAP Fiori app Case Management of SAP Supply Chain Control Tower. From this alert, a case can be defined, which can be assigned to a user; from there, comments and communications can be captured. Cases can be maintained and managed up to the moment they give a satisfactory answer.

Finally, SAP Supply Chain Control Tower offers business network collaboration. This capability allows you to share your business data with external partners via a native connection to the Ariba Network. It's managed via data sharing plans and arrangements, which connect to the SAP Ariba Supply Chain Collaboration capabilities of the Ariba Network.

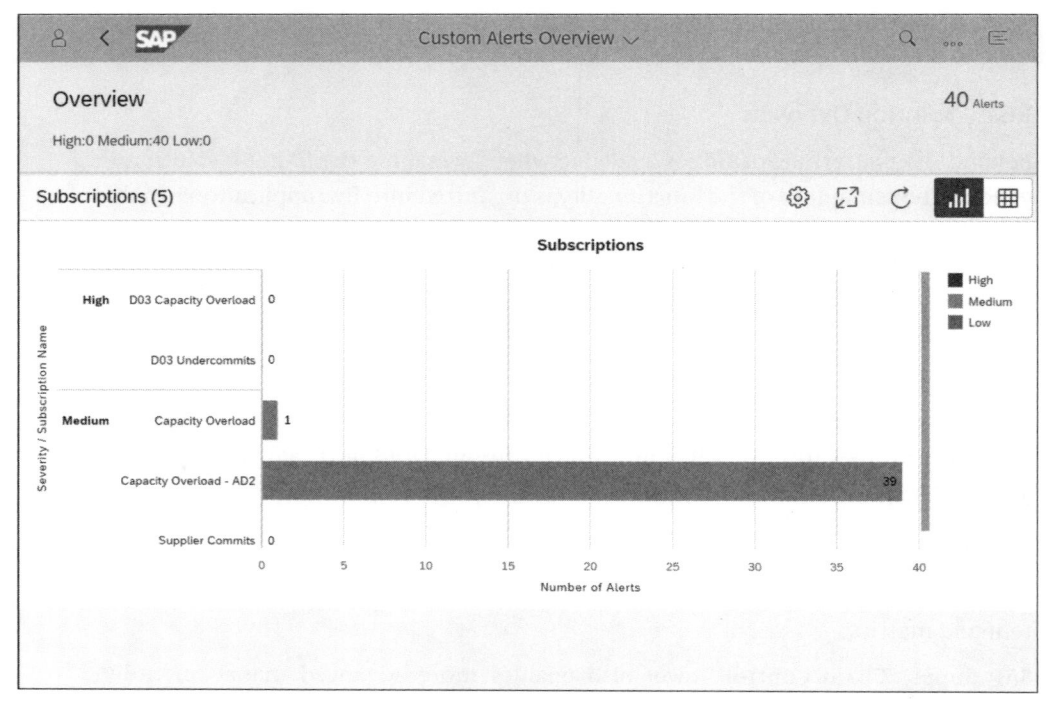

1   Introduction to Inventory Planning and Optimization

Figure 1.12 Custom Alerts: Overview

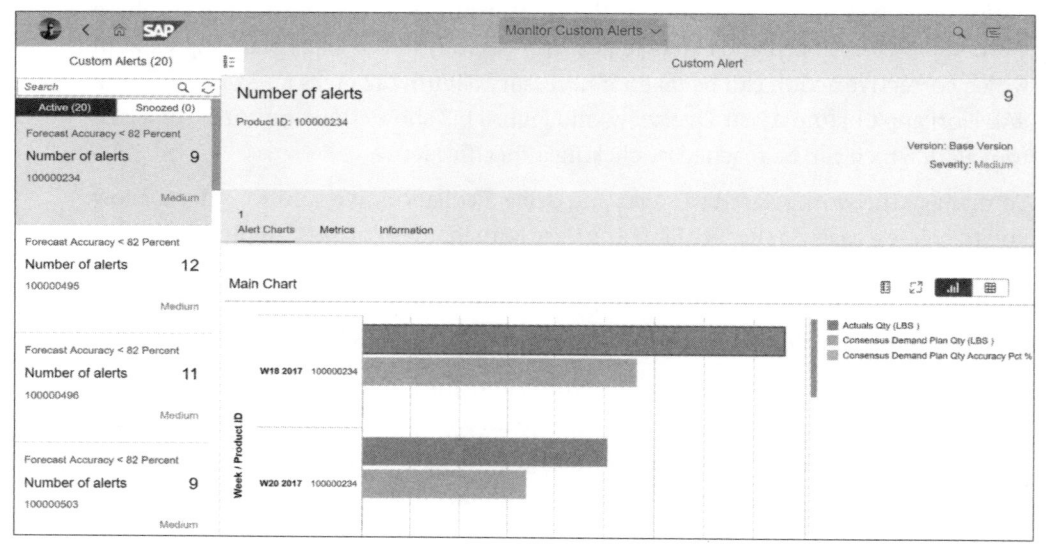

Figure 1.13 Custom Alerts: Forecast Accuracy

48

1.6 Introducing SAP Integrated Business Planning

SAP IBP for Sales and Operations

As mentioned in Section 1.6.1, the SAP IBP solution started as a pure S&OP-enabling platform. Therefore, SAP IBP for sales and operations is a core application many companies start their SAP IBP journey with. It delivers baseline capabilities in both demand planning and supply planning, supporting the key elements of the S&OP process.

On the demand planning side, SAP IBP for sales and operations offers a basic *statistical forecasting* capability. It enables the use of five statistical forecasting techniques and one postprocessing algorithm that can be used to calculate the root mean square error of the ex post forecast. The combination of these capabilities even allows for a best-fit selection of the five algorithms used. The statistical forecasting capability can be embedded in a thorough consensus demand planning process, in which multiple stakeholders can influence demand plans via the user-friendly Excel planning views.

On the supply planning side, SAP IBP for sales and operations enables the *multilevel supply planning time-series-based heuristic*, which performs infinite multilevel demand and supply planning, allowing you to identify capacity bottlenecks and issues with constraint materials. It comes with a supply propagation version of the heuristic, which allows you to propagate shortages through the supply chain and up to the customer-facing level. This provides visibility into the impact of constraints, either capacity or material, up to the customer-facing demand level.

Finally, SAP IBP for sales and operations aims to support the S&OP process by delivering the process management capabilities reflected in the upper section of Figure 1.10. These capabilities allow you to manage your S&OP process by maintaining process steps that have with owners and participants. This feature will generate tasks for participants in the process and can trigger planning jobs the moment all tasks are completed for a specific step. It provides process automation capabilities, as well as process monitoring, ensuring all stakeholders know exactly where the process is at.

SAP IBP for Demand

SAP IBP for demand deepens the capabilities in the demand planning space by delivering more advanced statistical forecasting techniques. The number of forecasting algorithms increases to 16 from the five available in SAP IBP for sales and operations. The algorithms include the Croston method, auto-ARIMA models, and Brown's linear exponential smoothing model. But beyond these statistical forecasting techniques, SAP IBP for demand enables a full array of pre- and postprocessing steps. In preprocessing, SAP IBP for demand enables you to perform outlier correction, missing value

1   Introduction to Inventory Planning and Optimization

substitution, and promotion sales lift elimination. On the postprocessing side, there are eight error calculations available for reporting and best-fit selection.

Building on this advanced statistical forecasting capability, SAP IBP for demand offers the demand-sensing algorithms that SAP acquired with the SmartOps acquisition. Demand sensing focuses on creating forecasts for shorter time horizons, typically 8–12 weeks, based on the consensus demand combined with the most recent demand signals retrieved from the backend ERP system, such as open sales orders. The sensed demand typically offers a big improvement in short-term-forecast accuracy.

Finally, SAP IBP for demand enables promotion analysis and integration to the trade promotion platform to model and analyze promotional lift implications on the forecast.

SAP IBP for Response and Supply

SAP IBP for response and supply deepens the capabilities of time-series-based supply planning, as well as enabling the order-based planning capabilities of the SAP IBP solution.

For time-series-based planning, SAP IBP for response and supply offers the multilevel optimizer. The optimizer provides a finite, cost-optimized plan. It aims to fulfill the demands, which can be prioritized, as best as possible under the given constraints, either material- or capacity-based. By planning the required production and transportation amounts while adhering to the modeled supply chain, the optimizer creates a feasible solution.

The response management side of SAP IBP for response and supply enables order-based planning algorithms, with the following key figures:

- **Constrained, priority-driven heuristic**
  This leverages rule-based demand and supply matching in a prioritization algorithm to derive a constrained plan.
- **Gating factor analysis**
  This explains the results of the planning by identifying constraining factors and visualizing them in a user-friendly fashion, as shown in Figure 1.14.
- **Planning with product allocations**
  This calculates the allocations and uses them as constraints in the constrained, priority-driven heuristic.

1.6 Introducing SAP Integrated Business Planning

- **Reconfirmation of sales orders**
  This leverages an order-pegging-based algorithm to find the exact timing with which orders can be fulfilled in case of supply disruptions.

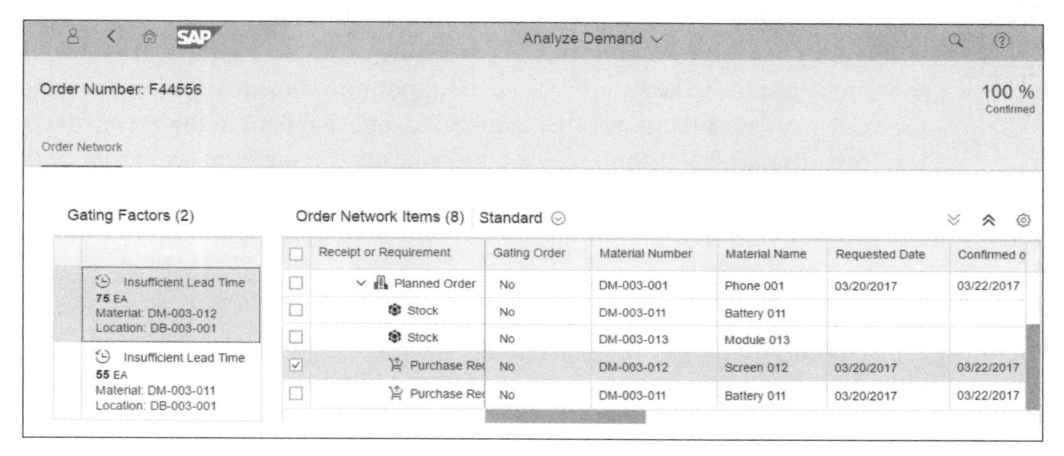

Figure 1.14 Gating Factor Analysis

Now that we've covered a high-level overview of the user interface for SAP IBP, the platform capabilities, and the various applications (excluding SAP IBP for inventory), let's look deeper into the network inventory planning capability, which the remainder of this book will teach you all about.

1.6.3 Network Inventory Planning

This entire book is about the network inventory planning capabilities that SAP IBP for inventory offers, but in this section we want to zoom into the high-level capabilities the inventory engine brings. The SAP IBP for inventory application enables five key operators:

- **Decomposed inventory optimization**
  The *decomposed*, or *single-stage, inventory optimization algorithm* will calculate the target inventory position locally for every location-product combination.

- **Global inventory optimization**
  The *global*, or *multistage, inventory optimization algorithms* will calculate the target inventory position across all products and locations in the supply chain. The objective is to minimize the total safety stock holding costs across the network while ensuring all customer service level targets are adhered to. The algorithms

1   Introduction to Inventory Planning and Optimization

will optimize safety stock simultaneously over all products and locations in the supply chain, considering demand and supply uncertainties, supply quantities, lead times, cost parameters, and target service levels.

To do this, the optimizer will propagate the demand through the network, for both the forecast and the forecast variability to ensure a complete picture. This is done in a similar fashion to how the S&OP heuristic performs the propagation, ensuring the same rules are adhered to. This propagation only happens in the global inventory optimization algorithm, so it's a prerequisite for the local inventory optimizer to run the global one first, ensuring the full demand is propagated through the network.

Note

More information on the decomposed inventory optimization algorithm and the global inventory optimization algorithm can be found in Chapter 5 on optimizing inventory.

- **Expected lost demand**
  Because inventory optimization algorithms plan to a specific service level, there's a likelihood of losing demand. You can use the expected lost demand calculation to calculate the expected lost demand quantity for a given inventory plan and distribution plan. The operator will estimate the opportunity loss for selected target service levels by calculating the average demand lost or average expedited demand.

Note

More information on the expected lost demand can be found in Chapter 8 on measuring inventory performance.

- **Calculated forecast error coefficient of variation**
  One of the inputs into the inventory optimization algorithms is the coefficient of variation for the forecast error, a depiction of the demand variability. To calculate the forecast error coefficient of variation, the SAP IBP for inventory application has an operator that leverages the forecast and actual key figures to calculate the coefficient of variation. The coefficient of variation determines the difference between the forecasted and actual demand. The better demand is forecasted, the less safety stock is required to meet inventory targets.

1.6 Introducing SAP Integrated Business Planning

Note

More information on the impact of forecast error and demand variability can be found in Chapter 2 on understanding inventory variables.

- **Calculate target inventory components**

  Finally, to correctly interpret the role of inventory in the organization, it's important to decompose the target inventory into its components. We covered the inventory types earlier in this chapter. SAP IBP for inventory offers an algorithm that helps you decompose the target inventory into components such as cycle stock, pipeline stock, and safety stock. It also calculates a reorder point, which can be used in a reorder-point-based planning approach.

Note

More information on the target inventory component calculation can be found in Chapter 6 on structuring inventory.

1.6.4 Demand-Driven MRP

Historically the multistage inventory optimization capability has formed the essence of SAP IBP for inventory, but recent releases have enabled strong inventory optimization capabilities that fit within the demand-driven MRP approach as defined by the Demand Driven Institute. Demand-driven MRP, or DDMRP, is a complete supply chain planning and execution method in itself. Although it's outside of the scope of this book to completely describe the approach and how SAP IBP for inventory enables it, we did want to introduce the basics in this section.

DDMRP is a multiechelon supply chain planning and execution methodology to protect and promote flow through the establishment of strategic inventory buffers. The Demand Driven Institute breaks DDMRP into position, protect, and pull segments, as shown in Figure 1.15:

- **Position**

  Strategically position inventory on deliberately determined decoupling points. The idea of decoupling is not new, but DDMRP provides a renewed focus on the explicit decision about where to buffer inventory. It focuses more on where to put inventory than on the prevalent decision of how much to buffer.

1   Introduction to Inventory Planning and Optimization

- **Protect**

  The strategic inventory positions will be buffered based on buffer inventory profiles and levels that determine the amount of protection. These inventory buffers are not meant to be static over time but should evolve up and down based on operating parameters, market changes, and planned future events.

- **Pull**

  This segment focuses on the day-to-day operations of the DDMRP logic, making it a demand-driven planning process in which supply orders (purchase/production/stock transfer) are generated exclusively based on actual customer orders and strategic buffers. Of course, the whole methodology has a visibility and collaboration overlay to provide clear prioritization and execution visibility.

Demand Driven Material Requirements Planning				
Strategic Inventory Positioning	Buffer Profiles and Levels	Dynamic Adjustments	Demand Driven Planning	Visible an Collaborative Execution
Position	Protect		Pull	
①	②	③	④	⑤

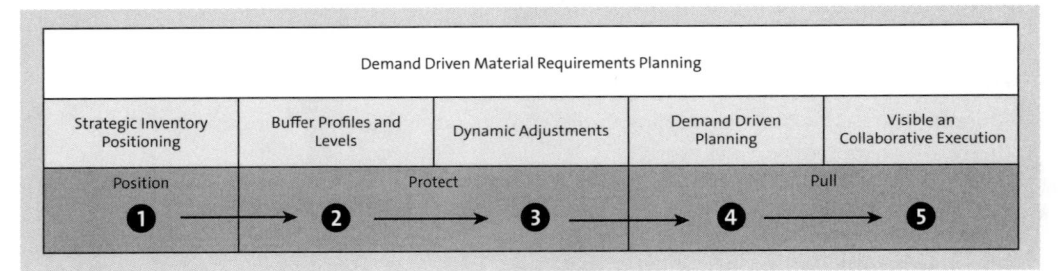

Figure 1.15 Demand Driven MRP

> **Note**
>
> More information on DDMRP can be found on the Demand Driven Institute's website at *https://www.demanddriveninstitute.com/*.

The SAP IBP for inventory application supports the first two components of the DDMRP logic—namely, strategic inventory positioning by creating decoupling points, and creating buffer profiles and maintaining buffer levels. The solution uses the underlying inventory optimization techniques to drive an optimal calculation for both steps and visualizes the results in the DDMRP Buffer Analysis app, shown in Figure 1.16.

In the DDMRP Buffer Analysis app, you can create scenarios in which you can influence the strategic inventory positioning and compare the results with the baseline. This allows you to visualize the delta between the baseline and the scenario in terms

1.6 Introducing SAP Integrated Business Planning

of decoupled lead time, average on-hand inventory, and the corresponding inventory value.

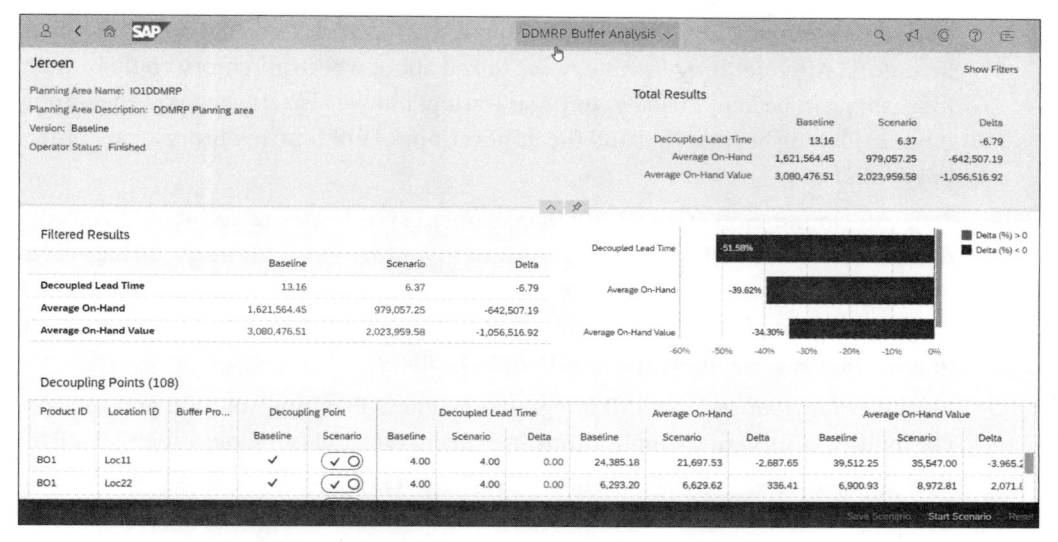

Figure 1.16 DDMRP Buffer Analysis App

To enable this capability, SAP IBP for inventory offers two planning algorithms to support the strategic inventory positioning and buffer calculation:

- *Recommendation of decoupling points*, which recommends where to strategically position inventory in the network and calculates the amount of inventory to buffer with
- *Calculation of DDMRP buffer levels*, which allows you to recalculate only the amount of inventory to buffer with, given the strategic decoupling points

SAP IBP for inventory focuses on making strategic decisions about where to position inventory and how much to position. From there, the results can be connected to SAP S/4HANA, which enables the other DDMRP steps.

> **Note**
>
> More information on DDMRP in SAP S/4HANA can be found in *Introducing Demand-Driven Replenishment (DDMRP) in SAP S/4HANA* (SAP PRESS 2017), by Ferenc Gulyássy and Jawad Akhtar, available at *www.sap-press.com/4569*.

55

1.7 Summary

In this chapter, we introduced the core concept of this book: what inventory is. We covered the purposes of inventory, the types of inventory, and why companies hold inventory. After defining inventory, we talked about where inventory could be held. Inventory can be kept inside your organization, but we also showed you the importance of looking beyond that and the implications of holding inventory at customers or suppliers.

To lay the foundation of inventory management systems, we talked about inventory control systems, in which we keep track of inventory, and inventory management approaches that will play a key role in moving toward inventory planning and optimization. We combined these systems with the objectives of inventory planning to define the role of technology in the inventory space.

Finally, we introduced the SAP Integrated Business Planning solution and the core capabilities of its various applications. We finally took a closer look at the SAP IBP for inventory application, which will make up the core of this book. We closed that section by mentioning the new DDMRP paradigm that's emerging.

In the next chapter, we'll take a much closer look at the variables driving inventory.

Chapter 2
Understanding Inventory Variables

Inventory is one of the biggest investments of any organization, but it's also a necessary evil. There's no doubt inventory is required to ensure steady operations, but too much of it can hamper your organization's growth. In this chapter, we'll discuss the variables that drive inventory and how you can take control of them and reduce overall inventory levels.

In the previous chapter, we explained that inventory serves an important purpose in the supply chain. Before setting up the inventory planning optimization model for your supply chain within SAP IBP, it's crucial for the inventory planners from your organization to understand the critical variables that impact inventory levels. You should know the inventory variables that make inventory go up or down. Knowing all these variables in greater detail will help you understand the reasons for inventory changes in your supply chain. Once you understand these variables, you'll be able to establish better control over your inventory levels. The variables being discussed in this chapter aren't just limited to the inventory optimization models that you'll set up within SAP IBP for inventory. These variables are used in any application that deals with supply chain inventory planning and optimization.

2.1 Primary Factors that Drive Inventory

In this section, we'll introduce the key factors that have an influence on inventory levels.

2.1.1 Demand Forecast

Demand forecasting and inventory planning go hand in hand. If you can master these two critical functions of supply chain planning, you can achieve higher levels of operational efficiency. Holding inventory and hoping that it will sell is a rudimentary method of forecasting. A good demand forecast can lower inventory levels considerably. If you're completely in a make-to-order environment—that is, you buy raw materials only when you receive a customer order, and your customers are willing to wait for your products to be built and shipped to them—then you don't need demand forecasting. You can have practically zero inventory because you buy/produce when you have an order. However, this is rarely the case. A customer may simply go to another supplier who's willing to deliver faster, and you could lose your competitive advantage. To make sure you can deliver to the customers whenever they want, you have to reduce lead time. Reducing lead time doesn't mean that you keep an inventory of almost everything, which would be unwieldy because the customer could ask for anything. This where a good demand forecast adds value to inventory decisions.

Demand forecasting is the process that predicts what and how much customers will purchase in the future. A demand forecast helps you determine how much inventory you should keep in your supply chain to meet your customer demand. This forecast can be categorized into two parts: independent demand and dependent demand. *Independent demand* is the demand for finished goods such as a television, car, laptop, cell phone, and so on. *Dependent demand* is demand derived from the demand for finished goods, such as demand for an LED screen for a television, engine for a car, memory chips for laptops, microchips for cell phones, and so on. The relationship between independent demand and dependent demand is represented in the bill of materials (BOM). Dependent demand can be derived by exploding the bill of the materials of the finished goods. This can be achieved by any simple MRP tool. Figure 2.1 shows an example of a bill of materials for a bike. Here you can see that one unit—one bike—needs, for example, two wheel assemblies and 200 spokes.

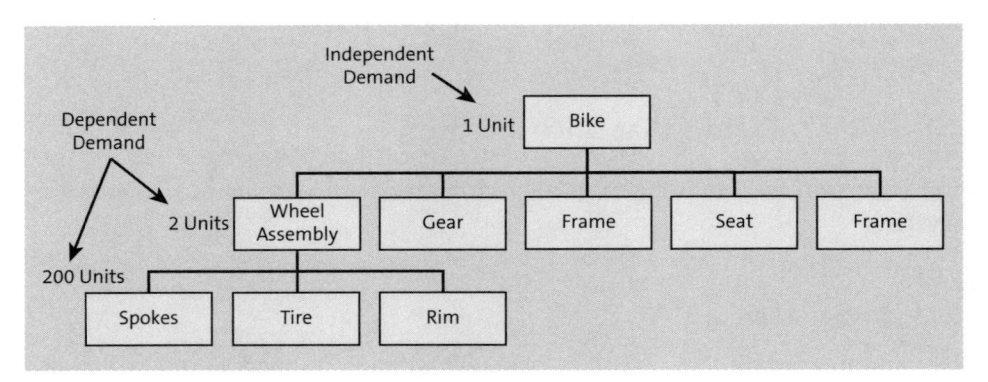

Figure 2.1 Bill of Materials Showing Independent Demand and Dependent Demand

Dependent demand can also be a dependent distribution demand. For example, a finished good is sold from a distribution center. The distribution center demand is fulfilled from a manufacturing plant. The demand for the finished good at the manufacturing plant is dependent on the independent demand for the finished goods at the distribution center, so it's a dependent demand as well.

Demand can be forecasted with a variety of methods, and a company needs to generate a forecast for every product. Companies usually invest their time in forecasting independent demand and rely on systems to generate a dependent forecast using MRP or advanced planning software. To forecast the independent demand, there are two major categorizations of demand forecasting methods: qualitative and quantitative methods. The *qualitative method* uses the judgment and expertise of the various stakeholders, such as suppliers, sales, marketing, and so on, to predict demand, whereas *quantitative methods* use scientific or statistical models to predict demand.

Quantitative methods can be categorized into time series techniques (predictions based on historical demand) and regression techniques (predictions based on causal factors). A lot of companies invest in advanced planning tools that help them generate a better quantitative forecast using advanced statistical algorithms. They often use this forecast as a baseline forecast. Planners usually adjust this baseline forecast to generate a final forecast for the materials.

Companies use both quantitative and qualitative methods to predict demand. Figure 2.2 shows some of the qualitative and quantitative forecast models.

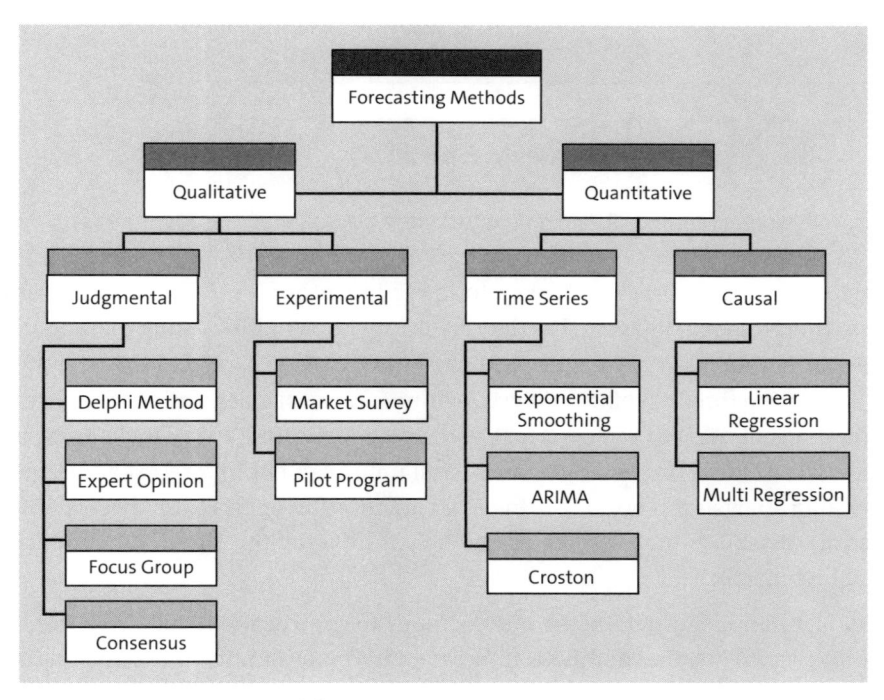

Figure 2.2 Forecasting Models

Based on the product life cycle, in the introduction phase planners usually rely on their judgment to predict demand, whereas they rely on statistical methods when the product is mature. Figure 2.3 shows the product life cycle graph and the typical forecasting methods used in each stage.

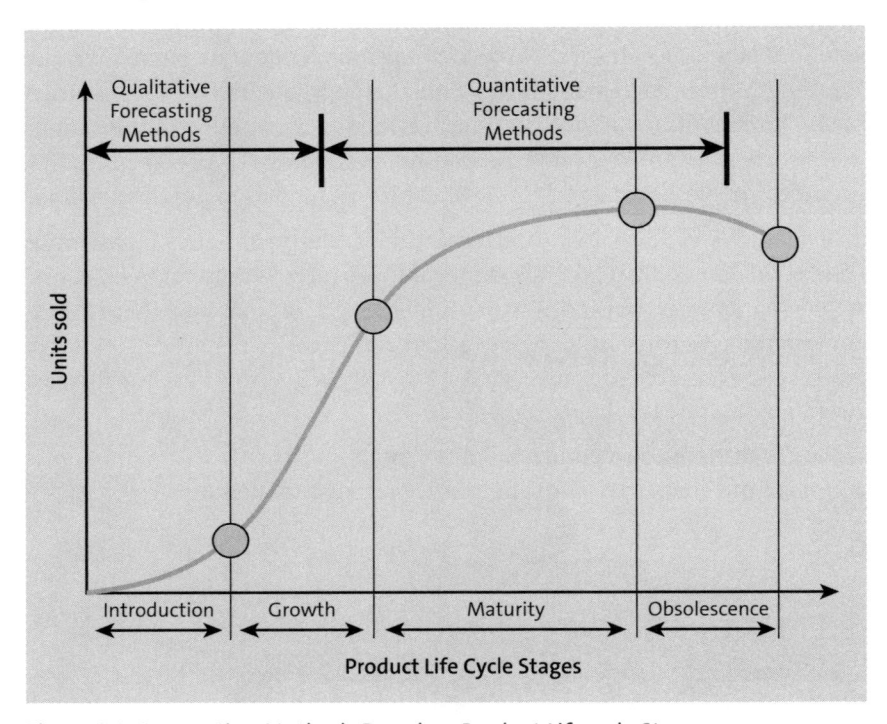

Figure 2.3 Forecasting Methods Based on Product Lifecycle Stage

An accurate demand forecast is the key to lower inventory levels, but companies should also invest in making sure that they are using the right forecasting methodology for a set of products. Maintenance of a good forecast for a product is usually the hardest part. Using forecastability analysis, planners can easily determine what forecasting methods should be employed for a given set of materials. They can determine what materials to focus on, leading to an overall improvement in forecast accuracy. Forecastability analysis can be done using ABC classification or Pareto analysis, along with the forecastability metric, such as coefficient of variation. Figure 2.4 shows a forecastability matrix.

Inventory planners can use the same methodology to control and reduce inventory. For example, for high-value and high-forecastability materials, inventory planners can rely completely on statistical forecasts to set up their replenishment strategies. Because the demand is highly predictable, a just in time (JIT) strategy can be used, helping them keep very low inventory for these high-value products. They can also share the forecast with their suppliers, who in turn can reduce the costs of production because they have a known demand for the material, thus reducing the overall inventory levels in the supply chain. For low-value products with unpredictable demand, inventory planners can keep high buffer stock. They can use a periodic review inventory control system for these products

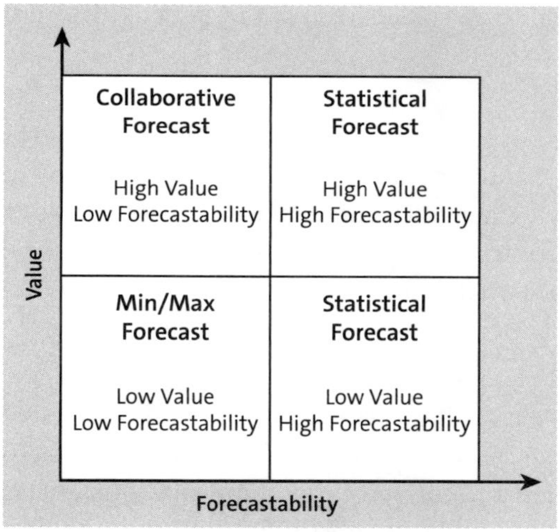

Value	Collaborative Forecast High Value Low Forecastability	Statistical Forecast High Value High Forecastability
	Min/Max Forecast Low Value Low Forecastability	Statistical Forecast Low Value High Forecastability

Forecastability

Figure 2.4 Forecastability Matrix

You must have heard it several times: the forecast is always wrong. So why should you bother even forecasting? The truth is that forecasts are accurate only to a certain degree. There's always an error component. Even though the forecast won't be 100% accurate, what you're attempting to do is get close to the actual demand. If you don't have a forecasting process in place, you might have a completely wrong estimate of customer demand, which leads to lost sales revenue, increased inventory levels, low service levels, and unhappy customers.

As important as forecast accuracy is, forecast errors are equally important. The *forecast error* is a control area that gives you an insight into how well you're forecasting. In quantitative forecasting methods, the error measurement can help you assign the correct forecasting model for a given product or group of products. The forecast error measure is also used to decide if you're forecasting at the right level of the hierarchy.

For example, you might have a lower error measurement when you forecast at a product family level compared to forecasting at a granular level.

There can be multiple reasons for forecast inaccuracy, some of which are well known:

- **Data**
  Statistical modeling is one of the most popular and effective ways of forecasting demand. For any kind of forecasting model, the first prerequisite is to have historical data. Because demand history is one of the key factors used in forecasting, the availability and accuracy of historical data becomes extremely important. There are multiple aspects of data that need to be considered with respect to historical data:

  - **What forms demand history?**
    A business should decide what type of customer orders should be considered as a basis for forecasting. This can include decisions like whether you want to include consignment orders and whether you want to include free-of-charge or sample sales in the forecasting process, as well as whether returns need to be included in the demand history and what dates need to be used.

  - **Demand data cleansing**
    It's important to make sure that the historical data is accurate. Inaccurate history means inaccurate demand forecasts. If the data being captured is outdated (i.e., contains obsolete products or locations), the history needs to be aligned to the new products to capture the demand correctly. Any cannibalization effects should be captured and the history should be corrected accordingly. Similarly, any other irregularities or outliers should be appropriately corrected to represent the most accurate demand history.

    For example, suppose you're in the raincoat business. You usually have your biggest sales in the summer period; sales are low in other seasons. This year there was a big hurricane in December, due to which your raincoat sales suddenly spiked. This is an exception event and such sales should not be used for forecasting demand.

  - **How much demand history to use?**
    In addition to defining what constitutes demand history, it's equally important to define how much history you need. If the products are seasonal in nature, it's important that at least three to four seasonal cycles are captured for statistical forecast models to calculate a forecast accurately. In most cases, at least two years of historical demand data is needed. Three is probably better.

- **Product life cycle**

  New product introductions, product phase-ins and phase-outs, and so on should be handled properly with respect to data. For example, if an existing product is being phased out and a new product is being phased in to replace it, the history of the old product should be transferred over to the new product to generate the forecast.

- **Using shipment data versus actual order data**

  This is the most common issue. Companies often use shipment data as historical data because it's easy to obtain. This gives the wrong indication of historical demand because, for example, the customer might have asked for a material in a certain month but you may have shipped it two months late due to production issues. The right practice for historical demand is to capture the customer order date and the date on which the customer requested delivery.

- **Forecast bias**

  Bias refers to the prejudice in the mind of the person giving the forecast input, and forecast accuracy is affected by that prejudice or bias. This is one forecasting issue that's widely prevalent across industries and is least admitted to. Because of this prejudice, the forecast is either consistently high or consistently too low.

  There are two main components of bias:

  - How much is the planner over- or underforecasting?
  - How many times in a row is the planner over- or underforecasting?

  One of the most common examples of bias is input from sales. The salesperson has to achieve his sales targets and ensure that the product being ordered by the customer is available. Thus, the forecast given by sales tends to have a positive bias—that is, the forecast will be greater than actual customer orders. Another reason for bias can be giving more importance to recent history than to total history. Recent trends may not be a true representation of future demand, which causes bias in the forecast.

  A *positive bias* means that the forecast is constantly higher than the actual demand. This means increased inventory because you're asking the organization to make more than you're selling. Similarly, *negative bias* means that the forecast is constantly lower than the actual customer demand. This means that you have a situation of constant stock-outs, missed customer orders, and low service levels. Because both positive and negative bias are undesirable, it's important that the organization strives to achieve zero bias.

- **Wrong level of forecasting**
  Forecasts generally are more accurate at the aggregate level than at the detailed level. At the most granular level, the demand is very erratic and irregular. There's too much noise at this level, and any forecast generated based on demand history at this level will be bad because of this excessive noise. At the aggregate level, the demand fluctuations or noise cancels out, and the demand or the history on which the forecast is based is more stable, leading to better forecasts.

  For example, you can probably generate a reasonably accurate forecast for a 12-month horizon at the product family level, but it's very difficult to achieve the same accuracy at the product-customer level. In other words, a top-down forecasting approach is more accurate than the bottom-up approach. Because one of the objectives of the forecast is to drive inventory, the organization should focus on finding the right middle level in the hierarchy to generate forecasts that are high enough to represent demand patterns and not so low as to cancel out the noise in the demand history. The forecast needs to contain enough details to provide a realistic view of the demand at the operational level.

- **Accountability**
  Holding the managers accountable for the forecast accuracy can help reduce forecast errors significantly. For example, the sales organization generally overforecasts to ensure material availability, which leads to higher inventory levels. If the sales organization isn't held accountable for that forecast, you'll be consistently driving higher inventory levels. Having a forecasting process in which all the stakeholders are held accountable for their contributions in generating the forecast can help in reduce forecast errors. This can be achieved by linking performance KPIs with forecast accuracy metrics.

2.1.2 Lead Time

Lead time is the time elapsed from the moment an order is placed to the moment an order is received. In any supply chain, there are three primary types of lead time:

- **Manufacturing lead time**
  For materials that are manufactured, the manufacturing lead time covers from the time a material is requested from the plant until the material is received. Manufacturing lead time is comprised of the following actions that have to be or may be taken:
  - Time to review the order
  - Time to generate or create an order

- Time to schedule an order
- Time for goods issue—collecting the components required to manufacture the product
- Time for any preproduction activity such as cleaning, setting up the machine, and so on
- Time for actual production
- Wait time—for example, drying paint
- Time for quality inspection
- Time for rework, if any
- Time for packaging
- Time for receiving the goods in the warehouse
- Time for any other administrative paperwork

As you can see, the manufacturing lead time consists of some administrative time along with actual production lead time. While setting up the manufacturing lead time, all these elements should be considered to produce an accurate actual lead time. The manufacturing lead time is somewhat in the control of the manufacturer. That is, the manufacturer can expedite an order if needed.

- **Supplier lead time**

    For materials that are purchased, the supplier lead time is the time from the PO placement to the time the goods are received. Supplier lead time is very critical to know. It's just not the transportation time from a location to your warehouse. Supplier lead time includes the following:

    - Time for decision and approvals before buying
    - Time to review the order
    - Time to place an order with the supplier
    - Time to receive an acknowledgment from the supplier
    - Time to receive the confirmation from the supplier
    - Time for the supplier to manufacture the material (the supplier manufacturing time would be like the manufacturing lead time)
    - Time to prepare shipping notes
    - Time to ship the order
    - Transportation time
    - Time to inspect the order
    - Time to receive the material in the warehouse
    - Expedition time, if any

Like manufacturing lead time, supplier lead time also consists of some administrative time along with actual lead time. While setting the supplier lead time for further use, these elements should be considered to have an accurate actual supplier lead time. Later in the chapter, we'll discuss how supplier lead time affects inventory levels.

- **Customer lead time**
  For the materials that are sold, the customer lead time covers from the time an item is requested by the customer until the customer receives the item. Like supplier lead time and manufacturing lead time, there are some administrative elements along with the actual delivery time to the customer. All these times should be considered while setting up the customer lead time.

As we explained in Chapter 1, any inventory in transit from one location to another or any inventory being worked on (work in progress) is known as *pipeline inventory* or *pipeline stock*. For example, when a supplier ships a material, the inventory is in transit until it reaches your warehouse. This inventory can't be used while in transit, but you may have to account for it in your inventory. Thus, the longer the lead time, the longer the pipeline stock.

For the materials that are purchased or manufactured, lead times have a direct impact on inventory levels. Consider a material with very low lead time. For such materials, companies can use the just-in-time strategy or Six Sigma very effectively. They can order or manufacture just enough material whenever there's a known demand, without any adverse effect on their operations. They therefore can reduce inventory levels considerably.

Lead time for manufactured or procured materials has a positive impact on inventory. Any increase in the lead time increases the inventory levels of the company. It increases the pipeline stock and hence the inventory levels. Figure 2.5 shows how the inventory levels increase with the increase in the lead time.

Very often, to gain a competitive advantage in the market companies want to reduce the lead time for delivery to the customer. To reduce this customer delivery lead time, companies keep inventory on hand for the finished goods for make-to-stock items and some semifinished goods for make-to-order items. They want to fulfill the customer order as soon as it arrives. But this comes at a cost. They must keep enough inventory on hand to fulfill the customer order, so customer lead times can have a negative impact on inventory. To reduce customer lead times, you must keep higher levels of inventory to be able to meet demand on time. In this scenario, a good demand forecast can help reduce inventory levels.

2.1 Primary Factors that Drive Inventory

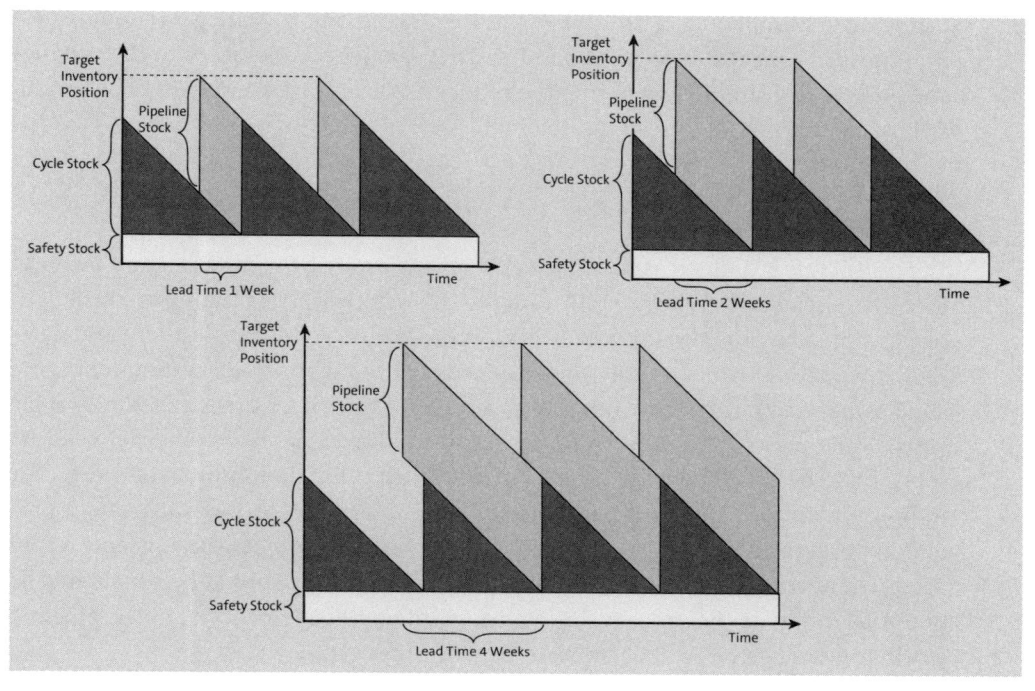

Figure 2.5 Effect of Lead Time on Inventory Levels

Lead times also have an indirect impact. For example, if the lead time of a product is three months, you would have to have a good forecast of the product three months ahead of time. As we all know, demand forecast is more accurate in the short term than in the long term, and longer lead times can put a great amount of pressure on inventory managers. They often assume the worst and order more inventory if they're not sure about the demand in the longer term.

All customers want lead times to be smaller than the total supply lead time. Knowing the accurate supply lead time is very important because you could end up stocking more. Companies usually take a supplier's word for the lead time. Sometimes the supplier also says the lead time is variable—for example, between 15 and 20 weeks. Should the inventory managers assume the worst and consider the supplier lead time to be 20 weeks? Consider this situation: the supply manager isn't too sure about the demand five months down the line. He adds a buffer to it because of uncertainty and procures more than the demand he anticipated because he doesn't want to be in a position where a stock-out might occur. All this stock is in the pipeline now, which leads to an increase in the total inventory level of the company.

2   Understanding Inventory Variables

Reducing the supplier lead time is even more necessary now. Managers should question the lead time the supplier is quoting. They should collaborate with the supplier and enter into a strategic agreement to reduce the lead time, which would be beneficial to both parties.

2.1.3   Order Cycle

The *order cycle* is defined as the time between one replenishment order and the next for a given material at a location in a supply chain network. Depending on the length of this time, the order cycle could be longer or shorter. For example, there are materials in your supply chain that you may order once every week, so the order cycle equals one week, and other ones you order maybe once a month, so the order cycle equals one month. The order cycle for a procured material from external vendors represents the time between the placement of two subsequent purchase orders; for in-house manufactured items, it represents the time between two subsequent production orders. In manufacturing scenarios, if you're leveraging the concepts of the production wheel or rhythm wheel in your planning, they should be considered as potential inputs to the order cycle. Inventory categories such as cycle stock, pipeline stock, and safety stock will be impacted by the order cycles.

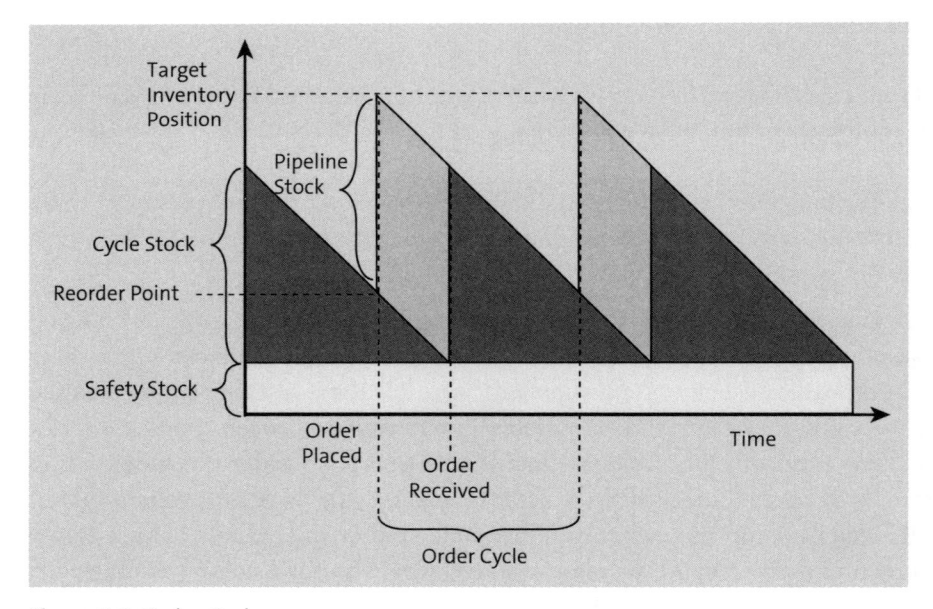

Figure 2.6 Order Cycle

Figure 2.6 shows an inventory diagram for a typical replenishment cycle. As you can see, the time between the two replenishment orders represents the order cycle. The order cycle and the order lead time are considered while calculating safety stock. As such, the order cycle length, when combined with other drivers that we'll discuss later in this chapter in detail, such as demand variability and customer service level, could increase the amount of safety stock to be carried during this period.

2.1.4 Variability

As we move toward globalization, supply chains are becoming increasingly complex in nature. There are uncertainties at every stage of the supply chain: suppliers, manufacturers, customers, distributors, and so on. There are two kinds of uncertainties in a supply chain: quantity and time. Uncertain quantities arise when the quantity of the demand or supply is variable; for example, the demand forecast quantity could be higher or lower than the quantity you expected to sell, or the supplier may send you a partial delivery, or part of the delivery may be damaged while in transit. Uncertain times arise when the delivery time of the demand or supply varies from the expected time. For example, you were expecting to receive a shipment on a certain day, but due to road work, you received your shipment five days late. *Variability* is defined as how much your actuals vary from your projections.

To protect against this variability in the supply chain, planners keep a buffer inventory so that downstream operations are not affected. This inventory is known as *safety inventory* or *safety stock*. The higher the variability, the higher the safety stock, and thus the higher the inventory levels. Uncertainty in demand and supply are by far the most critical factors that lead to an increase in inventory levels. We'll discuss variabilities and their impact in detail later in the chapter.

2.1.5 Service Level Target

A *service level* is defined as the probability of non-stock-out over a planning period. A service level also denotes the percentage of time you will fulfill your customer demands from inventory on hand before the next order arrives. Setting up the service level target is a strategic decision for the whole organization, not just inventory managers. Setting up the right service level can be very difficult because multiple factors can affect it. In the following sections, we'll look at some factors that affect this choice.

Current Service Levels

Knowing the current service levels and the current inventory position is very critical. Without knowing where you are, you can't decide where you want to be. There are multiple metrics that can be used to measure product availability, including the following:

- **Fill rate**
  The *fill rate* is defined as the percentage of product demand fulfilled from the current inventory. The fill rate is calculated over a specific volume of demand rather than time. For example, out of 1,000 units ordered by customers, 850 units were fulfilled from the inventory on hand, so the fill rate is 85%.

> **Fill Rate**
>
> The formula to calculate fill rate is as follows:
>
> *Fill rate = Demand fulfilled from inventory on hand ÷ Total demand*

- **Order fill rate**
  The *order fill rate*, also known as the *non-stock-out probability*, is defined as the percentage of customer orders delivered in full from available inventory. The order fill rate is calculated over a specific volume of customer orders received. For example, out of 100 orders received, 90 orders were delivered in full, so the order fill rate is 90%. If a company sells only one product, there isn't much difference between the order fill rate and the fill rate. The difference is noteworthy when the company sells multiple products to customers, however.

> **Order Fill Rate**
>
> The formula to calculate the order fill rate is as follows:
>
> *Order fill rate = Number of orders fulfilled from inventory on hand ÷ Total number of orders*

- **Cycle service level**
  The *cycle service level* is defined as the percentage of the replenishment cycles in which the customer demand was fulfilled in full. The *replenishment cycle* is defined as the time between two successive replenishment deliveries. This metric should

be calculated over various replenishment cycles. Let's consider an example of a retail store in which inventory is replenished every Thursday evening. Over the past 10 weeks, items went out of stock before Thursday three times. If a customer came by on Wednesday in any of those weeks for the out-of-stock item, they had to wait until Friday morning to get it. This means that 3 out of 10 cycles there will be a stock-out situation, so the cycle service level is 70%.

> **Cycle Service Level**
>
> The formula to calculate cycle service level is as follows:
>
> *Cycle service level = Number of replenishment cycles in which customer demand was met ÷ Total number of replenishment cycles*

Often there's a question about what the right measure is for your kind of business. If you're in a complete B2B type of environment, then it makes sense to use fill rate to measure your service level because your customers can accept partial delivery of an order to make sure that their operations continue.

Cost of Inventory

The cost of servicing the customer is a very important metric that needs to be considered when you're setting up your target service level. As is evident from the definition of service levels, if you want higher customer service levels, you need to keep higher inventory levels. The cost is usually associated with higher safety stocks and thus higher inventory cost. Other costs associated with the cost of inventory are the holding cost, ordering cost, and obsolescence cost. The inventory holding cost is the cost to hold inventory. Ordering costs are the costs associated with ordering materials, such as the cost to raise a purchase requisition, cost of phone calls to the vendors, cost of shipments, and so on. Obsolescence costs are costs incurred if inventory isn't sold. This is most common in industries involving perishable products. For example, if food isn't sold by its expiration date, it's considered waste.

Inventory is a form of investment—a necessary investment—and it ties up the working capital. This tied-up money could have been used for a new promotion, to invest in a production facility, for research and development, to create a new product, or for financial instruments. Inventory costs are therefore opportunity costs as well.

Figure 2.7 shows the relationship between the cost of inventory and the service level.

2   Understanding Inventory Variables

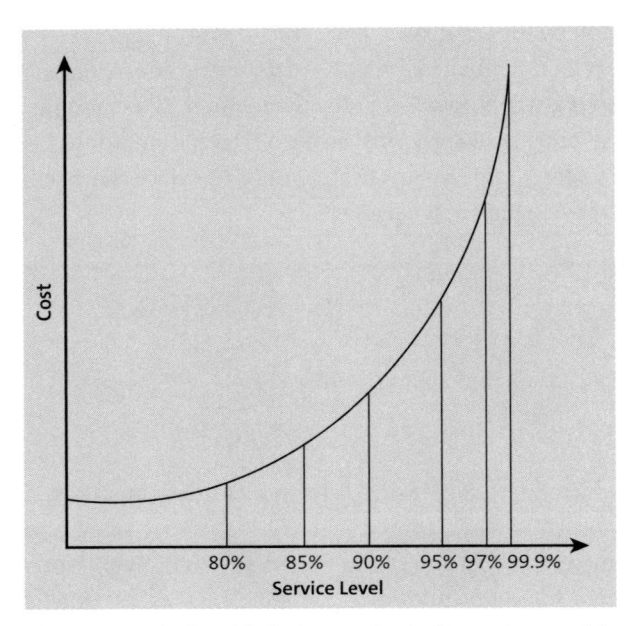

Figure 2.7 Relationship between Cost of Inventory and Service Level

As you can see, going from a 95% service level to a 97% service level involves a considerable amount of cost. Achieving a 100% service level is almost impossible. Companies need to create a balance between cost of inventory and service levels.

Cost of Lost Sales or Order Expedition Cost

In the case of a stock-out situation, another cost element to measure is the cost of lost sales or cost of expediting delivery of an order. Lost sales are defined as missed sales when you were out of stock of a product when the customer wanted it. Lost sales value is calculated as a margin loss when the sale is missed. For example, say a product sells for 20 dollars and the profit margin on that product is about 20%. Lost sales are calculated as 20% of 20 dollars, or 4 dollars.

Some organizations have a policy not to lose sales when customer orders come in; they do everything possible to meet the customer demand. Companies try to speed up the upstream operations and activities to deliver to the customer. These costs are also considered when setting up the target service level. These costs could include the cost of shifting to a costlier mode of transport, for example. Figure 2.8 shows the relationship between the cost of lost sales or the cost of expediting an order and the service level offered.

2.1 Primary Factors that Drive Inventory

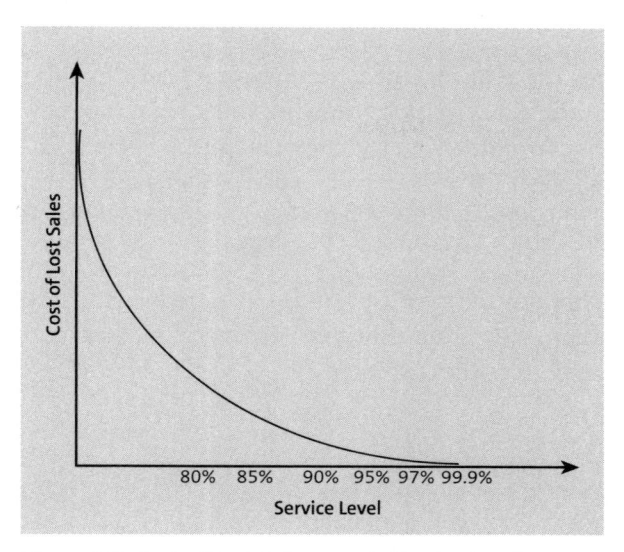

Figure 2.8 Cost of Lost Sales versus Service Level

Adding the cost of lost sales or expedition to the cost of service, you get the total cost to serve the customer. Figure 2.9 depicts the total cost to serve versus the service level. The optimal service level is the lowest sum of cost of services plus cost of lost sales or expediting orders.

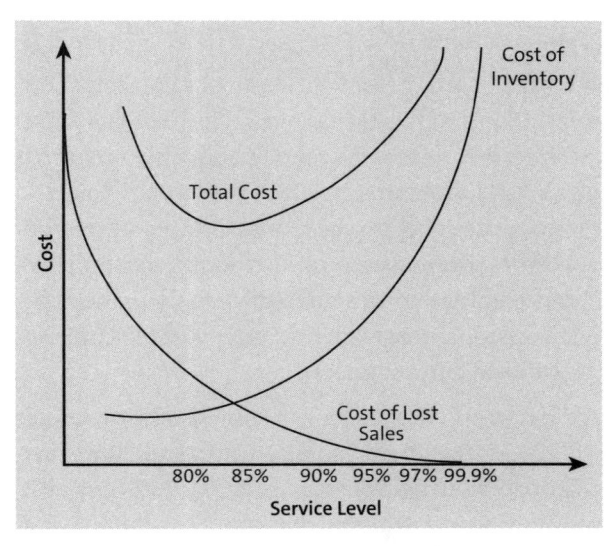

Figure 2.9 Total Cost versus Service Level

Lead Time

When deciding on a service level, the replenishment strategy and lead time play important roles. They help you make your decision by giving you insight into how much time would it take to come out of a stock-out situation and the cost of expediting service. When lead times are longer for a product, companies generally have a higher service level because it's difficult to get out of the stock-out situation once it arises on those items.

When companies have multiple options for means of transport to reduce the lead time in case of a stock-out situation, they often shift to costly means of transport such as air freight to deliver the product to the customer.

Market Competition

Market competition can also influence your choice of target service level. Take a grocery store, for example: if you can't get food you want in one store, you go to another one because you need food and you have other options. This could lead to a customer loyalty shift to the competing store, thus leading to the loss of the customer completely. In this situation, grocery stores need to have enough stock to meet customer demands and ensure that the customer doesn't shop instead at the neighboring store. In a B2B environment, this is very important: you risk of losing a chunk of your business to a competitor if you can't meet customer demand.

Differential Customer Service Levels

Service level setting is one of the most important strategic decisions you can make. To achieve a balance between the cost to serve and service levels, you can have differentiated customer service level strategies for different segments of customers. For example, consider airline and hotel loyalty programs, in which they award points to the customer based on the miles flown or nights stayed along with the number of dollars spent. There are different customer tiers based on the points accumulated. You may have witnessed the difference in the services offered when you travel on a plane or are waiting for check-in. The customers at higher tiers get the first choice of seats or room preference, plus a plethora of extra services.

Segmentation of customers can be based on the volume of business each customer gives you. You can have a higher service level for high-value customers and lower service levels for customers who order occasionally. Sometimes to win new business, companies have higher service levels for new customers that could be strategic customers in the future.

2.2 Breakdown of Variability Drivers

As we discussed in the previous section, safety stock is the inventory that's required to mitigate the variability in the supply chain. Determining the variability is more valuable than the accuracy of demand or delivery by the supplier. Variability has a more direct impact on the inventory levels compared to the actual forecast itself. There are three different types of variability that drive safety stock:

- Demand variability
- Lead time variability
- Service variability

We'll be discussing each of these variabilities in detail ahead and their impact on inventory levels, primarily safety stocks.

2.2.1 Demand Variability

Imagine you could predict the future and you know exactly what's going to happen: you could be the richest person on the planet. You could predict the stock prices, or you could predict what cards the dealer is going to draw in blackjack, or the result when you roll the dice in craps. You could predict when there would be a natural disaster and save millions of lives. In reality, however, you know that nobody can predict the future accurately.

Demand uncertainty or variability occurs when you can't predict accurately how much your customers need. There can be many reasons you can't predict the demand. It could be the nature of your business, or it could be external factors beyond your control. Consider a retail store selling clothes and fashion accessories: You could see a sudden drop in sales because there's a new style on the market and customers want to buy it. Or another store may have had a friends and family sale, which led to a drop in your sales. In the recent past, people reported a battery flaw in Samsung phones, and ultimately the phone was banned everywhere, especially on flights. This led customers to shift to Apple phones, and suddenly there was a demand for iPhones that was unprecedented. Demand can fluctuate up or down. The fluctuations could be even greater when you increase your demand horizon.

To manage these fluctuations in the short term, companies need to keep safety stock. They often face the dilemma of how much safety stock they need. Consider an example of an electronic retail store that sells noise-cancelling headphones and smart TVs. To save on the ordering costs and get a bulk discount for headphones, the retailer

2   Understanding Inventory Variables

orders 500 headphones and 500 smart TVs, and it takes about three weeks for the manufacturer to deliver the order. The average demand for headphones and smart TVs is the same: 100 units per week. For the smart TV, the retailer had a massive issue with stock-outs at some points and sometimes had excess stock; for headphones, he didn't have much of problem. The retailer decided to keep a buffer stock of 100 units each. He solved the problem of the stock-out but faced a risk: if the manufacturer came up with a new version or a competitor released a new product, he would have to sell the units at a loss. So how much safety stock should he keep?

In the following sections, we'll discuss how to measure the demand variability based on the past historical demand pattern and the impact of this variability on the safety stock.

Measuring Demand Variability

Let's look at the demand variability by looking at the historical actual sales of both products. Table 2.1 shows the historical demand of the smart TVs and headphones.

Week	Smart TV	Headphones
1	110	90
2	90	50
3	95	150
4	95	60
5	101	140
6	102	130
7	101	70
8	105	60
9	110	140
10	99	110
11	102	120
12	90	80

Table 2.1 Actual Sales History of Two Products

Week	Smart TV	Headphones
13	93	115
14	102	95
15	105	90
Total	1500	1500
Average	100	100

Table 2.1 Actual Sales History of Two Products (Cont.)

As you can see in Figure 2.10, even though both the products have an average demand of 100 units per week, the demand fluctuations are higher in the case of headphones as compared to smart TVs. The demand for smart TVs varies from 90 to 110 units per week, whereas for headphones the demand varies from 50 to 150 units.

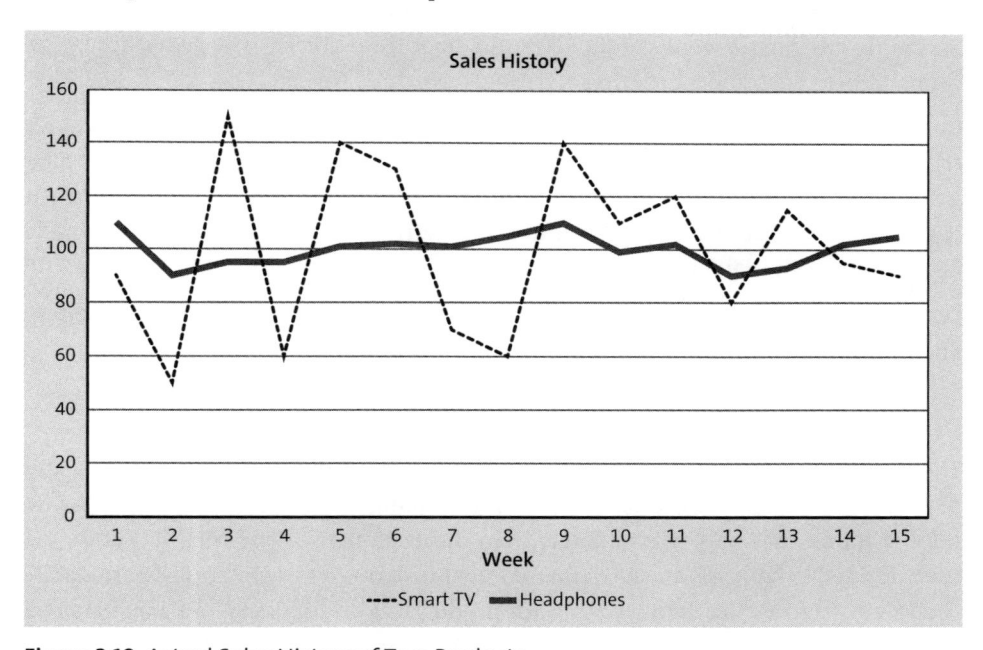

Figure 2.10 Actual Sales History of Two Products

The lead time is three weeks for both products, so considering that the average demand is 100 per week, the retailer needs to order whenever he's left with 300 units.

2 Understanding Inventory Variables

Over three weeks, if the retailer sells exactly 300 units, he shouldn't have a stock-out or excess situation. Let's look how many of each product can he sell over three weeks in Table 2.2.

Product	Minimum Demand	Maximum Demand
Smart TVs	270	330
Headphones	150	450

Table 2.2 Range of Demand for Headphones and Smart TVs

If the demand for headphones was 450 for those three weeks, the retailer would have lost the margin on 150 units, provided they had no safety stock. If the real demand was 150 units for the headphones, the retailer would be carrying an excess of 150 units along with the order of 500 units he already placed.

So, should the retailer keep a safety stock inventory of 150 units of headphones, assuming customers would order 450 units over three weeks? The answer is in the probability of customers ordering 450 units over three weeks.

Consider the weather forecast. It never says it's going to rain or not; it always states the probability of precipitation. If the weather forecast says the probability of precipitation is 5% you wouldn't even bother to carry an umbrella or change your plans. But if it said the probability of precipitation is 80%, then you would carry an umbrella because there's a high probability that it will rain.

Let's look at how this probability can be applied in the context of demand planning and how it can be used to determine the safety stock.

Demand Distribution

The retailer decides to analyze an additional historical demand for smart TVs and headphones he sold in the past two years. Looking at the historical demand, the retailer found that only two or three times did customer orders total 150 units. He then decided to look at how the demand was spread out for the historical periods. He found a pattern in the demand for both products. Both products had a bell-shaped curve, as shown in Figure 2.11 and Figure 2.12. However, the spread of the bell curve is larger for headphones as compared to smart TVs. This means the demand for headphones has much more variability as compared to the demand for smart TVs.

2.2 Breakdown of Variability Drivers

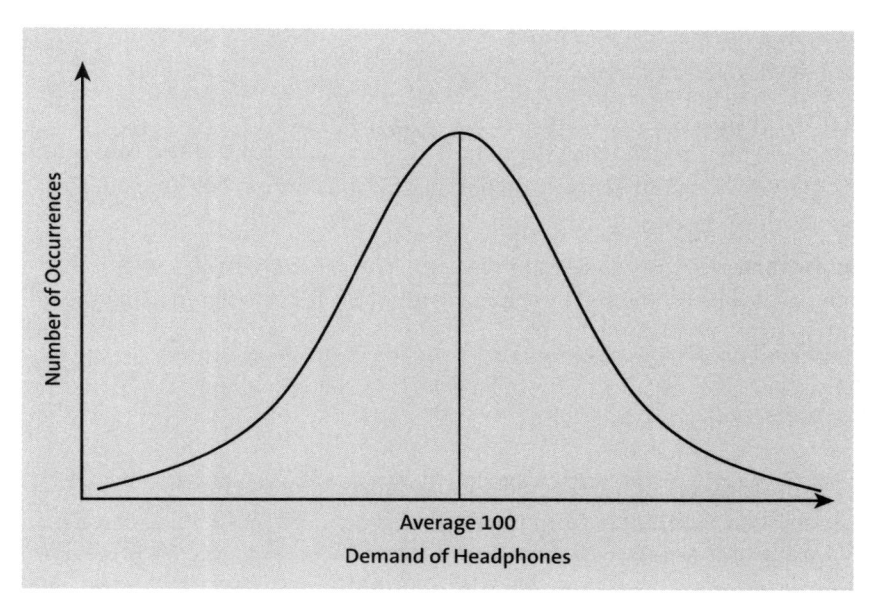

Figure 2.11 Historical Demand Distribution for Headphones

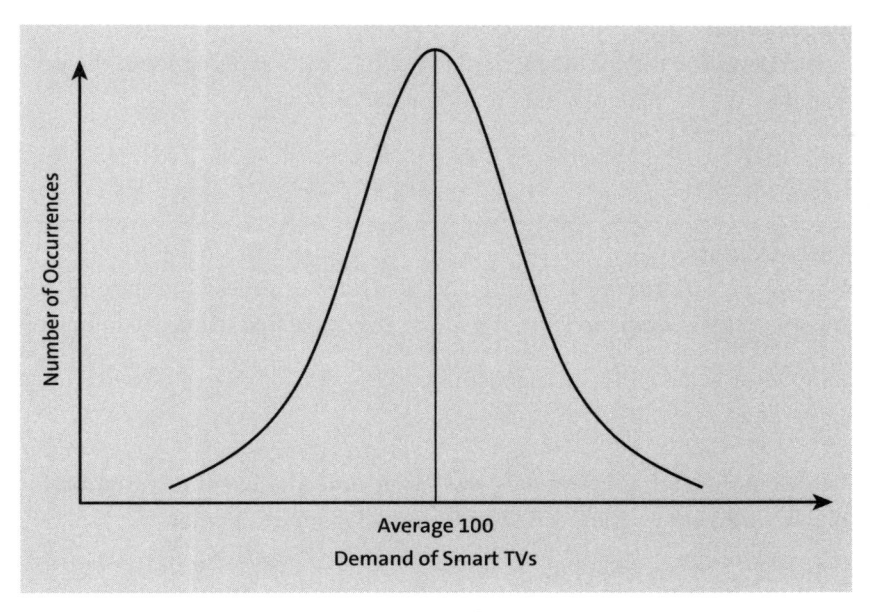

Figure 2.12 Historical Demand Distribution for Smart TVs

79

Let's go over what normal distribution is and how to calculate the safety stock using the standard deviation and mean:

- **Normal distribution**
  In a *normal distribution*, most of the data is concentrated toward the center and the rest tapers down symmetrically on both sides. The curve is bell-shaped. This is the most common form of distribution.

  Mean or average
  The *mean* or *average* is denoted by the mu symbol (μ). It's calculated using the following formula:

  $$\mu = \frac{\sum x}{N}$$

- **Variance**
  Variance is the measure of how spread out the data is from the mean. It's the average of the squared differences from the mean. It's denoted by sigma squared (σ^2), and its formula is as follows:

  $$\sigma^2 = \frac{\sum (x - \mu)^2}{N}$$

- **Standard deviation**
  The *standard deviation* is denoted by sigma (σ), and it's the square root of the variance calculated. It's calculated using the following formula:

  $$\sigma = \sqrt{\frac{\sum (x - \mu)^2}{N}}$$

- **Coefficient of variation**
  The *coefficient of variation of demand* (CV) is a dimensionless measure of the extent of variability of demand from the mean. It's calculated using the following formula:

  $$CV = \frac{\sigma}{\mu}$$

Let's now calculate the variance, standard deviation, and coefficient of variation for our example. Table 2.3 shows these values calculated for smart TV sales.

Week	Smart TVs Sold	Difference from Mean	Square of Difference
1	110	10	100
2	90	-10	100
3	95	-5	25
4	95	-5	25
5	101	1	1
6	102	2	4
7	101	1	1
8	105	5	25
9	110	10	100
10	99	-1	1
11	102	2	4
12	90	-10	100
13	93	-7	49
14	102	2	4
15	105	5	25
Total	1500	0	564
Average	100	0	37.6
Standard Deviation			6.13
Coefficient of Variation			0.06 or 6%

Table 2.3 Mean, Variance, Standard Deviation, and Coefficient of Variation for Smart TV Sales

Table 2.4 shows these values calculated for headphone sales.

2   Understanding Inventory Variables

Week	Headphones Sold	Difference from Mean	Square of Difference
1	90	-10	100
2	50	-50	2500
3	150	50	2500
4	60	-40	1600
5	140	40	1600
6	130	30	900
7	70	-30	900
8	60	-40	1600
9	140	40	1600
10	110	10	100
11	120	20	400
12	80	-20	400
13	115	15	225
14	95	-5	25
15	90	-10	100
Total	1500	0	14550
Average	100		970
Standard Deviation			31.14
Coefficient of Variation			0.31

Table 2.4 Mean, Variance, Standard Deviation, and Coefficient of Variation for Headphone Sales

The coefficient of variation is used to compare variability between the two sets of demand or between two different SKUs with completely different sales patterns and average demands. As you can see, the headphones have a coefficient of variation of 0.31 or 31%, compared to 6% for smart TVs. This means the demand for headphones is more variable than the demand for smart TVs.

2.2 Breakdown of Variability Drivers

Finally, let's discuss the empirical rule. In statistics, the *empirical rule*, also known as the *three standard deviation rule* or the *68–95–99.7 rule*, states that almost all data will fall within three standard deviations. Empirical rules in terms of demand forecast state the following:

- Demand will fall within ±1 standard deviation 68% of the time.
- Demand will fall within ±2 standard deviations 95% of the time.
- Demand will fall within ±3 standard deviations 99.7 % of the time.

Figure 2.13 shows the empirical rule in a normal distribution curve.

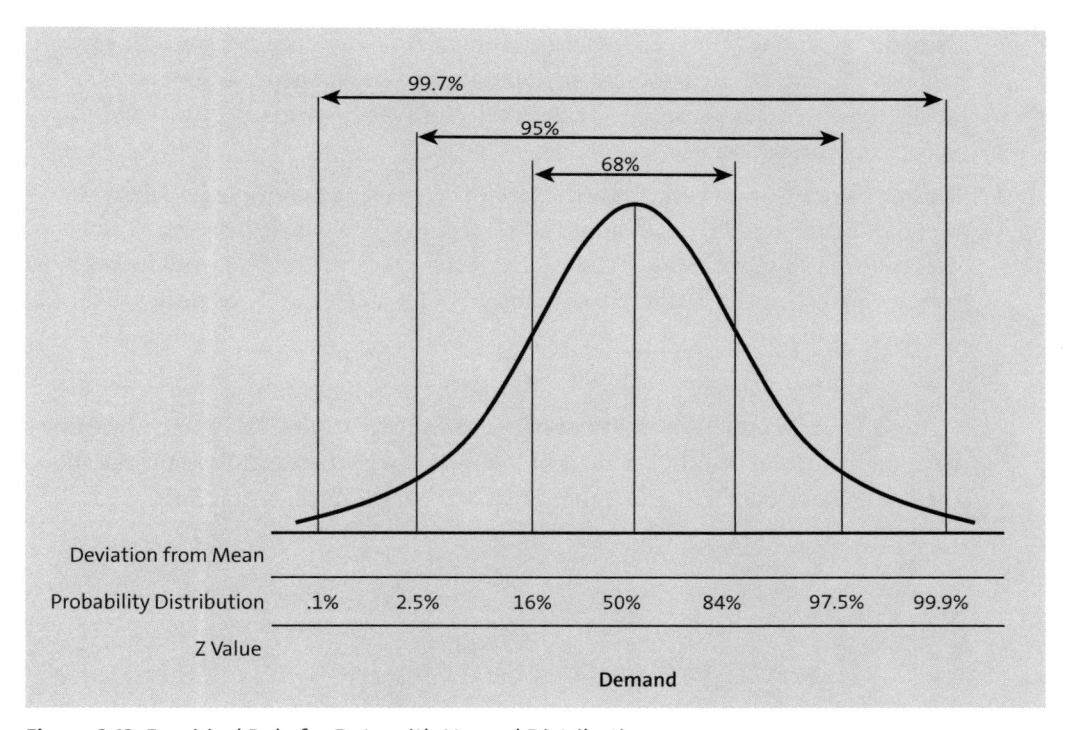

Figure 2.13 Empirical Rule for Data with Normal Distribution

The number of standard deviations away from the mean is known as the *z-score* or *service factor*. The relationship between Z, standard deviation, and mean is shown in the following formula:

$$Z = \frac{X - \mu}{\sigma}$$

2 Understanding Inventory Variables

The service factor is used as a multiplier with the standard deviation to calculate a specific quantity to meet a specific service level.

X is the deviation from the mean. Using the empirical rule along with the the *z-score*, we can come up with the value of deviation from the mean via the following formula:

$$X = Z\sigma + \mu$$

Safety Stock

Let's consider the demand distribution curve for headphones and smart TVs. In any week, if you don't keep any safety stock, 50% of the time you can fulfill your customer demand, assuming you keep inventory equivalent to average demand. This means you're servicing your customers at a 50% service level. There's a 50% chance that you'll receive customer orders greater than the average demand of 100 and thus a 50% chance of stock-outs.

Now let's say you want to increase the service level. Using the empirical rule, we know that 68% of demand for headphones and smart TVs would be in between ±1 standard deviation. At +1 sigma, 50% + 34% = 84% of the times the demand will be below +1 sigma. Calculating the maximum demand at Z = 1 (for 84%), we once again use the following formula:

$$X = Z\sigma + \mu$$

Figure 2.14 shows the probability of demand and stock-outs. The green area shows what demands can be fulfilled at an 84% service level, whereas the white area shows the risk of stock-outs if the customer's requests exceed available product.

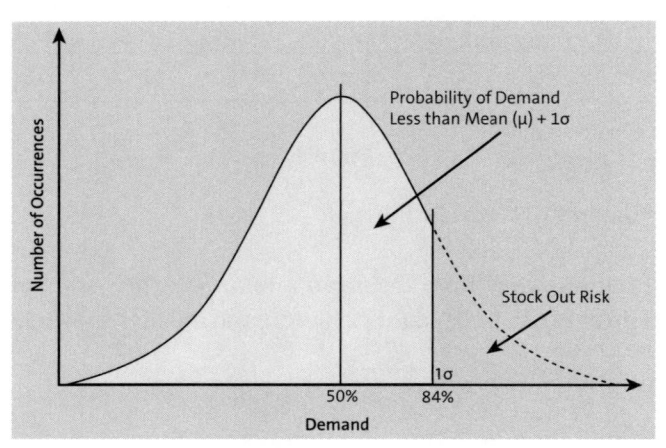

Figure 2.14 Probability of Demand and Stock-Out Risk at 84% Service Level

For Smart TVs	For Headphones
X = 100 + × 6.1	X = 100 + × 31.1
X = 106.1	X = 131.1

Table 2.5 Demand Calculation

Table 2.5 shows the calculation of average demand plus one standard deviation. This means during any given week, 84% of the customer demand would be below 131 for headphones and below 106 for smart TVs. There's a 16% chance of having a stock-out situation if you have a starting inventory equivalent to this number. Because the lead time is three weeks, we need to account for variability of demand in that time. Assuming the demands during these three weeks are independent of each other, the following formula can be used:

Average Demand During Lead Time = Lead Time × μ_{Demand}

The standard deviation during the three weeks would be calculated as follows:

$\sigma_{Demand\ during\ lead\ time} = \sqrt{Lead\ Time} \times \sigma_{Demand}$

The safety stock to achieve the target of an 84% service level over three weeks would be equal to the following:

Safety Stock = Z × $\sqrt{Lead\ Time} \times \sigma_{Demand}$

For the headphones, then, the calculation would be as follows:

Safety Stock = 1 × √3 × 31.1 ~ 54

For smart TVs, the calculation would be as follows:

Safety Stock = 1 × √3 × 6.1 ~ 11

Therefore, to achieve an 84% service level, we need a safety stock of 54 units of headphones and 11 units of smart TVs. If a retailer uses the reorder point method to replenish his stock, his reorder point would be the sum of the average demand during the lead time and safety stock required:

- *For headphones:* Reorder point = 300 + 54
- *For smart TVs:* Reorder point = 300 + 11

Using the same methodology, let's compare the safety stock required at different service levels, as shown in Table 2.6.

Service Level	Z-Score	Safety Stock for Smart TVs	Safety Stock for Headphones
70%	0.52	5	28
75%	0.67	7	36
84%	1.00	11	54
85%	1.04	11	56
90%	1.28	14	69
93%	1.48	16	80
95%	1.65	17	89
97%	1.88	20	101
99%	2.33	25	126
99.5%	2.58	27	139
99.9%	3.00	32	162

Table 2.6 Safety Stock Requirements at Different Service Levels

In Table 2.6, you can see that any marginal increase beyond a 97% service level results in a huge amount of safety stock. This is where the organization needs to make a judgment call about service levels and safety stock to keep.

Seasonality in Demand

In our example, we used variability in the demand to calculate the safety stock, and we used the standard deviation of the demand to come up with the safety stock. This is accurate only when the demand for the product is constant throughout the year. Now let's consider a toy store. During the holiday season, the toy store sells the largest number of toys. Its sales in the holiday season are higher than the sales during the rest of the year. There's an inherent variability in the demand if you consider seasonality. Figure 2.15 shows an example of seasonality in demand. If we use the standard deviation of this highly variable demand to calculate the safety stock, we'd be stocking a lot of toys all year. In such a situation, forecast and forecast errors can be used to calculate the safety stock, as we'll explain in the next section.

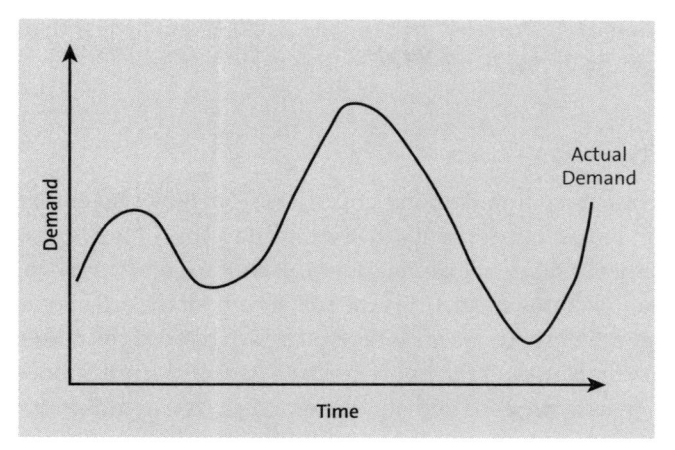

Figure 2.15 Seasonal Demand Pattern

Forecast and Forecast Error in Safety Stock Calculation

As we discussed, forecast error is just as important as the forecast. In our toy store example, we noted that if we just take the demand as is, the variability could be very high. Now let's assume the toy store predicted the seasonality and the owner places orders with manufacturers based on the demand he predicts. In that case, the variability of the demand from the forecast would be lessened. In Figure 2.16, you can see that the toy store forecast was very close to the actual demand. If you measure the variability of demand each week individually from the demand he forecasted, it would be much lower, meaning he doesn't have to keep very high levels of inventory to avoid a stock-out situation.

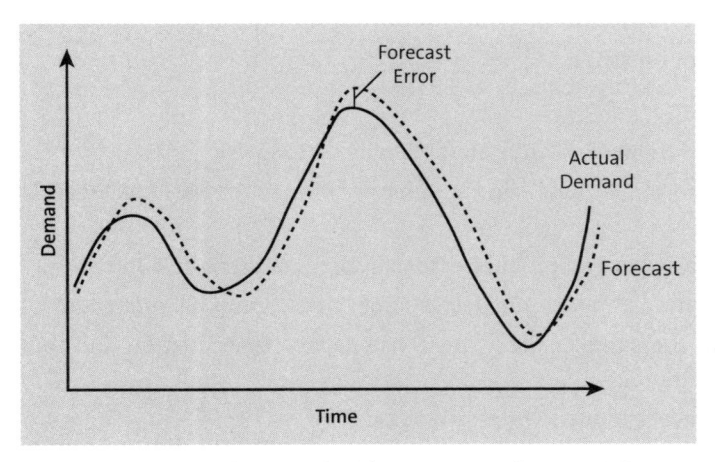

Figure 2.16 Seasonal Demand with Forecast and Forecast Error

87

Thus, if the standard deviation of the forecast error is calculated, it will be less than the standard deviation of just the demand, resulting in lower safety stock.

2.2.2 Lead Time Variability

In the previous section, we discussed how demand uncertainty can affect inventory levels, but it isn't always the demand uncertainty that we need to consider. We also need to consider the supply uncertainty. For example, for a cell phone manufacturer in China, a supplier in Brazil manufactures and delivers the LED screen for the cell phone. For some reason, the shipment of the LED screens is delayed, which halts all cell phone production. The manufacturer exhausts all the safety stock he has for the cell phones because the safety stock only accounted for demand uncertainty. The manufacturer didn't consider supply uncertainty when deciding on an amount for safety stock.

As you know, there are two kinds of supply uncertainty: quantity and lead time. In this section, we'll focus on lead time uncertainty—that is, variability in the lead time, the time within which the product will be delivered. Managers need to account for lead time variability when setting safety stock targets. Lead time variability can be either production lead time variability or supplier lead time variability.

Some of the reasons for production lead time variability are as follows:

- A machine breaks down, causing delays.
- MRO supplies are not available or delayed for any kind of repair.
- Delays occur in issuing goods for production.
- A component used in the production process isn't available, so all production is on hold.
- Delays occur in quality inspections.
- Labor is unavailable or on strike.
- Union issues arise.

Some of the reasons for supplier lead time variability are as follows:

- A truck used to transport materials from a supplier location to the warehouse breaks down.
- Weather issues can delay your shipments, especially air or sea freight shipments.
- International shipments are most often delayed due to customs and border control.
- Production issues at the supplier plant can cause delays in production and thus delays in fulfilling your order.
- Variations in lead time occur due to human error.
- Shipments can be lost while in transit.

2.2 Breakdown of Variability Drivers

- Damage while in transit can lead to delays because you have to reorder materials after you receive a shipment.
- Natural disasters like earthquakes or hurricanes can delay shipments.

The most prominent reasons for variability in supplier lead time are production issues at the supplier and shortages at the supplier. If the suppliers have stock on hand, they ship it right away. The only time needed is the transportation time. If the supplier doesn't have the stock or production is in progress at the supplier location, the lead time is highly variable. As soon as the supplier manufactures the product, the supplier ships it. Many suppliers quote the lead time much higher than actual transportation time because it also includes the manufacturing lead time.

All these reasons contribute to the variability in the lead time. This variability should also be accounted for before deciding on safety stock requirements. Unfortunately, many organizations don't do a good job of calculating lead time variability: they don't track the date an order was placed, the requested delivery date on that order, the actual delivery date of the order, the number of times they requested expedited shipping, and so on. They receive multiple orders every week or every two weeks from the same vendor, which adds to the problem of calculating the deviation in the lead time. The procurement manager also doesn't track incoming shipments until she sees a material shortage. A good system is required to track and calculate the lead time variability instead of taking the supplier's word for it or any other approximation because it affects the amount of safety stock you need.

Variability of lead time has an impact on safety stock during lead time. Figure 2.17 shows the effect of lead time variability.

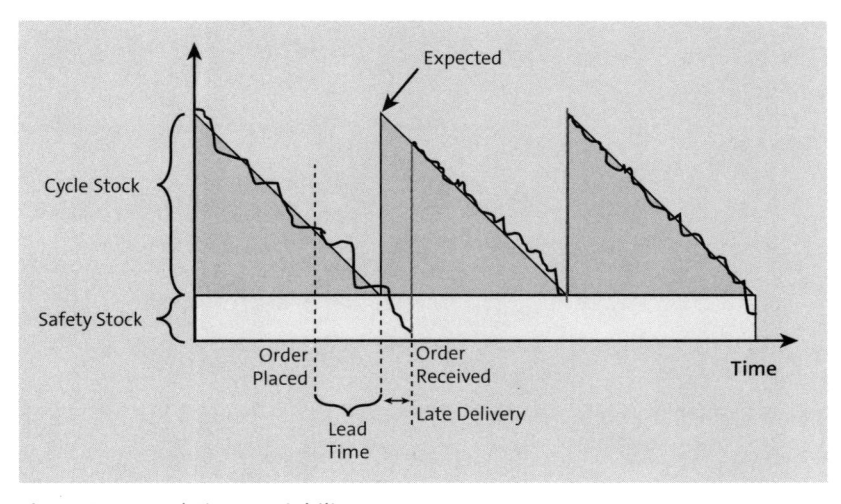

Figure 2.17 Lead Time Variability

2   Understanding Inventory Variables

As you can see, the probability of a stock-out situation is at the end of the lead time—that is, around the time that you're expecting the order to be received. If the order isn't received on time, that can delay your downstream operations or fulfillment of customer demand.

In our previous example, while calculating the demand uncertainty we assumed that the supplier had a constant lead time of three weeks. The retailer also recorded the lead time for each order he placed. He recorded the lead times for headphones and smart TVs separately.

In Table 2.7, you can see that the lead time variability for smart TVs is much higher than the lead time variability for headphones.

Order	Smart TVs Lead Time in Weeks	Headphones Lead Time in Weeks	Difference for Smart TVs	Difference for Headphones
1	3.1	3.1	0.1	0.1
2	3.2	3.2	0.2	0.2
3	4	2.9	1	-0.1
4	3.2	2.8	0.2	-0.2
5	3.4	2.9	0.4	-0.1
6	2.4	3.2	-0.6	0.2
7	2.6	3.1	-0.4	0.1
8	2.2	2.9	-0.8	-0.1
9	2.9	2.8	-0.1	-0.2
10	3	3.1	0	0.1
Total	30	30		
Average	3	3		
Variance			2.42	0.22
Standard Deviation			1.55	0.47

Table 2.7 Lead Time Variability for Smart TVs and Headphones

Assuming that the lead time is normally distributed, just like the demand distribution, then 68% of the time lead time is ±1 standard deviation, 95% of time the lead time is ±2 standard deviations, and 99.7% of the time the lead time is ±3 standard deviations.

The standard deviation of the demand variability and lead time variability is defined as follows:

$$\sigma_{Demand\ during\ lead\ time} = Z \times \sqrt{Lead\ Time \times \sigma_{Demand}^2 + \mu_{Demand}^2 \sigma_{Lead\ time}^2}$$

The safety stock is then defined as follows:

$$Safety\ Stock = Z \times \sqrt{Lead\ Time \times \sigma_{Demand}^2 + \mu_{Demand}^2 \sigma_{Lead\ time}^2}$$

Using this formula, let's calculate the safety stock for headphones and smart TVs at an 84% percent service level, as follows:

- For headphones:

$$Safety\ Stock = 1 \times \sqrt{3 \times 6.1^2 + 100^2 \times 1.55^2} \sim 155$$

$$Safety\ Stock = 1 \times \sqrt{3 \times 31.1^2 + 100^2 \times .47^2} \sim 71$$

- For smart TVs:

$$Safety\ Stock = Z \times \sqrt{Lead\ Time \times \sigma_{Demand}^2 + \mu_{Demand}^2 \sigma_{Lead\ time}^2}$$

As you can see, by just including the lead time variability, the safety stock requirement has become very high. Compared to demand uncertainty, lead time variability has a much greater impact in this example. If we used demand uncertainty, the headphones had a higher safety stock requirement, but after including the lead time variability in the calculation, smart TVs have a greater risk of stock-out.

2.2.3 Service Variability

So far, we've focused on the customer service level, demand, and supply uncertainty. However, there's another element that influences the safety stock requirements. In today's global supply chain, all organizations have multiple satellite warehouses that supply products to customers. They have plants supplying a central warehouse, which in turn supplies these satellite warehouses. A plant or a central warehouse services either the customer directly or satellite warehouses. The service level for the internal fulfillment of orders is known as the *internal service level*. Variability in internal fulfillment of orders is known as *service level variability*.

Figure 2.18 shows a multiechelon supply chain network. A supplier supplies the central warehouse, which in turn supplies customers.

Figure 2.18 Service Levels in Multiechelon Network

If you want to serve the customer at a 95% service level, the warehouse should be servicing the customer-facing warehouse at a 100% or 99.9% service level.

If the central warehouse serves at a lower internal service level or if the internal service level is variable, the customer-facing node might have to account for this variability and keep additional safety stock to account for this internal service level variability.

In Chapter 5 and Chapter 6, we'll explain the significance of internal service levels and the concept of risk pooling.

2.3 Additional Factors that Influence Inventory

In addition to the factors we discussed in the previous sections, there are many other factors that influence inventory. Some center on policies or strategies chosen by an organization, and some arise due to inherent product characteristics. In the following sections, we'll discuss the various other factors affecting inventory.

2.3.1 Service Level Type

In Section 2.1.5, you learned about different service level types. The choice of service level types affects the safety stock you carry. In this section, we'll compare the cycle service level and the fill rate. As we discussed, the cycle service level is the just the frequency of stock-outs, without any regard for volume, whereas the fill rate is about the volume of demand fulfilled. As shown in Figure 2.19, when the demand variability is low and the lead time variability is low, fill rate is almost 100%, but the cycle service rate is 0% because we had a stock-out situation in every cycle. In such a scenario, the fill rate will suggest a lower safety stock compared to the cycle service rate.

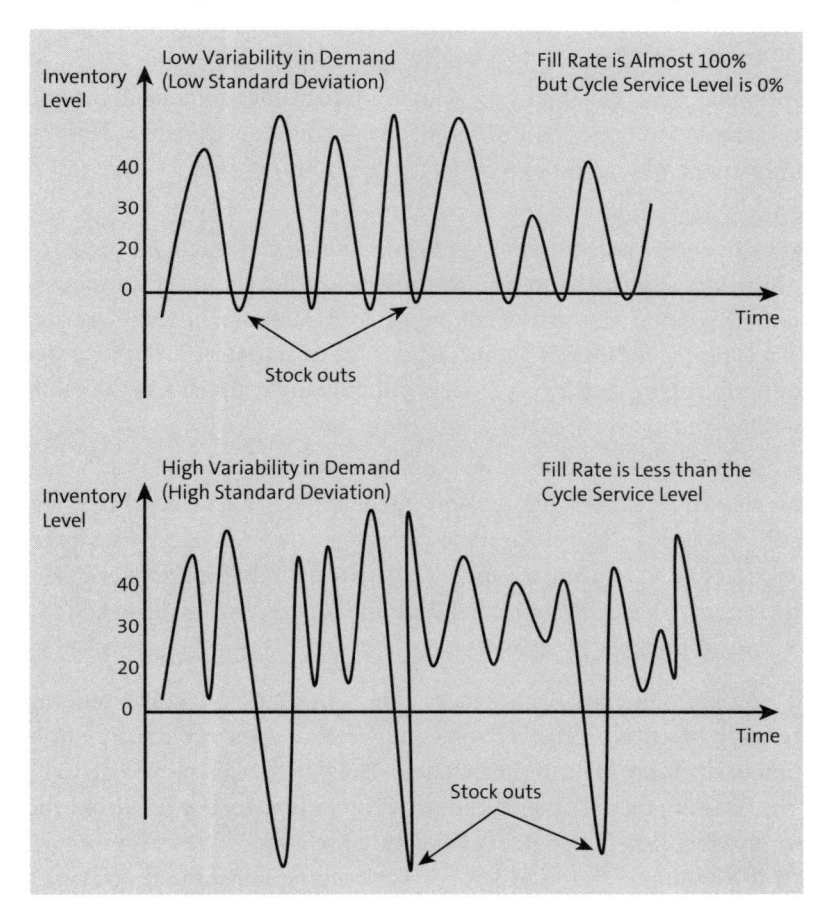

Figure 2.19 Comparision of Cycle Service Level and Fill Rate

However, when there is higher variability in demand, the fill rate and cycle service level will be low, but the fill rate could be significantly lower than the cycle service level due to higher variability in demand. Higher safety stock will be required in both cases.

Usually, using a fill rate results in less safety stock than using the cycle service level. Fill rate is most widely used service level type because it gives a clear idea of the volume of demand fulfilled.

Any increase in lot size or reorder point can increase the fill rate, but the cycle service level isn't affected.

2.3.2 Replenishment Strategy

Inventory replenishment refers to refilling stock to fulfill customer demand and avoid stock-outs. There are two fundamentally different replenishment strategies, depending on the inventory control systems explained in Chapter 1:

- **Fixed quantity**
  This strategy is also known as *continuous replenishment* and is used in perpetual or continuous inventory control systems. The inventory levels are continuously monitored, and as soon as the stocks fall below a predetermined level (reorder point), an order is placed for a fixed quantity, usually equal to the economic order quantity. Economic order quantity is the ideal order quantity (i.e., it has the minimum total holding and ordering cost).

- **Fixed time**
  This strategy is also known as *periodic replenishment* and is used in periodic review inventory control systems. The inventory levels are reviewed at fixed time intervals, and an order is placed to bring the inventory up to a predetermined level. The order quantity is equal to the difference between the predetermined level and the on-hand inventory at the time of review.

For an example of a periodic replenishment system, consider a beverage vending machine. The vending machine is stocked once per week, and the replenishment is based on the number of empty slots in the machine. The machine is stocked up to its full capacity at the time of replenishment. The target inventory level is fixed, but the quantity of the order is variable. Periodic replenishment strategies work best for low-value SKUs with low volume. The products for periodic replenishment strategies have higher safety stock. If the items are critical, a higher safety stock buffer may be required.

As compared to continuous replenishment, there is no need to calculate the order quantity or economic order quantity in periodic replenishment strategy. This is because you always fill up to the maximum target inventory level. Figure 2.20 shows a comparison of continuous and periodic replenishment strategies. As you can see, in the continuous model the order size is the same; in the periodic model, the order size varies.

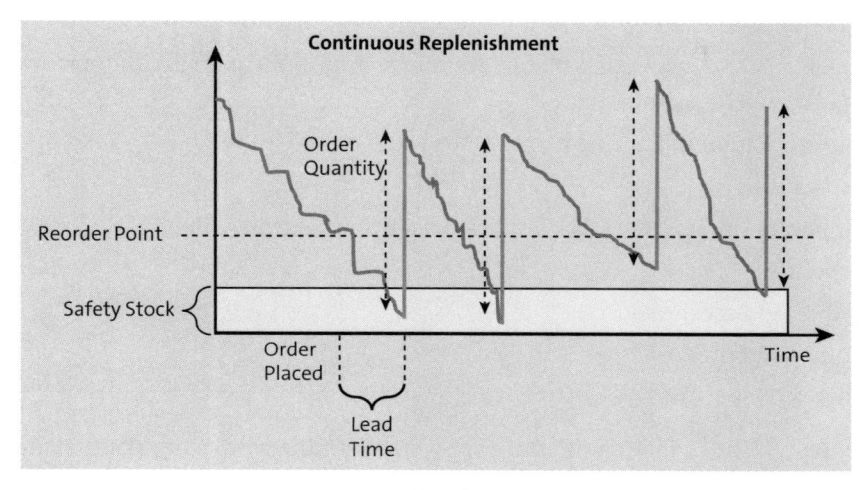

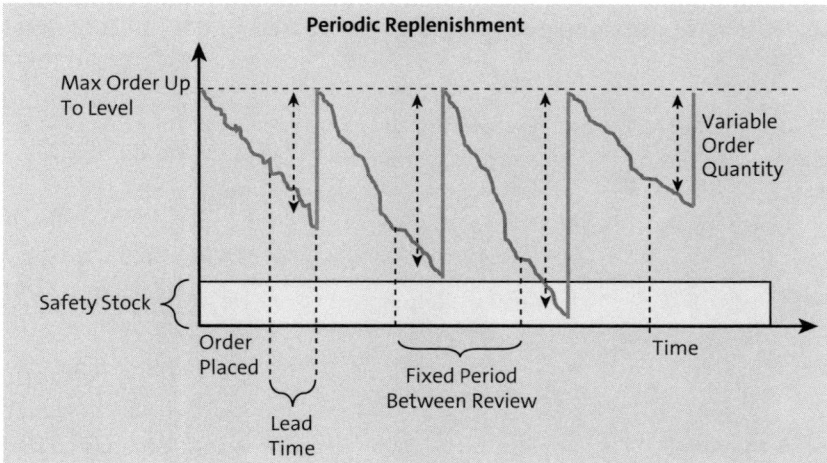

Figure 2.20 Continuous and Periodic Replenishment Strategies

2.3.3 Stocking Policy

As companies increasingly become global, they're subject to a more dynamic environment and turbulence. It's very important for companies to have a stocking strategy defined to handle supply chain unpredictability and swings. The key to establishing a successful inventory policy is to try to achieve a balance between customer service levels and cost incurred to maintain the inventory, which essentially blocks working capital. Some of the key elements of inventory policies include the following:

- Which products to stock
- How much stock to maintain—that is, defining a minimum and maximum stock level that should be maintained
- Where to stock (manufacturing plant versus warehouse)
- Safety stock levels
- Reorder points—that is, the stock levels at which you want to replenish
- Review periods
- Excess and obsolescence criteria
- Drop shipment criteria
- Customer service criteria

There are many factors that come into play while defining a stocking policy. One common method is ABC classification, along with XYZ (or runner, repeater, stranger) criteria. Table 2.8 shows an example of a stocking policy based on ABC and XYZ classification.

A	<ul><li>Low safety stock</li><li>Continuous inventory system</li><li>Auto replenishment</li></ul>	<ul><li>Low safety stock</li><li>Continuous inventory system</li><li>Auto and manual replenishment</li></ul>	<ul><li>No safety stock</li><li>No inventory</li><li>Make to order</li></ul>
B	<ul><li>Low safety stock</li><li>Periodic review system</li><li>Auto replenishment</li></ul>	<ul><li>Varying safety stock</li><li>Periodic review system</li><li>Auto and manual replenishment</li></ul>	<ul><li>No safety stock</li><li>No inventory</li><li>Make to order</li></ul>
C	<ul><li>Low safety stock</li><li>Periodic review system</li><li>Auto replenishment</li></ul>	<ul><li>High safety stock</li><li>Periodic review system</li><li>Auto replenishment</li></ul>	<ul><li>High safety stock</li><li>Periodic review system</li><li>Auto replenishment</li></ul>
	X (Runner)	Y (Repeater)	Z (Stranger)

Table 2.8 Stocking Policy Based on ABC and XYZ Classification

Lead time is an important factor to consider while defining the stocking policy for a material. If the lead time for the material is low—say, a few days—you don't need to maintain a lot of stock for that material. But if the material has a long lead time and high service level, you'll need to maintain stock.

The shelf life of the product also influences the stocking policy. Life sciences and the pharmaceutical industry typically have a lot of shelf-life-bound materials. The shelf life period will also play an important part in determining how much stock you want to hold on to for that material. For instance, you won't keep a lot of stock for materials with short shelf lives.

While defining stocking policy for a raw material or semifinished material, you need to evaluate how critical it is to production. For example, if there's a raw material that can cause the manufacturing operation to shut down if it's not available, you would probably want to maintain stock for that material. You also have to evaluate the trade-off between maintaining stock for such a material and the cost of downtime. In the case of semifinished materials or materials in between two manufacturing processes, you may not want to keep any stock at all for these materials but instead process them further and store them at the finished goods or assembly level.

The number of distribution centers and manufacturing plants also plays an important role in setting up the stocking policy. For example, manufacturing plants may have limited storage area, so they may want to move stock to distribution centers as soon as it's produced. In the case of a central warehouse and satellite warehouses, planners may need to keep most of the stock in the central warehouse to achieve flexibility.

2.3.4 Sourcing Decisions

Sourcing managers are mainly responsible for obtaining the right product in the right quantity at the right time and price. Sourcing decisions have a significant impact on the total inventory of an organization. Sourcing managers often enter into agreements with suppliers on the following elements that impact inventory levels:

- **Replenishment lead time**
  As discussed in the previous section, this is the by far the most important agreement with the supplier. Managers must be accurate in their forecasting during the lead time.

- **On-time performance**
  Any variability in the lead time warrants keeping additional inventory to ensure smooth downstream operations. Sourcing managers enter into agreements for their performance. If it's below a certain threshold, they penalize the supplier. The on-time performance metric also gives an idea of how reliable your supplier is.

- **Minimum order size and delivery frequency**
  Some suppliers deliver every week; others might deliver every month. Delivery frequency and minimum order size have an impact on the total inventory of the organization. It increases the average cycle stock.

- **Maximum order size or maximum capacity**
  In addition to minimum order size, suppliers also enter agreements for the maximum order size. This helps an organization plan if they see a huge surge in demand. They can look for alternate sources if the preferred supplier can't deliver.

- **Flexibility**
  Some degree of flexibility to change the purchase order quantity once an order has been placed also plays an important role. Companies can change the quantity if the customer demand changes drastically or the mix changes.

- **Order expedition cost**
  The buyer and seller agree on the cost to expedite an order.

- **Price**
  The cost of the material defines the inventory value carried, so it's a critical element that influences your inventory strategy.

- **Ownership of the inventory**
  Sourcing managers enter into an agreement on the ownership of the inventory. Whether the organization takes ownership when the order ships or when it's received affects the ownership of the pipeline stock.

- **Freight cost**
  In some cases, the buyer has to pay freight charges, which increases the cost of inventory. The buyer and supplier enter into an agreement on freight costs and preferred shipment modes.

- **Volume discounts**
  The supplier often offers a volume discount, which affects the economic order quantity and thus the total cost of inventory.

- **Buyback and rebates**
  If companies can't sell inventory, they often enter into an agreement with the supplier for buyback or they offer a manufacturer's rebate on the selling price. This helps companies to reduce inventory levels. This is most common in a retail or wholesale business model.

In addition, the sourcing manager is also responsible for finding an alternate source for a material if the preferred supplier can't deliver. To maintain a steady supply, they enter into contractual agreements with multiple suppliers for the same part, sometimes at a higher price. They often have a quota arrangement to split the demand across multiple suppliers. This helps them maintain healthy relationships with multiple suppliers, helping ensure the option to switch to another supplier if one is unable to deliver.

2.3.5 Bill of Materials

The BOM, also referred to as a *product structure*, is a list of raw materials, subcomponents, subassemblies, components, and assemblies. The product structure also has an impact on inventories that need to be carried by the company. Consider a home appliance manufacturer. There are hundreds of parts that go into making up one appliance. The product structure has many components and assemblies that make up one unit. The product structure is like that of a tree. These are mainly made-to-stock items.

An example BOM is shown in Figure 2.21. This BOM shows a many-to-one relationship—that is, many components and subassemblies make one finished product. Automobiles and appliances fit into this category. They have a typical A-shaped (or a pyramid-shaped) BOM. In this case, the demand for components and raw materials is very much dependent on the demand for the finished product, and the mix of finished goods can change the dependent demand of the components significantly.

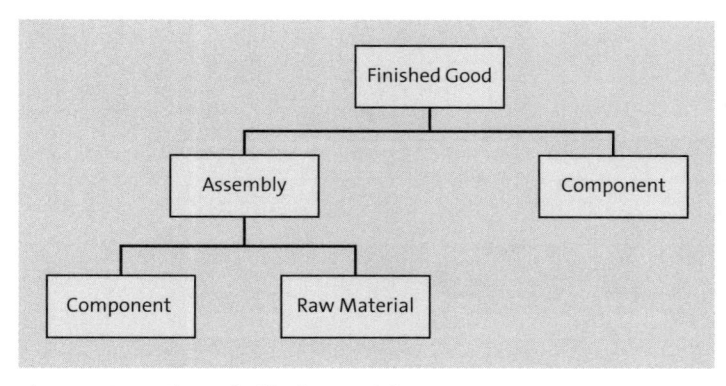

Figure 2.21 A-Shaped Bill of Materials

The second kind of BOM shows one-to-many relationships. Here there are very few components or raw materials, but many finished goods can be built from just those few components. Think of the oil industry: Crude oil is transformed into multiple finished goods. There is only one component, crude oil, but it can be transformed into various finished products, such as fuel oil, lubricating oil, paraffin, and gas.

Another example is the meat industry or milk industry. Figure 2.22 shows a one-to-many product structure, forming a V-shaped BOM.

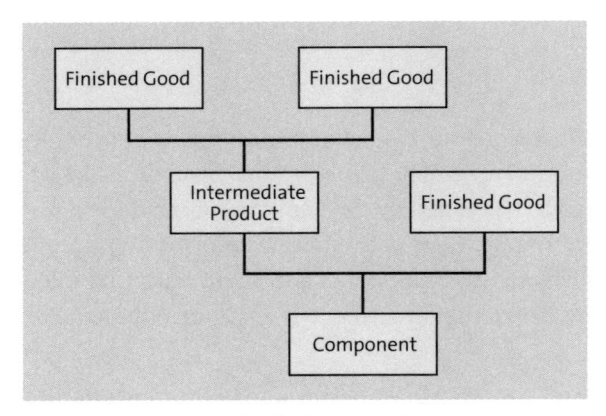

Figure 2.22 V-Shaped Bill of Materials

Another kind of product structure with one-to-many relationships forms a T-shaped BOM, as shown in Figure 2.23. This is most common in jewelry, paper, or steel industries. One component can have multiple finished goods. For example, a sheet of paper can be cut into different sizes.

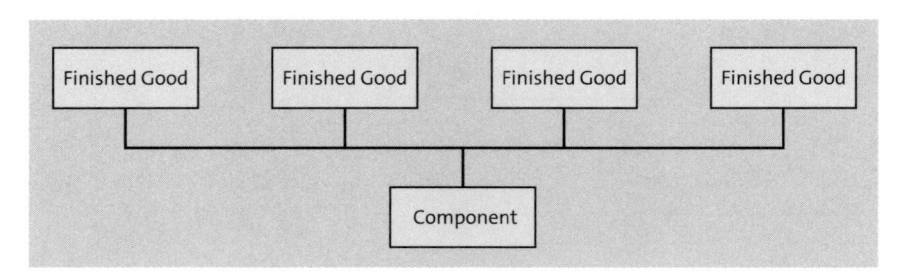

Figure 2.23 T-Shaped Bill of Materials

Finally, there's a configurable or modular product structure with many-to-many relationships. Think of a laptop. A laptop can have many different configurations based on the choice of the hard disk drive, memory, graphics card, processor, motherboard, speakers, screen, and any other optional features. These product structures are very common in make-to-order industries. They have X-shaped BOMs, as shown in Figure 2.24.

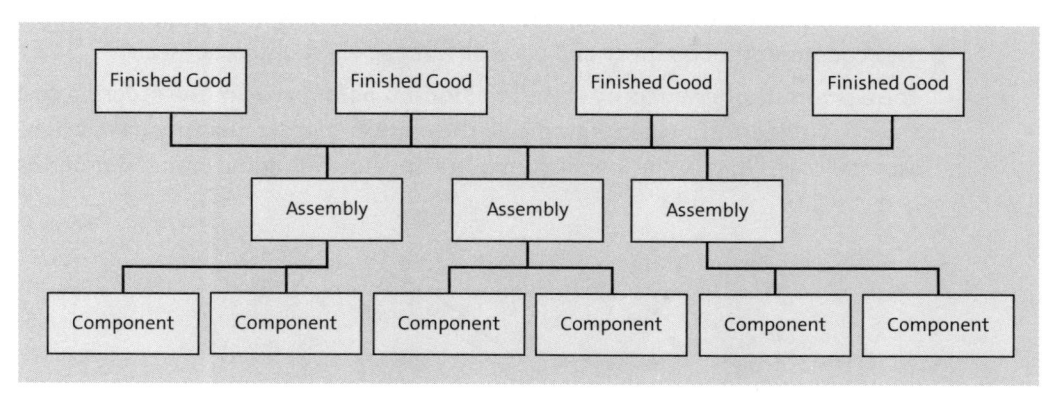

Figure 2.24 X-Shaped Bill of Materials

Inventory managers tend to keep inventory at the BOM level whenever there are fewer items and whenever it allows maximum flexibility. For example, computer company Dell keeps stock at the assembly level: that is, it has different assembly options in stock for the hard drive, memory, processors, and motherboards. This gives the company more flexibility to make the finished product per customer demand while also keeping fewer parts in inventory compared to the individual components.

In short, the product structure often drives where you keep inventory.

2.3.6 Lot Size and Economic Order Quantities

Lot size or batch size influences the total amount of inventory and safety stock you need to keep. There are three different lot size strategies:

- **Lot for lot**
  An order is placed for the exact quantity required to fulfill demand. This strategy is common in a just in time (JIT) environment or in lean manufacturing. This method is often used for expensive items and items for which demand occurs intermittently. It can also be used for ordering products with low shelf life, like produce. This method essentially results in low to near-zero inventory levels but increases the ordering cost.

- **Fixed order quantity**

    An order is placed for a fixed quantity. This strategy is used in continuous replenishment systems. This method works well when a fixed order quantity is equal to the economic order quantity and takes advantage of economies of scale.

    The economic order quantity is the equilibrium point between the ordering cost and carrying cost, shown in Figure 2.25. The economic order quantity has the lowest total cost—that is, the lowest sum of the inventory holding cost and ordering cost.

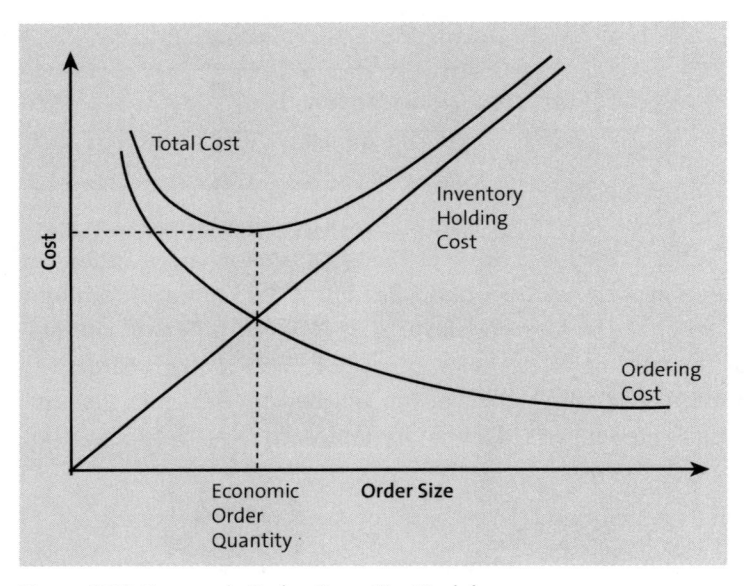

Figure 2.25 Economic Order Quantity Model

The economic production quantity, also known as the manufacturing quantity, is like the economic order quantity. It balances the fixed order costs (e.g., changeover cost) with a variable cost of production.

- **Period order**

    The period order is also known as the dynamic lot size. An order is placed for a quantity that covers n future periods of demand.

Consider a continuous replenishment system in which you order when you go below the reorder point. As shown in Figure 2.26, any increase in the lot size increases the cycle stock, so the average inventory increases. It also reduces the frequency of orders. As we discussed, the exposure to a stock-out situation is maximized when you're about to receive orders; as you increase the order lot size, the number of stock-out situations decreases due to a reduction in the frequency of orders.

Theoretically, the batch size has no effect on the safety stock levels because it's independent of variability in demand or supply. However, in a multiechelon environment, batch size can reduce the overall safety inventory. This is because batch size can act as a safety stock in a multiechelon network. Figure 2.26 shows the effect of the batch size on inventory. The number of exposure periods are reduced when the batch size increases.

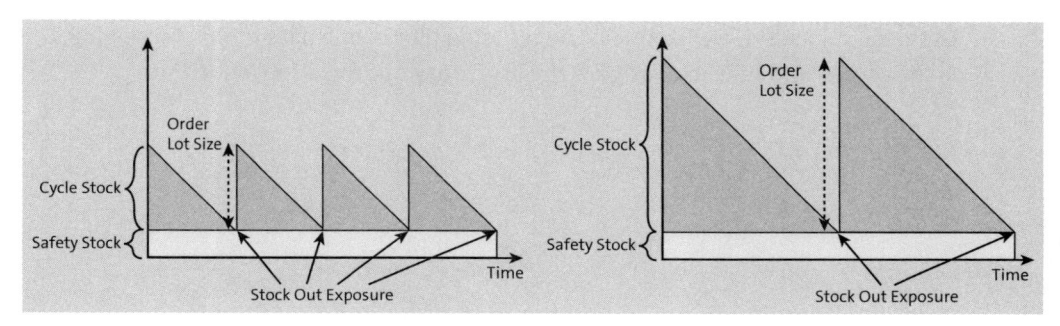

Figure 2.26 Effect of Batch Size on Inventory

2.3.7 Inventory Holding Cost

Holding inventory isn't free. There are costs incurred by carrying inventory. There are two main types of inventory holding costs: capital and noncapital.

Noncapital costs include warehousing, insurance, obsolescence, shrinkage, and labor, among others. *Capital costs* refer to the money tied up in the inventory. Typically, this is valued using the weighted average cost of capital (WACC), but in less risky industries the capital cost can be valued using the borrowing rate.

Inventory holding costs affect a company's decision about holding inventory to fulfill demand. If for a given service level the cost of holding inventory is more than the lost sales that would occur due to a stock-out situation, companies may choose to have a lower service level.

Inventory holding costs also affect the economic order quantity. The higher the inventory holding cost, the lower the order quantity, and therefore the lower the cycle stock.

2.4 Summary

In this chapter, we explained the various factors that affect inventory levels. Lead time and demand forecast, along with forecast error, are critical variables affecting the overall inventory levels of the organization. We looked at the different service level types used by organizations and how the choice of service level target affects inventory levels. We analyzed the impact of the service level target, demand, and lead time on the safety stock requirements. Finally, we explained the additional factors that affect inventory, such as stocking policies, sourcing decisions, replenishment strategies, and inventory holding costs.

In the next chapter, we'll explain the building blocks of a data model in SAP IBP, the architecture, and how to configure the inventory optimization algorithm.

Chapter 3
Configuring SAP IBP for Inventory

SAP Integrated Business Planning provides extensive flexibility when modeling various business requirements for planning. This allows customers to model their unique business processes and consolidate planning data across different levels. This chapter focuses on the building blocks of a planning model and the configuration steps.

In any planning solution implementation, the first step is to create a planning model based on business requirements and populate it with data. A planning model should be a good representation of business planning processes. In this chapter, we'll introduce the key concepts that enable planning processes across SAP IBP applications. We'll focus on the building blocks used to build a planning model, such as attributes, time profiles, planning areas, planning levels, key figures, and versions. We'll also cover the steps to configure these different entities and how to use the content pre-delivered by SAP IBP to build your planning model.

3.1 Architecture

Before we explain the building blocks of the planning model and how the planning model is configured, it's important to discuss the architecture of SAP Integrated Business Planning, as illustrated in Figure 3.1.

The left-hand side of Figure 3.1 depicts the stakeholders from areas such as sales and marketing, demand planning, supply planning, finance, and inventory planning. As we explained in Chapter 1, planners interact with SAP IBP through three types of user interface: Microsoft Excel, a web-browser-based UI, and a mobile web interface.

To model business requirements, SAP IBP provides an intuitive UI to configure a planning model. All data is stored and calculated in an in-memory SAP HANA database in the backend. SAP IBP also provides an administrator area to manage user

3   Configuring SAP IBP for Inventory

access and content administration and to monitor day-to-day planning processes and jobs.

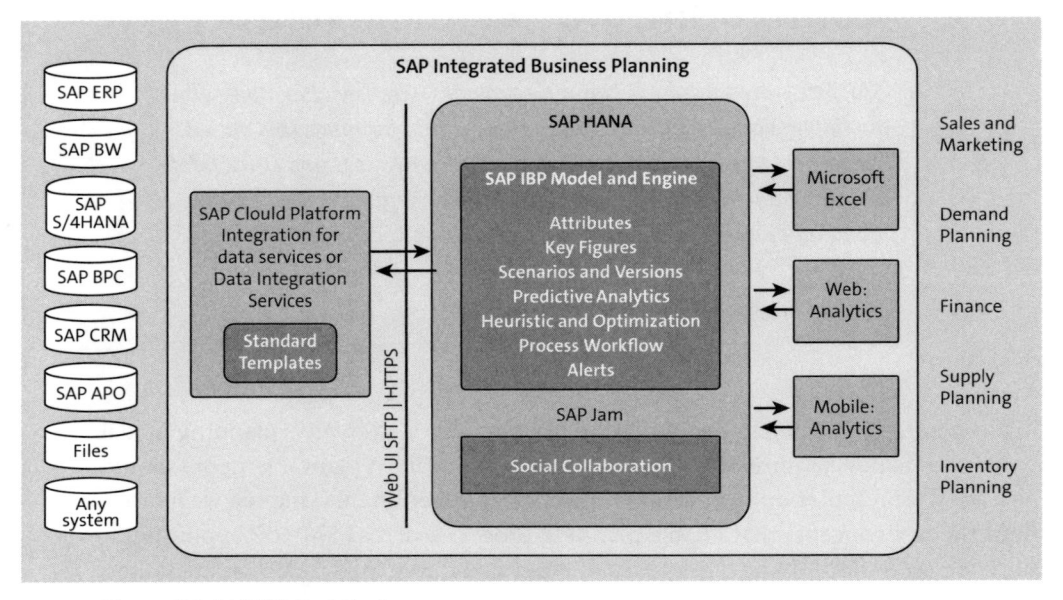

Figure 3.1 SAP IBP Architecture

Social collaboration is enabled via SAP Jam. SAP Jam allows easy, secure collaboration among internal and external stakeholders for planning activities.

On the left-hand side of Figure 3.1, you can see various data stores that can be integrated with SAP IBP for data transfers. Data can be transferred to and from external systems using cloud platform integration for data services or other data services. Chapter 10 explains each available data integration technology in more depth.

3.2   Building Blocks

One of the key success factors for the successful implementation of any advanced planning tool is correct and consistent modeling of business processes and business requirements. SAP Integrated Business Planning provides extensive functions for creating, updating, and capturing information in a plan, which is configured using a planning model.

A planning model is a well-defined structure of your business plan in terms of data and calculations. It defines how data is stored, calculated, and aggregated in the system. Based on your planning model, you can create planning views and work on your data using SAP Integrated Business Planning, add-in for Microsoft Excel.

In technical terms, a *planning model* is a collection of master data, transaction data, and associated calculations to manage and optimize a supply chain network. Every organization is different in terms of its business processes and supply networks, so a planning model is unique to an organization. SAP IBP lets you configure and customize your own planning models to address your unique business requirements. The basic building blocks to model these business requirements remain the same.

All the planning models consist of the following entities:

- Attributes
- Master data types
- Time profiles
- Planning areas
- Planning levels
- Key figures (including snapshots)
- Versions
- Calculations
- Miscellaneous additional entities such as global configuration parameters, planning operators, and reason codes

Figure 3.2 illustrates the relationships between the main configuration entities. In the subsequent sections, we'll explain each of these entities in detail.

The model configuration group in the web user interface consists of all SAP Fiori apps for viewing, configuring, and maintaining the configurable entities. To construct the planning model, the high-level flow is as follows:

1. Create attributes
2. Create a time profile
3. Create master data types
4. Create a planning area by assigning the time profile, master data types, and attributes

3   Configuring SAP IBP for Inventory

5. Create planning levels
6. Create key figures
7. Create version
8. Create planning operators or planning profiles and assign them to the planning area
9. Activate the planning model
10. Load the data in the newly constructed planning model

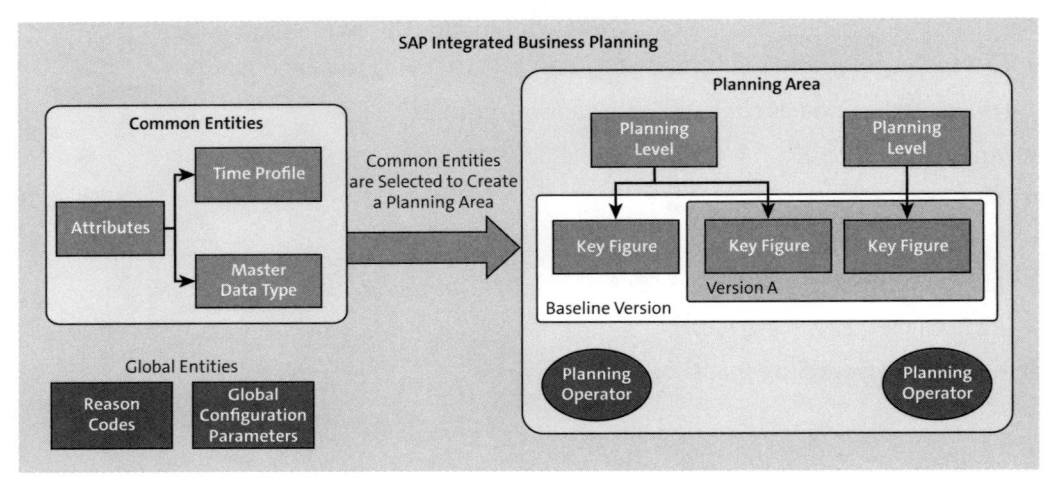

Figure 3.2 Relationships between Main Configuration Entities

3.2.1   Attributes

An *attribute* is a basic element that carries information about a business entity. Multiple attributes can be grouped logically to define a *master data type*, which represents a supply chain or business entity. Attributes define the characteristics of master data types; for example, a product that an organization manufactures and sells has attributes such as a product identification number, size, color, brand, product group, product family, business unit, and so on. To model a supply chain network, the first step in the design phase is to identify all the attributes that are relevant to the planning model.

Based on the properties of an attribute, it can contain numeric, string, or date-type information.

In SAP IBP, the following types of attributes are supported:

- **Character (nvarchar)**
  Characters are the most widely used attribute type, used to represent character information such as the product description, market type, customer name, resource name, and so on.

- **Decimal**
  Decimal attributes are used for maintaining numerical values that remain the same across a time horizon. They're primarily used to model the attributes as key figures. If the numeric value of an information element remains the same for all time periods, mapping it as a decimal attribute with an attribute as a key figure can be considered. For example, standard cost, static safety stock target, capacity supply, consumption rate, currency conversion exchange rate, and more can be defined as attributes as key figures so that the same numerical values can be used for all time periods.

- **Integer**
  Integer values are used to represent information such as lead time, period of coverage, or system setting values for lot size policy indicators, period IDs, and so on. These information elements are created as integer-type attributes in SAP IBP.

- **Timestamp**
  There are many information elements that require data to be maintained as dates or times. These information elements are created as timestamp attributes. For example, the product introduction or discontinuation date, promotion start date, phase in date, phase-out date, material availability date, and more can be captured through timestamp attributes.

After completion of attribute configuration, every attribute for the planning model design is created and is available to use in SAP IBP.

To create an attribute, click the **Attributes** SAP Fiori app tile under the catalog group **Model Configuration**. Figure 3.3 shows how to access the app and create a new attribute. You can see all the existing attributes. Using the filter options, you can narrow the results to a specific attribute or group of attributes. To create a new attribute, click the new attribute, then enter its ID, description, data type, and length (if relevant). Click **Save** to save it in SAP IBP, **Save and New** to create another attribute, or **Save and Copy** to create a copy of the attribute you just created. Figure 3.4 shows the attribute creation screen.

3   Configuring SAP IBP for Inventory

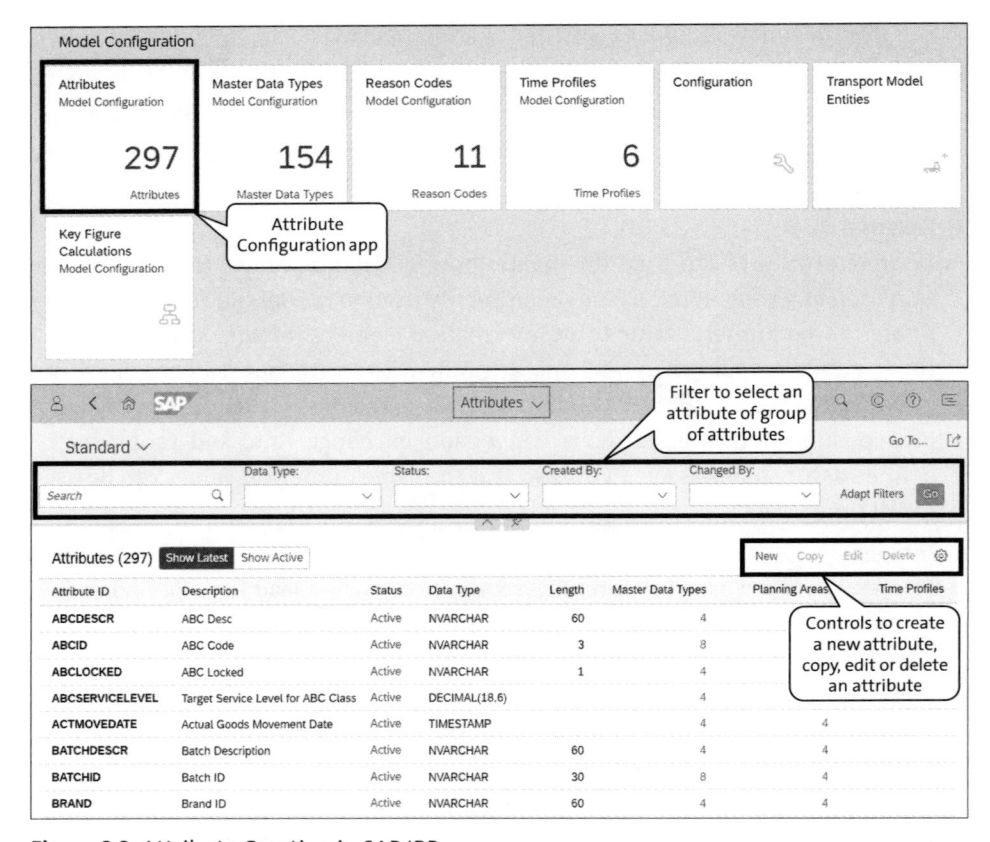

Figure 3.3 Attribute Creation in SAP IBP

Figure 3.4 Create New Attribute

110

3.2.2 Master Data Type

Master data is used to segment and organize planning information. It represents categories of information, such as customer, location, product, or resource. Different master data types can be combined to represent planning-relevant information. A typical example is sales history, the number of products sold from a plant or a distribution center against a customer's requirements. Here the product, location (plant or distribution center), and customer are examples of master data types, and the combination of these master data types is used to define the sales history.

A master data type is a logical grouping of multiple attributes to define an entity. For example, a product is a master data type, and it contains attributes that define a product, such as product ID, product description, product family, product group, the base unit of measure, standard cost, and so on.

For any given master data type, there's always a minimum of one key attribute, which should have a unique value. In our previous example for the product master data type, the product ID is a key attribute, which will always contain a unique value that is not null. An attribute also can be marked as a required attribute, which means that it should contain a value other than null. By default, a key attribute is a required attribute. Any other attribute in a master data type can be a nonkey attribute or non-required attribute, and you can store a null value in these attributes.

To view or create a master data type, click the **Master Data Types** SAP Fiori app tile in the **Model Configuration** group (Figure 3.5). You can view all the existing master data types in the system, and you can also filter to view a specific master data type or a group of master data types. Using the control buttons, you can create a new master data type or **Copy, Edit, check, activate, delete**, or **Restore Active Instance** to restore an active version master data type.

In SAP IBP, there are five different master data types:

- **Simple master data type**
  A *simple master data type* represents one independent master data element—for example, product, location, customer, or resource. Figure 3.6 shows a simple master data type for a product. The product ID is the key, required attribute, which means this attribute can't have a null value; it must have a unique value. All the other attributes can have a null value; that is, it's not mandatory to set a value for these attributes.

3 Configuring SAP IBP for Inventory

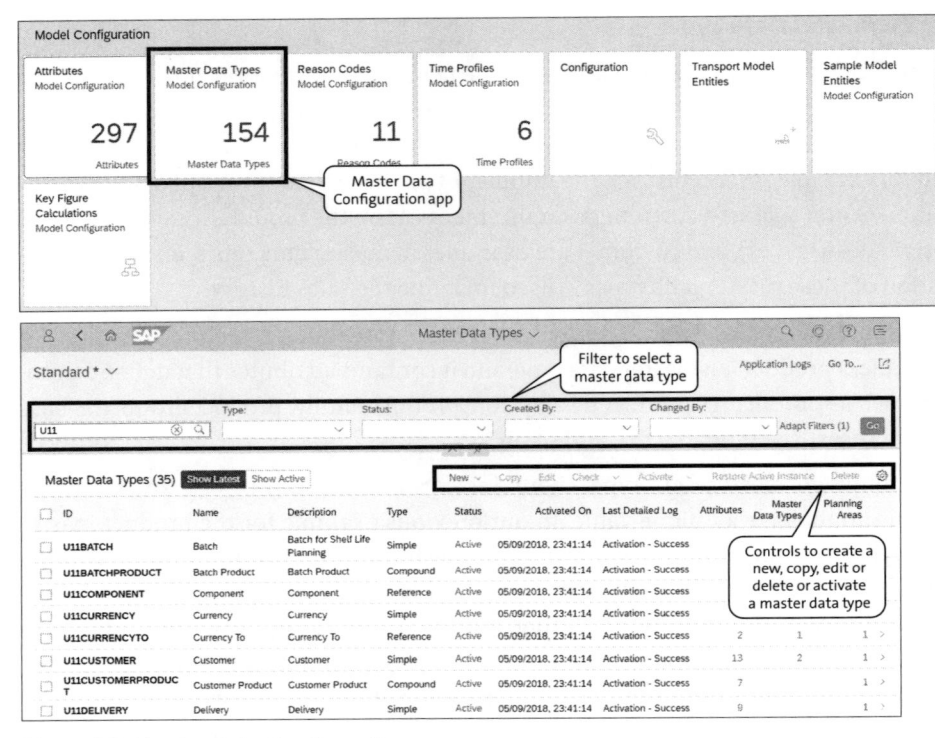

Figure 3.5 Master Data Configuration

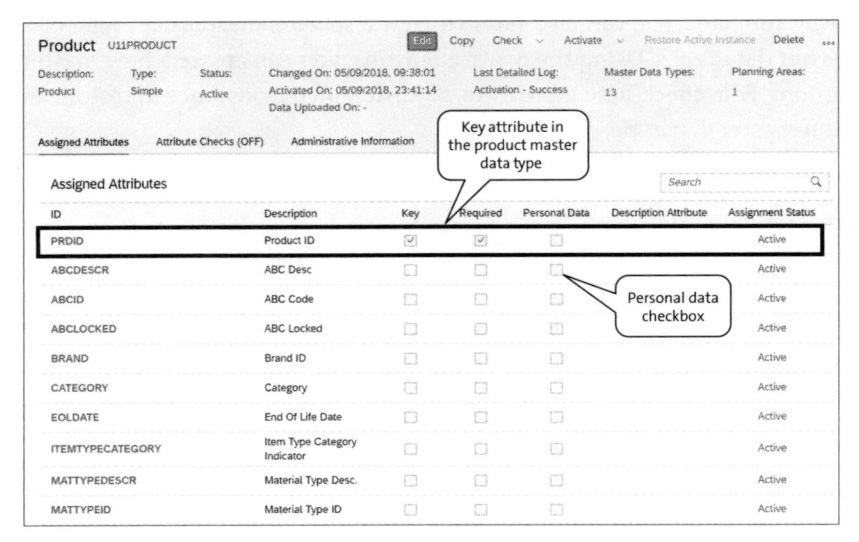

Figure 3.6 Selection of Attributes to Create Master Data Type

- **Compound master data type**
 Compound master data represents a combination of two or more simple master data types. A product and location individually represent the characteristics of a material and a location through simple master data, but some attributes are defined as a product and location combination. For example, safety stock can be different for a product at two different locations. A compound master data type consisting of a location and a product can be created to represent a valid combination. Compound master data is created by selecting associated simple master data. By default, all attributes assigned to the simple master data types can be used for the combination. However, additional attributes relevant to the combination are added to the compound master data type. For example, a safety stock target attribute can be added as an attribute that's valid for a product-location combination. Figure 3.7 shows examples of compound master data types.

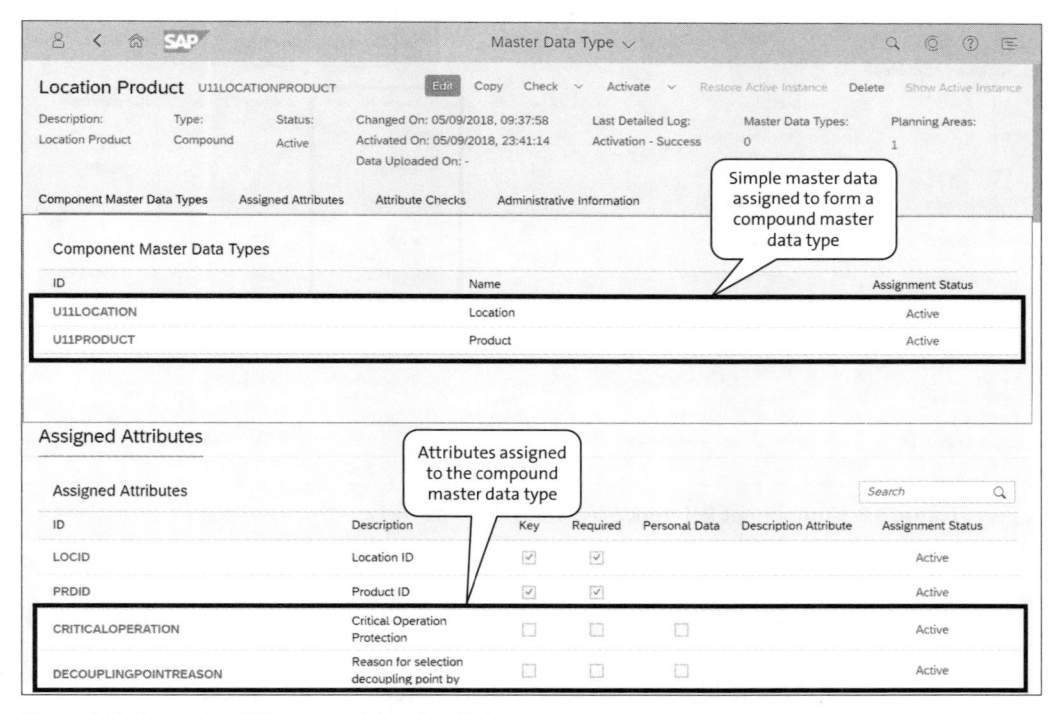

Figure 3.7 Example of Compound Master Data

- **Reference master data type**
 A *reference master data type* refers to another master data element and doesn't

3   Configuring SAP IBP for Inventory

require a separate data load of its own. Reference master data is used when the primary data elements of a set of data are the same as or a subset of another set of data. For example, every component is also a product, so a component can be created as reference master data that refers to product master data. When creating a reference master data type, all assigned attributes should refer to attributes of the referenced master data type. Figure 3.8 shows the reference master data type for a component. As you can see, component ID refers to product ID, the component description refers to the product description, and so on.

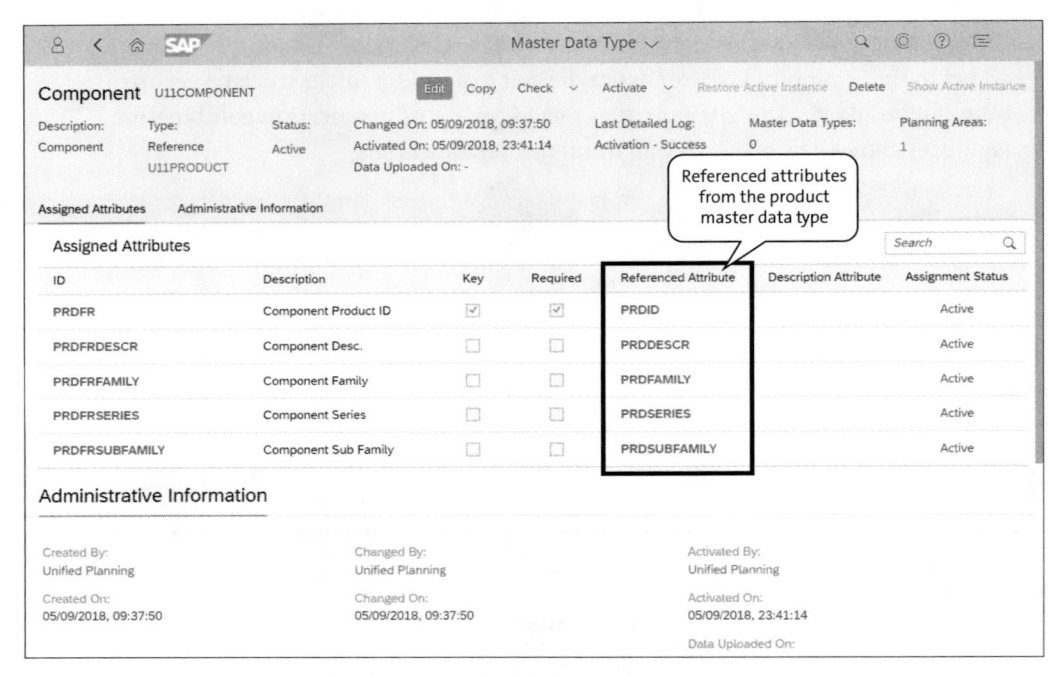

Figure 3.8 Component Reference Master Data Type

- **Virtual master data type**
  The *virtual master data type* doesn't store any data. It's used to join two or more master data types so that the attributes of one master data type are available for the other. This enables you to create joins between two or more master data types that otherwise have no connection to each other. Virtual master data can be built by joining two or more simple, compound, or reference master data types through a join condition, which can be a common attribute of different master data so that other attributes are also available. The join conditions you define between these

referenced master data types determine the set of data the virtual master data type uses.

- **External master data type**
External master data is used to integrate the master data content from external SAP ERP or SAP S/4HANA systems. It allows near-real-time integration of the master data elements from the source system into SAP IBP. For external master data types, an external data source table is used, and the characteristics of the master data are mapped to the reference attributes of the source table from an external master data system. So before you can use external master data types, the database tables they retrieve their content from must be integrated from SAP ERP into SAP HANA database tables inside SAP IBP. For SAP IBP for response and supply, it's mandatory to use an external master data type for some master data elements, such as product, location, and so on. When you set up your planning model, you define an external master data type referring to a table that contains the predefined content. The integration runs in batch mode, so the external master data entries are updated on a regular basis from SAP ERP according to the preferences you've set. There's no need for a manual data upload.

To create a master data type, click the **New** button and select which kind of master data you want to create: simple, compound, reference, virtual, or external. For a naming convention, we recommend using a two- or three-letter prefix in the master data type name. This name can be the company's stock symbol, business unit, or any other text related to the organization. The expectation is that the same three-letter prefix will be used for other relevant SAP IBP items. The sample planning areas delivered with SAP IBP use the prefix *IBP* in their master data type IDs.

Figure 3.9 shows the master data type creation screen. Enter the **Master Data ID**, **Name**, and **Description**. In our example, we chose the prefix *IP*. Add the relevant attributes by clicking the **Add** button. You can also create new attributes to be added to the master data type directly from this screen by clicking **New**. Mark the attributes that are **Key** or **Required**. At least one attribute should be a key in a master data type. Any attribute that might contain personal data should be marked as **Personal Data**. The description attributes can be linked to an ID by selecting them. You can also define an attribute check for the master data. Attribute checks help to check the relevancy of data before it's loaded into the system. Any invalid value in the checked attribute of a master data type will be rejected during load, thereby maintaining the consistency of the data. For example, you can add a check to validate the location from the location master data before loading it into the location product master data.

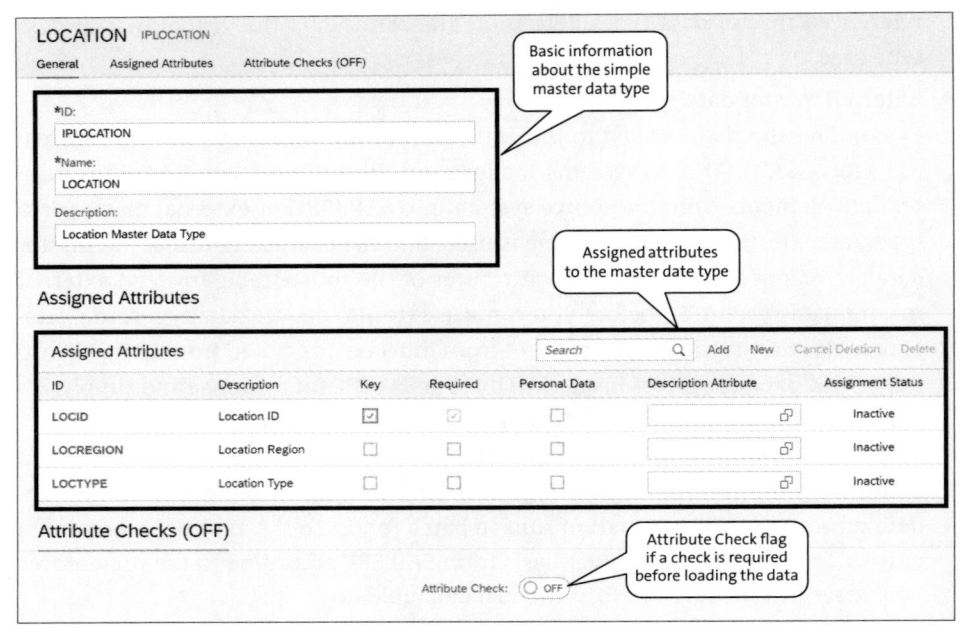

Figure 3.9 Configuration of Simple Master Data Type

3.2.3 Time Profiles

Time profiles define the time dimension used for managing planning data. They define the various levels of time buckets in which planning data can be managed. A time profile is made up of time profile levels (e.g., days, weeks, months, quarters, or years). Each level is made up of periods, which are identified by a number (integer) and describe the start and end time of the time bucket. The time profiles can be customized based on business requirements—for example, to use financial years instead of calendar years.

If you want to perform aggregation or disaggregation along time dimensions, then the periods on different levels need to form a hierarchy. Figure 3.10 shows an example of a hierarchy. In this hierarchy, time profile levels can have multiple parents, and there can be time profile levels without a parent level.

Time profiles can be accessed through the Time Profiles SAP Fiori app. Figure 3.11 shows a sample time profile. The smallest time bucket (a day, in our example) is assigned level 1, the next smallest (a technical week) is level 2, and so on up. For all levels other than the smallest level, you also must assign the base level.

3.2 Building Blocks

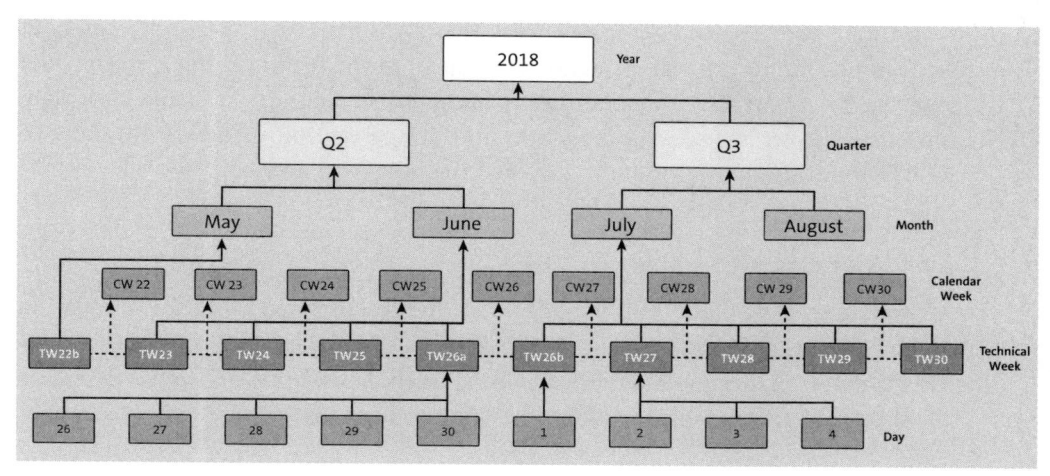

Figure 3.10 Time Profile Hierarchy Structure

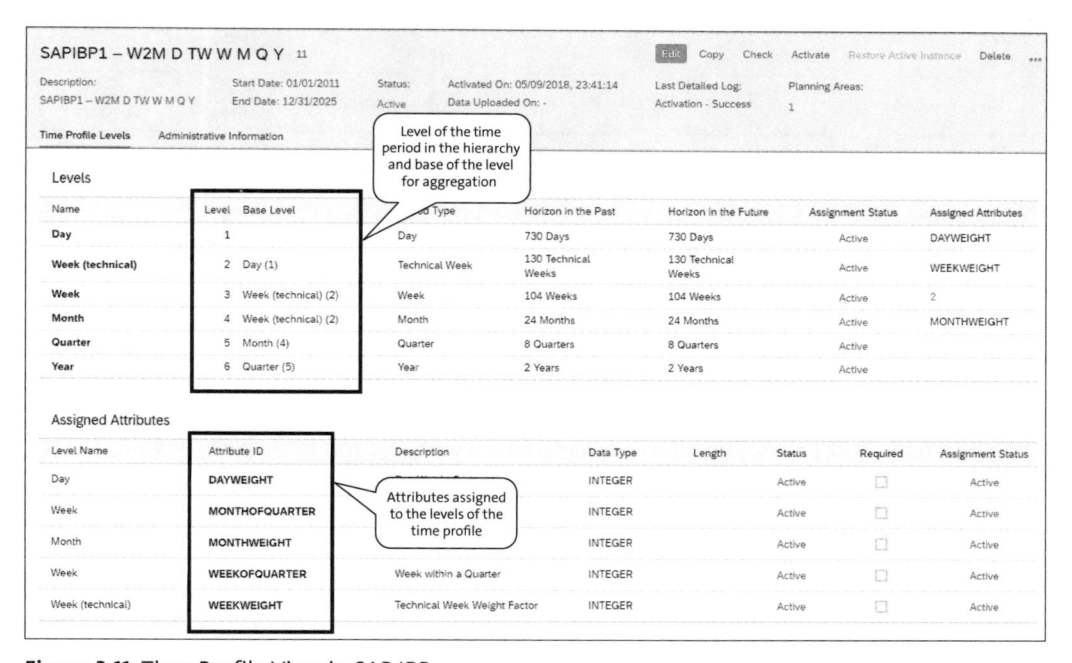

Figure 3.11 Time Profile View in SAP IBP

The base level defines from which level you want to aggregate the data. For example, the technical week is aggregated from the day, so the base level for that time period is 1.

117

A calendar week is also aggregated from the day, so the base level for a calendar week is also 1. A month can be aggregated up from the technical week, so the base level for the month is 2. The relationship hierarchy of planning level and base planning level allows seamless aggregation and disaggregation of data from daily to weekly, monthly, quarterly, and yearly, and the other way around.

3.2.4 Planning Area

A *planning area* is a model entity that defines the structure and forms the foundation of the planning process. A planning area consists of other entities such as time profile, attributes of master data types, planning levels, key figures, and versions. Figure 3.12 shows the relationships among these common entities.

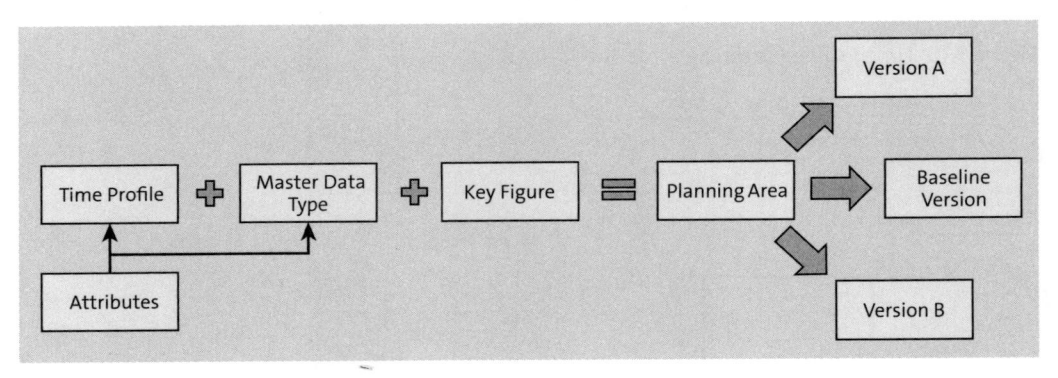

Figure 3.12 Planning Area Structure

Planning areas can contain multiple planning data sets—that is, a base version data set plus additional version data sets. The versions are for alternative plans or to support what-if plans. The alternate version plan can be for all or part of what's in the base version and needs to be configured and activated. The Excel planning view of SAP IBP is connected to one planning area at a time. For project implementation and infrastructure management purposes, an organization can choose to create a single planning area or multiple planning areas for configuration, test, and active environments. Transactional data can be transferred automatically between two planning areas using a planning operator.

For each planning process, such as demand planning, supply and response planning, S&OP, and inventory optimization, SAP IBP provides sample planning areas, as well

3.2 Building Blocks

as a unified planning area that is a superset of the individual sample planning areas. The sample planning areas provides the recommended definitions for time profiles, master days, and key figures. It also assigns the relevant operators for each of the SAP IBP applications. In Section 3.3, we'll explain in detail the content delivered with SAP IBP and how to use it to start your implementation.

To view or create a planning area, click the **Planning Areas** SAP Fiori app tile in the **Model Configuration** group. Figure 3.13 shows the Planning Areas SAP Fiori app. Here you can view all the existing planning areas in the system. Using the control buttons, you can create a new planning area, copy, edit, check, activate, or delete a planning area, or restore to a previously active version of the planning area.

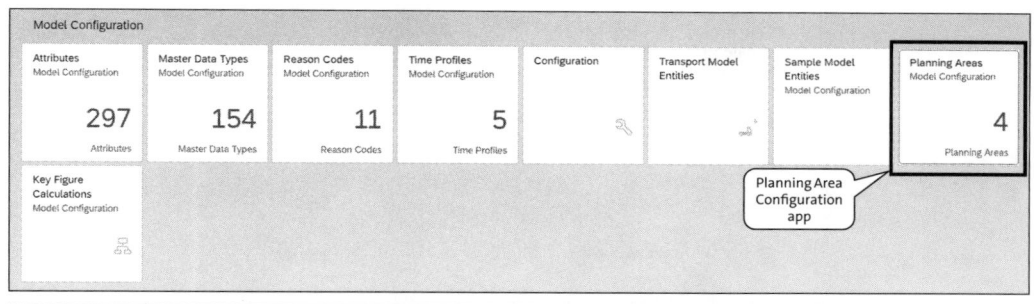

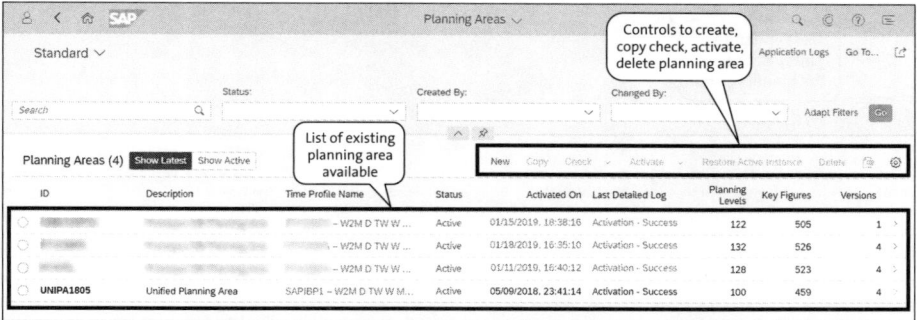

Figure 3.13 Planning Areas App

Figure 3.14 shows a sample planning area definition screen. At the top, you can view the tabs for all the different entities assigned to the planning area. For example, the **Attributes** tab shows all the attributes assigned to the planning area. The initial screen shows the planning area settings, the time profile assigned to the planning

119

3   Configuring SAP IBP for Inventory

area, and administrative information such as the user who created the initial planning area and the user who changed the planning area last along with time stamps.

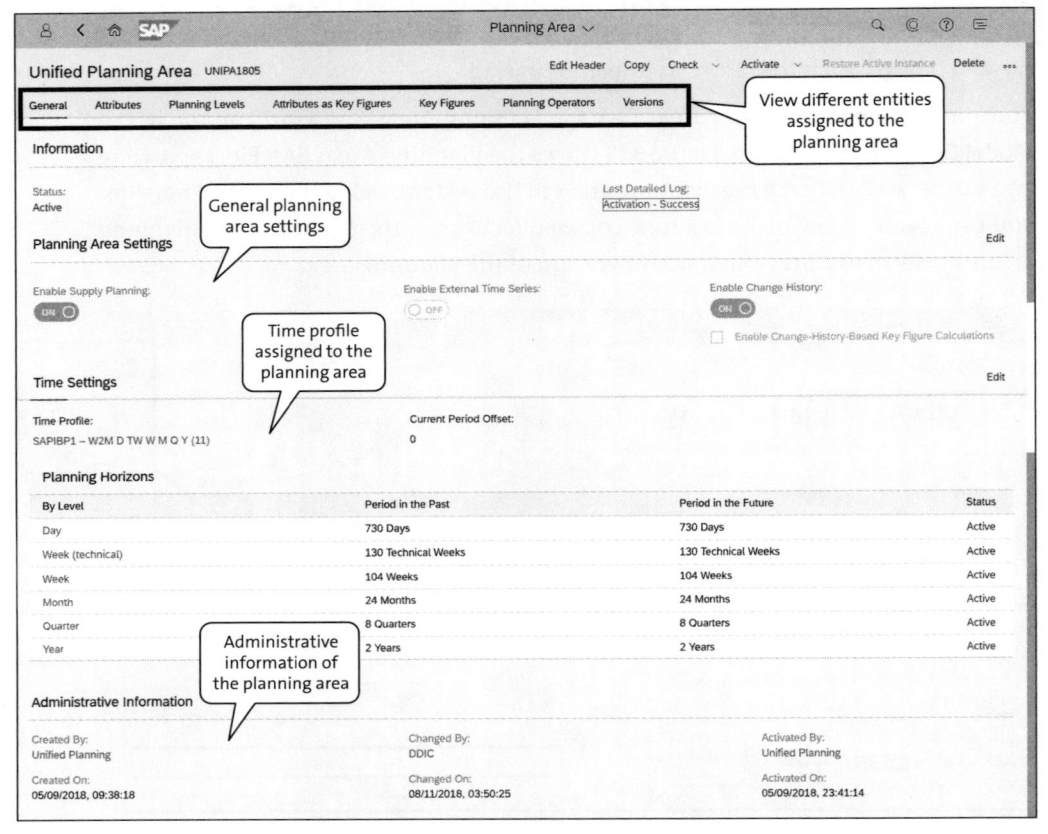

Figure 3.14 Planning Area Definition Screen

3.2.5 Planning Levels

A *planning level* is a set of attributes that identifies and labels key figure values. It enables slicing and dicing the data along different dimensions in SAP IBP. Only the attributes that have been assigned to the planning area are available to form planning levels. Planning levels can also have time profile levels, as well as the attributes assigned to the time profile levels.

A planning level enables you to analyze and plan at a specific aggregation level. It sets the boundaries for integrated business planning, which are used to set up the information tables. For example, the period-product-customer planning level provides data analysis tied to the time period, customer, and product or a combination product-customer.

A planning level can be used as the base planning level of a key figure. The *base planning level* specifies the most granular level at which the value of the key figure is defined. Key figures are calculated or stored at specific planning levels, and their values can be queried at these planning levels. Depending on the planning level—that is, the specific set of attributes used in a key figure query—different calculation and/or aggregation steps are performed to compute the key figure numbers at that level. These calculation/aggregation steps are specified in the calculation definitions of the key figure.

In a planning level, there are many types of root attributes and nonroot attributes:

- **Root attributes**
  These are necessary as keys to identify (find) individual key figure values. They define the independent dimensions in which the key figure values exist. The root attributes are often also the keys of master data types, but this is not a necessary condition.

- **Nonroot attributes**
  These are also associated with the key figure values but don't on their own uniquely identify what the key figure value is for. They can be thought of as labels (sometimes hierarchies) to aggregate key figure values.

For example, the forecast key figure is defined and stored at the technical week-product-customer planning level, and this key figure can be aggregated by other nonroot attributes of the time dimension, such as week, month, quarter, or year; of the product dimension, such as product family or group; and of the customer group dimension, such as customer region or customer country. A planning area typically includes key figures of multiple planning levels, and these can be linked with calculations, often resulting in key figures at additional planning levels.

Figure 3.15 shows the sample planning level defined as the technical week, product, location, and customer.

3   Configuring SAP IBP for Inventory

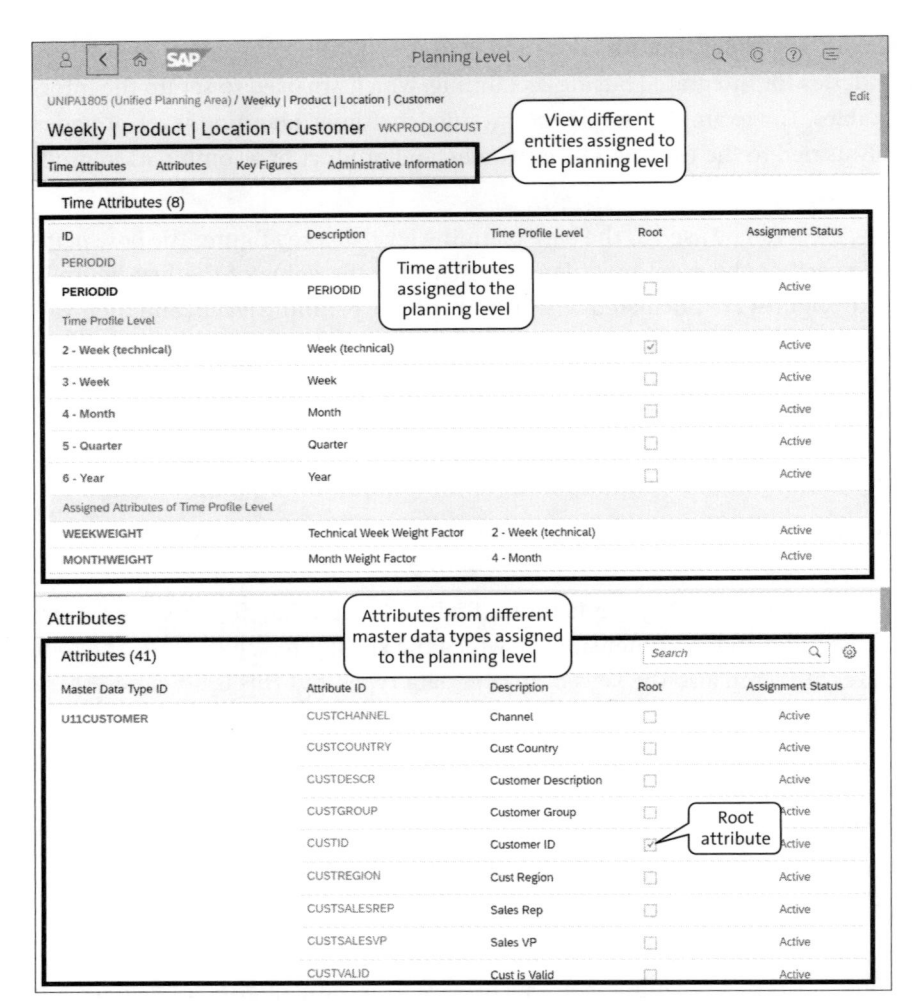

Figure 3.15 Example of Planning Level

Planning levels can be accessed by clicking the **Planning Area** tile and then navigating to the **Planning Levels** tab. To create a new planning level, click the **New** button, as shown in Figure 3.16. You'll have to select the lowest time profile at which the data will be stored or calculated. After you select the time profile level, a new screen will open on which you'll enter the ID and the description of the new planning level. All the time-profile-related attributes are added automatically, and the root is selected as per the lowest time profile level you selected on the previous screen. Add all the attributes from the master data types for the planning level by clicking the **Add** button.

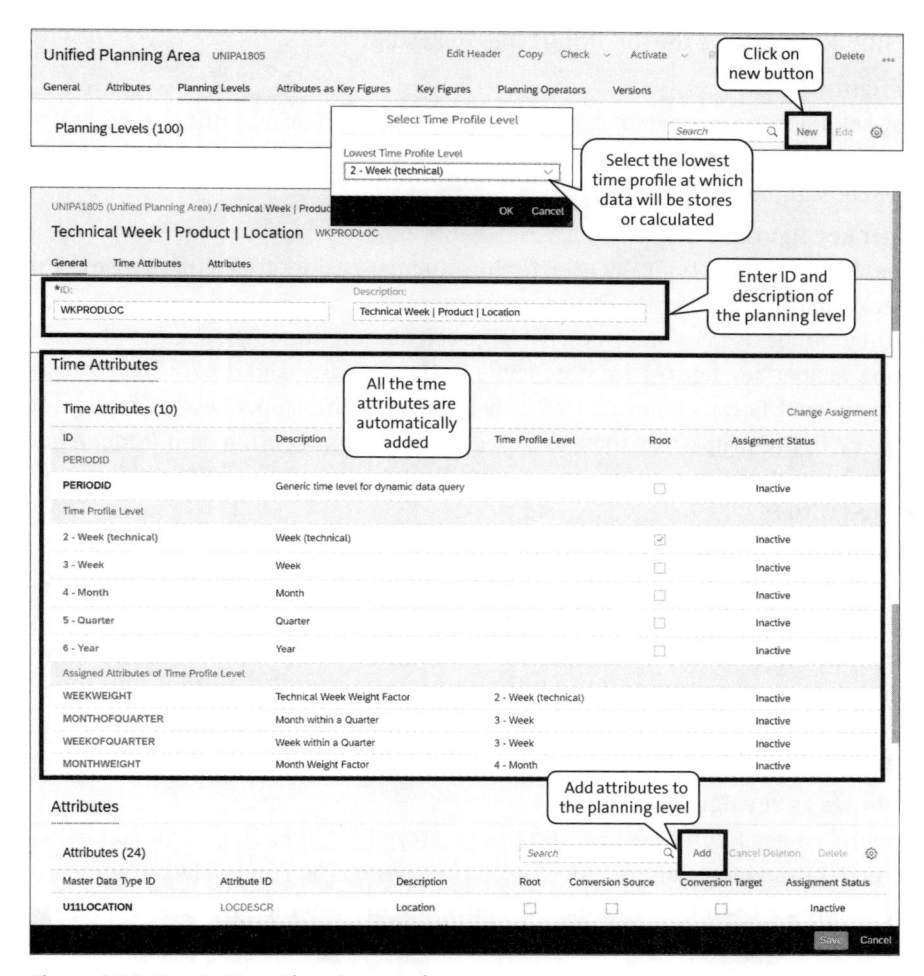

Figure 3.16 Create New Planning Level

3.2.6 Key Figures

Key figures are a series of numbers over time in which each number corresponds to a particular time period value. Transaction data in SAP IBP is represented by key figures. Examples of key figures include sales forecast, consensus demand plan, time-phased safety stock, shipment history, open sales orders, and others.

Key figures are associated with a *key*, which is a combination of attributes from one or more master data objects. Every key figure has a base planning level at which its value is stored, calculated, or manually edited.

In SAP IBP, you can have the following types of key figures:

- **Key figure**
  Most key figures are created as *standard key figures*. The values for these key figures can be stored, calculated, or edited. These key figures can be accessed through the Excel planning view and analytics.

- **Helper key figure**
  Helper key figures are typically used for intermediate values for an otherwise complex calculation in a regular key figure or in another helper key figure. For example, they can be used to break down a large calculation into manageable subcalculations. Helper key figures are not visible to the end user and do not have a base planning level. Because they're used only in calculations, helper key figures do not have key figure properties such as *stored*, *editable*, *aggregation*, and *disaggregation*. As a standard practice for ease of identification, helper key figures are usually prefixed with *H*.

- **Attribute transformation**
  An *attribute transformation key figure* is used for changing the value of an attribute based on a calculation expression, which can be used for further calculation or analysis. For example, a time period ID—say, for a week—is represented by an attribute value, PERIODID. Through attribute transformation, you can transform the value of this attribute using a calculation, such as adding an offset for lead time.

- **Attributes as key figures**
  Attributes as key figures are special types of stored key figures that are loaded as master data and have a single value for all time periods. For example, the standard cost of a product can be a decimal-type attribute in a product. While selecting the decimal attribute for the planning area, you must assign whether it's an attribute as a key figure or not. When you assign the attribute as a key figure, the system will ask you to create a new planning level or select an existing planning level. This ensures that the value is stored as a key figure in a database and is visible as a key figure in a planning view. These costs also can be used in other key figure calculations.

- **Alert key figure**
  Alert key figures help in monitoring and managing the exceptions in a business plan based on user-defined criteria. These key figures are always calculated; they can't be stored or edited. Alert key figures can only have the values 0 or 1, meaning that the alert itself is either on or off. Alerts typically check conditions on other key figures, such as safety stock versus previous cycle safety stock greater than 10%.

3.2 Building Blocks

- **Snapshot key figure**
  Snapshot key figures are system-generated key figures created when a snapshot is defined for a key figure in a planning area. There are two kinds of snapshots: original snapshots and lag-based snapshots.

After you've created attributes, master data types, time profiles, and planning areas and levels, you'll define the key figures you want to include in your planning model. To create a new key figure, go to the key figure configuration by clicking **Manage Key Figures** on the initial screen of the Configuration app or by clicking a key figure directly. Figure 3.17 shows how to access key figures.

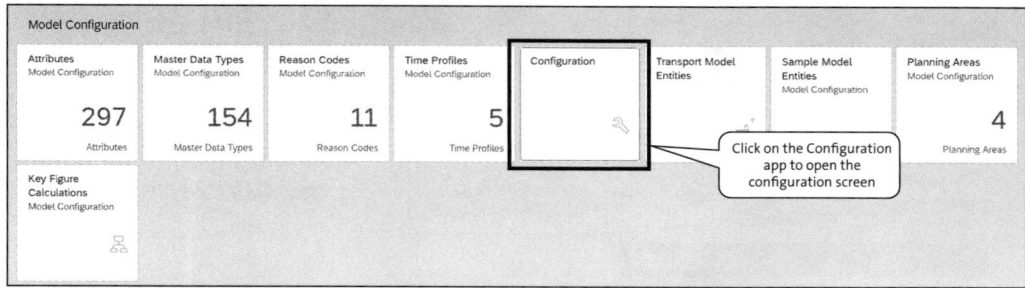

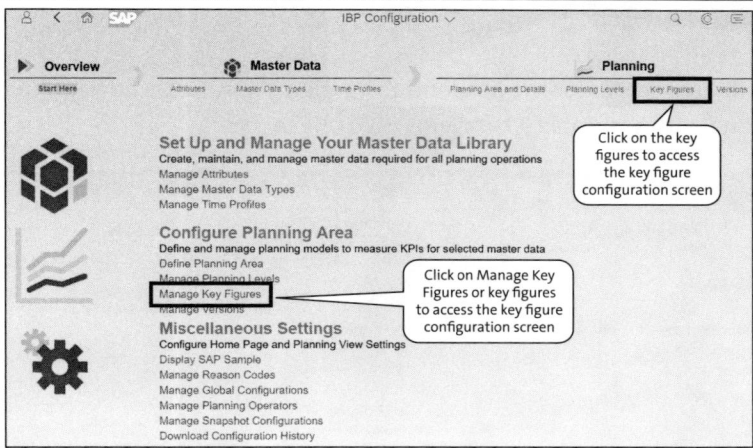

Figure 3.17 Access Key Figures Configuration Screen

On the key figure screen, you'll see the list of key figures in the planning area. To create a new key figure, click the **New** button and select the type of key figure you want to create. Select the **Key Figure** radio button to create a key figure used in analytics or Excel. Enter the **Key Figure ID**, then select the **Base Planning Level**, as shown in Figure 3.18.

125

3   Configuring SAP IBP for Inventory

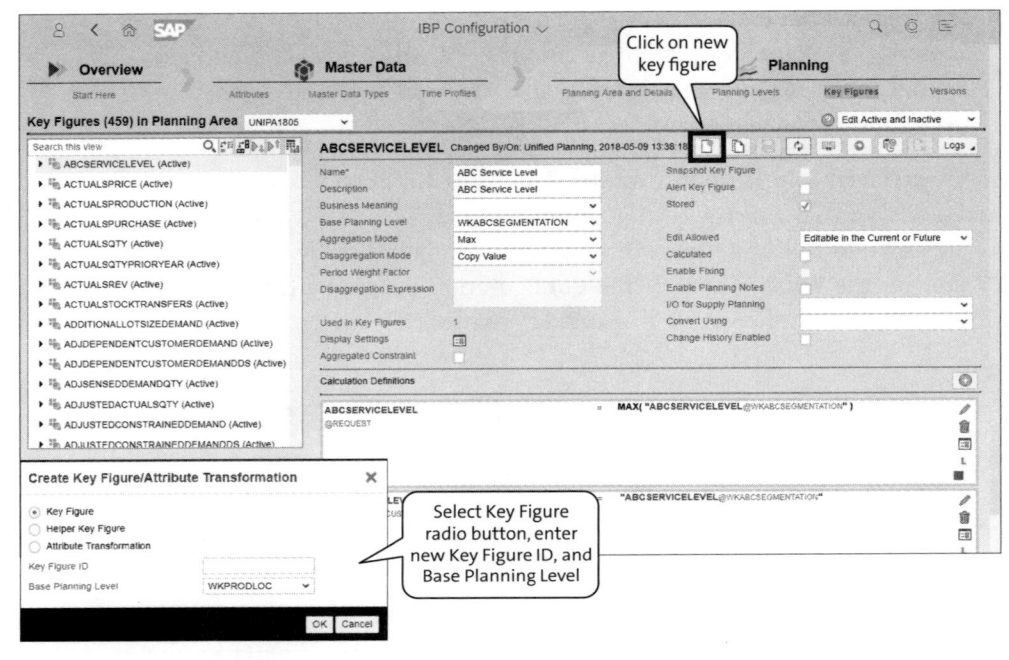

Figure 3.18 Create New Key Figure

Based on the key figure type, enter the header information. Figure 3.19 shows all the header information fields, and Table 3.1 explains each one in detail.

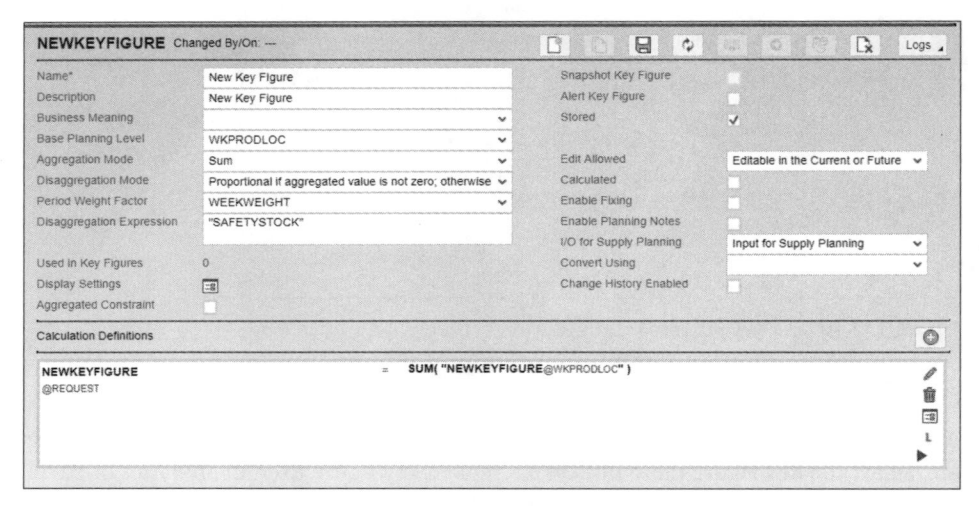

Figure 3.19 Key Fields on Key Figure Configuration Screen

Field	Explanation
Name	Name of the key figure, shown in the Excel planning view.
Description	Description of the key figure name.
Business Meaning	In the configuration, you can assign a business meaning to attributes and key figures and the code. The use of a business meaning replaces the need to use hard-coded attributes and key figure IDs. When setting business meanings for attributes, keep in mind the following: You can use a business meaning once in a planning area. If you select a description business meaning for an attribute, you must also select its corresponding ID business meaning for a different attribute in the planning area.
Base Planning Level	Shows the planning level you selected earlier.
Aggregation Mode	There are five aggregation modes: **SUM** (default value), **MIN, MAX, AVG, CUSTOM**. You use aggregation mode **CUSTOM** in the following cases: - When a key figure has a complex calculation at a request level—for example, unit price, which has inputs at the request level. - When the planning level used in the request level calculation is different from both the base planning level of the key figure and from the planning level that is used in the unit of measure or currency conversions.
Disaggregation Mode	Disaggregation mode is available only for key figures for which **Edit Allowed** or **System Editable** is selected. The following disaggregation modes are available: - **Proportional if aggregated value is not zero; otherwise, equal distribution**. Typically used for quantity and revenue key figures. - **Copy Value**. - **Equal Distribution**. - **Proportional if aggregated value is not zero; otherwise, copy value to**. Typically used for price and cost key figures—for example, the key figure COSTPERUNIT.

Table 3.1 Key Figure Configuration Fields and Explanations

Field	Explanation
Period Weight Factor	This disaggregation setting is used for disaggregation across different time levels. Used to enable a proportional distribution according to the period weight factor. This option can only be used for the disaggregation modes **Equal Distribution** and **Proportional if aggregated value is not zero; otherwise, equal distribution** and if the time profile contains the relevant attribute of the data type INTEGER. For example, week to technical split or month to week split.
Disaggregation Expression	Used to enter a disaggregation expression—that is, a mathematical expression that disaggregates the values entered for a key figure defined using other attributes and key figures. The following conditions apply to disaggregation expressions: - All the key figures in the expression must be stored and must have the same base planning level as the key figure for which the expression is defined. - All the attributes must be from the base planning level of the key figure for which the expression is defined.
Display Setting	Determines how the key figure is displayed in analytics (web user interface only), as follows: - **Decimal Places**: Specify the number of decimal places required. The default setting is six decimal places. This setting also controls rounding in disaggregation for those key figures that use SUM or AVG aggregation mode. - **Display as Percentage**: Select to display the key figure as a percentage.
Aggregate Constraint	Determines whether the key figure is used to store the aggregate constraint value. This is used for the supply planning optimizer only.
Snapshot Key Figure	By default, this field is grayed out. However, if the key figure was created from the **Manage Snapshot** window, then the field **Snapshot Key Figure** in the **Key Figure** window is enabled. Note that snapshot key figures are system-generated and are always stored.

Table 3.1 Key Figure Configuration Fields and Explanations (Cont.)

Field	Explanation
Alert Key Figure	Calculated key figures with user-defined criteria that monitor and manage the execution of business plans. Alert key figures must be calculated. They cannot be stored or edited.
Stored	Indicates a key figure in which data is stored at a defined base planning level.
Edit Allowed	If a key figure is only calculated, its values can't be edited. The values of stored key figures and key figures that are both stored and calculated can be changed. The **Edit Allowed** field controls by which of the above means a key figure value can be changed in the system. The following options are available: - **Not Editable**: You can't edit the key figure in the Excel planning view. - **System Editable**: Any kind of planning algorithm—for example, the forecasting algorithm—can change the key figure for the complete time horizon. - **Editable in the Current or Future**: System users and planning algorithms can both change the key figure, but only in the current period or for future periods. - **Editable in the Past**: System users and planning algorithms can both change the key figure, but only in the past periods. - **All Editable**: Any of the above changes are possible.
Calculated	Key figures in which values are always calculated based on user-defined formulae (e.g., Revenue = Qty × Price). Key figure calculations (for calculated key figures) are made at a defined planning level, which can be different from the level at which a user requests to view the key figure. An SAP IBP planning area typically includes key figures from multiple planning levels, which can be linked with calculations that often result in key figures at additional planning levels.
Enable Fixing	This option enables you to fix the values of an editable key figure. You can only have 20 key figures in a planning area in which fixing can be enabled.

Table 3.1 Key Figure Configuration Fields and Explanations (Cont.)

3   Configuring SAP IBP for Inventory

Field	Explanation
Enable Planning Notes	Select this checkbox if you want to use planning notes for a specific key figure as Excel comments. You can only have 20 key figures in a planning area in which planning notes functionality can be enabled.
I/O for Supply Planning	Indicates an input and/or output key figure for supply planning. If the planning area is enabled for supply planning, this field determines whether the key figure is used as an I/O for supply planning.
Convert Using	Used for disaggregation of conversion key figures. Required only for key figures that are editable. Select the key figure that you want to use to convert the current key figure.
Change History Enabled	Indicates that changes to the key figure will be tracked.

Table 3.1 Key Figure Configuration Fields and Explanations (Cont.)

3.2.7   Key Figure Calculation

For any key figure, calculation logic is always required. All key figures that an end user can see and use from the user interface must have a calculation at the request level because the system determines how to calculate the key figure starting from this calculation. The request level calculation most often uses aggregation logic (sum, minimum, maximum, average, or custom). The sum is the most popular request level aggregation logic used in SAP IBP because generally the roll-up of the planning level works with the sum logic. For example, if the sales forecast is at the product location customer level, the request calculation would be as follows:

```
SALESFORECAST@REQUEST = SUM("SALESFORECAST@WKPRODLOCCUST)
```

This means that when a sales forecast is pulled into a planning view or analytics view—say, at the product family and month level—it will aggregate the forecast by summing the all detailed values. The detailed values for sales forecast for example could be all the time periods, products, locations, and customers which fall under the requested product family and month.

For any safety-stock-related key figure, there's a complex calculation in which you can't just sum up the values across the time periods or use any other aggregation method available. For example, if the safety stock per week is 10 units, the safety stock data at a month level can't be 40. You can't just sum the values for each week in

3.2 Building Blocks

that month. In such cases, you need to have the last period aggregation method, which shows the values from the last week of the month when the data is viewed in monthly buckets, or from the last month of the quarter, when the data is viewed at the quarter level. This complicated calculation is achieved using helper key figures and attribute transformations. In such cases, the request level calculation would point to a helper key figure to do these calculations on the fly when viewing the data.

Key figures that are calculated also have a calculation other than the request level calculation. For example, the on-hand-stock value is calculated as *on-hand stock × cost per unit*. An example of the key figure calculation is shown in Figure 3.20.

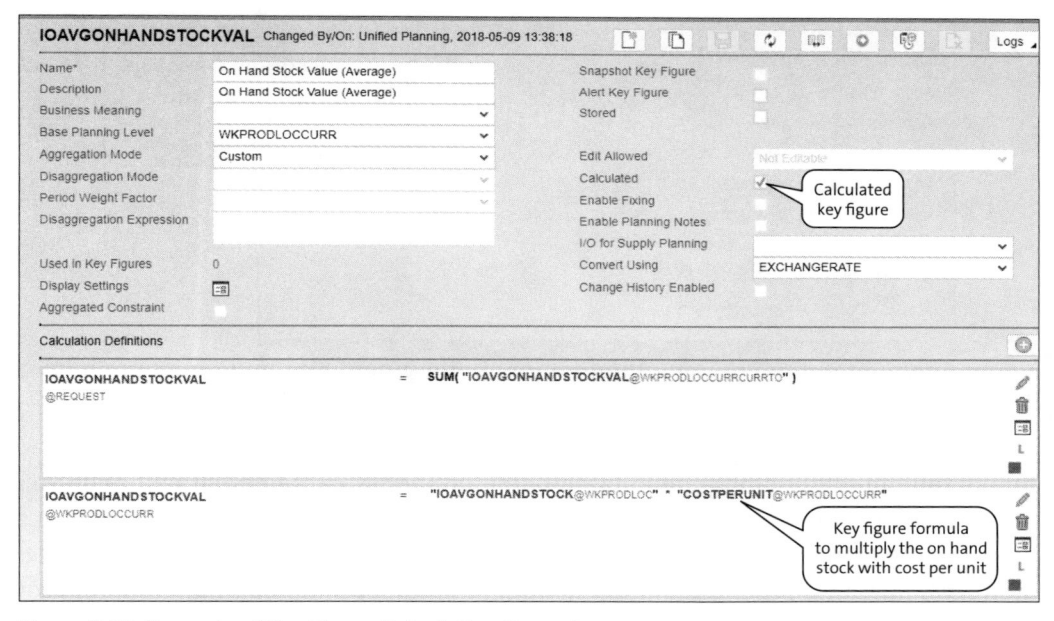

Figure 3.20 Example of Key Figure Calculation Formula

To add a calculation, click the plus icon (**+**), the **Add Calculation Icon** in the calculation definition. Select the planning level for the left side of the calculation. This can be the request level ("@REQUEST") or another planning level.

Place the cursor on the expression editor (to the right of the equals [=] sign) and type your calculation expression. When you enter the double quote (") character, a drop-down menu appears from which you can select the desired key figure. For example, for the on-hand value calculation, enter the following:

```
"IOAVGONHANDSTOCK@WKPRODLOC" * "COSTPERUNIT@WKPRODLOCCURR"
```

131

After entering the formula, when you click the **Validate** checkbox, an input key figure screen opens up in which you validate whether the values of the key figures used in the calculation are stored values. In our example, both the key figures used are stored key figures. Figure 3.21 shows the **Input Key Figures** screen after clicking **Validate**. Note that both the key figures have a **Stored Value** flag. If you use any calculated key figure as an input to the key figure calculation, then you shouldn't select this flag.

Figure 3.21 Input Key Figure Screen after Clicking Validate

You can also see the graphical view of the calculation in the Key Figure Calculation app (found in the **Model Configuration** group). To view the calculation graph, enter the planning area and the key figure for which you want to view it. Figure 3.22 and Figure 3.23 show the calculation graph of a key figure. You can toggle between the root attributes view and calculation view. Figure 3.22 shows the root attribute view of the key figure calculation; Figure 3.23 shows the calculation view of the key figure calculation.

SAP IBP supports many different calculation expressions. SAP IBP supports mathematical operators such as +, -, *, /, >, <, =, >=, <=, !=, **, %, AND, OR, and NOT. SAP IBP also supports expressions such as IF, ISNULL, CASE, ABS(), ROUND(), DAYSBETWEEN, ROUNDOWN(), ROUND(), FLOOR, CEIL, LTRIM(String), RTRIM(String) and TRIM. You can also use attributes in both conditional expressions and calculation expressions, such as the following:

KEYFIGURE1 = IF(ATTRIBUTE = "VALUE", KEYFIGURE * 2, KEYFIGURE, * 3)

3.2 Building Blocks

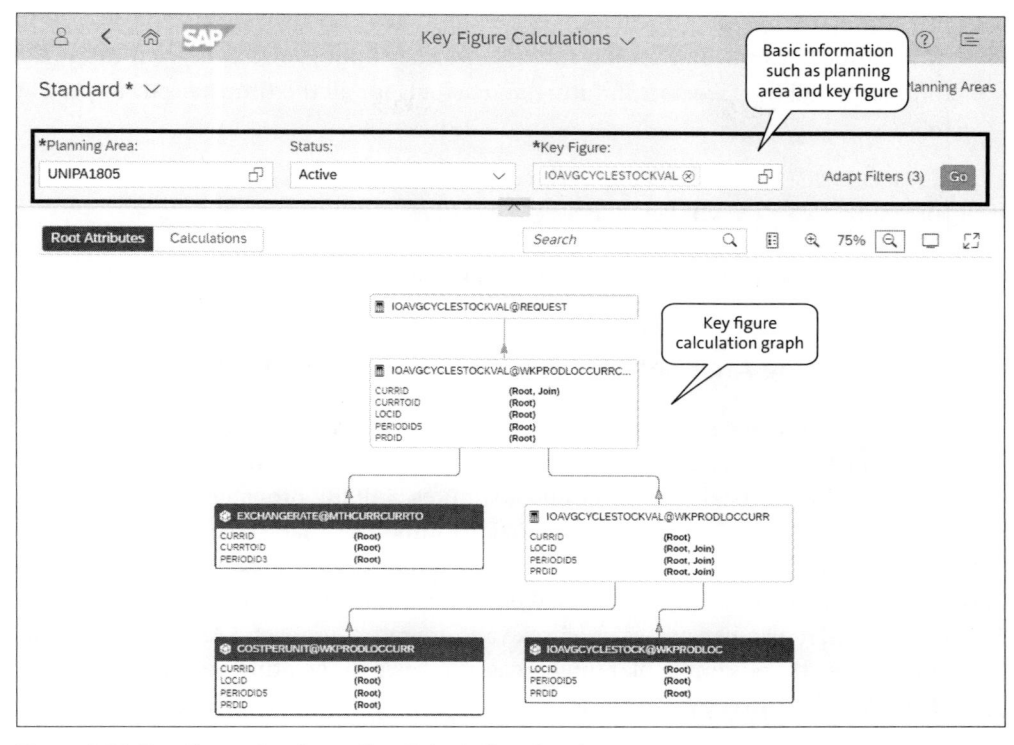

Figure 3.22 Key Figure Configuration Calculation Graph

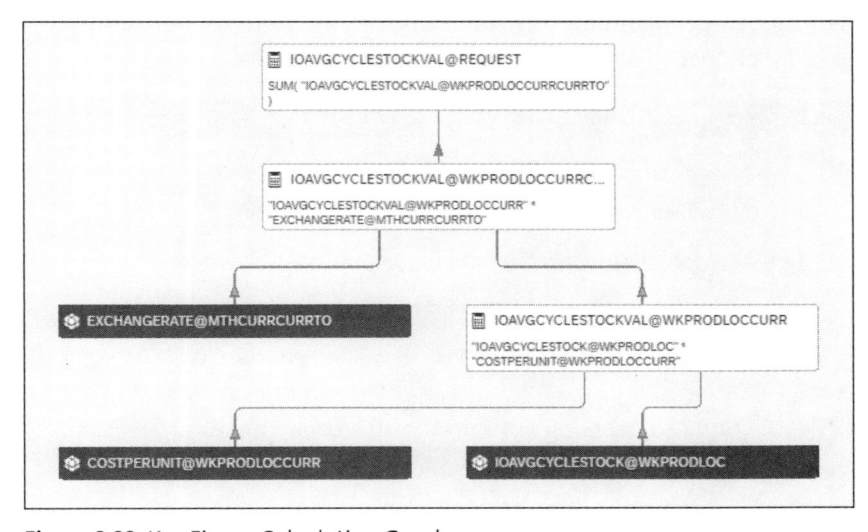

Figure 3.23 Key Figure Calculation Graph

133

Just like attributes in a calculation expression, you can also use criteria related to time periods in a calculation. For example, in a key figure you might want to use the forecast for all the forecasts in future and actuals for all the time periods in past, as follows:

KEYFIGURE@BASEPLANNINGLEVEL=IF(PERIODIDn>=$$PERIODIDCUn$$,
FORECAST@BASEPLANNINGLEVEL,ACTUALS@BASEPLANNINGLEVEL)

Here, $$PERIODIDCUn$$ is the fixed current period and PERIODIDn is the time period.

3.3 Planning Area Setup Using Predelivered Content

In SAP IBP, to run the inventory operators and time-series-based supply planning algorithms, you must use specific technical IDs defined by SAP for the relevant key figures and for master data types and attributes. SAP IBP provides sample planning areas for each module, as well as a unified planning area that is a superset of the individual sample planning areas. The sample planning areas provided by SAP provides all the mandatory and recommended definitions for time profiles, master data, and key figures. It also has preassigned relevant operators for each SAP IBP application. You can use these sample planning areas as a basis for creating your own planning areas. You also can copy one of the planning areas and extend it as necessary to meet your business needs, and you can modify the planning area after copying it—for example, to add your own master data types, key figures, calculations, or attributes.

Table 3.2 lists the sample planning areas pre-delivered with SAP IBP, along with the application or functional area represented by each planning area.

Sample Planning Area	Application or Function
SAP3	Inventory optimization
SAP3B	Demand-driven material requirement planning
SAP4	Supply (time-series-based supply planning algorithms)
SAP4c	Business network collaboration
SAP4S	Time-series-based shelf life planning, heuristic only
SAP5	SAP Supply Chain Control Tower
SAP6	Demand planning and demand sensing

Table 3.2 Sample Planning Areas Delivered by SAP

3.3 Planning Area Setup Using Predelivered Content

Sample Planning Area	Application or Function
SAP7	Order-based planning
SAP74	Order-based planning and time-series-based supply planning
SAPIBP1	Unified planning area, a comprehensive sample planning area that supports an integrated planning process covering all of the following: - Demand planning - Demand sensing - Inventory optimization - Supply planning (time-series-based supply planning algorithms) - Sales and operations planning - SAP Supply Chain Control Tower

Table 3.2 Sample Planning Areas Delivered by SAP (Cont.)

To access the sample planning areas, go to the Sample Model Entities SAP Fiori app (in the **Model Configuration** group), as shown in Figure 3.24.

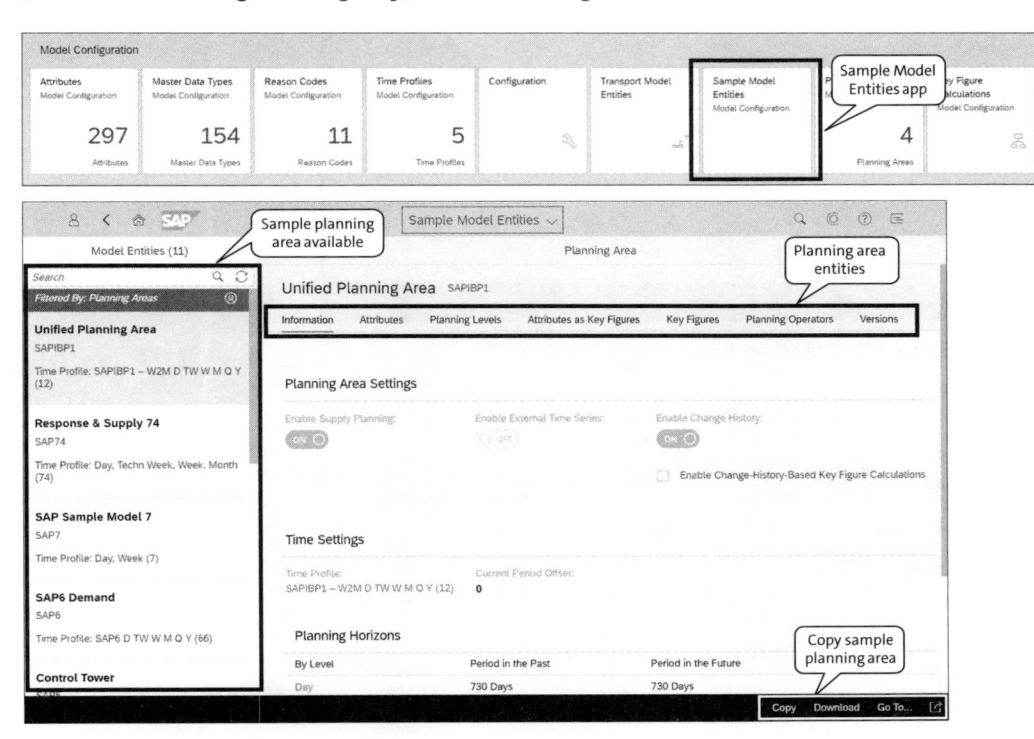

Figure 3.24 Sample Model Entities Delivered by SAP

135

3 Configuring SAP IBP for Inventory

On the left-hand side are all the sample planning areas delivered by SAP. You can view all the entities assigned to the planning area in the middle section. You can see all the attributes, time profiles, master data types, key figures, planning operators and versions assigned to the planning area by clicking on the relevant tabs.

To copy a planning area, select the planning area you want to copy and click the **Copy** button in the bottom toolbar. After you click **Copy**, you'll see four options (Figure 3.25).

Copy Planning Area
Create New with Dependencies
Creates an exact copy of the source planning area with a new ID and copies the master data types and the time profile of the planning area as well.
Merge with Existing
Combines two planning areas into a single planning area. Keeps the configuration of the target planning area, adds new configuration from the source planning area, and updates the intersect configuration in the target planning area based on the source planning area.
Replace Existing
Updates the target planning area based on the source planning area while keeping the ID of the target planning area.
Replace Existing Including Dependencies
Updates the target planning area and master data types based on the source planning area while keeping the IDs of the target planning area and master data types.

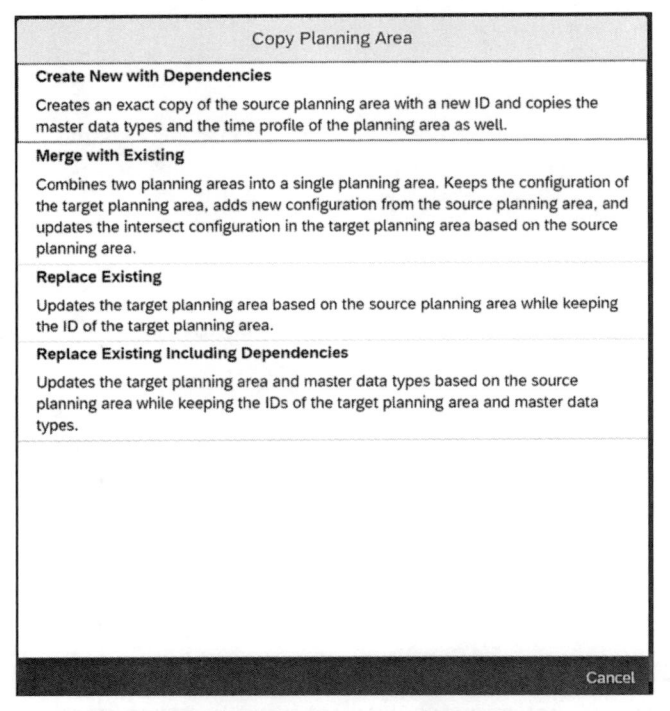

Figure 3.25 Planning Area Copy Options

The four options to copy the planning area are described in Table 3.3.

Copy Option	Description
Create New with Dependencies	This option creates an exact copy of the source planning area with a new ID and copies the master data types and the time profile of the planning area as well.

Table 3.3 Options to Copy Planning Areas

Copy Option	Description
	This option should be used to copy a sample planning area if you want to copy the attributes, the master data types, and the time profile associated with it. You can also use this option to copy a nonsample planning area if you want to create a planning area with a different set of master data types and that uses a different time profile.
Merge with Existing	This option combines two planning areas. It keeps all the configuration in the target planning area, adds everything new from the source planning area, and updates the intersect configuration based on the source configuration.
	This option is used to combine two planning areas that contain different planning area settings but are based on the same set of master data types. You can also merge a sample planning area with a nonsample planning area, or you can merge two nonsample planning areas if the source and target planning areas include the same set of master data types; that is, the master data types have the exact same ID and configuration in both planning areas.
Replace Existing	This option updates the existing target planning area based on the source planning area while keeping the ID of the target planning area.
	You can use this option if you want to recreate a planning area with an ID that's already in use. This option is used to create a copy of the source planning area in an existing target planning area—that is, delete configuration in the target planning area that isn't included in the source planning area, add the new configuration from the source planning area, and update the existing configuration in the target planning area based on the source planning area.
Replace Existing Including Dependencies	This option updates an existing target planning area and its master data types based on the source planning area and its master data types.
	You can use this option if you want to recreate a planning area with an ID that is already in use and you also want to update the master data types in the target planning area.

Table 3.3 Options to Copy Planning Areas (Cont.)

3   Configuring SAP IBP for Inventory

When you copy the unified planning area, SAPIBP1, you can also do a partial copy, selecting which application you want to copy. For example, if you have demand planning and inventory optimization in scope, you can copy SAPIBP1 and select the applications you want to copy, as shown in Figure 3.26.

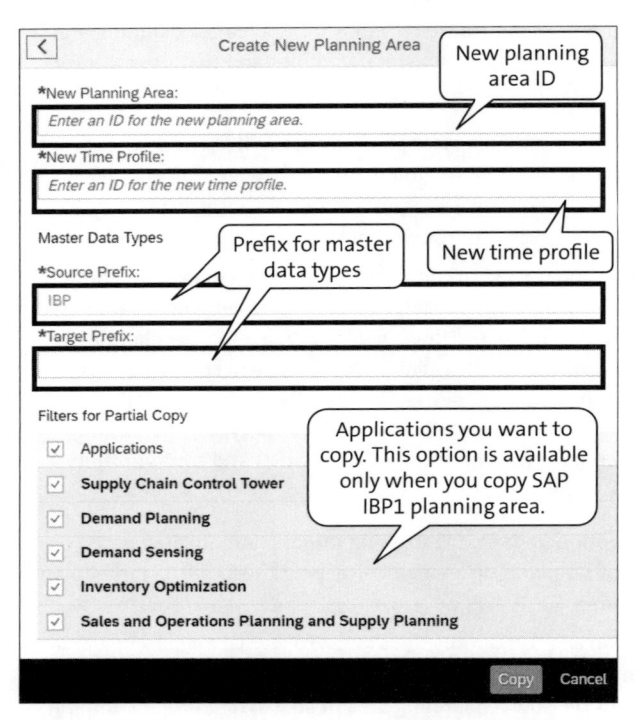

Figure 3.26 Copy Parameters Input Screen before Copying Planning Area

Once the planning area is copied from the sample planning area, it's mandatory to activate the master data, time profile, and planning area. The planning area can't be used unless it's been activated in SAP IBP. The activation needs to follow a sequence and can be started via the **Activate** button. As shown in Figure 3.27, in the Configuration app, click **Planning Area and Details**, type the planning area ID into the **Search** bar, select the planning area from the left side of the screen, and click the **Activate** icon. Check the box for **Include Related Time Profile and Master Data Types** in the pop-up and click **Activate** to confirm. This creates the necessary tables in the database for storing time data and master data records (as covered in Section 3.2.2, Section 3.2.6, and Section 3.2.7).

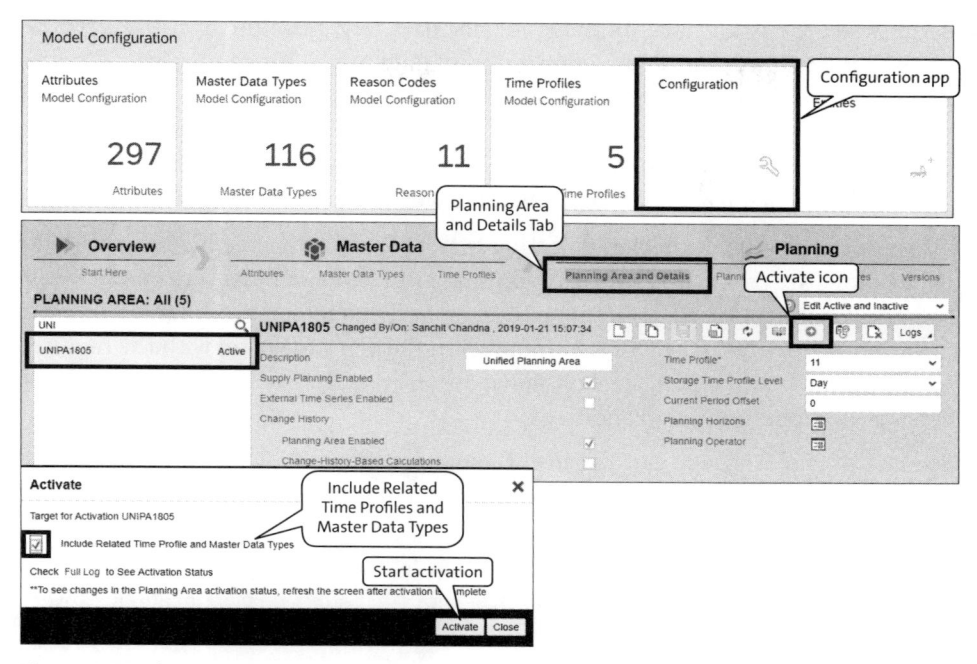

Figure 3.27 Planning Area Activation

3.4 Versions

Versions in SAP IBP let you create and manage alternate plans and perform what-if planning. You can also use the scenario functionality in SAP IBP for what-if planning, which we'll discuss in the next section. The *base version* is the inherent active version of the SAP IBP system, which is used for the active plan and data integration. You can configure additional simulations in your planning area to support alternate plans.

Versions can be defined using all or subsets of the key figures of the planning area, including calculated key figures. If a version doesn't contain all the key figures from the base planning version, you can still have references to the base version key figures so that they can be used in calculations within the version.

Versions can have version-specific master data. Those that don't have version-specific master data share their master date with the base version. You can copy key figures and/or master data (where applicable) between versions—for example, copy the data before the planning cycle (perhaps a daily or weekly cycle) into a different version to analyze and compare against the previous cycle plan.

Because versions can have different master data, organizations can use versions when they must model a completely different data model for simulation purposes. For example, you may be expanding in the future and adding lots of plants and resources to extend your capacity. To model such a scenario, you can utilize the version capability to model additional master data and plans for the capacity extension. You can compare the results with the baseline version in a planning view.

Versions are configuration elements; that is, not all users can create a version on the fly. Versions are configured by the IT administrator. For example, versions are available to all planners based on authorization roles set up by security. Planning data in a version is available to every other member in the planning team with the required authorization to work in the version, and it doesn't require an essential sharing of the version from one planner to another.

For what-if planning, you can also use scenario functionality in SAP IBP. The ways in which scenarios and versions differ are described in Table 3.4.

	Scenario	**Version**
Purpose	On-the-fly what-if scenarios.	Alternate plans maintained over time.
Created by	Planner or end user (dynamically when using the system).	Administration user at time of configuration. The number of versions is defined during configuration.
Created from	Microsoft Excel add-in by choosing **Create** in the **Scenarios** group.	Configuration app by choosing **Versions**, then **Create New**.
Changed method	*Delta:* The system keeps track of all changes to key figure values as delta records inside the scenario. If changes are made in the base version at the same time, they're visible in the scenarios—unless there are conflicting scenario deltas, in which case those take precedence.	*Copy:* Customers copy data between versions. As a result, a version is based on a copy (or an overlay of multiple copies) and not on a collection of deltas. Changes to the base version (or to another version that you copied from) are not transferred automatically to the target version. You will have to recopy the data from the source version to the target version.

Table 3.4 Differences between Scenarios and Versions

3.4 Versions

	Scenario	Version
Population	When created or saved.	Via copy process in Excel UI.
Promotion to baseline	Scenarios can only be promoted to baseline version.	Version data can be copied to any other version.
Key figures included	All.	Selectable.
Visibility	Excel and dashboards.	Excel and dashboards.
Master data changes	No.	Configurable.

Table 3.4 Differences between Scenarios and Versions (Cont.)

A planning version for an alternate plan needs to be configured in SAP IBP by an IT administrator. As shown in Figure 3.28, to navigate to the version, go to the Configuration app in the **Model Configuration** group. Click the **Version** tab and select the planning area from the left-hand side for which you want to view the versions. To create a new version, click the **New** button, enter the ID of the version you want to create and click **OK**. Select all the key figures you want to be version-specific. If you want to have version-specific master data, select the corresponding checkbox.

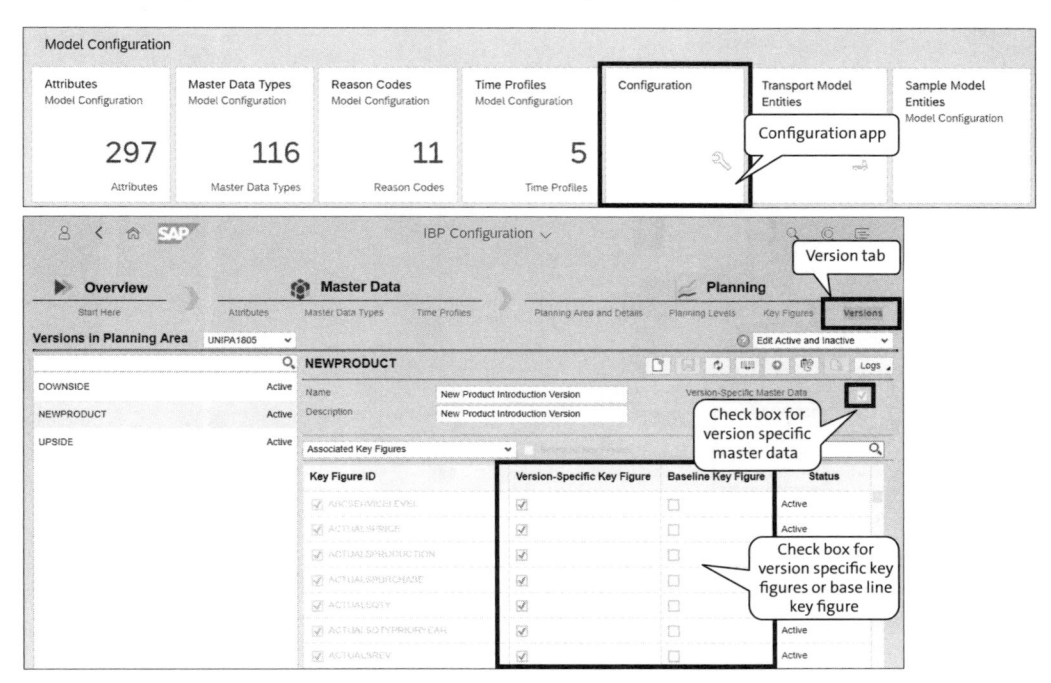

Figure 3.28 Steps to Create Version

141

3 Configuring SAP IBP for Inventory

3.5 Scenarios

Scenarios allow what-if planning in SAP IBP. Planners can use scenarios to create simulations on the fly. As explained in the previous section, there's a huge difference between a scenario and a version. Planning versions are created through configuration activity and require planning area activation. It isn't easy to create or delete a version on an ad hoc basis. Scenarios, on the other hand, can be created by a business planner without any IT support.

Scenarios are used to simulate how the user's changes to the key figure data affect other parts of the plan, and the planner can create what-if simulations to see how certain changes to the planning data affect the plan. When a planner creates a simulation and saves it as a scenario, the simulation data in a scenario is only available to the planner who has created the scenario or with whom he or she has shared the scenario. A baseline scenario is provided in the system, which contains the data in the active database.

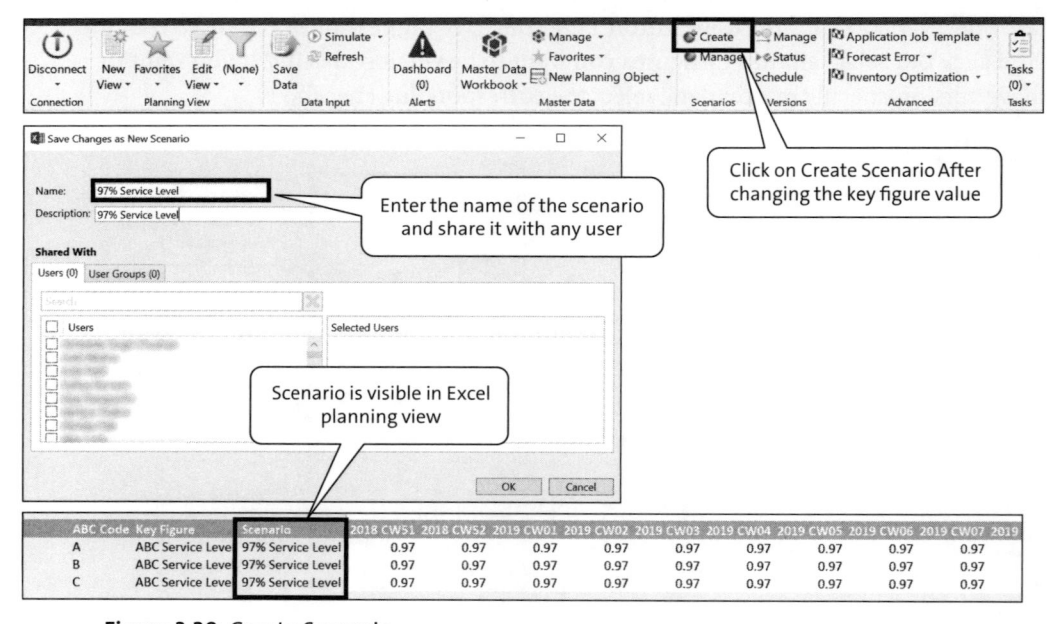

Figure 3.29 Create Scenario

Scenarios only save the delta changes made by the planner in a simulation. For example, if the planner changes the forecast for a simulation, SAP IBP only records and saves what changed in the data. The data for all other key figures, such as supply and inventory, is taken from the base scenario and doesn't change. The system keeps track of all changes to key figure values as delta records inside the scenario. If changes are made in the base version at the same time, they're visible in the scenarios—unless there are conflicting scenario deltas, in which case those take precedence.

Figure 3.29 shows how to create a scenario. To save a simulation as a scenario, click **Create** under the **Scenarios** group in Excel. After you click **Create**, you'll see the screen on which to enter the scenario details. You can also select the users with whom you want to share the scenario. In Chapter 9, we'll talk in detail about scenarios and how to perform what-if analysis.

3.6 Planning Operators

Planning operators are algorithms used to compute large amount of key figure data through defined logic in a single planning session. A simple example of using planning operators is copying one key figure to another key figure. Other examples of planning operators include statistical forecasting, supply heuristics, and inventory optimization.

Planning operators can be triggered interactively or can be scheduled to run in the background in batch mode. Interactive mode allows the operator to work in a planning simulation without saving the data in the table. Data can be saved by a user by clicking the **Save** button manually after she's satisfied with the result of the calculations. The batch mode executes in the background and saves the results in the table through the same method.

For some planning operators, you can define a filter to run the operator only for a subset of data. Not all operators can work with filters. A few operators can only be triggered in a batch mode through application job templates in SAP IBP. Every planning operator has a set of parameters, which allow you to influence the planning algorithm to achieve the desired results. Some parameters are mandatory, and others can be blank. For example, in a copy planning operator planner you must specify mandatory parameters such as source key figure, target key figure, and duration. Period offset is an optional parameter in a copy operator, which lets you copy past data.

There are several parameters delivered by SAP, which are detailed in Table 3.5.

3   Configuring SAP IBP for Inventory

Planning Operator Type	Operator Name	Usage
ABC	ABC classification	Categorize attributes as A, B, or C. The Manage ABC/XYZ Segmentation Rules app can be used to specify your segmentation settings, and the ABC/XYZ segmentation application job template can run the segmentation.
ADVSIM	Advanced simulation	Preprocessing and postprocessing operations for the simulation.
COPY	Copy	Copy values of source key figures to target key figures in the same version (base or other) of a planning area.
DISAGG	Copy and disaggregate key figure data	Copy and disaggregate values of source key figures to target key figures in the same version (base or other) of a planning area. This operator is also used to copy data between two planning areas.
IBPFORECAST	Statistical forecasting	Allows you to run the statistical forecast for the defined model in simulation or batch mode by making the statistical forecasting controls available in Excel. Statistical forecasting models are defined in the Manage Forecast Models SAP Fiori app, and statistical forecast models can be executed using the statistical forecast job template.
IO	IO (inventory optimization)	Run inventory optimization algorithms for a given supply chain network. All the algorithms for inventory optimization are automatically assigned when this operator is assigned to the planning area. The inventory optimization algorithms are as follows: - Single-stage inventory optimization - Multistage inventory optimization - Expected demand loss

Table 3.5 Planning Operators Delivered by SAP

3.6 Planning Operators

Planning Operator Type	Operator Name	Usage
		<ul><li>Forecast error CV calculator</li><li>Calculate inventory components</li><li>Forecast error calculation</li><li>Calculate DDMRP buffer levels</li><li>Recommend decoupling points (solve)</li></ul>
SCM	S&OP	Run global supply planning across your supply chain network. This is for time-series-based supply planning algorithms like the heuristic, optimizer, and network consistency check. The supply planning operators are managed through the S&OP Operator Profiles app.
SNAPSHOT	Snapshot for a predefined set of key figures	Take a snapshot of a predefined set of key figures in a batch process. When you define a snapshot on the **Manage Snapshot Configurations** screen of the Configuration app, the system automatically creates a snapshot planning operator and a redo snapshot planning operator for the definition.
SNAPSHOTREDO	Redo snapshot	Generate a new snapshot by overwriting the most recent snapshot for the predefined set of key figures.
KPI_PROFILE	Forecast error	Set up forecast error calculations for a selection of your data.

Table 3.5 Planning Operators Delivered by SAP (Cont.)

To create a planning operator on the initial screen of the Configuration app, select **Manage Planning Operators**. Select a planning operator type from the list of planning operator types on the left side of the screen. To add a new planning operator, select **+** (**Add Planning Operators**). Specify the planning operator name and description and the required modes (one or more of interactive, batch, or filter), along with the planning operator parameters, as shown in Figure 3.30.

145

3   Configuring SAP IBP for Inventory

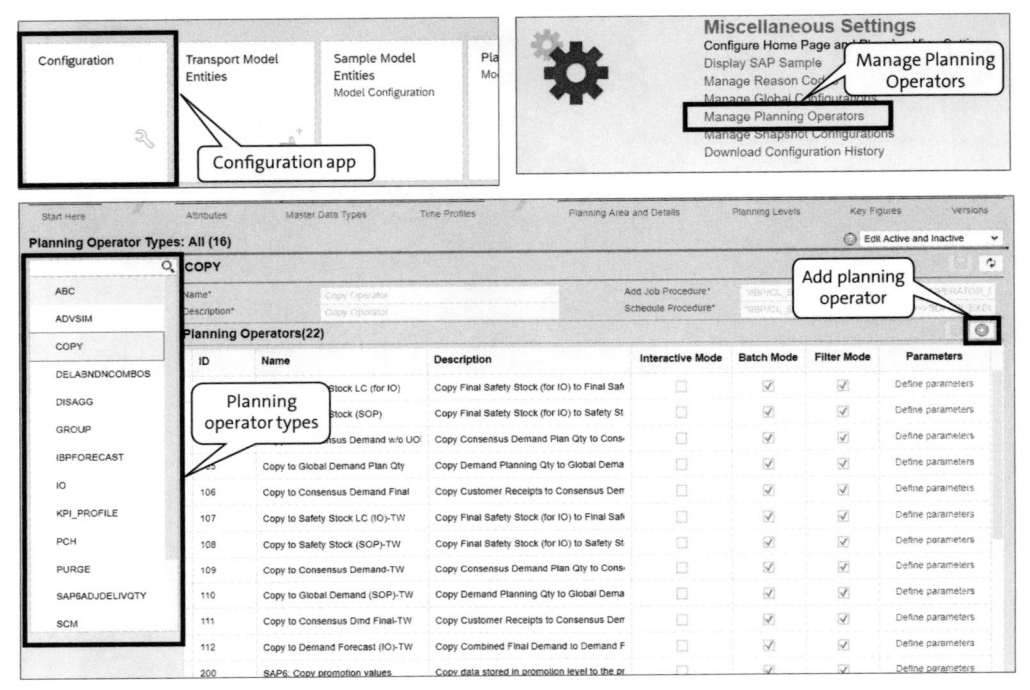

Figure 3.30 Create Planning Operators in SAP IBP

3.7   Reason Codes

Reason codes refer to a set of tags that you can use to keep track of the decisions and changes made throughout the planning process in the Excel add-in. When a user changes some data in the Excel planning view, he or she can select a reason code, provide a comment, and share it with an existing SAP Jam group. Reason codes are also recorded as a part of change history. Figure 3.31 shows the reason code pop-up window that opens when you change any data value in SAP IBP.

SAP provides a set of default reason codes, and you can set up your own reason codes per your business processes. Reason codes pop up every time any data value is changed, and they are defined at a global level. So for any planning area, whenever the data is changed by a planner, the same reason codes can apply. During the solution design phase, it's recommended to identify potential reason codes for collaboration and tracking. To create a reason code, on the initial screen of the Configuration app, select **Manage Reason Codes**. You'll see the list of reason codes already configured. To create a new reason code, click the **New** button (see Figure 3.32).

3.7 Reason Codes

Figure 3.31 Reason Code Pop-Up Screen in Excel

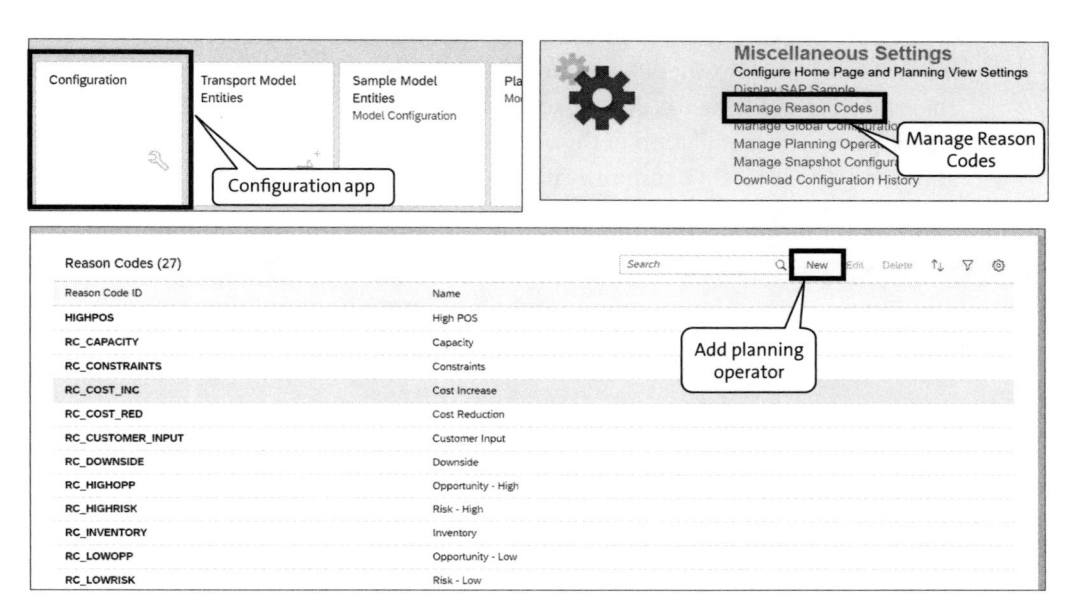

Figure 3.32 Configure Reason Codes

147

3.8 Data Integration

SAP IBP can be integrated with various SAP and non-SAP ERP and planning systems to extract the master data and transaction data required for planning. There are four broad categories of integration technologies available to integrate with SAP IBP:

- SAP Cloud Platform Integration for data services
- Open API based on SAP HANA smart data integration
- Manual data integration using the web UI in SAP IBP
- Integration using OData services

Chapter 10 explains all these integration technologies in detail and how you can load data into your planning model.

3.9 Planning Views

The primary interface to plan and interact with SAP IBP is Microsoft Excel. The advanced capabilities of SAP IBP combined with the familiarity and flexibility of Microsoft Excel makes SAP IBP the planners' tool of choice. Planners can review and edit planning data and master data using Excel planning views.

Before you start using Microsoft Excel for planning, the very first step is to download the SAP Integrated Business Planning, add-in for Microsoft Excel to your computer. This add-in is available for download from within SAP IBP or through SAP Service Marketplace. The installation of the add-in can also be pushed to all the PCs in your network by your local IT administration. Once you install the add-in, a new **IBP** tab appears in the Excel ribbon (see Figure 3.33).

Figure 3.33 SAP IBP Add-In for Microsoft Excel

To review your planning data, you need to first establish a secure connection between Microsoft Excel and SAP IBP. A connection will establish access to a specific planning area in a specific SAP IBP system, which is unique to an organization. Once the connection is established, the different buttons of the **IBP** tab in the Excel ribbon become active.

3.9 Planning Views

3.9.1 Connection to SAP IBP System

To create a connection, click **Log On**. You can either chose an existing connection or create a new one. To view the connection manager, click the icon showing three horizontal dots. To create a new connection, click **Create** (see Figure 3.34).

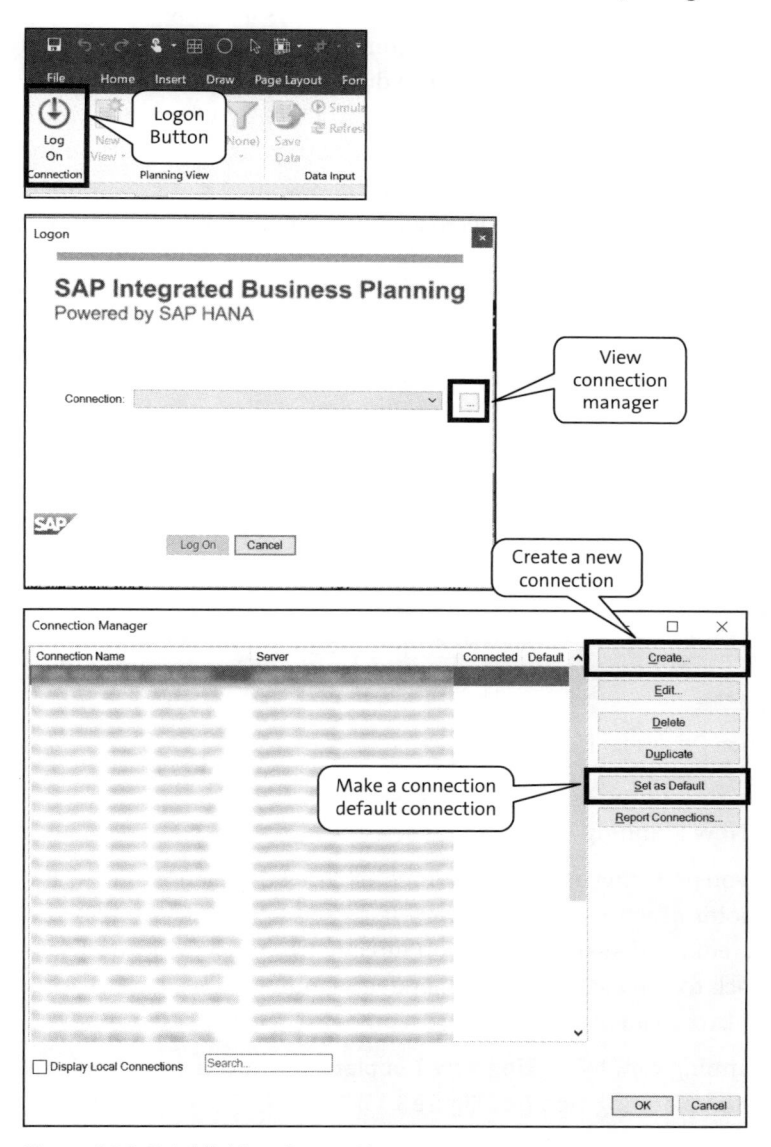

Figure 3.34 Establishing Connection

As shown in Figure 3.35, enter the connection details: the **Connection Name** and SAP IBP's **Server URL**. Then click the **Look Up Planning Areas** button and select the planning area to which you want to login via this connection. Click **OK** and a connection will be created. To make it a default connection, click the **Set as Default** button. To log in to the planning area, click the **Log On** button. Once you log on, all the buttons that were grayed out earlier in the Excel ribbon will become active. When logging off, you can choose to log off from the planning area or to disconnect from the SAP IBP system. If you choose the log off option, you log off from the SAP IBP system, which means that the remember me setting is deleted, along with your credentials for the identity provider used by your company. However, if you choose the disconnect option, the **Remember Me** setting is not deleted and you should be able to log back in without typing your credentials.

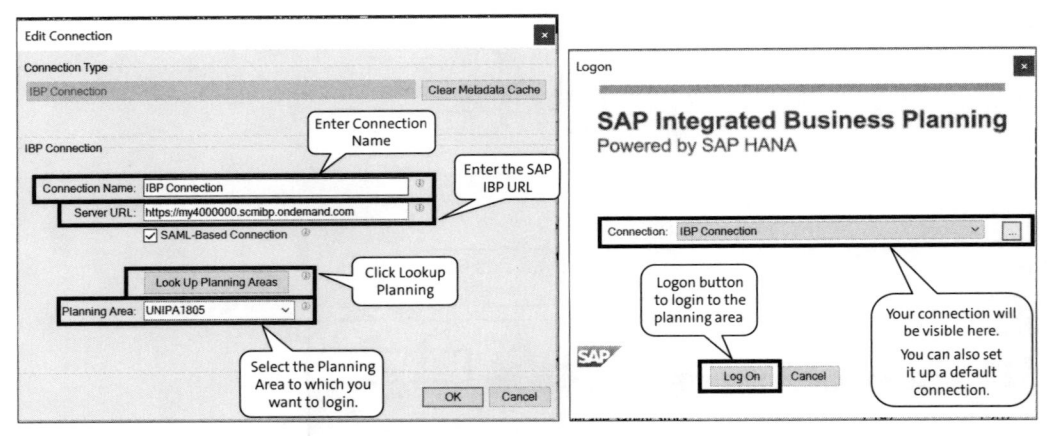

Figure 3.35 Connection Details for Excel Add-In

3.9.2 Creating a New Planning View

Planning views let you perform your daily planning activities as a planner in SAP IBP. From a technical point of view, a *planning view* is a user-defined data report that allows you to view, edit, and share information directly from the application database and save it back to the database. All generated planning views can be stored locally as Microsoft Excel data files or shared with other users in the system.

You can create a planning view by clicking **New Template**. When you do so, you'll see five options to create a planning view (see Figure 3.36):

3.9 Planning Views

- **From Template**
  With this option, you can create a planning view based on a template created by an administrator. This option is most commonly used by business users. We recommend that you use an available template. If you don't use a template, your data won't be formatted. If no templates are available, contact your administrator.

- **Without Template**
  With this option, you can create a planning view without any template. This option is most commonly used by template administrators. If you're a business user, use this option with caution.

- **Change History View on Current Sheet**
  This option is used to create a change history view. This view can only be made for a key figure for which change history capture mode is enabled. This is most commonly used by business users.

- **Copy Current Sheet**
  This option is to create copies of the current planning view worksheet, including all content, sheet-specific code, and SAP IBP definitions. This is most commonly used by business users.

- **Copy Current Workbook w/o Formatting**
  This option copies the current planning view without conditional formatting, local members, or sheet options. This option is meant to be used for support purposes only.

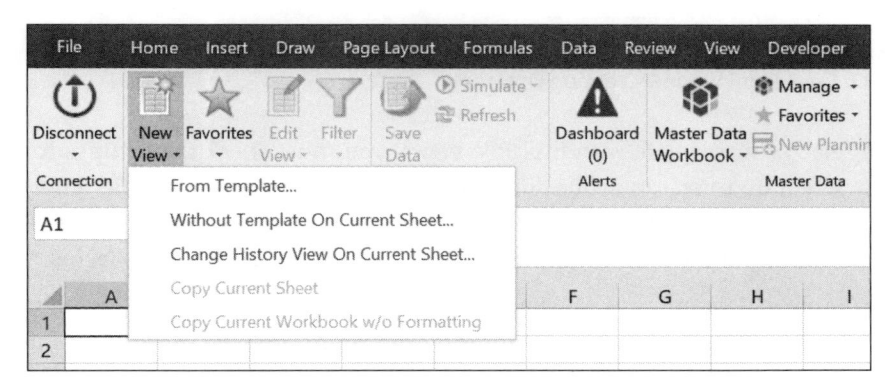

Figure 3.36 Creating New Planning View in Excel

To create a planning view from a template, in the **Planning Views** group, choose the arrow next to **New View** and select **From Template**. Select the template from which you want to create a view. The version and scenario have the default values from the base version and baseline scenario, respectively. Check the settings (key figures, planning level, etc.) derived from the selected template; if you're not using a template, make the required settings. Figure 3.37 shows how to create a new planning view.

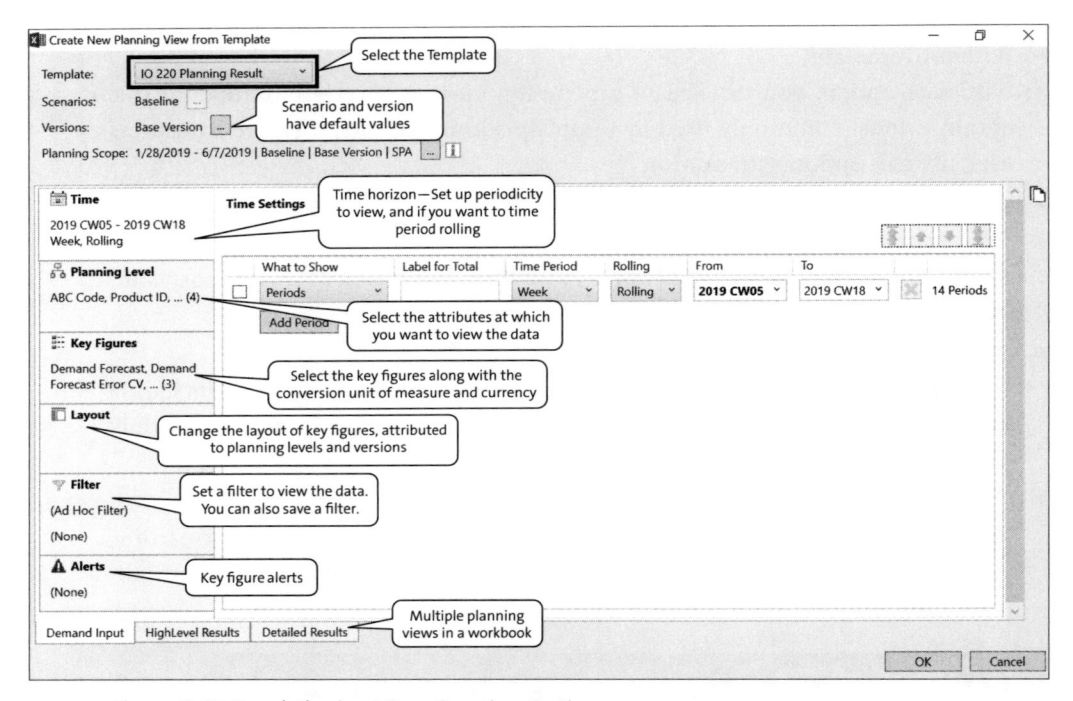

Figure 3.37 Excel Planing View Creation Options

If you've selected a template with multiple views, you must check the settings for each view. If required, you can define different settings per view—for example, different planning levels or key figures. If you change the time and key figures in a template, note that any chart or key figure formatting in the template may be affected.

Once you've created planning views, you can edit the data according to your business needs and save the changes to the database. Figure 3.38 shows a sample planning view.

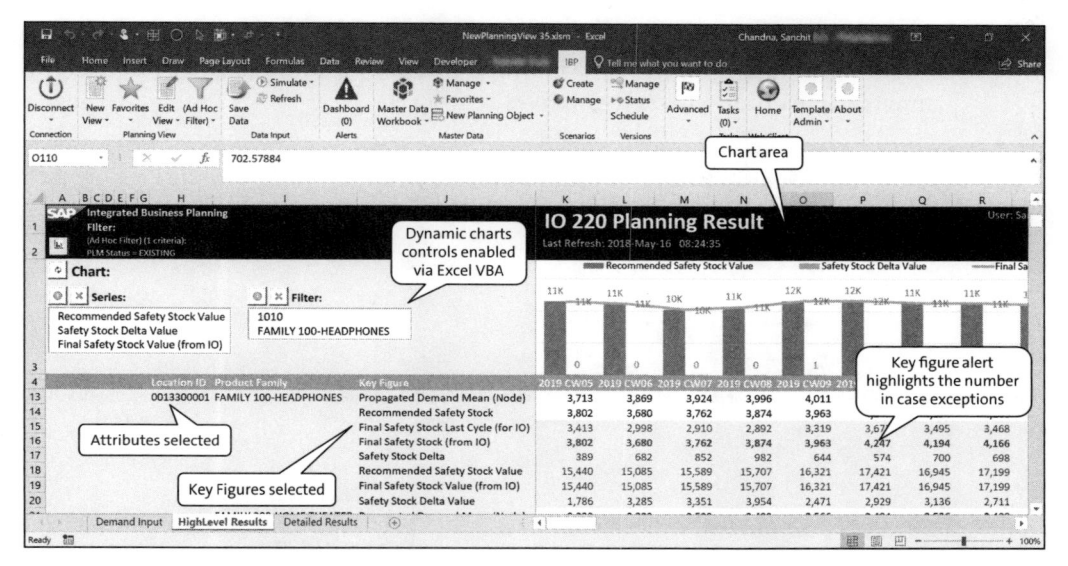

Figure 3.38 Excel Planning View

3.10 Dashboard and Analytics

In addition to Excel planning views, SAP IBP lets you analyze and visualize data in the form of charts. Certain apps enable you to view planning data in SAP IBP:

- **Analytics—Advanced**
  This app lets you view and analyze your data in SAP IBP. You can view the data in a tabular format or create a chart.
- **Dashboards—Advanced**
  This app lets you organize and present charts and other information of your choice in a single user interface to allow for convenient access.
- **Supply Chain Network**
  This app allows you to create network visualization charts that help you analyze and visualize the flow of inventory and information through the supply network. We'll discuss this app in detail in the next chapter.

3   Configuring SAP IBP for Inventory

These apps can be accessed in SAP IBP in the **General Planner** area of the SAP Fiori launchpad, as shown in Figure 3.39. All these apps are very user-friendly, allowing planners to create any charts themselves.

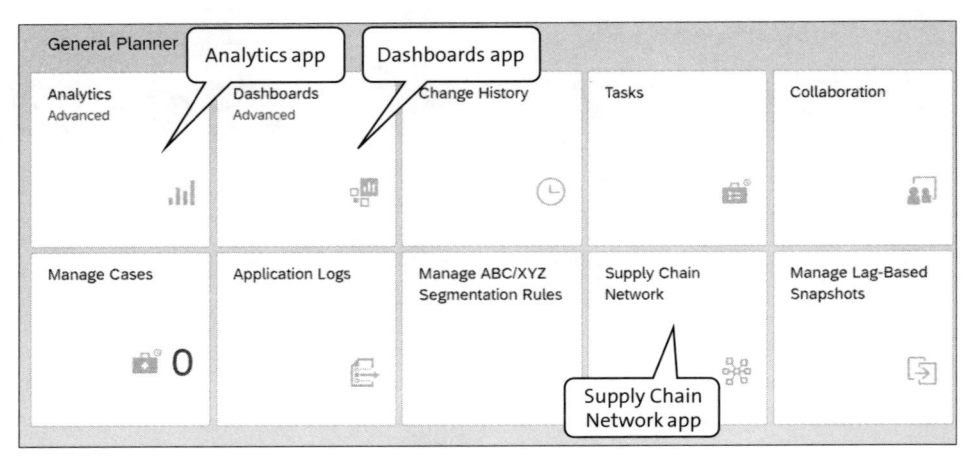

Figure 3.39 Dashboard and Analytics App

Figure 3.40 shows how to create an analytics chart. When you open the Analytics app, a list of the charts that you have permission to view will appear. From this list, you can manage your charts or create or edit charts in **Analytics Details**. To create a new chart, click **Create**, then enter the **Basic** information, select the chart type, and enter the filter criteria to display the chart. You can also select the tabular view as a chart type to view the data in tabular format. You can save your chart to access it later, and to add the chart to the dashboard you must save it first.

A dashboard shows all the charts you're most interested in. You can flexibly add charts, customize the layout of your dashboard, and share it with other users or user groups. To create a dashboard, open the Dashboards app. When you open the app, you'll see a list of all dashboards that you've created or that were shared with you. To create a dashboard, click the **New** button. Your first step will be to add analytics objects by clicking the **Add Analytics Objects** dropdown and selecting the charts you want to see. You can change the width and height of the chart added to your dashboard as needed. Figure 3.41 shows how to create a dashboard.

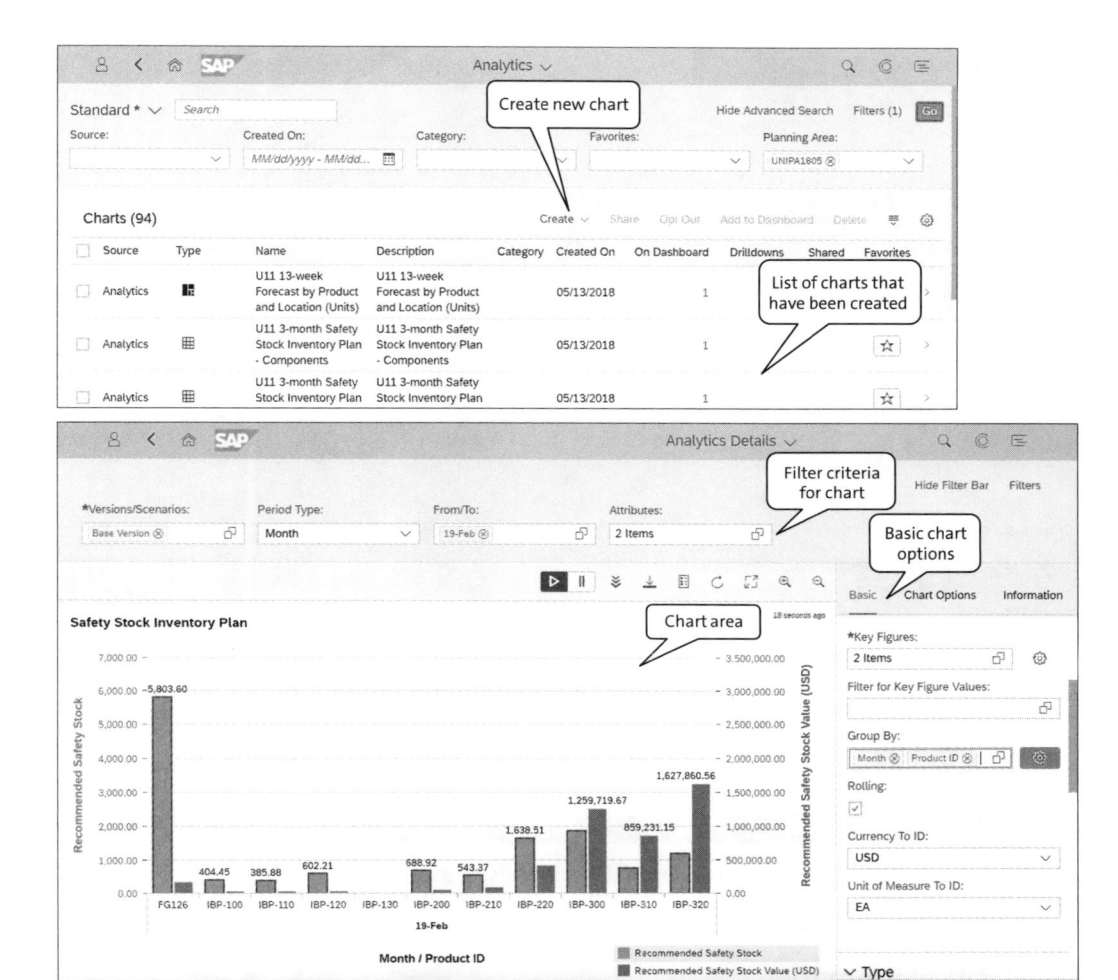

Figure 3.40 Create Charts Using Analytics App in SAP IBP

3   Configuring SAP IBP for Inventory

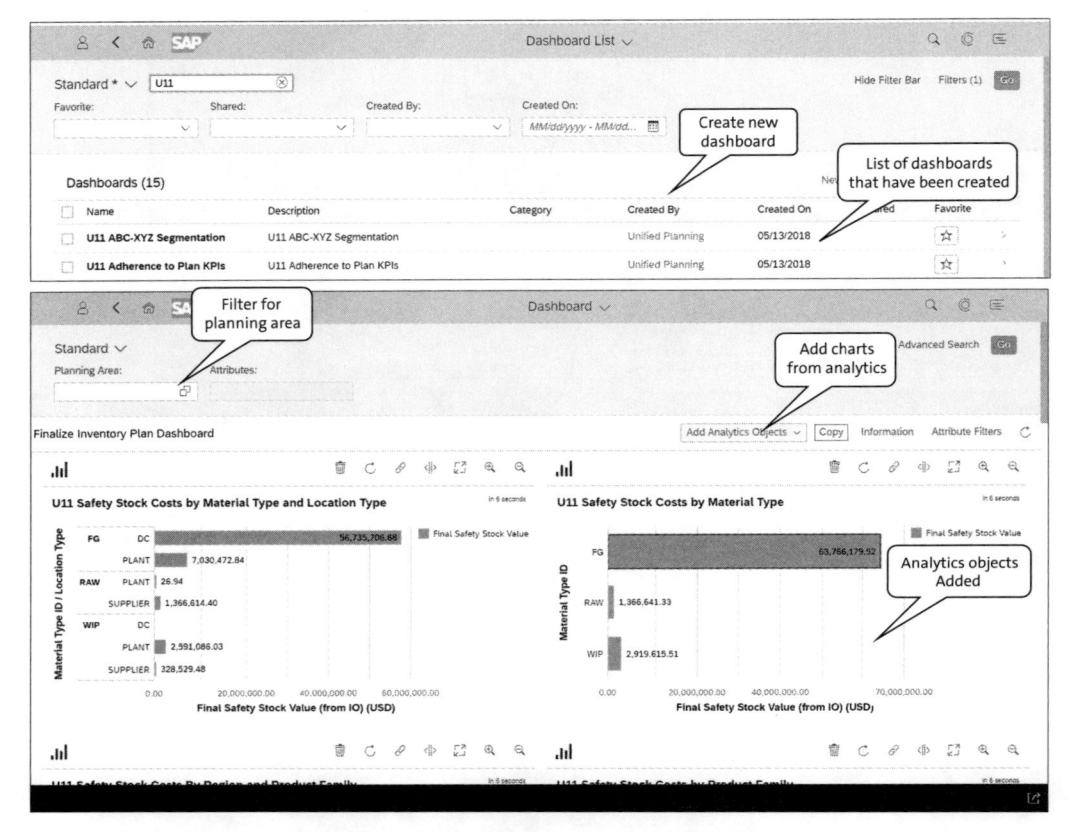

Figure 3.41 Create Dashboard Using Dashboards App in SAP IBP

3.11 Summary

In this chapter, we covered the building blocks of SAP IBP, along with the configuration of planning area and its core planning elements, like attributes, key figures, master data types, versions, and time profiles. We also covered how you can start your implementation project by copying the standard-delivered content as your starting point. Finally, we discussed other configuration elements of SAP IBP, such as planning operators, reason codes, planning views, dashboards, and analytics. In the next chapter, we'll explain the supply network and its elements in detail. We'll also cover the different master data types to model a supply network in SAP IBP and techniques to visualize the supply network in SAP IBP.

Chapter 4
Modeling a Supply Network

One of the most important aspects of a supply network is its physical structure, consisting of distributions centers, manufacturing facilities, customers, suppliers, products, and bills of materials. In this chapter, we'll discuss supply network design, which can have a significant impact on the performance of an organization and its ability to generate profit.

This chapter covers the essence of modeling a supply network, which will form the foundational structure in which our multiechelon inventory optimization algorithms will operate. We'll start this chapter with an introduction to supply networks, followed by an in-depth description of every element of a supply network. We'll cover some points to consider with respect to the complexity of supply networks, as well as techniques to visualize them in SAP IBP.

4.1 Introduction to Supply Networks

A *supply network*, as we will use the term in the context of this book, documents the flow of material, from the source of the raw material through the finished product for the end consumer. Supply networks don't need to be limited to your own organization. They can cover multiple organizations—for example, including subcontracting or contract manufacturing flows. In general, we can distinguish between two types of supply networks:

- *Physical supply networks* model the physical flow of goods as they go from raw materials to sellable products in your organization.
- *Document-based supply networks* follow the document flow, which often could become more complicated than one would expect—for example, accommodating intercompany transfers and the like.

4 Modeling a Supply Network

In supply chain planning, we aim to stay as close to the physical flow as we can, ensuring we plan the supply chain activities involved in sourcing, manufacturing, and selling products.

Modeling a supply network requires us to consider all steps required to go from acquiring a raw material to delivering a sellable product to the customer. The complexity of the supply network depends on the organizational competitive strategy, industry, and types of products being sold. For example, convenience stores aim to have their products easily available to their customers, so they have multiple warehouses or stores in their network. The perishables product industry aims to have a shorter supply network to maximize shelf life. Discount stores tend to have fewer but larger warehouses to provide lower prices to the customer. Retail companies which also operate online have a complex supply network to cater to customers.

A supply network exists in two formats: single-stage networks and multistage networks. Imagine an independent customer who orders products from a supplier for his own consumption. The customer here represents a single stage—an individual who orders products from suppliers. A multistage network is an extension of the single-stage network and includes suppliers, manufacturing plants, and distribution warehouses.

Consider a retail store that a customer enters to buy a product to consume. The supply chain begins with the customer and their demand for the product. The retail store keeps inventory of the product, which it sources from a regional warehouse. The regional warehouse sources the finished good product from the manufacturing plant. The manufacturing plant produces the finished product using one raw material and one semifinished product. The raw material is sourced from a supplier, but a semifinished product is produced using two other raw materials. These raw materials that produce the semifinished products are sourced from two different suppliers. Together, all these stages form a multistage supply network. With an increase in the number of stages, the complexity of the supply network increases exponentially because many stages and relationships need to be managed.

A multistage supply network can be represented by arcs and nodes, as shown in Figure 4.1. The supply network nodes represent the facilities where the products are stored, transformed, or sold to the customer, and the arcs that connect the nodes represent the production flow or transportation route. A production flow represents how the product is transformed—for example, from a semifinished to a finished product. A transportation route represents the movement of material between two facilities—for example, movement of a material from a plant to a distribution center.

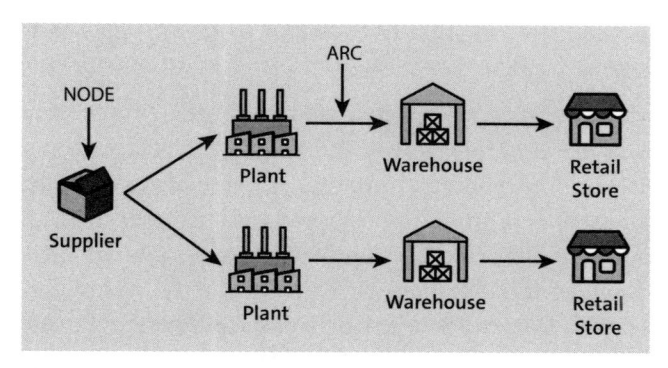

Figure 4.1 Supply Network Represented by Nodes and Arcs

4.2 Supply Network Complexity

In any given supply chain, many companies interact simultaneously with many customers, suppliers, and business partners. They interact through information sharing and material flows to create a balance between supply and demand. A *chain* suggests that there is a linear relationship between these entities, but it's not a simple one-to-one, linear relationship. Rather, it's a complex network of interconnected and interrelated entities. The number of entities and the interdependencies among them increases day by day, and managing these interactions is becoming complex.

Supply network design is dependent on an organization's competitive strategy and how supply networks can support that strategy. Firms can be either highly responsive or highly cost-efficient. A supply network is *responsive* when it can respond to changes in demand, handle demand from different markets, have shorter lead times to service the customer, handle a wide range of products, manage supply uncertainty, be able to introduce new products into markets, and service the customer at a very high service level. Being responsive comes at a cost. For example, to meet shorter lead times, you need to have many facilities closer to the customer and appropriate inventory levels at each of these facilities, which could be costly. So managers must make a trade-off between responsiveness and the cost to serve the customer.

The choice of distribution network also adds to the complexity of the supply chain. The distribution strategy and distribution network play an important role in an organization's profitability. *Distribution* refers to the movement of product between any two facilities or from facilities to the customers. An appropriate distribution network can help an organization achieve its strategic objective—that is, to have a highly cost-efficient or highly responsive supply chain.

For example, Apple sells its products through an online channel, through Apple Store locations, and through resellers like Best Buy, Target, and Walmart. A customer can get products through any distribution channel. On the other hand, companies like Dell do not own any stores and sell their products directly to the customer through an online channel and through resellers like Best Buy, Target and Walmart. Dell, through its online channel, provides its customers with high flexibility in configuring their own PCs, but this also adds to the lead time to deliver the product to the customer. Canyon bicycles, a German manufacturer, sells directly to the end consumers. They do not sell through any local reseller or stores. They have stores only for testing. An online retailer such as Amazon sells the majority of their products online and has a strong distribution network with a small number of large warehouses. It can deliver a wide variety of products to its Amazon Prime customers within two days. No other online retailer can beat this for the variety of products that Amazon offers. Some discount stores such as Costco and Sam's Club follow a different strategy for their distribution networks. They offer a smaller variety of products at a lower cost to their customers.

Retailers like Macy's and Nordstrom also take online orders from their customers, and when they do not have the product in stock, the product is shipped directly from the supplier to the customer. This is also known as drop-shipping: the product is sold through a reseller but shipped directly from the supplier. This reduces the response time, and at the same time retailer doesn't have to carry any inventory for the product. As you can see from these examples, there are many distribution strategies that an organization can adopt to achieve its strategic objectives. Some organizations follow multiple strategies for different customer groups, which adds to the complexity of their supply networks.

In today's world, the complexity of a supply network is increasing due to demanding customers and more competition. Essentially, in any supply network, there are two types of complexities in any supply chain: static and dynamic.

4.2.1 Static Sources

Static sources of complexity are part of the structural complexity of the supply network and include the following:

- **Network complexity**
  The network complexity of a supply network is a function of the following:
  - **Number of nodes in a supply network**
    The higher the number of nodes in a supply network, the higher the complexity. So if there are many distribution centers or plants or suppliers, the supply network becomes very complex. Figure 4.2 shows the simplest possible supply network with very few nodes.

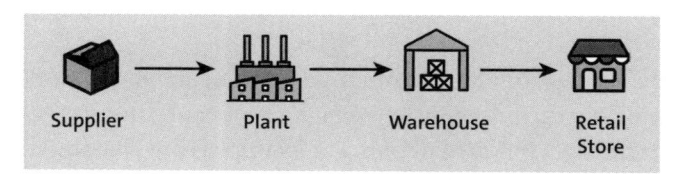

Figure 4.2 Simple Supply Network with Small Number of Nodes

  - **Number of linkages**
    The higher the number of linkages or arcs between the nodes of the supply network, the higher the complexity. For example, if there are many suppliers supplying the same component or different components to multiple plants, the complexity is higher than when one supplier supplies one plant. Figure 4.3 shows the complexity in a supply network with a high number of linkages.

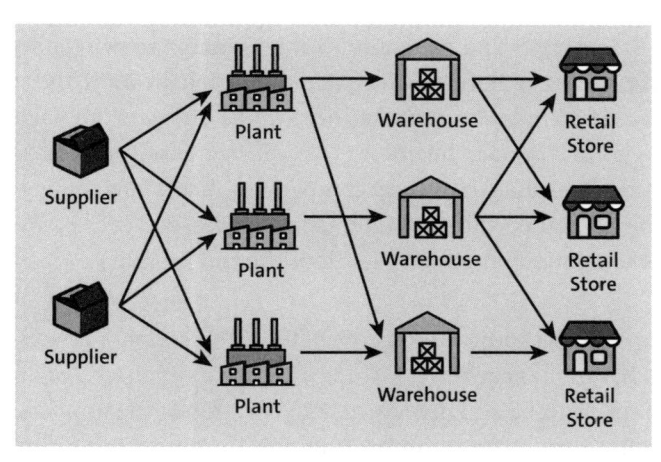

Figure 4.3 Supply Network with High Number of Linkages

- **Product mix**

    The variety of products an organization offers is one of the most significant sources of complexity in a supply chain. The smaller the number of products the organization offers, the lower the complexity. The variants of the same products offered by an organization also add to the complexity. For example, an automobile manufacturer offers multiple variants of the same car, with wheel options, technology options, interior options, and color options. The larger the number of variants an organization offers, the greater the complexity in the supply network.

- **Product complexity**

    The type and design of the product can be a significant source of supply network complexity. Product complexity can arise due to the high number of components or assemblies or raw materials in a bill of materials. For example, consider an airplane engine, which requires more than a thousand components to assemble.

- **Demand for customization**

    In today's world, customers don't just expect to receive a product or services on time; they also want choices and customizations for the products and services an organization offers. For example, each customer may want to place an order at a different frequency or different order size or different delivery schedule. The cost of serving different customers can be significantly higher with increased choices and customizations.

- **Standards and regulations**

    Organizations must follow local laws and regulations in their manufacturing processes and to sell products in certain markets. With increasing globalization, these laws and regulations can add complexity because they can be different for each country in which the organization does business. This can increase the cost to serve the customer. For example, pharmaceutical companies must follow the regulations and standards to sell their products in different countries, and each country may have different labeling requirements by law for different products.

- **Supplier base**

    The number of suppliers can also add to the complexity of the supply network because the organization has to manage relationships with these suppliers. For an agile supply chain, there needs to be a high level of collaboration with suppliers. For example, in the retail industry, there are many suppliers that supply products to be sold in retail stores, and all these suppliers require active relationship management.

4.2.2 Dynamic Sources

Dynamic complexity refers to operational complexity and the complexity of the operating environment. It also refers to complexity due to the amount of uncertainty generated by different components of the supply chain network. Some of the sources of dynamic complexity are as follows:

- **Process complexity**

  To manage any supply chain, there are several internal and external process steps to complete an activity. The larger the number of steps, the more it is prone to failure because of handoffs between the process steps. For example, to deliver the product to the customer, there may be steps like packing the product, putting it on a pallet, moving the pallet to the shipping point, preparing shipping documents, preparing insurance, posting the transaction in the ERP system, loading the truck, handing off documents to the carrier, monitoring the delivery, and so on. Although some of these steps are non-value-adding, without these steps the activity won't be complete. All these process steps also add to the lead time to fulfill the customer demand, and any failure in any one of the process steps adds to the variability of the process.

- **Parallel interactions**

  Parallel interactions with the supplier is another source of complexity in the supply network. Parallel interactions are commonly observed in the automobile or aerospace industry. For example, if the final assembly of the engine is made up of four different modules supplied by four different suppliers, any failure from any of the suppliers could lead to production halting, and that affects the entire supply chain, including other, on-time suppliers.

- **Demand amplification**

  Demand amplification is the most significant source of complexity. Demand amplification is also called the *bullwhip effect*, a term first used by the retailer Proctor and Gamble to describe demand amplification and supply distortions. Proctor and Gamble analyzed the demand of its bestselling product and noticed that sales at retail stores were variable but not excessively variable. However, the distributor orders, tied to independent entities, had a higher degree of variability. Upstream, the orders to the suppliers were even more variable. Considering that customers used the product at an almost steady rate, the degree of variability at the supplier level was huge. This pattern is called the bullwhip effect.

  Figure 4.4 shows the pattern of sales to the customer, the order pattern from retail to distributors, from a distributor to a manufacturer, and from a manufacturer to a supplier. As you can see, the variation in sales to a customer isn't huge, but the retailer order pattern has higher variability. This leads to increased or insufficient inventory at the nodes because planners tend to exaggerate demand swings, and this effect increases as we move upstream.

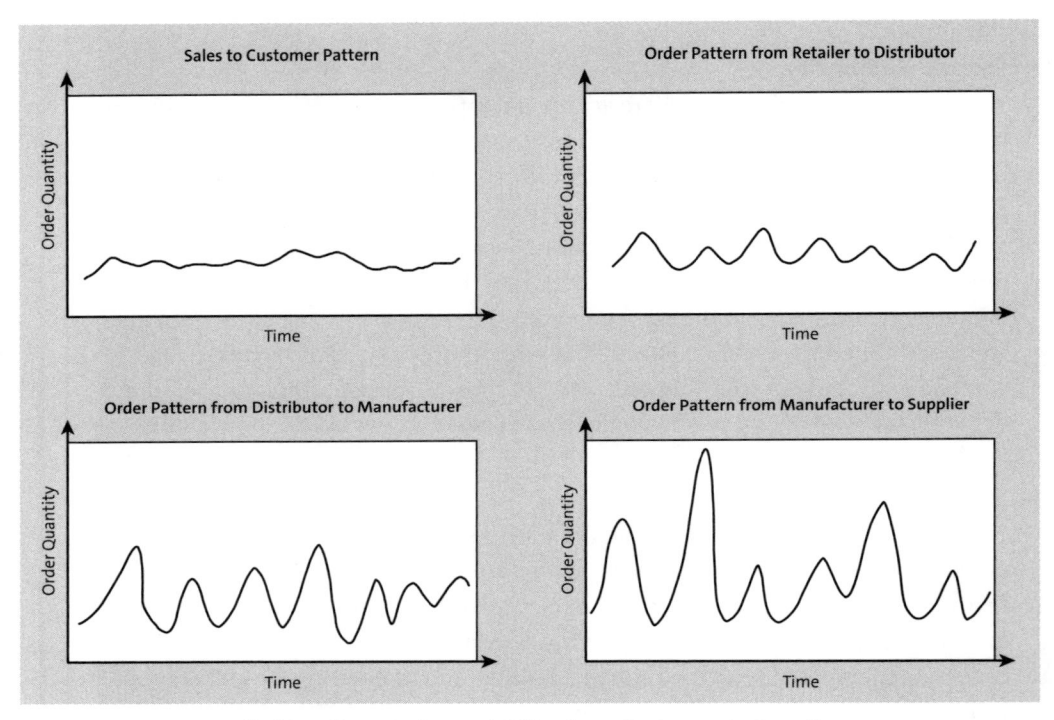

Figure 4.4 Bullwhip Effect: Order Variability from Customer to Supplier

In the next section, we'll explain various elements of a supply network and how the supply network can be modeled in SAP IBP. We'll also explain how the complexity of the supply network can influence inventory management decisions. After setting up the model in SAP IBP, in Section 4.4 we'll explain how the supply network can be visualized by leveraging SAP Fiori.

4.3 Elements of a Supply Network

In the previous chapter, you learned about the basic building blocks of the planning model, such as master data types, attributes, key figures, time profile, planning level, and so on. The planning model is the foundation of SAP IBP. All these entities together can be used to model the structure of an organization's supply network and the material flows in the network.

In this section, we'll cover how the basic building blocks of a planning model can be used to represent the supply network, which is built from locations, distribution centers, manufacturing facilities, customers and suppliers, products, and bills of materials.

4.3.1 Locations

A *location* is an actual, physical location in a supply network where products or resources are managed. There are two main categories of location in any supply network: distribution centers or warehouses, where a product is stored or packaged; and production plants, where a product is produced or assembled. In any organization, the number of locations or facilities depends on the level of complexity of the network and the organizations' objectives.

For example, to have a lower response time to fulfill a customer demand, an organization would have many warehouses or distribution centers to make the product easily available for the consumer. It's very critical for any organization to identify the location in its network that will play an inventory optimization role. For example, a cloth manufacturer that outsources all its production to contractors may want to plan inventory at the contractor locations to reduce the overall working capital. An organization may or may not want to include the cross-docking location while running inventory optimization.

In SAP IBP, a physical location is represented by the location master data type. A location is a physical place in the supply network. A location master data type has the following attributes:

- **LOCID (location ID)**
  The location ID is a unique identifier for a location in a supply network. This is a required field for the master data type.

- **LOCREGION (location region)**
  This attribute represents the region the location belongs to. For example, a location may belong to the North America or Europe region. This attribute is used mainly for reporting purposes or reviewing the data at an aggregate location region level in SAP IBP.

- **LOCTYP (location type)**
  This attribute represents the type of location; for example, a location may be a

distribution center or a plant. This attribute is also used to differentiate a vendor or a supplier location from a distribution center or warehouse location. This attribute is mainly used for reporting purposes or reviewing the data at an aggregate level in SAP IBP.

- **HOLDINGCOSTPCT (holding cost percentage)**
  This attribute represents the holding cost percentage by location. This is the cost of carrying inventory expressed as a percentage by location.

- **GEOLATITUDE (geographical latitude)**
  This attribute represents the latitude of the address of the location. This information is used for geoanalytics in the Analytics SAP Fiori app.

- **GEOLONGITUDE (geographical longitude)**
  This attribute represents the longitude of the address of the location. This information is used for geoanalytics in the Analytics SAP Fiori app.

- **LOCBUPAID (location business partner ID)**
  This attribute represents the ID of a business partner. For example, if you've modeled a subcontractor in your network, this field captures the ID of the location as in your business partner's IT system.

- **LOCVALID (location validity)**
  This attribute represents the validity of the location. This information is used for reporting purposes only.

4.3.2 Suppliers

A *supplier* or a *vendor* is an entity that supplies a material or service to an organization. Traditionally, a supplier is defined as an entity that supplies materials and subcontractors, and a contractor is an entity that provides both materials and services. Depending on the business, there can be many suppliers. For example, a very large manufacturing firm manufacturing an expensive product, such as Boeing, will have a large number of suppliers. Resellers such as Amazon also have a lot of suppliers.

Some suppliers are also classified as business partners. Organizations have tailored business relationships based on trust with their partners. Partners share risks with their customers, and their relationships are often fluid to accommodate any changes. Usually, key suppliers are modeled in the supply network for planning.

In SAP IBP, suppliers are modeled as locations. As described in the previous section, they are differentiated from the plants or distribution centers through the attribute location type and/or business partner ID. If the supply network ends at a supplier, then the location type value V is used for that location to denote the end of the supply network.

Figure 4.5 shows an example of location master data in SAP IBP.

Location ID	Geo Latitude	Geo Longitude	Location	Location Region	Location Type	Location Validity	Location Business Partner ID	Holding
0010300001	51.741168	7.255851	Inlandslieferant DE 1	EMEA	SUPPLIER	X		
0013300001	31.373596	121.256862	Supplier 1 Shanghai	APJ	SUPPLIER	X		
0013300002	31.095008	121.175048	Supplier 2 Shanghai	APJ	SUPPLIER	X		
0013300003	30.761794	121.356535	Contract Manufacturer 3 Shanghai	APJ	SUPPLIER	X		
1010	50.11056	8.685997	Plant Frankfurt	EMEA	PLANT	X		
1310	39.914325	116.426271	Plant Beijing	APJ	PLANT	X		
1710	33.749996	-84.396573	Plant Atlanta	AMERICAS	PLANT	X		
1720	47.605504	-122.340718	DC Seattle	AMERICAS	DC	X		
3710	51.924564	4.475977	DC Rotterdam	EMEA	DC	X		
6210	22.407141	114.109337	DC Hong Kong	APJ	DC	X		

Figure 4.5 Example of Location Master Data

4.3.3 Products

A *product* or *material* is a tangible or intangible good that is part of the business activities of a company. It's produced, transported, stored, and sold in the supply network. Products can be of different types: finished products, raw materials, intermediates, components, packaging, and so on. Often the focus of inventory target setting will be on critical products only. Planners need to decide whether they want to plan all the products using a sophisticated inventory optimization tool or only the important ones.

In SAP IBP, a product is represented by the product master data type (PRODUCT). It represents all the materials relevant for inventory planning. The product master provides you with all the information about the products that your company purchases, manufactures, and sells. It's the central source from which product-specific information can be retrieved. Product master data is also used in demand, supply, and S&OP planning processes. Some of its attributes are as follows:

- **PRDID (product ID)**
  The product ID is a unique identifier for each product.
- **ABCID (ABC code)**
  This attribute represents the ABC classification ID. The product's ABC classification can be used to look up the service level.
- **XYZID (XYZ code)**
  This attribute represents the XYZ classification ID. The product's XYZ classification can be used to create a differentiated process.

4   Modeling a Supply Network

- **PRDDESCR (product description)**
  The product description gives basic, high-level information about the product.
- **PRDFAMILY (product family)**
  The product family is a product attribute for reporting at an aggregate level.
- **BRAND (brand)**
  The product brand is a product attribute for reporting at an aggregate level.
- **MATTYPEID (material type ID)**
  This attribute represents the material type—for example, finished good, semifinished, or raw material. This is a product attribute for reporting at an aggregate level.
- **CATEGORY**
  The product category is a product attribute for reporting at an aggregate level.

Figure 4.6 shows an example of the product master data in SAP IBP.

Product ID	ABC Code	XYZ Code	Brand ID	Category	Material Type Desc.	Material Type ID	PLM Status	Product BU	Product Desc	Product Family
FG126	B	X	BRND400	SP	FINISHED	FG	EXISTING	BU 400	FIN126,MTS-DI,PD,SerialNo	FAMILY 400-SMARTPHONES
IBP-100	C	X	BRND100	SP	FINISHED	FG	EXISTING	BU 100	IBP-100	FAMILY 100-HEADPHONES
IBP-101-R			BRND100	RA	RAW	RAW	EXISTING	BU 100	IBP-101-R	FAMILY 100-HEADPHONES
IBP-101-S			BRND100	CP	SEMI-FINISHED	WIP	EXISTING	BU 100	IBP-101-S	FAMILY 100-HEADPHONES
IBP-102-R			BRND100	RA	RAW	RAW	EXISTING	BU 100	IBP-102-R	FAMILY 100-HEADPHONES
IBP-103-R			BRND100	RA	RAW	RAW	EXISTING	BU 100	IBP-103-R	FAMILY 100-HEADPHONES
IBP-110	C	X	BRND100	SP	FINISHED	FG	EXISTING	BU 100	IBP-110	FAMILY 100-HEADPHONES
IBP-111-R			BRND100	RA	RAW	RAW	EXISTING	BU 100	IBP-111-R	FAMILY 100-HEADPHONES
IBP-111-S			BRND100	CP	SEMI-FINISHED	WIP	EXISTING	BU 100	IBP-111-S	FAMILY 100-HEADPHONES
IBP-112-R			BRND100	RA	RAW	RAW	EXISTING	BU 100	IBP-112-R	FAMILY 100-HEADPHONES
IBP-113-R			BRND100	RA	RAW	RAW	EXISTING	BU 100	IBP-113-R	FAMILY 100-HEADPHONES
IBP-120	C	X	BRND100	SP	FINISHED	FG	EXISTING	BU 100	IBP-120	FAMILY 100-HEADPHONES
IBP-121-R			BRND100	RA	RAW	RAW	EXISTING	BU 100	IBP-121-R	FAMILY 100-HEADPHONES
IBP-121-S			BRND100	CP	SEMI-FINISHED	WIP	EXISTING	BU 100	IBP-121-S	FAMILY 100-HEADPHONES
IBP-122-R			BRND100	RA	RAW	RAW	EXISTING	BU 100	IBP-122-R	FAMILY 100-HEADPHONES
IBP-123-R			BRND100	RA	RAW	RAW	EXISTING	BU 100	IBP-123-R	FAMILY 100-HEADPHONES
IBP-130	A	X	BRND100	SP	FINISHED	FG	NEW	BU 100	IBP-130	FAMILY 100-HEADPHONES
IBP-1X0			BRND100	SP	SEMI-FINISHED	WIP	PROPOSED	BU 100	IBP-1X0	FAMILY 100-HEADPHONES
IBP-1X1-R			BRND100	RA	RAW	RAW	PROPOSED	BU 100	IBP-1X1-R	FAMILY 100-HEADPHONES
IBP-1X1-S			BRND100	CP	SEMI-FINISHED	WIP	PROPOSED	BU 100	IBP-1X1-S	FAMILY 100-HEADPHONES

Figure 4.6 Example of Product Master Data

4.3.4 Customers

A *customer* is a business partner with whom a business relationship exists, involving the issue of goods or services. As we move toward customer-centric supply chains, for some industries it's of the utmost importance to model all individual customers as part of the supply network because they're like business partners. Mostly in a B2B environment, all customers are modeled to enable differential planning. For an organization that sells its product to thousands of customers, it may not make sense to include all individual customers but instead include groups of customers.

In SAP IBP, a customer is represented by a customer master data type. A customer is modeled as an individual customer in a supply network. The customer ID in SAP IBP can correspond to, for example, the customer number, sold-to party, or ship-to party in the on-premise system. Other attributes, such as description, region code, and so on, are optional. A customer master data type has the following attributes:

- **CUSTID (customer ID)**
  The customer ID is a unique identifier for a customer in a supply network. This is a required field for the master data type.

- **CUSTCHANNEL (channel)**
  This attribute represents the channel through which a product is sold to a customer. This attribute is for reporting only.

- **CUSTCOUNTRY (customer country)**
  This attribute represents the country to which the customer belongs. For example, a customer may belong to a country in North America (Canada) or a country in Europe (France). This attribute is used mainly for reporting purposes or for reviewing the data at an aggregate customer region level in SAP IBP.

- **CUSTGROUP (customer group)**
  This attribute is used to sort customers into logical segments or groups. This attribute is required for inventory optimization to set target service levels at the group level. The groups can include industry, wholesale, retail, and so on.

- **CUSTREGION (customer region)**
  This attribute represents the region which the customer belongs to. For example, a customer may belong to the North America or Europe region. This attribute is mainly used for reporting purposes or reviewing the data at an aggregate region level in SAP IBP.

- **CUSTSALESREP (customer sales rep)**
  This attribute represents the sales rep who has a business relationship with the customer. This attribute is mainly used for reporting purposes or reviewing the data at an aggregate sales rep level.

- **CUSTSALESVP (sales VP)**
  This attribute represents the sales reps' manager. This attribute is mainly used for reporting purposes or reviewing the data at an aggregate sales VP level.

- **CUSTVALID (customer validity)**
  This attribute represents the validity of the customer's location. This information is used for reporting purposes only.

- **GEOLATITUDE (geographical latitude)**
  This attribute represents the latitude of the address of the customer. This information is used for geoanalytics in the Analytics app.

4   Modeling a Supply Network

- **GEOLONGITUDE (geographical longitude)**
  This attribute represents the longitude of the address of the customer. This information is used for geoanalytics in the Analytics app.

- **CUSTBUPAID (customer business partner ID)**
  This attribute represents the ID of the business partner. For example, if you've modeled a customer in your network, this field captures the ID of a customer as in your business partner's IT system.

- **KEYACCOUNT (key account)**
  This attribute represents whether the customer is a key account. This information is used for reporting purposes only.

Figure 4.7 shows an example of customer master data in SAP IBP.

Customer ID	Channel	Customer Country	Customer Desc.	Customer Group / Segment	Customer Region	Sales Rep.	Sales VP	Customer Valid	Geo Latitude	Geo Longitude	Key Account (Y)
0010100001	Direct	DE	Berlin	Industry	EMEA	Smith	David	X	52	13	
0011100001	Direct	GB	London	Wholesale	EMEA	Brown	David	X	51	7	
0012100001	Direct	FR	Paris	Retail	EMEA	Brown	David	X	48	21	
0013100001	Direct	CN	Beijing	Wholesale	APJ	Miller	Rodriguez	X	39	116	
0017100001	Direct	US	Chicago	PrivateCustomer	AMERICAS	Johnson	Garcia	X	41	87	
0017100002	Direct	US	Phoenix	Retail	AMERICAS	Johnson	Garcia	X	33	112	
0017100003	Direct	US	Seattle	Wholesale	AMERICAS	Jones	Garcia	X	47	122	
0018100001	Direct	IN	Bangalore	PrivateCustomer	APJ	Williams	Rodriguez	X	12	77	
0037100001	Direct	NL	Binnenlandse klant NL 1	Trading	EMEA	ZZZ	ZZZ	X	52.372	4.89	
0037100002	Direct	NL	Binnenlandse klant NL 2	Trading	EMEA	ZZZ	ZZZ	X	52.23	4.76	
0061100001	Direct	SG	Singapore	Industry	APJ	Miller	Rodriguez	X	1	103	
0062100001	Direct	CN	Domestic HK Customer 1	Trading	APJ	ZZZ	ZZZ	X	22	114	
0062100003	Direct	CN	Domestic HK Customer 3	Trading	APJ	ZZZ	ZZZ	X	22	114	

Figure 4.7 Example of Customer Master Data

Note that SAP IBP for inventory uses customer group attributes for flexibility rather than customer ID attributes. This is because SAP IBP for response and supply and/or SAP IBP for sales and operations often need to model individual customer ship-to locations as customer IDs, whereas SAP IBP for demand and other demand planning systems create forecasts at an aggregate customer group level. This flexibility supports the following three use cases:

- Demand planning forecasts and service levels are set a product-location level. In this case, all customer IDs are assigned to a "dummy" customer group.

- Demand planning forecasts and service levels are set for each individual product-location-customer ID level. In this case, the customer group attribute for each customer record can be set to be the same as the customer ID.

- Demand planning forecasts and service levels are set at an aggregate customer-attribute level.

4.3.5 Source Customer Group

Source customer group master data (SOURCECUSTGROUP) represents the inventory flow to the customer group from the customer-facing stocking nodes, also referred to as the *demand stream*. This data is specific to a product at a customer-facing location to meet the demand for a customer group. You also define the customer-service-level-target input for each demand stream, and a record must exist for each demand stream for which there is demand key figure data (forecast or sales).

The source customer group nonroot attribute is TARGETSERVICELEVEL, which represents the customer service level (between 0.5 and 1). The customer service level input is used to calculate inventory targets. The root attributes are CUSTGROUP, PRDID, and LOCID, which we defined previously. Figure 4.8 shows an example of source customer master data attributes.

Customer Group / Segment	Location ID	Product ID	Target Service Level
Industry	3710	IBP-100	0.90
Industry	3710	IBP-110	0.90
Industry	3710	IBP-120	0.90
Industry	6210	IBP-200	0.90
Industry	6210	IBP-210	0.90
Industry	6210	IBP-220	0.90
PrivateCustomer	1720	IBP-100	0.95
PrivateCustomer	1720	IBP-110	0.95
PrivateCustomer	1720	IBP-120	0.95
PrivateCustomer	6210	IBP-100	0.95
PrivateCustomer	6210	IBP-110	0.95
PrivateCustomer	6210	IBP-120	0.95
Retail	1720	IBP-200	0.92
Retail	1720	IBP-210	0.92
Retail	1720	IBP-220	0.92
Retail	3710	IBP-200	0.92
Retail	3710	IBP-210	0.92
Retail	3710	IBP-220	0.92
Trading	3710	FG126	0.95
Trading	6210	FG126	0.95

Figure 4.8 Example of Demand Stream Master Data

4.3.6 Location Product

In a supply network, a node is represented by a combination of a customer product or a location product. Because the inventory optimization model works at the customer group level, neither a customer product node nor any of its attributes are required for inventory optimization. Each location-product combination can have a different planning strategy. For example, a product at the plant may not be stored due to storage space limitation. As soon as the product is manufactured, it's moved to a nearby warehouse in which all the products are stored. Two locations may also have a different product replenishment strategy for the same product; for example, a warehouse on the East Coast may order more frequently than a warehouse on the West Cost.

A supply network node that's a location-product combination is represented by the location-product master data (LOCATIONPRODUCT) in SAP IBP. The attributes of the location-product combination also represent how a product's inventory is held at a location and how the information about that product flows through that location. LOCID and PRDID were previously defined, but the other attributes are as follows:

- **PLUNITID (planning unit or subnetwork ID)**
  The planning unit ID or subnetwork ID to which this location-product is assigned, also referred to as a *subnetwork ID*, is used to split the supply network and execute inventory operators on that limited scope. Because you'll be executing multiechelon inventory optimization on the network, make sure that you that you select the scope of the individual supply chains that are independent of each other.

- **STOCKINGNODETYPE (stocking node type)**
  This attribute represents the stocking node type indicator (S or N). S refers to a stocking node (inventory is held), and N refers to a nonstocking node (inventory flows through). S is the default value.

- **SERVICELEVELTYPE (service level type)**
  This attribute represents the service-level-type indicator (A or F). A refers to the available in full, type 1, or non-stockout-probability service level metric. F refers to fill rate or type 2. A is the default value.

- **PBR (periods between review)**
  The periods between review, also known as the *order cycle*, is the time interval (in weeks) between two consecutive order or manufacturing run decisions. It's typically one day (1/5 or 1/7 weeks) for distribution DCs, the inverse of run frequency at plants, and the inverse of ordering frequency at procurement. It shouldn't be based on the minimum order quantity (MOQ).

- **SAFETYSTOCKPOLICY (safety stock policy)**
  This attribute represents the safety stock allocation policy (F, I, or D). This attribute is relevant for how safety stock targets are calculated at hybrid stocking nodes (with both external customer demand and internal dependent demand). The options are as follows:

  - *F:* Refers to first come, first served (no allocation) and implies that the total demand at the hybrid stocking node is set to the customer service level target. It's set as the default.
  - *I:* Refers to independent demand and indicates that safety stock is calculated for only the external customer demand at the customer service level target. You might use this when, for example, a plant has limited storage capacity.
  - *D:* Refers to divide and indicates that safety stock is calculated separately (no risk pooling) for each demand at its own service level target.

- **MAXINTERNALSERVICELEVEL (maximum internal service level)**
  This attribute represents the maximum value as a constraint for the internal service level (between 0.5 and 1). A key step in the end-to-end inventory planning process is multiechelon inventory optimization (MEIO), the outcome of which is coordinated inventory targets for each node of the supply network for each period of the planning horizon. To achieve this, the MEIO solver must calculate the optimal internal service levels at each of the internal stocking points while using the customer service level targets as constraints. This attribute acts as an upper-bound constraint on the optimal internal service level.
- **MININTERNALSERVICELEVEL (minimum internal service level)**
  This attribute represents the minimum value as a constraint for the internal service level (between 0.5 and 1). Like MAXINTERNALSERVICELEVEL, this attribute acts as a lower-bound constraint on the optimal internal service level.

Figure 4.9 shows an example of location-product master data in SAP IBP.

Location ID	Product ID	Distribution Type (G or N)	Lot-Sizing Procedure	Periods Between Replenishment	Subnetwork ID	Stocking stock policy indicator for calculation (F or D	Service Level Type Indicato	Stocking Node Type In
0010300001	RM20	G		1	SPA	F	F	S
0010300001	SG25	G		1	SPA	F	F	S
0013300001	IBP-101-R	G		1	SPA	F	F	S
0013300001	IBP-103-R	G		1	SPA	F	F	N
0013300001	IBP-112-R	G		1	SPA	F	F	N
0013300001	IBP-121-R	G		1	SPA	F	F	N
0013300001	IBP-123-R	G		1	SPA	F	F	S
0013300001	IBP-1X1-R	G		1	SPA	F	F	S
0013300001	IBP-1X3-R	G		1	SPA	F	F	S
0013300001	IBP-202-R	G		1	SPA	F	F	N
0013300001	IBP-211-R	G		1	SPA	F	F	N
0013300001	IBP-212-R	G		1	SPA	F	F	N
0013300001	IBP-221-R	G		1	SPA	F	F	S
0013300001	IBP-223-R	G		1	SPA	F	F	S
0013300001	IBP-301-R	G		1	SPA	F	F	S
0013300001	IBP-302-R	G		1	SPA	F	F	N
0013300001	IBP-311-R	G		1	SPA	F	F	N
0013300001	IBP-313-R	G		1	SPA	F	F	N
0013300001	IBP-322-R	G		1	SPA	F	F	S
0013300001	RM20	G		1	SPA	F	F	S
0013300001	SG25	G		1	SPA	F	F	S
0013300002	IBP-102-R	G		1	SPA	F	F	N
0013300002	IBP-111-R	G		1	SPA	F	F	N
0013300002	IBP-113-R	G		1	SPA	F	F	N
0013300002	IBP-122-R	G		1	SPA	F	F	

Location Product

Figure 4.9 Example of Location-Product Master Data

4 Modeling a Supply Network

4.3.7 Ship-From Location and Ship-To Location

In a supply network, there are many locations that supply to another location or multiple locations. For example, a manufacturing plant supplies a product to different distribution centers. So for any given location-product combination, a product can be sourced from a plant or can be supplied to a different distribution center.

In SAP IBP, the supplying location is represented by the ship-from location master data (LOCATIONFR). This is a reference master data type that references the location master data type. It isn't an independent master data type and doesn't require separate data loading. It represents a sourcing location that ships to other locations. Its root attribute is LOCFR, which represents the ship-from location ID. Its values are referenced from the LOCID attribute.

Just like the ship-from location, the receiving location in SAP IBP is represented by ship-to location master data (LOCATIONTO). This is a reference master data type that references the location master data type. Like ship-from location master data, it isn't an independent master data type and doesn't require separate data loading. It represents a receiving location that receives the product from other locations. Its root attribute is LOCTO, which represents the ship-to location ID. Its values are referenced from the LOCID attribute.

Figure 4.10 shows an example of ship-from location reference master data in SAP IBP, and Figure 4.11 shows an example of ship-to location reference master data in SAP IBP.

Ship-From Loc. ID	Ship-From Loc. Desc.	Ship-From Loc. Region	Ship-From Loc. Type
0010300001	Inlandslieferant DE 1	EMEA	SUPPLIER
0013300001	Supplier 1 Shanghai	APJ	SUPPLIER
0013300002	Supplier 2 Shanghai	APJ	SUPPLIER
0013300003	Contract Manufacturer 3 Shanghai	APJ	SUPPLIER
1010	Plant Frankfurt	EMEA	PLANT
1310	Plant Beijing	APJ	PLANT
1710	Plant Atlanta	AMERICAS	PLANT
1720	DC Seattle	AMERICAS	DC
3710	DC Rotterdam	EMEA	DC
6210	DC Hong Kong	APJ	DC

Ship-From Location

Figure 4.10 Example of Ship-from Location Master Data

Ship-To Location ID	Ship-To Location Desc	Ship-To Location Region	Ship-To Location Type
0010300001	Inlandslieferant DE 1	EMEA	SUPPLIER
0013300001	Supplier 1 Shanghai	APJ	SUPPLIER
0013300002	Supplier 2 Shanghai	APJ	SUPPLIER
0013300003	Contract Manufacturer 3 Shanghai	APJ	SUPPLIER
1010	Plant Frankfurt	EMEA	PLANT
1310	Plant Beijing	APJ	PLANT
1710	Plant Atlanta	AMERICAS	PLANT
1720	DC Seattle	AMERICAS	DC
3710	DC Rotterdam	EMEA	DC
6210	DC Hong Kong	APJ	DC

Figure 4.11 Example of Ship-to Master Data

4.3.8 Location Sourcing

Location sourcing rules determine how the demand is fulfilled at a location other than the customer. A location sourcing rule represents an arc that connects two locations in a supply network. Location sourcing rules are used to represent how the stock moves between different locations—for example, a stock transfer from a manufacturing location to a distribution center.

Location sourcing rules also have a location sourcing ratio, which determines the split by which the demand at the location is fulfilled from two different sourcing locations. The location sourcing ratio can be constant or time-phased. To depict a constant location sourcing ratio, the location transport ratio in the master data type can be maintained (TRATIO). If the location sourcing ratio should vary over time, the time series flag will be set in the master data type (RATIOTS = 'X'), resulting in the use of the transport ratio key figure by the inventory optimization operator.

Lead times are also available in location sourcing rules to account for the transportation time between the sending and receiving locations. Because lead time provides the only opportunity to do so, you must capture the time offset between the availability of stock at a source location and receipt of stock at the destination location.

4   Modeling a Supply Network

Various factors should be considered while modeling transportation lead times. Some examples of times that may add up to overall transportation lead times are as follow:

- The time required to pick, pack, and load the product at the source location
- Physical transportation time between source and destination locations
- Other time considerations for receiving the product at the destination location, such as the time at customs

In SAP IBP, transportation sourcing information for each product, ship-from location (source), and location (target) is represented by the source location master data. SOURCELOCATION represents the PRDID, LOCFR, and LOCID root attributes, which we defined previously. The nonroot attributes are as follows:

- **RATIOTS (ratio time series indicator)**
  This attribute represents a time-series/static indicator for sourcing quotas. This indicates if time-series values (if set to X or x) or static quota values should be used for transportation sourcing quotas.

- **TRATIO (location sourcing ratio)**
  This attribute represents the static transportation sourcing quota value. If RATIOTS is set to static, this value is used as the sourcing quota for all periods for the transportation lane.

- **TLEADTIME (transportation lead time)**
  This attribute represents the transportation lead time in weeks (can be fractional). It includes any ordering time, picking time, and so on.

- **TLEADTIMEVARIABILITY (transportation lead time error CV)**
  This attribute represents the transportation lead time coefficient of variation (CV) in weeks. This is the ratio of the standard deviation of lead time to the average lead time in weeks.

- **TMINLOTSIZE (minimum transportation lot size)**
  This attribute represents the minimum lot size for the transportation lane in the base unit of measure of the product.

- **TINCLOTSIZE (incremental lot size)**
  This attribute represents the incremental lot size for the transportation lane in the base unit of measure of the product.

- **TSHIPMENTFREQUENCY (transportation shipment frequency)**
  This attribute represents the number of shipments received per week. This is the inverse of the shipment frequency per week. This attribute is optional and should

be used only in specific advanced scenarios, such as when shipments are received more frequently than the ordering frequency—for example, if orders are placed once a week but the product is shipped daily in smaller batches. This doesn't impact safety stock requirements but does have an impact on the cycle stock (inventory to cover forecast or known net requirements). This defaults to the inverse of PBR when no value is provided (recommended).

- **TDELIVERYTYPE (transportation delivery type indicator)**
  This attribute represents the indicator for the impact of late deliveries. This attribute is optional and should be used only in specific advanced scenarios related to lead time variability. It specifies how two consecutive shipments are assumed to behave when the first shipment is late:
  - S or s indicates sequential; that is, the second shipment always arrives after the first shipment (more conservative safety stock). This is the default.
  - C or c indicates cross-over; that is, the two shipments are independent, and the second shipment can arrive before the first shipment (less conservative safety stock).

Figure 4.12 shows an example of location-source master data in SAP IBP.

Version	Ship-From Loc. ID	Location ID	Product ID	Transportation Lead Time	Transportation Leadtime Error CV	Location Sourcing Ratio	Transportation Shipment Frequency
Base Version	0013300001	1010	IBP-101-R	1	0.1	1	
Base Version	0013300001	1010	IBP-103-R	1	0.1	1	
Base Version	0013300001	1010	IBP-112-R	1	0.1	1	
Base Version	0013300001	1010	IBP-121-R	1	0.1	1	
Base Version	0013300001	1010	IBP-123-R	1	0.1	1	
Base Version	0013300001	1010	IBP-1X1-R	1	0.1	1	
Base Version	0013300001	1010	IBP-1X3-R	1	0.1	1	
Base Version	0013300001	1010	IBP-202-R	1	0.1	1	
Base Version	0013300001	1010	IBP-211-R	1	0.1	1	
Base Version	0013300001	1010	IBP-212-R	1	0.1	1	
Base Version	0013300001	1010	IBP-221-R	1	0.1	1	
Base Version	0013300001	1010	IBP-223-R	1	0.1	1	
Base Version	0013300001	1010	IBP-301-R	1	0.1	1	
Base Version	0013300001	1010	IBP-302-R	1	0.1	1	
Base Version	0013300001	1010	IBP-311-R	1	0.1	1	
Base Version	0013300001	1010	IBP-313-R	1	0.1	1	
Base Version	0013300001	1010	IBP-322-R	1	0.1	1	
Base Version	0013300001	1310	IBP-101-R	1	0.1	1	
Base Version	0013300001	1310	IBP-103-R	1	0.1	1	
Base Version	0013300001	1310	IBP-112-R	1	0.1	1	
Base Version	0013300001	1310	IBP-121-R	1	0.1	1	
Base Version	0013300001	1310	IBP-123-R	1	0.1	1	
Base Version	0013300001	1310	IBP-1X1-R	1	0.1	1	
Base Version	0013300001	1310	IBP-1X3-R	1	0.1	1	
Base Version	0013300001	1310	IBP-202-R	1	0.1	1	
Base Version	0013300001	1310	IBP-211-R	1	0.1	1	
Base Version	0013300001	1310	IBP-212-R	1	0.1	1	
Base Version	0013300001	1310	IBP-221-R	1	0.1	1	
Base Version	0013300001	1310	IBP-223-R	1	0.1	1	
Base Version	0013300001	1310	IBP-301-R	1	0.1	1	

Location Source

Figure 4.12 Example of Location-Source Master Data

4.3.9 Production Sourcing

In any supply network, at a manufacturing location where a product is produced, one of the key requirements is to have a bill of materials for the product. A bill of materials is a complete, formally structured list of the components that make up a product or assembly. The list comprises the material number of each component, together with the quantity and unit of measure. A BOM can be single level or multilevel. For example, a finished material would contain semifinished materials as components, which in turn would contain raw materials as components in the next level. There can also be different alternative BOMs for a product depending upon the lot sizes, validity dates, and different production methods.

BOMs are also used in production planning for semifinished goods and in purchase planning for raw materials by propagating the demand through a BOM explosion.

In SAP IBP, a single bill of materials is represented by a production source header and production sourcing item master data. The production source header (SOURCEPRODUCTION) is the header information for each product, location, and source header. This can be from a manufacturing BOM or sourced from an external vendor. The source header (SOURCEID) must be unique for each product and location if it represents a BOM (has component products). PRDID and LOCID were defined previously. Scenarios in which a product can be made at a plant and simultaneously sourced from another plant are supported. The additional source production attributes are as follows:

- **SOURCEID (source ID)**
  This attribute represents the production source header ID. This is a unique indicator for each source production record.

- **OUTPUTCOEFFICIENTTS (output product coefficient time series indicator)**
  This attribute represents the output coefficient time series indicator. This is an optional attribute that indicates whether the output coefficient is a time series (X or x) or static (any other value). It defaults to static if no value is provided.

- **OUTPUTCOEFFICIENT (output product coefficient)**
  This attribute represents the output coefficient value. This is an optional attribute (it defaults to 1 if no value is provided) used as the output coefficient in every period if the corresponding indicator is set to static. The component coefficient in the BOM is divided by this value when determining the BOM multiplier for the components.

- **PRATIO (production sourcing ratio)**
  This attribute represents the static production sourcing quota value. If PRATIOTS is set to static, this value is used as the sourcing quota for all periods for the production source headers.

- **PRATIOTS (production ratio time series indicator)**
  This attribute represents a time series/static indicator for sourcing quotas. This indicates if time series values (if set to X or x) or static quota values should be used for production-sourcing quotas.

- **PLEADTIME (production lead time)**
  This attribute represents the production lead time in weeks (can be fractional). It includes any ordering time, picking time, goods issue time, and so on.

- **PLEADTIMEVARIABILITY (production lead time CV)**
  This attribute represents the production lead time CV in weeks. This is the ratio of the standard deviation of lead time to the average lead time in weeks.

- **PMINLOTSIZE (minimum production lot size)**
  This attribute represents the minimum lot size for production in the base unit of measure of the product.

- **PMAXLOTSIZE (maximum production lot size)**
  This attribute represents the maximum lot size for production in the base unit of measure of the product.

- **PINCLOTSIZE (production incremental lot size)**
  This attribute represents the incremental lot size for the production source in the base unit of measure of the product.

- **PSHIPMENTFREQUENCY (production shipment frequency)**
  This attribute represents the number of shipments received per week. This is the inverse of the order frequency per week. This attribute is optional and should be used only in specific advanced scenarios, such as when orders are produced more frequently than the ordering frequency—for example, if orders are placed once a week but the product is produced daily in smaller batches. This doesn't impact safety stock requirements but does have an impact on the cycle stock (inventory to cover forecast or known net requirements). This defaults to the inverse of PBR when no value is provided (recommended).

- **PDELIVERYTYPE (production delivery type)**
  This attribute represents the indicator for the impact of late orders. This attribute is optional and should be used only in specific advanced scenarios related to lead time variability. It specifies how two consecutive production orders are assumed to behave when the first order is late:
  - S or s indicates sequential; that is, the second order always finishes after the first order (more conservative safety stock). This is the default.

4   Modeling a Supply Network

- C or c indicates cross-over; that is, the two orders are independent, and the second order can be completed before the first order (less conservative safety stock).

- **SOURCETYPE (source type)**
This attribute represents the production source type indicator (P, U, or C). This indicates if the source production record represents a primary output of a BOM (P), if the product is sourced from an external vendor (U), or if it is a secondary coproduct output of a BOM (C). Coproducts are ignored in inventory target planning, and an external vendor represents a supply end point in the network.

Figure 4.13 shows an example of production source header master data in SAP IBP.

Location ID	Product ID	Source ID	Output Product Coefficient	Output Product Coefficient Time Series Indicator	Production Delivery Type	Production Incremental Lot Size	Production Source Inva
1010	IBP-101-S	1010_IBP-101-S	1		C		1
1010	IBP-110	1010_IBP-110	1		C		1
1010	IBP-111-R	1010_IBP-111-R	1		C		1
1010	IBP-111-S	1010_IBP-111-S	1		C		1
1010	IBP-112-R	1010_IBP-112-R	1		C		1
1010	IBP-113-R	1010_IBP-113-R	1		C		1
1010	IBP-120	1010_IBP-120	1		C		1
1010	IBP-121-R	1010_IBP-121-R	1		C		1
1010	IBP-121-S	1010_IBP-121-S	1		C		1
1010	IBP-122-R	1010_IBP-122-R	1		C		1
1010	IBP-123-R	1010_IBP-123-R	1		C		1
1010	IBP-1X0	1010_IBP-1X0	1		C		1
1010	IBP-1X1-S	1010_IBP-1X1-S	1		C		1
1010	IBP-200	1010_IBP-200	1		C		1
1010	IBP-201-S	1010_IBP-201-S	1		C		1
1010	IBP-202-R	1010_IBP-202-R	1		C		1
1010	IBP-203-R	1010_IBP-203-R	1		C		1
1010	IBP-210	1010_IBP-210	1		C		1
1010	IBP-211-R	1010_IBP-211-R	1		C		1
1010	IBP-211-S	1010_IBP-211-S	1		C		1
1010	IBP-212-R	1010_IBP-212-R	1		C		1
1010	IBP-213-R	1010_IBP-213-R	1		C		1

Figure 4.13 Example of Production Source Header Master Data

4.3.10   Production Sourcing Item

Component master data (COMPONENT) is a reference master data type that references the product master data type. It represents the component products in a BOM that are used to manufacture or build or assemble the output product. Its root attribute is PRDFR, which represents the component product ID. Its values are referenced from the PRDID attribute.

Production source item master data (PRODUCTIONSOURCEITEM) represents the BOM information for each source production record of type P. PRDID and SOURCEID were defined previously. COMPONENTCOEFFICIENTTS and COMPONENTCOEFFICIENT are like OUTPUTCOEFFICIENTTS and OUTPUTCOEFFICIENT, respectively.

Figure 4.14 shows an example of production source item master data in SAP IBP.

4.4 Visualizing Supply Networks in SAP IBP

Product ID	Source ID	Component Coefficient	Component Coefficient Time Series Indicator	Component Offset	Source Item ID
IBP-101-R	1010_IBP-101-S	1			10
IBP-101-R	1310_IBP-101-S	1			10
IBP-101-R	1710_IBP-101-S	1			10
IBP-101-S	1010_IBP-100	1			10
IBP-101-S	1310_IBP-100	1			10
IBP-101-S	1710_IBP-100	1			10
IBP-102-R	1010_IBP-101-S	1			20
IBP-102-R	1310_IBP-101-S	1			20
IBP-102-R	1710_IBP-101-S	1			20
IBP-103-R	1010_IBP-100	1			20
IBP-103-R	1310_IBP-100	1			20
IBP-103-R	1710_IBP-100	1			20
IBP-111-R	1010_IBP-111-S	1			10
IBP-111-R	1310_IBP-111-S	1			10
IBP-111-R	1710_IBP-111-S	1			10
IBP-111-S	1010_IBP-110	1			10
IBP-111-S	1310_IBP-110	1			10
IBP-111-S	1710_IBP-110	1			10
IBP-112-R	1010_IBP-111-S	1			20
IBP-112-R	1310_IBP-111-S	1			20

Figure 4.14 Example of Production Source Item Master Data

4.4 Visualizing Supply Networks in SAP IBP

In SAP IBP, you can visualize the supply network you've modeled using the Supply Network Visualization SAP Fiori app. This app is available for all SAP IBP applications, but there are only specific planning areas with supply network data that can be used to visualize supply networks. This app allows planners to build a graphical representation of the supply network, from the vendor to the customer. The network visualization can be used by the planners to validate the overall supply network for accuracy, along with material flows across the supply chain.

The sample planning areas delivered by SAP that have the required master data and attributes to support the supply network visualization are as follows:

- The unified planning area (SAPIBP1)
- SAP IBP for sales and operations (SAP2)
- SAP IBP for supply (SAP4)
- SAP IBP for inventory (SAP3)

For an active model with master data attributes and generated key figures, the network chart can be created in SAP IBP by opening the Supply Network Visualization app. This app can be accessed from the **General Planner** area. Figure 4.15 shows where to find the Supply Network Visualization app, and Figure 4.16 shows the page that opens when you select the app.

181

4   Modeling a Supply Network

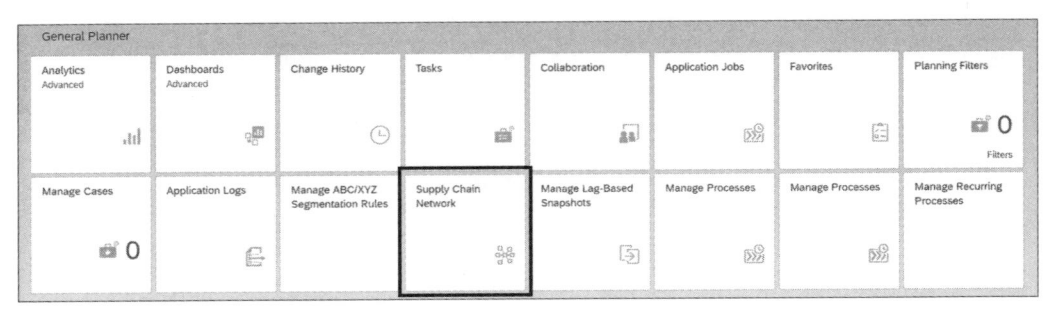

Figure 4.15 Supply Network Visualization App

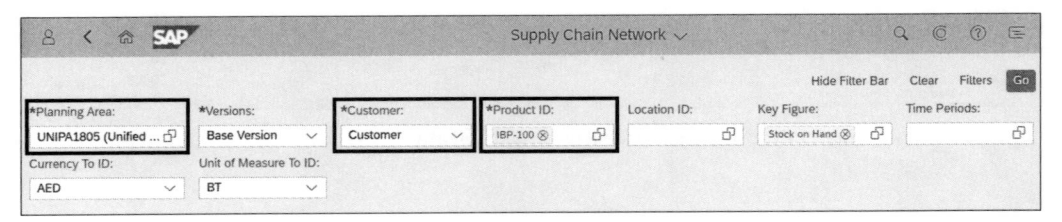

Figure 4.16 Selection Area

You must select the **Planning Area**, **Customer Group**, and a **Product ID**, as shown in Figure 4.16. Additional filter data can be provided to filter the selection of chart generation in the **Filter Data** area, such as a **Location** and **Key Figure**. The network represented in Figure 4.17 shows the end-to-end supply network of the organization, for which we've selected the finished product sold to the customer. Note that all other nodes, like the components and other facilities, are automatically selected, giving you an end-to-end network view.

As you can see in Figure 4.17, different icons are used in the chart to represent various parties, including suppliers, manufacturing nodes, warehouse nodes, nonstocking nodes, and vendors. You can view these icons by clicking the **Legend** button. The legend offers a value legend and a symbol legend. Key figure values in the chart can be displayed by hovering over the chart area at the nodes or arcs of the network. To view a key figure value, you must first select the key figure in the filter criteria.

You can also view the end-to-end network in a tabular view. To view the network in the tabular view, click the **Table** button, as shown in Figure 4.17. Figure 4.18 shows the tabular view of the supply chain network.

4.4 Visualizing Supply Networks in SAP IBP

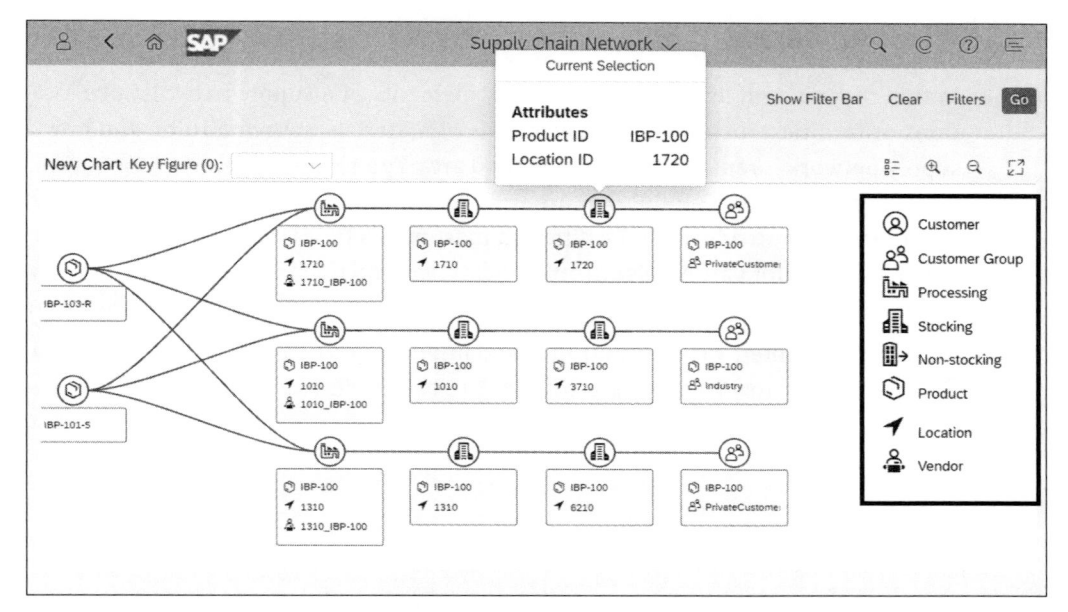

Figure 4.17 Supply Chain Network Chart Visualization

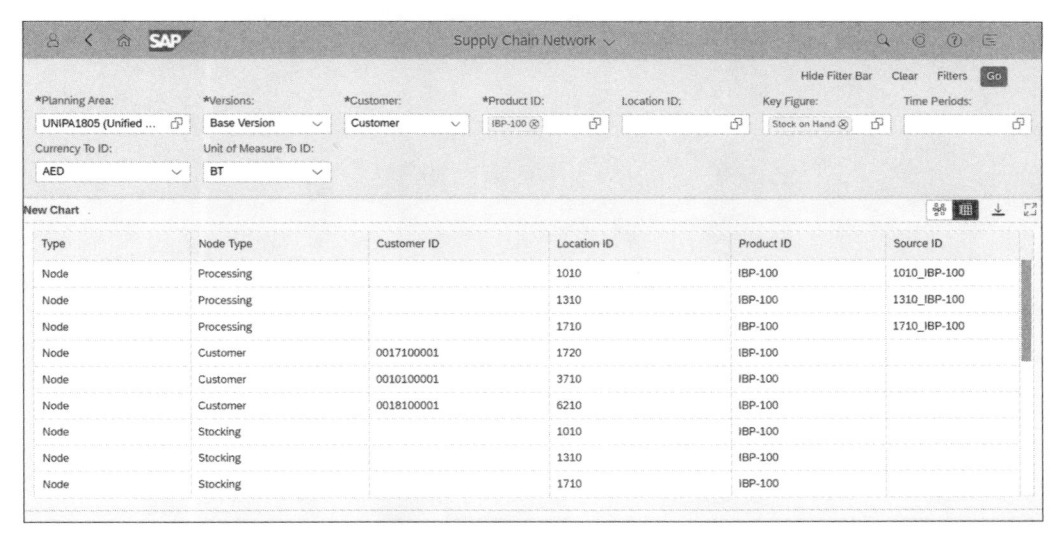

Figure 4.18 Tabular View of Supply Chain Network in SAP IBP

183

4.5 Summary

In this chapter, you learned about the key elements of a supply network, like locations or facilities, customers, products, bills of materials, sourcing rules, and how a supply network is represented by nodes and arcs. You also learned about the various master data types in SAP IBP that are used to represent a supply network. We also covered various attributes of the different master data types that are used for reporting or as inputs for various algorithms. Finally, we explained the reason for the complexity of the supply network and how to visualize a supply network within SAP IBP.

In the next chapter, we'll explain the fundamentals of the inventory optimization algorithms and how they're used to calculate the inventory targets across the network.

Chapter 5
Optimizing Inventory in SAP IBP

In this chapter, we'll explain the fundamentals of the inventory optimization algorithms used to calculate the inventory targets across the network simultaneously.

As discussed in Chapter 1, inventory is the consequence of many different strategic and tactical choices across an organization. Inventory optimization is the science of making these choices more rational, more profitable, and automatic. The main objective of this chapter is to provide an understanding of the fundamentals of inventory optimization algorithms in SAP IBP.

In this chapter, we'll start by defining network inventory optimization in SAP IBP, explaining its objectives, constraints, and decision variables. We'll then review the single-stage inventory calculation and discuss the impact of primary drivers on inventory targets as building blocks before introducing multiechelon inventory optimization. Finally, we'll cover the fundamentals of the underlying algorithms used to calculate the optimal inventory targets across the network simultaneously step by step.

5.1 What Is Network Inventory Optimization in SAP IBP?

Let's start with a simple description of a supply chain network. Figure 5.1 shows a typical consumer products supply chain. Suppliers, indicated by S, supply raw materials and components inventory to inventory locations at the frontend of the manufacturing location. Inventory stocking points, places where inventory is held, are represented by triangles. The bill of materials (BOM) relationship, the process of manufacturing a product, is represented by a rectangle. Finished goods are made and stored at the plant distribution center (DC) and then sent to forward-deployed customer-facing distribution centers, which serve end customers (C).

5   Optimizing Inventory in SAP IBP

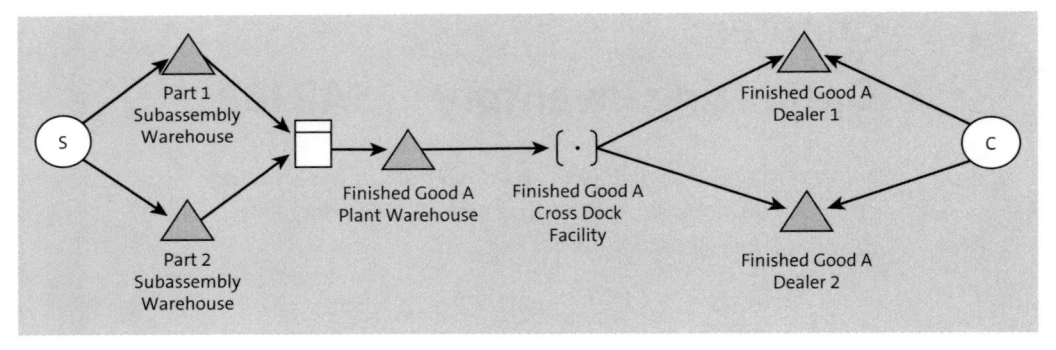

Figure 5.1 Example Consumer Products Supply Chain Network

The business problem we attack here is this: In a multistage supply chain network, how do you best deploy or allocate inventory that meets the end customer service level target? How much inventory should you hold for each product, and what is the most cost-efficient point at which to store that inventory in multiple planning periods?

The traditional approach tends to manage inventory at each individual stage independently, but the network inventory optimization in SAP IBP aims to set the inventory targets up and down the supply chain on a simultaneous basis.

The objective of the network inventory optimization algorithm in SAP IBP is to find an inventory plan that minimizes total safety stock holding costs across all locations and products of the supply chain over the entire optimization horizon.

The network optimization algorithm is subjected to the hard constraint of meeting desired customer service levels. The following planning parameters and replenishment constraints are also factored into the calculation of inventory requirements:

- Uncertain, time-varying demands
- Lead-time and lead-time variability
- Periods between reviews
- Minimum and incremental lot size
- Stocking/nonstocking policy
- Sourcing
- Bill of materials
- Order delivery handling

In addition, the optimization takes the inventory holding cost rate key figure as input.

The network inventory optimization is performed via a transformation of the inventory data model in a nonlinear objective function, where the decision variables are the internal service levels. A proprietary search algorithm then searches for the combination of internal service levels that meets the desired target customer service level and minimizes safety stock holding costs. We'll explain the concept of internal service levels in Section 5.3.

5.2 Building Blocks for Inventory Calculation

Before delving into the difficulties of calculating the inventory targets in more than one echelon, let's review the single-echelon inventory calculation as a building block. In this environment, suppliers supply distribution centers, which supply customers.

In this single-echelon situation, the target inventory positions need to be calculated to meet the desired service levels at distribution centers for demand fulfillment. To understand the purpose of target inventory positions and what goes into calculating the inventory targets, we need to explore the inventory replenishment process.

5.2.1 Inventory Replenishment Process Definitions

Replenishment is an operation that brings the inventory level up to ensure enough stock to produce goods and/or fulfill orders. The inventory replenishment process needs to define a review period for reordering and an ordering quantity. Based on how the review period and order quantities are defined, replenishment can be driven by the following choices:

- **Continuous review versus periodic review**
  The frequency of review determines when orders can be placed for reordering. In the continuous review process, the inventory levels are continuously monitored, and once the stocks fall below a reorder point (or reorder level), a replenishment order is placed. Under periodic review, the inventory levels are reviewed at a predetermined frequency—for instance, once per week or once per month. At the time of review, if the stock levels are below a predetermined level, then a replenishment order is placed; otherwise, an order isn't placed until the next cycle.

- **Fixed order quantity versus order-up-to level**
  These parameters determine how much is ordered when a replenishment order is placed. With the first option, the order quantity is fixed for all replenishment orders. For the second option, the actual order quantity is determined as the difference between the inventory position, which is on-hand plus on-order stock at the time of review, and the pre-determined order-up-to level. So as soon as the replenishment order has arrived, the inventory position will be brought up to the

5   Optimizing Inventory in SAP IBP

predetermined order-up-to level. The order quantity in this process can differ from one replenishment order to another depending on the inventory position and/or the order-up-to level at the time of review.

Based on these two parameters, a replenishment process can be deployed in different ways. To better understand the purpose of target inventory positions (e.g., the predetermined order-up-to level) and how they should be calculated, we'll assume a periodic review process in which the inventory level is reviewed in every period: periods between reviews (PBR) is one period, and the lead time between the distribution center and its supplier is also one period. Figure 5.2 depicts an example inventory replenishment process.

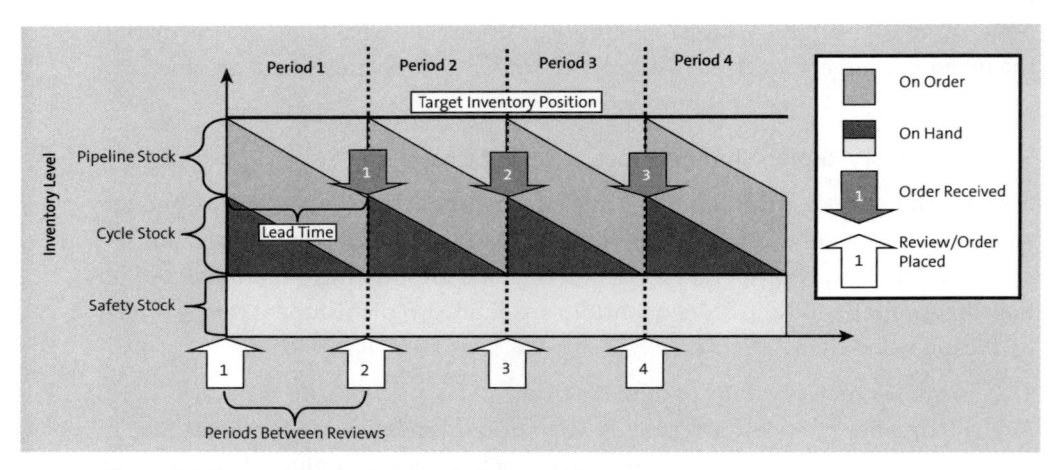

Figure 5.2 Example Inventory Replenishment Process

At the beginning of period 1, a replenishment order is placed. As time passes, customer demand consumes the on-hand inventory. At the start of period 2, the previously placed order arrived, which is the pipeline stock from the previous period, and it manages to meet the demand for period 2. The next shipment doesn't arrive until the start of period 3. In short, the right target inventory position depends on the following:

- Inventory needed to meet current period demand (cycle stock)
- Inventory needed to meet future demand until next order is received (pipeline stock)
- Inventory needed to hedge against uncertainty (safety stock)

5.2.2 Impact of Primary Drivers on Inventory Targets

In this section, we'll explain the impact of some primary drivers on different types of inventory targets. Table 5.1 describes the inventory drivers for a SKU located at a distribution center.

Inventory Drivers	Description
Demand	Demand forecast
Forecast error	Forecast demand standard deviation
Periods between reviews	Replenishment review frequency
Lead time	Expected time delay between ordering and receiving new shipment available to fulfill demand
Lead time variability	Fluctuation in the lead time from order to order
Minimum and incremental lot size	Transportation or production lot size
Target service level	The distribution center's service commitment to end customers

Table 5.1 Primary Inventory Drivers for SKU Located at a Distribution Center

As noted in Section 5.2.1, the right target inventory position can depend on three types of inventory targets. Now, let's discuss the impact of the corresponding inventory drivers for each type of inventory target.

Impact of Inventory Drivers on Cycle Stock

Cycle stock needs to meet the demand forecasts of all periods until the next review. Therefore, cycle stock is driven by the replenishment frequency or lot sizes. The cycle stock key drivers are as follows:

- Periods between review
- Demand forecast
- Lot sizes

For instance, a less frequent inventory review or a longer review cycle (monthly vs. weekly) or larger lot sizes can lead to higher cycle stock requirements. Figure 5.3 shows cycle stock increases as PBR increases.

5 Optimizing Inventory in SAP IBP

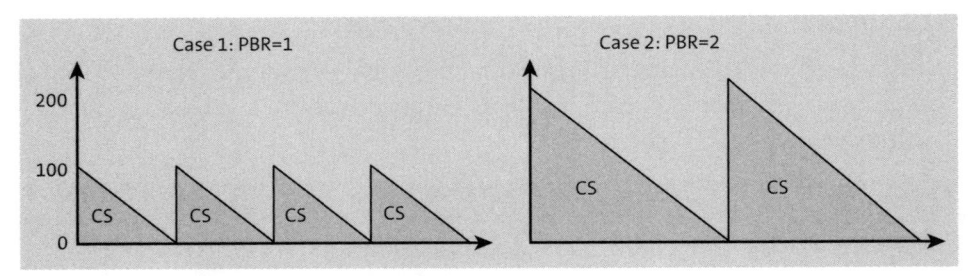

Figure 5.3 Cycle Stock Increases with PBR

Impact of Inventory Drivers on Pipeline Stock

Pipeline stock needs to meet future demand until the next order is received. Pipeline stock is based on the inventory requirements of all periods over the lead time. The pipeline stock key drivers are lead times and demand forecasts.

When lead times become longer, more outstanding orders can stay in transit and account for pipeline stock. Figure 5.4 shows how pipeline stock increases with lead time.

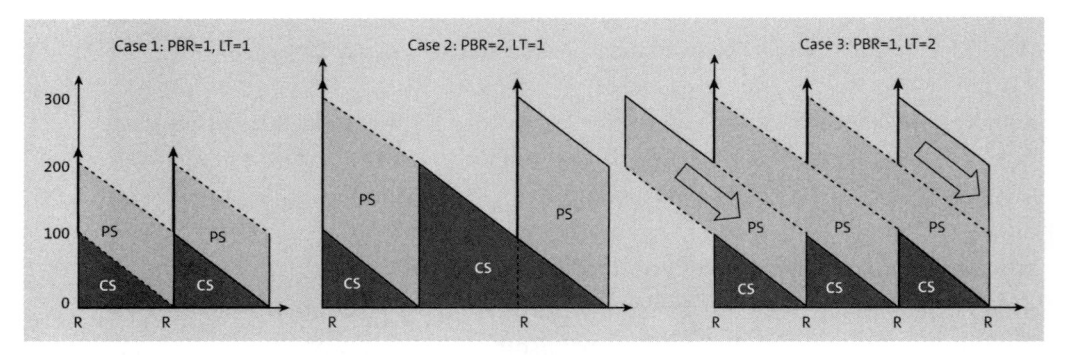

Figure 5.4 Pipeline Stock Increases with Lead Time

Impact of Inventory Drivers on Safety Stock

Safety stock is dependent upon the uncertainty during the exposure period. The safety stock drivers in the context of single-stage calculation include the following:

- Forecast error
- Lead time error/variability
- Target service level
- Exposure period

5.2 Building Blocks for Inventory Calculation

In particular, a single-stage safety stock can be calculated using the following equation when demand is static over time:

$$\text{Safety Stock} = z \times \sqrt{(PBR + LT) \times \sigma_D^2 + \sigma_{LT}^2 \times \mu_D^2}$$

The elements in this equation represent the following:

- *PBR + LT* is referred to as the *exposure period*
- μ_D is forecast demand; σ_D is forecast error standard deviation
- σ_{LT} is lead time error standard deviation
- *z* is the safety factor corresponding to the nonstockout probability service level target. Table 5.2 is a sample safety factor lookup table.

Target Service Level	Safety Factor
50%	0
77%	0.7388
80%	0.8416
84.13%	1.0000
90%	1.2816
92%	1.4051
94%	1.5547
95%	1.6449
98%	2.0537
99%	2.3263
99.9%	3.0903
99.99%	3.7194

Table 5.2 Safety Factor Lookup Table Based on Normal Distribution

So far, we've covered the three types of inventory components that make up the target inventory position. To sum up, *target inventory position* can be calculated as *exposure demand mean plus safety stock*. We can use the following equation to calculate target inventory position when demand is static over time. In this calculation,

5 Optimizing Inventory in SAP IBP

PBR times μ_D represents the cycle stock, while lead time × μ_D accounts for the pipeline stock:

$$Target\ Inventory\ Position = (PBR + LT) \times \mu_D + z \times \sqrt{(PBR + LT) \times \sigma_D^2 + \sigma_{LT}^2 \times \mu_D^2}$$

> **Note**
>
> These simple formulas are only valid for single-echelon, demand during an exposure period under the normal approximation, and nonstockout probability service level metrics.

Next we'll focus on safety stock and take a close look at the impact of probability distributions for demand, service level metrics (nonstockout probability vs. fill rate), lead time uncertainty, and lot sizes on safety stock in detail.

Probability Distributions for Demand during Exposure Period

The probability distribution of demand during the exposure period is an important characteristic in determining the safety stocks. In practice, the demand during the exposure period or lead time is often modeled as a discrete, nonnegative random variable, provided that the demand is reasonably low. If the demand is large, a continuous probability distribution should be chosen.

Most textbooks assume that demand for a product is formed from many smaller demands from individual customers. Therefore, the resulting demand is continuous and follows a normal distribution. According to the central limit theorem, under mild conditions the normal distribution can be used to approximate a large variety of distributions in large samples.

The normal distribution has two parameters, usually denoted by μ and σ^2, which are the mean and the variance. The standard deviation is σ. The coefficient of variation for the normal distribution is $\sigma \div \mu$. The probability density function of the normal distribution is given by using the following formula:

$$f(x|\mu, \sigma^2) = \frac{1}{\sqrt{2\pi\sigma^2}} e^{-\frac{(x-\mu)^2}{2\sigma^2}}$$

In Figure 5.5, we plot the probability density function of normal distributions with μ = 100 and various σ values.

The normal distribution is very tractable and can be approximately correct in many cases, but using the normal distribution for a demand distribution can be questioned because the distribution has a small but positive probability of negative demand. This effect is more pronounced when the coefficient of variation of demand is high. As a result, it can't be used in computer simulations because negative demand may be generated at random.

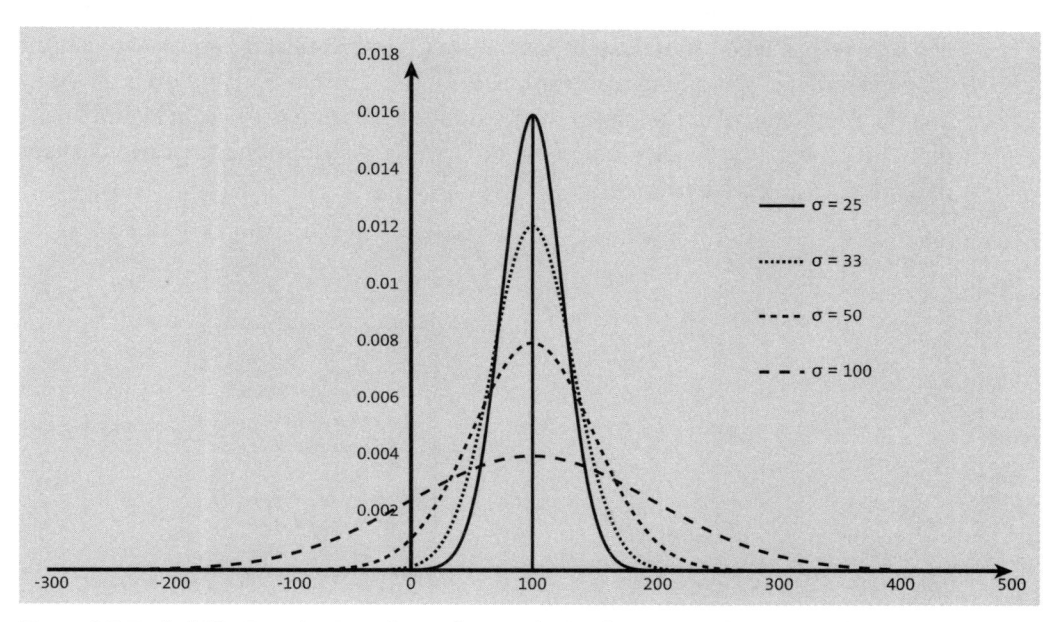

Figure 5.5 Probability Density Functions of Normal Distributions with μ=100 and Various σ Values

In general, the distribution of the demand during exposure period or lead time has the following characteristics:

- It exists only for nonnegative values.
- As the mean demand increases, the distribution changes from monotonic, decreasing to unimodal distribution heavily skewed to the right, and finally to normal distribution.

These features can be satisfied by the Gamma distribution. The Gamma distribution is defined by two positive parameters, $\lambda > 0$ and $\alpha > 0$. The probability density function of the Gamma distribution is given by the following formula:

$$f(x|\lambda, \alpha) = \frac{\lambda^\alpha}{\Gamma(\alpha)} x^{\alpha-1} e^{-\lambda x} \quad (0 < x < \infty)$$

5 Optimizing Inventory in SAP IBP

In this formula, $\Gamma(\alpha)$ is a gamma function, which itself can be calculated as follows:

$$\Gamma(\alpha) = \int_0^\infty t^{\alpha-1} e^{-t} dt$$

The mean μ and variance σ^2 for the Gamma distribution are given by $\mu = \alpha \div \lambda$ and $\sigma^2 = \alpha/\lambda^2$ respectively. The constant λ is the scale parameter, and the constant α is the shape parameter. The standard deviation, σ, for the Gamma distribution is $\sigma = \sqrt{\alpha} \div \lambda$ and the coefficient of variation for the Gamma distribution is $1 \div \sqrt{\alpha}$. In Figure 5.6, we plot the probability density functions of Gamma distributions for various shape parameters α and scale parameters λ.

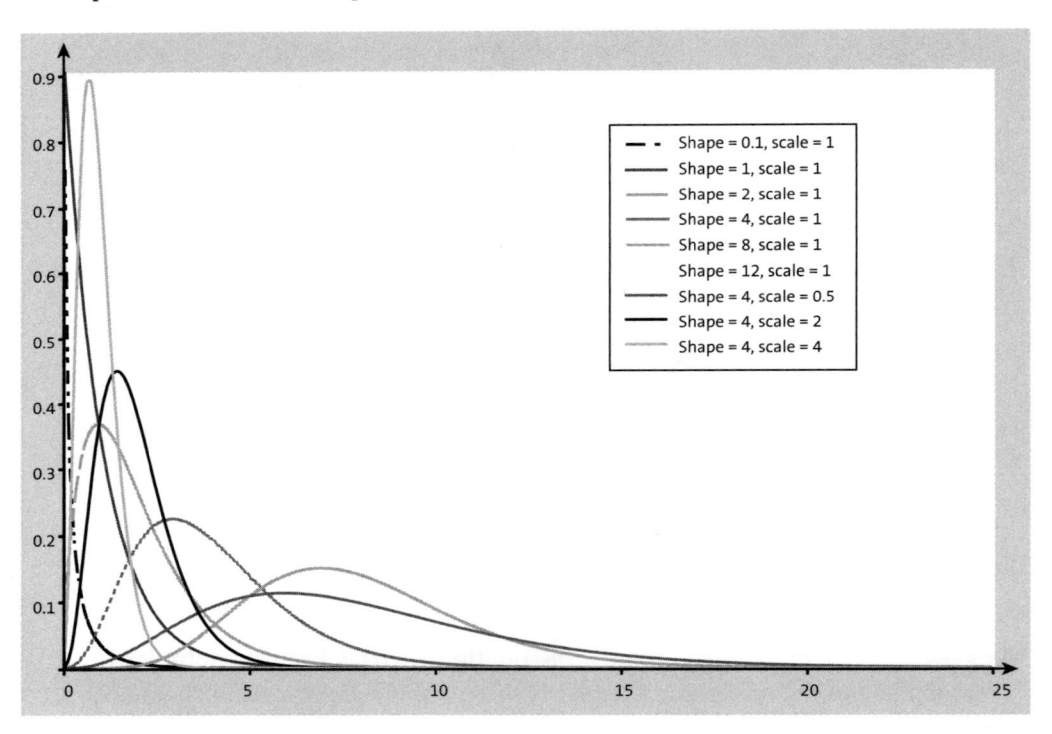

Figure 5.6 Probability Density Functions of Gamma Distributions with Various Shape and Scale Parameters

As shown in Figure 5.6, when the mean demand ($\mu = \alpha \div \lambda$) increases, the distribution changes from an L-shaped distribution to a right-skewed distribution with a long tail, and finally to a symmetric, bell-shaped distribution. Other advantages of using Gamma distribution include the following:

5.2 Building Blocks for Inventory Calculation

- Demand that follows a Gamma distribution is always positive and continuous.
- When the shape parameter α equals 1, Gamma distribution simplifies to exponential distribution; that is, exponential distribution is the special case of Gamma distribution. The exponential distribution is also a good approximation of the demand, especially for demand of slow-moving items.

Given the mean µ and the variance σ^2 of demand over the exposure period, we fit a Gamma distribution to the mean and the variance of the exposure period demand. The parameters of the corresponding Gamma distribution are given by $\alpha = \mu^2 \div \sigma^2$ and $\lambda = \mu \div \sigma^2$.

The DISTRIBUTIONTYPE attribute for the location-product master data type is used to specify the distribution type for SAP IBP for inventory to model the exposure period demand distribution. The value of the attribute can be either G (gamma distribution, the default) or N (normal distribution).

Impact of Service Level Metrics

SAP IBP for inventory supports two different service level types in the calculation of inventory targets. The SERVICELEVELTYPE attribute for the location-product master data type is used to specify the service type. For instance, the service level type for a location-product can be specified as A (available in full) or F (fill rate, the default).

Available in full or nonstockout probability, α, a type-1 service level, measures the probability that all customer orders arriving within a given time interval will be completely delivered from stock on hand—that is, without delay.

Now, let X denote a random variable representing the demand in a period and let s be the stock on-hand available. The nonstockout probability, α, can be written as $\alpha = \text{Prob}(X \leq s)$, where $\text{Prob}(\cdot)$ represents the probability of a given event.

Fill rate, or β, a type-2 service level, measures the percentage of demand in a period which is delivered without delay from stock on hand. Using the same notation above, the fill rate, β, can be written as $\beta = E[\min(X, s) \div X]$, where $E[\cdot]$ represents the expected value. By the definitions, comparing service levels, we have $\alpha \leq \beta$ given the same stock on hand. This happens because when $X \leq s$, the partially satisfied demand is also credited to the fill rate service level measure. In addition, for a given service level value, the nonstockout probability metric requires higher inventory than the fill rate metric in achieving the service level, as shown in Figure 5.7.

5   Optimizing Inventory in SAP IBP

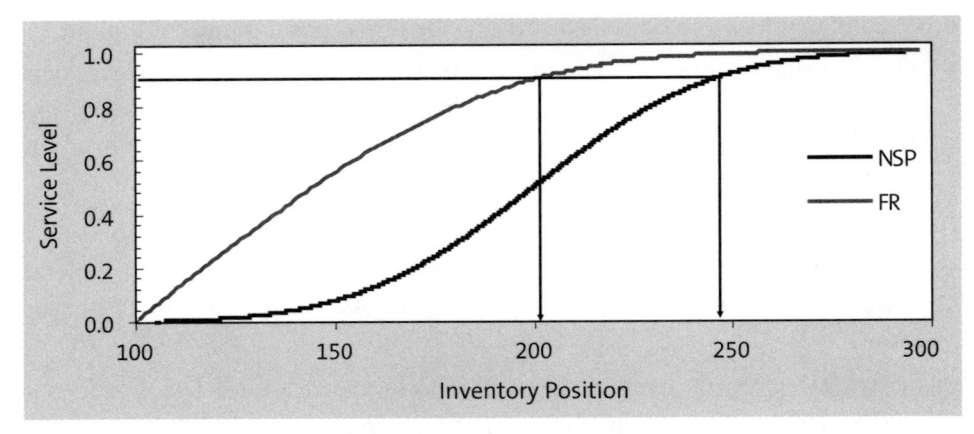

Figure 5.7 Impact of Service Level Metrics on Inventory Requirement

Previously, we showed that inventory targets—for example, safety stock—can be calculated based on the nonstockout probability via a safety factor. Although fill rate is chosen as the service level type, the calculation in SAP IBP for inventory needs to convert the service level metric from fill rate to nonstockout probability as a prerequisite step. Next we'll explain conceptually how the conversion from fill rate to nonstockout probability works in SAP IBP for inventory through a simple example.

In the example, we'll plan for one SKU for a period with an instantaneous lead time and a PBR of one period. We assume the demand, denoted as D, is normally distributed, with demand mean $\mu = 100$ and demand standard deviation $\sigma = 25$. The target service level is a 95% fill rate. Recall that for a 95% nonstockout probability, safety stock can be calculated as $z_{95\%} \times \sigma = 1.6449 \times 25 \approx 41$.

For a 95% fill rate, the calculated nonstockout probability is 61.66% and safety stock is $z_{61.66\%} \times \sigma = 0.2966 \times 25 \approx 7$ according to SAP IBP for inventory. Let's first show how the 61.66% nonstockout probability is equivalent to a 95% fill rate. With safety stock of seven, the expected on-hand stock available will be 107 (= 100 + 7). In Table 5.3, for each possible scenario of demand realization listed in the first column, we can calculate its probability in the second column based on the normal distribution and evaluate the fill rate in the third column. For instance, for demand realization 110 < d <= 120, the probability that it happens is about 13%, and the fill rate is calculated as $107 \div 115 \approx 93\%$. In the end, we take the calculated fill rate multiplied by its probability to obtain the expected fill rate of 95%.

Demand Realization	Probability	Calculated Fill Rate
d <= 100	50%	100%
100 < d <= 107	11%	100%
107 < d <= 110	5%	99%
110 < d <= 120	13%	93%
120 < d <= 130	10%	86%
130 < d <= 140	6%	80%
140 < d <= 150	3%	74%
150 < d <= 160	1%	69%
160 < d <= 170	0.6%	65%
170 < d <= 180	0.2%	61%
180 < d <= 190	0.1%	58%
d > 190	0.02%	57%
Expected fill rate		95%

Table 5.3 Evaluate Fill Rate for Normally Distributed Demand with μ = 100 and σ = 25 and Expected On-Hand Stock Available of 107

In SAP IBP for inventory, an iterative search is used to determine the correct value of the nonstockout probability corresponding to a fill rate as follows:

1. Assume a starting nonstockout probability service level.
2. Calculate the safety stock and expected on-hand available.
3. Evaluate the expected fill rate (which is conceptually explained in Table 5.3).
4. If the expected fill rate matches the target fill rate, then stop; otherwise, follow steps 1–3 again.

Impact of Lead Time Uncertainty: Sequential versus Crossover

Safety stock is required to hedge against uncertainty in transportation and production lead times—that is, deviation from requested dates and/or promised dates for planned order receipts. To properly calculate the safety stock requirements in SAP

IBP for inventory, lead time variability input should capture variations in lead times due to natural, external forces, including but not limited to the following:

- Transportation delays and scheduling issues
- Customs delays (for international shipments)
- Issues surrounding labor (e.g., strikes)
- Weather
- Mistakes in data entry/processing or in routing
- Security

However, lead time variability input shouldn't include the effects of expediting and advanced order placements (we don't plan to expedite) and shouldn't include the effects of upstream material unavailability, which is a different measurement in SAP IBP for inventory.

The TLEADTIMEVARIABILITY for master data type source location and PLEADTIMEVARIABILITY for master data type source production attributes as key figures are used to define the variability in transportation and production lead times. In addition, the TDELIVERYTYPE attribute for master data type source location or the PDELIVERYTYPE attribute for master data type source production can be used to specify how order crossover should be considered or not in the calculation of safety stock requirements in the presence of lead time variability input.

Order crossover occurs when replenishment orders are not received in the same sequence in which they were placed. A couple of examples of order crossover are shown in Figure 5.8. Whenever a second order is received prior to the replenishment that should have occurred due to a prior first order, the inventory level when the first order arrives is greater than if no crossover had occurred. The risk of the first order being late is capped. When this happens, order crossover can provide higher protection against stockouts, thereby reducing safety stock requirements. The value of TDELIVERYTYPE/PDELIVERYTYPE can be either s or c. The s value represents sequential, which is the default, whereas c indicates crossover is allowed.

The frequency with which order crossover occurs can depend on inventory review frequency, transportation, and production policies. For instance, if a single supplier is used, or if the time between orders is long in comparison to the variability in the lead time, then crossover may be unlikely. However, shorter ordering intervals, a greater number of suppliers, and adoption of more variable transportation modes (e.g., less than load [LTL] trucking) may cause replenishment orders to cross over one another.

5.2 Building Blocks for Inventory Calculation

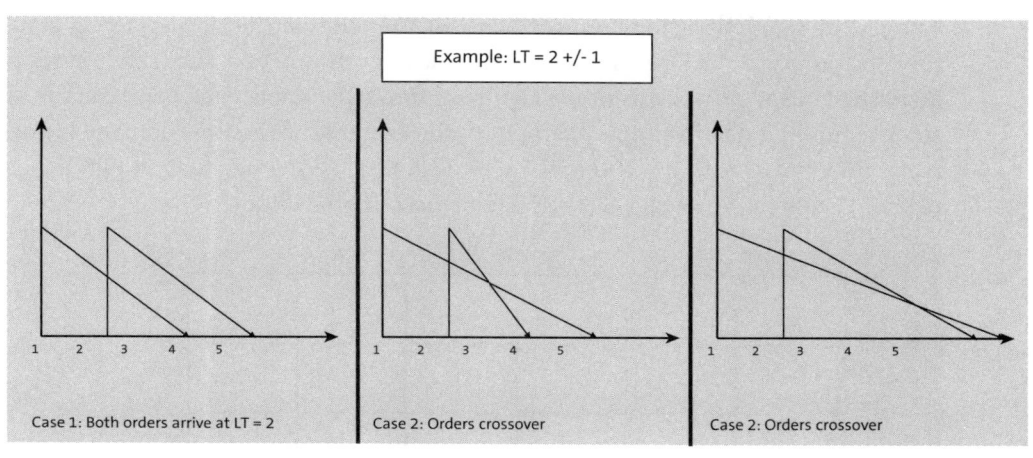

Figure 5.8 Examples of Order Crossover

Table 5.4 shows the impact of order crossover on safety stock targets with different inventory review frequencies through a simple example. In the example, we assume demand is normally distributed, with demand mean µ = 100 and demand standard deviation σ = 30; lead time is uncertain with the mean of one period and lead time standard deviation of one period. The target service level is a 95% nonstockout probability. When orders are placed in every period, order crossover leads to a lower safety stock target than the sequential option. However, when orders are placed in every four periods order crossover is unlikely, so both options result in the same safety stock requirements.

Recommended Safety Stock	Sequential	Crossover
PBR = 1	179	141
PBR = 4	198	198

Table 5.4 Impact of Order Crossover on Safety Stock Targets with Different PBRs

Impact of Lot Sizes

In SAP IBP for inventory, minimum lot size and incremental lot size are input parameters that production or order quantities need to respect. For example, if minimum lot size is 1,000 and incremental lot size is 100, then order quantity can be 0, 1000, 1100, 1200, and so on. Extra orders due to lot sizes will increase cycle stock but can serve as a buffer to reduce safety stock requirements. Total inventory will increase.

5 Optimizing Inventory in SAP IBP

To calculate safety stock requirements with lot sizes, the distribution of target inventory positions with lot sizes is modeled and the opportunity to reduce safety stock is quantified in SAP IBP for inventory. Figure 5.9 shows the impact of lot sizes on safety stock requirements in a simple example. In the example, we assume demand is normally distributed with $\mu = 100$ and $\sigma = 25$, lead time is one period, and PBR is one period. The target service level is a 95% nonstockout probability.

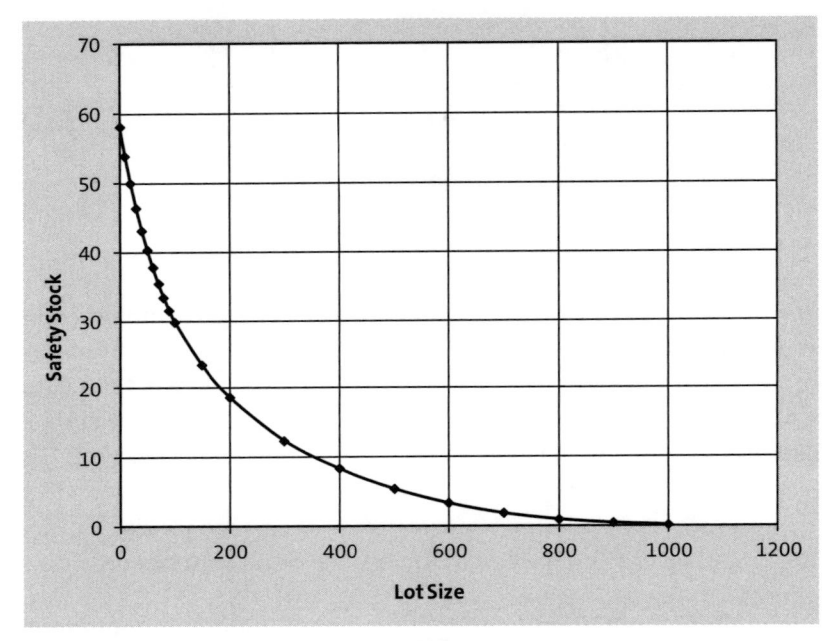

Figure 5.9 Impact of Lot Sizes on Safety Stock Requirment

5.2.3 Impact of Time-Varying Demand

It's very important to consider time-varying demand when setting optimal inventory targets. For example, supply chains in various industries have many products with a seasonality element. If we only consider time-average values in determining safety stock, we could end up keeping the higher inventory level throughout the time horizon or the year. Now let's discuss how time-varying demand can be incorporated into the calculation of safety stock and target inventory position. Let $\mu_{D,t}$ denote time-varying demand and $\sigma_{D,t}$ denote time-varying forecast error standard deviation, where t represents the time index. μ_D is still the average demand across the exposure (PBR + lead time) periods. The time-varying safety stock can be calculated as follows:

$$Time-Varying\ Safety\ Stock = z \times \sqrt{\sigma_{D,1}^2 + \sigma_{D,2}^2 + \cdots + \sigma_{D,PBR+LT}^2 + \sigma_{LT}^2 \times \mu_D^2}$$

As you can see in the calculation of safety stock via the preceding equation, the total variability over exposure periods is calculated based on the time-varying demand standard deviations through the exposure periods. Please note that the variability due to lead time uncertainty can still be calculated as $\sigma_{LT}^2 \times \mu_D^2$ here. The time-varying target inventory position can be calculated respectively as follows:

$$Time-Varying\ Target\ Inventory\ Position = (\mu_{D,1} + \mu_{D,2} + \cdots + \mu_{D,PBR+LT}) +$$
$$z \times \sqrt{\sigma_{D,1}^2 + \sigma_{D,2}^2 + \cdots + \sigma_{D,PBR+LT}^2 + \sigma_{LT}^2 \times \mu_D^2}$$

Similarly, the calculations of demand over exposure periods in the time-varying target inventory position also consider the time-varying demand over PBR and lead time, respectively, as shown in the preceding equation.

5.3 Network Multiechelon Inventory Calculation

Now let's consider a multiechelon network that includes regional distribution centers (RDCs) in between the suppliers and the distribution centers. In this situation, we have supplier to regional distribution center to distribution center to customer. The same inventory drivers described in the previous section apply for the SKU at the regional distribution center location. However, some significant issues emerge:

- What is the proper measure of demand for the regional distribution center, and should this demand be forecasted?
- How do we measure the forecast error at the regional distribution center?
- What's the optimal service level goal between the regional distribution center and its customers, which are the distribution center?
- How do the inventory drivers at the regional distribution center, such as lead time, periods between review, and the service level goal, affect inventory and service levels at the distribution center level?
- If there are multiple downstream distribution centers, when faced with a limited supply situation at the regional distribution center, how should we allocate product down to the distribution centers?
- Do the external supplier lead time and lead time variation still play a role in the distribution centers' inventory decisions?

5 Optimizing Inventory in SAP IBP

In this section, we'll explain how the network multiechelon inventory calculation works in SAP IBP to resolve each of these issues.

5.3.1 Constructing the Network Topology

The multiechelon calculation starts by building the supply chain network topology based on the following master data inputs:

- Demand stream (IBPSOURCECUSTGROUP)
- Location product (IBPLOCATIONPRODUCT)
- Location source (IBPSOURCELOCATION)
- Production source header (IBPSOURCEPRODUCTON)
- Production source item (IBPPRODUCTIONSOURCEITM)

The topology creation process creates customer-facing stocking points based on demand stream data and creates supply paths and internal stocking points further upstream along the supply chain based on location source and production source data. The topology creation process creates process points based on production source item (or bill of materials) data, and finally connects vendor-facing stocking points to an external vendor. The outcome of the process is the representation of the supply chain as a network of stocking points at which the inventory is planned/managed, process points at which components are assembled, and supply paths through which stock is supplied. Table 5.5 summarizes the building blocks of supply chain network topology.

Building Blocks of Supply Chain Network	Representation in Supply Chain Model	Icon
Customer	End customer	C
Stocking point	Inventory storage of a product at a location	Prod A / Loc 1
Process point	Plant or other assembly point	

Table 5.5 Building Blocks of Supply Chain Network Topology

5.3 Network Multiechelon Inventory Calculation

Building Blocks of Supply Chain Network	Representation in Supply Chain Model	Icon
Supply path	Logistics connection	↓
Supplier	External provider of inventory or raw material	Ⓢ

Table 5.5 Building Blocks of Supply Chain Network Topology (Cont.)

For instance, Figure 5.10 shows a couple of example process and distribution supply chains.

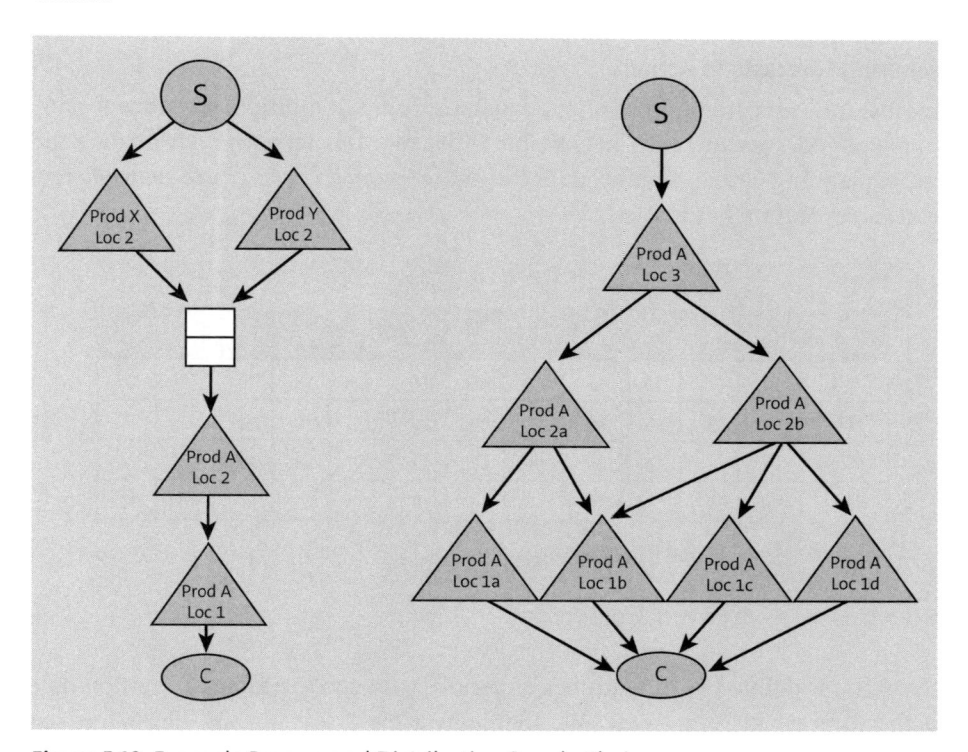

Figure 5.10 Example Process and Distribution Supply Chains

It's worth mentioning that the topology creation process also decomposes the entire supply chain into separate, disconnected supply networks—for example, by products

203

5   Optimizing Inventory in SAP IBP

if they don't have shared raw materials. These supply networks are naturally disconnected, which should be addressed separately. The benefit, of course, is in performance and scalability.

5.3.2   Historical Forecast Accuracy for Customer Demand

As described in the previous sections, forecast error is one of the key inputs into safety stock planning. In this section, we'll explain the major processing steps in the calculation of historical forecast error and/or historical forecast accuracy in SAP IBP. The corresponding calculation settings will be highlighted in each of the steps. For a period in the given historical horizon, we use A_t to denote actual sales in period t and F_t as the forecast in period t for a given lag. Note that we introduce lag here and will explain it in the following sections.

Comparing Forecasts to Actuals

Typically, forecasts are periodically updated, resulting in multiple revisions for any demand period. We show such an example with a monthly forecast revision date and forecast planning date in Figure 5.11. In the figure, every column in the example represents an evolution of forecast.

	JAN	FEB	MAR	APR	MAY	JUN	JUL	AUG	SEP	OCT	NOV	DEC
JAN	10	20	10	15	12	16	18	12	15	-	-	-
FEB	-	24	15	20	15	20	20	15	20	22	-	-
MAR	-	-	14	18	14	18	19	14	18	25	30	-
APR	-	-	-	19	14	18	19	15	25	30	40	50

Forecast Planning Date (columns); Revision Date (rows); Evolution of Forecast

Figure 5.11 Example of Evolution of Forecast

Forecast lag is defined as the number of periods between the forecast revision date and the forecast planning date. We highlight a lag-0 forecast and lag-3 forecast respectively for the same example in Figure 5.12.

Each set of forecasts will likely have different forecast errors, depending on the forecast lag. Normally, because of the nature of the forecast, we will have better results in the near-term horizon; that is, the larger the lag, the larger the forecast error or the lower the forecast accuracy. The right lag forecast we should use when measuring forecast accuracy is the forecast for which the time lag matches when important business decisions are made. In the calculation of safety stock requirements, the relevant lag is usually the lead time for a product. Ahead, we assume all calculations are carried out for a given lag.

	\multicolumn{12}{c	}{Forecast Planning Date}
Revision Date		JAN	FEB	MAR	APR	MAY	JUN	JUL	AUG	SEP	OCT	NOV	DEC
	JAN	10	10	10	15	12	16	18	12	15	-	-	-
	FEB	-	24	15	20	15	20	20	15	20	22	-	-
	MAR	-	-	14	18	14	18	19	14	18	25	30	-
	APR	-	-	-	19	14	18	19	15	25	30	40	50

Lag -0 Forecast   Lag -3 Forecast

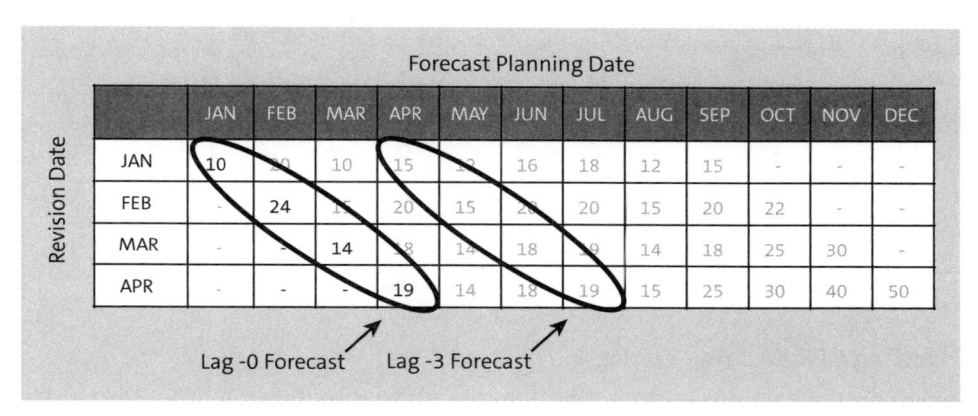

Figure 5.12 Lag-0 Forecast and Lag-3 Forecast

Table 5.6 shows a sample path of a historical forecast (for a given lag) and actual sales, which we also plot in Figure 5.13. Forecast error is the difference between the forecast and actual sales. Forecast error variability is the variability of this difference over time. Under a different approach, historical demand variability is the variability of the demand over time. For this example, the forecast error coefficient of variation is 0.16, and the demand variability CV is 0.35. It's important that safety stock targets be driven by forecast error rather than only by demand variability. When there exist time-varying forecasts, the evaluation of historical demand variability CV can either overestimate or underestimate the forecast error CV, which can result in excess safety stock requirements or service level risks.

Week	1	2	3	4	5	6	7	8	9	10	11	12	13	14
Sales A_t	80	110	60	180	170	140	165	200	185	140	90	80	110	105
Forecast F_t	75	95	100	140	150	160	165	180	175	170	100	90	105	100
Forecast − Sales $(F_t - A_t)$	-5	-15	40	-40	-20	20	0	-20	-10	30	10	10	-5	-5

Table 5.6 Comparing Forecasts to Actuals

5   Optimizing Inventory in SAP IBP

Although this comparison could be done at any level/granularity, accounting for variability in the same time granularity as the planning period enables a more accurate calculation of safety stock requirements.

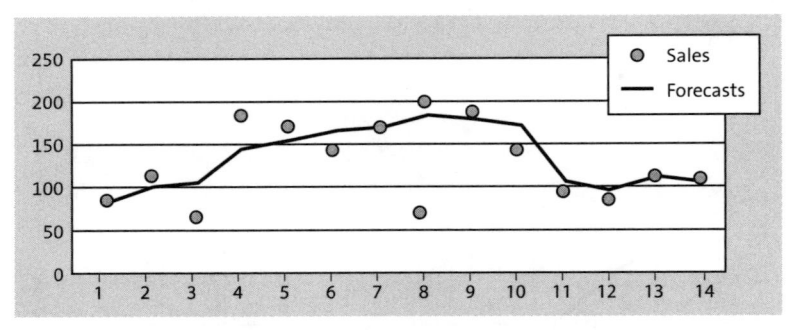

Figure 5.13 Sample Path of Historical Forecast and Sales

Handling Missing Data/Filtering

In general, there is no order for zero quantity; the data point simply does not exist. How missing data is handled can be crucial to calculations. In SAP IBP, the algorithm recognizes periods with no data and can compute forecast error measures based on the two calculation settings shown in Table 5.7. Please note that all the calculation settings discussed in Section 5.3.2 can be specified in a forecast error profile that can be created and managed by the Manage Forecast Error Calculations – Inventory Optimization app in SAP IBP.

Calculation Settings	Description
Replace Null Values by Zero	If you select this checkbox, the system replaces null values with zeroes. The algorithm disregards periods that have null values for either forecast or sales or that have zeroes for both forecast and sales.
Start History from First Sales Period	If you select this checkbox, the system takes the first period for which data for sales history exists and uses this period as the first period in the calculation of forecast error measures.

Table 5.7 Calculation Settings Relevant for Handling Missing Data

Such an example is shown in Figure 5.14. In the initial analysis, periods of missing sales data are assumed as zero sales in the calculation. If **Replace Null Values by Zero** is not selected, the algorithm can recompute forecast error CV based solely on periods with sales and forecasts. As a result, the forecast error CV changes from 0.90 to 0.42.

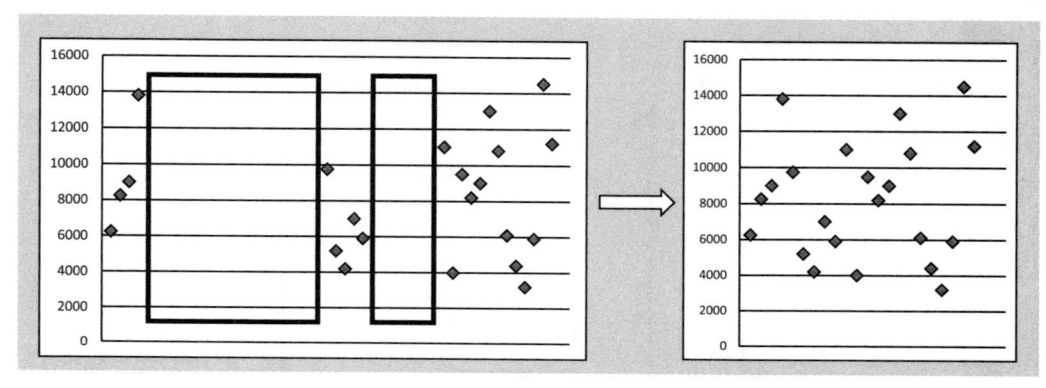

Figure 5.14 Handling Missing Data in Calculation of Forecast Error Measures

Outlier Detection and Exclusion

Outliers are historical data points that are very different from other data points. Typically, outliers represent rare events that should not influence planning decisions. SAP IBP provides outlier detection and exclusion capabilities through the two calculation settings shown in Table 5.8.

Calculation Settings	Description
Exclude Outliers from Forecast Error	Determines whether the algorithms should exclude outliers in the calculation of forecast error measures
Outlier Multiplier	Number of standard deviations used to identify outliers

Table 5.8 Calculation Settings Relevant for Outlier Detection and Exclusion

In the calculation of forecast error measures, outlier detection is performed based on the mean and standard deviation of the forecast error. It uses the **Outlier Multiplier** setting to determine what multiple of standard deviation to use. The default value is 3. For example, the outlier periods are defined using the 3-σ rule; that is, the periods with forecast errors three standard deviations away from the mean forecast error (including both positive and negative sides) are outlier periods. In addition, outlier detection is done iteratively; that is, if outlier periods are detected and excluded, then

5   Optimizing Inventory in SAP IBP

the mean and standard deviations of forecast error and outliers are calculated again from the remaining data until no further outliers are found. In the example in Figure 5.15, two outliers are detected iteratively. As a result, the forecast error CV changes from 0.63 without outlier detection to 0.56 with outlier detection.

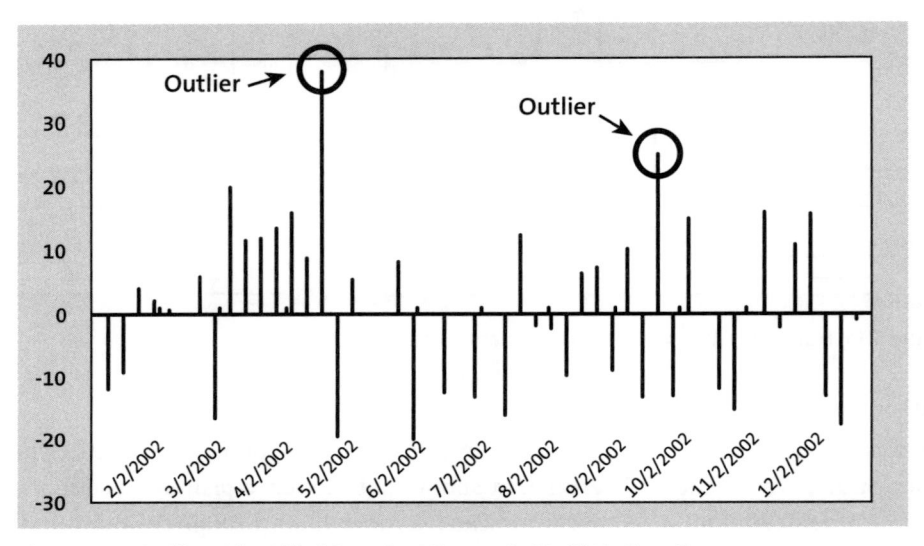

Figure 5.15 Outliers Identified Based on Errors via Multiple Iterations

Forecast Bias Estimation and Correction

Forecast bias represents a consistent tendency to overforecast (or underforecast) customer demand. A positive forecast bias reflects a tendency to inflate forecasts and a negative forecast bias reflects a tendency to deflate forecasts. Two examples with positive forecast bias (top) and negative forecast bias (bottom) are illustrated in Figure 5.16.

Overforecasting can result in excess cycle stock and overestimation of forecast error and therefore an excessive safety stock requirement. Underforecasting may lead to holding less inventory than required and therefore to service level misses. It's crucial to measure the forecast bias reliably and correct it for the historical forecasts properly in the calculation of forecast error measure. The outputs from the process include calculated bias and used bias (in the bias correction for historical forecasts). The settings in Table 5.9 are used in the forecast bias estimation and correction.

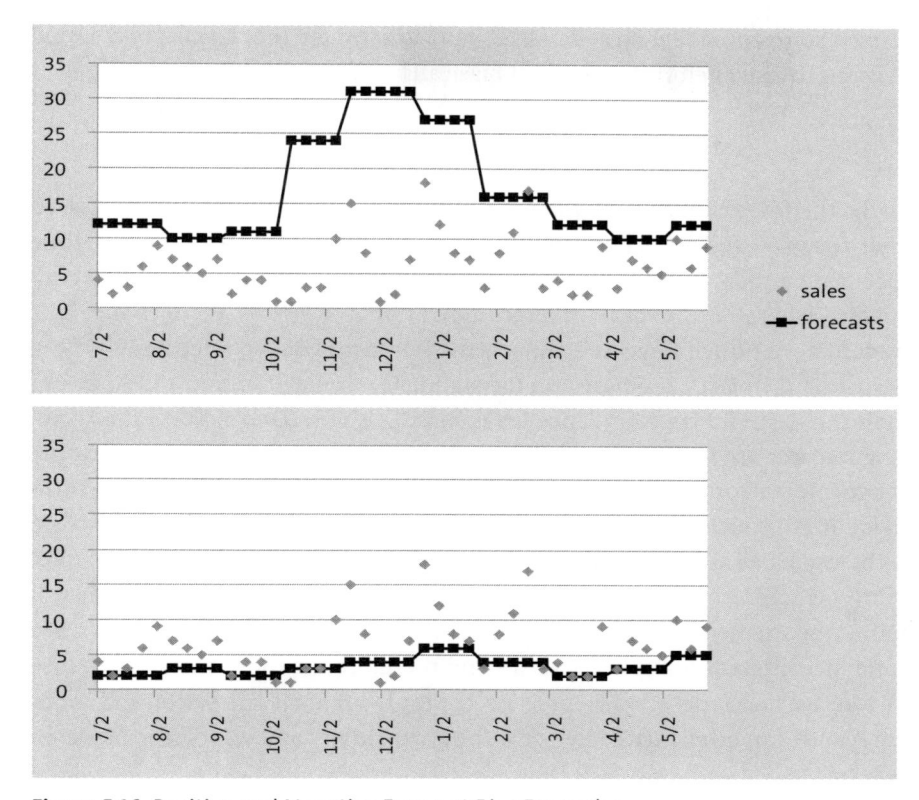

5.3 Network Multiechelon Inventory Calculation

Figure 5.16 Positive and Negative Forecast Bias Examples

Calculation Settings	Description
Adjust Bias of Forecast	Determines whether the system applies the bias adjustment to historical forecasts in the calculation of forecast error measures
Bias Adjustment Method	Determines the types of forecast bias adjustment: **Adjust Positive Bias, Adjust Negative Bias, Adjust Positive and Negative Bias**
Bias Confidence Level	Determines level of confidence required in estimating bias
Maximum Positive Bias Value	Specifies the upper bound limit for the bias
Minimum Negative Bias Value	Specifies the lower bound limit for the bias

Table 5.9 Calculation Settings Relevant for Forecast Bias Estimation and Correction

Let's discuss some more technical details of how to estimate the forecast bias. Using the notations defined before, the forecast bias can be calculated as follows:

$$1 - \frac{\sum_{t=1}^{n} A_t}{\sum_{t=1}^{n} F_t}$$

Essentially, the forecast bias is *1 – the ratio of total sales in the historical horizon to total forecasts in the historical horizon*. To ensure the forecast bias is estimated at the user-specified confidence level, a confidence interval for forecast error can be constructed by $\bar{e}$, where $\bar{e}$ is the mean of forecast error; that is, $\bar{e} = \frac{1}{n}\sum_{t=1}^{n}(F_t - A_t)$, σ_e is the standard deviation of forecast error, n is the number of data points, and $\frac{Z_{(1+biasCL)}}{2}$ is the *z-score* at *(1 + biasCL) ÷ 2* based on the standard normal distribution. For example, when the desired bias confidence level, biasCL, is 0.9, 0.95, or 0.99, the corresponding z-scores are 1.645, 1.96, or 2.576, respectively. We then need to check if the confidence interval for the forecast error contains zero. If it does, we don't have sufficient evidence to conclude that the forecast bias is different than zero and therefore output the used bias as zero. In addition, note that if the standard deviation of forecast error σ_e is fixed, the lower the desired confidence level or larger the number of data points, the smaller the range of the confidence interval and the lower the chance the confidence interval will contain zero—and therefore the more likely the chance that the forecast bias is detected. In practice, the trade-off of bias detection and confidence in results can be evaluated by performing sensitivity analysis on the bias confidence level.

After a forecast bias is detected, the correction of forecast bias in historical forecasts is performed based on the user-specified bias-adjustment method. Positive forecast bias is corrected only if **Adjust Positive Bias** or **Adjust Positive and Negative Bias** is selected as the bias adjustment method. Negative forecast bias is adjusted only if **Adjust Negative Bias** or **Adjust Positive and Negative Bias** is specified. Figure 5.17 shows an example of positive forecast bias adjustment. In the figure, the detected positive bias is 0.63 and the bias-adjusted forecast is *the original forecast × (1 – forecast bias)*. After the forecast bias correction, the forecast error CV is changed from 1.2 to 0.74. The smaller forecast error CV will result in a lower safety stock requirement, which can help prevent excess inventory in the overforecasting situation.

In the underforecasting situation, the detected negative forecast bias would be corrected if **Adjust Negative Bias** or **Adjust Positive and Negative Bias** is specified as the bias adjustment method. In Figure 5.18, the detected negative bias is -0.84. The forecast error CV is changed from 1.25 to 0.54 after the bias correction, which can result in lower safety stock requirements. However, underforecasting already results in insufficient cycle stock and therefore possible service level misses, which should have been compensated for by higher safety stock requirements. We recommend that users carefully evaluate the different bias adjustment methods provided by SAP IBP. The default bias adjustment method is **Adjust Positive Bias** (only). In the presence of negative bias, we recommend measuring the bias and correcting the forecasting process/future forecast routinely—that is, correct the cycle stock first rather than adjust the negative bias for historical forecast error.

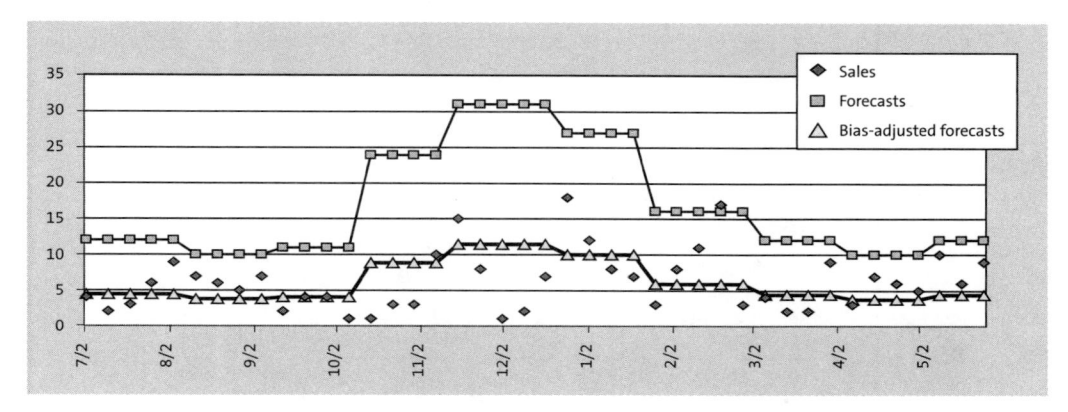

Figure 5.17 Adjust Positive Forecast Bias for Historical Forecasts

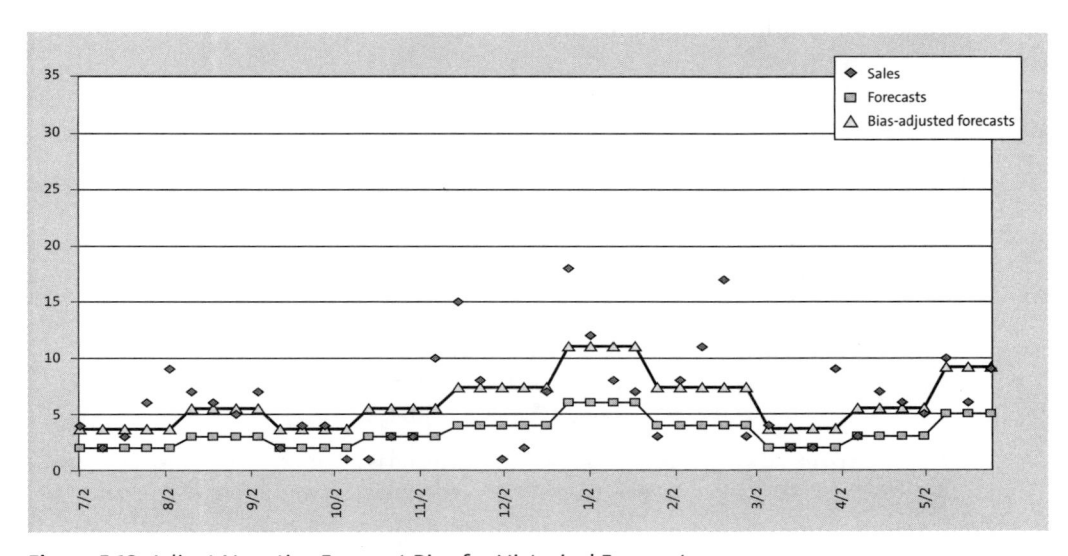

Figure 5.18 Adjust Negative Forecast Bias for Historical Forecasts

5   Optimizing Inventory in SAP IBP

Aggregate Sales and Forecast for Intermittent Demand

Intermittent demand occurs at random, with some time periods having no demand at all. Moreover, when demand appears, the demand size also varies. Intermittent demand is often referred to as *lumpy*, *sporadic*, or *erratic* demand in the academic literature. An example SKU with intermittent demand is shown in Figure 5.19.

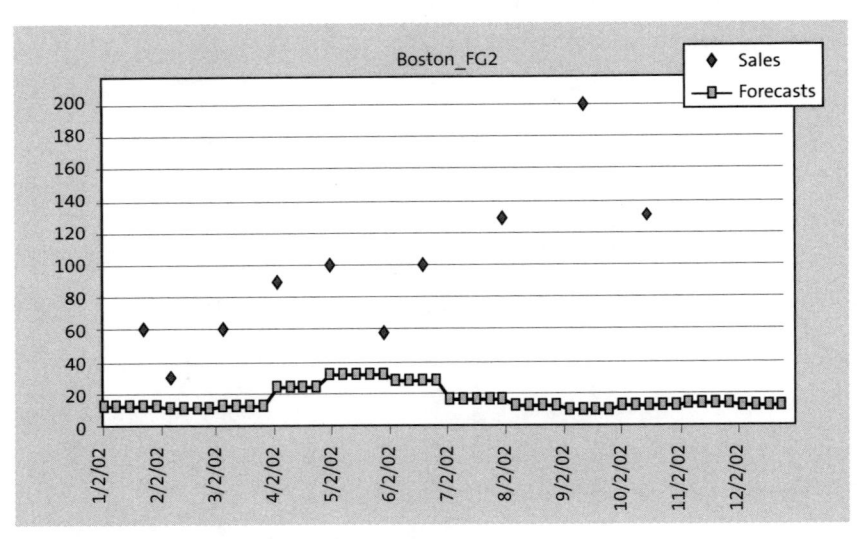

Figure 5.19 Example SKU with Intermittent Demand

In the calculation of forecast error measures, the calculation settings shown in Table 5.10 are used for intermittent demand classification.

Calculation Settings	Description
Consider Intermittency of Sales History	Determines whether the system aggregates historical forecast and sales over an average demand interval for intermittent demand in the calculation of forecast error CV.
Minimum Intermittent Demand Interval (IDI)	Specifies minimum value for the ratio of length of horizon to number of periods with positive sales below which the demand is classified as nonintermittent.
Minimum Demand Switch Frequency	Determines whether demand is intermittent or seasonal based on how many times historical sales switch from zero to nonzero (or back). A higher value indicates demand is less likely to be classified as seasonal.

Table 5.10 Calculation Settings Relevant for Intermittent Demand Classification

Calculation Settings	Description
Maximum Forecast Timing Accuracy	Defines the maximum value for forecast timing accuracy as a percentage ratio used for intermittent demand classification.
Minimum Number of Periods with Sales	If the number of periods with positive sales is fewer than the number specified by this setting, the system considers demand as frequent demand with insufficient information, and the forecast error CV is considered the default CV.

Table 5.10 Calculation Settings Relevant for Intermittent Demand Classification (Cont.)

A demand is classified as intermittent if the following criteria are met:

- Average demand interval (ADI) exceeds minimum intermittent demand interval. ADI is calculated as the ratio of length of the historical horizon to the number of periods with positive sales.
- Not classified as seasonal based on how many times historical sales switch from zero to nonzero (or back).
- Does not have sufficient forecast timing accuracy.

For the example shown in Figure 5.19, the historical horizon is 52 weeks, and we can assume the other relevant calculating settings are defined as follows:

- Minimum intermittent demand interval is 4.
- Minimum demand switch frequency is 0.5.
- Maximum forecast timing accuracy is 0.5.
- Minimum number of periods with sales is 5.

The demand for this SKU is identified as intermittent because of the following criteria: The number of positive sales is 10. ADI is calculated as 52/10 = 5.2 > 4. Demand switch frequency for this example is 1 > 0.5 (it doesn't have two sales in a row at all). Moreover, there are 10 weeks with both forecast and sales positive, so the forecast timing accuracy is 10 / 52 < 0.5.

SKUs with truly intermittent demand must be buffered from both quantity and timing variabilities. In the remainder of this section, we'll focus on how forecast quantity error is calculated for intermittent demand.

In the calculation of forecast error for intermittent demand, forecast quantity error is separated from forecast timing error by comparing aggregate forecast and sales. The ADI is used to determine how many weeks of sales and forecasts to aggregate. Let's walk through Figure 5.20 to show how the aggregation of forecasts and sales is performed.

Week	1	2	3	4	5	6	7	8	9	10	11	12	13	14
Sales	0	0	0	60	0	30	0	10	0	60	0	0	0	90
Forecast	12	12	12	12	12	10	10	10	10	11.5	11.5	11.5	11.5	24
Error	12	12	12	-48	12	-20	10	0	10	-48.5	11.5	11.5	11.5	-66
K-period Sales	60	90	90	100	40	100	70	70	60	150	90	90	90	90
K-period Forecast	60	58	56	54	52	51.5	53	54.5	56	70	82.5	95	107.5	127.6
Error	0	-32	-34	-46	12	-48.5	-17	-15.5	-4	-80	-7.5	5	17.5	37.6

Figure 5.20 Aggregate Forecasts and Sales for Intermittent Demand

In this example, ADI = 5, so sales and forecasts are summed across five periods. The aggregated forecasts and sales are then used in the calculation of the forecast error measure for intermittent demand.

Forecast Error Measure Calculation

Now that we've explained all the preprocess steps, including filtering, outlier detection and exclusion, bias detection and correction, and demand classification, let's discuss the forecast error measures available in SAP IBP, listed in Table 5.11. Note that for all the percentage errors (or relevant errors), the basis of percentage error is configurable between forecast and actual sales. Here we assume the basis of percentage error is for actual sales for convenience purposes only.

Forecast Error Measure	How to Calculate
Mean absolute deviation (MAD)	$MAD = \dfrac{1}{n}\sum_{t=1}^{n} |A_t - F_t|$
Mean absolute percentage error (MAPE)	$MAPE = \dfrac{1}{n}\sum_{t=1}^{n} \left|\dfrac{A_t - F_t}{A_t}\right|$
Forecast accuracy	$Max(100\% - MAPE, 0)$

Table 5.11 Forecast Error/Accuracy Measures Available in SAP IBP

Forecast Error Measure	How to Calculate
Weighted MAPE (wMAPE)	$wMAPE = \dfrac{\sum |A_t - F_t|}{\sum A_t}$
Mean percentage error (MPE)	$MPE = \dfrac{1}{n} \sum_{t=1}^{n} \dfrac{F_t - A_t}{A_t}$
Mean squared error (MSE)	$MSE = \dfrac{1}{n} \sum_{t=1}^{n} (A_t - F_t)^2$
Root mean squared error (RMSE)	$RMSE = \sqrt{MSE} = \sqrt{\dfrac{1}{n} \sum_{t=1}^{n} (A_t - F_t)^2}$
Mean absolute scaled error (MASE)	$MASE = \dfrac{1}{n} \sum_{t=1}^{n} \left(\dfrac{|A_t - F_t|}{\dfrac{n}{n-1} \sum_{i=2}^{n} |F_{i+1} - F_i|} \right)$
Total absolute error (TAE)	$TAE = \sum_{t=1}^{n} |A_t - F_t|$
Total error (TE)	$TE = \sum_{t=1}^{n} (F_t - A_t)$

Table 5.11 Forecast Error/Accuracy Measures Available in SAP IBP (Cont.)

The calculation settings in Table 5.12 are also relevant for the forecast error measure calculation.

Calculation Settings	Description
Basis of Percentage Error	Determine whether forecast or actual is used as basis in the calculation of percentage error
Default Percentage Error for One Period	Specifies the default percentage error for a period where both historical forecast and sales are zero

Table 5.12 Calculation Settings Relevant for Percentage-Based Forecast Error Measures and Forecast Error CV

Calculation Settings	Description
Maximum Percentage Error for One Period	Specifies the maximum percentage error for a period where forecast error is strictly greater than zero and the basis value of percentage error is zero
CV Computation Method	Choose MAD- or MAPE-based calculation

Table 5.12 Calculation Settings Relevant for Percentage-Based Forecast Error Measures and Forecast Error CV (Cont.)

Finally, the forecast error CV in SAP IBP can be calculated using two options based on the CV computation method: if MAD-based computation method is chosen, *forecast error CV = 1.25 × MAD ÷ Max (Average Forecast, Average Sales)*; otherwise forecast error CV can be calculated based on MAPE using *forecast error CV = 1.25 × MAPE*.

5.3.3 Future Demand Forecast and Variability

In time-phased inventory planning, we need to scale historical forecast error variability relative to the future forecast at all customer-facing locations. The forecast error CV is a constant scaling factor to calculate the time-phased forecast error standard deviation for the entire future planning horizon. SAP IBP for inventory can consume any forecast input—for example, an unconstrained demand plan from SAP IBP for demand, a constrained supply plan from SAP IBP for sales and operations, or any other non-SAP IBP systems. In summary, the forecast error standard deviation in period t is the future forecast in period t times the forecast error CV for any period t in the future planning horizon.

5.3.4 Demand Forecast Variability Propagation

In this section, we'll discuss how the demand and demand variability are calculated for every echelon of a multiechelon supply chain network. For instance, recall the simple multiechelon network we introduced in the beginning of Section 5.3 where inventory moves from the supplier to the regional distribution center, to the distribution center, and then to the customers. We want to address the following two questions:

- What is the proper measure of demand for the regional distribution center, and should this demand be forecasted?
- How do we measure the forecast error at the regional distribution center?

How should demand forecasts be created for the regional distribution center? One traditional approach is to calculate demand based on historical orders/consumptions from the distribution centers to the regional distribution center. Another approach is to simply "pass up" the end customer demands from distribution centers. Both approaches are imperfect, as you'll see.

The first approach falls into the bullwhip trap by using multiple independent demand forecasts in different echelons. Much has been written about the bullwhip effect and the way it distorts demand information as the information is transmitted up a supply chain. In supply chain management classes, a thought exercise called the Beer Game is often used to explain the bullwhip effect. As shown in Figure 5.21, four managers representing the retailer, wholesaler, distributor, and factory comprise a supply chain team responsible for moving beer from the supply point to the customer. Only the retail manager can see the actual customer demand and places orders to the wholesaler. The manager of the wholesaler observes "demand" from the retailer and places orders with the distributor, and so on. This theoretical simulation demonstrates that small changes in actual customer demand can result in an amplified, whip-like effect on upstream estimation of customer demand. The bullwhip effect causes increased demand variation between the regional distribution center and the distribution center. This results in unnecessary inventory at the regional distribution center.

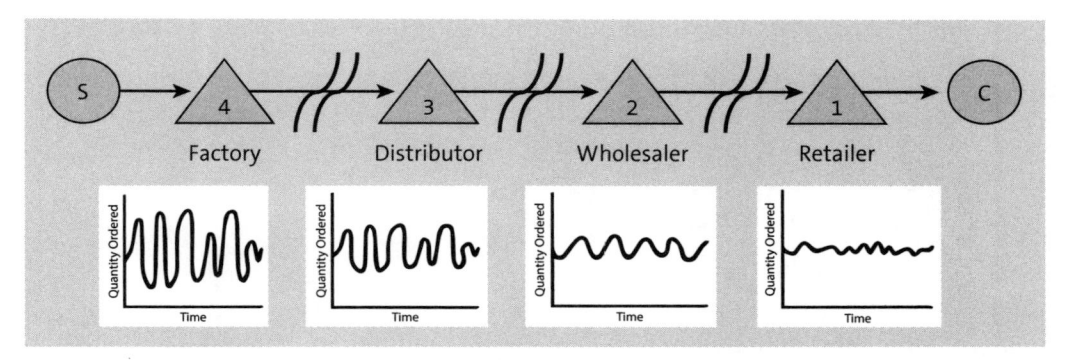

Figure 5.21 Beer Game Thought Experiment

In the second approach, the end customer demand is simply "passed up" from the distribution center to the regional distribution center. For example, using the standard material requirements planning (MRP) approach, the end-customer forecasts are combined with safety stock requirements and available on-hand stock information to get net requirements at the distribution center. The time-phased dependent demand at the regional distribution center is then calculated by offsetting the distribution

5   Optimizing Inventory in SAP IBP

center net requirements by the RDC → DC lead time. This approach certainly avoids multiple independent forecast updates in each echelon, but its major shortcoming is that the requirements passed up to the regional distribution center include no uncertainty; there's no rigorous method for determining safety stock.

In SAP IBP for inventory, both the end customer demand forecast and demand forecast error are propagated up through the supply chain. All stages of the supply chain execute based on a forecast or plan and on replenishment quantities calculated from the plan adjusted by actual demand. The calculation of demand propagation considers the following factors when propagating end customer demand and demand uncertainty upstream:

- Review frequency (PBR)
- Lead time
- Stocking policy
- Sourcing decisions
- Bill of materials
- Minimum lot size and/or incremental lot size (Q)

The demand forecast is propagated up through the supply chain using the standard MRP logic. At each echelon of a supply chain, net requirements are propagated upstream by lead time to arrive downstream on time, as illustrated in Figure 5.22.

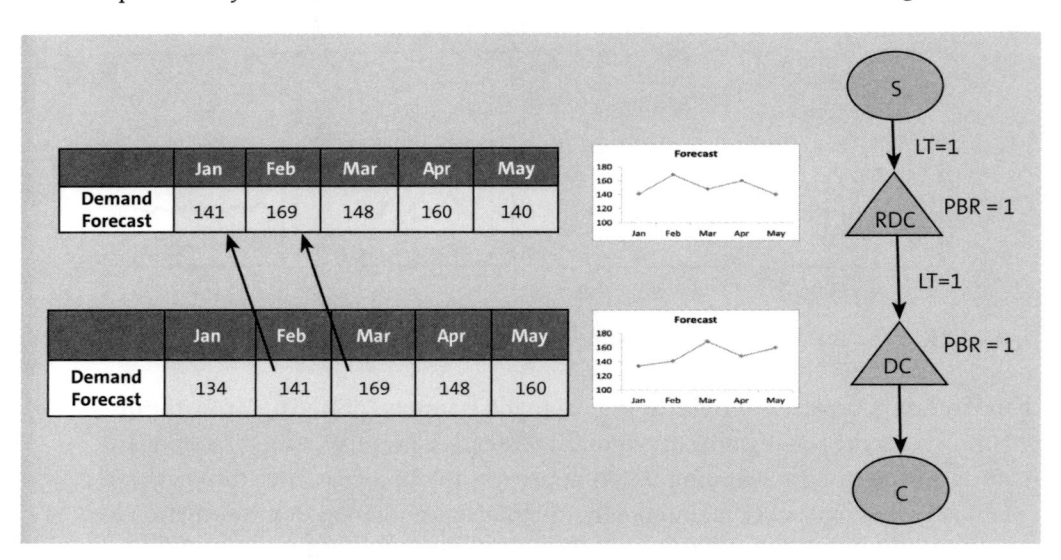

Figure 5.22 Net Requirements Propagated Upstream by Lead Time

5.3 Network Multiechelon Inventory Calculation

The demand forecast uncertainty must likewise be propagated up through the supply chain. However, the uncertainty is experienced during replenishment—for instance, after a period of high demand—so must be propagated by PBR forward. High demand downstream in period t results in a higher upstream replenishment order for the following period, $t + PBR$, as downstream safety stocks are replenished. Similarly, during ramp-down demand, a lower upstream replenishment order can be placed for the following period because there is expected to be leftover stock from the current period, so a reduced forecast error is propagated (see Figure 5.23).

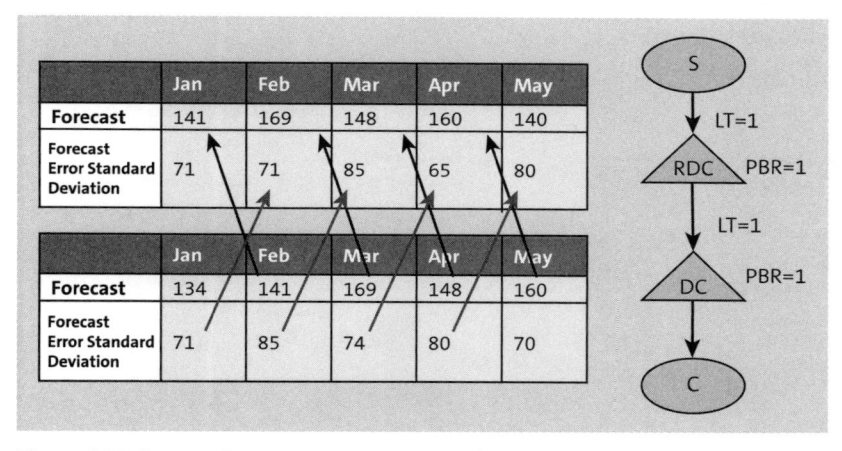

	Jan	Feb	Mar	Apr	May
Forecast	141	169	148	160	140
Forecast Error Standard Deviation	71	71	85	65	80

	Jan	Feb	Mar	Apr	May
Forecast	134	141	169	148	160
Forecast Error Standard Deviation	71	85	74	80	70

S → LT=1 → RDC (PBR=1) → LT=1 → DC (PBR=1) → C

Figure 5.23 Demand Uncertainty Propagated Upstream by PBR

Figure 5.24 shows an additional example to highlight the impact of PBR > 1 and lead time > 1 on demand propagation.

t	1	2	3	4	5	6	7	8	9	10	11	12	13	14	15
Forecast	200	0	200	0	200	0	200	0	200	0	200	0	200	0	200
Forecast Error Stdev	14	0	14	0	14	0	14	0	14	0	14	0	14	0	14

In order to arrive downstream on time, mean demand must be considered upstream LT earlier, "grouped" by PBR ... But uncertainty is experienced *after* a period of high demand, and propagates PBR later, "grouped" by PBR

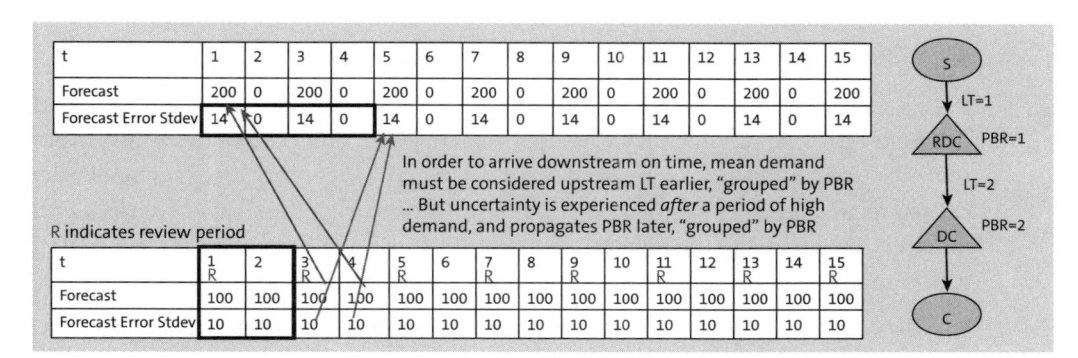

R indicates review period

t	1R	2	3R	4	5R	6	7R	8	9R	10	11R	12	13R	14	15R
Forecast	100	100	100	100	100	100	100	100	100	100	100	100	100	100	100
Forecast Error Stdev	10	10	10	10	10	10	10	10	10	10	10	10	10	10	10

S → LT=1 → RDC (PBR=1) → LT=2 → DC (PBR=2) → C

Figure 5.24 Impact of PBR and LT on Demand Propagation

219

5   Optimizing Inventory in SAP IBP

As you can see, the calculation of demand forecast and demand forecast variability propagation considers all complexities of real-world supply chains without making simplifying assumptions. The following select complexities are also illustrated in Figure 5.25:

- Multisourced stocking nodes
- Multidownstream nodes
- Nonstocking nodes
- Hybrid nodes—that is, stocking nodes that supply both internal demand and external customer demand
- Bill of materials

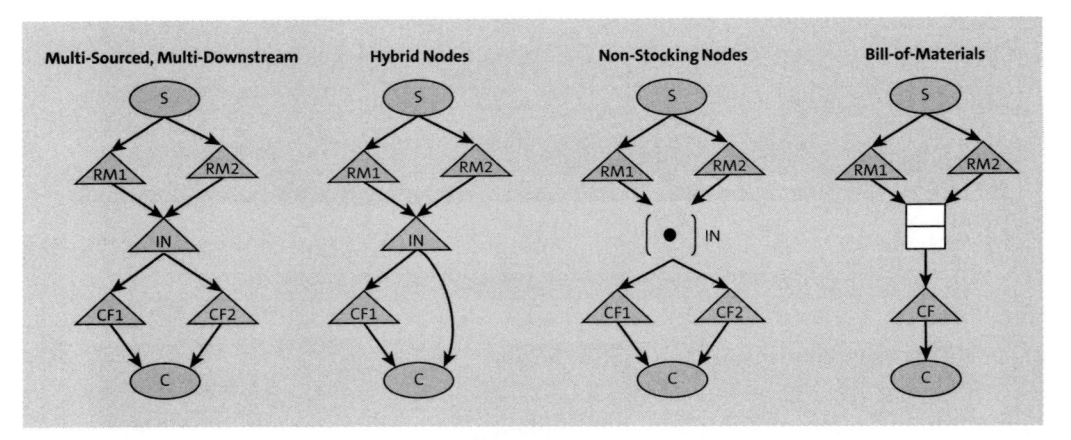

Figure 5.25 All Complexities Considered in Calculation of Demand Propagation

5.3.5   Estimating Service Variability from Source Location

In this section, we'll focus on how the linkage is created between safety stocks across different echelons up and down the supply chain. This is crucial to network inventory optimization because it can make optimally balancing inventory across echelons become practicable. Once again, we'll build the intuition using the simple multiechelon network introduced in the beginning of Section 5.3: supplier to regional distribution center to distribution center to customer. We want to address the follow questions:

- How do the inventory drivers at the regional distribution center, such as lead time, periods between review, and the service level goal, affect inventory and service levels at the distribution center level?

5.3 Network Multiechelon Inventory Calculation

- If there are multiple downstream distribution centers, when faced with a limited supply situation at the regional distribution center, how should we allocate product down to the distribution centers?
- Do the external supplier lead time and lead time variation still play a role in the distribution centers' inventory decisions?

In a multiechelon supply chain network, echelons/stages are all linked together. Orders placed by the downstream node create demand for product upstream. Service level goals at the upstream node have an impact on the ability to meet service levels downstream. The network inventory optimization in SAP IBP for inventory allows the internal service level of the upstream echelon and the backlog between the upstream echelon and downstream echelon to be modeled at the downstream stage and ensure that downstream service level targets are met.

The *backlog* is the portion of the order that can't be met from current on-hand inventory. It exists because of inventory decisions/product availability at internal stocking points (regional distribution centers), and it impacts inventory decisions at downstream stocking points (distribution centers). Figure 5.26 shows the impact of the internal service level on the safety stocks between the regional distribution center and distribution center and how the backlog links the safety stock between two echelons.

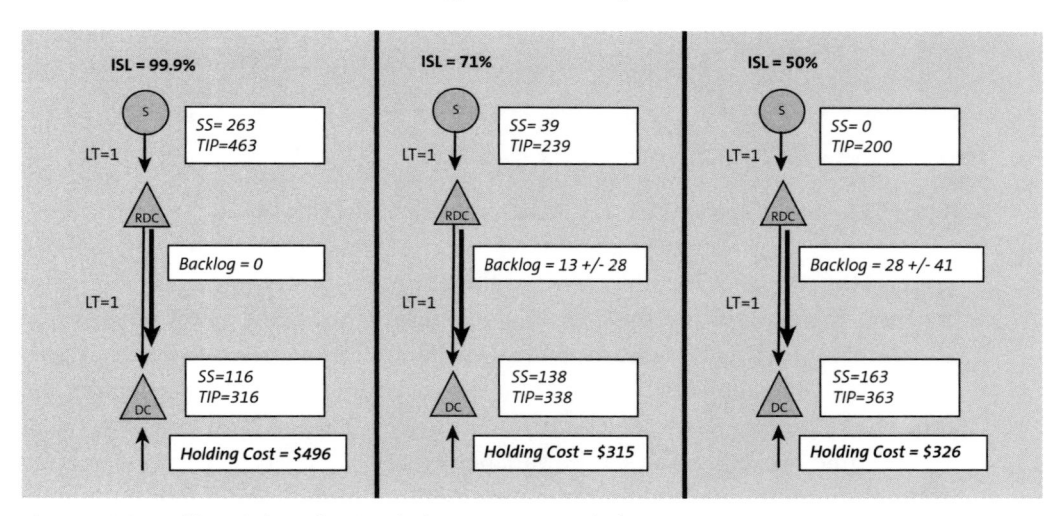

ISL = 99.9%	ISL = 71%	ISL = 50%
LT=1, S, SS=263, TIP=463	LT=1, S, SS=39, TIP=239	LT=1, S, SS=0, TIP=200
RDC	RDC	RDC
Backlog = 0	Backlog = 13 +/- 28	Backlog = 28 +/- 41
LT=1, DC, SS=116, TIP=316	LT=1, DC, SS=138, TIP=338	LT=1, DC, SS=163, TIP=363
Holding Cost = $496	Holding Cost = $315	Holding Cost = $326

Figure 5.26 Backlog Links Safey Stocks between Two Echelons

How is the backlog distribution quantified in terms of backlog mean and backlog standard deviation? In SAP IBP for inventory, the algorithms compare the target

5   Optimizing Inventory in SAP IBP

inventory position calculated for a given internal service level to the total exposure demand distribution at an internal stocking node and apply the stochastic calculation to characterize the backlog distribution. For instance, we illustrate how the backlog is calculated when the regional distribution center maintains an internal service level of 71% nonstockout probability in Figure 5.27. In addition, simulation is also widely used in practice to measure the backlog distribution. The simulation is usually created in an Excel spreadsheet for a fixed supply chain network, such as the simple supplier to regional distribution center to distribution center to customer network. The simulation randomly generates demand and captures the unmet demand distribution across multiple replications. The simulation can be used to verify the backlog distribution calculated by the analytical approach in SAP IBP for inventory.

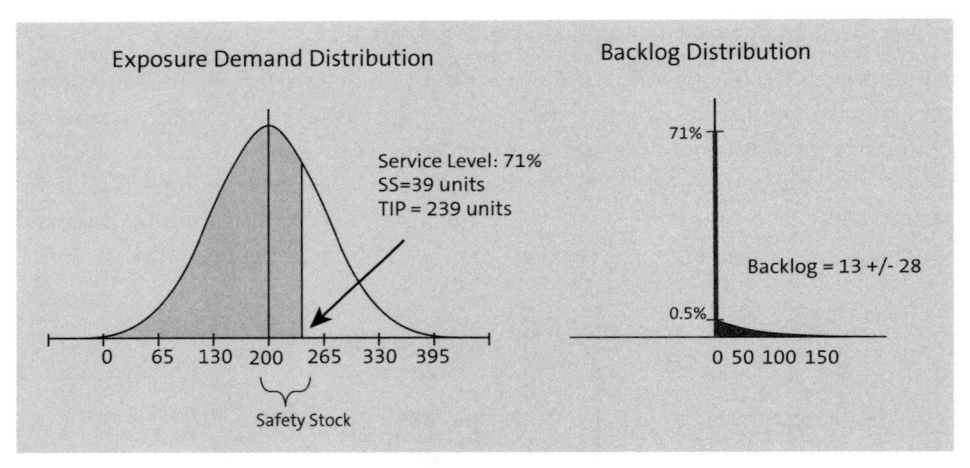

Figure 5.27 Quantifying Backlog Distribution at Internal Stocking Nodes

The backlog results in late shipments at the downstream stocking node and hence increases the exposure of the downstream stocking node. The safety stock at the downstream stocking node, such as the distribution center, needs to hedge against not only the demand variability but also the backlog. In SAP IBP for inventory, we also refer to backlog as *service variability*. The algorithms pool the demand variability, lead time variability, and service variability (backlog) together to calculate safety stocks at every stocking node in the supply chain. In Figure 5.26, a safety stock of 116 units is enough to hedge against demand variability. Additional safety stocks are needed to hedge against service variability/backlog. Safety stocks at the distribution center increase from 116 to 138, and to 163 finally as backlog mean and backlog standard deviation increase.

5.3 Network Multiechelon Inventory Calculation

To answer the questions asked at the beginning of this section, consider the primary drivers of backlog at the upstream node (the regional distribution center; we explain their impact on backlog in Figure 5.28):

- Internal service level
- Internal demand variability
- Exposure (PBR + lead time)

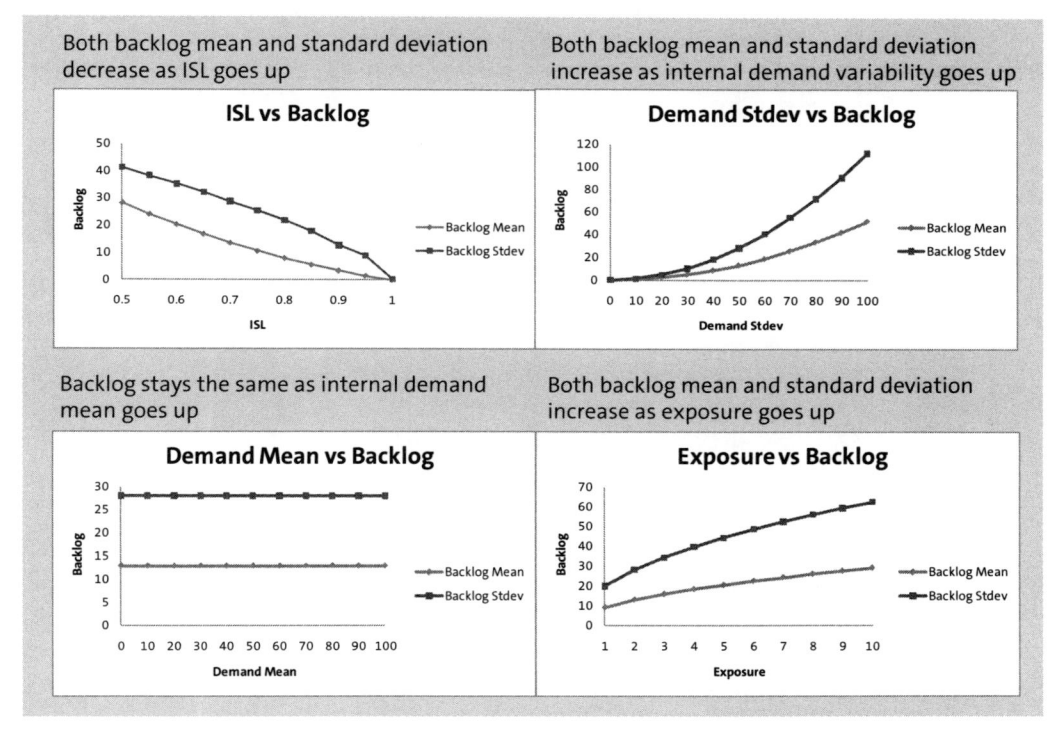

Figure 5.28 Primary Drivers of Backlog

There are several additional complexities in the calculation of backlog:

- **Three or more echelons**

  In network inventory optimization, the algorithms traverse the network and calculate the backlog in a top-down manner. The backlog is first calculated at the top echelon/vendor-facing echelon, then propagated down along the supply chain until the calculation reaches the bottom echelon/customer-facing echelon. The backlog calculated at a downstream stocking node incorporates all the (incoming) backlogs calculated at all its upstream stocking nodes. This is illustrated on the right side of Figure 5.29.

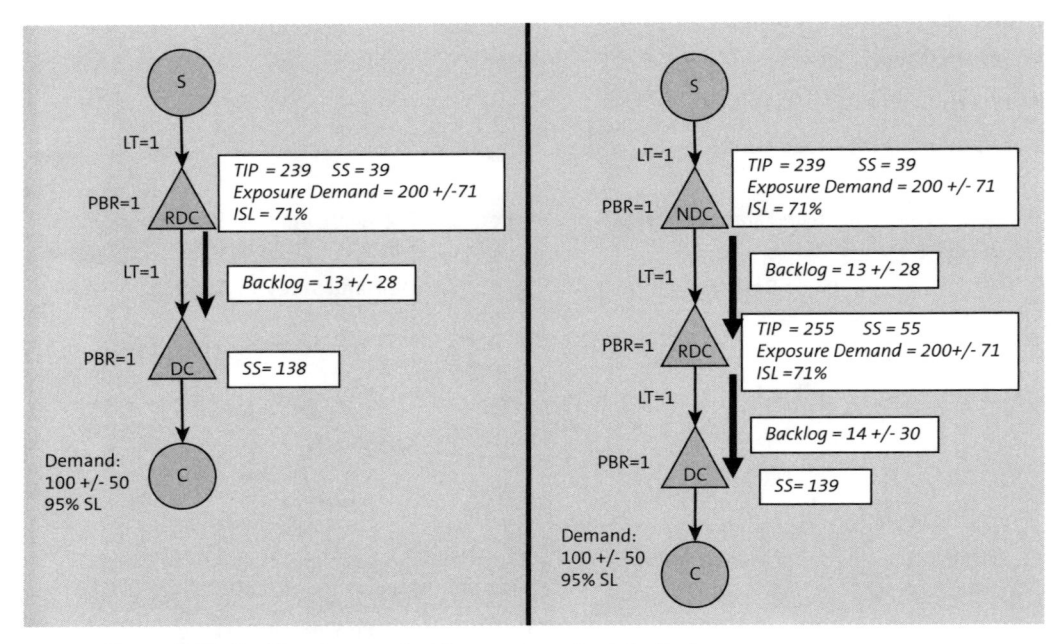

Figure 5.29 Backlog Propagated Down along Supply Chain

- **Impact of lead time variability**
  In the presence of lead time variability, for a given internal service level, the backlog at the upstream stocking node increases and therefore the safety stock at the downstream node goes up to meet its service level target. For example, see the right side of Figure 5.30.

- **Multiple downstream stocking nodes**
  If there are multiple downstream stocking nodes, the total backlog calculated at the upstream node needs to be allocated across its downstream stocking nodes. In SAP IBP for inventory, the backlog allocation is proportional to the corresponding downstream demand standard deviation, as shown in Figure 5.31.

  In the example on the left side, the total backlog is equally divided between DC1 and DC2 because they have the same demand standard deviation. In the example on the right side, because the ratio of demand standard deviation between DC1 and DC2 is 2:1, two-thirds of the total backlog is allocated to DC1 and the remaining one-third is allocated to DC2. Note that here we assume that orders from DC1 and

5.3 Network Multiechelon Inventory Calculation

DC2 are fulfilled at the regional distribution center on a first-come, first-serve basis and thus the backlog allocated to DC1 and the backlog allocated to DC2 are completely correlated. Therefore their means and standard deviations are simply summed up to the total backlog mean and standard deviation at the regional distribution center.

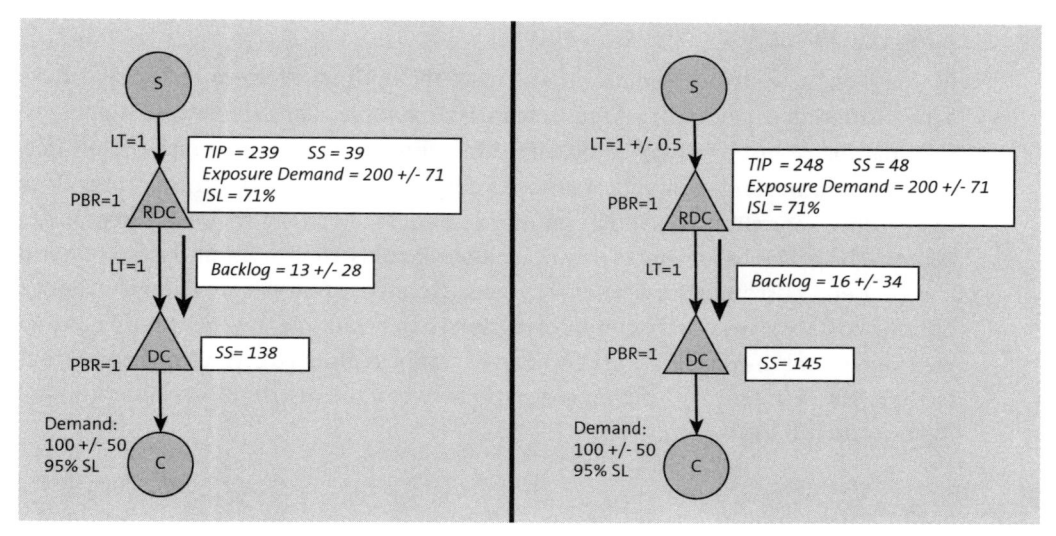

Figure 5.30 Larger Backlog In Presence of Lead Time Variability

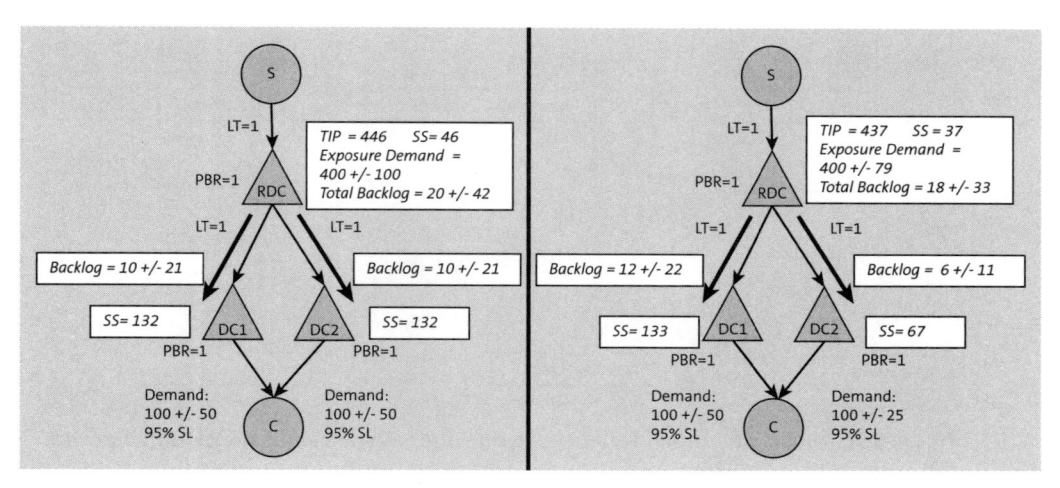

Figure 5.31 Allocate Backlog across Multiple Downstream Stocking Nodes

5 Optimizing Inventory in SAP IBP

You've seen now that backlog/service variability is a result of inventory decisions, demand variability, and supply variability. Backlog should be accounted for by downstream nodes in safety stock calculations to maintain service level targets. Multistage interactions and replenishment policies should be considered in backlog calculation.

5.3.6 Finalizing the Inventory Targets

In this section, we'll focus on how to calculate the optimal allocation of safety stocks across different echelons of a supply chain. For example, using the simple supplier to regional distribution center to distribution center to customer multiechelon network, should we deploy or allocate more safety stock at the distribution center close to customers, or should we push up more safety stock to the regional distribution center? The goal is to minimize the total network safety stock holding costs while still meeting end customer service level targets. Note that to evaluate the safety stock holding costs, we've added extra information to the example. The inventory holding cost rate is $2 at the distribution center and $1 at the regional distribution center; that is, there's a 2:1 inventory holding cost ratio between the distribution center and the regional distribution center.

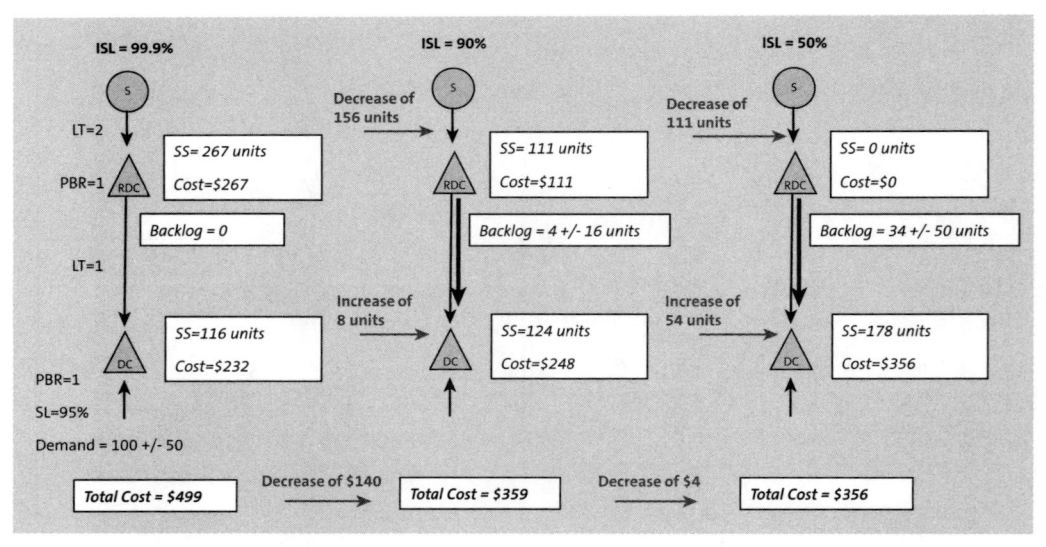

Figure 5.32 Impact of Internal Service Level on Total Network Safety Stock Holding Cost

5.3 Network Multiechelon Inventory Calculation

In the prior section, we showed that different service level goals at the regional distribution center result in different allocations of safety stocks between the regional distribution center and the distribution center and therefore different total network costs. In Figure 5.32, we vary the internal service level from the almost perfect 99.9% to 90% and finally 50%, push all the safety stock to the distribution center, and evaluate the total network cost. As shown, pushing all the safety stock to the distribution center leads to the lowest total network cost among the three scenarios.

However, is this scenario the best overall? In SAP IBP for inventory, the algorithms apply fast and sophisticated optimization techniques to find the optimal internal service levels, resulting in the lowest total network safety stock holding costs. For the simple example we've provided, the optimal internal service level is 72%, as shown in Figure 5.33.

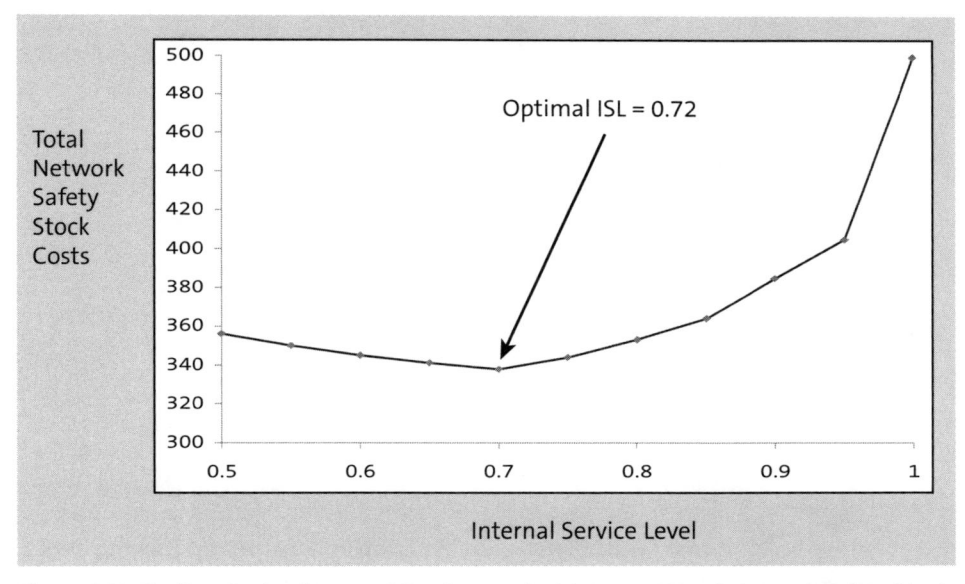

Figure 5.33 Finding Optimal Internal Service Level with Lowest Total Network Safety Stock Holding Cost

As soon as the optimal internal service levels are found, the algorithms finalize the inventory targets for all locations and products of the supply chain for all the periods

5   Optimizing Inventory in SAP IBP

in the planning horizon. This step is conceptually shown in Figure 5.34 with the simple supplier to regional distribution center to distribution center to customer example.

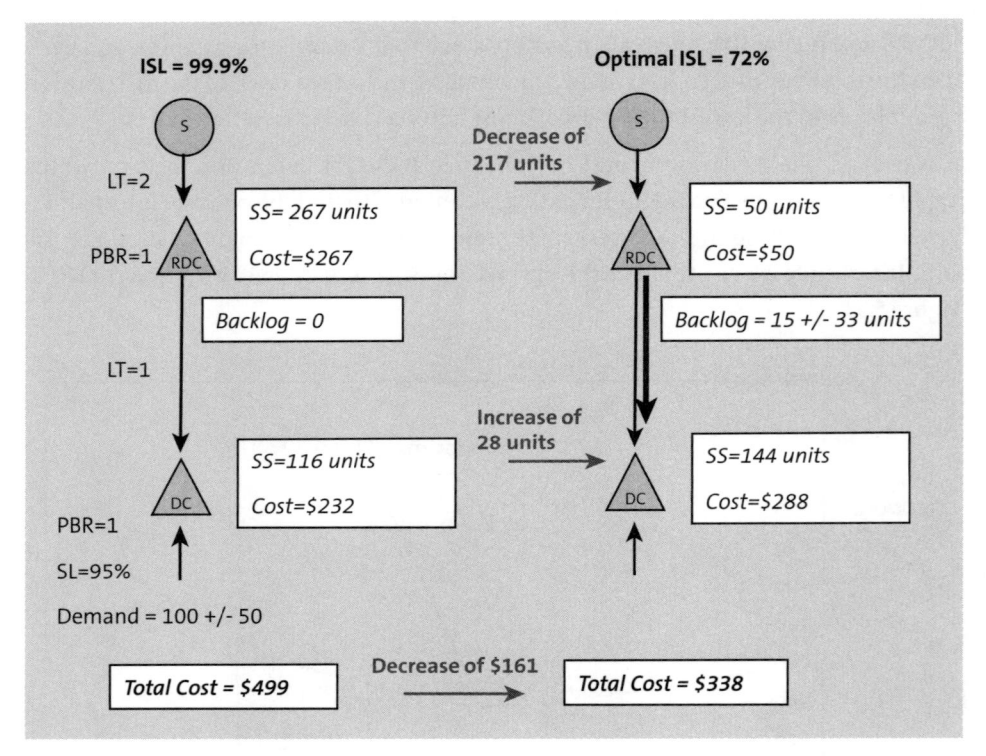

Figure 5.34 Finalized Safety Stock Targets Based on Optimal Internal Service Level

The following are several drivers of the optimal internal service level:

- **Inventory holding cost ratio between downstream and upstream stocking nodes**
  Increasing inventory carrying costs downstream moves safety stock upstream, away from high-cost nodes. As shown in Figure 5.35, the higher the inventory holding cost ratio, the higher the optimal internal service level and the more safety stock is held upstream.

5.3 Network Multiechelon Inventory Calculation

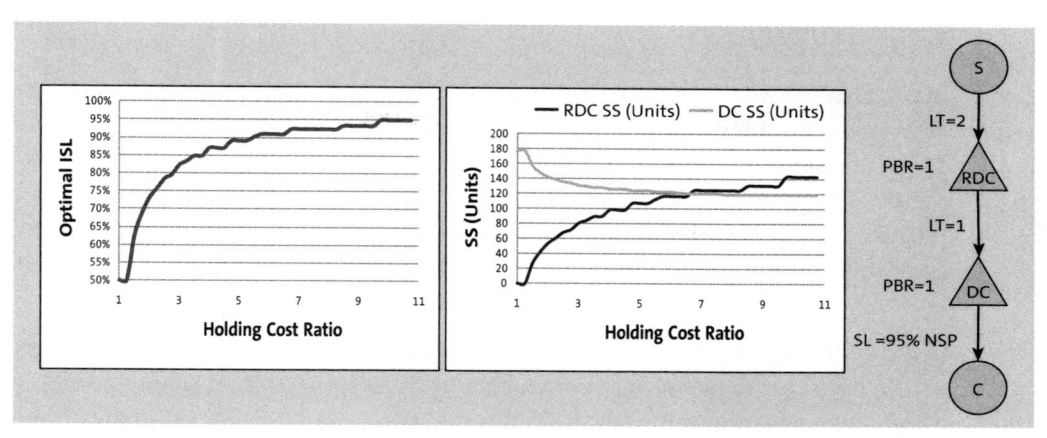

Figure 5.35 Optimal Internal Service Level Increases as Carrying Inventory Becomes More Expensive Downstream

- **Customer service level**

  In Figure 5.36, as the desired end customer service level increases, of course, the total network safety stock holding cost increases. As shown by the blue (lower) line, the optimal internal service level also increases, with more safety stocks allocated to the upstream stocking nodes.

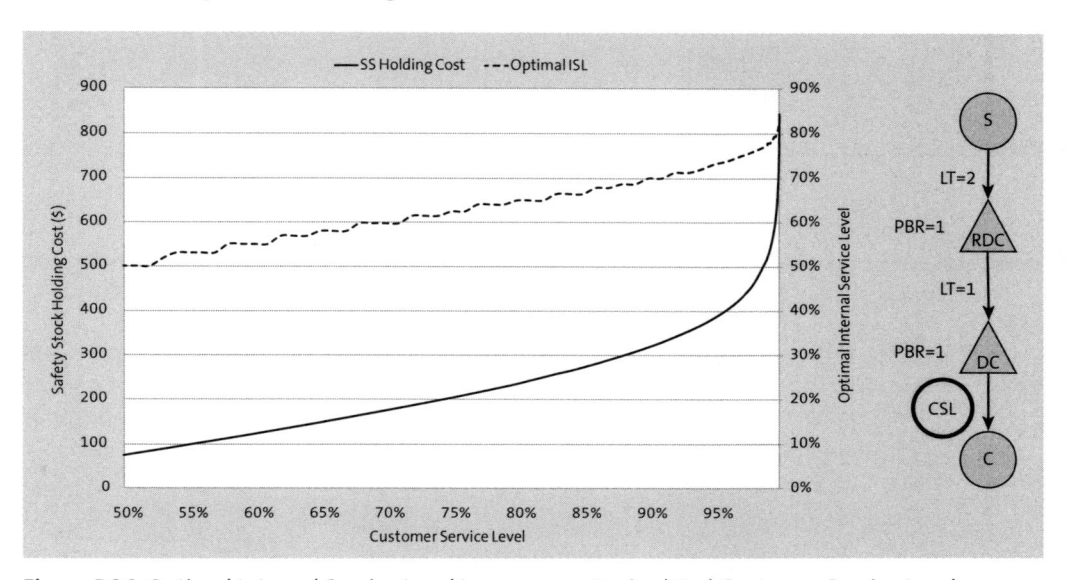

Figure 5.36 Optimal Internal Service Level Increases as Desired End Customer Service Level Increases

5.4 Summary

In this chapter, we discussed network inventory optimization in SAP IBP by defining its objectives, constraints, and decision variables. Before delving into the difficulties of calculating the inventory targets in a multiechelon supply chain network, we reviewed the single-echelon inventory calculation as a building block to introduce the inventory replenishment process and analyze the impact of primary drivers on inventory targets. Then we discussed all the crucial calculations in the multiechelon inventory optimization in SAP IBP step by step.

In the next chapter, we'll look beyond calculating the safety stock and provide more details about other inventory components, such as cycle stock, pipeline stock, and merchandising stock. A further breakdown of safety stock by sources of variability will be also discussed in detail.

Chapter 6
Structuring Inventory

Supply chain planners executing replenishment decisions based on total inventory need complete visibility into its components. In this chapter, we'll discuss how SAP IBP for inventory calculates all components of inventory based on inventory forms and purposes across the entire supply chain network and planning horizon.

In Chapter 5, we explained the fundamentals the inventory optimization algorithm in SAP IBP uses to calculate the optimal safety stock targets across the network simultaneously.

In this chapter, we'll take a close look at the other components that make up an organization's inventory beyond the safety stock. We'll describe the different types of inventory based on inventory forms and purposes and explain how to calculate them in SAP IBP for inventory. This together with the previous chapters will provide a good foundation for you to move to designing your inventory planning process.

6.1 Types of Inventory

As introduced in Chapter 1, inventory across the entire supply chain can be classified by forms/flow of materials and by purposes/functions. We'll start this section by discussing classifying inventory by the flow of materials and by purpose. Next, we'll dive into specific details of the different inventory types (cycle stock, pipeline stock, safety stock, merchandizing stock, and prebuild stock) that will form the basis of the discussion of structuring inventory throughout this chapter.

6 Structuring Inventory

6.1.1 Flow of Materials and Purpose

Inventory types can be grouped into four classifications by the flow of materials across the supply chain, as depicted in Figure 6.1:

- **Raw materials**
  Raw materials are inventory items that are purchased but haven't entered the production process. They include purchased materials, component parts, and subassemblies. Typically, raw materials are commodities such as ore, grain, minerals, petroleum, chemicals, paper, wood, paint, steel, and food items. However, items such as nuts and bolts, ball bearings, key stock, casters, seats, wheels, and even engines may be regarded as raw materials if they are purchased from outside sources.

  In most cases, raw materials are used in the manufacture of components. These components are then incorporated into the final product or become part of a subassembly. Subassemblies are then used to manufacture or assemble the final product.

- **Work in process (WIP)**
  Work in process is made up of all the materials, components, assemblies, and subassemblies that have entered the manufacturing process and are being worked on or waiting to be worked on. This usually includes all materials, from raw materials that have been released for initial processing up to materials that have been completely processed and are awaiting final inspection and acceptance before inclusion in finished goods.

- **Finished goods**
  Finished goods are the finished products of the production process that are ready to be sold as completed items. These goods have passed final inspection requirements so that they can be transferred out of work in process and into finished goods inventory. From this point, finished goods can be sold directly to their final users, sold to retailers, sold to wholesalers, sent to distribution centers, or held in anticipation of a customer order.

- **Maintenance, repair, and operating supplies**
  Maintenance, repair and operating supplies (MROs) are inventory items that are used in production but do not become part of a product. MRO items may include consumables (e.g., cleaning supplies), industrial equipment (e.g., valves, compressors, and pumps) and plant upkeep supplies (e.g., gaskets, lubricants, and repair tools), as well as computers, furniture, and so on.

6.1 Types of Inventory

Figure 6.1 shows an example of a flow of materials that includes movement of goods from supplier to consumer and transformation between different types of inventory.

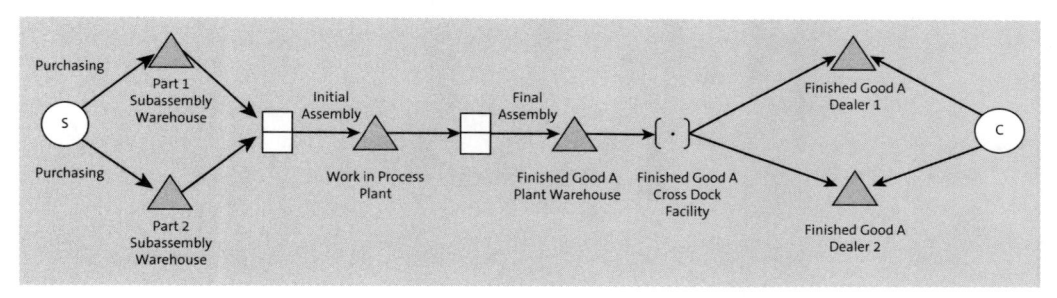

Figure 6.1 Inventory Classified by Flow of Materials

Inventory can also be classified according to the purpose it serves. These inventory types may include the following:

- **Cycle stock**
  Inventory needed to meet current demand until the next order can be placed
- **Pipeline stock**
  Inventory needed to meet future demand until the next order can be received
- **Safety stock**
  Inventory needed to hedge against risk and uncertainty
- **Merchandizing stock**
  Additional "display" stock needed on hand in each period
- **Prebuild stock**
  Inventory that ensures against predictable demand variability

Note that prebuild stock can be modeled and calculated by SAP IBP for response and supply. Except for prebuild stock, SAP IBP for inventory provides complete visibility into all other components of inventory based on inventory forms and purposes across the entire supply chain network and planning horizon (as shown in Figure 6.2). The multiechelon inventory model in SAP IBP for inventory allows multiple types of inventory, including cycle stock, pipeline stock, and merchandising stock, along with safety stock, to be properly modeled across the supply chain. This opens tremendous opportunities to improve supply chain performance and lower total inventory.

In the following sections, we'll elaborate more on the five types of inventory classified by their purposes and explain the drivers of each one.

6   Structuring Inventory

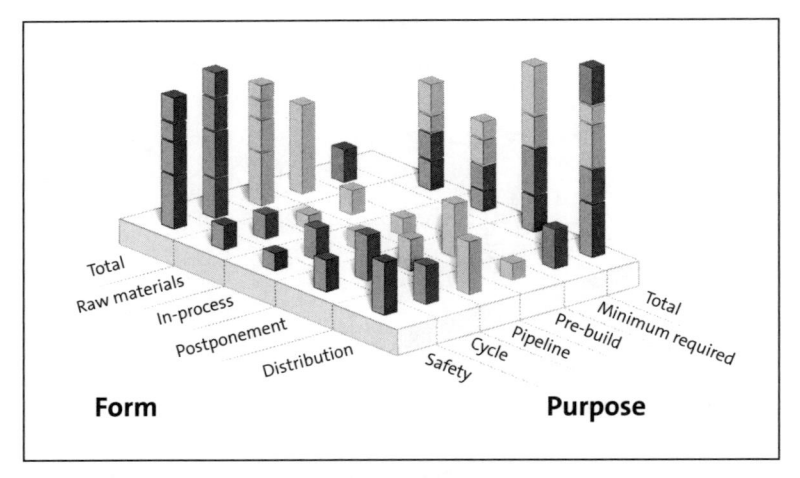

Figure 6.2 Complete Visibility into Various Types of Inventory

6.1.2   Cycle Stock

Cycle stock is the amount of inventory that is planned to be used to meet current demand during a period until the next order can be placed. This time is often defined as *periods between review* (PBR). It's either the time between orders (for raw materials) or the time between production cycles (for work in process and finished goods). The quantity of cycle stock inventory is equal to the total on-hand inventory minus the safety stock inventory.

Key drivers of cycle stock are demand forecast, replenishment frequency, and lot sizes. For example, cycle stock increases with PBR, as shown in Figure 6.3.

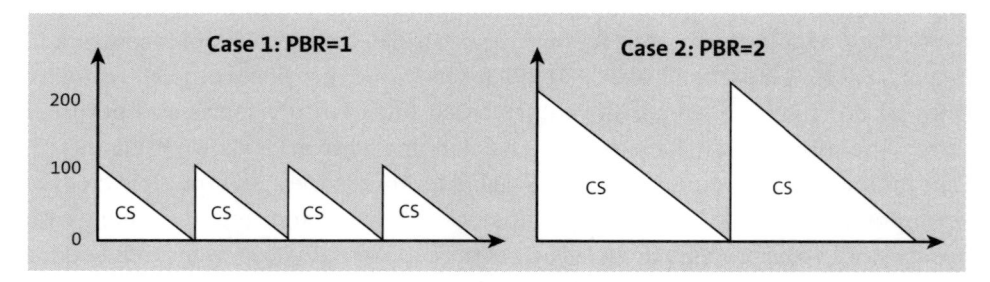

Figure 6.3 Cycle Stock Increases with Period between Reviews

Cycle stock inventory serves an important function in a company's accounting. As a business sells its cycle stock inventory and replenishes it, its cash flow accounts for the income it receives and the payments it makes. Cycle stock inventory is also part of a company's total assets on its balance sheet. To determine the cost of cycle stock inventory, a business can use the last-in, first-out method or the first-in, first-out method, which base the price of items in the cycle stock on the most recent or oldest prices paid, respectively.

6.1.3 Pipeline Stock

Pipeline stock is in-transit stock that is planned to be used to meet future demand. For example, pipeline stock consists of items that are in the transit pipeline between locations, such as those en route from the warehouse to the retail outlet. While the items are in transit, they are still considered to be part of the shipper's inventory if the recipient has yet to pay for them. When the recipient pays for the items, even if that recipient has not taken physical custody of the items, that pipeline inventory goes on the recipient's inventory list.

Key drivers of pipeline stock are demand forecast and production or transportation lead time. Pipeline stock should cover the total planned receipts of all periods during the lead time. Therefore, pipeline stock increases with lead time as shown in Figure 6.4.

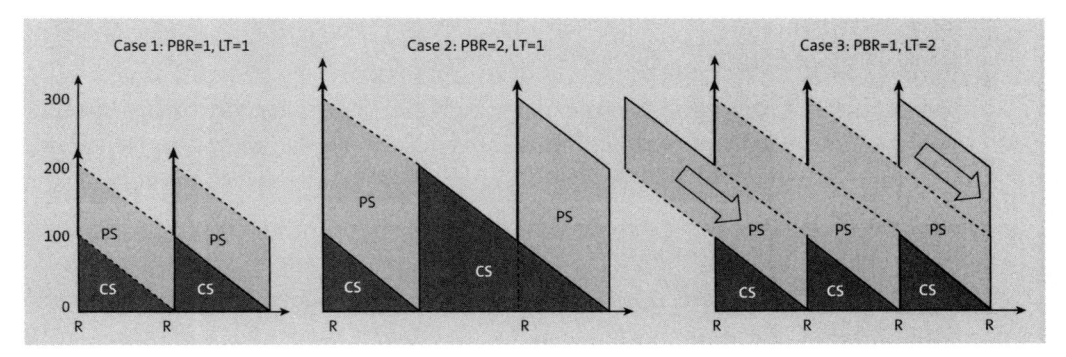

Figure 6.4 Pipeline Stock Increases with Lead Time

6.1.4 Safety Stock

Safety stock is the buffer used to hedge against risk and uncertainty, such as loss of production due to plant shutdown, late deliveries, or unexpectedly high demand. We have covered a lot about how safety stock can be calculated and its primary drivers in Chapter 5. We'll further discuss different components of safety stock in Section 6.2.

6 Structuring Inventory

6.1.5 Merchandizing Stock

Merchandizing refers to the variety of products available for sale and displaying those products in such a way as to stimulate interest and entice customers to make a purchase. In SAP IBP for inventory, merchandizing stock is calculated as the difference between the minimum stock requirement and safety stock in each period. Therefore the merchandizing stock reflects additional display stock needed on-hand in that period. Table 6.1 illustrates how merchandising stock is calculated given safety stock and minimum stock requirements.

Period	1	2	3	4	5
Forecast	100	200	300	200	50
Minimum Stock Requirement	250	250	250	250	250
Safety Stock	116	184	297	297	168
Merchandising Stock	134	66	0	0	82

Table 6.1 Merchandizing Stock: Difference between Minimum Stock and Safety Stock Requirements

6.1.6 Prebuild Stock

Prebuild stock is the amount of inventory built due to capacity constraints in anticipation of future demand. Prebuild stock is needed when a demand for a given period exceeds capacity. If this occasion arises, additional inventory in the previous period(s) must be produced or stored in anticipation of the period with a demand higher than maximum capacity.

In the following example, let's assume the maximum production capacity of a product is 100 units per week. The demand for this product as per each week in January is given in Table 6.2.

Simply producing as per the demand in each week would result in a demand of 150 units being unfulfilled in Week 4. However, by prebuilding some units in the previous weeks, all the demand can be satisfied.

Thus, prebuilding 100 units in week 2 and 50 units in week 3 allows fulfillment of the full 250 unit demand in week 4, even though production was limited to 100 units in week 4.

Period	Demand	Production	Prebuild Stock
Week 1	25	25	0
Week 2	0	100	100
Week 3	50	100	150
Week 4	250	100	0

Table 6.2 Prebuild Stock: Inventory Built to Address Capacity Constraints in Anticipation of Future Demand

6.2 Further Decomposition of Safety Stock

In SAP IBP for inventory, in addition to total recommended safety stock for each product location in a period, a few additional safety stock components are also calculated that can give a comprehensive breakdown by sources of safety stock:

- Safety stock due to demand variability
- Safety stock due to service variability
- Safety stock due to supply variability
- Safety stock reduction due to lot sizes

The further decomposition of safety stock can help supply chain planners better understand the drivers of safety stock; link safety stock requirements to important factors such as service level, forecast accuracy, lead time variability, and so on; and identify inventory reduction opportunities. The safety stock reduction due to lot sizes accounts for the decrease of total safety stock because of minimum or incremental lot size inputs, which cause excess cycle stock. We'll elaborate on the three remaining safety stock components and summarize the primary reasons for companies to carry safety stock in the following sections.

6.2.1 Safety Stock Due to Demand Variability

Safety stock due to demand variability accounts only for the single-stage demand variability, which is calculated based on the sum of demand variabilities during exposure (PBR + LT) periods. Therefore, the drivers of safety stock due to demand variability are PBR, lead time (LT), forecast error, and service level requirement. Figure 6.5 shows the impact of major drivers on safety stock due to demand variability using simple examples.

6   Structuring Inventory

As shown in Figure 6.5, lower forecast accuracy can lead to a higher safety stock requirement. Many companies are investing or plan to invest in improving demand forecast accuracy. Performing sensitivity analysis of forecast accuracy on safety stock in SAP IBP for inventory can help identify the value that can be created from an accurate forecast.

In addition, the higher desired service level, the longer the lead time and review cycle and the higher the safety stock requirement. In practice, companies use different approaches to find an optimum service level for each individual product, ranging from heuristics like ABC analysis to determine an adequate service level for groups of products to advanced service level optimization techniques.

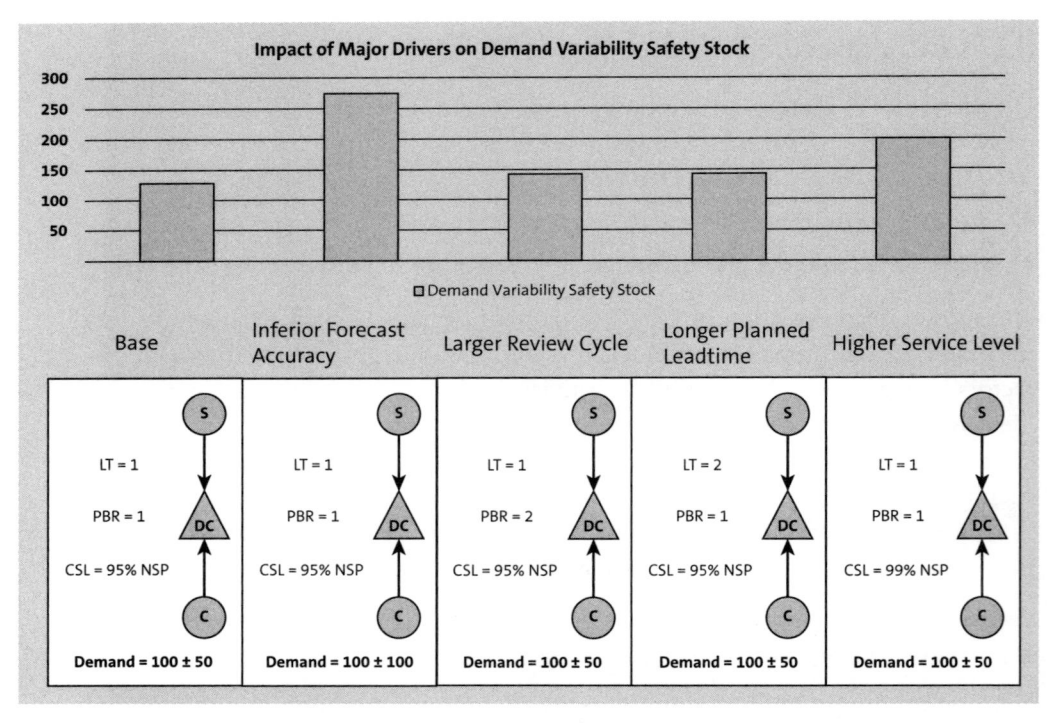

Figure 6.5 Impact of Major Drivers on Demand Variability Safety Stock

6.2.2   Safety Stock Due to Supply Variability

Safety stock due to supply variability accounts for the uncertainty in supply due to lead time variability. In SAP IBP for inventory, supply variability safety stock is defined as the additional amount of safety stock needed on top of demand variability

6.2 Further Decomposition of Safety Stock

safety stock to cover for lead time variability. To calculate supply variability safety stock, a safety stock amount based on total demand variability and supply variability is calculated first, then demand variability safety stock is subtracted from it. The difference is interpreted as the incremental units of safety stock needed to cover for supply variability, as shown in Figure 6.6.

In Figure 6.6, the additional safety stock represented by the orange bar is required to cover the 50% lead time error we add to the originally constant lead time. Performing sensitivity analysis of lead time variability on safety stock can help identify the value that can be created from better managing lead time and lead time variability.

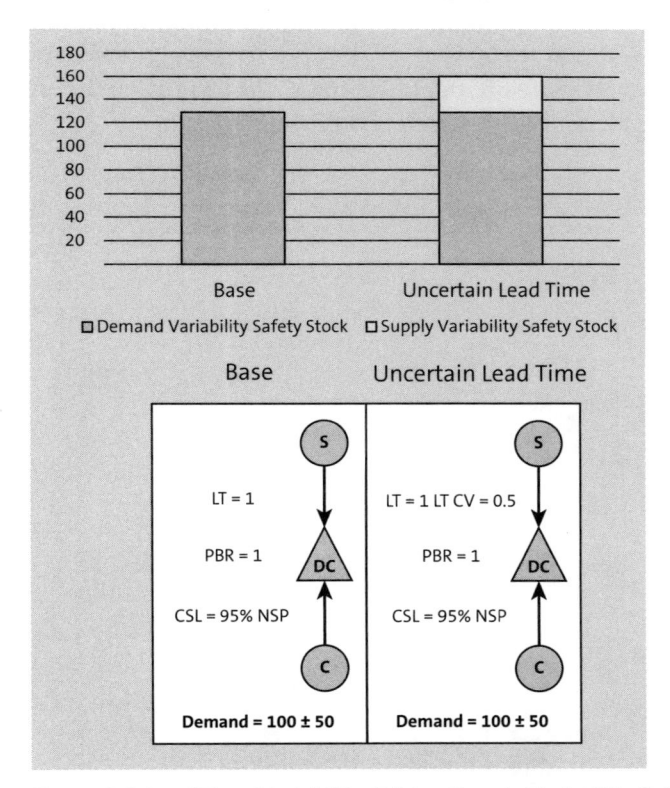

Figure 6.6 Lead Time Variability Driving Supply Variability Safety Stock

6.2.3 Safety Stock Due to Service Variability

Safety stock due to service variability accounts for the variability due to imperfect upstream service levels. More details can be found in Chapter 5 about how the service

6   Structuring Inventory

variability can be quantified and what the primary drivers are for it. In SAP IBP for inventory, service variability safety stock is defined as the additional amount of safety stock needed on top of demand variability safety stock plus supply variability safety stock to cover for service variability. Therefore, it's calculated as the difference between total recommended safety stock and the sum of demand variability safety stock and supply variability stock, as shown in Figure 6.7.

In Figure 6.7, the additional safety stock represented by the red bar is required to cover the imperfect service level of 50% at the upstream product location. In SAP IBP for inventory, the upstream service level is calculated by the network inventory optimization algorithms (subjected to user-specified minimum and maximum service levels) to minimize the total safety stock holding costs across the supply chain. The higher the internal service level upstream, the lower the service variability safety stock and therefore the lower the total safety stock at the downstream node.

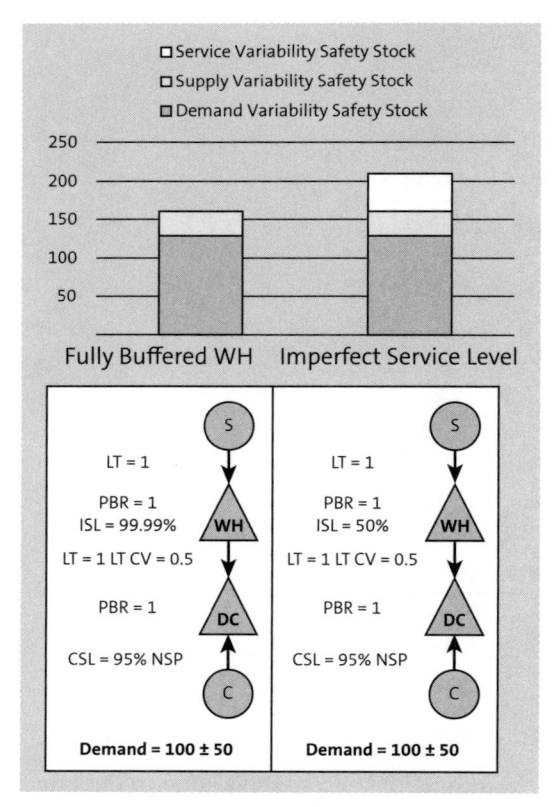

Figure 6.7 Service Variability Safety Stock Driven by Imperfect Service Level

In conclusion, you can see that the primary reasons for companies to carry safety stock are as follows:

- To compensate for forecast inaccuracies
- To avoid stockouts and maintain desired customer service and satisfaction levels
- To prevent disruptions in manufacturing or deliveries
- To hedge against imperfect service level/stockout risks from upstream suppliers

6.3 Calculating Inventory Components

In this section, we'll explore in more detail the SAP IBP for inventory operator that calculates all inventory components across the supply chain and cover the inputs and outputs of inventory component calculation.

6.3.1 Operator to Calculate Inventory Components

The SAP IBP for inventory *calculate target inventory components operator* performs the following steps to calculate all inventory components across the entire supply chain:

1. Starts from the bottom of the supply chain and propagates the customer demand forecast to the customer-facing product locations.
2. Calculates net inventory requirements, incorporating the demand forecast requirement, safety stock requirement, and ending inventory from the previous period. The final net inventory requirements are also adjusted to respect minimum or incremental lot size inputs.
3. Propagates the final net inventory requirements upstream along the supply chain using the standard MRP heuristic. For example, the final net inventory requirements are shifted by lead time and calculated as propagated demand mean at an upstream production location.
4. Calculates the various forms of inventory as target (beginning of period) and average (average of period) in quantity and days.

For larger and complex supply chains, all these calculations need to be processed in a timely manner. We'll walk through two examples of how SAP IBP for inventory supports scalability.

6   Structuring Inventory

The calculate target inventory components planning operator supports the use of planning units (subnetworks), as shown in Figure 6.8. Users can separate/filter the whole network by region and/or product family into planning units so that they can run them separately.

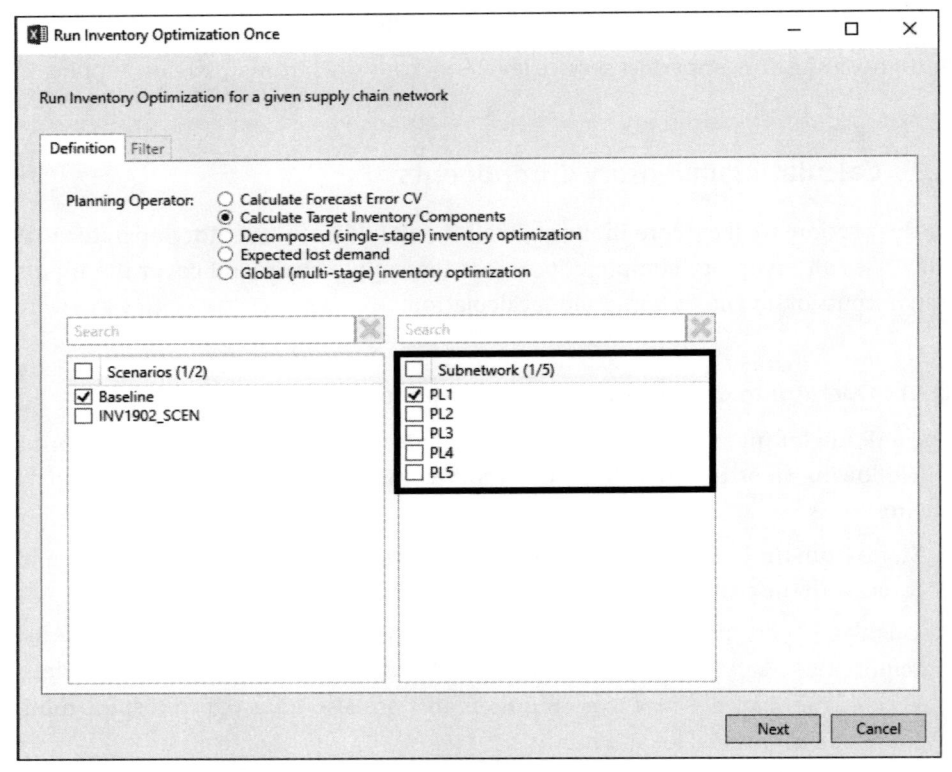

Figure 6.8 Calculate Target Inventory Components Operator: Subnetworks

In addition, the calculate target inventory components planning operator supports the planning horizon as an operator parameter, as shown in Figure 6.9. This feature supports cases in which users want to (1) use planning horizons different than the standard planning area planning horizons and (2) apply different planning horizons at the planning unit level.

Now let's review the recommended sequence for running the inventory planning operators in batch mode to generate a comprehensive inventory plan. We'll cover with more details of where this fits into the end-to-end inventory planning process and how to review key inputs and outputs of the inventory plan in Chapter 8.

6.3 Calculating Inventory Components

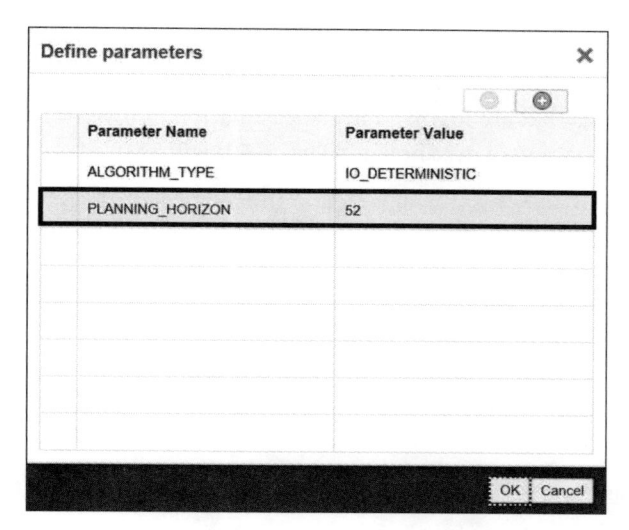

Define parameters	
Parameter Name	Parameter Value
ALGORITHM_TYPE	IO_DETERMINISTIC
PLANNING_HORIZON	**52**

Figure 6.9 Calculate Target Inventory Components Operator: Planning Horizon as Parameter

As shown in Figure 6.10, the forecast error calculation is performed first to assess the historical forecast error and provide it as a primary input for multistage inventory optimization. This is followed by global (multistage) inventory optimization to optimize safety stock globally and simultaneously across all products and locations in the supply chain. We've covered the fundamentals of the first two processes in Chapter 5. Finally, the calculate target inventory components operator takes the optimal safety stock targets that are calculated by global inventory optimization and calculates target and average quantities of complete inventory components, such as inventory position, on-hand stock, cycle stock, pipeline stock, and merchandizing stock.

Manage Forecast Error Calculations – Inventory → Global (Multistage) Inventory Optimization → Calculate Target Inventory Components

Figure 6.10 Running Sequence of Inventory Planning Operators in Batch Mode

6.3.2 Inputs to Calculate Inventory Components

In this section, we'll cover some details of the inputs to calculate inventory components. As shown in Figure 6.10, the calculation requires a successful run of the global inventory optimization operator. This is because for optimal safety stock targets, one

243

6   Structuring Inventory

key input for the inventory component calculation is the result of the multistage inventory optimization.

To cover all the inputs and outputs that are involved in the calculation of inventory components, the sample supply chain network shown in Figure 6.11 will be used.

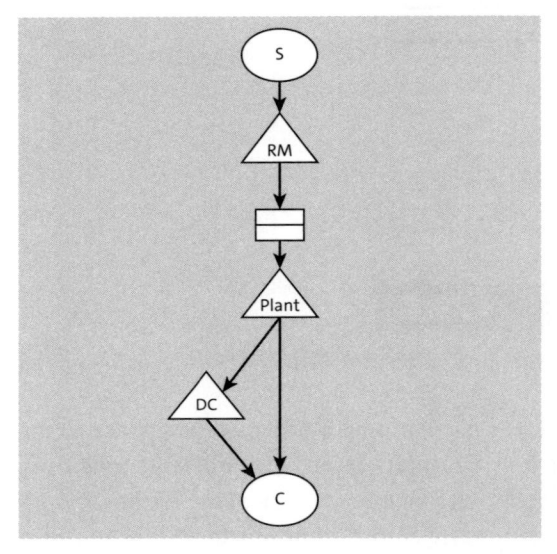

Figure 6.11 Sample Network for Explaining Inputs and Outputs

The sample supply chain network shown in Figure 6.11 consists of the following stages or processes:

- The customer node (C) represents the end customer of the supply chain. Demand forecasts from customers can be fulfilled from various locations in the network.
- The distribution center (DC) is the customer-facing stocking point in the network, fulfilling customer demand while ordering from the plant.
- The plant represents a production facility where finished goods are produced. Plants fulfill customer and distribution center demand while producing and hence require raw materials.
- Raw materials (RM) are the stocking points holding raw materials and supplying plants.

Now we can group the inputs into three categories: the inputs that drive net inventory requirements, the inputs that specify inventory policy parameters, and the inputs that come from the supplier side.

Net Inventory Requirements Inputs

To propagate customer demand upstream along the supply chain, to the DC, plant, and RM, net inventory requirements need to be evaluated at each product-location and every period in the planning horizon. Inventory requirements consist of forecasted or propagated dependent demand, safety stock requirements, and minimum stock requirement:

- **IOFORECAST (demand forecast)**
  This input key figure represents independent/external customer demand that's an outcome of the demand planning process. In SAP IBP for inventory, the input key figure is defined at the product-location-customer group level or the demand stream level. For example, given the sample supply chain network, demand forecasts need to be provided at both product-DC-customer demand stream and product-plant-customer demand stream levels.

- **RECOMMENDEDSAFETYSTOCK (recommended safety stock)**
  This key figure represents the safety stock requirement per product and location. It's the output of the global inventory optimization operator. In the sample supply chain network, recommended safety stock is given at the DC, plant, and RM in every period.

- **IOMINSTOCKREQUIREMENT (minimum stock requirement)**
  This input key figure represents a user-specified minimum stock level in a given period per product and location.

> **Note**
> The net inventory requirement in a period can be calculated as *demand forecast or propagated demand requirement + max (safety stock requirement, minimum stock requirement) – available inventory in the beginning of the period.*

Inventory Policy Parameters Inputs

Inventory policy parameters outline stocking and replenishment policies to ensure that inventory is properly controlled and that losses or shortages are prevented. It applies to all types of inventory, including raw materials, work in progress, and finished goods. Inventory policy parameters are typically business decisions and usually are not fully available in an ERP system. The following inputs represent inventory policy parameters—for example, periods between reviews, stocking vs non-stocking decisions, and shipment frequency:

6　Structuring Inventory

- **PBR (periods between review)**
  This defines the periods between replenishments for product-locations, such as DC, plant, and RM in the sample network. Note that this input is an attribute as a key figure, which allows users to perform what-if simulation on it directly in a planning view. PBR can be defined based on locations. For example, in our sample supply chain network, PBR is one week at the customer-facing DC, but less frequent at plant or RM locations at four weeks. PBR can also be determined by demand characteristics. For example, high-volume, fast-moving products need more frequent review than low-volume, slow-moving products.

- **STOCKINGNODETYPE (stocking node type)**
  This attribute specifies the strategy decision for stocking versus not stocking for a given product-location. At a nonstocking product location, inventory components such as on-hand stock, cycle stock, merchandising stock, and safety stock will be zero. However, pipeline stock and target inventory position will be calculated.

- **TSHIPMENTFREQUENCY (transportation shipment frequency)**
  This attribute defines the transportation shipment frequency per location source. The transportation shipment frequency is independent of review frequency (i.e., PBR). Planners may review inventory for multiple periods but can receive multiple shipments over the review cycle. For example, inventory is reviewed and orders are placed once a month, but shipments arrive every week as trucks are filled up.

- **PSHIPMENTFREQUENCY (production shipment frequency)**
  This attribute defines the production shipment frequency per production source.

Supplier-Side Inputs

The following inputs specify the planning parameters from the supplier side—for example, lead time, lot size, supply ratios, and bill of materials data:

- **TLEADTIME (transportation lead time)**
  This attribute as a key figure defines the transportation lead time for source-locations. In the calculation of demand propagation, the net inventory requirement is shifted by lead time and calculated as the propagated demand mean at an upstream product location. Note that currently only the value in the current period of this key figure is considered by SAP IBP for inventory operators. This also applies for the following attribute as key figure inputs.

- **TMINLOTSIZE (transportation minimum lot size)**
  This attribute as a key figure defines the transportation minimum lot size (in units) for source-locations.

- **TINCLOTSIZE (transportation incremental lot size)**
  This attribute as a key figure defines the transportation incremental lot size (in units) for source-locations.
- **TRATIO (transportation ratio)**
  This attribute defines the static transportation ratio for source-locations.
- **RATIOTS (transportation ratio time series indicator)**
  If the sourcing is time-dependent, then set RATIOTS to "X" and the LOCATIONRATIO key figure will be used to specify the time-dependent transportation ratio.
- **LOCATIONRATIO (location ratio)**
  This key figure defines the time-dependent transportation ratio for source-locations.
- **PLEADTIME (production lead time)**
  This attribute as a key figure defines the production lead time for source-production combinations.
- **PMINLOTSIZE (production minimum lot size)**
  This attribute as a key figure defines the production minimum lot size (in units) for source-production combinations.
- **PINCLOTSIZE (production incremental lot size)**
  This attribute as a key figure defines the production incremental lot size (in units) for a source-production combination.
- **PRATIO (production ratio)**
  This attribute defines the static production ratio for source-production combinations.
- **PRATIOTS (production ratio time series indicator)**
  If a product can be produced or procured by more than one SOURCEID, the same mechanism as with TRATIO applies here for PRATIO and PRATIOTS (the key figure is PRODUCTIONRATIO).
- **PRODUCTIONRATIO (production ratio)**
  This key figure defines the time-dependent production ratio for source-production combinations.
- **COMPONENTCOEFFICIENT (component coefficient)**
  The quantity of a component in a BOM can be modeled as time-independent or time-dependent as a key figure. Note that this attribute is required for a base quantity of a finished product.

- **COMPONENTCOEFFICIENTTS (component coefficient time series indicator)**
  If the component coefficient is time-dependent, the flag can be set to "X" and the COMPONENTCOEFFICIENT key figure used to specify the time-dependent component coefficient.

- **OUTPUTCOEFFICIENT (output product coefficient)**
  This defines the base quantity produced of a finished product. It can be modeled as time-independent or time-dependent as a key figure.

- **OUTPUTCOEFFICIENTTS (output product coefficient time series indicator)**
  If the output product coefficient is time-dependent, the indicator can be set to "X" and the OUTPUTCOEFFICIENT key figure used to specify the time-dependent output product coefficient.

- **SOURCETYPE (source type)**
  The source type in the production source header table can be defined as P (production) or U (unspecified). U is specified when the source of supply to meet the demand is not required to be modeled explicitly.

6.3.3 Outputs of Inventory Components Calculation

In this section, we'll focus on the outcome of inventory components calculation. The outputs construct a comprehensive inventory plan, providing visibility into all types of inventory components across all the products and locations over the entire planning horizon. We'll review each output with certain details about what it represents and how it's calculated. We'll cover in more detail where they fit into the end-to-end inventory planning process and how to review some of the key outputs in Chapter 8.

Ahead, we'll group the outputs into three categories: visibility into future independent and dependent product demand across the end-to-end supply chain, types of inventory components in units, and inventory components in days of supply.

Future Independent and Dependent Product Demand

There's really only one output in this category, as follows:

- **PROPAGATEDDEMANDMEAN (propagated demand mean)**
  This output represents future independent and dependent demand at a given product location. For example, propagated demand is equal to customer demand forecast at a customer-facing product location. At an internal product location,

propagated demand mean is the dependent demand propagated from downstream product locations. The output is calculated for all types of inventory, including raw materials, work in process, and finished goods.

The primary reason for a company to hold inventory is to be ready to fulfill future customer demand. Companies must make sure that the inventory investments they make will provide the best possible return. Having visibility into future independent and dependent product demand across the end-to-end supply chain is an important beginning point for measuring inventory performance. We'll cover more details of this topic in Chapter 8.

Types of Inventory Components in Units

Most outputs represent target and average quantities of various types of inventory components, including inventory position, on-hand stock, cycle stock, pipeline stock, and merchandising stock:

- **IOTARGETONHANDSTOCK (target on-hand stock)**
  Target on-hand stock represents the beginning period on-hand stock. Target on-hand stock is the sum of target cycle stock, safety stock, and merchandising stock.

- **IOAVGONHANDSTOCK (average on-hand stock)**
  Average on-hand stock is the time-average on-hand stock for a period that can be calculated as target on-hand stock minus propagated demand mean divided by 2.

- **IOTARGETCYCLESTOCK (target cycle stock)**
  Target cycle stock is the beginning period cycle stock, which can be calculated as target on-hand stock minus recommended safety stock and merchandising stock.

- **IOAVGCYCLESTOCK (average cycle stock)**
  Average cycle stock is the time-average cycle stock, which can be calculated as average on-hand stock minus recommended safety stock and merchandising stock.

- **IOTARGETPIPELINESTOCK (target pipeline stock)**
  Target pipeline stock is the beginning period on-order stock, which can be calculated as the sum of future planned receipts or net requirements over lead time.

- **IOAVGPIPELINESTOCK (average pipeline stock)**
  Average pipeline stock is the time-average on-order stock for a period.

- **IOMERCHANDISINGSTOCK (merchandizing stock)**
  Merchandizing stock is calculated as the difference between minimum stock requirements and safety stock in each period.

- **IOTARGETINPROCESSSTOCK (target in-process stock)**
  This output represents the beginning period quantity of in-process stock defined by processing or manufacturing lead time at the product-location level.

- **IOAVGINPROCESSSTOCK (average in-process stock)**
  This output represents the time-average quantity of in-process stock defined by processing or manufacturing lead time at the product-location level.

- **IOTARGETVENDORTRANSITSTOCK (target vendor transit stock)**
  This output represents the beginning period quantity of in-transit stock defined by (external) vendor lead time at the product-location level.

- **IOAVGVENDORTRANSITSTOCK (average vendor transit stock)**
  This output represents the time average quantity of in-transit stock defined by processing or manufacturing lead time at the product-location level.

- **IOENDONHANDSTOCK (ending on-hand stock)**
  The ending on-hand stock represents the on-hand stock level at the end of a period, which is also equal to the on-hand stock level at the beginning of the next period before shipments arrive. Ending on-hand stock is the target on-hand stock minus propagated demand mean.

- **ROP (reorder point)**
  Reorder point (ROP) planning is a consumption-based MRP procedure. Under the procedure, a replenishment order or production is triggered when the total amount of on-hand and on-order stock falls below the reorder point. The order or production quantity is typically determined based on minimum order quantity or target inventory position. The reorder point is calculated as the propagated demand mean over the replenishment lead time plus current period safety stock.

- **TARGETINVENTORYPOSITION (target inventory position)**
  Target inventory position is the optimal order-up-to inventory level for a product location, which can be calculated as total propagated demand mean over the exposure periods plus safety stock.

- **IOAVGINVENTORYPOSITION (average inventory position)**
  Average inventory position is the time-average inventory position for a period, which can be calculated as the sum of average cycle stock, average pipeline stock, recommended safety stock, and merchandising stock.

Inventory Components in Days of Supply

Inventory in days of supply is an efficiency ratio that measures the average number of days the company holds its inventory before selling it. This metric often is used to measure inventory performance. We'll cover more details of the topic in Chapter 8. Ahead we'll show one example to explain how the safety stock days of supply is calculated in SAP IBP for inventory. Other inventory components in days of supply are available, including target on-hand, average on-hand, and ending on-hand:

- **IOSAFETYSTOCKDAYSOFSUPPLY (safety stock days of supply)**
  Safety stock days of supply is calculated as the number of days of future forecasts that can be covered by the safety stock. We show how safety stock in periods can be converted from safety stock in units in Table 6.3. For example, safety stock in period 6 is 45, which covers propagated demand mean in period 6 (40) completely and covers 5 of 50 of the propagated demand mean in period 7. Therefore, the periods of supply are 1.1. The same approach can be applied to all the relevant inventory target in periods calculations.

	1	2	3	4	5	6	7	8	9	10
Propagated Demand Mean	0	0	10	20	30	40	50	60	70	80
Safety Stock (Units)	0	0	8.2	18.4	30.8	45.0	60.4	76.3	92.3	108.5
Safety Stock (Periods)	0	0	0.8	0.9	1.0	1.1	1.2	1.2	1.3	1.3

Table 6.3 Safety Stock in Units and in Periods

- **IOTGTONHANDDAYSOFSUPPLY (target on-stock stock days of supply)**
  This output represents target on-hand stock days of coverage for a period.
- **IOAVGONHANDDAYSOFSUPPLY (average on-hand stock days of supply)**
  This output represents average on-hand stock days of coverage for a period.
- **IOENDONHANDDAYSOFSUPPLY (ending on-hand stock days of supply)**
  This output represents ending on-hand stock days of coverage for a period.

6.4 Summary

In this chapter, we covered the details of different inventory components that make up a company's inventory. They're classified either by forms/flow of materials or by purposes/functions. Supply chain planners need complete visibility into inventory components to better understand the drivers of inventory requirements and be able to meet desired customer service levels and identify inventory reduction opportunities. SAP IBP for inventory calculates all the inventory components across the supply chain and provides comprehensive visibility into them. We explored the operator that calculates the inventory components and covered the inputs and outputs of inventory component calculation.

In the next chapter, we'll provide more best practices and recommendations for how to define the inventory planning process. We'll go into more detail about, for example, the advantages and disadvantages of centralized versus decentralized inventory planning teams, the frequency of the inventory planning cycle, and the sequence of the planning tasks in inventory planning.

Chapter 7
Designing Your Inventory Planning Process

Each organization has its own inventory planning process. This chapter provides recommendations for how to define an inventory planning process, from analyzing the planning results to performing scenario analysis to providing a feedback loop to other planning teams.

Now that we've covered the core aspects of how SAP IBP for inventory provides the number-crunching capabilities to reduce your inventory, in this chapter we'll focus on how you enable this math in an integrated inventory planning process. We'll start by introducing the difference between centralized and decentralized planning processes, with some considerations of driving factors that influence what makes sense. Next we'll talk about the frequency of the inventory planning cycle, weighing the advantages and disadvantages of periodic inventory planning as opposed to a more continuous planning cycle. We'll look at proactive and reactive planning tasks and sequencing in an integrated inventory planning process. After covering segmentation in some more detail, we'll close the chapter with some considerations of the role of an inventory planner in a modern supply chain organization.

7.1 Centralized and Decentralized Inventory Planning Teams

When designing inventory planning processes, the personnel aspect is key in driving your process design. There are two prevalent ways of organizing your inventory planning teams: as centralized teams for product groups, regions, or business units, or as decentralized teams responsible for individual segments of the supply network.

Centralization or decentralization of planning teams can be defined along various dimensions—typically either per product dimension, such as product groups, or regionally. In both cases, the level of integration typically drives how supply chain planning and operations teams—and hence inventory planning teams—develop.

Centralized inventory planning teams are most common in either smaller organizations or teams with a tightly integrated global supply chain. If there are a lot of dependencies in the supply chain and the different stages need to be tightly synchronized, having a centralized team is the most logical choice. These dependencies can be either regional, such as if manufacturing is done only in one location, or product-based, such as when the same (constraint) components are used to make different product groups.

When there is little dependency, such as for regional manufacturing of products that share little between product groups, companies tend to grow more toward regional—or decentralized—planning teams. This description mainly applies to how companies organically organize themselves when they grow. The following are the advantages and disadvantages of centralization and decentralization of inventory planning teams:

- **Decentralized planning teams**
  Decentralized planning teams are closer to their markets, whether geographically or with respect to the products they manage. Consequently, there's more room for incorporating local market intelligence when establishing inventory planning strategies. In other words, when planners are close to their markets, there will be more direct input from local functions like sales, marketing, and operations, allowing inventory planners to more proactively consider these elements in inventory planning parameterization.

  Local teams tend to have little visibility into the upstream supply consistency, however, which often leads them to overprotect their markets. Combined with the fact that decentralized planning teams often have little visibility into or accountability over the total inventory in the organization, this typically results in higher service levels with higher inventory profiles.

- **Centralized planning teams**
  Centralized planning teams accommodate exactly two aspects: with visibility into the full supply chain and the total inventory numbers, they tend to have better information to perform true multiechelon inventory optimization. This often requires trade-offs and key decisions about which segments will not attempt to provide perfect customer service due to cost-benefit assessments and considering the global inventory level of the organization.

  But operating a centralized inventory planning team requires information about individual markets to seamlessly flow through in a systematic fashion to ensure that it can be considered. When there is an integrated trade promotion management system that provides clear and detailed information about promotions being planned, that information can be considered by the centralized planning team. However, if promotions are not well structured and hence planners have to rely on informal information, there's a likelihood that planning results will suffer.

These descriptions already allude to the idea of trying to combine the best of both worlds with a hybrid team in which there are people responsible for the global inventory planning capability. Often this includes a level of multiechelon inventory optimization, which sets the baseline inventory targets for the product groups and/or regions. This can be completed with in-market inventory planners who can adjust their targets to account for local market events they're aware of. These teams can also fine-tune the exact mix of products being stocked based on their deeper insights into the market.

Managing hybrid teams requires a clear segregation of duties, with a clear governance structure for the local teams, ensuring they do not just ignore the centralized inventory planning targets. This can be achieved by providing budgets for additional safety stock targets in regions and providing clear performance indicator monitoring that demonstrates the impact of deviating from the centralized targets. Monitoring these KPIs allows the centralized targets to improve and allows the in-market inventory planners to trust the targets more.

Of course, these hybrid teams, with their duplicate roles, require a certain scale of organization to be effective.

7.2 Frequency of the Inventory Planning Cycle

Now let's consider how often we should recalculate safety stock targets. Consider two extreme cases: you can recalculate stock targets every day or just once a year. Both cases have advantages and disadvantages.

If you recalculate stock targets daily, the downside is that every day the execution results—the actual orders you calculate—would fluctuate based on the changed inventory targets. Yet those fluctuations would be very small because it's unlikely that major shifts in results would appear overnight. Therefore you would have continuous but very small adjustments to safety stock targets, which would have the inventory targets very quickly adopt shifts in demand patterns. If products became more popular, they would get higher safety stock targets; if products became less popular, you'd gradually release safety stocks from them.

If we assess the opposite example, with a yearly review, we get much bigger fluctuations. Of course, the next time you do the calculation, there's a high likelihood that some products have slowed down, others increased, suppliers might have become more or less reliable, and lead times might have become more or less widely distributed around their average. You're very likely to see major shifts in inventory targets in this case. Yet throughout the year, this means there's a lot more stability in safety stocks. This stability could be incredibly important—for example, to allocate the right amount of warehouse space to specific products, to make sure that the executional systems run in a stable manner, and to ensure that signals to suppliers or manufacturing do not fluctuate more than necessary. Of course, if patterns emerge in which products slow down, reliability of upstream supply deteriorates (or improves), or lead times change, it takes until the next iteration to incorporate these changes in parameters in the design.

You can see that both extreme cases are unlikely to form an ideal way of performing inventory optimization in your organization. Today, the most successful implementation of inventory planning and optimization capabilities have a periodic recalculation of inventory planning targets. The periodicity is mostly quarterly or monthly. The frequency of recalculation should be driven by the following factors:

- **Volatility in market**
  What's the length of your product's lifecycle? The shorter the product lifecycles, the more frequently you should recalculate your inventory targets to make sure the targets correctly reflect changes in maturity of the products.

- **Reliability of supply**
  How much do your suppliers fluctuate? If suppliers are stable and their reliability is stable, you can survive with less frequent inventory recalculations.

- **Automation, quality of data inputs, and manual review required**
  If the inputs require a significant manual intervention, running inventory optimization very often can become very time-consuming.

- **Approval levels and scrutiny on inventory investments**
  If the process of approving or rejecting increases or decreases in inventory targets requires a long internal approval and review cycle, it's impractical to review too often.

If you are, for example, renewing target inventory levels for raw materials flowing into the production line, the products themselves are fairly stable in terms of which go into the manufacturing process. The volumes can fluctuate based on supplier variability or demand variability, but the impact of small fluctuations in the bins is of little impact. In such cases, more frequent reviews would be adequate, and weekly or monthly cadences might be most appropriate.

If your decision has bigger implications—for example, which products to put on the shelf in a warehouse or even a retail location—the impact of changes is more impactful and requires more backend work. This can include creating shelf space, labeling, and organizing the other products in such a way that the total space—which is fixed in nature—is optimally leveraged. In such cases, slower cadences, such as quarterly, might make more sense.

7.3 From Reactive to Proactive Planner Tasks

In traditional environments with a lack of strong digital support for inventory planning and optimization, planners tend to spend a lot of their time on reactive, "firefighting" tasks. These include performing root-cause analyses on stockouts, placing and tracking emergency orders to address stockouts, and reacting to implications of disruptions such as late delivery notifications from suppliers.

The next step in maturity in inventory planning and optimization aims to drive planners from this reactive management to a more proactive approach. There are various drivers enabled by the SAP IBP for inventory application that enable this shift.

Performing inventory planning and optimization drives better inventory results, which should dramatically reduce the likelihood of disruptions impacting customer service and hence the number of stockouts. For example, it will measure the inbound service levels of suppliers and consider the variability of supply as a key element in setting safety stock targets. It will measure the variability and forecastability of demand and consider it in setting inventory targets, allowing for more buffer where the likelihood of stockouts is highest.

It also will allow an easier way of performing reactive tasks. If stockouts still occur, the analysis capabilities of the SAP IBP platform allow for a quicker, more accurate analysis based on one integrated platform that provides all data in an easy-to-consume format. Analyzing the cause of stockouts still occurring or responding to inquiries made by higher management about why service wasn't maintained for specific orders can be handled in a more scientific way, pointing to, for example, sudden erratic behavior by clients in case of an outlying order or the deliberate choice to set the target service level such that it allowed the stockout to occur. If stockouts occur due to the choices that have been made, those choices can be substantiated by factual data; for example, reducing the likelihood of these stockouts to occur may incur a certain additional investment in safety stock, which can be quantified and valorized.

Finally, the SAP IBP platform leveraging SAP Supply Chain Control Tower allows for additional capabilities to structure these root-cause investigations. Custom alerts can be enabled to identify cases that require further analysis, and case management can be leveraged to ensure that an observation is closely followed, documented, and made available for future record.

All these capabilities drive planners to act more in a proactive way when performing inventory planning and optimization. The logic by which the inventory planning process will be established will actively include all observations of the parameters that form the basis for the inventory optimization algorithms, such as historical supplier and production lead times, erratic customer behaviors, and deliberate choices such as service levels. Planners can see the impact these inputs have on inventory values and build scenarios to plan proactively.

7.4 Inventory Planning in Sales and Operations Planning

Inventory planning and optimization is not a process that can be executed in a vacuum. It's a crucial part of the sales and operations planning cycle that companies go through on a regular cadence. However, if you look at most frameworks and definitions of sales and operations planning, you can recognize the following steps, as depicted in Figure 7.1:

1. **Product/portfolio review**
   Assess the performance of your product portfolio, including new products, phase-out products, and the product roadmap.

Product Review → Demand Review → Supply Review → Operational S&OP → Executive S&OP

Figure 7.1 S&OP Process

2. **Demand review**
   Establish and agree on the unconstrained consensus demand signal that forms the basis for the S&OP horizon.

3. **Supply review**
   Leverage the consensus demand planning signal and propagate it through the supply network in the organization to establish a constrained plan for production and transport.
4. **Operational S&OP review (integrated reconciliation)**
   Bring all aspects of the plan together to ensure there is one consolidated, agreed-upon plan for the organization, considering demands and their priorities, available supply, and financial feasibility.
5. **Executive S&OP review**
   Make sure the agreed-upon number is endorsed and supported by the executive leadership in the organization, allowing a consistent execution.

> **Note**
>
> For more details about the S&OP process in SAP IBP, check out the book *Sales and Operations Planning with SAP IBP* (SAP PRESS, 2018), by Jandhyala, Kusters, Mane, and Sinha, available at *www.sap-press.com/4589*.

Looking at this process flow, you could ask where inventory planning and optimization fits in. The most logical answer is that it fits into the supply review process because it shares a dependency with the rest of supply planning on a finished demand signal, and it forms a key input to supply network planning because it sets the inventory targets.

Finally, the perhaps somewhat hidden nature of inventory planning and optimization has been called out by some companies that have renamed their S&OP process to SIOP—for sales, inventory, and operations planning—making it more explicit that inventory is a critical item in their S&OP cycle.

In advanced supply network planning scenarios, there can be more intricate interdependencies at play between supply network optimization and inventory optimization. Although inventory optimization is dependent on a supply network in which the sourcing rules are uniquely defined, supply network optimization attempts to redefine the flows in the network. Yet for supply network optimization to do so, it requires a firm grip on the inventory targets. In other words, running inventory optimization and supply network optimization sequentially might result in nonconvergence—that is, a solution that doesn't yield a single solution and instead flips back and forth between solutions.

7   Designing Your Inventory Planning Process

In SAP IBP, you should run three operators to make a complete run, as depicted in Figure 7.2.

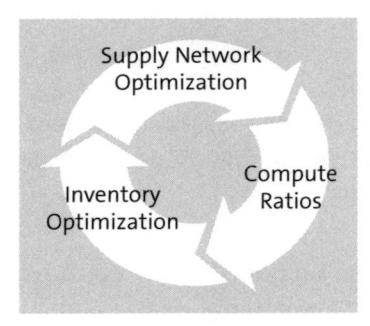

Figure 7.2 Interdependencies between Supply Network Optimization and Inventory Optimization

Say the process starts with supply network optimization (assuming the inventory targets from the previous cycle). In this case, the network propagation will be performed based on the cost optimization engine available in SAP IBP for response and supply. To make sure the multiechelon inventory optimization engine runs on the "correct" sourcing rules, there is an algorithm available that computes the sourcing rations (customer sourcing, location sourcing, and production sourcing) based on the results of the supply network optimization algorithm. This paves the way for inventory optimization to determine the "correct" new inventory targets based on the renewed network flows.

However, when the inventory targets change, the supply network optimization should be run again to make sure it accounts for the inventory targets. There are various ways out of this vicious circle, which can be analyzed during your implementation to make sure your approach is aligned to your corporate objectives.

In this section, we covered how inventory planning and optimization fits within the recurring S&OP process. In the next section, we'll detail the steps of the inventory planning and optimization approach itself.

7.5 Sequence of Planning Tasks

As described earlier, the inventory planning process typically is executed monthly or quarterly, depending on your organization.

7.5 Sequence of Planning Tasks

The inventory planning process typically is decomposed into the steps shown in Figure 7.3. You can use the process modeling made available in SAP IBP for sales and operations to model your inventory planning process. Let's assume you run a monthly process, in which case you could create a process template that looks like Figure 7.3.

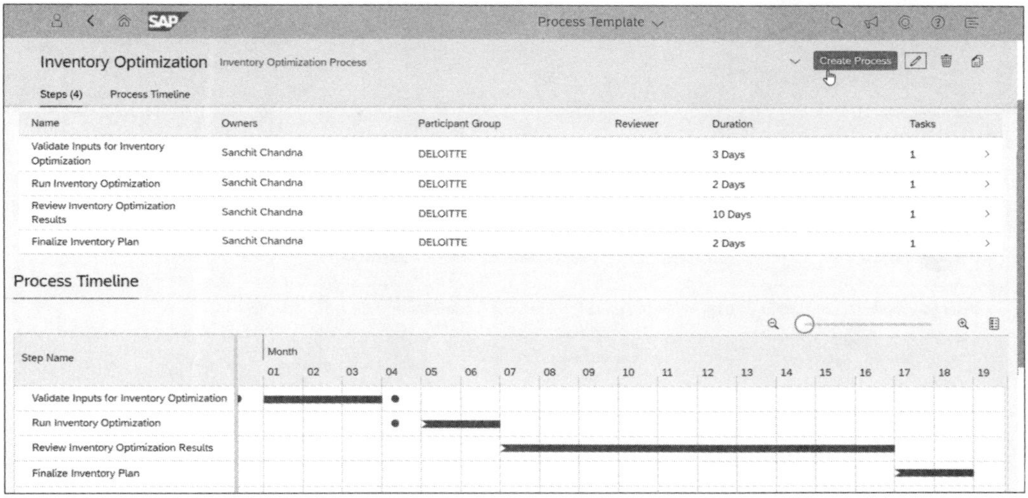

Figure 7.3 Inventory Optimization Process Template

The process management capability of SAP IBP for sales and operations allows you to start the process at the beginning of the month and assign tasks to users at the start of every step. It's possible to leverage the status of the steps—for example, the start or end of every step—to automatically trigger planning operators in the system. In other words, you could automatically trigger the run of the inventory optimization planning job upon completion of the first step: **Validate Inputs for Inventory Optimization**.

The process can be instantiated every month and hence be shown in a dashboard. From there, the process owner can start the different steps in the process, which will generate tasks for the step owners. They can complete their tasks, which will inform the process owner and might trigger planning jobs depending on the configuration. Figure 7.4 shows the process in the dashboard.

Before going into the individual steps, it's important to mention the importance of management by exception. A lot of the steps in the inventory planning and optimization process—especially in organizations with a lot of products and locations—needs

261

to be executed in a management-by-exception fashion. It's practically impossible for planners to periodically review the vast array of all product-location combinations and their inventory components. When going through the process flow, we'll focus on aspects of management by exception in some more detail.

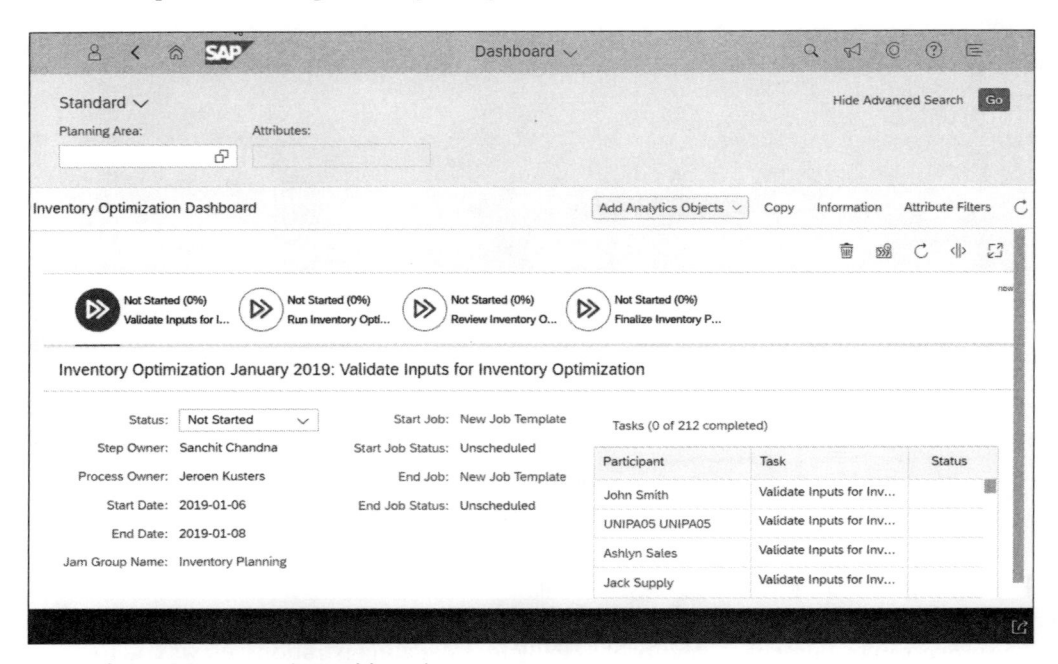

Figure 7.4 Process in Dashboard

7.5.1 Step 1: Validate Inputs for Inventory Optimization

In the first step of the process, make sure all the parameters are set correctly for the inventory planning run. This step of the process starts a few days before the algorithms are run—typically in a batch run—to calculate all aspects of the supply network.

The first check that should be performed is to make sure the supply network is accurately established. Chapter 4 gave an in-depth discussion of how to set up the supply network, including locations, products, and bills of materials. Chapter 4, Section 4.4 in particular provides an easy way to assess a supply network by visualizing it in a dashboard. Looking at the dashboards for specific product groups allows you to easily visually assess if the inventory planning supply network is complete. Figure 7.5 shows an example of a supply network.

7.5 Sequence of Planning Tasks

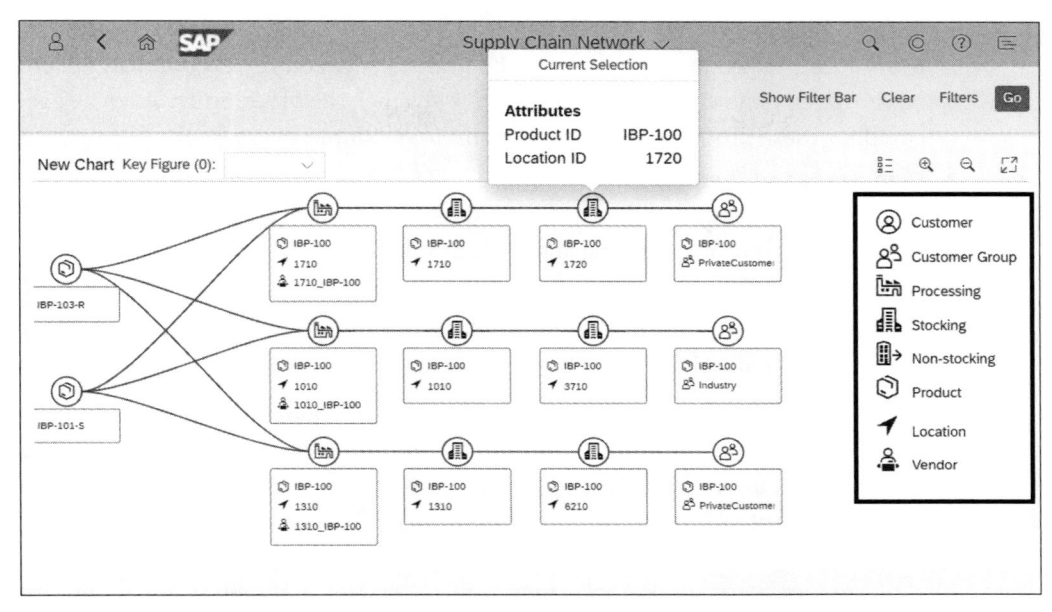

Figure 7.5 Supply Network Visualization in Dashboard

If you're using SAP IBP for sales and operations or SAP IBP for response and supply, it's possible to leverage the supply network consistency checking algorithms delivered with those applications. The check network algorithm allows the system to validate internally if the full network is complete, which means every product and location has a source of supply for customers and at every stage. The algorithm produces a log that can be leveraged to identify and resolve gaps in your supply network.

Our examples focus on identifying exceptions. When identifying such exceptions—given that most supply networks are established via interfaces—it's important to trace the root cause of the error. Upon identification of the root cause, you should ensure that the data integration model establishes a consistent supply network model in the SAP IBP system.

Once the supply network is validated, you need to make sure that key parameters are available to run the inventory planning algorithms:

- **Target service level**
  Target service levels are assigned to customer groups, so for this step you need to check that all customers have a customer group assigned and that all groups have a target service level assigned.

263

7 Designing Your Inventory Planning Process

- **Periods between review**
  Every location product should have the periods between review populated. Periods between review refers to the frequency at which the ordering cycle can be executed for these products at these locations, for example, every week.

- **Lead times and their variability**
  Lead time is described in depth in Chapter 2 and should be updated at the beginning of the inventory planning and optimization cycle.

- **Forecast and its variability**
  The forecast comes from the demand planning side of SAP IBP, and the variability can be calculated by leveraging the coefficient of variation from the forecast error.

In most cases, the review of the inventory planning parameters will be performed in a management-by-exception way. The most logical way of managing exceptions is by creating custom alerts. The functionality of customer alerting is embedded in SAP Supply Chain Control Tower, but is very valuable in inventory planning and optimization. The process of creating a custom alert was described in Chapter 3. Some examples of custom alerts that might help you check the parameters for inventory planning and optimization include the following:

- Identification of big spikes in demand. Compare the current cycle's demand signal with a snapshot of the previous cycle to determine why demands have shifted drastically (e.g., more than 100% or more than 10 units).
- Identification of strong increases in variability, in lead times as well as forecast, compared to previous cycles.

Another approach that can be leveraged is working with Excel workbook lists. In this case, you can define a key figure that gives a value only if the condition you're trying to check for is true. For example, if the target service level is null, the key figure would have a value of 1 in the current bucket. This allows you to suppress null and zero results in the Excel planning view and get a list of only those product-customer-group combinations with no target service level assigned.

7.5.2 Step 2: Running Inventory Optimization

Once the inputs have been validated, the inventory optimization algorithms should be run. Depending on the data volume and the corresponding run times, this either can happen as a batch-based process that runs overnight or can be triggered by the planner.

As you've learned so far, with the configuration in Chapter 3 and the details about optimization algorithms in Chapter 5, running inventory optimization requires a sequence of steps—or planning operators—to be executed. Figure 7.6 shows the standard way inventory planning operators should be structured to get all elements calculated accurately.

Calculate Forecast Error CV → Multi-Stage Inventory Optimization → Calculate Target Inventory Components → Expected Lost Demand Calculation

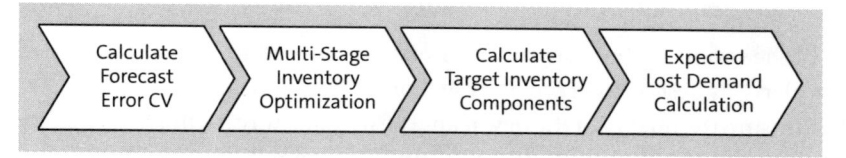

Figure 7.6 Inventory Optimization Sequence

The following steps are typically part of a complete inventory optimization run:

1. Calculate the forecast error CV, which we mentioned in the first step as a validation element. Typically you would include this step in the end-to-end run.
2. Run the global (multistage) inventory optimization, which optimizes the stock globally and simultaneously over all products and locations, considering all drivers for safety stock, as described in previous chapters. The global run also makes sure that all the propagated demands are calculated, which might be required by subsequent operators.
3. Calculate target inventory components such as cycle stock, pipeline stock, merchandising stock, and the average inventory position.
4. Finally, the expected loss demand calculation allows you to estimate the opportunity loss for the selected target service levels by calculating the average lost demand quantity (or average expedited quantity) under a given inventory plan and demand distribution.

Optionally, you can store the previous cycle values of inventory optimization in a set of key figures with previous cycle in the name—for example, Previous Cycle Target Inventory. This allows the planner to compare the newly calculated results to the previous ones. This operator, of course, should only be executed once, at the start of the cycle.

As mentioned in the beginning of this section, upon completion of the first step of validation of inputs, this job can be triggered automatically. Alternatively, planners can trigger it manually from the Excel add-in, by pressing **Run** in the **Advanced** section, and selecting **Inventory Optimization**.

7 Designing Your Inventory Planning Process

7.5.3 Step 3: Analyze Inventory Optimization Results via Scenario Planning

Once the inventory planning numbers have been calculated, the planner can engage in a detailed review of the results. Chapter 8 on measuring the performance of inventory planning and Chapter 9 on building intuition and performing scenario planning will provide all the techniques required for the planner to analyze the inventory planning and optimization results.

The analysis of the results of the inventory optimization algorithms can be performed by leveraging alerts, as described in previous sections. Alerts and Excel planning views allow you to measure the quality of the new plan. The baseline way in which the quality or impact of a new inventory optimization run can be measured is by comparing it to the previous iteration. This can be done by taking a snapshot (a copy) of the previous inventory components and comparing it to the newly calculated results.

If the relative change is dramatic, it's worth spending time to analyze it. The relative change typically has two angles; on the one hand, you could look at the percentage difference—for example, if the inventory rises 20% for a particular product, that might be a cause for analysis. On the other hand, it's typically important to overlay this with a dollar-change amount. Especially in cases where the inventory numbers are low, a change from 1 to 2, for example, in safety stock might represent a 100% change, but if the value of the product is one dollar while other products have a value of thousands of dollars, this plays an important role in prioritizing which products to spend time on. Figure 7.7 gives an example of an Excel planning view that provides a comparison of inventory values and immediately visualizes it.

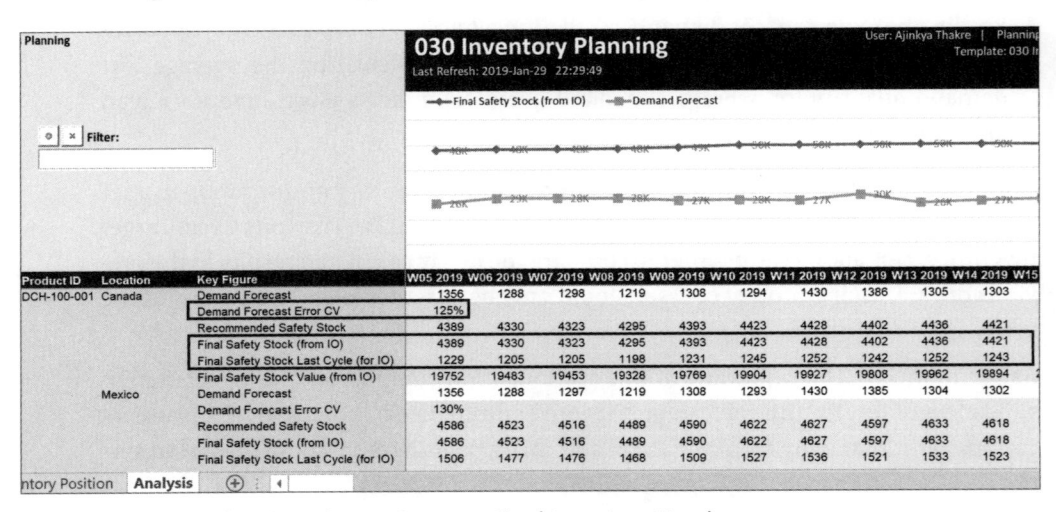

Figure 7.7 Planning View to Compare Final Inventory Numbers

7.5 Sequence of Planning Tasks

You can complement this approach of using Excel planning views by adding custom alerts, which can provide additional charts to immediately assess some of the key drivers. For example, you could add a chart with the demand pattern for this product, which would immediately tell you if there was an uptick in demand in the previous cycle that triggered the increase in safety stock. An example of a custom alert is shown in Figure 7.8, which shows the cases in which inventory is higher than in previous cycles via the demand forecast CV.

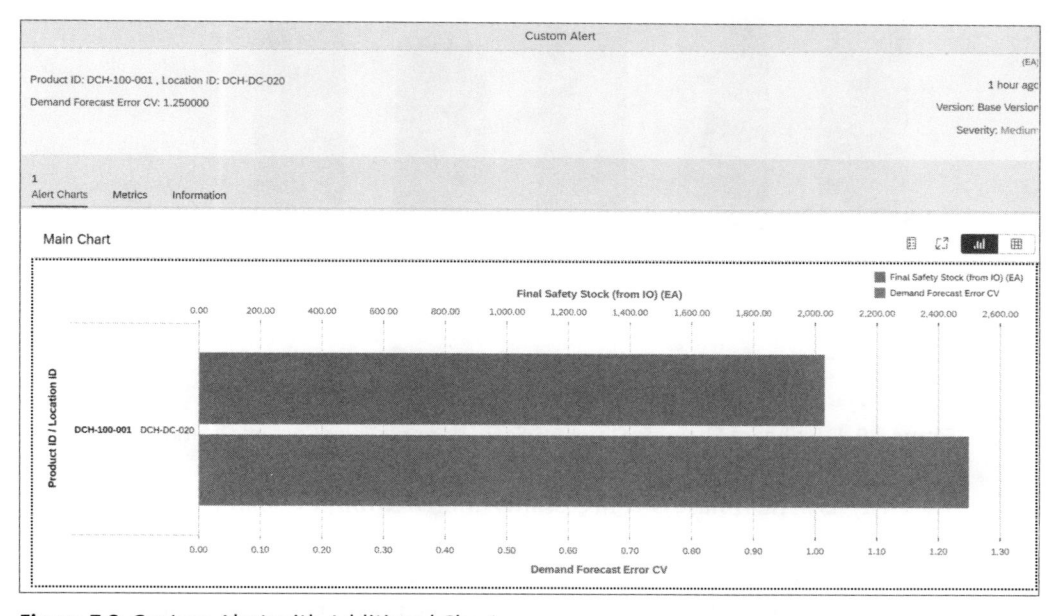

Figure 7.8 Custom Alert with Additional Chart

Beyond alerts and evaluations of specific product-related increases, you can leverage dashboards, which provide a comprehensive overview of all key performance indicators for the newly calculated inventory plan. It's good practice to create multiple scenarios that allow planners to compare results and pick a scenario that aligns closest to the business imperative of the product group, region, or organization.

As we'll explore more in Chapter 9, planners can create multiple scenarios to simulate the impact of increasing service levels. The system can calculate the corresponding expedite costs and add them to the safety stock to find the minimum. The example in Figure 7.9 demonstrates that setting a service level of 97% provides the lowest cumulative cost of expedited shipments and safety stock.

7   Designing Your Inventory Planning Process

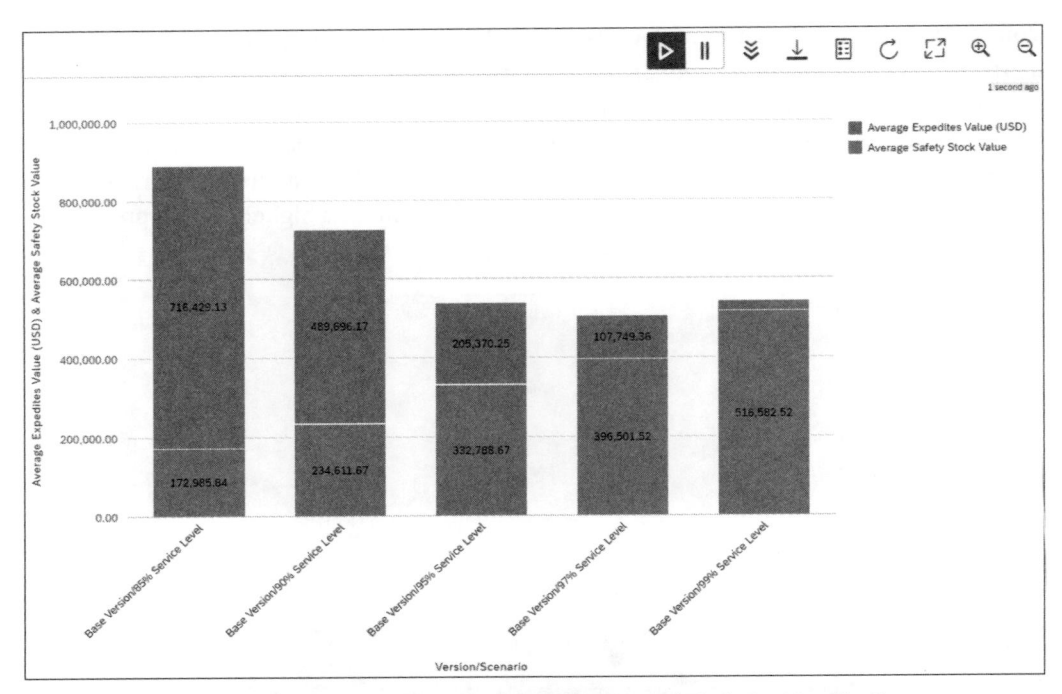

Figure 7.9 Dashboard Showing Different Scenarios and Their Cost Implications

The analysis in this phase isn't necessarily limited to only evaluating parameters that are under the direct control of the inventory planner. The analyses are aimed at reducing the total cost of inventory while maintaining the desired level of customer service. Analyses can be performed to determine the cost of the variance in customers' ordering patterns. A higher coefficient of variance in the demand will lead to a higher safety stock, so if there is little knowledge about the ordering pattern the customer will exhibit, you need to buffer your supply network with extra inventory to account for this. In industries in which customers are connected to the company for a long duration, there can be room to engage with customers in collaborative planning, which allows you to reduce the uncertainty.

For example, if a customer was to provide a customer forecast and adhere to it closely, you could reduce safety stock while maintaining the same customer service. The same can be said of the supplier side: if you can build a better supplier collaboration capability, this will reduce the inventory cost in the network. Inventory simulations allow you to provide quantitative and value-based information to support such initiatives.

7.5 Sequence of Planning Tasks

Concluding this step includes selecting which scenario will form the baseline of the inventory plan moving forward, making adjustments to inputs where root-cause analyses call for it, and confirming that the overall metrics of the newly optimized inventory plan look good.

7.5.4 Step 4: Finalize Inventory Plan

The last step in the inventory planning process finalizes the process, making sure all updates are made based on analyses and providing the inventory planning results to the downstream processes—typically, the supply planning process.

In this step, manual adjustments can be performed to change the outcome, and the outcome is copied into the right key figures for downstream processes. Reports are published, and the overall process is closed in the process management view of the dashboard. Since the 1902 release of SAP IBP, it's possible to leverage the web-based planning capability to make these final edits, as shown in Figure 7.10, which shows the web-based planning view for the inventory numbers for a series of products.

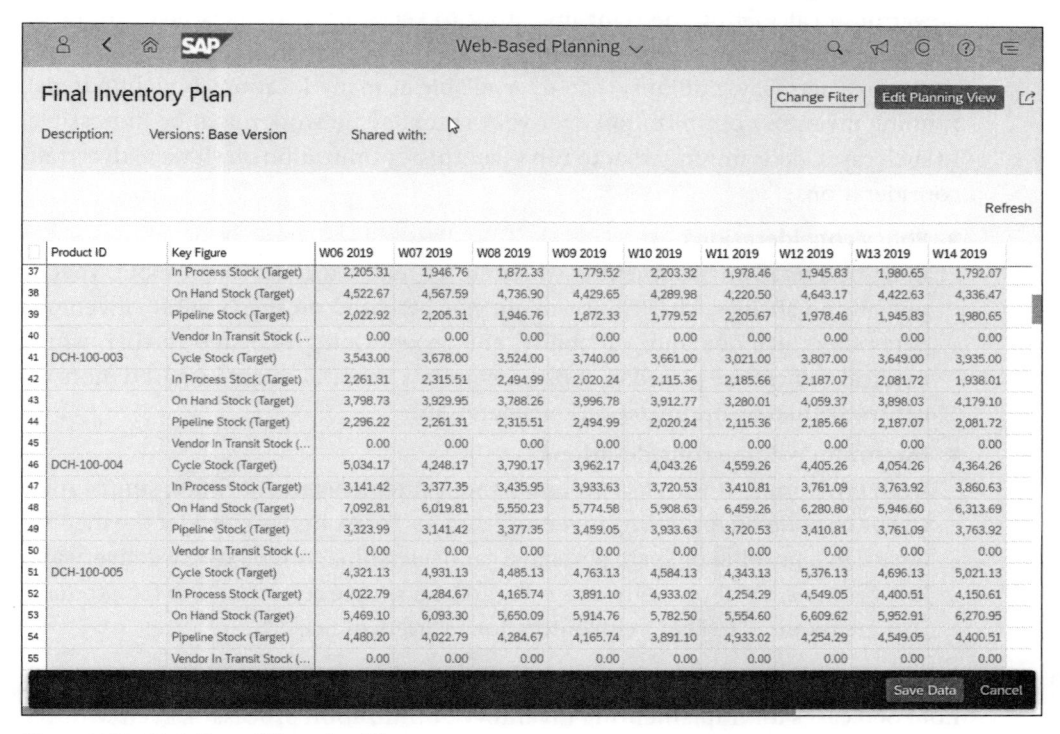

	Product ID	Key Figure	W06 2019	W07 2019	W08 2019	W09 2019	W10 2019	W11 2019	W12 2019	W13 2019	W14 2019
37		In Process Stock (Target)	2,205.31	1,946.76	1,872.33	1,779.52	2,203.32	1,978.46	1,945.83	1,980.65	1,792.07
38		On Hand Stock (Target)	4,522.67	4,567.59	4,736.90	4,429.65	4,289.98	4,220.50	4,643.17	4,422.63	4,336.47
39		Pipeline Stock (Target)	2,022.92	2,205.31	1,946.76	1,872.33	1,779.52	2,205.67	1,978.46	1,945.83	1,980.65
40		Vendor In Transit Stock (...	0.00	0.00	0.00	0.00	0.00	0.00	0.00	0.00	0.00
41	DCH-100-003	Cycle Stock (Target)	3,543.00	3,678.00	3,524.00	3,740.00	3,661.00	3,021.00	3,807.00	3,649.00	3,935.00
42		In Process Stock (Target)	2,261.31	2,315.51	2,494.99	2,020.24	2,115.36	2,185.66	2,187.07	2,081.72	1,938.01
43		On Hand Stock (Target)	3,798.73	3,929.95	3,788.26	3,996.78	3,912.77	3,280.01	4,059.37	3,898.03	4,179.10
44		Pipeline Stock (Target)	2,296.22	2,261.31	2,315.51	2,494.99	2,020.24	2,115.36	2,185.66	2,187.07	2,081.72
45		Vendor In Transit Stock (...	0.00	0.00	0.00	0.00	0.00	0.00	0.00	0.00	0.00
46	DCH-100-004	Cycle Stock (Target)	5,034.17	4,248.17	3,790.17	3,962.17	4,043.26	4,559.26	4,405.26	4,054.26	4,364.26
47		In Process Stock (Target)	3,141.42	3,377.35	3,435.95	3,933.63	3,720.53	3,410.81	3,761.09	3,763.92	3,860.63
48		On Hand Stock (Target)	7,092.81	6,019.81	5,550.23	5,774.58	5,908.63	6,459.26	6,280.80	5,946.60	6,313.69
49		Pipeline Stock (Target)	3,323.99	3,141.42	3,377.35	3,459.05	3,933.63	3,720.53	3,410.81	3,761.09	3,763.92
50		Vendor In Transit Stock (...	0.00	0.00	0.00	0.00	0.00	0.00	0.00	0.00	0.00
51	DCH-100-005	Cycle Stock (Target)	4,321.13	4,931.13	4,485.13	4,763.13	4,584.13	4,343.13	5,376.13	4,696.13	5,021.13
52		In Process Stock (Target)	4,022.79	4,284.67	4,165.74	3,891.10	4,933.02	4,254.29	4,549.05	4,400.51	4,150.61
53		On Hand Stock (Target)	5,469.10	6,093.30	5,650.09	5,914.76	5,782.50	5,554.60	6,609.62	5,952.91	6,270.95
54		Pipeline Stock (Target)	4,480.20	4,022.79	4,284.67	4,165.74	3,891.10	4,933.02	4,254.29	4,549.05	4,400.51
55		Vendor In Transit Stock (...	0.00	0.00	0.00	0.00	0.00	0.00	0.00	0.00	0.00

Figure 7.10 Web-Based Planning View

Just like in the Excel planning views, users can use the web-based planning views to visualize and edit data. In other words, the inventory planner or the inventory planning manager can make the changes directly in the web browser, save their changes, and complete the inventory plan.

7.6 Segmentation

Thus far in this book we've focused on inventory optimization, without distinguishing whether it's relevant for all products. In this section, we'll first tackle whether inventory optimization is equally important for all products. Then, for products for which we decide inventory optimization makes sense, we can leverage segmentation to set some of the parameters rather than setting them at the individual products (location) level.

Typically, there are a couple of characteristics that drive whether inventory optimization will be impactful for a given product. Although inventory optimization is very powerful in calculating the right inventory to keep, it's a complex algorithm that requires time and computing power to complete. If you're in an environment with many products (say, millions) that are available at many locations (say, hundreds), running inventory optimization over your complete network might be impossible. In such cases, determining what to run inventory optimization on starts with certain considerations:

- **Policy considerations**
  Imagine a retail environment in which stores make clear decisions about what to put on the shelves. That choice might not be based on the "typical" inventory parameters like demand, variability, and so on. Going one step further, which medical devices are placed in consignment in a hospital might be based more on contracts than on optimization considerations.

- **Minimum volume considerations**
  In an environment with low volumes and fast replenishment times, simple rules can be considered for setting inventory targets. For example, consider the medical device in a hospital or spare parts in a car dealership. With next-day delivery and low volumes, a sell-one, buy-one rule can be a simple rule of thumb for products that are required to kept in inventory for a variety of reasons.

This doesn't mean companies which have a smaller set of products or locations are not good cases for implementing inventory optimization processes. Even within a company with strong business cases for inventory optimization, there are still considerations to be made about what to include and what not to include when running inventory optimization. For example, the medical devices company placing products in consignment at hospitals might have a clear advantage when implementing inventory optimization for distribution centers, but not so much for calculating targets in consignment locations. The retail environment might opt to run inventory optimization only for products with a velocity above a certain sales amount—for example, above one order quantity per week. Implementing this type of simple rule for inventory optimization will ensure the heavy computing power required remains scalable and impactful for the products for which the biggest value can be realized.

Within products that are considered relevant for optimization, further segmentation can be performed to automate the entry of parameters. ABC segmentation is the most common approach, which is implemented in the SAP3 sample planning area delivered with SAP IBP for inventory. In the SAP3 sample model, the target customer service level is defined for each product-location-customer group combination.

In practice, you may want to segment your demand at some aggregate level (by product, customer, brand-region, etc.) into classes. This is also referred to as ABC segmentation, in which demand is segmented into different classes such as A, B, and C (or more, but three is typical). The segmentation can be based on any number of key figures, such as revenue, total profit, and so on. Then the service level is assigned at this aggregate class level, and you can use this service level for inventory operators. For example, you can segment your finished products into A, B, and C classes based on total revenue across all markets. Figure 7.11 demonstrates what an ABC segmentation looks like from the perspective of the number of products in the classes making up the total volume.

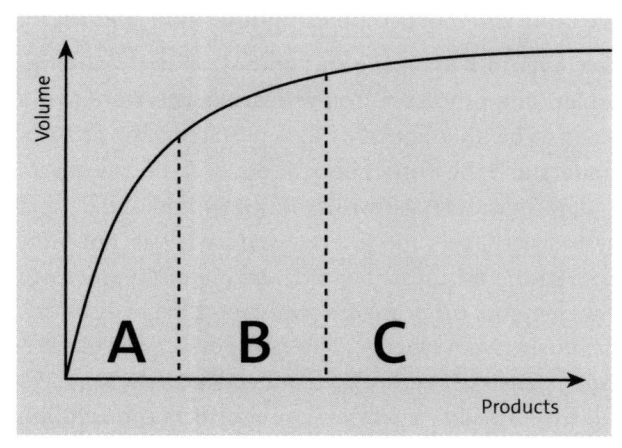

Figure 7.11 Inventory Segmentation

Based on the segmentation, you could determine that A, B, and C products receive 99%, 97%, and 95% service levels, respectively. This allows you to leverage a more rule-based approach to setting inventory targets, which is likely to drive better performance. In Chapter 9, we'll provide a more detailed example of this, in which we'll use the ABC classes to assign different service levels in scenarios and drive better overall inventory optimization performance.

7.7 Role of the Inventory Planner

Central to the whole inventory planning process as we have described it in this chapter is the inventory planner. The inventory planner and his direct management carries the responsibility for designing the inventory planning processes, parameterizing the inventory optimization technology, and controlling the results of the process in terms of inventory, working capital implications, and supply chain reliability—of which inventory is typically perceived as the key.

Over time, the role of the inventory planner has changed considerably. Originally inventory planners were close to the inventory control process, with a primary understanding of the exact materials going into the business and building simple inventory control rules for which products needed to be stored close to the production line, in the regional distribution centers, or even put forward to customers in retail stores. Like most elements in modern supply chain management, a lot of this "tribal" knowledge has evolved to become much more scientifically based. Inventory planning and optimization is no different and requires more and more understanding of advanced mathematical constructs, being statistically savvy, and having the underlying knowledge to operate more and more complex optimization engines.

In this book, we've described the inventory planning and optimization capabilities that govern modern inventory planning processes. You've learned there are many statistics and parameters that need to be understood as they pertain to the process. For example, it's important to understand the impact periods between review has on the inventory buffers, understand normal and Poisson distributions, and understand the difference between customer service levels and internal service levels. But none of this takes away the importance of the business in which the planning processes occur. Introducing all these new elements often makes companies believe the science will win in all cases over the business knowledge. This isn't correct: it's important for the inventory planner and manager to keep a close connection to the business reality around them, which will drive a reality check on the numbers the solution spits out.

Taking the inventory planner complexity away from the business reality can lead to hilarious planning results. For example, during the testing of an implementation of inventory planning for a retail store selling paint, algorithms easily predict that there is only one product required: white paint! That sells best, and though the algorithms try to fill up the store, they suggest doing so with only white paint. Would you go to a store with only white paint? Other examples can be found in car dealerships, for which inventory algorithms easily suggest keeping various bumpers in stock. Given the size of car bumpers and the size of the average car dealership, this isn't practical.

In conclusion, the profile of a good inventory planner combines a scientific savviness, an appetite for data analysis, and a good dose of common sense to validate the results of the algorithms. In many cases, assessing the practicality of the results allows the inventory planner to translate them back into updates of parameters, improving the performance of the algorithms over time.

7.8 Summary

In this chapter, we covered the way inventory planning and optimization processes can be established and how the approach of the inventory planning organization should evolve from reactive to proactive. We demonstrated how to establish an inventory optimization process and how to segment your products into optimization-relevant products to ensure an efficient inventory planning process.

The next chapter will dive into measuring inventory performance, demonstrating the key performance indicators that can be established to continuously improve your parameter settings and drive an optimal inventory profile.

Chapter 8
Measuring Inventory Performance

Inventory planning usually affects a company in several ways, such as determining its cash flow and its profit margins particularly for those that have an over-reliance on fast turnovers of materials and goods. Therefore, inventory planning is an important aspect of any business's success, as we'll discuss in this chapter.

In this chapter, we'll use the fictitious ABBFI company to showcase an approach to setting up a monthly network inventory planning process. In the detailed case study, we'll introduce some key performance indicators for inventory planning and optimization. Then we'll look at more details of how ABBFI's inventory team can perform the inventory planning process steps in SAP IBP for inventory, which we introduced in Chapter 7.

8.1 Example Supply Chain for Inventory Planning

In this section, we will introduce an example supply chain for AB Breakfast Inc. (ABBFI), which we'll reference throughout the rest of the chapter. We'll introduce the company's fully centralized approach to inventory planning and its inventory center of excellence (CoE) team.

ABBFI makes and sells products in three categories—cereals, breakfast protein bars, and frozen breakfast—in four different regions—North America, Europe, Asia, and Oceania. The global supply chain network of ABBFI is shown in Figure 8.1.

The finished products are manufactured and may be copacked in three plants: Puerto Rico, Poland, and the Philippines. From there, they're shipped to the different distribution centers (DCs) in each region, which in turn ship the finished products to ABBFI customers (typically grocery stores). The sourcing relationships are shown in Figure 8.1 with arrows.

8   Measuring Inventory Performance

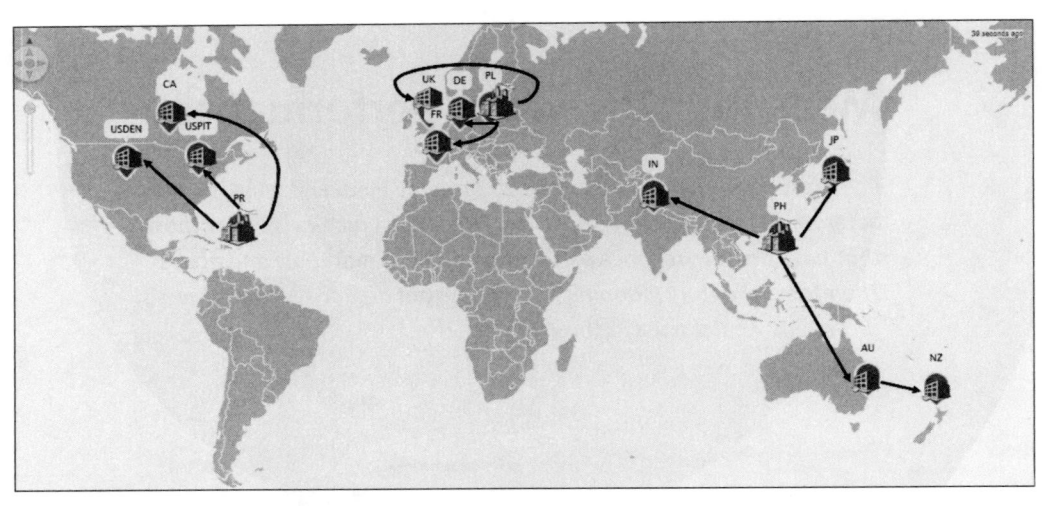

Figure 8.1 Global Supply Chain Network of ABBFI

Each finished product has a BOM that shows its ingredients and packaging materials and respective quantities of each. Ingredients and packaging materials are in turn sourced from external suppliers unique to each plant.

ABBFI has a fully centralized approach to inventory planning. Its network inventory planning process contains the following steps:

1. **Inventory targets review**
   In this step, the inventory targets are calculated simultaneously for the end-to-end network. The results are reviewed and finalized by a central team. The targets review contains the following steps:
   - Validate data inputs
   - Review inventory plan
   - Assess inventory drivers
   - Update inventory plan
   - Perform what-if analysis requests

2. **Inventory planning collaboration**
   In this step, the central team communicates the finalized inventory plan from the previous step to the supply planners and other end users. Ad hoc change requests from end users are reviewed and approved or rejected. This collaboration contains the following steps:

- Report planning decisions to end users
- Respond to what-if analysis requests from end users
- Engage regional teams with planning questions

3. **Inventory performance review**
   The goal of this step is to have a feedback loop based on historical inventory performance to continuously improve on the first two steps. The performance review follows these steps:
   - Review historical inventory performance key performance indicators (KPIs) and metrics
   - Review projected inventory KPIs

ABBFI has an inventory CoE team consisting of one or more inventory analysts and support from supply chain IT analysts. This team is responsible for the inventory planning process. That is, the team provides an end-to-end network view of the ABBFI supply chain and determines the inventory targets across the board. It validates the drivers for the inventory targets and analyzes the data quality of such drivers. It also performs scenario analyses that can be tactical (impact of demand uptick) or strategic (impact of increasing the customer service level, adding or closing a plant or DC, etc.).

We defined the planning tasks for inventory planning and optimization in Chapter 7. In the next few sections, we'll showcase how ABBFI's CoE team can perform these steps in SAP IBP for inventory, supported by dashboards, charts, planning views, custom alerts, and more. As we do so, we'll emphasize how the inventory optimization steps fit into the entire supply chain planning process in terms of input and output integration points. We'll cover more data flows and integration topics for SAP IBP for inventory in Chapter 10.

As shown in Figure 8.2, a global demand plan as an outcome of long- to mid-term demand planning and short-term demand sensing, together with segmented product information from, say, ABC-XYZ segmentation, is fed as an input into inventory optimization. In the end, an optimal inventory plan resulting from inventory optimization fits into the supply review process of sales and operations planning by specifying optimal inventory targets for the process. (More details of inventory planning in sales and operations planning were covered in Chapter 7.) Moreover, the optimal inventory targets are fed to external operational planning and execution processes to support, for example, the replenishment order process.

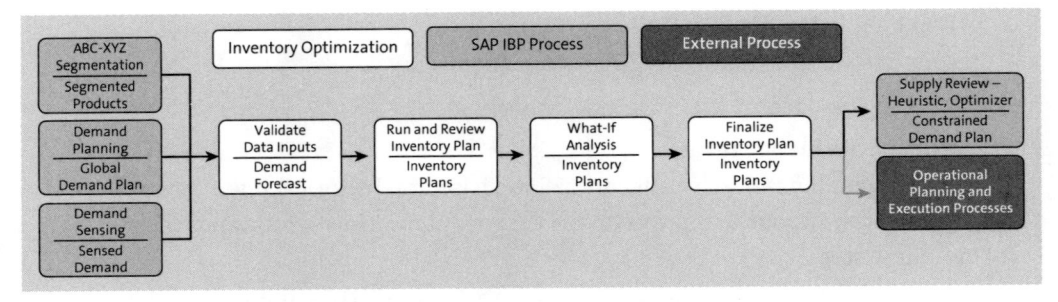

Figure 8.2 Inventory Optimization in Supply Chain Planning Process

For collaboration, the team is responsible for communicating the inventory plan to end business users by region (inventory managers) and by region and product category (supply planners, customer service representatives, S&OP users). The CoE team responds to any questions and what-if requests from end users and collaborates with them to finalize an inventory plan. (We'll cover more details of SAP IBP's what-if capabilities in Chapter 9.) In the end, any adjustments made by end users to the recommended plan are documented with reason codes and measured.

This team is also responsible for publishing a report of the company's inventory health periodically relative to the inventory plan, both historically (based on actuals) and forward-looking (based on projected inventory). We'll cover some key performance indicators for inventory planning and optimization in the next section. In addition, the team should publish a periodic report on opportunity areas for reducing inventory based on the drivers of inventory (demand and supply).

The inventory planning collaboration and inventory performance indicators steps of the process are typically performed on an ad hoc basis during the month, as analyses are requested by end users and/or supply chain leaders.

Optionally, some companies may choose to have more than one CoE team separated by region (e.g., ABBFI may have a CoE team responsible for North America and a second team responsible for Europe and Asia-Pacific [APJ]). However, best practice is to have one CoE team, perhaps virtually located. Some companies have successfully extended the role of central demand planners to demand and inventory planners. This is because of two recent trends:

- Increased automation from statistical forecasting and demand-sensing tools (such as SAP IBP for demand) and implementation of S&OP tools (such as SAP IBP for sales and operations) reduce the effort required for demand planners to create forecasts.

- Efforts focusing only on improving forecast accuracy KPIs in isolation from inventory KPIs and inventory drivers have not brought the desired inventory reduction or business value due to SKU proliferation and increasing number of sales channels.

8.2 Key Performance Indicators for Inventory Optimization

In this section, we'll discuss some key performance indicators for inventory optimization before detailing the individual steps of the inventory planning process.

A *key performance indicator* (KPI) is a measurement of the performance within a given area toward a specific goal. By giving an organization clear milestones to hit every week, quarter, or year, KPIs help greatly in eliminating guesswork. Much has been written about commonly used inventory KPIs, their purposes, their traits, and how to calculate them in best practices.

> **Note**
>
> For a comprehensive overview of key performance indicators in SAP IBP, we recommend the book *Sales and Operations Planning with SAP IBP* (SAP PRESS, 2018), by Jandhyala, Kusters, Mane, and Sinha, available at *www.sap-press.com/4589*.

Some commonly used inventory KPIs including the following:

- Inventory turnover or days of supply
- Average days to sell inventory
- Average inventory
- Inventory holding costs
- Service level by stock-out probability, fill-rate percentage, on-time delivery, or perfect order rate
- Lead time
- Inventory accuracy

SAP IBP provides rich analytics features to build different analytics charts and group them into a dashboard. Figure 8.3 shows an example dashboard that can be built in SAP IBP with some inventory planning and optimization KPIs.

8 Measuring Inventory Performance

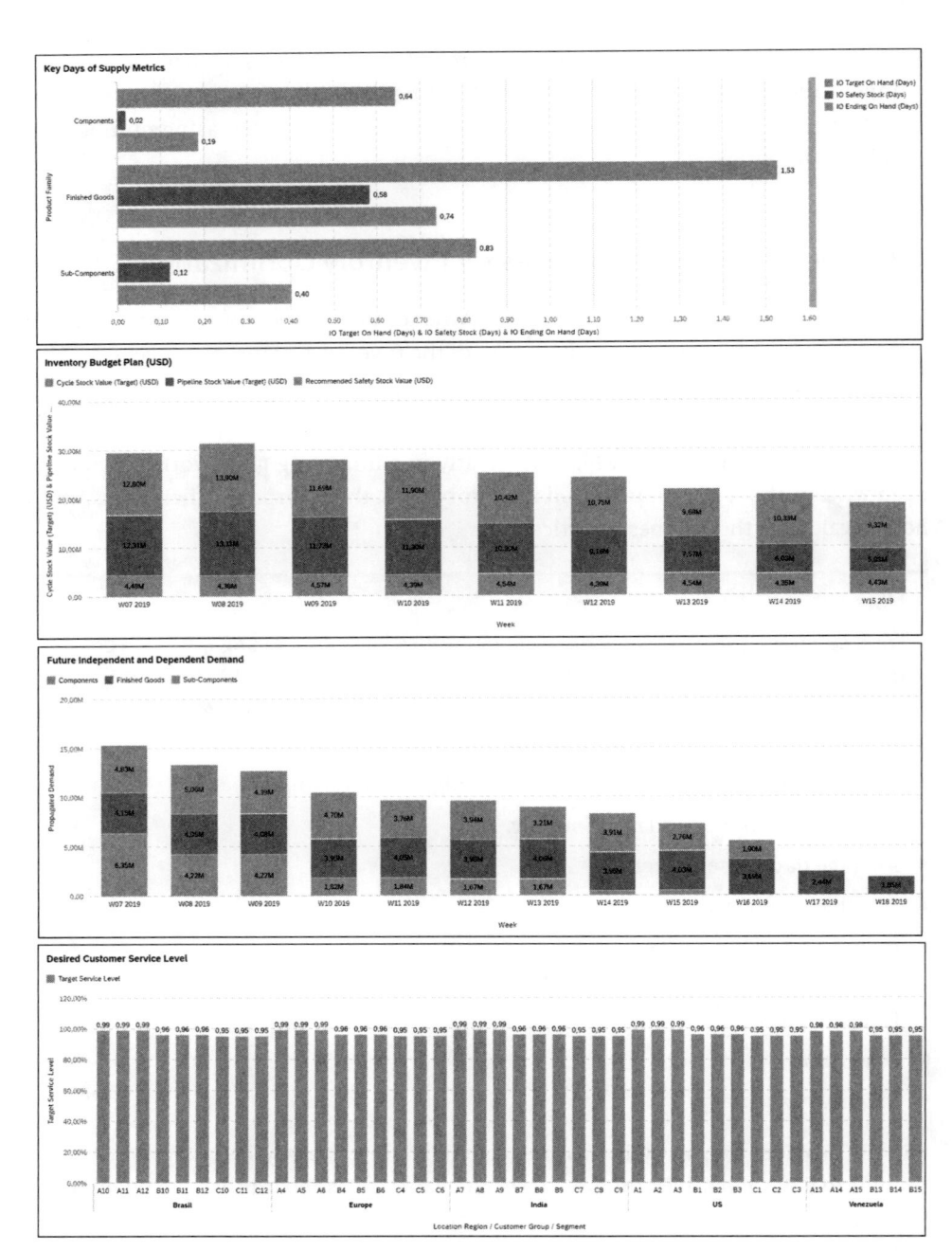

Figure 8.3 Dashboard and Analytics for Sample Inventory Planning and Optimization KPIs

> **Note**
>
> A Gartner research note discussed building performance indicators for inventory health evaluation (see Gartner research note ID G00325925, by Pukkila, at *https://www.gartner.com/doc/3729917/build-capability-inventory-health-assessment*; a subscription is required). This research note suggested that comparison of an item's current inventory against its own or other products' historical levels (e.g., inventory turns) is considered a lagging metric. It offers little insight about opportunities to improve inventory performance relative to future demand.

Some of the recommendations for KPIs are as follows:

- Develop visibility into future independent and dependent product demand across the end-to-end supply chain. In Chapter 6, we noted that the future independent and dependent product demand are calculated across the supply chain in SAP IBP for inventory for raw materials, work in process, and finished goods.
- Establish coverage objectives for inventory SKUs (product-location combinations). In Chapter 6, we covered some details about the inventory target outputs in days of supply.
- Develop reporting capabilities to assess the health of current inventory holdings by comparing them with the future product requirements. All the calculations of the performance indicators of inventory health assessment in the research note can be configured in SAP IBP in a straightforward manner. Note that in SAP IBP such reports can be configured both historically based on actuals and forward-looking based on projected inventory.

In the next few sections we'll focus on the steps in the inventory planning process performed by ABBFI's CoE team.

8.3 Validate Input Quality

In the first step of the process, the *CoE* team reviews the quality of the input data prior to the production batch job run of the inventory operators. This task is often overlooked in companies, but it's important because of the garbage in, garbage out issue: if input data quality is poor and not identified, the *CoE* team may end up spending cycles on root-cause analysis of nonintuitive inventory recommendations.

8   Measuring Inventory Performance

SAP IBP provides dashboarding and analytics capabilities in the web UI that can be leveraged for quality review.

There are several inventory drivers (inputs), and a single dashboard to determine the quality of all the drivers may not be usable. As discussed in Chapter 6, safety stock due to demand variability, safety stock due to supply variability, and safety stock due to service variability provide the breakdown of total safety stock for demand variability over exposure periods, lead time variability, and impact of imperfect upstream service level, respectively, in relative units. End users may want to see these values as percentage contributions to support root-cause analysis. We call this the *uncertainty index*. It can be calculated via the configuration shown in Listing 8.1 by introducing three new calculated key figures with base planning level WKPRODLOC.

```
SAFETYSTOCKDEMANDVARPCT @ REQUEST =
"SAFETYSTOCKDEMANDVAR @ REQUEST" / RECOMMENDEDSAFETYSTOCK @ REQUEST"

SAFETYSTOCKSERVICEVARPCT @ REQUEST =
"SAFETYSTOCKSERVICEVAR @ REQUEST" / RECOMMENDEDSAFETYSTOCK @ REQUEST"

SAFETYSTOCKSUPPLYVARPCT @ REQUEST =
"SAFETYSTOCKSUPPLYVAR @ REQUEST" / RECOMMENDEDSAFETYSTOCK @ REQUEST"
```

Listing 8.1 Calculation for Uncertainty Index Key Figures

By maintaining the calculation at the request level, SAP IBP will aggregate the numerator and denominator separately first, then take the ratio.

The uncertainty index groups the input drivers into three different dashboards: demand, forecast error, and supply. It's important to keep the dashboards at a simple and easy-to-understand level. Detailed analysis can be achieved by starting from the higher-level analytics and drilling down to the details, which is well supported by SAP IBP analytics and Excel. This helps standardize the templates and the work across the *CoE* team and end users while allowing for deep analysis by power users.

Before we look closer at the dashboard examples ahead, Figure 8.4 will show how to navigate to the list of dashboards available in the web UI via the Dashboards SAP Fiori app, found on the home page.

8.3 Validate Input Quality

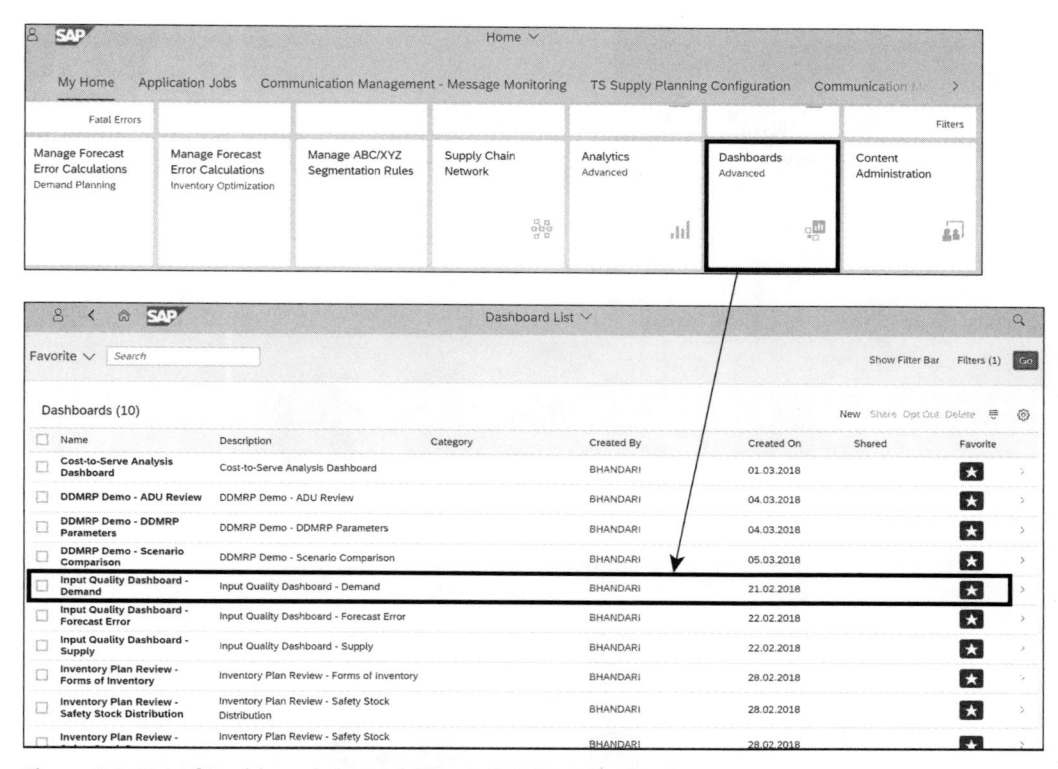

Figure 8.4 List of Dashboards in Dashboards SAP Fiori Application

The first input-quality dashboard reviewed by the ABBFI CoE team focuses on demand. An example of such a dashboard is shown in Figure 8.5.

Inventory analysts can determine and validate the largest market by volume, the largest product category by region, and the distribution of demand volume by product and location for a given product category and region quickly. They can deep-dive into any information by clicking the chart in the dashboard and drilling down by any parameter. For example, say that you notice from the last chart in the dashboard that Frosted Cereal in the US East region has a high demand in the month of March. By selecting the corresponding bar and clicking the drill-down option (downward-pointing arrow) in the **Chart** menu, you can look closer to see the demand by week in that month, as shown in Figure 8.6.

283

8 Measuring Inventory Performance

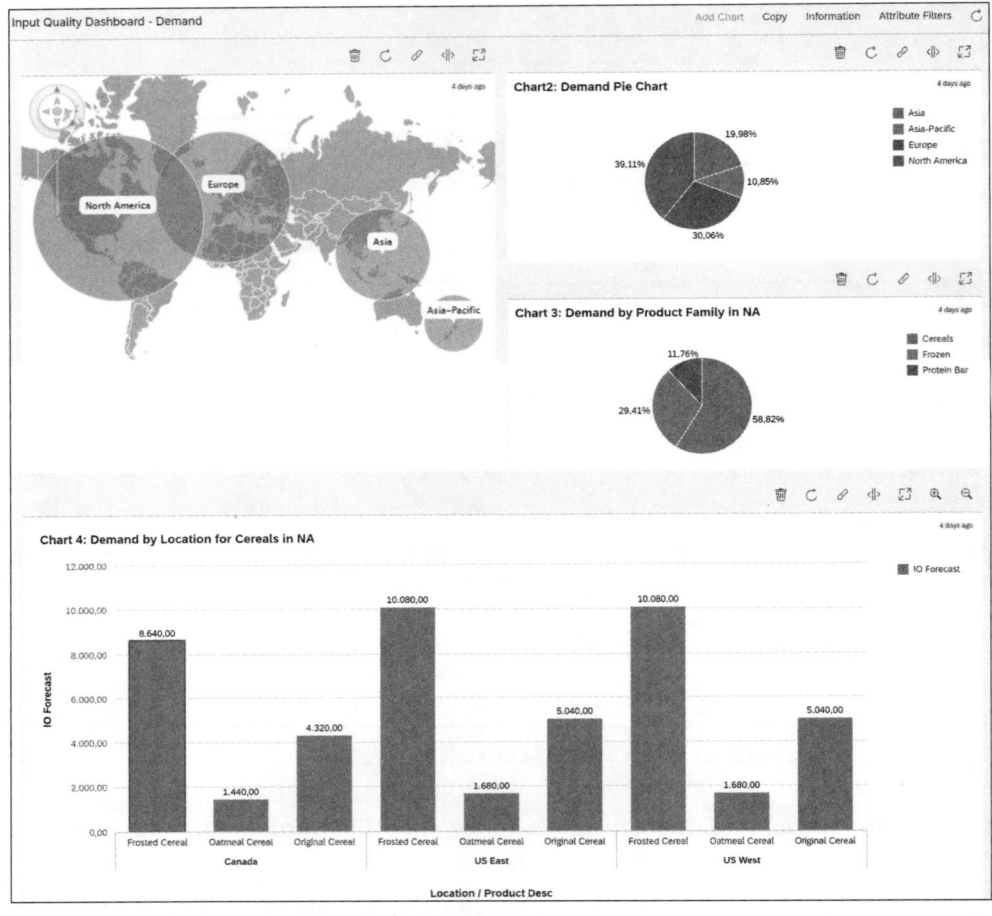

Figure 8.5 ABBFI Input-Quality Dashboard for Demand

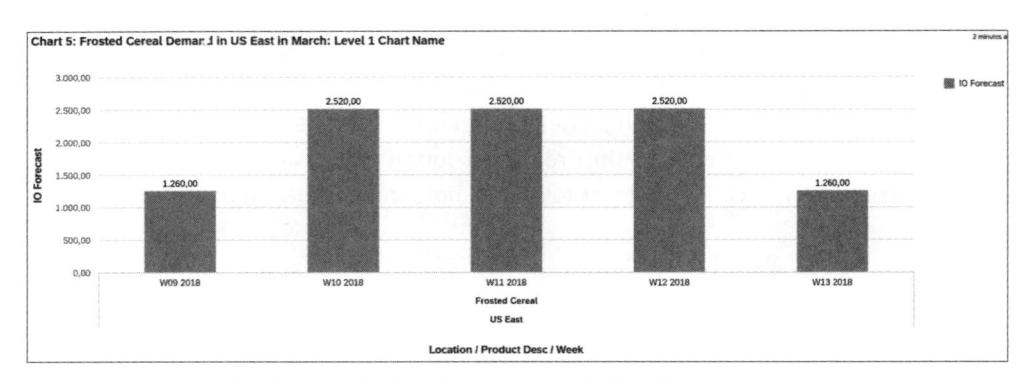

Figure 8.6 Weekly Demand for Frosted Cereal in US East in March

8.3 Validate Input Quality

The second input-quality dashboard focuses on the forecast error analytics for inventory optimization (see Figure 8.7). An inventory analyst can rank the finished products by the forecast error (or accuracy), as shown in **Chart 1**, and drill down into the product-location granularity in **Chart 2**. **Chart 3** shows the weekly historical forecast and sales for her favorite product-location, and she can also look at the heat maps for overforecasting and underforecasting bias in **Chart 4** and **Chart 5**.

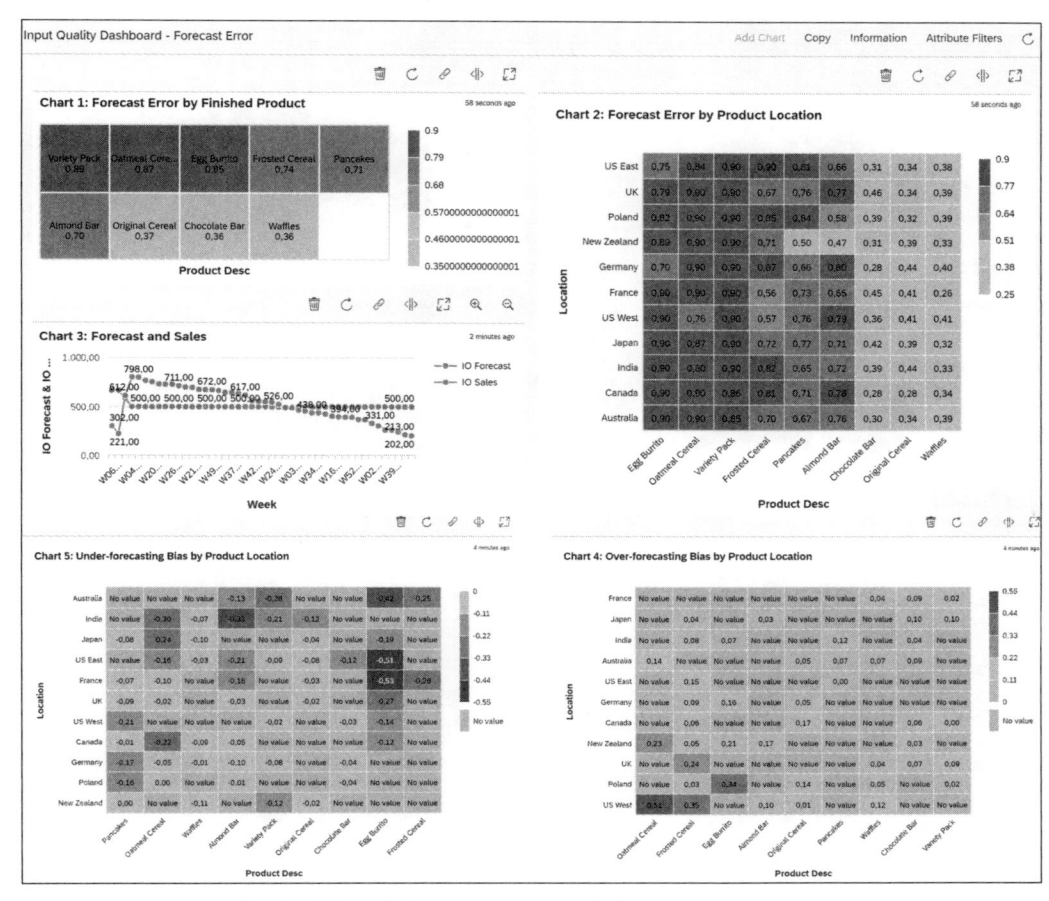

Figure 8.7 Input-Quality Dashboard: Forecast Error Analytics

Finally, the third input-quality dashboard should focus on supply parameters (see Figure 8.8). An analyst can review and validate the lead time and lead time variability for the DCs (transportation), plants (production), and raw material sourcing (vendor). She can also validate the lot sizes between locations and for production, as well as the order cycles by product family at each location.

8   Measuring Inventory Performance

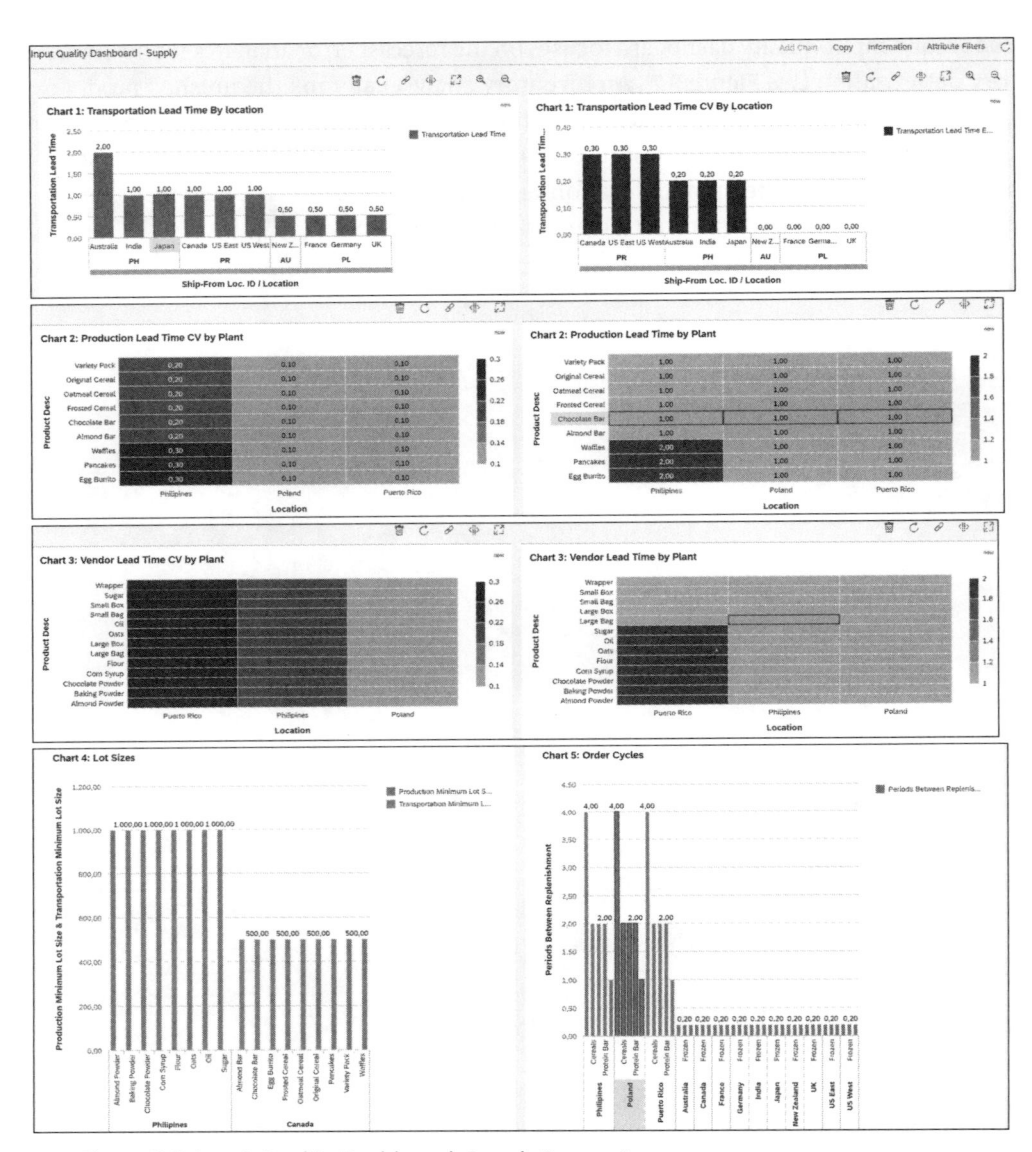

Figure 8.8 Input-Quality Dashboard: Supply Parameters

Note that SAP IBP dashboards and analytics charts support user filters and visibility filters. By keeping the dashboards at an aggregate attribute level and combining them with the use of filters, the CoE team can break up its work. We recommend that inventory operators be scheduled to run automatically at a certain frequency. The CoE team is responsible for completing the input-quality-review step before the operators run.

8.4 Review Inventory Plan

In this section, we'll show how the CoE team can review the inventory plan recommendations from the inventory operators using SAP IBP dashboards and analytics. This is done once the inventory operators have been run as part of a production batch job and after the input-quality dashboard review. These templates also can be shared with end users such as inventory managers and planners with suitable predefined visibility filters. Also, any user can further drill down into the template dashboards by using his favorite attributes as filters.

We recommend that the first dashboard for inventory plans be identical to the first input-quality dashboard for demand, except that demand is replaced by recommended safety stock cost, as shown in Figure 8.9.

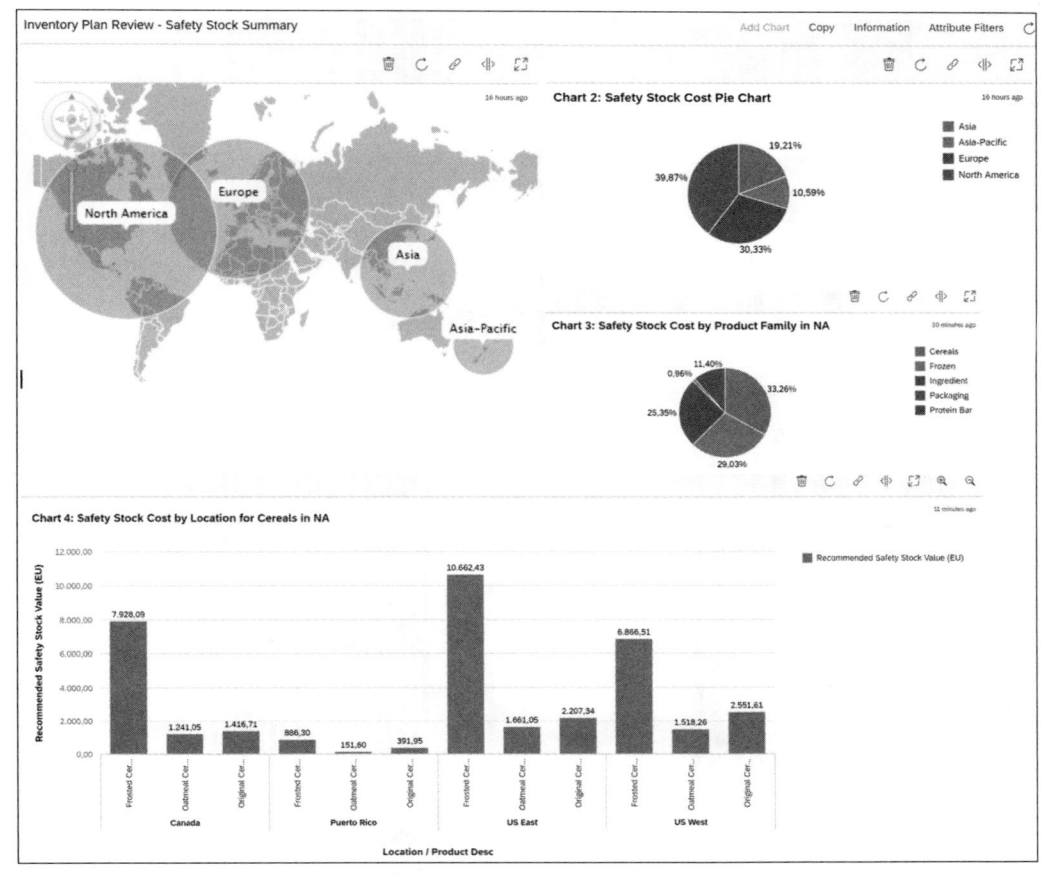

Figure 8.9 Inventory Plan Review Dashboard for Safety Stock Summary

287

8 Measuring Inventory Performance

In the dashboard shown in Figure 8.9, the inventory analyst can quickly determine and validate the largest safety stock region by cost, the largest safety stock product category by region, and the distribution of safety stock cost by product and location for a given product category and region. She can deep-dive into any information by clicking on the chart in the dashboard and drilling down by any parameter. For example, you might notice from the last chart in the dashboard that Frosted Cereal in US East has high safety stock in the month of March and want to get more details.

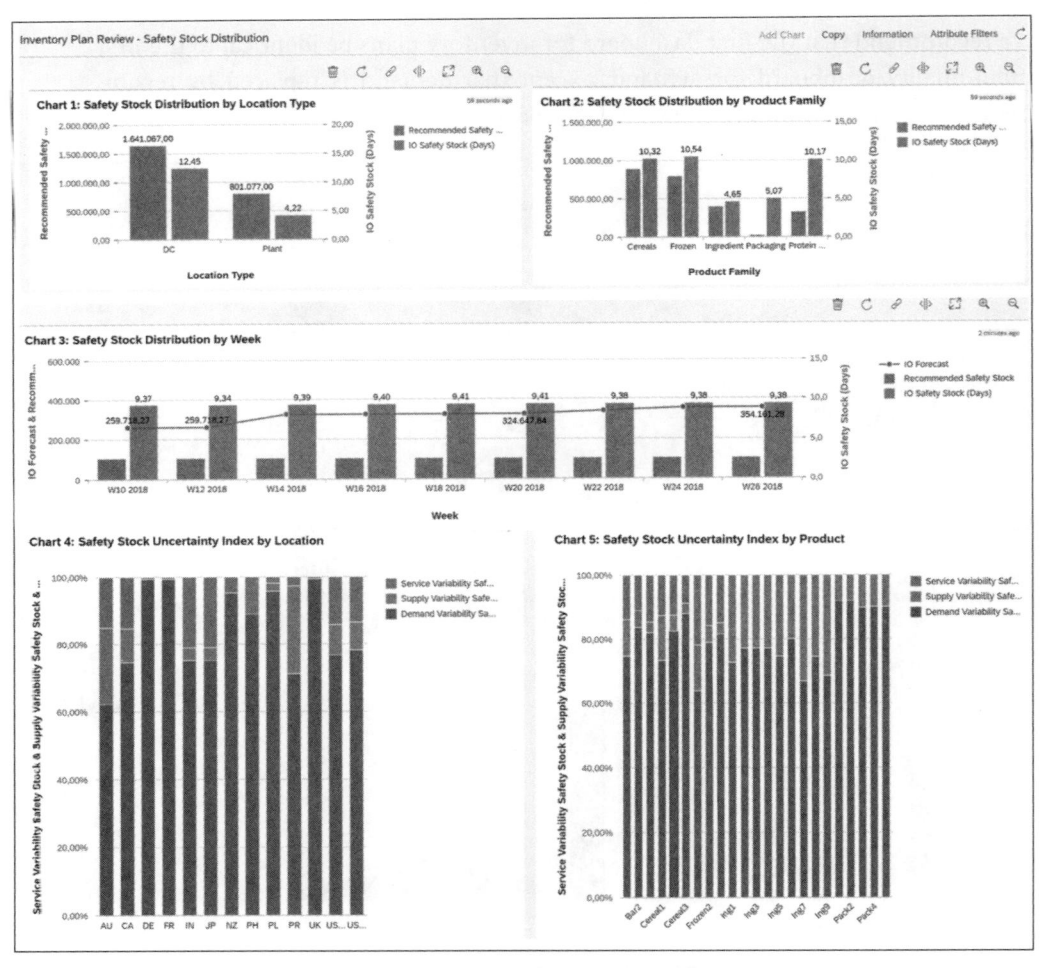

Figure 8.10 Inventory Plan Review Dashboard for Safety Stock Distribution

The second dashboard for reviewing inventory plans should focus on distribution of safety stock by location type (DCs vs. plants), by product family (finished goods vs. ingredients vs. packaging), by driver of safety stock (demand variability vs. lead time variability vs. service variability), and by weeks in cost and days of coverage. This is shown in Figure 8.10.

Figure 8.11 shows the third dashboard, which we recommend for reviewing inventory plans. It shows the distribution of the min-max levels (safety stock and target inventory position) and forms of inventory.

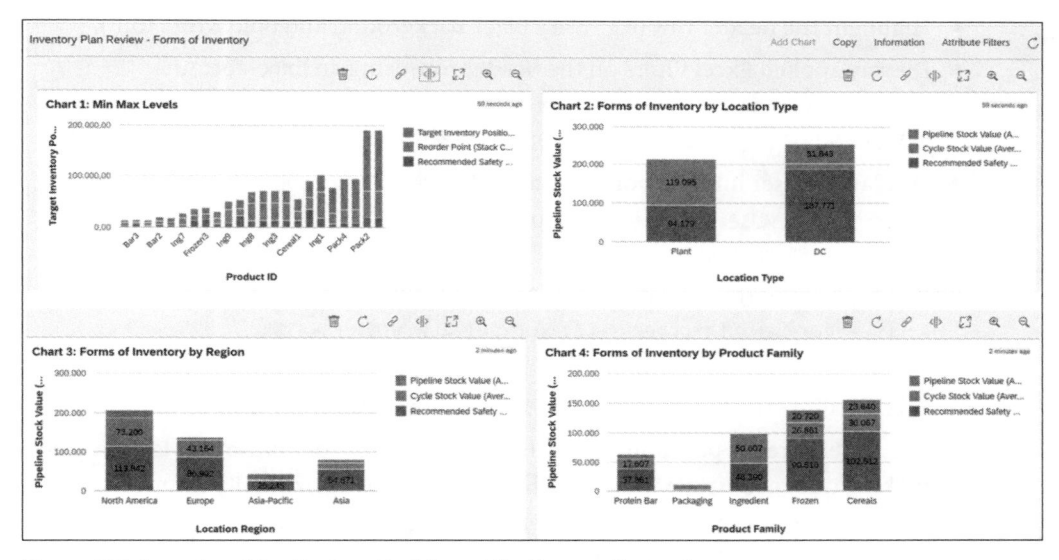

Figure 8.11 Inventory Plan Review Dashboard for Forms of Inventory

After reviewing the inventory plan by region or by product family in a high level of the hierarchy, the CoE team can drill down to detailed results in planning views to understand the drivers of any specific inventory target recommendations or big changes from the last cycle run in the next step.

8.5 Assess Inventory Drivers

In this section, we'll discuss some Excel templates that the CoE team can use as planning views for root-cause analysis to explain the inventory target recommendations from inventory operators. Root-cause analysis in the context of this section is a systematic process to identify the inventory drivers for holding inventory. The goal of the step is to help the CoE team link the inventory drivers to any specific inventory target recommendations or big changes from the last cycle run.

We'll make changes to the EPM formatting sheet associated with the planning view (*https://bit.ly/2BoeXWg*) and add a corporate logo as examples of how to standardize the Excel templates. You can then modify the content of the Excel planning view using the provided standard Excel template. Some ideas for creating an Excel template are as follows:

- Highlight the header row (e.g., use a black background and bold white font).
- Display applied Excel filters on the header row using an Excel formula:
  `"=SOP_Filter_Name&" ("&SOP_Filter_Criteria_Count&" criteria):"&" "&IFERROR(INDEX(SOP_Filter,1),"")&""&IFERROR(INDEX(SOP_Filter,2),"")&"""`
- Display the user information on the header row using an Excel formula:
  `"="User: "&EPMUser()&" | Planning Area: "&IFERROR(SOP_Planning_Area, "Offline")&" "&"Template: "&IFERROR(SOP_Template_Name,"none")"`
- Display the last time the planning view was refreshed using an Excel formula:
  `=" Last Refresh: "&IFERROR(YEAR(SOP_Refresh_Timestamp)&"-"&TEXT(SOP_Refresh_Timestamp,"MMM")&"-"&DAY(SOP_Refresh_Timestamp)&" "&TEXT(SOP_Refresh_Timestamp,"HH:MM:SS"),"Offline")`
- Use Excel's freeze panes feature, which allows a row or column to lock in place, making it always visible when scrolling vertically or horizontally through an open document. You can freeze the header row as well as the attribute columns. Format the data using the EPM formatting sheet.

In our example, we've highlighted the header row, used Excel filters on the header row, used the freeze panes feature, and formatted the data. We call the resulting template Analysis View (Figure 8.12). The top two rows also show the current user, when the view was last refreshed, and information from the SAP IBP filter applied. Finally, for attributes as key figures, we display the current period value in default format but gray out all the other periods to signal to the user that inventory operators read the current period value only for such input key figures.

Then, you can save this as a standard Excel template for any user by clicking on **Template Admin** in the **IBP** tab, selecting **Templates** followed by **Add**, and providing a name for the template.

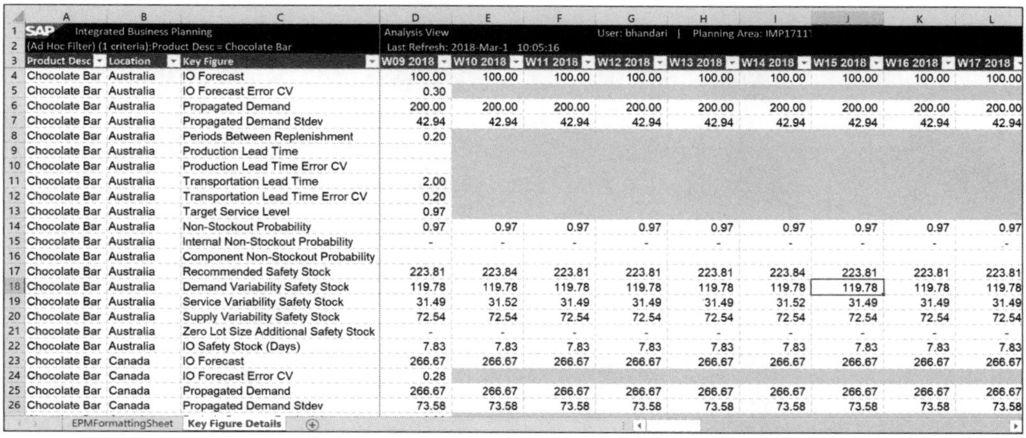

SAP Integrated Business Planning — Analysis View — User: bhandari | Planning Area: IMP1711T

(Ad Hoc Filter) (1 criteria):Product Desc = Chocolate Bar — Last Refresh: 2018-Mar-1 10:05:16

Product Desc	Location	Key Figure	W09 2018	W10 2018	W11 2018	W12 2018	W13 2018	W14 2018	W15 2018	W16 2018	W17 2018
Chocolate Bar	Australia	IO Forecast	100.00	100.00	100.00	100.00	100.00	100.00	100.00	100.00	100.00
Chocolate Bar	Australia	IO Forecast Error CV	0.30								
Chocolate Bar	Australia	Propagated Demand	200.00	200.00	200.00	200.00	200.00	200.00	200.00	200.00	200.00
Chocolate Bar	Australia	Propagated Demand Stdev	42.94	42.94	42.94	42.94	42.94	42.94	42.94	42.94	42.94
Chocolate Bar	Australia	Periods Between Replenishment	0.20								
Chocolate Bar	Australia	Production Lead Time									
Chocolate Bar	Australia	Production Lead Time Error CV									
Chocolate Bar	Australia	Transportation Lead Time	2.00								
Chocolate Bar	Australia	Transportation Lead Time Error CV	0.20								
Chocolate Bar	Australia	Target Service Level	0.97								
Chocolate Bar	Australia	Non-Stockout Probability	0.97	0.97	0.97	0.97	0.97	0.97	0.97	0.97	0.97
Chocolate Bar	Australia	Internal Non-Stockout Probability	-	-	-	-	-	-	-	-	-
Chocolate Bar	Australia	Component Non-Stockout Probability									
Chocolate Bar	Australia	Recommended Safety Stock	223.81	223.84	223.81	223.81	223.81	223.84	223.81	223.81	223.81
Chocolate Bar	Australia	Demand Variability Safety Stock	119.78	119.78	119.78	119.78	119.78	119.78	119.78	119.78	119.78
Chocolate Bar	Australia	Service Variability Safety Stock	31.49	31.52	31.49	31.49	31.49	31.52	31.49	31.49	31.49
Chocolate Bar	Australia	Supply Variability Safety Stock	72.54	72.54	72.54	72.54	72.54	72.54	72.54	72.54	72.54
Chocolate Bar	Australia	Zero Lot Size Additional Safety Stock	-	-	-	-	-	-	-	-	-
Chocolate Bar	Australia	IO Safety Stock (Days)	7.83	7.83	7.83	7.83	7.83	7.83	7.83	7.83	7.83
Chocolate Bar	Canada	IO Forecast	266.67	266.67	266.67	266.67	266.67	266.67	266.67	266.67	266.67
Chocolate Bar	Canada	IO Forecast Error CV	0.28								
Chocolate Bar	Canada	Propagated Demand	266.67	266.67	266.67	266.67	266.67	266.67	266.67	266.67	266.67
Chocolate Bar	Canada	Propagated Demand Stdev	73.58	73.58	73.58	73.58	73.58	73.58	73.58	73.58	73.58

EPMFormattingSheet | Key Figure Details

Figure 8.12 Analysis View Template for Assessing Inventory Drivers

Next, to display the content of the planning view, click **New View** in the **IBP** tab and select **From Template**, which brings up the **Create New Planning View from Template** Excel window box. Select the previous template in the **Template** dropdown selector. Then use the following selections for each section:

- The **Planning Level** is a combination of product description (or ID) and location (or ID).
- For **Time Settings**, utilize a calendar week bucket ranging from the current week to the current week plus the planning horizon (this can be shortened).
- Use a product description (or ID) **Filter**; you can save frequently used filters.
- We recommend that the **Key Figures** in Table 8.1 be used in the Analysis View template.
- Use the default **Layout**.

Finally, click on **OK**.

Type	Key Figure ID	Description
Input	IOFORECAST	Weekly forecast or consumption of a product at a location for a customer group
Input	IOFORECASTERRORCV	Weekly customer forecast error coefficient of variation as a normalized measure of demand forecast variability

Table 8.1 Key Figures to Use in Analysis View Template

8　Measuring Inventory Performance

Type	Key Figure ID	Description
Output	PROPAGATEDDEMANDMEAN	Analytical output that provides the total demand at each product location
Output	PROPAGATEDDEMANDSTDDEV	Analytical output that provides the total demand variability at each product location
Input	PBR	Time interval (in weeks) between two consecutive order or manufacturing run decisions
Input	PLEADTIME	Total production lead time in weeks
Input	PLEADTIMEVARIABILITY	Production lead time coefficient of variation (CV) in weeks
Input	TLEADTIME	Total transportation lead time in weeks
Input	TLEADTIMEVARIABILITY	Transportation lead time CV in weeks
Input	TARGETSERVICELEVEL	Customer-service-level input to calculate inventory targets
Output	AVAILABLEINFULL	Customer service level as nonstockout probability calculated from target service-level input (fill rate or nonstockout probability)
Output	INTERNALAVAILABLEINFULL	Upstream transportation source internal service level in nonstockout probability
Output	INTERNALLOCTOPRDAIF	Upstream production internal service level from components in nonstockout probability
Output	RECOMMENDEDSAFETYSTOCK	Buffer stock recommended to mitigate the uncertainties in supply and demand
Output	SAFETYSTOCKDEMANDVAR	Analytical output for contribution of demand variability over the lead time and order cycle to RECOMMENDEDSAFETYSTOCK
Output	SAFETYSTOCKSUPPLYVAR	Analytical output for contribution of lead time variability to RECOMMENDEDSAFETYSTOCK
Output	SAFETYSTOCKSERVICEVAR	Analytical output for contribution of the upstream source's variability from its optimal internal service level to RECOMMENDEDSAFETYSTOCK

Table 8.1 Key Figures to Use in Analysis View Template (Cont.)

Type	Key Figure ID	Description
Output	SAFETYSTOCKLOTSIZE	Analytical output that informs the user of how much additional safety stock would be needed if the lot size was reduced to zero
Output	IOSAFETYSTOCKDAYSOFSUPPLY	Analytical output that provides the recommended safety stock in days of supply in terms of future coverage

Table 8.1 Key Figures to Use in Analysis View Template (Cont.)

This view provides sufficient information to the user for an initial root-cause analysis. In most scenarios, this view is sufficient to explain the safety stock recommendations of the inventory operator (80/20 rule—that is, 80% of the effects come from 20% of the causes). In the remaining scenarios, this view will yield information about further avenues of investigation. ABBFI doesn't have multiple sourcing; for a company in which multiple sourcing is common, the Analysis View template can be enhanced by adding another Excel worksheet and creating an Excel planning view that shows the sourcing details, as shown in Figure 8.13. In this example, we added the ship-from location and source ID to the planning level. The key figures in this view are restricted to lead time, lead time variability, lot sizes, sourcing quota (inputs), and the calculated internal service level (output). This Excel planning view is useful in addition to the previous one, not in isolation.

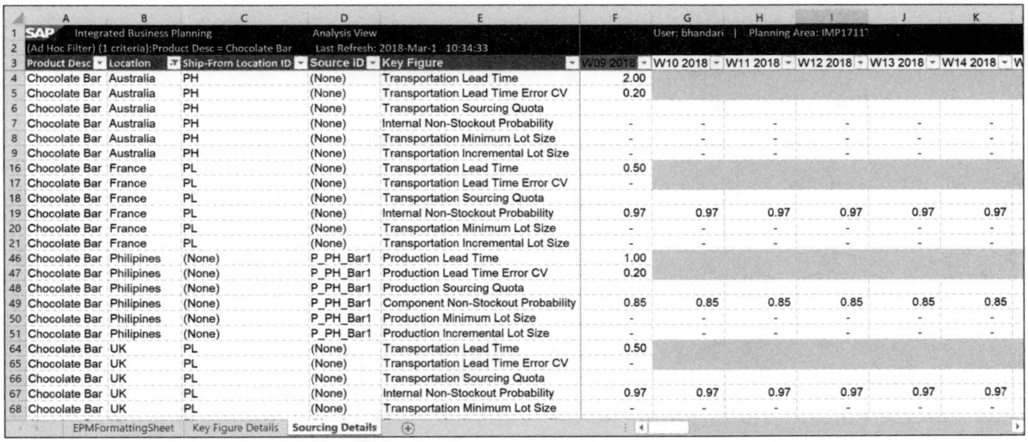
SAP Integrated Business Planning — Analysis View — User: bhandari | Planning Area: IMP1711
(Ad Hoc Filter) (1 criteria):Product Desc = Chocolate Bar — Last Refresh: 2018-Mar-1 10:34:33

	Product Desc	Location	Ship-From Location ID	Source ID	Key Figure	W09 2018	W10 2018	W11 2018	W12 2018	W13 2018	W14 2018
4	Chocolate Bar	Australia	PH	(None)	Transportation Lead Time	2.00					
5	Chocolate Bar	Australia	PH	(None)	Transportation Lead Time Error CV	0.20					
6	Chocolate Bar	Australia	PH	(None)	Transportation Sourcing Quota						
7	Chocolate Bar	Australia	PH	(None)	Internal Non-Stockout Probability	-	-	-	-	-	-
8	Chocolate Bar	Australia	PH	(None)	Transportation Minimum Lot Size	-	-	-	-	-	-
9	Chocolate Bar	Australia	PH	(None)	Transportation Incremental Lot Size	-	-	-	-	-	-
16	Chocolate Bar	France	PL	(None)	Transportation Lead Time	0.50					
17	Chocolate Bar	France	PL	(None)	Transportation Lead Time Error CV	-					
18	Chocolate Bar	France	PL	(None)	Transportation Sourcing Quota						
19	Chocolate Bar	France	PL	(None)	Internal Non-Stockout Probability	0.97	0.97	0.97	0.97	0.97	0.97
20	Chocolate Bar	France	PL	(None)	Transportation Minimum Lot Size	-	-	-	-	-	-
21	Chocolate Bar	France	PL	(None)	Transportation Incremental Lot Size	-	-	-	-	-	-
46	Chocolate Bar	Philipines	(None)	P_PH_Bar1	Production Lead Time	1.00					
47	Chocolate Bar	Philipines	(None)	P_PH_Bar1	Production Lead Time Error CV	0.20					
48	Chocolate Bar	Philipines	(None)	P_PH_Bar1	Production Sourcing Quota						
49	Chocolate Bar	Philipines	(None)	P_PH_Bar1	Component Non-Stockout Probability	0.85	0.85	0.85	0.85	0.85	0.85
50	Chocolate Bar	Philipines	(None)	P_PH_Bar1	Production Minimum Lot Size	-	-	-	-	-	-
51	Chocolate Bar	Philipines	(None)	P_PH_Bar1	Production Incremental Lot Size	-	-	-	-	-	-
64	Chocolate Bar	UK	PL	(None)	Transportation Lead Time	0.50					
65	Chocolate Bar	UK	PL	(None)	Transportation Lead Time Error CV	-					
66	Chocolate Bar	UK	PL	(None)	Transportation Sourcing Quota						
67	Chocolate Bar	UK	PL	(None)	Internal Non-Stockout Probability	0.97	0.97	0.97	0.97	0.97	0.97
68	Chocolate Bar	UK	PL	(None)	Transportation Minimum Lot Size	-	-	-	-	-	-

EPMFormattingSheet | Key Figure Details | Sourcing Details

Figure 8.13 Sourcing Details Planning View Added to Analysis View Template

8 Measuring Inventory Performance

8.6 Finalize Inventory Plan

In this section, we'll discuss how to enable end users to finalize inventory plan recommendations for the products and locations that they manage. We'll discuss how planners can be allowed to propose changes with reason codes and how inventory managers can review the proposed changes before approving or rejecting them. The configuration setup was discussed in Chapter 3.

First, create an Excel template called *Days Coverage Alert* that contains two sheets. In the first sheet, labeled *Days Coverage Alert Indicator*, you want to see only those product-locations for which the recommended safety stock in days is out of range (see Figure 8.14). Use the following settings in the Excel planning view setup:

- **Time Settings**
  Month; current month to planning horizon
- **Planning Level**
  Location and product description
- **Key Figures**
  Alert safety days out of range
- **Layout**
  Default
- **Filter**
  Default
- **Alerts**:
  - **Base Calculation**
    Alert safety days out of range
  - **Highlighted Key Figure**
    Inventory optimization safety stock (days) in red
  - **Scenario**
    Baseline
  - **Version**
    Base version

> **Note**
>
> You can go to the **Edit View** screen to add/modify the alerts under the **Alerts** section. We'll explain how to configure the alert key figures used in the current section in the next section.

In our case study example, you can see that the recommendation is out of range from March 2018 to July 2018 for some of the products in New Zealand.

	A	B	C	D	E	F	G	H	I	J
1	SAP Integrated Business Planning			Days Coverage Alert			User: bhandari	Planning Area: IMP171	
2	(Ad Hoc Filter) (1 criteria):Location Type = DC			Last Refresh: 2018-Mar-1 12:31:43						
3	Product Desc	Location	Key Figure	MAR 2018	APR 2018	MAY 2018	JUN 2018	JUL 2018	AUG 2018	SEP 2018
20	Chocolate Bar	New Zealand	Alert safety days out of range	1.00	1.00	1.00	1.00	1.00		
30	Egg Burrito	New Zealand	Alert safety days out of range	1.00	1.00	1.00	1.00	1.00		
40	Frosted Cereal	New Zealand	Alert safety days out of range	1.00	1.00	1.00	1.00	1.00		
50	Oatmeal Cereal	New Zealand	Alert safety days out of range	1.00	1.00	1.00	1.00	1.00		
60	Original Cereal	New Zealand	Alert safety days out of range	1.00	1.00	1.00	1.00	1.00		
80	Variety Pack	New Zealand	Alert safety days out of range	1.00	1.00	1.00	1.00	1.00		
90	Waffles	New Zealand	Alert safety days out of range	1.00	1.00	1.00	1.00	1.00		

Figure 8.14 Alert Indicator in Days Coverage Alert Template

Next, the *Finalize Plan* sheet highlights scenarios in which safety stock is below the minimum value in red and above the maximum value in blue. Use the following settings in the Excel planning view setup:

- **Time Settings**
  Month; current month to planning horizon

- **Planning Level**
  Location and product description

- **Key Figures**
  Minimum safety stock (Days) (IOMINSAFETYDAYS), IO safety stock (days) (IOSAFETYSTOCKDAYSOFSUPPLY), maximum safety stock (days) (IOMAXSAFETYDAYS), propagated demand (PROPAGATEDDEMANDMEAN), recommended safety stock (RECOMMENDEDSAFETYSTOCK), planner safety stock quantity (override) (PLANNERADJUSTEDSAFETYSTOCK), inventory manager override approval (MANAGERAPPROVEOVERRIDE), final safety stock quantity (FINALSAFETYSTOCK)

- **Layout**
  Default

- **Filter**
  Default

- **Alerts**
  - Alert 1:
    - **Base calculation**
      Alert safety days below minimum
    - **Highlighted Key Figure**
      Inventory optimization safety stock (days) in red

8   Measuring Inventory Performance

- Scenario
  Baseline
- Version
  Base version

– Alert 2:
  - Base calculation
    Alert safety days above maximum
  - Highlighted Key Figure
    Inventory optimization safety stock (days) in blue
  - Scenario
    Baseline
  - Version
    Base version

In Figure 8.15, you can see that for Chocolate Bar, the safety stock at four days is below the minimum value at six days; for Egg Burrito, the safety stock at 14 days is above the maximum value at 10 days.

Product Desc	Key Figure	MAR 2018	APR 2018	MAY 2018	JUN 2018	JUL 2018	AUG 2018	SEP 2018	OCT 2018	NOV 2018
Chocolate Bar	Minimum Safety Stock (Days)	6.00	6.00	6.00	6.00	6.00				
	IO Safety Stock (Days)	4.01	4.01	4.01	4.01	4.01	4.01	4.01	4.01	4.01
	Maximum Safety Stock (Days)	10.00	10.00	10.00	10.00	10.00				
	Propagated Demand	400.00	500.00	400.00	400.00	500.00	400.00	450.00	450.00	400.00
	Recommended Safety Stock	228.95	286.19	228.95	228.95	286.19	228.95	257.57	257.57	228.95
	Planner Safety Stock Qty (Override)									
	Inventory Manager Override Approval									
	Final Safety Stock Qty	228.95	286.19	228.95	228.95	286.19	228.95	257.57	257.57	228.95
Egg Burrito	Minimum Safety Stock (Days)	6.00	6.00	6.00	6.00	6.00				
	IO Safety Stock (Days)	13.77	13.77	13.77	13.77	13.77	13.77	13.77	13.77	13.77
	Maximum Safety Stock (Days)	10.00	10.00	10.00	10.00	10.00				
	Propagated Demand	1,000.00	1,250.00	1,000.00	1,000.00	1,250.00	1,000.00	1,125.00	1,125.00	1,000.00
	Recommended Safety Stock	1,967.73	2,459.68	1,967.73	1,967.73	2,459.64	1,967.73	2,213.68	2,213.68	1,967.73
	Planner Safety Stock Qty (Override)									
	Inventory Manager Override Approval									
	Final Safety Stock Qty	1,967.73	2,459.68	1,967.73	1,967.73	2,459.64	1,967.73	2,213.68	2,213.68	1,967.73

Figure 8.15 Detailed Alert Indicator in Days Coverage Alert Template

Next, imagine you open the Analysis View template with filter values set to Chocolate Bar and Egg Burrito for products and New Zealand for location (see Figure 8.16). You can see right away that the forecast error coefficient of variation (CV) is much lower for Chocolate Bar (31%) than for Egg Burrito (89%) in New Zealand. This explains when the safety days of coverage is higher for Egg Burrito than Chocolate Bar and why it's outside the range provided as an input: because it was based on a 50% forecast error CV. Note that in both cases the recommended safety stock is primarily due to demand variability and determined by reviewing the safety stock due to demand variability key figure relative to the recommended safety stock key figure.

	A	B	C	D	E	F	G	H	I	J	K	L
1	SAP Integrated Business Planning			Analysis View			User: bhandari | Planning Area: IMP1711T					
2	(Ad Hoc Filter) (2 criteria):Product Desc = Chocolate Bar; Egg Burrito; Panc			Last Refresh: 2018-Mar-1 12:47:04								
3	Product Desc	Location	Key Figure	W09 2018	W10 2018	W11 2018	W12 2018	W13 2018	W14 2018	W15 2018	W16 2018	W17 2018
4	Chocolate Bar	New Zealand	IO Forecast	100.00	100.00	100.00	100.00	100.00	100.00	100.00	100.00	100.0
5	Chocolate Bar	New Zealand	IO Forecast Error CV	0.31								
8	Chocolate Bar	New Zealand	Periods Between Replenishment	0.20								
11	Chocolate Bar	New Zealand	Transportation Lead Time	0.50								
12	Chocolate Bar	New Zealand	Transportation Lead Time Error CV	-								
13	Chocolate Bar	New Zealand	Target Service Level	0.97								
17	Chocolate Bar	New Zealand	Recommended Safety Stock	57.24	57.24	57.24	57.24	57.24	57.24	57.24	57.24	57.2
18	Chocolate Bar	New Zealand	Demand Variability Safety Stock	55.38	55.38	55.38	55.38	55.38	55.38	55.38	55.38	55.3
19	Chocolate Bar	New Zealand	Service Variability Safety Stock	1.86	1.86	1.86	1.86	1.86	1.86	1.86	1.86	1.8
20	Chocolate Bar	New Zealand	Supply Variability Safety Stock	-	-	-	-	-	-	-	-	-
21	Chocolate Bar	New Zealand	Zero Lot Size Additional Safety Stock	-	-	-	-	-	-	-	-	-
22	Chocolate Bar	New Zealand	IO Safety Stock (Days)	4.01	4.01	4.01	4.01	4.01	4.01	4.01	4.01	4.0
23	Egg Burrito	New Zealand	IO Forecast	250.00	250.00	250.00	250.00	250.00	250.00	250.00	250.00	250.0
24	Egg Burrito	New Zealand	IO Forecast Error CV	0.89								
27	Egg Burrito	New Zealand	Periods Between Replenishment	0.20								
30	Egg Burrito	New Zealand	Transportation Lead Time	0.50								
31	Egg Burrito	New Zealand	Transportation Lead Time Error CV	-								
32	Egg Burrito	New Zealand	Target Service Level	0.97								
36	Egg Burrito	New Zealand	Recommended Safety Stock	492.00	491.91	491.91	491.91	492.00	491.91	491.91	491.91	492.0
37	Egg Burrito	New Zealand	Demand Variability Safety Stock	470.80	470.80	470.80	470.80	470.80	470.80	470.80	470.80	470.8
38	Egg Burrito	New Zealand	Service Variability Safety Stock	21.19	21.11	21.11	21.11	21.19	21.11	21.11	21.11	21.1
39	Egg Burrito	New Zealand	Supply Variability Safety Stock	-	-	-	-	-	-	-	-	-
40	Egg Burrito	New Zealand	Zero Lot Size Additional Safety Stock	-	-	-	-	-	-	-	-	-

Figure 8.16 Analysis View for Chocolate Bar and Egg Burrito in New Zealand

You can further validate this by changing the filter to Pancakes in New Zealand, which has a forecast error CV of 50% and for which the recommended safety stock of seven days is within the range of six to 10 days (see Figure 8.17).

	A	B	C	D	E	F	G	H	I	J
1	SAP Integrated Business Planning			Analysis View			User: bhandari | Planning Area: IMP1711T			
2	(Ad Hoc Filter) (2 criteria):Product Desc = Chocolate Bar; Egg Burrito; Panc			Last Refresh: 2018-Mar-1 12:47:04						
3	Product Desc	Location	Key Figure	W09 2018	W10 2018	W11 2018	W12 2018	W13 2018	W14 2018	W15 2018
42	Pancakes	New Zealand	IO Forecast	250.00	250.00	250.00	250.00	250.00	250.00	250.00
43	Pancakes	New Zealand	IO Forecast Error CV	0.50						
46	Pancakes	New Zealand	Periods Between Replenishment	0.20						
49	Pancakes	New Zealand	Transportation Lead Time	0.50						
50	Pancakes	New Zealand	Transportation Lead Time Error CV	-						
51	Pancakes	New Zealand	Target Service Level	0.97						
55	Pancakes	New Zealand	Recommended Safety Stock	248.39	248.36	248.36	248.36	248.39	248.36	248.36
56	Pancakes	New Zealand	Demand Variability Safety Stock	240.44	240.44	240.44	240.44	240.44	240.44	240.44
57	Pancakes	New Zealand	Service Variability Safety Stock	7.95	7.92	7.92	7.92	7.95	7.92	7.92
58	Pancakes	New Zealand	Supply Variability Safety Stock	-	-	-	-	-	-	-
59	Pancakes	New Zealand	Zero Lot Size Additional Safety Stock	-	-	-	-	-	-	-
60	Pancakes	New Zealand	IO Safety Stock (Days)	6.95	6.95	6.95	6.95	6.95	6.95	6.95

Figure 8.17 Analysis View for Pancakes in New Zealand

Finally, say that you decide not to change the safety stock of Egg Burrito because lowering it may impact customer service level negatively. However, imagine that you override the safety stock quantity for Chocolate Bar to 350 units from March 2018 to July 2018. For the inventory manager's benefit, you can document this change by entering a comment. Enter "Temporarily increasing safety stock until minimum

8   Measuring Inventory Performance

safety stock (days) is adjusted to reflect forecast error CV." in the **Comment** field, then click the **Save** button (see Figure 8.18).

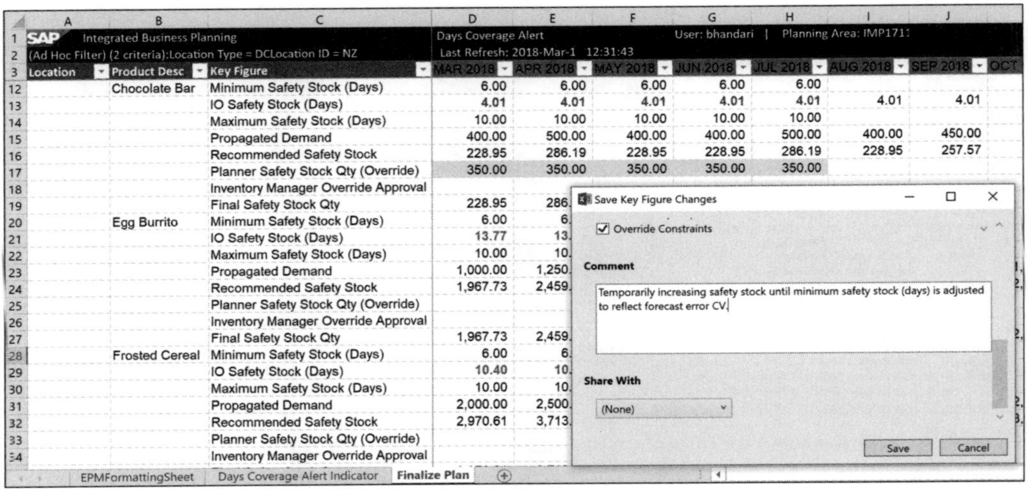

Figure 8.18 Increasing Safety Stock for Chocolate Bar in New Zealand

We also recommend enabling change history on the **Planner Safety Stock Qty (Override)** key figure (in the **Planning Area and Details** configuration screen for **Key Figures**) so that the manager can use the Change History report in SAP IBP to review all the changes and the impact to cost.

Assume that you're the inventory manager. You've used the Change History report to review the changes and are now ready to approve the planner's override in the Finalize Plan sheet. You decide to approve the override for March and April, but not for May to July because you would like the planner to readjust the minimum safety stock (days) level by the end of March. You can approve the override by entering the same value in the **Inventory Manager Override Approval** key figure row and clicking the **Save Data** button in the **IBP** tab in Excel. You'll be prompted to enter a reason for the approval. Enter a message in the **Comment** field and click the **Save** button, as shown in Figure 8.19. Once you save these changes, the final safety stock key figure is automatically updated. We will explain how to configure this review and approval process in the next section.

Finally, the CoE team is responsible for creating a summary report of the changes to the recommendations using the Change History report. This report is available via

8.7 Create Custom Inventory Alerts

the Change History SAP Fiori app in the web UI. It includes a summary of the reasons for changes, the cost impact of the changes, and a list of follow-up action items. It's also recommended to provide this summary by planner and inventory manager, location region, and business unit.

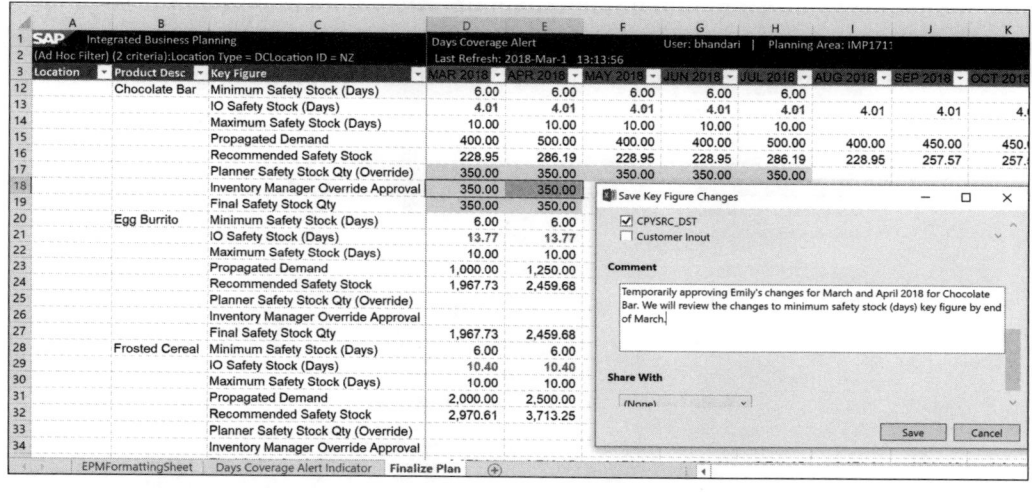

Figure 8.19 Inventory Manager's Approval of Override

8.7 Create Custom Inventory Alerts

In this section, we'll introduce two options to create and manage custom inventory alerts in SAP IBP. One is through alert key figures, and the other is through the Custom Alert app in SAP IBP. Note that the second option requires a license for SAP Supply Chain Control Tower.

8.7.1 Inventory Alerts Key Figures

As we discussed in the previous section, the CoE team and the end users (planners and inventory manager) will want to review the safety stock recommendations and finalize the plan. Typically, they have minimum and maximum safety days as a business rule at an aggregate level—say, product category and location type levels. For example, ABBFI's finished goods planners in New Zealand have minimum and maximum safety days policies of six days and 10 days, respectively. In this section,

299

8   Measuring Inventory Performance

we'll discuss how to add a configuration to alert users when safety stock recommendations may be out of the minimum-maximum range suggestions and allow planners to provide override recommendations for review by the inventory manager.

First, configure the minimum and maximum safety stock days at the WKPRODLOC planning level, with **Disaggregation Mode** set to **Copy Value** so that users can set these values at any aggregated level (month, product family, location region, etc.; see Figure 8.20 and Figure 8.21).

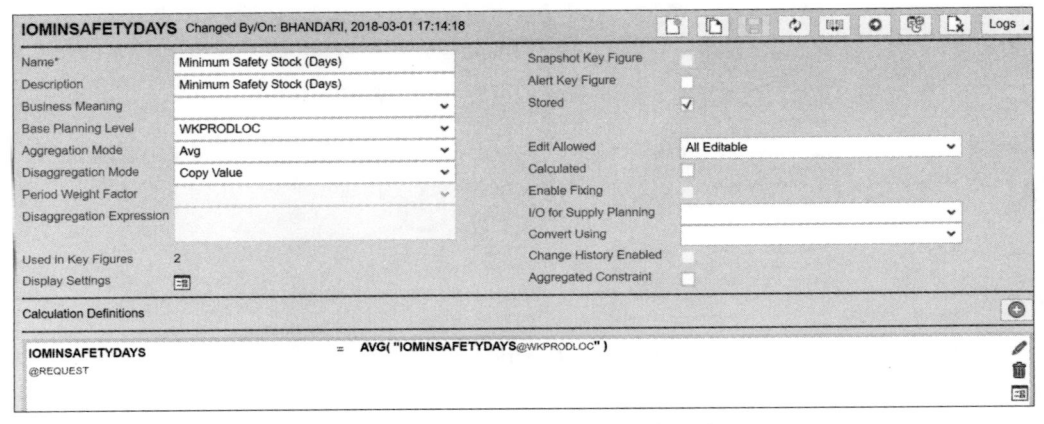

Figure 8.20 Configuration for Minimum Safety Stock (Days)

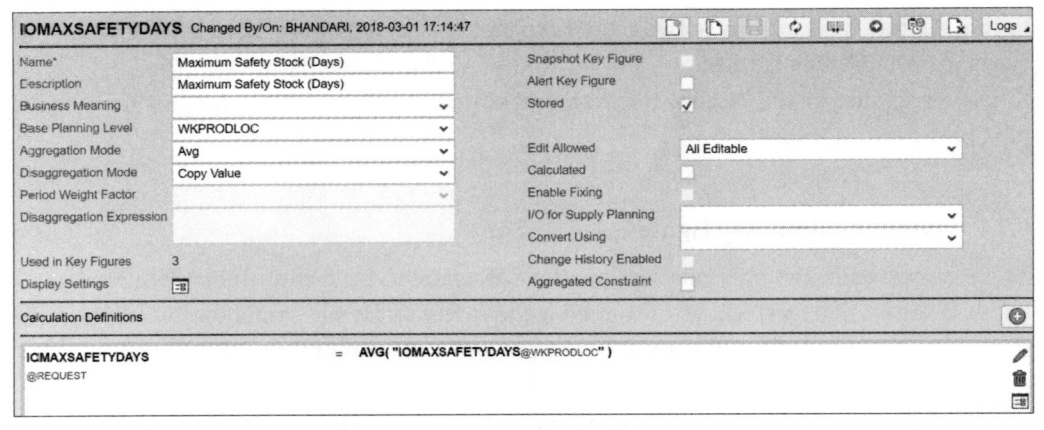

Figure 8.21 Configuration for Maximum Safety Stock (Days)

8.7 Create Custom Inventory Alerts

Next, configure three alert key figures to show when the recommended safety stock in days is out of range, when it's specifically below the minimum, and when it's specifically above the maximum (see Figure 8.22, Figure 8.23, and Figure 8.24, respectively).

Configure these calculated key figures at the WKPRODLOC planning level, with **aggregation Mode** set to **Max**. The calculations at the base planning level are as follows:

- **Safety stock out of range**
  ALERTSAFETYDAYS @ WKPRODLOC = IF(" IOSAFETYSTOCKDAYSOFSUPPLY @ WKPRODLOC " < " IOMINSAFETYDAYS @ WKPRODLOC " , 1 , IF (" IOSAFETYSTOCKDAYSOFSUPPLY @ WKPRODLOC " > " IOMAXSAFETYDAYS @ WKPRODLOC " , 1 , NULL))

- **Safety stock below the minimum**
  ALERTSAFETYDAYSMIN @ WKPRODLOC = IF (" IOSAFETYSTOCKDAYSOFSUPPLY @ WKPRODLOC " < " IOMINSAFETYDAYS @ WKPRODLOC " , 1 , NULL)

- **Safety stock above the maximum**
  ALERTSAFETYDAYSMAX @ WKPRODLOC = IF (" IOSAFETYSTOCKDAYSOFSUPPLY @ WKPRODLOC " > " IOMAXSAFETYDAYS @ WKPRODLOC " , 1 , NULL)

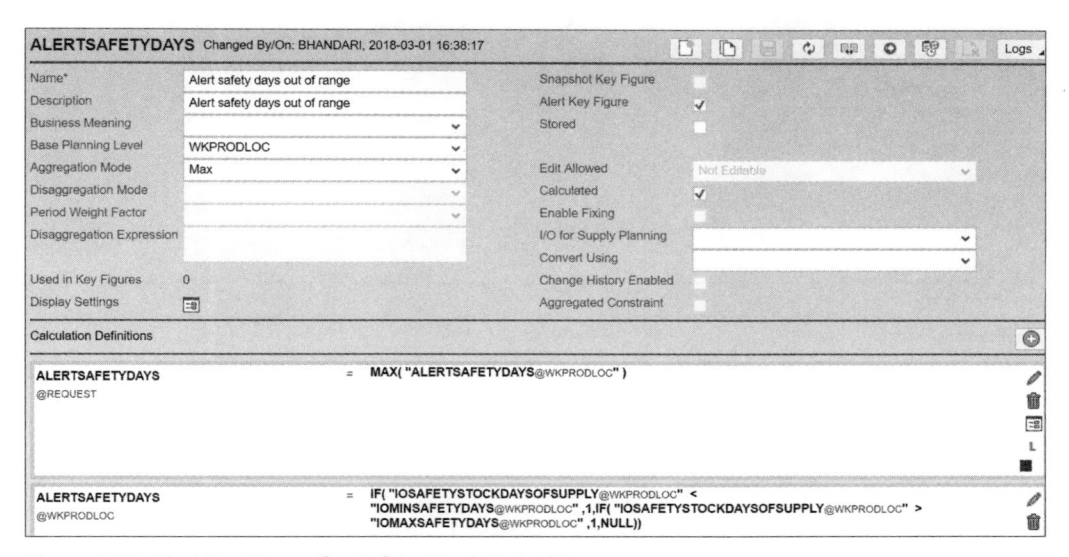

Figure 8.22 Alert Key Figure for Safety Stock Out of Range

8 Measuring Inventory Performance

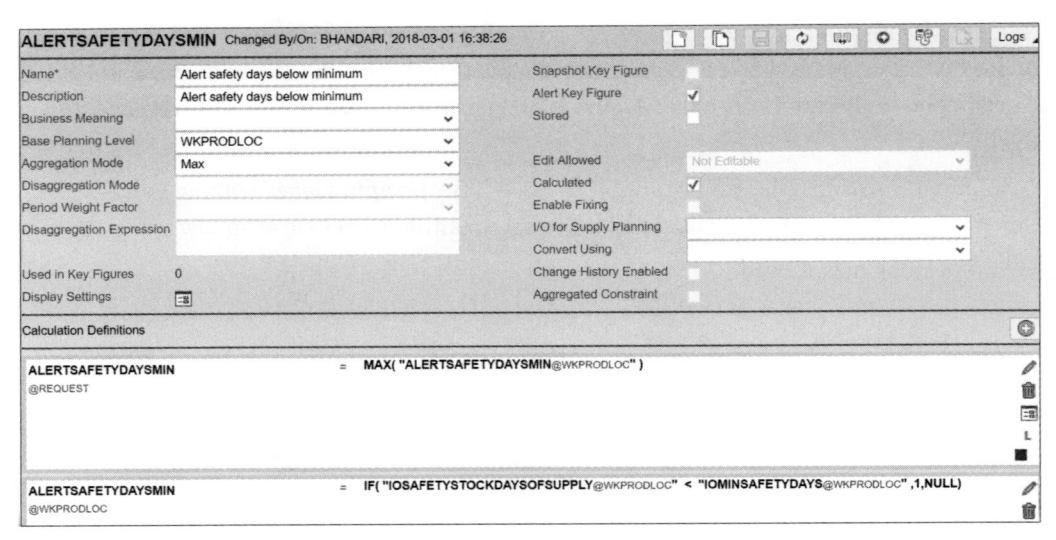

Figure 8.23 Alert Key Figure for Safety Stock Days below Minimum Value

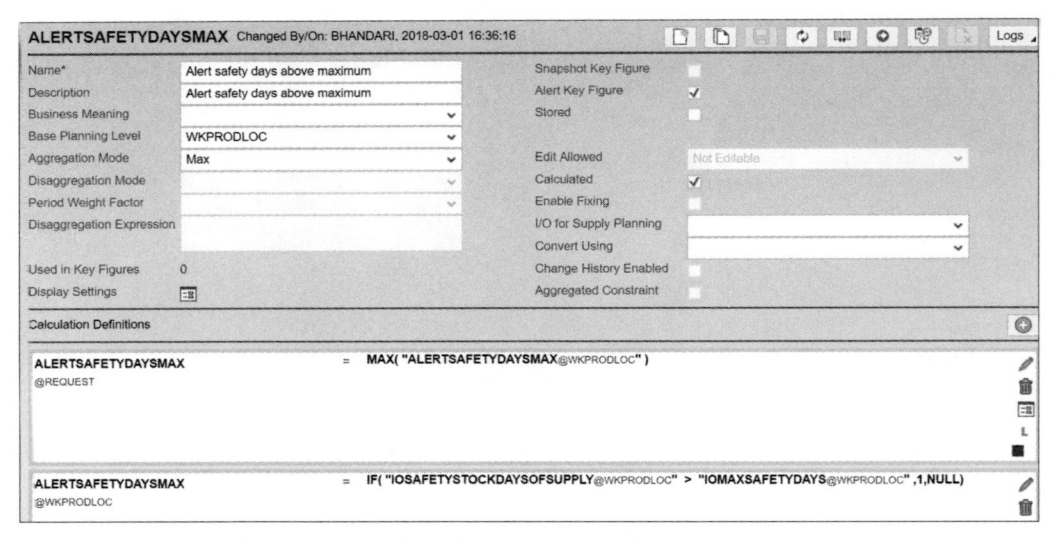

Figure 8.24 Alert Key Figure for Safety Stock Days above Maximum Value

Finally, configure a key figure for planners to provide a safety stock quantity override recommendation (Figure 8.25), a key figure for the inventory manager to approve the planners' overrides (Figure 8.26), and a final safety stock key figure set to the override when approved and to the recommended safety stock otherwise (Figure 8.27).

8.7 Create Custom Inventory Alerts

Configure the first two as **Stored** and **All Editable** key figures at the WKPRODLOC planning level, with **Aggregation Mode** set to **Sum**. The final safety stock key figure is configured as a **Calculated** key figure at the WKPRODLOC planning level, with **Aggregation Mode** set to **Sum**. The calculations at the base planning level are shown in Listing 8.2.

```
FINALSAFETYSTOCK @ WKPRODLOC =
IF(ISNULL("MANAGERAPPROVEOVERRIDE@WKPRODLOC"),
"RECOMMENDEDSAFETYSTOCK@WKPRODLOC",
IF(ISNULL("PLANNERADJUSTEDSAFETYSTOCK@WKPRODLOC"),
"RECOMMENDEDSAFETYSTOCK@WKPRODLOC","PLANNERADJUSTEDSAFETYSTOCK@WKPRODLOC"))
```

Listing 8.2 Calculations at Base Planning Level for Safety Stock Override Recommendation

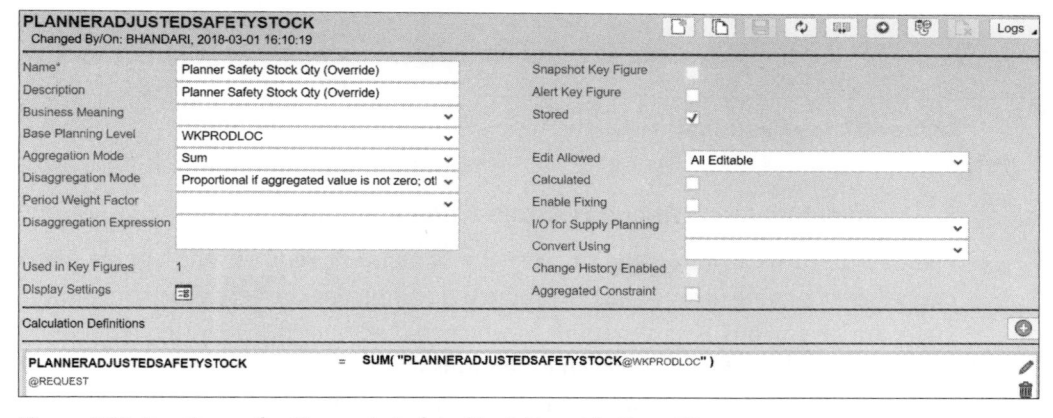

Figure 8.25 Key Figure for Planner's Safety Stock Override Quantity

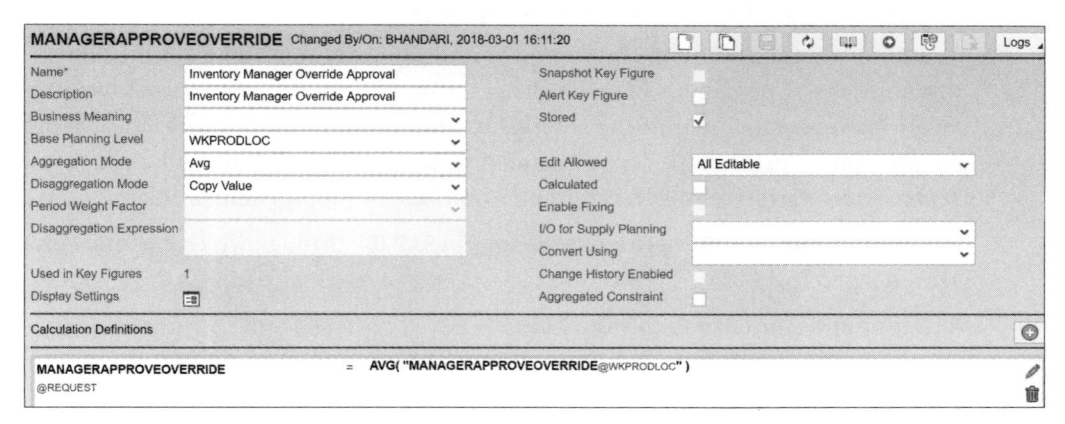

Figure 8.26 Key Figure for Inventory Manager to Approve Overrides

8 Measuring Inventory Performance

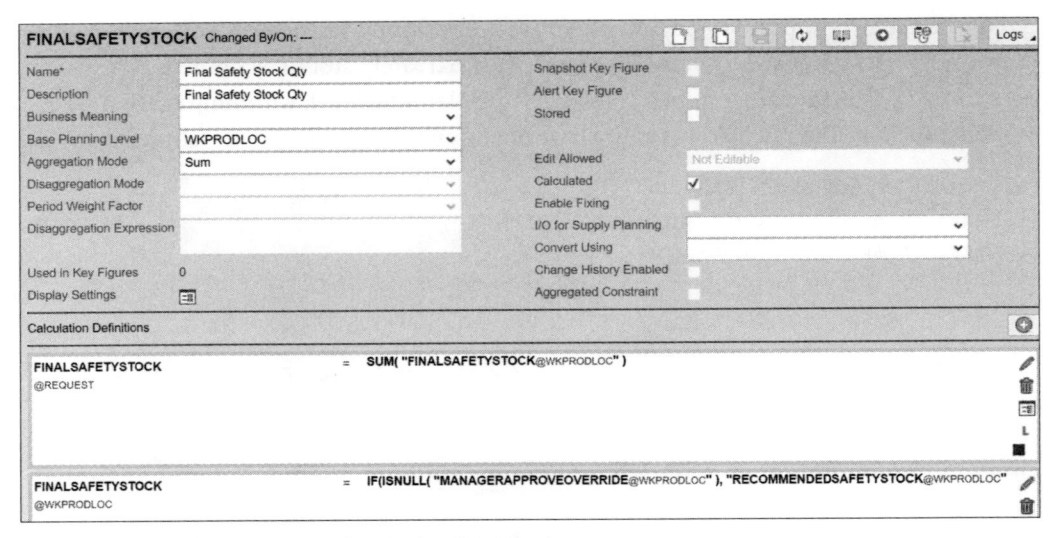

Figure 8.27 Key Figure for Final Safety Stock

8.7.2 Inventory Alerts through Custom Alerts Application

Planners need to monitor and analyze the demand, inventory, and supply plans every day, but going through all the products/locations can be very time-consuming. There are several business situations in which planners need to identify, report, and resolve exceptions. Managing such exceptions efficiently and on time is critical for supply chain processes in any organization. To facilitate these tasks, custom alert functionality in SAP IBP can be used. Planners can identify exceptional situations using custom alerts and resolve them using cases.

Custom alerts are used to find important or critical supply chain issues such as inventory shortages, a demand supply imbalance, or any unexpected changes in inventory levels. Planners can fine-tune the criteria for alert generation to mitigate issues in the supply chain. Custom alerts are integrated with cases in SAP Supply Chain Control Tower, which facilitates the tracking and resolution of supply chain problems.

As shown in Figure 8.28, there are three apps in SAP IBP through which custom alerts are managed:

- Define and Subscribe to Custom Alert
- Custom Alerts Overview
- Monitor Custom Alerts

8.7 Create Custom Inventory Alerts

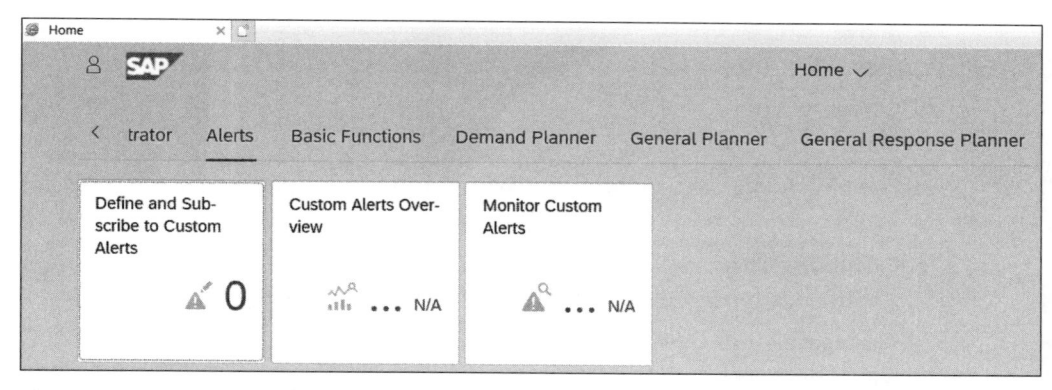

Figure 8.28 Custom Alerts App in SAP IBP

Let's walk through how to define and subscribe to custom alerts to warn users of large safety stock changes from the last cycle:

1. Open the Define and Subscribe to Custom Alerts app by choosing the corresponding tile on the SAP Fiori launchpad.
2. Choose the **+** icon (on the bottom-left side of the screen) as shown in Figure 8.29.

Figure 8.29 Add New Alert

3. In the **Information** section, enter the following data, as shown in Figure 8.30:
   – **Name**
     "Safety Stock Change from Last Cycle"
   – **Description**
     Alert users on large safety stock changes from last cycle run

305

8   Measuring Inventory Performance

- **Active**
  Check
- **Category**
  Blank
- **Planning Area**
  \<Your planning area\> (e.g., ZSAPIBP1)
- **Calculation Level**
  LOCID (location ID), PRDID (product ID), PERIODID4 (week)
- **Aggregate Alerts Over Time Horizon**
  Blank (uncheck)
- **Time Horizon**
  Week
- **Time Horizon From**
  \<The current week\>
- **Time Horizon To**
  \<Fifty-two weeks into the future\>
- **Rolling**
  Check

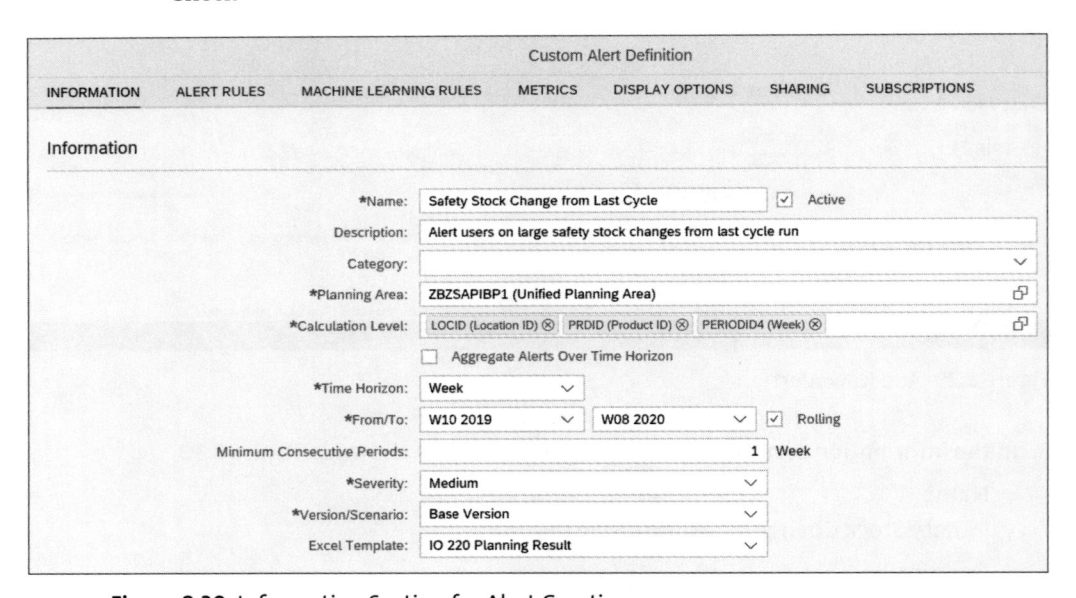

Figure 8.30 Information Section for Alert Creations

8.7 Create Custom Inventory Alerts

- **Minimum Consecutive Periods**
  One (week)
- **Severity**
  Medium
- **Version**
  Base version
- **Excel Template**
  <Your Excel template> (e.g., Inventory Optimization 220 Planning Result)

4. In the **Alert Rules** section, enter the following data, as shown in Figure 8.31:
   - **Group Condition**
     Select **All Rule Groups are Satisfied**
   - **Rule Group 1**
     - Rule 1
       Final Safety Stock (from IO) > 120% Final Safety Stock Last Cycle (for IO)
     - Rule 2 (use the + icon to add a new rule)
       Final Safety Stock (from IO) < 80% Final Safety Stock Last Cycle (for IO)
   - **Condition**
     Select **Any Rule Is Satisfied**

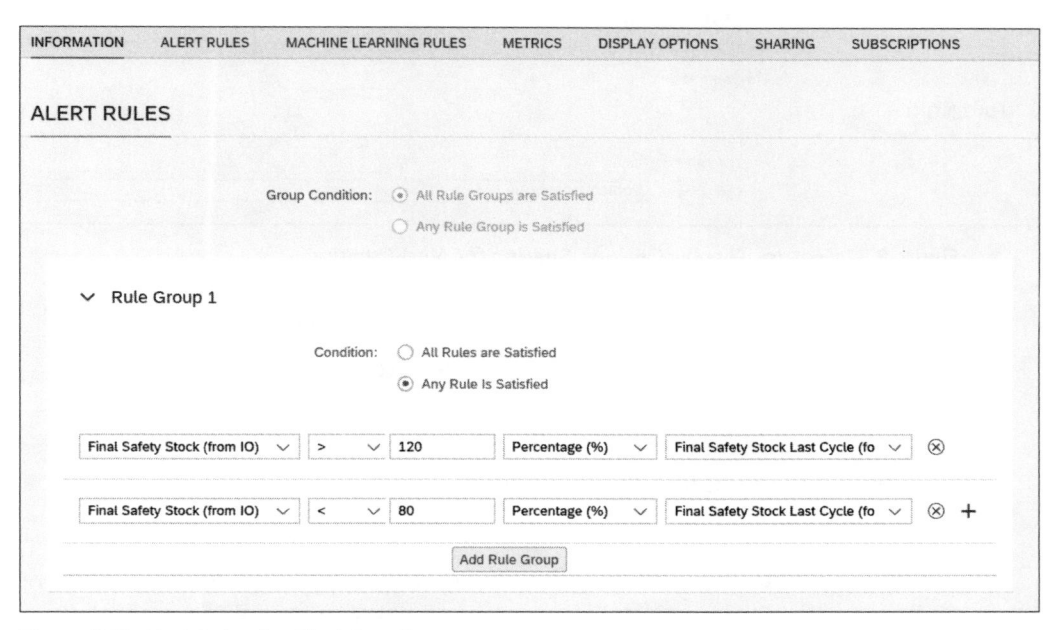

Figure 8.31 Alert Rules for Alert Creation

8   Measuring Inventory Performance

5. In the **Metrics** section, enter the following data, as shown in Figure 8.32:
   - **Final Safety Stock (from IO)**
   - **Final Safety Stock Last Cycle (for IO),**
   - **Recommended Safety Stock and Safety Stock Adj. (from IO)**

6. In the **Display Options** section, enter the following data, as shown in Figure 8.32:
   - **Target UoM**
     EA
   - **Target Currency**
     Blank
   - **Default Chart Type**
     Bar
   - **Complementary Charts**
     Blank

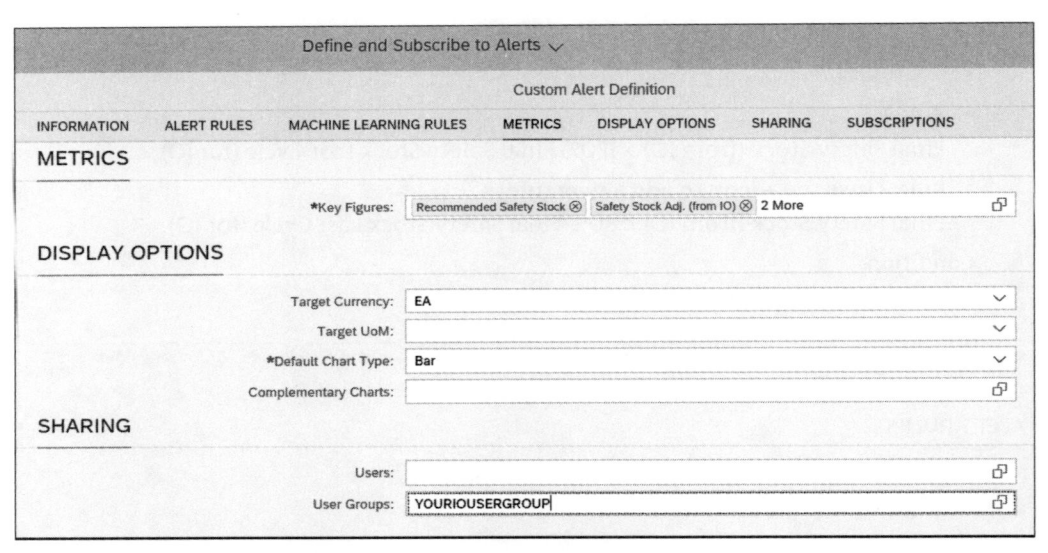

Figure 8.32 Metrics, Display Options, Sharing for Alert Creation

7. In the **Sharing** section, enter the following data, as shown in Figure 8.32:
   - **Users**
     Blank
   - **User Groups**
     "YOURIOUSERGROUP"

8. Subscribe to custom alert definitions and add filters if needed to restrict or further customize the alerts that will be triggered.

9. Click **Save**.

The Custom Alerts Overview app gives planners a graphical summary of alerts. Planners can use the Custom Alerts Overview app to view a summary of current alerts in

8.7 Create Custom Inventory Alerts

the form of a bar chart, and the alerts are clustered by subscriptions and either severity or category. The overview allows you to visualize which alerts will be triggered if the Monitor Custom Alerts app is executed. Planners can use filters to prioritize which alerts need to be processed first.

The Monitor Custom Alerts app allows users to calculate on-the-fly alerts to which they are subscribed to and display them in a comprehensive chart or table. With custom alerts, planners can analyze the charts and metrics to identify and resolve potential issues. They can also create a new alert or link an existing case to an alert to follow up on issues, delegate them, and resolve them. They can also filter custom alerts by case. Figure 8.33 shows the Custom Alerts Overview and Monitor Custom Alerts apps.

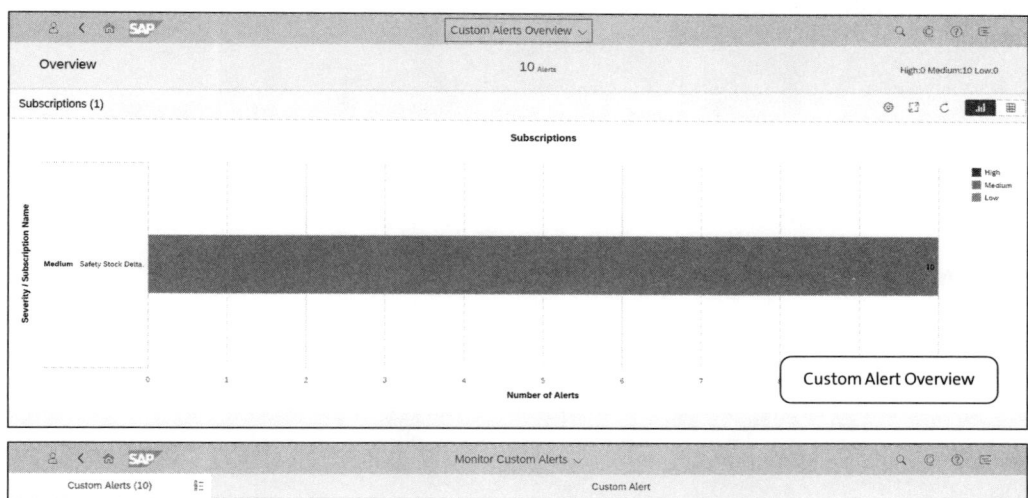

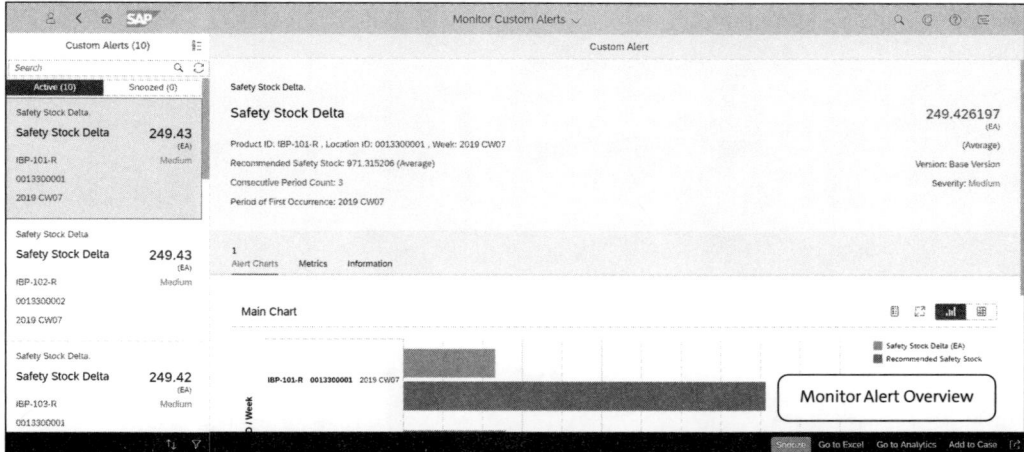

Figure 8.33 Custom Alerts Overview and Monitor Custom Alerts

309

8.8 Summary

In this chapter, we used the fictional ABBFI company to demonstrate how to execute the monthly inventory plan setup step by step in SAP IBP, from validating input to reviewing and root-cause analysis of inventory targets to proposing changes to finalizing the inventory plan. We discussed how to use analytics tools such as Excel templates, analytics charts, dashboards, and custom alerts to evaluate the success of the recurring inventory planning process. We noted some important references for commonly used inventory KPIs and inventory health assessments. In the next chapter, we'll focus on SAP IBP's what-if capabilities and show you how to evaluate the impact and sensitivity of the inventory drivers on your organization's inventory investment and strategy.

Chapter 9
Building Intuition and Conducting What-If Analysis

In a complex supply network, the intuition-based decision-making process can play a significant role in the choices we make. You build intuition with experience, but if you can simulate situations and analyze the results, as we'll discuss in this chapter, you can build your intuition and manage crises better.

Managing inventory can be an intimidating task for an organization with thousands of materials located at hundreds of facilities around the world. It is even tougher when the facilities are at different echelons of the organization's supply network. Managing inventory in a multiechelon network versus a single-stage network presents major challenges. Inventory managers try to balance the conflicting pressures of reducing inventory costs and operating costs, improving customer service levels and customer satisfaction, and at reducing lost sales.

As explained in Chapter 5, the inventory optimization operator, with a sophisticated algorithm in the background, helps you achieve lower inventory targets and safety stocks in a multiechelon environment. The inventory optimization algorithm balances the inventory costs and customer service levels across the multiple echelons in the supply network and recommends an optimal safety stock target. However, as the environment changes, the inventory strategies need to be revisited to find the optimal balance again. Any change to an inventory strategy at a single facility could lead to a far greater impact on inventory in the whole supply network. There are a lot of what-if strategies that inventory managers may think of, but they often rely on their gut feelings about what should be a starting point or what strategies they want to test.

Using SAP IBP for inventory, planners can create multiple scenarios and versions to test different inventory management strategies and do a comparative analysis against the current strategy or alternative strategies. This helps planners validate if

9   Building Intuition and Conducting What-If Analysis

their inventory strategies will work or not before implementing them. Inventory managers can also provide these alternative strategies and their assumptions to their management for approval, backed by the analytical power of SAP IBP.

In this chapter, we'll explain how a planner can create multiple scenarios and versions by changing the input parameters to the inventory optimization operator. We'll also explain how you can use Excel charts, SAP IBP analytics, and dashboard apps to compare the results of these scenarios and versions to help you make a better decision.

9.1   What-If Analysis with Versions and Scenarios

As explained in Chapter 3, versions and scenarios are the two features of SAP IBP that can help you perform what-if analysis. Both versions and scenarios can be used for what-if analysis, but which one you choose depends on the kind of simulation that you want to perform. For example, if you just want to create a simulation based on different supply variability or supplier lead time, you can choose a scenario for your what-if planning because it just involves changing the key figures for lead time and lead variability. However, if you want to model a completely a new facility, such as adding a new warehouse, or you want to set a node as stocking or nonstocking, or you want to change the safety stock policy, you may want to use a different version to allow for comparison with the baseline version. You can configure a version that allows different master data, so versions can help you model a completely different supply network or different safety stock policies for your simulations and help you evaluate the impact of the strategies you want to try.

Some organizations operate with three versions of demand: baseline, pessimistic, and optimistic demand. These versions of demand also affect the safety stock required to meet the desired safety stock level. Therefore, to evaluate the impact of the optimistic and pessimistic demand on inventory position and the supply capability of the organization, they operate with three versions of demand, inventory targets, and supply plans. In SAP IBP, these are configured as versions because they're required for every cycle by every business user. They also serves as input for sales and operations planning review meetings.

Most of the parameters that are inputs for inventory optimization, such as production minimum lot size, production incremental lot size, transportation minimum lot size, transportation incremental lot size, service level, and so on, can be managed via key figures instead of changing the master data. Therefore, you can use the scenarios feature in SAP IBP for most of your inventory management simulations. As explained in Chapter 3, scenarios offer ease of use and you can create as many scenarios as you want. You don't need any IT support, unlike for versions; a new version can only be created by your IT team via configuration. With the latest version of SAP IBP, you can also view scenarios and compare them with the baseline scenarios in the web-based Analytics SAP Fiori app.

In the subsequent sections, we'll explain how you can create multiple simulations in SAP IBP for your what-if analysis and how you can compare these simulations with the baseline scenario. We'll primarily be using the scenario feature of SAP IBP to create different simulations and using Excel and the Analytics app to compare against the baseline scenario.

9.2 Perform What-If Analysis

To perform any what-if analysis, an inventory manager should be aware of her organization's supply network. As explained in Chapter 4, there are many different types and levels of complexity of supply networks. Understanding the supply network plays an important role in intuition building. If the supply network is more distribution-focused, strategies to reduce inventory may be different compared to those for manufacturing-focused supply networks. It's also important to understand the competitive strategy of your organization because it also affects inventory decisions. For example, some organizations have higher inventory at customer-facing distribution centers to achieve the lowest lead time for a customer order.

For all what-if simulations and analysis in this chapter, we'll use an example of an electronic consumer goods company. Figure 9.1 shows the illustrative supply network of the company, which has one manufacturing plant in Beijing, China, supplying three distribution centers: Seattle in the Americas region, Berlin in the Europe region, and Hong Kong in the Asia Pacific region. The Seattle and Berlin distribution centers supply mostly retail customers, whereas the Hong Kong distribution center supplies industrial customers. There are two suppliers supplying the plant in Beijing.

Figure 9.2 shows the illustrative product structure of three finished goods sold from the three distribution centers. All finished products are manufactured in the plant in Beijing and are made of one raw material and one semifinished product. The semifinished products are made of two raw materials, which are provided by the two suppliers in Shanghai.

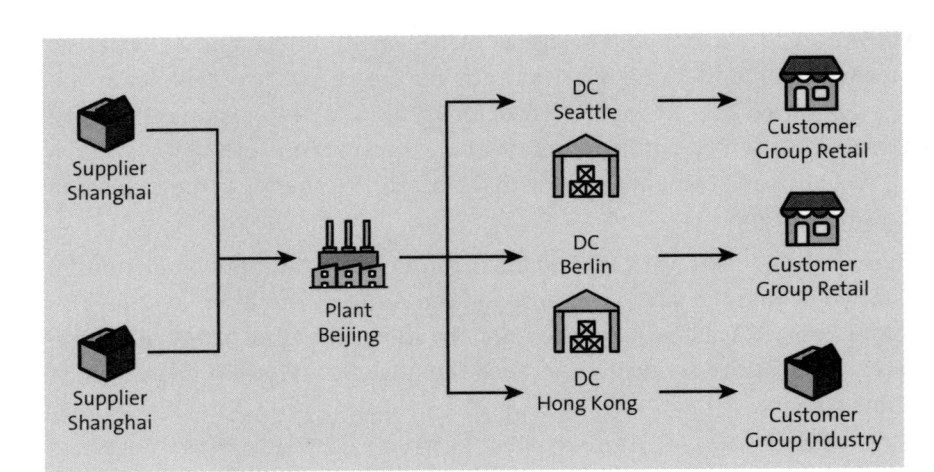

9   Building Intuition and Conducting What-If Analysis

Figure 9.1 Illustrative Supply Chain Network

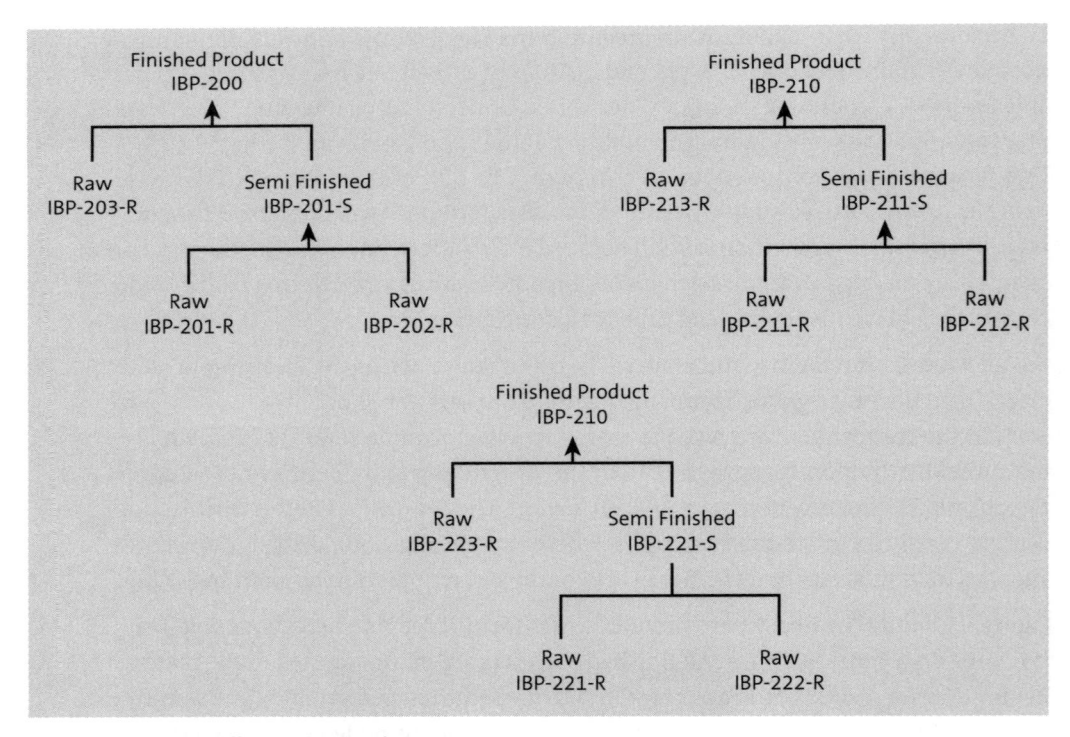

Figure 9.2 Illustrative Product Structure

As explained in Chapter 4, you can also view the supply chain network in the Supply Chain Network app using the web user interface of SAP IBP. Figure 9.3 shows the supply network in the Supply Chain Network app.

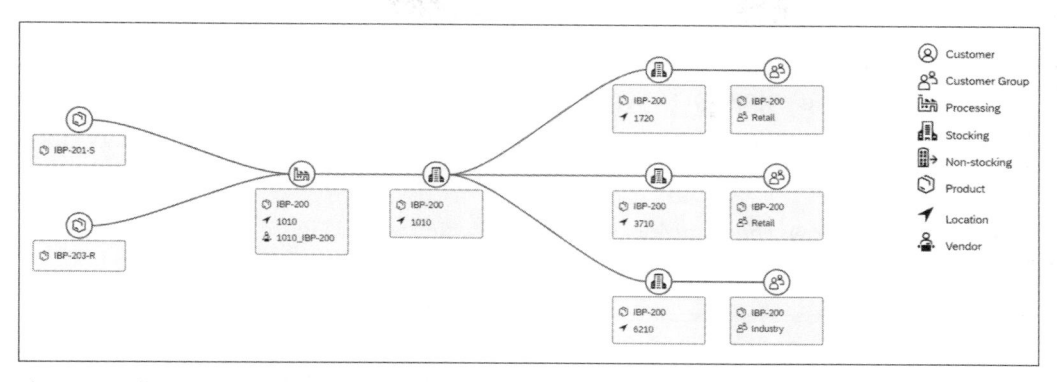

Figure 9.3 Illustrative Supply Chain Network Visualization in Supply Chain Network App

For this network, for the baseline version, the following key input parameters are considered:

- A customer service level of 99% for all customer groups and all the products.
- The inventory holding cost is the same for all the products, at the distribution center and at the plant.
- The Manage Forecast Error Calculations app will be used for inventory optimization to determine the forecast error.
- Transportation lead time is three weeks from Hongkong to Seattle, two weeks from Hong Kong to Berlin, and one week from Hong Kong to Singapore. All the locations have a transportation variability of 10%.
- The production lead time for each step is one week, with a variability of 10% error CV.

For the purposes of the evaluation, we'll use the standard key figures available: average expedites and average expedites value. For the safety stock, we'll use a configured key figure that averages the safety stock across the time periods. We've used a special configuration to average the safety stock and safety stock value. To configure an average across time key figure, follow these steps:

1. Create a copy of the WKPRODLOC planning level as WKPRODLOCWOROOT and remove the PRDID and LOCID as roots from this level.

9   Building Intuition and Conducting What-If Analysis

2. Set the average safety stock key figure equal to the recommended safety stock at the WKPRODLOC level.
3. Create an aggregate calculation of average safety stock at WKPRODLOCWOROOT as the sum of average safety stock at WKPRODLOC from the previous step.
4. For the request level calculation, create an average aggregation of average safety stock at the WKPRODLOCWOROOT level.
5. Repeat steps 1–4, but this time creating a configuration for the average safety stock value key figure instead of the average across time key figure.

Figure 9.4 shows the planning level of the key figure, and Figure 9.5 shows the key figure configuration of the average safety stock.

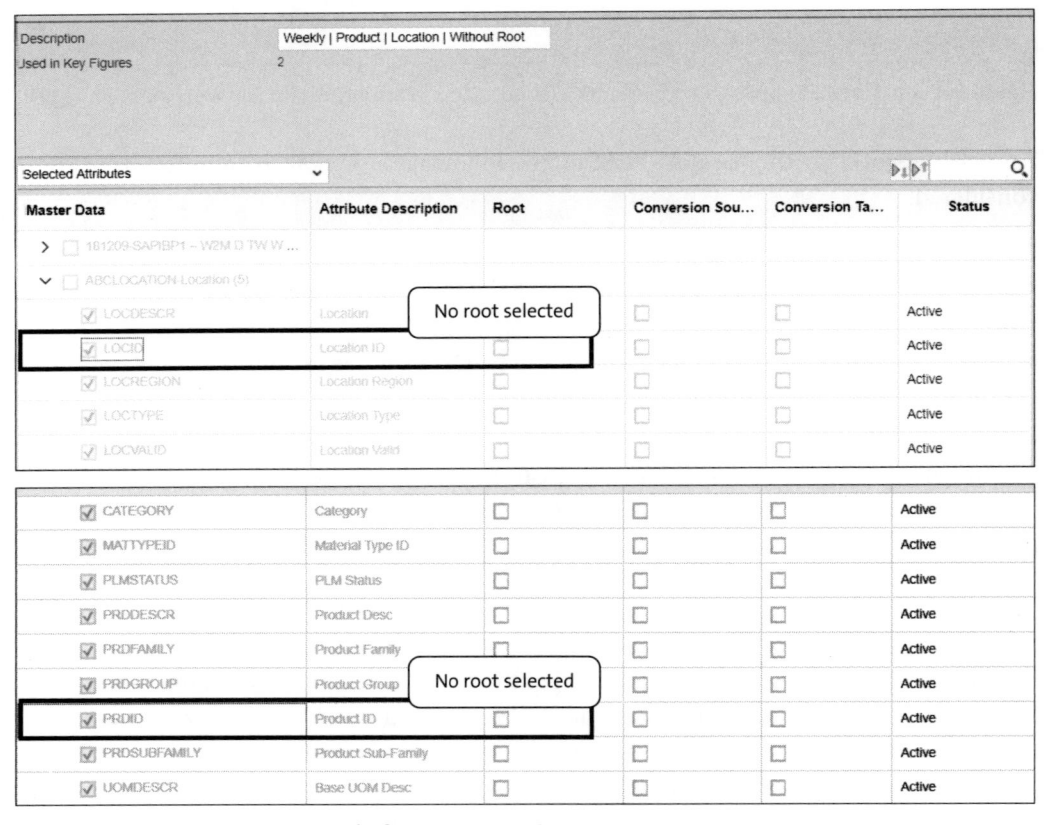

Figure 9.4 Planning Level of Average Key Figure

9.2 Perform What-If Analysis

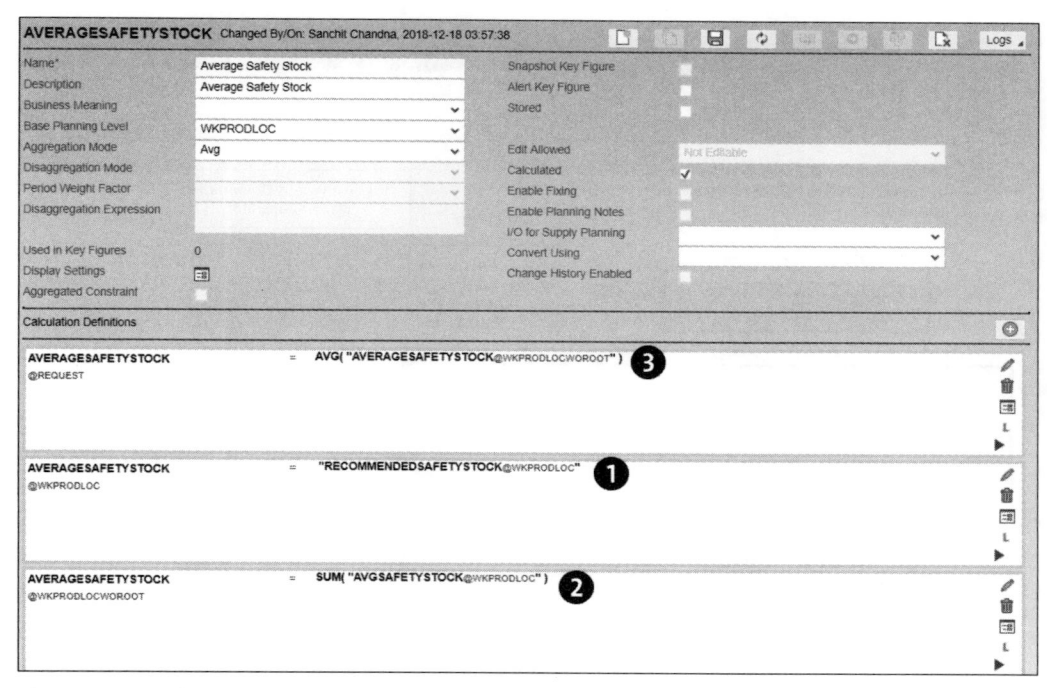

Figure 9.5 Configuration for Average Safety Stock Key Figure

To generate the safety stock and average expedites, you'll have to execute the following operators: global inventory optimization, calculate inventory target component, and expected lost demand. Figure 9.6 shows how to execute the planning operators. To execute the inventory optimization algorithms, click the **Inventory Optimization** button; select the operators you want to execute; select the scenario, version, and planning unit for which you want to execute the algorithm; and click **Next**. Once the baseline scenario is generated, review the recommended safety stock, average safety stock, and average expedite for the baseline scenario.

Figure 9.7 shows the planning view, which is a summary view of the safety stock at the product family level.

To have an average view of the safety stock for one year and average expedites, you can use the yearly period. Note that recommended safety stock, when aggregated, will take the safety stock from the last period, whereas average safety stock will be an average of safety stock across time periods. Average expedites are summed over time periods. For our simulation analysis, we'll be focusing on a yearly bucket, which will make the analysis of results easier.

317

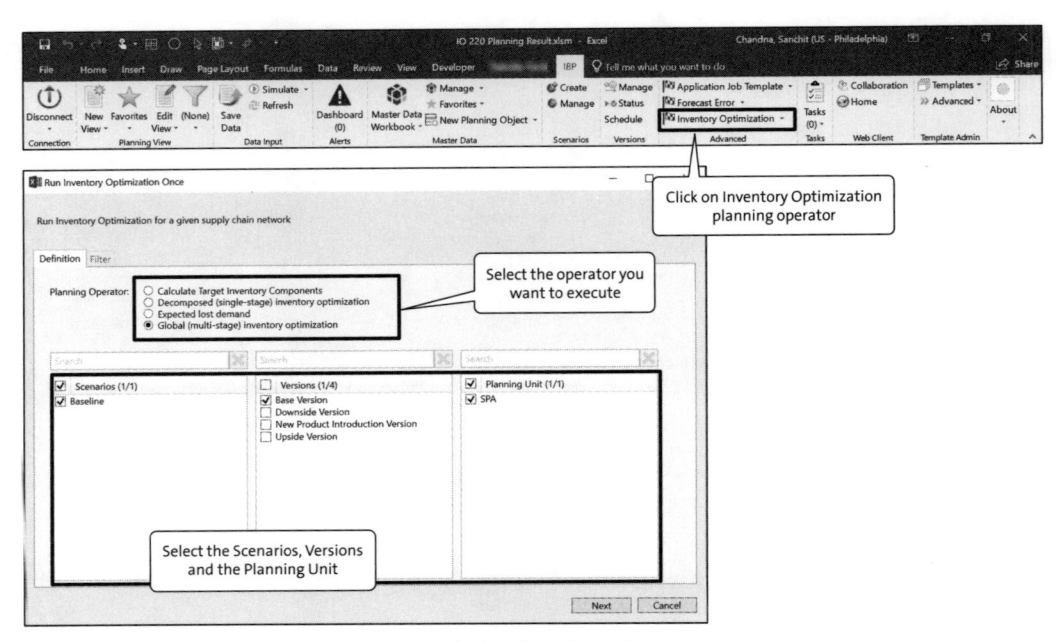

9 Building Intuition and Conducting What-If Analysis

Figure 9.6 Execute Inventory Optimization Algorithms

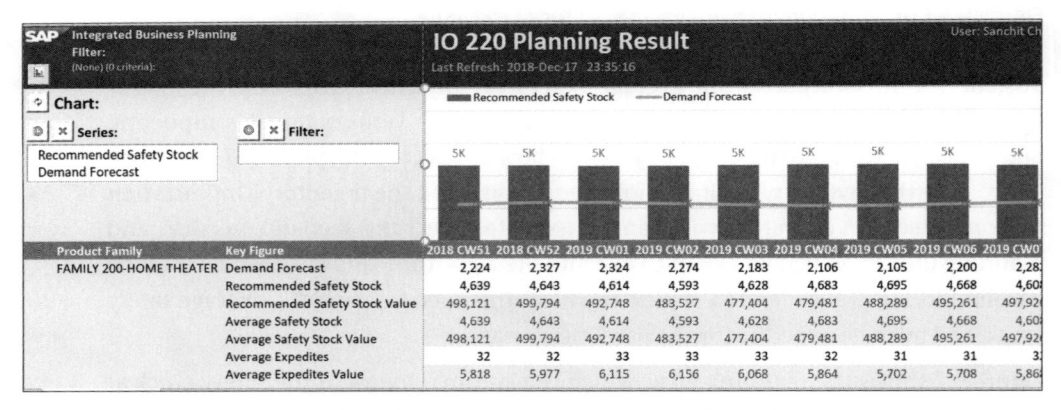

Figure 9.7 Summary View of Safety Stock at Product Family Level

Figure 9.8 shows the results in yearly buckets. Note that the average safety stock and average safety stock key figures are an average of recommended safety stock across the time periods in a year, whereas the recommended safety stock is the safety stock from the last bucket of the year.

9.3 Simulating Situations

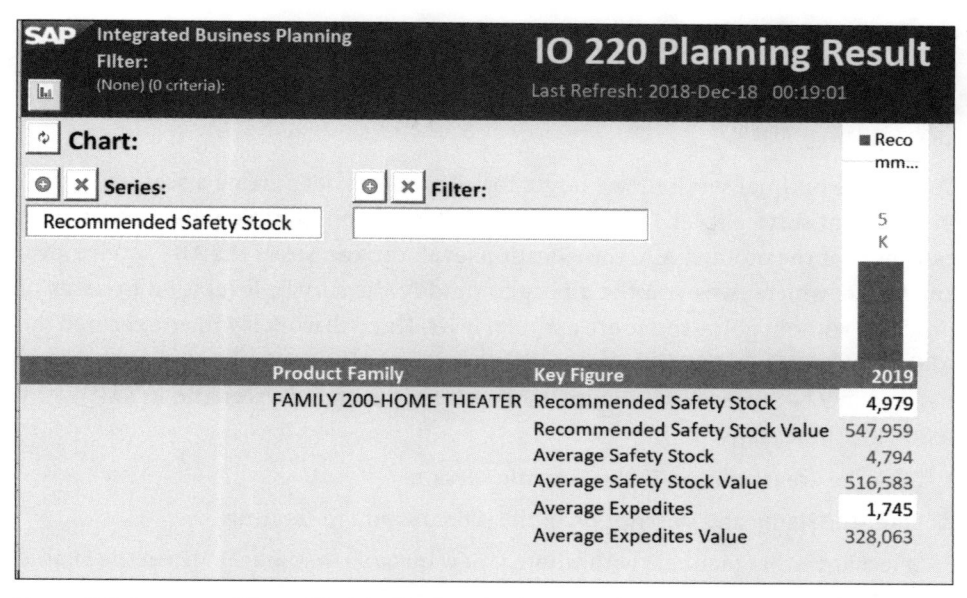

	2019
Product Family	
FAMILY 200-HOME THEATER	
Recommended Safety Stock	4,979
Recommended Safety Stock Value	547,959
Average Safety Stock	4,794
Average Safety Stock Value	516,583
Average Expedites	1,745
Average Expedites Value	328,063

Figure 9.8 Summary View of Safety Stock at Product Family Level in Yearly Bucket

9.3 Simulating Situations

In any planning organization, planners strive to be well informed about unforeseen and complex situations that might occur in future. There can be numerous situations and alternative plans of action that planners might want to analyze before presenting options to their management in their review meetings. In this section, we'll explain how you can create different scenarios for your analysis and how you can build your intuition along the way.

9.3.1 Service Level

In our baseline scenario, we set up the service level to be 99% for all products. In Figure 9.7, you can see that we carry a huge amount of safety stock, which is almost double the demand in units when we operate at a service level of 99%. If you've been given the task to reduce the total cost of inventory, you'll have to think through a lot of different scenarios to reduce the inventory cost. Recall that in Chapter 2 we talked about the relationship between the cost of inventory and service level. The cost of inventory increases exponentially when you try to increase the service level.

9   Building Intuition and Conducting What-If Analysis

As an inventory manager, you may have an intuition that reducing the service level will lead to a decrease in the safety stock and hence the inventory cost will reduce. You may want to start by finding the optimal balance between safety stock and average expedites.

To find the optimal service level target for all products, let's create a scenario with a 97% percent service level. In the standard-delivered configuration, the service level can be set at the product ABC classification level. You can select the ABC service level key figure, which gives you the ability to modify the service level for all classes of products without going to a more granular level. This will work if you've executed the ABC classification in SAP IBP. We'll use the standard ABC service level to create a scenario for a 97% service level. Figure 9.9 shows how to create a scenario in SAP IBP by following these steps:

1. Click the **Create** button in the **Scenario** section.
2. Enter the **Name** and **Description** of the scenario you're creating.
3. Select any other planners with whom you want to share the scenario in the **Shared With** area and click **OK**.

You'll see a **Scenario** column added to your planning view.

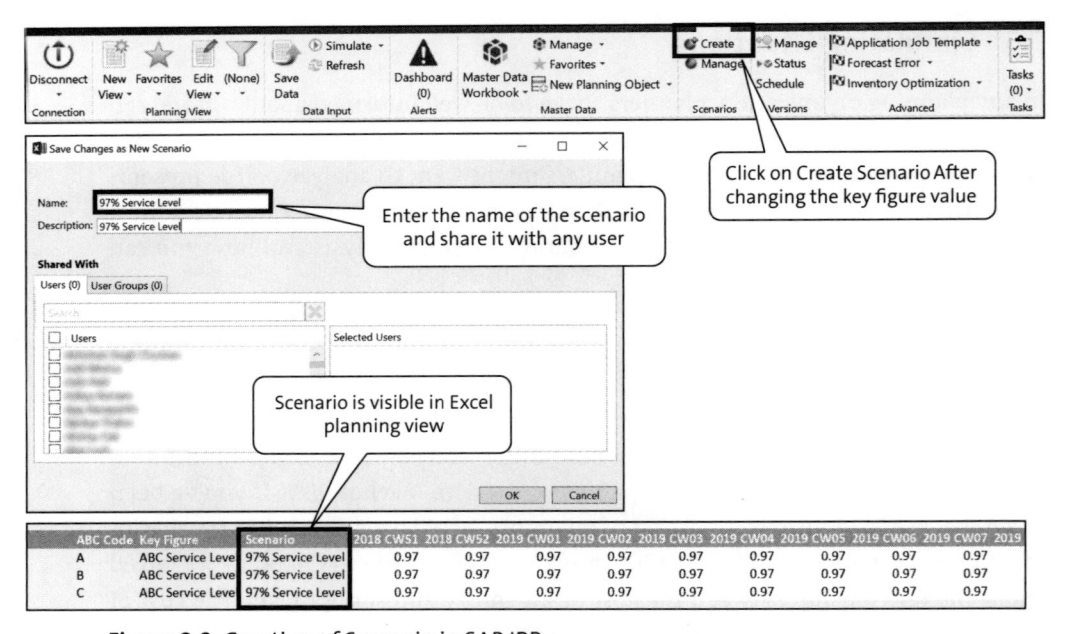

Figure 9.9 Creation of Scenario in SAP IBP

9.3 Simulating Situations

Similarly, you can create multiple scenarios for different service levels. By clicking the **Inventory Optimization** button, you can execute the operator for multiple scenarios simultaneously as well. Figure 9.10 shows the selection screen of the inventory optimization planning operators to execute the operator for multiple scenarios. Click the **Inventory Optimization** button in the **Advanced** section; select the invenoty optimization **Planning Operator** you want to execute; select all the **Scenarios** for which you want to execute the algorigthm, along with the **Versions** and the **Planning Unit**; and click **Next**.

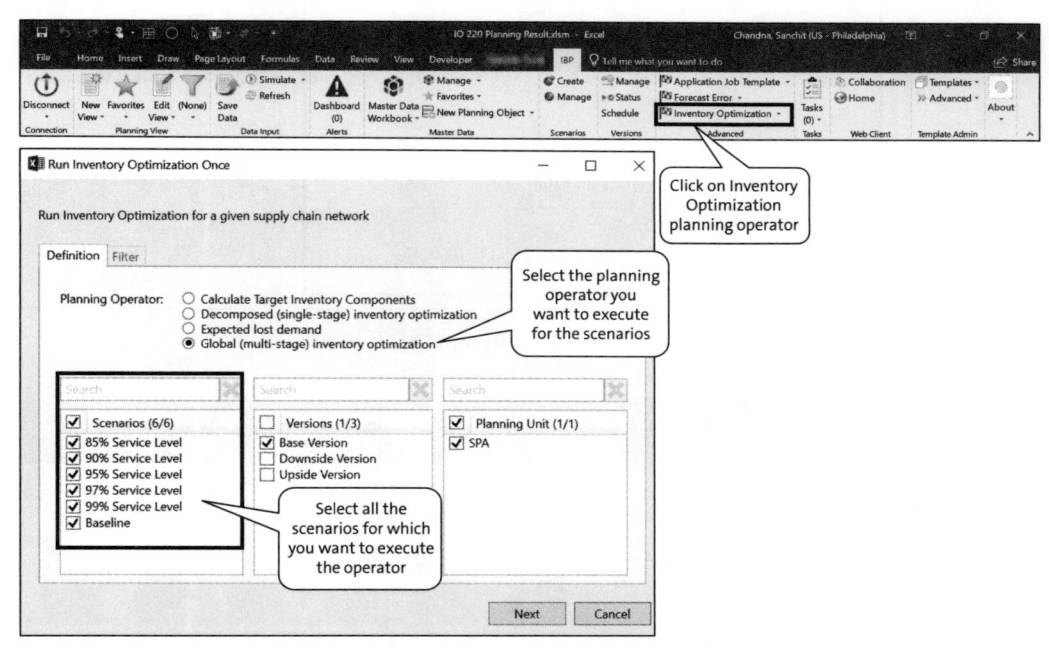

Figure 9.10 Execution of Planning Operator for Different Scenarios

To do a comparison in Excel, you can select all the scenarios you created in the edit planning view. Figure 9.11 shows how to create a planning view and change the layout for an easy comparison. To create a comparison view, click **Edit Planning View**, click the **Scenario** button, select the scenarios you want to view for comparison, click **Layout** and change the layout if required, and click **OK**.

Figure 9.12 shows the comparison of the scenarios we've created. In our example, you can see that our ideal service level should be around 97%. This is the service level at which we achieve an optimal balance between safety stock cost and average expedites.

321

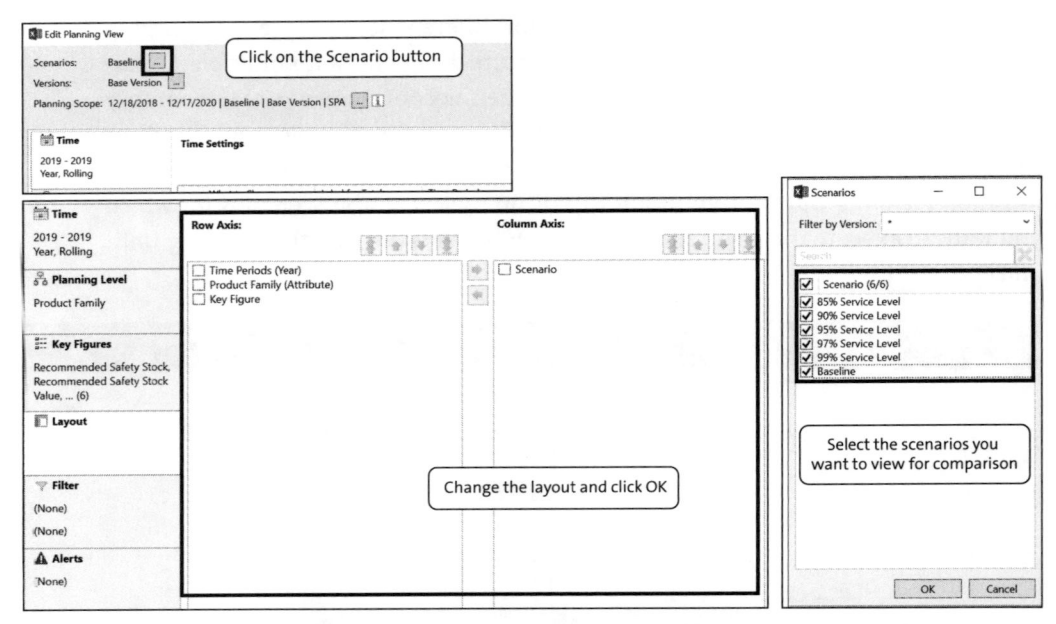

9   Building Intuition and Conducting What-If Analysis

Figure 9.11 Planning View Configuration to Compare Different Scenarios Easily

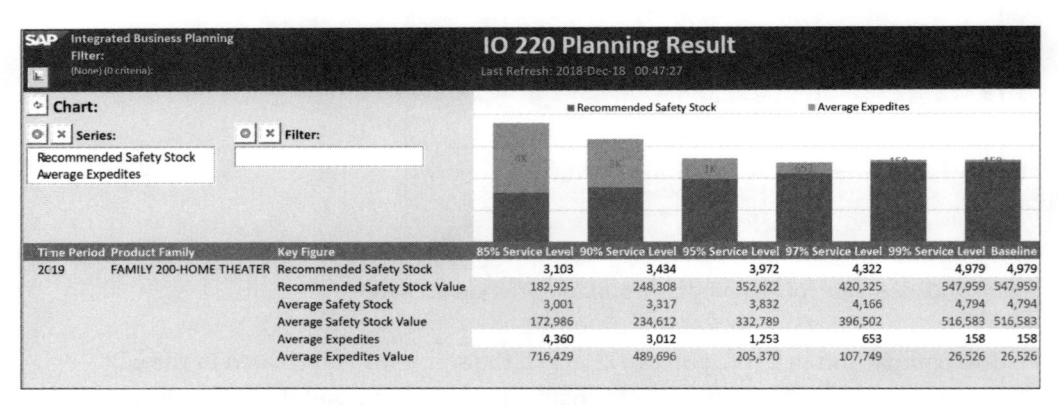

Time Period	Product Family	Key Figure	85% Service Level	90% Service Level	95% Service Level	97% Service Level	99% Service Level	Baseline
2019	FAMILY 200-HOME THEATER	Recommended Safety Stock	3,103	3,434	3,972	4,322	4,979	4,979
		Recommended Safety Stock Value	182,925	248,308	352,622	420,325	547,959	547,959
		Average Safety Stock	3,001	3,317	3,832	4,166	4,794	4,794
		Average Safety Stock Value	172,986	234,612	332,789	396,502	516,583	516,583
		Average Expedites	4,360	3,012	1,253	653	158	158
		Average Expedites Value	716,429	489,696	205,370	107,749	26,526	26,526

Figure 9.12 Comparison of Different Scenarios in Excel Planning View

You can also create an analytics chart in the web user interface to view these scenarios and compare them with the baseline.

Figure 9.13 shows the chart in the Analytics app. This is a stacked column chart in the SAP Fiori app.

9.3 Simulating Situations

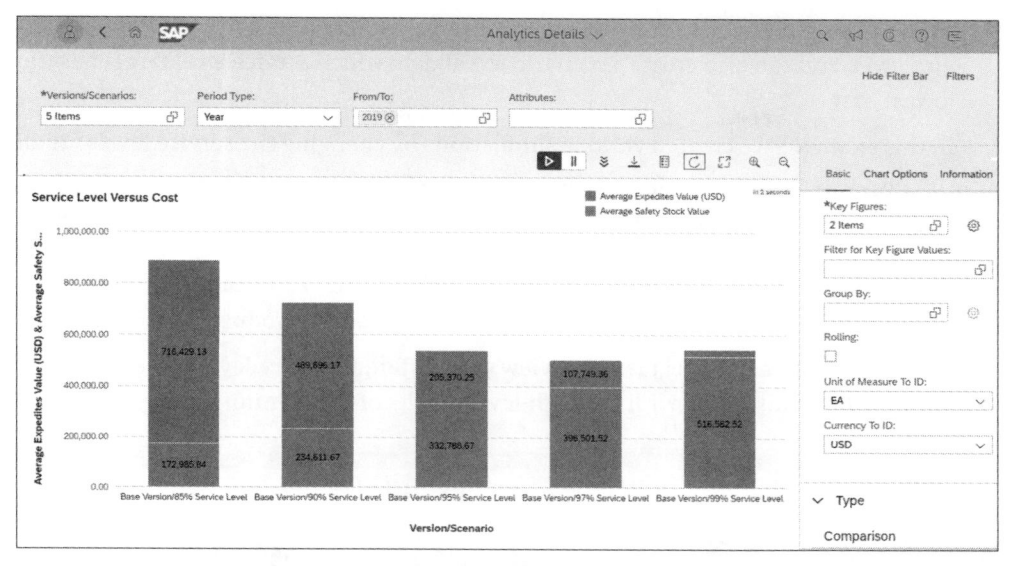

Figure 9.13 Scenario Comparison Chart in Analytics App in Web UI

Figure 9.14 shows the same information with a different chart type. The chart type in Figure 9.14 is a dual-axis line chart.

Figure 9.14 Scenario Comparison Dual-Axis Line Chart in Analytics App in Web UI

323

9   Building Intuition and Conducting What-If Analysis

In our example, it's clear that the organization should really have a 96% to 98% service level. You can also create a scenario to validate which service level target has the lowest cost.

In this example, we created various simulations by changing the service levels for all the products across the organization. Some organizations use differential management strategies in which all products or customers are treated not equally but based on the revenue they generate. For example, many organizations use ABC classifications for products with differential service levels. In this classification system, products classified as A have a higher service level than B and C products.

Figure 9.15 shows an Excel planning view with different service levels based on product classifications, along with the high-level results of the planning run.

ABC Code	Key Figure	Scenario	2018 CW51	2018 CW52	2019 CW01	2019 CW02	2019 CW03	2019 CW04	2019 CW05	2019 CW06	2019 CW07	2019 CW08
A	ABC Service Level	ABC Service Levels	0.99	0.99	0.99	0.99	0.99	0.99	0.99	0.99	0.99	0.99
B	ABC Service Level	ABC Service Levels	0.95	0.95	0.95	0.95	0.95	0.95	0.95	0.95	0.95	0.95
C	ABC Service Level	ABC Service Levels	0.92	0.92	0.92	0.92	0.92	0.92	0.92	0.92	0.92	0.92

SAP Integrated Business Planning
Filter:
(None) (0 criteria)

Chart:
Series: Recommended Safety Stock Value, Average Safety Stock Value
Filter:

Scenario Comparison
Last Refresh: 2018-Dec-18 17:34:04

■ Average Safety Stock Value
■ Recommended Safety Stock Value

Time Period	Product Family	Key Figure	ABC Service Levels	Baseline
2019	FAMILY 200-HOME THEATER	Recommended Safety Stock	4,023	4,979
		Recommended Safety Stock Value	323,384	547,959
		Average Safety Stock	3,898	4,794
		Average Safety Stock Value	307,601	516,583
		Average Expedites	1,102	158
		Average Expedites Value	252,515	26,526

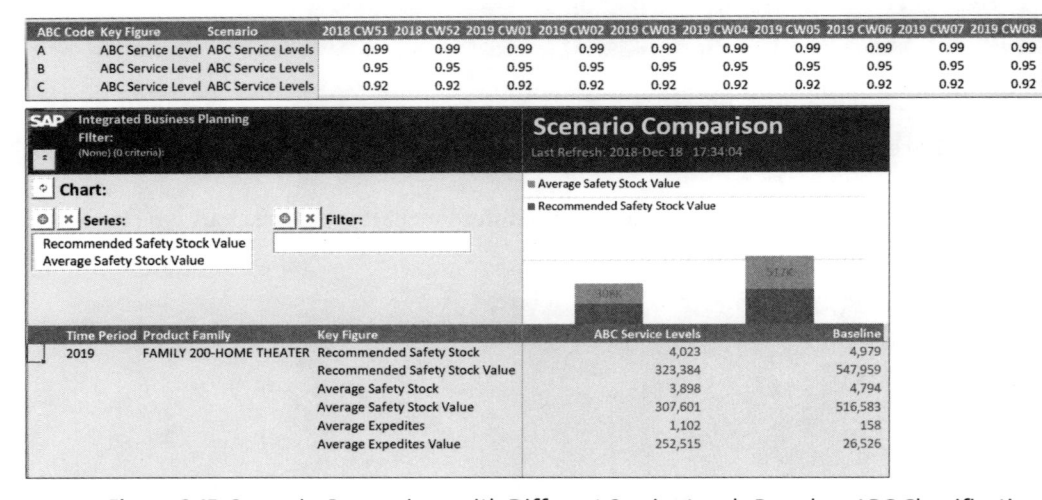

Figure 9.15 Scenario Comparison with Different Service Levels Based on ABC Classification

As you can see in Figure 9.15, the cost is significantly lower than our baseline, which had the same service level for all products. You can also create an analytics chart in the Analytics SAP Fiori app in the web user interface, as explained in Chapter 3. Figure 9.16 shows the analytics chart in the web user interface, comparing the safety stock value and average expedites value across different classes of products. Figure 9.17 shows the same comparison in units.

9.3 Simulating Situations

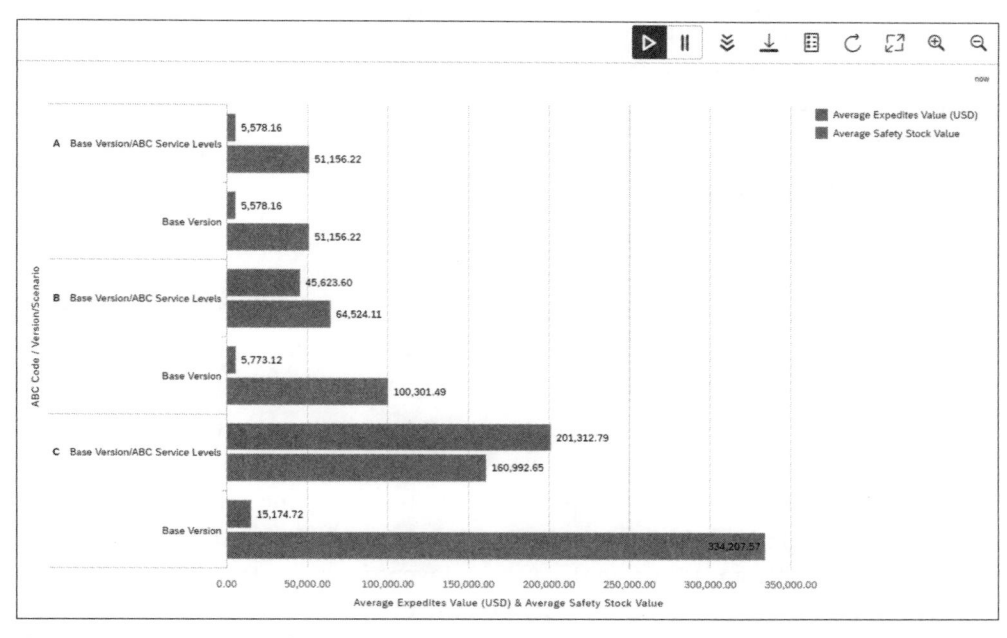

Figure 9.16 Comparison of Average Safety Stock Value and Average Expedites Value in USD

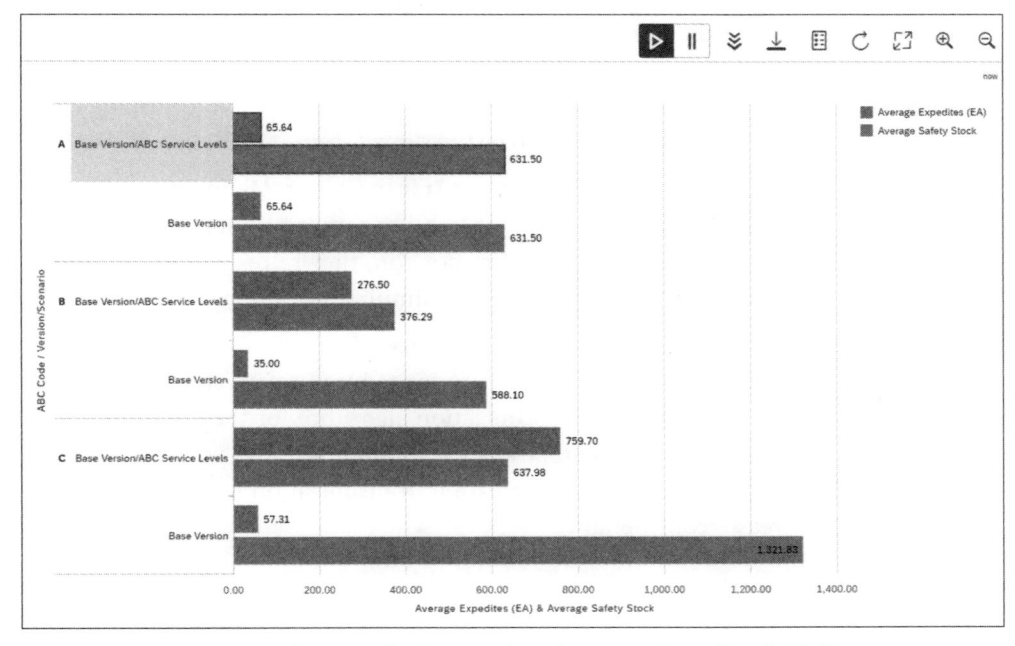

Figure 9.17 Comparison of Average Safety Stock and Average Expedites in Units

325

9 Building Intuition and Conducting What-If Analysis

Note the recommended safety stock in this simulation for the different service levels: A is the same as for the A product, and the safety stock for C products is considerably lower compared to the baseline version.

9.3.2 Distribution Lot Size

So far we've focused on the service level for all our simulations, but the service level isn't the only reason to increase safety stock. As explained in Chapter 2 and Chapter 5, there are numerous drivers that lead to higher or lower safety stock. Inventory managers can evaluate the impact of each of these drivers and take action on the parameters that are impacting the safety stock quantity.

Let's consider distribution lot size. For the shipments to the United States and Europe, the lead times are three and two weeks, respectively. The logistics team has shown potential savings in shipping cost by increasing the minimum shipment quantity to 50 units. As you saw in Chapter 2 and Chapter 6, increasing the transportation lot size has an impact on the average inventory you carry, but this is also an opportunity to reduce the safety stock because the distribution lot size can act as a buffer.

Let's evaluate the model with minimum shipping quantitites of 50, 100, 150, and 200 to see the impact on the safety stock in the whole network. For this scenario, we'll change the transport minimum lot size key figure and transport incremental lot size to these quantities. Note that the transport minimum lot size and transport incremental lot size don't necessarily have to be the same.

Figure 9.18 shows the changed values for the **Transportation Minimum Lot Size** and **Transportation Incremental Lot Size** key figures. For simulation purposes, you don't have to change these values for the entire horizon; they're read from the current bucket only. This makes it very easy to create a simulation.

Let's look at the average recommended safety stock for these scenarios. Increasing the transportation lot size is an opportunity for reduced safety stocks. Figure 9.19 shows the results of the inventory optimization algorithm for these scenarios with different minimum and incremental transportation lot sizes. As you can see in the scenario comparison view, with the increase in transportation lot size, the average safety stock decreases considerably.

9.3 Simulating Situations

Ship-From Loc. Desc.	Location	Product ID	Key Figure	Scenario	2018 CW51	2018 CW52	2019 CW01
Plant Beijing	DC Hong Kong	IBP-200	Transportation Minimum Lot Size	Lot Size 50	1	1	1
			Transportation Incremental Lot Size	Lot Size 50	1	1	1
		IBP-210	Transportation Minimum Lot Size	Lot Size 50	1	1	1
			Transportation Incremental Lot Size	Lot Size 50	1	1	1
		IBP-220	Transportation Minimum Lot Size	Lot Size 50	1	1	1
			Transportation Incremental Lot Size	Lot Size 50	1	1	1
	DC Rotterdam	IBP-200	Transportation Minimum Lot Size	Lot Size 50	50	1	1
			Transportation Incremental Lot Size	Lot Size 50	50	1	1
		IBP-210	Transportation Minimum Lot Size	Lot Size 50	50	1	1
			Transportation Incremental Lot Size	Lot Size 50	50	1	1
		IBP-220	Transportation Minimum Lot Size	Lot Size 50	50	1	1
			Transportation Incremental Lot Size	Lot Size 50	50	1	1
	DC Seattle	IBP-200	Transportation Minimum Lot Size	Lot Size 50	50	1	1
			Transportation Incremental Lot Size	Lot Size 50	50	1	1
		IBP-210	Transportation Minimum Lot Size	Lot Size 50	50	1	1
			Transportation Incremental Lot Size	Lot Size 50	50	1	1

Figure 9.18 Changes to Transportation Minimum and Incremental Lot Size for Simulations

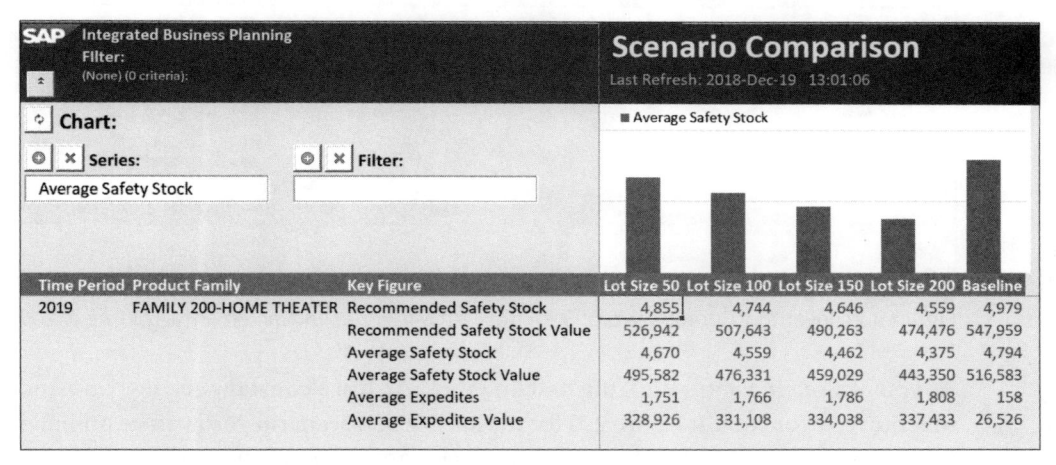

Time Period	Product Family	Key Figure	Lot Size 50	Lot Size 100	Lot Size 150	Lot Size 200	Baseline
2019	FAMILY 200-HOME THEATER	Recommended Safety Stock	4,855	4,744	4,646	4,559	4,979
		Recommended Safety Stock Value	526,942	507,643	490,263	474,476	547,959
		Average Safety Stock	4,670	4,559	4,462	4,375	4,794
		Average Safety Stock Value	495,582	476,331	459,029	443,350	516,583
		Average Expedites	1,751	1,766	1,786	1,808	158
		Average Expedites Value	328,926	331,108	334,038	337,433	26,526

Figure 9.19 Comparison of Scenarios with Different Minimum and Incremental Transportation Lot Size

Now let's look at the impact of the increased distribution lot size on the other inventory components. As you learned in Chapter 6, in SAP IBP for inventory you can calculate the inventory components using the planning operator. Let's compare the scenario with a lot size of 200 with the baseline. Figure 9.20 shows the graphical view of the inventory components: recommended safety stock, cycle stock, pipeline stock, and on-hand average stock. On-hand average in this particular example is equal to the sum of recommended safety stock, cycle stock, and pipeline stock. Similarly, Figure 9.21 shows the inventory components key figure for the scenario with a lot size of 200.

327

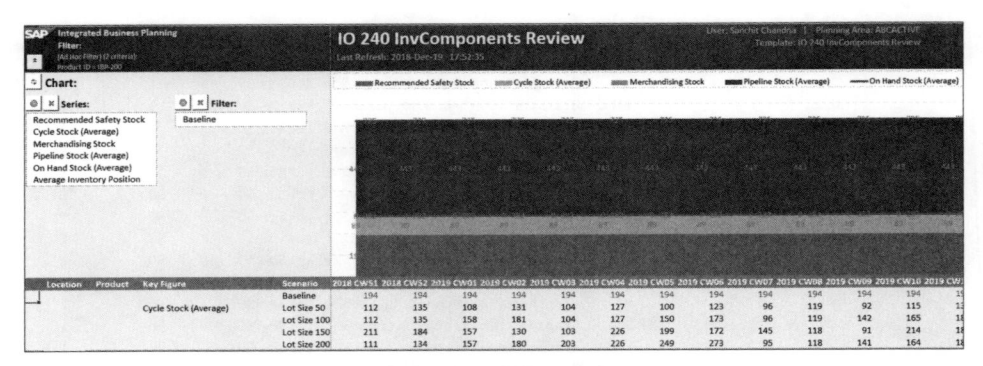

9   Building Intuition and Conducting What-If Analysis

Figure 9.20 Inventory Components of Baseline Scenario

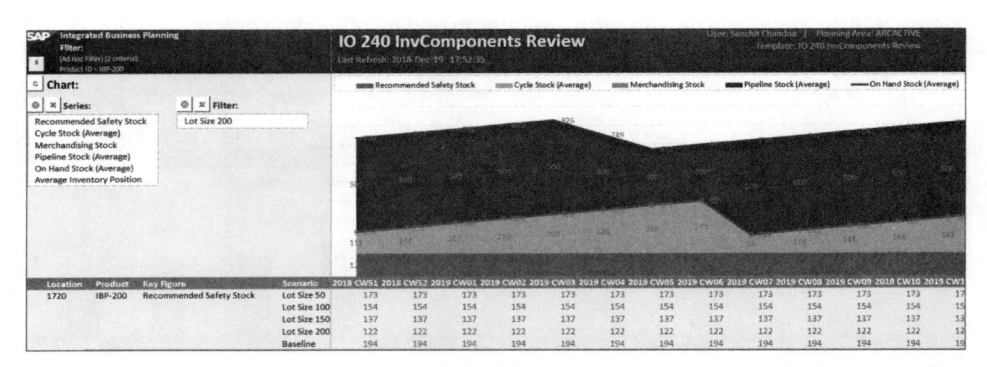

Figure 9.21 Inventory Components of Scenario with Minimum and Incremental Lot Size of 200

As you can see in Figure 9.20, the baseline scenario has a constant average on-hand inventory; if you look at Figure 9.21 for the lot size 200 scenario, the average on-hand fluctuates. The latter scenario has a lower recommended safety stock, but the on-hand inventory is quite due to dips and high points. The cycle stock in the baseline scenario is a constant value and lower than the scenario with the increased lot size. Note in the lot size 200 scenario that the cycle stock almost doubles in quantity in some weeks when compared to the lowest value of the cycle stock in the horizon.

9.3.3   Periods between Review

So far we've shown the impact of customer service level and distribution lot size on safety stock. One of the other drivers for increased safety stock is periods between review (PBR). In our baseline scenario, we had a constant PBR of one for all products. This parameter is totally in our control. Organizations use differential strategies for

PBRs as well, with ABC and XYZ classifications as the most commonly used methods. As discussed in Chapter 2, you can have different strategies to handle these segments of products. Class A items can have a lower PBR compared to C class items.

Let's change the PBR of all finished goods to 2, 3, 4, and 5 and compare these scenarios to understand the impact of PBR on the network-level safety stock. To change the PBR for the scenarios, add the periods between reviews key figure in your planning view. As for distribution lot size, you have to change the PBR of the items at the location level for the first period only. While running the operator, the first period is read to generate the recommended safety stock. This is true for almost all the input parameters for the Inventory Optimization operator. This makes scenarios easy to use for inventory optimization in SAP IBP.

Figure 9.22 shows the PBR changed to two weeks for the finished products at the DCs in our representative supply network. The PBR is changed for the current bucket only. Similarly, we'll change the PBR to 3, 4, and 5 weeks and create separate scenarios for different PBRs.

Location ID	Material Type ID	Product ID	Key Figure	Scenario	2018 CW51	2018 CW52	2019 CW01	2019 CW02	2019 CW03
1720	FG	IBP-200	Periods Between Reviews	PBR 2 Weeks	2	1	1	1	1
		IBP-210	Periods Between Reviews	PBR 2 Weeks	2	1	1	1	1
		IBP-220	Periods Between Reviews	PBR 2 Weeks	2	1	1	1	1
3710	FG	IBP-200	Periods Between Reviews	PBR 2 Weeks	2	1	1	1	1
		IBP-210	Periods Between Reviews	PBR 2 Weeks	2	1	1	1	1
		IBP-220	Periods Between Reviews	PBR 2 Weeks	2	1	1	1	1
6210	FG	IBP-200	Periods Between Reviews	PBR 2 Weeks	2	1	1	1	1
		IBP-210	Periods Between Reviews	PBR 2 Weeks	2	1	1	1	1
		IBP-220	Periods Between Reviews	PBR 2 Weeks	2	1	1	1	1

Figure 9.22 PBR Changed to Two Weeks for Scenario

Now let's compare the results of the different periods between review. We'll compare the recommended safety stock across the time periods for simplicity. To do this comparison, you can create an analytics chart in the Analytics SAP Fiori app with the appropriate filters. Figure 9.23 shows a graphical comparison of recommended safety stock filtered for the finished products at the distribution center. As the PBR increases, the variability in the recommended safety stock for the finished products increases; that is, there is a larger degree of fluctuations in the amount of safety stock carried across time periods. There is no direct relationship between the amount of increase in the safety stock and an increase in PBR. This is because PBR has implications for pooling of inventory, especially at a fill rate service level.

Figure 9.24 shows the comparison of recommended safety stock for the entire supply chain with no filter for products. As the PBR increases, the variability grows across the supply chain.

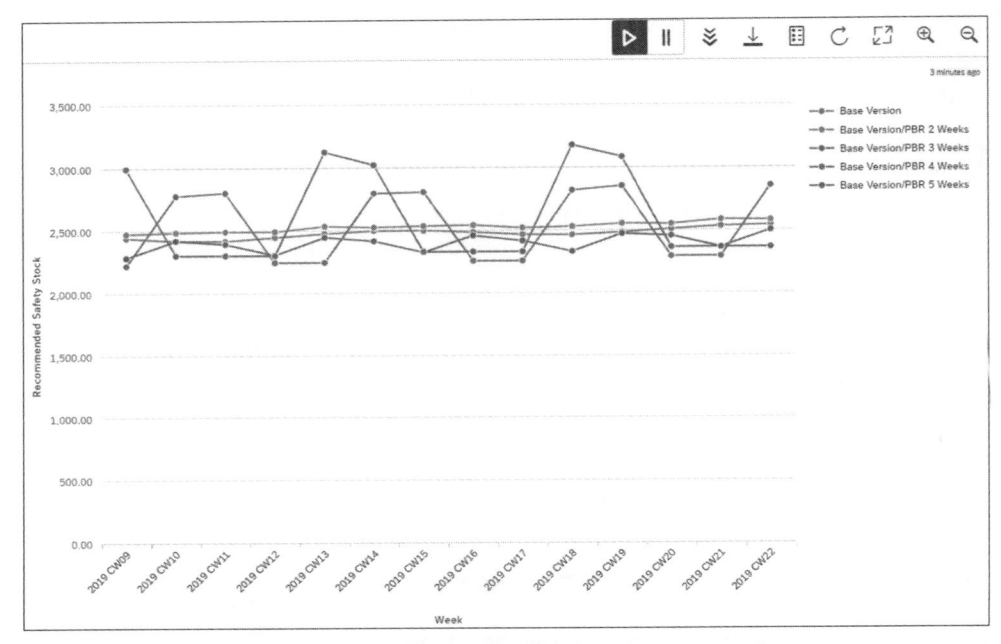

9   Building Intuition and Conducting What-If Analysis

Figure 9.23 Comparison of Recommended Safety Stock for Finished Goods at DCs

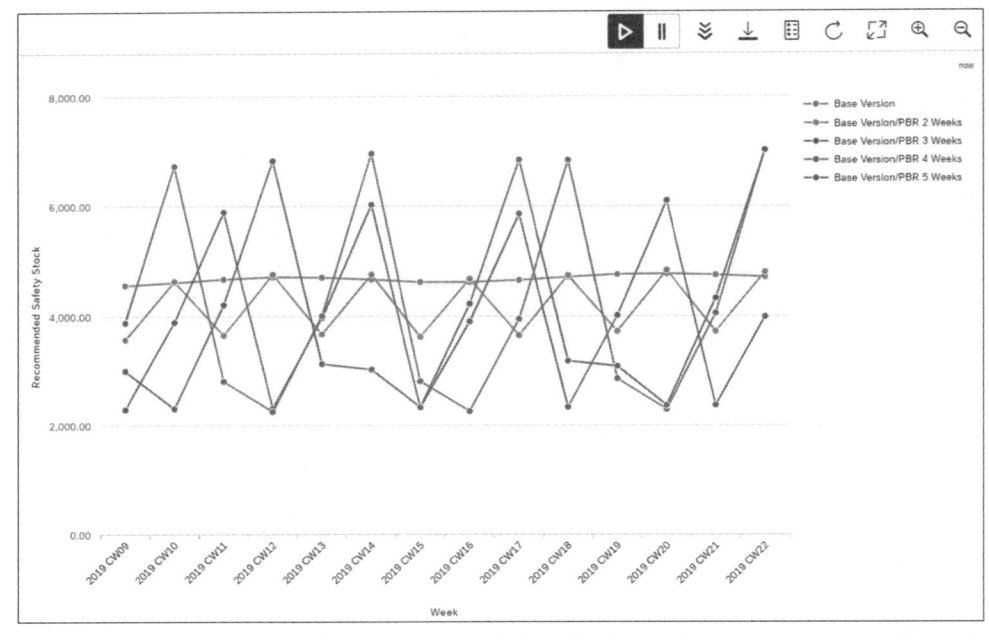

Figure 9.24 Comparison of Recommended Safety Stock for All Products in Supply Network

330

9.3 Simulating Situations

Although there is a lot of fluctuation across the time buckets, let's compare the average safety stock in a year for all scenarios. To do this, you can create an analytics bar chart with a filter for the year and compare the relevant scenarios. Figure 9.25 shows the comparison of the average safety stock in units and value.

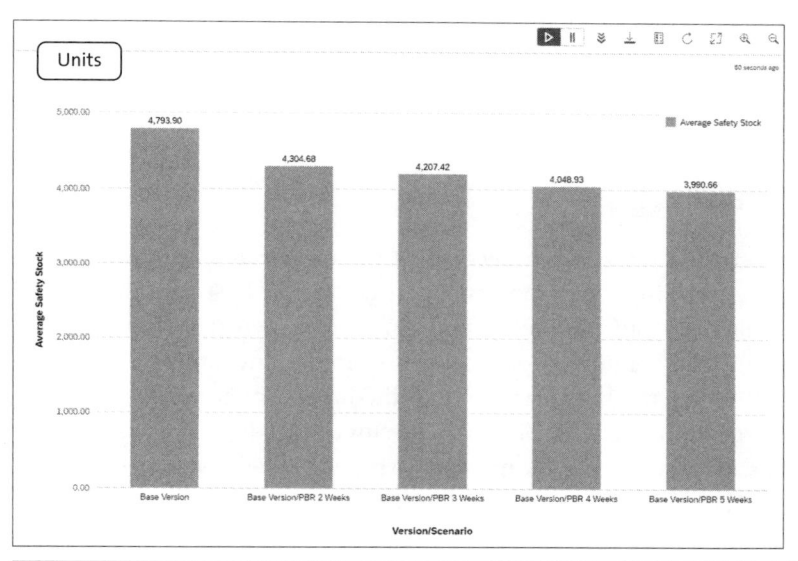

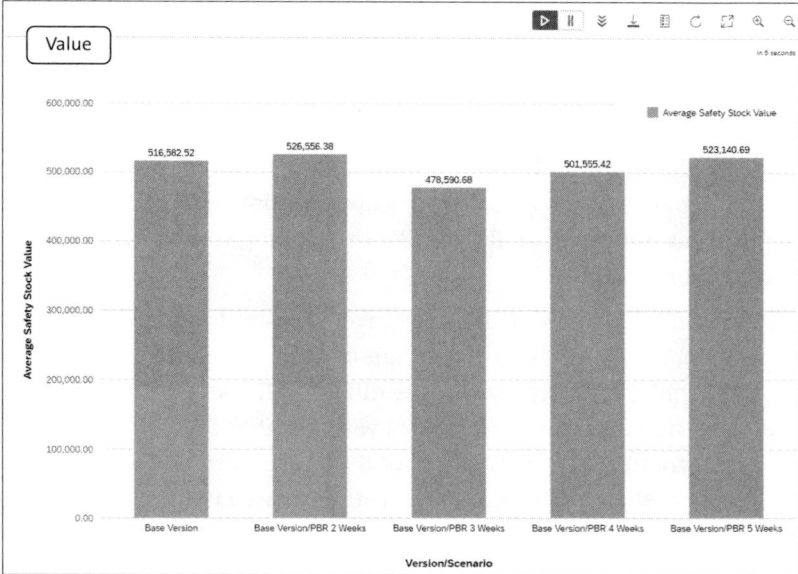

Figure 9.25 Comparison of Average Safety Stock and Average Safety Stock Value Based on Changed Parameters

331

The average safety stock for a year in units decreases as PBR increases, whereas the average value of the safety stock for a year is almost the same.

Before creating a simulation to see what input parameters could impact the safety stock, it's important to understand what's contributing to the safety stock. Is it the supply variability or demand variability that's affecting the recommended safety stock values? The safety stock due to different variabilities is captured in the demand variability, service, and supply variability key figures.

9.4 Intuition Building

As you've seen from the simulations in Section 9.3, you can create a lot of simulations with any variation of the input parameters. With the increase in supply chain nodes and arcs, the number of input parameters you can change to create simulations just grows. As you change any of these input parameters for the inventory optimization algorithm, SAP IBP finds the best place to hold the inventory at the item location level based on the changed scenario. The change in inventory target isn't as simple to assess as it is to assess in a single-stage model. The sophisticated inventory optimization algorithm will always try to find the cheapest way to set up the inventory target, which is hard to predict in a complex supply network. So the target will be different for any strategy you choose, and the results may surprise you.

Some of the results of inventory optimization with changes to input parameters are intuitive while others may not be. The inventory optimization results for a single-stage inventory optimization always follow the theoretical concepts we discussed in Chapter 2, but the results of multiechelon inventory optimization are quite different. This is because of the way in which the inventory optimization algorithm solves the mathematical problems; for example, factors like risk pooling come into play while the algorithm sets inventory targets.

As you'll recall from Chapter 2, in a single-stage inventory optimization model, the PBR has a direct impact on the safety stock. But this concept can't be extended easily to a multiechelon supply chain network. For the different PBR scenarios we built in the previous section, the average inventory held with a higher PBR was lower than our baseline scenario that had a PBR of one. SAP IBP's inventory optimization was able to find the lowest safety stock possible, even with increased PBR, for the finished product with risk pooling. So for every organization, the results of the inventory optimization with changes in the parameters can be very different from the baseline results.

In a multiechelon supply network, an inventory manager has to spend some time understanding each of the inputs for the algorithm and finding the right parameters for their supply chain, those that influence the recommended safety stock significantly. But how do you find these different parameters? This is where your intuition comes into play. When you experiment with a lot of simulations based on different parameters, your brain will constantly learn the different parameters you tweaked and the results associated with them. So when you're faced with a situation in the future, your brain behaves as a predictive machine and makes decisions based on your past experience and current experience. This phenomenon is known as your intuition. Your intuition will help you decide how to approach the situation. Because there are many parameters that can be tweaked for an inventory optimization run, to find the right safety stock for a simulation your intuition will help you conceptualize an approach and decide which parameter to tweak first to produce a significant change.

As you simulate, simulate, and resimulate, SAP IBP helps you align your intuition with your supply network data. SAP IBP doesn't just help you navigate the complexity of your supply network data: it also helps you get answers to the questions you might have. While creating simulations for inventory optimization, you also need a common metric by which you can compare different scenarios. SAP IBP gives you the capability to monetize inventory, which helps in comparison of the simulations or situations you might encounter, helping you make a better decision for your supply network.

When you're evaluating the inventory optimization results, it's also important to measure all the inventory components to help you make a better decision. For example, when we increase the lot size for distribution, it leads to a decrease in the safety stock, but other inventory components such as cycle stock and pipeline stock increase. We achieve lower recommended safety stock, but the average on-hand inventory increases.

Table 9.1 lists all the parameters that can change and the effect of the changes to these parameters on safety stock and other inventory components. Some of the changes to the parameters have a direct relationship with the safety stock and inventory components, whereas the results of some of the other parameter changes have to be evaluated using simulations. The results of these simulations are dependent on the supply network you have and the position of nodes and arcs of the supply network for which the parameters were changed.

9   Building Intuition and Conducting What-If Analysis

Input Parameter Change	Impact on Safety Stock	Impact on Cycle Inventory	Impact on Pipeline Stock
Increase in demand quantity	Increases	Increases	Increases
Increase in demand variability	Increases	May or may not increase	May or may not increase
Increase in customer service level	Increases	May or may not increase	May or may not increase
Increase in transit lead time	Increases	May or may not increase	Increases
Increase in transit lead time variability	Increases	May or may not increase	May or may not increase
Increase in periods between review (PBR)	May or may not increase	Increases	May or may not increase
Increase in distribution lot size	Decreases	Increases	May or may not increase
Increase in production batch size	Decreases	Increases	May or may not increase
Increase in internal service level	May or may not increase	May or may not increase	May or may not increase

Table 9.1 Impact of Changes to Input Parameters on Safety Stock, Cycle Stock, and Pipeline Stock

9.5   Strategic What-If Analysis

In supply chain management, there are three levels of decision-making in a planning process: strategic, tactical, and operational. Figure 9.26 shows the levels of decision-making in the planning process, and the key planning activities at each level are as follows:

- **Strategic**
  - Strategic S&OP plan
  - Strategic inventory policies
  - Long-term capacity planning
  - Network design and policy setup

- **Tactical**
  - Tactical S&OP planning
  - Inventory target setting
  - Demand supply match
  - Inventory allocation
- **Operational**
  - Short-term order prioritization
  - Order planning
  - Demand sensing
  - Deployment planning

At the strategic level, an organization focuses on the long-term horizon of two to five years into the future. Organizations form policies and guidelines for where the organization wants to be for the next few years. These plans are developed by top management after consulting with middle management and operational management. These strategies are often influenced by external factors such as government policies, market competition, socioeconomic factors, future investments, growth plans, and the like. Strategic planning focuses on the following:

- Strategic S&OP planning
- Network design and policy setup
- Strategic inventory policies based on the current and future network design
- Long-term capacity planning
- New product introduction
- Policies related to customer service level

Figure 9.26 Levels of Planning in Supply Chain Planning Process

9   Building Intuition and Conducting What-If Analysis

SAP IBP provides valuable input during the strategic planning processes. A large amount of inventory in the supply chain ties up working capital, thereby restricting an organization's ability to capitalize any new opportunities for growth. Amount of inventory is also an important indicator for investors and shareholders of how the organization is performing. Inventory is an important metric to measure the health of an organization and thus a critical topic for strategic planning.

Inventory managers are constantly evaluating different strategies to reduce inventory and safety stock in their supply chains. Before creating a strategy, inventory managers need to understand the drivers of inventory in their supply networks. SAP IBP's inventory optimization algorithms help inventory managers understand the inventory components and the variabilities that lead to safety stock. Inventory managers can determine if demand variability or supply variability is impacting the safety stock and they can decide if there is too much inventory tied up in cycle stock or pipeline stock, leading to high average on-hand inventory.

The what-if capabilities of SAP IBP help inventory managers evaluate different scenarios and present the alternatives to higher management for policy setting. For strategic what-if analysis, we recommend creating a parallel version that allows the creation of independent master data for simulation. Some of the typical strategic what-if scenarios at the strategic level are as follows:

- **New facilities**
  Sometimes, to achieve customer service levels, an organization may evaluate whether to add new facilities closer to customers to reduce lead time. Inventory managers can evaluate the impact on total inventory these new facilities may have.

- **Merge or shut down facilities**
  When a company acquires another company, often it must decide whether to merge or shut down a facility. You can model these situations in SAP IBP and both evaluate the alternatives and present these alternatives to higher management.

- **Customer service levels**
  Inventory managers evaluate different customer service levels by doing a trade-off analysis between the cost of inventory and average expedites or lost sales. They can present the alternatives to the higher management to set the service levels for the entire organization. Inventory managers can create different simulations by applying differential management strategies such as ABC classification of the products or the customers and evaluating the inventory and recommended safety stock for these simulations.

- **Stocking versus nonstocking nodes**
  Inventory managers can evaluate if a facility should be a pass-through (nonstocking) facility or a stocking facility. They can evaluate the inventory position for any location.
- **Service level type**
  An inventory manager can evaluate the use of different service level types, such as available in full or fill rate.

9.6 Tactical What-If Analysis

In the supply chain planning process, the second level of planning is the tactical level. At the tactical level, an organization focuses on the horizon of 2 to 24 months. All the planning and decisions made at this level are as per the guidelines from the strategic planning process. Decisions made are focused on cost-saving and minimizing risks. At this level, the focus is on meeting customer demand in the most efficient way possible. Tactical planning focuses on the following:

- Demand supply match
- Setting up inventory targets based on the network
- Creating a master production schedule and distribution requirement plan
- Inventory projections
- Capacity planning

Using SAP IBP's inventory optimization capabilities, inventory managers can do more proactive analysis rather than be reactive. Inventory managers can generate inventory targets in each planning cycle, so inventory targets are improvised in each cycle with the changing demand plan and supply strategies.

For tactical what-if simulations, inventory managers can use the scenarios capability in SAP IBP; most of the tactical what-if simulations can be created by changing the input key figure values. As explained in Section 9.2, as long as there is no need for new master data or changes to the master data for the simulation, it's easier to create ad hoc scenarios using the scenarios capability rather than the version feature in SAP IBP. Some of the what-if simulations performed at the tactical level are as follows:

1. Evaluate the impact on safety stock due to anticipated demand shift or change.
2. Evaluate the impact on safety stock due to changes in the sourcing decisions or changes to the sourcing ratios.

3. Evaluate the impact on safety stock due to increased lead time variability from suppliers.
4. Evaluate the impact on safety stock due to increased or decreased lot sizes.
5. Evaluate the impact on safety stock with varying internal service levels.
6. Evaluate the impact on safety stock due to different periods between review.

9.7 Summary

In this chapter, you learned about the importance of what-if analysis in inventory optimization. We discussed the versions and scenarios features in SAP IBP and how these can be utilized to conduct various strategic and tactical what-if simulations. We looked through sample simulations created using the scenarios feature in SAP IBP and how these simulations and scenarios can be compared to the baseline scenario using SAP IBP Excel planning views and the Analytics app. Finally, you learned about the intuition building process and different strategic and tactical scenarios that inventory managers can create using SAP IBP.

In the next chapter, we'll explain all the integration technologies available by which you can populate the master data and transaction data required for SAP IBP from the different systems in your IT landscape.

Chapter 10
Integrating SAP IBP for Inventory

> *Every organization has several information systems to manage its day-to-day business processes, and it's important to have data from these systems in the planning process. SAP IBP provides a variety of integration mechanisms to connect with SAP and non-SAP external information systems, as we'll discuss in this chapter.*

In Chapter 3, we explained how to configure a planning model and its entities in SAP IBP. However, before starting to use the planning model, data needs to be loaded into it to enable the planning process. In Chapter 4, we covered various data elements required to run the multiechelon inventory optimization algorithm. As with any planning system, planning results are also required to be fed back into the ERP system or other systems for day-to-day activities.

SAP IBP offers multiple integration technologies to help you integrate with on-premise or other cloud systems. Master data and transaction data, required for planning in SAP IBP, can be extracted from any system in your landscape. In this chapter, we'll cover all the integration mechanisms available within SAP IBP by which you can populate the required master data and transactions for inventory optimization.

We'll begin by focusing on manual data integration using the data integration services in SAP IBP. Manual data integration is usually not recommended when the data volume is significant. We'll then focus in detail on using SAP Cloud Platform Integration for data services for SAP IBP for inventory. Next we'll discuss integrations with specific systems, rather than the methods of integration. Finally, we'll discuss how OData services can be used to export results from SAP IBP.

10.1 Data Integration Technologies

SAP IBP can be integrated with various SAP and non-SAP ERP and planning systems to extract the master data and transaction data required for planning. There are four broad categories of integration technologies available to integrate with SAP IBP:

10   Integrating SAP IBP for Inventory

- SAP Cloud Platform Integration for data services
- An open API based on SAP HANA smart data integration
- Manual data integration using the web UI in SAP IBP
- Integration using OData services

Figure 10.1 shows the data integration technologies available. On the left side are the on-premise source system data stores to which you can connect SAP IBP. On the right side is the SAP IBP system on the cloud and all the integration technologies available.

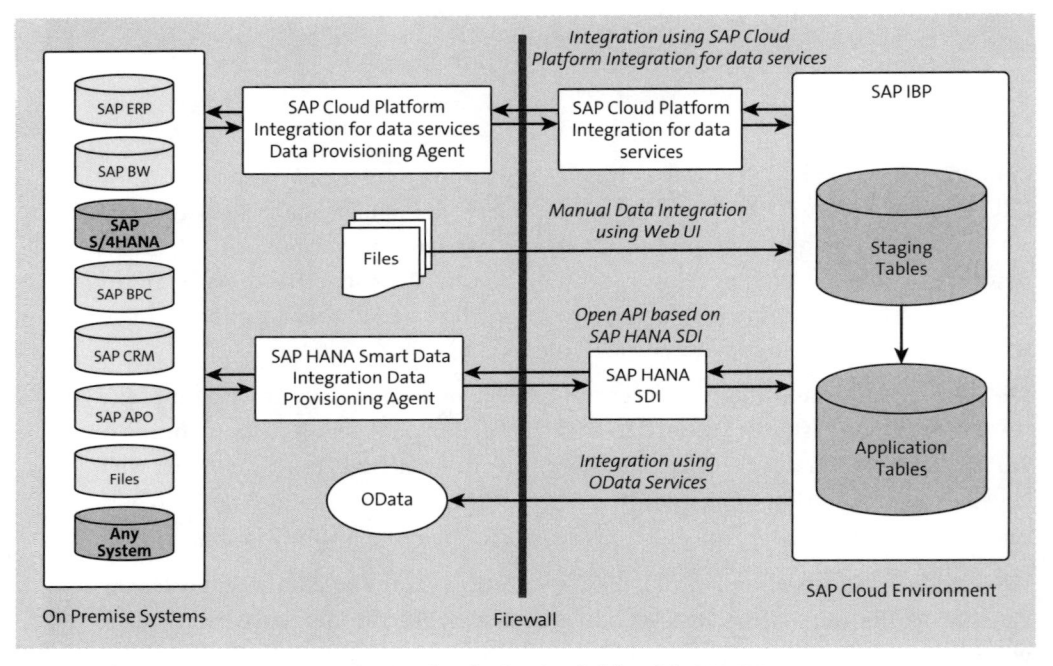

Figure 10.1 Data Integration Technologies Available with SAP IBP

SAP Cloud Platform Integration for data services and the open API based on SAP HANA smart data integration are the two most commonly used integration technologies for planning in SAP IBP. Depending on the planning process, you can choose which integration technology will suit your requirements.

As discussed in Chapter 1, SAP IBP provides the capability to support mid- to long-term tactical planning and short-term operational planning. For tactical planning, the data model should be highly configurable to allow for high flexibility in modeling different scenarios for planning across different business units or organizations.

However, for operational planning the data model should be consistent with the ERP data model with low flexibility.

For operational planning, the data is required to be at the lowest granularity possible. Operational planning is often order-based, and the time granularity required for operational planning can be as low as a second or a minute. On the other hand, tactical planning is often time-series-based bucket planning, and the time bucket granularity is weekly or monthly, depending upon the planning scenario.

SAP Cloud Platform Integration for data services is usually used for tactical time-series-based planning in SAP IBP. This is the preferred mode of integration for all applications in SAP IBP except for SAP IBP for response and supply. SAP Cloud Platform Integration for data services supports an automatic periodic transfer of data from any source system. It also supports the periodic extraction of data from SAP IBP to be used for any downstream execution process.

The open API based on SAP HANA smart data integration is usually used for operational order-based planning. Order-based planning requires tight integration with ERP systems such as SAP S/4HANA, SAP ERP, or any other external ERP system. SAP IBP for response and supply allows integration through SAP HANA smart data integration only. Master data objects and transaction data sourced from a source system using SAP HANA smart data integration usually are not modifiable in SAP IBP.

Table 10.1 highlights the differences in the planning process along with the choice of integration technology with respect to different applications available in SAP IBP.

	Tactical Planning	**Operational Planning**
SAP IBP applications	All applications in SAP IBP except for SAP IBP for response and supply	SAP IBP for response and supply
Planning process	Time-series-based planning	Order-based planning
Time granularity	Buckets (weekly/monthly)	Minutes
Technology used for integration	SAP Cloud Platform Integration for data services	Open API based on SAP HANA smart data integration

Table 10.1 Choice of Integration Technology Based on Planning Use Cases

As discussed in Chapter 4 and Chapter 5, the key data objects required to run inventory optimization are highlighted in Table 10.2.

Object Type	Object
Master data	Product
	Location
	Location product
	Customer
	Source customer group
	Source location
	Source production
	Production source item
Transaction data	Demand forecast
	Historical sales
	Historical production orders (to calculate the variability and lead time)
	Historical stock transfer orders (to calculate the lead time variability and lead time)
	Current safety stock

Table 10.2 Key Data Objects Required by SAP IBP for Inventory Optimization

As you saw in Table 10.1, integration using SAP Cloud Platform Integration for data services is the preferred option for all applications within SAP IBP, except for SAP IBP for response and supply. We'll look at this integration in more detail in Section 10.3, but first let's look at manual data integration.

10.2 Manual Data Integration Using the Web UI

SAP IBP provides the Data Integration Jobs SAP Fiori app to import data manually using a CSV file. This app supports data imports into generated tables or configurable data objects for master data, time profiles, key figures, and snapshots only. This self-service SAP Fiori app does not support downloading or exporting data from the SAP IBP system.

In the following sections, we'll first discuss the integration process that is supported by the Data Integration Jobs app and then discuss the three main types of objects supported by this process.

10.2 Manual Data Integration Using the Web UI

> **Note**
> You can only use the Data Integration Jobs app to transfer data for tactical planning purposes (generated tables for master data, time profiles, key figures, and snapshots). It doesn't support the transfer of external master data.

10.2.1 Integration Process

This method of data integration is recommended for a low volume of data and during the initial phase of implementation or testing product features. In the production environment, this method can be used by super users to upload data on an exception basis. You should always try to have data integration scenarios supported by SAP Cloud Platform Integration for data services.

Figure 10.2 shows the manual data integration architecture. The files are uploaded by the users from their machines to SAP IBP using the data integration job apps. The data is loaded into the staging tables before being loaded into application core tables.

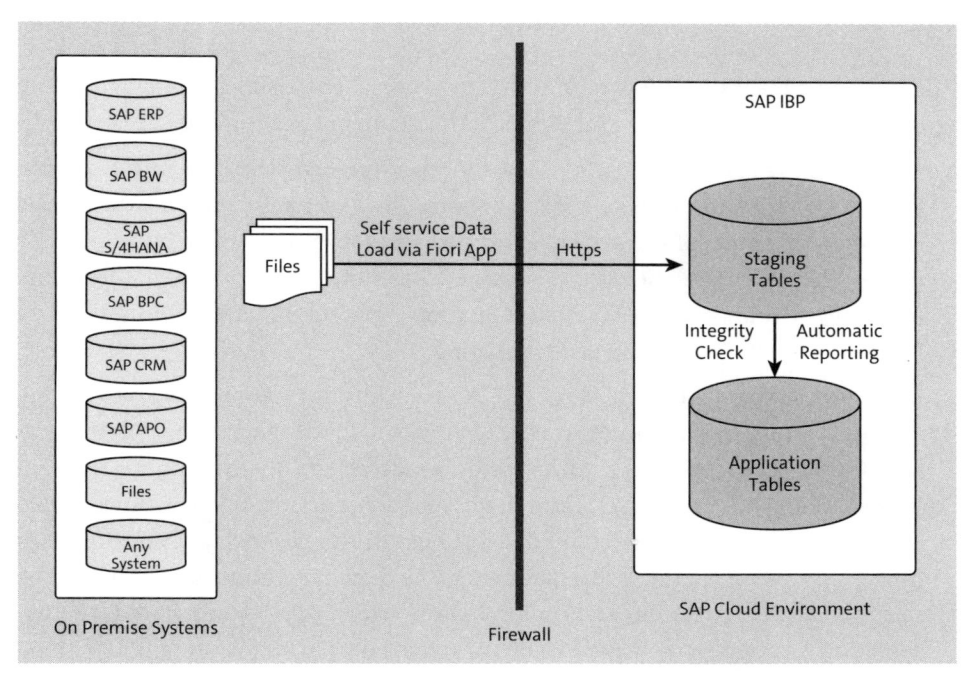

Figure 10.2 Integration Architecture when Using Manual Data Integration via Web UI App

343

10 Integrating SAP IBP for Inventory

The Data Integration Jobs app can be accessed from the **Administrator** group in the web UI. Figure 10.3 shows how to navigate to the Data Integration Jobs app. The key features of this app are as follows:

- Download templates for time periods, master data, key figures, and snapshots
- Import time periods, master data, key figures, and snapshots

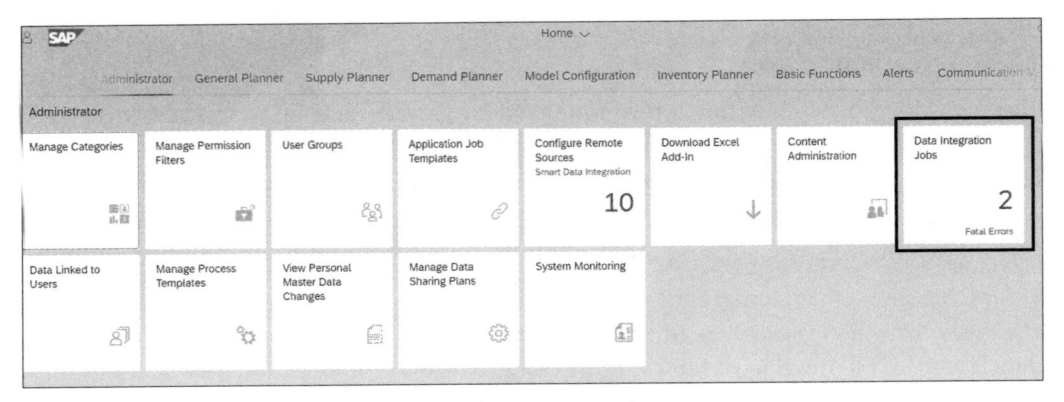

Figure 10.3 SAP Fiori App for Manual Data Integration

There are two stages in the data integration process. The following stages are also applicable to data loads using SAP Cloud Platform Integration for data services:

1. The system reads the contents of the CSV file and loads the data into a staging table, which is an intermediate storage space. The files can be rejected during this stage—for example, if the system can't parse a file. Some of the common errors during this stage are the columns in the files not being correct or separators unable to be found. For SAP Cloud Integration Platform for data services, the data is loaded directly into the respective staging tables.

2. In the second stage, the data is moved from the intermediate staging table to the application tables. Sometimes records are rejected in this phase. The possible reasons for rejection can include corresponding master data not existing, records failing referential integrity checks, and so on. When this occurs, the rejection appears as a rejection code. SAP IBP retains data load reports for seven days by default. This can be changed using the global parameter. The data integration jobs status can be seen on the main data integration **Job Details** screen. The import status is represented by a colored icon. A green icon means the data load was successful with no errors, yellow signifies that the import was processed with errors, and red signifies

10.2 Manual Data Integration Using the Web UI

that the data load was not successful. Figure 10.4 shows the main screen of the Data Integration Jobs app.

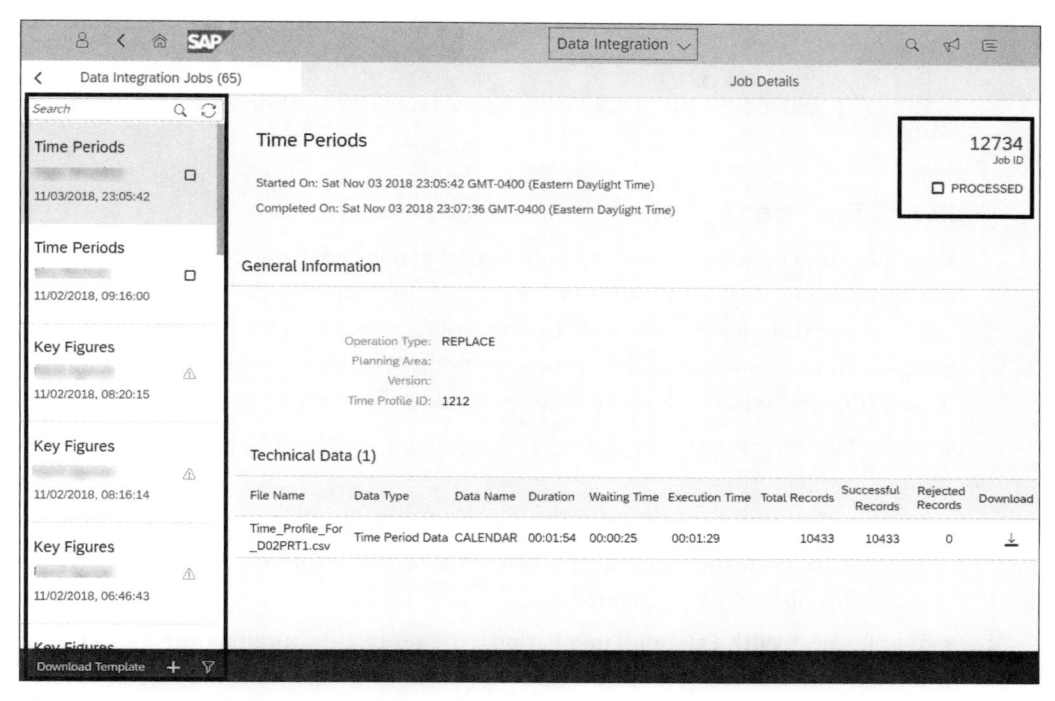

Figure 10.4 Web UI for Data Integration Jobs App

The data must be imported in the following sequence, or the integration process will fail:

1. Time periods
2. Master data related to master data objects
3. Key figures
4. Snapshots

The data can be uploaded to active data objects only, and the data must be in CSV format before it can be loaded into SAP IBP. You can also download the template for any of the objects mentioned in the preceding list using the Data Integrations Jobs app. To download a template, click the **Download Template** button in the Data Integration

Jobs app, select the data type, enter the required information, and click the **Download** button. We discuss each data object in more detail in the rest of this section.

> **Note**
>
> You can't upload time-independent key figure data using the key figures data type.

10.2.2 Time Periods

Typically, time periods for a time profile can be generated using the Create Time Periods for Time Profiles application job template, but this doesn't generate the attributes in the time profile, so most implementation projects end up using the Data Integration Jobs app to upload the time periods. When you download the template for the time periods, you'll see three options to prefill the time profiles:

- If you leave the **Prefill Template** dropdown blank, the template won't contain any time profiles.
- If you select **With New Time Periods**, the template contains the time periods in accordance with the value in the **Time Profile** field. Note that if periods already exist, this option is grayed out.
- If you select **With Existing Time Periods**, the template contains time periods that already exist in the system for the time profile—for example, because they have been uploaded at a previous point in time.

Usually this activity is done one time, but it can be used to extend the time horizon in the file to include new time periods in the future or to populate the attributes to time periods that help disaggregate data from a higher time period level to a lower time period level—for example, a month to week split, YTD calculation, and so on.

Figure 10.5 shows the option for downloading the **Time Periods** template from SAP IBP on the left-hand side, and on the right-hand side it shows the option for uploading the time profile into SAP IBP. When you upload time periods, the system always performs a load in the replace mode and not an INSERT_UPDATE upload. This means that any existing time periods in your system will be deleted. To avoid this, prefill the template with the existing periods and add your new periods to it. If you upload a period that previously existed in your system with a different period ID, the key figure values associated with the time period will become inconsistent.

10.2 Manual Data Integration Using the Web UI

Figure 10.5 Data Integration for Time Periods of Time Profile

10.2.3 Master Data

As explained in Chapter 3, there are five different master data types: simple, compound, reference, virtual, and external. You can only load master data into simple or compound master data types using the Data Integration Jobs app or using SAP Cloud Platform Integration for data services. You can download the template for master data in a similar way as you did for time periods.

Figure 10.6 shows the option for downloading the **Master Data** template from SAP IBP on the left-hand side, and on the right-hand side it shows the option for uploading the master data into SAP IBP.

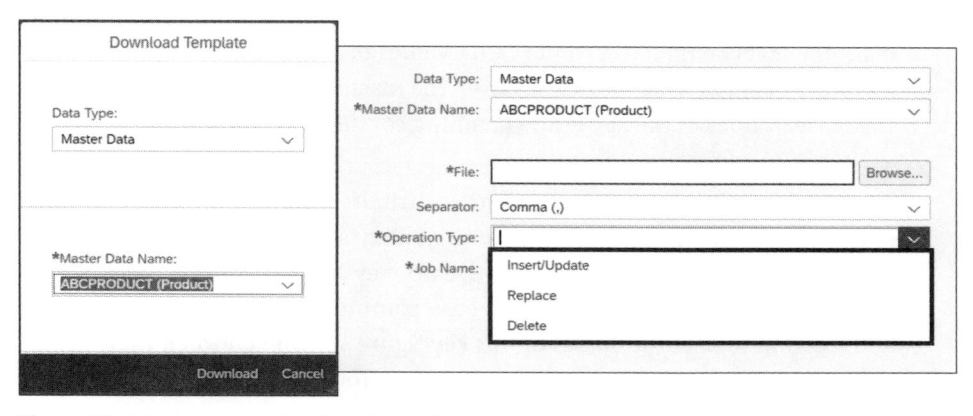

Figure 10.6 Data Integration for Master Data

347

When you upload the master data to SAP IBP via the Data Integration Jobs app or through SAP Cloud Platform Integration for data services, there are the following three operation types:

- **Insert/Update**
  If you select this operation type, the operation updates existing master data and inserts new records into SAP IBP.

- **Delete**
  This operation type deletes the master data from SAP IBP. It deletes only the records in the CSV file. Deleting master data for a master data object (e.g., a set of products or customers) affects all master data objects and related time series data linked to the deleted master data objects. The delete operation cascades to dependent master data objects and/or key figure data for related planning areas.

  To explain the cascading of the dependent master data, consider an example of a master data object, location, with the key LOCID (location ID); a product with key PRDID (product ID); and location-product, which is a compound of the master data objects location and product with keys LOCID from location and PRDID from product. Deleting PRODUCT data with PRDID = "PROD_1" deletes all rows of the related compound master data object location-product with PRDID = "PROD_1", and any value for location ID.

  The key figure values are deleted from the planning areas only if the planning area contains the related master data object. Values are deleted from the key figure if they relate to the deleted master data object data in one of the following ways:

  - The master data type key attributes are the same as or are a subset of the key figure base planning level root attributes. For example, for a master data object product with a key attribute PRDID and a key figure with root attributes of its planning level being PRDID and LOCID, values of the key figure are deleted for all values of PRDID that are deleted from the master data. This is independent of the LOCID values of the key figure planning combinations.

  - Nonkey attributes of the master data object are the same as or are a subset of the key figure base planning level root attributes, and no other master data object rows remain that have the same nonkey attributes. For example, for a simple master data object product with a nonkey attribute product group and a key figure with root attributes of its base planning level being product group and location region, the values of this key figure are deleted when there are no more products for the corresponding product group. This is independent of the location region values.

- **Replace**

    The **Replace** option updates master data that overlaps with existing data in the system. This option should be used with caution as you risk deleting data unintentionally. The **Replace** option does not provide a delta function. This means that if you upload a small subset of your data using the **Replace** option, all the other data in your system will be deleted, including dependent data such as planning objects and key figures.

    Any data in the CSV file that doesn't already exist in the system is inserted. Data (master data and related transaction or key figure data) that already exists in the system but isn't included in the CSV file is deleted. Data that is included in the CSV file and that already exists in the system is updated.

    For example, if the product master data type in SAP IBP has existing data for Product 1 through Product 10 and your CSV file has Product 1 and Product 2 only, the system will update Product 1 and Product 2 as per your CSV file and will delete Product 3 through Product 10 from SAP IBP, along with any dependent master and key figure data. This is because the Product 3 through Product 10 were weren't in the CSV file.

10.2.4 Key Figures

Similar to master data upload, key figure data also can be loaded using SAP Cloud Platform Integration for data services or using the Data Integration Jobs app. Key figure data can only be loaded into stored key figures. You can download the template for master data in a similar way as you did for time profile. By default, you can upload key figure values at an aggregated time level. To do so, specify the time profile level for the import job. If you want to upload the key figure values at the base planning level of the key figure, leave this field empty.

Figure 10.7 shows the option for downloading the **Key Figures** template from SAP IBP on the left-hand side, and on the right-hand side it shows the option for uploading the key figure data into SAP IBP.

When you upload the key figure data to SAP IBP via the Data Integration Jobs app or through SAP Cloud Platform Integration for data services, there are three operation types:

- **Insert/Update**

    This operation updates existing data and inserts new records into SAP IBP.

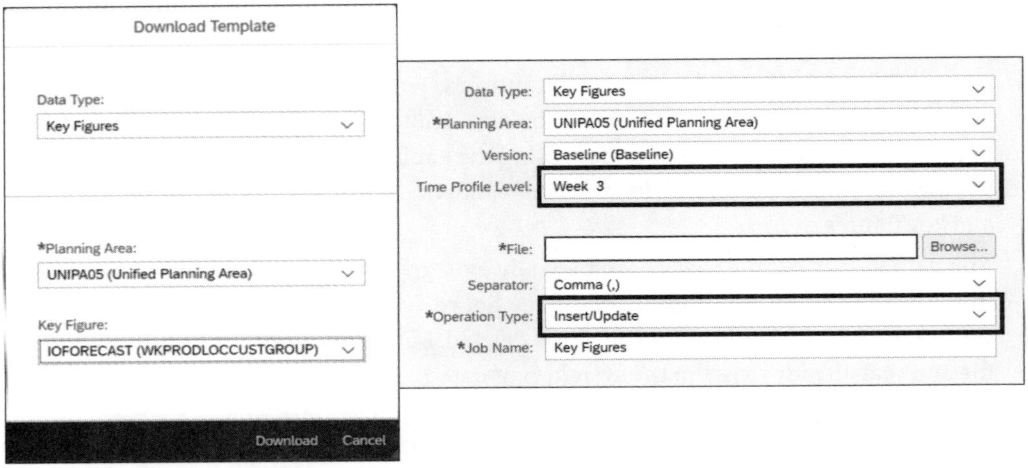

10   Integrating SAP IBP for Inventory

Figure 10.7 Data Integration for Key Figure Data

- **Delete**
  This operation clears all the key figure values for the records or values specified in the CSV file.

- **Replace**
  This option works in a similar way as the replace option for master data. It updates key figures that overlap with existing data in the system.

  Key figure data for combinations present in the CSV file that don't already exist in the system is inserted. Any existing key figure data in the system that isn't also included in the CSV file is erased (i.e., the key figure and any related transaction data is updated with NULL). Key figure values for the combinations that are present in CSV file and that already exist in the system are updated. The replace operation is generally used for transaction data such as inventory on hand, purchase orders, open orders, and production orders

10.3   Integration using SAP Cloud Platform Integration for Data Services

SAP Cloud Platform Integration for data services is a cloud-based data-integration tool offered by SAP to every SAP IBP customer. This is the most common integration technology used for batch/scheduled data integration between an external on-premise application and any cloud applications. It can integrate with a variety of external SAP and non-SAP systems with ease.

Some of the key features of SAP Cloud Platform Integration for data services are as follows:

- Direct access to multiple SAP ERP or SAP S/4HANA sources, with predefined templates to extract, transform, and load data into SAP IBP.
- A dedicated user-friendly, wizard-based web UI to design and create transformations and execute and monitor data loads.
- Manage data integration flows from anywhere using a secure browser.
- Graphical views of the data flows and mapping.
- Reads and writes from/to multiple sources, such as databases (SAP HANA, DB2, Oracle, SQL Server) and files (XML or delimited).
- Ability to schedule the data loads or extractions using the inbuilt scheduler.
- Central administration and monitoring of the data loads.
- Provides email notification alerts to users in case of failure of data loads.

In the following sections, we'll first look at the architecture of SAP Cloud Platform Integration for data services as it relates to integrating with SAP IBP. Then we'll examine some of the predefined content that SAP Cloud Platform Integration for data services provides. Finally, we'll walk you through what creating your first integration with SAP Cloud Platform Integration for data services will look like at a high level, including a look at the scripts, global variables, and functions that are involved.

10.3.1 Architecture

Figure 10.8 shows the basic architecture to integrate SAP IBP with external systems using SAP Cloud Platform Integration for data services. The left side of Figure 10.8 depicts the systems within the organization's IT systems landscape, and the right side depicts SAP IBP and the integration UI.

As shown, the SAP Data Services agent must be installed within your organization's firewall. SAP Cloud Platform Integration for data services interacts with your local SAP landscape via the SAP Data Services agent and secure HTTPS and RFC connections. The SAP Data Services agent enables the secure transfer of data between your on-premise data sources and SAP Cloud Platform Integration for data services. The

10   Integrating SAP IBP for Inventory

SAP Data Services agent is also used to provide metadata browsing functionality for on-premise sources to the web-based UI to design the data extraction flow. At run time, the SAP Data Services agent will trigger the extraction of the data from the IT systems in your landscape and push it into SAP IBP.

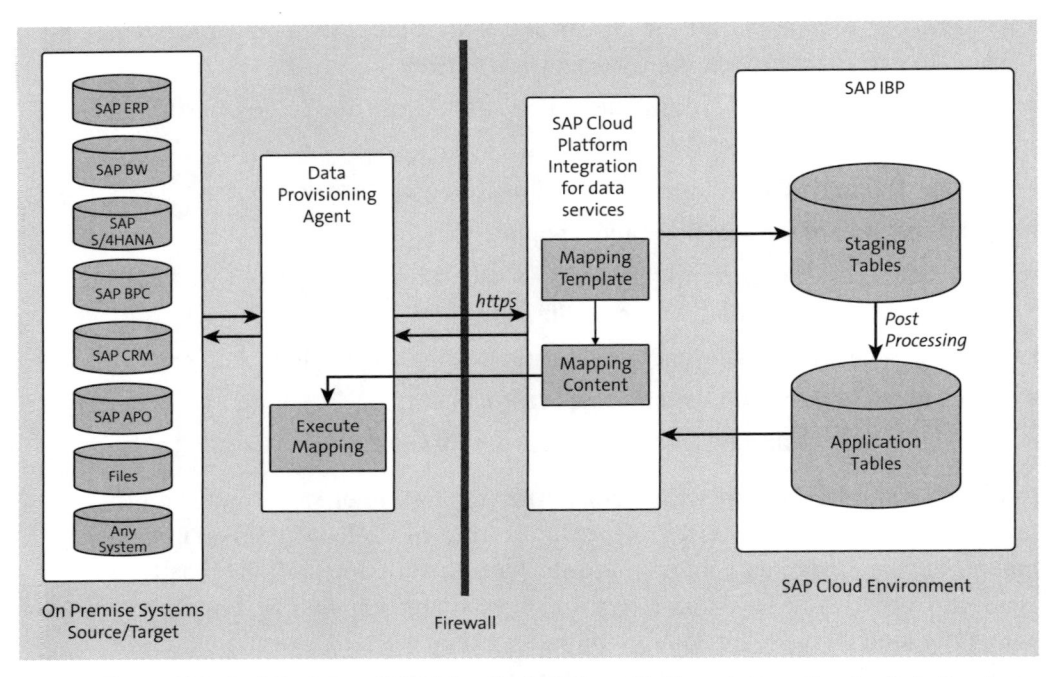

Figure 10.8 Architecture of SAP IBP with SAP Cloud Platform Integration for Data Services

The SAP Data Services agent can also be configured to connect securely with other applications using standards like SOAP, REST, and OData. The SAP Data Services agent is also used to extract the data from SAP IBP and push it into your on-premise systems. The SAP Data Services agent always initiates the request for a data transfer from SAP IBP. The SAP Data Services agent uses long polling: it places a request with the server and waits for a response when a task is ready to execute.

SAP Cloud Platform Integration for data services uses data stores to extract data. Data stores are the objects that connect SAP Cloud Platform Integration to your cloud and on-premise applications and databases. Through these connections, SAP Cloud Platform Integration can access metadata from and read and write data to your applications and databases. SAP Cloud Platform Integration supports data stores for the following types of applications and databases:

10.3 Integration using SAP Cloud Platform Integration for Data Services

- SAP Business Suite applications
- SAP BW sources
- SAP HANA cloud applications
- Applications that have prepackaged or user-written adapters
- Databases such as MySQL, DB2, Teradata, and so on
- File format groups
- SOAP and REST web services

On the right-hand side of Figure 10.8, there are two systems: SAP IBP and SAP Cloud Platform Integration for data services. Both systems are on the cloud, and the two systems are accessed via separate URLs. SAP Cloud Platform Integration for data services is a packaged integration tool that includes predelivered content to help you get started with your integration needs. The prepackaged templates let you connect directly to on-premise systems such as SAP APO, SAP ERP, or SAP S/4HANA. The prepackaged content is delivered to connect to SAP S/4HANA on-premise only and not SAP S/4HANA Cloud. SAP Cloud Platform Integration for data services lets you browse the metadata of the source tables and lets you design integration flows. It also provides a variety of predefined functions and scripts to do a light transformation of data at runtime, and it also can extract data from SAP IBP and send it to on-premise systems.

Before getting started with SAP Cloud Platform Integration for data services, there are four critical steps that you must perform:

1. Download, install, and configure the SAP Cloud Platform data services agent on your on-premise system—preferably an independent machine.
2. Register the agent with SAP Cloud Platform.
3. Create data stores in SAP Cloud Platform Integration for data services.
4. Import metadata objects into your data stores—that is, add tables and filenames from your source and target database applications to your datastores.

Once these steps are done, you can set up one or more integration projects. The following are the steps to set up your mapping content:

1. Create a project.
2. Create a task using a predefined template or start from scratch.
3. Add a data flow to the task. If using the predefined template, the data flow is created automatically.

4. Execute the task.
5. Promote the task to production.
6. Schedule the task to load the data to the production environment.
7. Monitor the data loads.

10.3.2 Predefined Content

In SAP Cloud Platform Integration for data services, there are templates available that provide predefined content to enable data flows from SAP APO or SAP ERP or SAP S/4HANA. This predefined content serves as the starting point for populating your SAP IBP applications or for transferring data from SAP IBP. The templates are designed to meet the specific requirements of SAP IBP data and reduce the time needed to get up and running. You're likely to customize this out-of-the-box content to meet your objectives, but using the templates has many advantages over creating them from scratch.

The templates provide a framework for how the integration works, thereby reducing your integration time. The predefined content contains critical global variables and preload and postload scripts that can be used rather than defining them from scratch. The templates provided follow the best practice design for optimal integration performance.

Three types of templates are available in SAP Cloud Platform Integration for data services:

- **General-purpose templates**
  General-purpose templates contain information required by SAP IBP to process data after it's loaded. The general-purpose templates contain global variables, preload scripts, and postload script.

- **Master data templates**
  Templates serve to transfer master data from the source system (SAP S/4HANA, SAP ERP, or SAP APO) to SAP IBP applications.

- **Key figure templates**
  Templates serve to transfer key figure values from the source system (SAP S/4HANA, SAP ERP, or SAP APO) to SAP IBP applications.

10.3 Integration using SAP Cloud Platform Integration for Data Services

10.3.3 Creating Your First Integration

SAP Cloud Platform Integration for data services is accessed via a separate URL provided by SAP. When you log in to SAP Cloud Platform Integration for data services, the first screen you will see is the SAP Cloud Platform Integration for data services dashboard, shown in Figure 10.9. The dashboard allows you to monitor the status of data integration services tasks. It provides a summary of the tasks that have failed or have been successful.

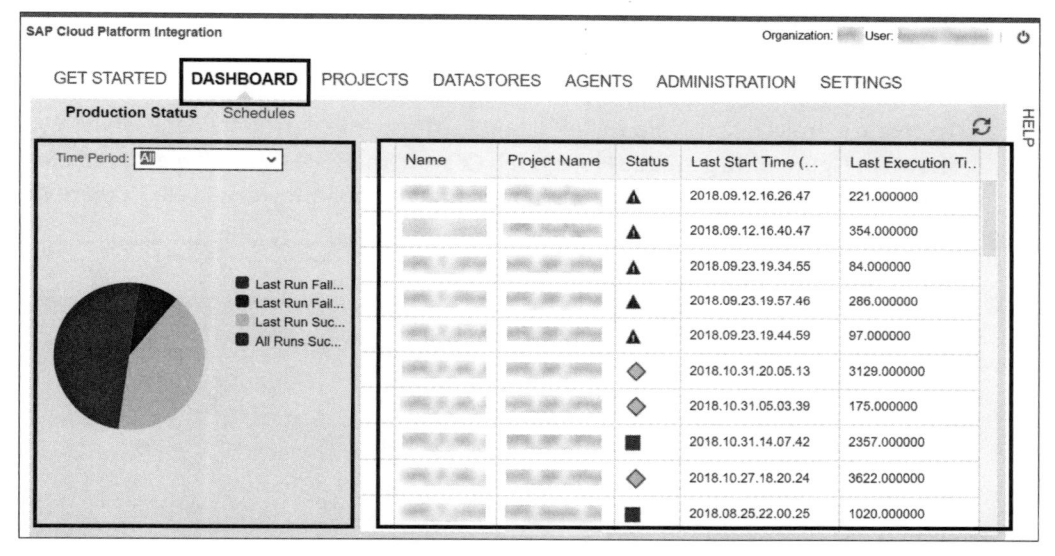

Figure 10.9 SAP Cloud Platform Integration for Data Services Dashboard

As mentioned earlier, the first step in creating the integration flow is to create a project. A *project* is a container that groups related tasks and processes. A *task* is a collection of one or more data flows that extract, transform, and load data to specific targets and the connection and execution details that support those data flows. You can create tasks from scratch or from predefined templates. A *data flow* defines the movement and transformation of data from one or more sources to a single target. Within a data flow, *transforms* are used to define the changes to the data that are required by the target. When the task or process is executed, the data flow steps are executed in a left-to-right order. The relationships between projects, tasks, and data flows are illustrated in Figure 10.10.

10 Integrating SAP IBP for Inventory

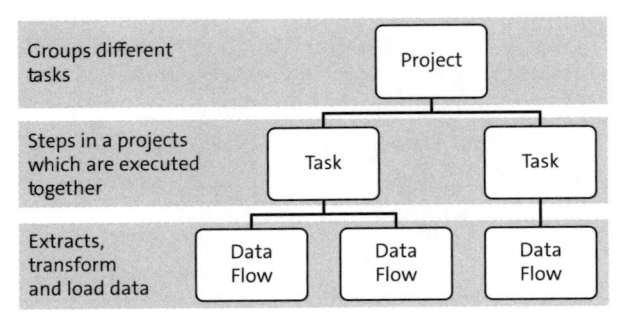

Figure 10.10 Relationships between Projects, Tasks, and Data Flows

To create a project, first login to SAP Cloud Platform Integration for data services. As shown in Figure 10.11, go to the **Projects** tab ❶. From there, click **New Project** to create a new project ❷. Enter a **Name** and **Description** for your new project and click **Create** ❸.

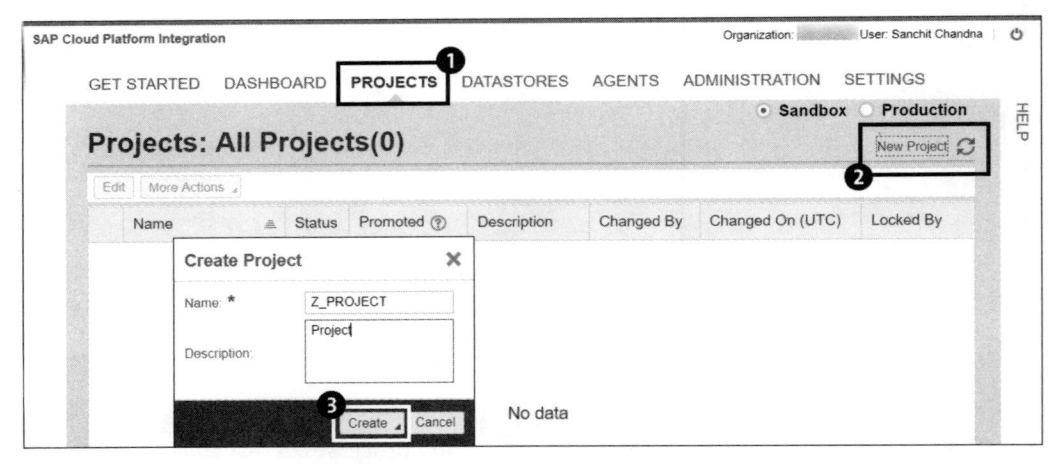

Figure 10.11 Create Project in SAP Cloud Platform Integration for Data Services

Once a new project is created, you can create a new task under the project. As shown in Figure 10.12, select the project you created ❶ and click **Create Task** ❷. Enter the **Name** of the task ❸. You can choose to create the task using a predefined template by selecting the **Use Template** checkbox ❹ or you can create a task from scratch. Click the **Next** button to complete the initial setup of the task.

10.3 Integration using SAP Cloud Platform Integration for Data Services

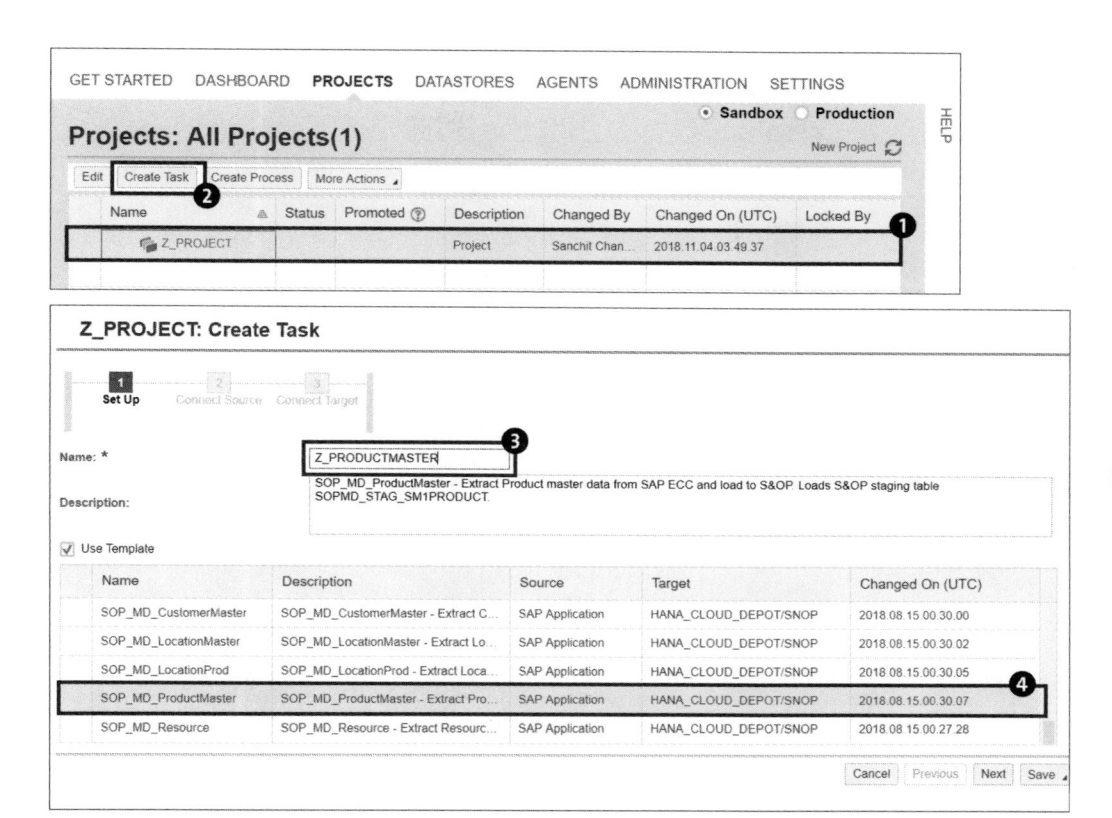

Figure 10.12 Create Task in SAP Cloud Platform Integration for Data Services Using Predelivered Template

After the initial setup of the task, select its source and target. All the data stores configured are available to select from. Figure 10.13 shows the selection of a source system for a task. After you click **Next**, you have to select the target system. Figure 10.14 shows the selection of the target system for the task.

As shown in Figure 10.14, expand the **Save** button options and select **Save and Edit** data flow. A data flow is automatically created when using a template. If you didn't select a template, then a blank screen will open, allowing you to create the data flow from scratch. In our example, we're using the product master, and as you can see in Figure 10.15, a data flow is automatically created. You can edit the data flow mapping by clicking the **Mapping** button and editing the data flow. An example of editing could be you want to concatenate two fields from the source data before sending it to

357

10 Integrating SAP IBP for Inventory

SAP IBP. There are a lot of functions available to convert the data from the source data stores before sending it to the target data stores.

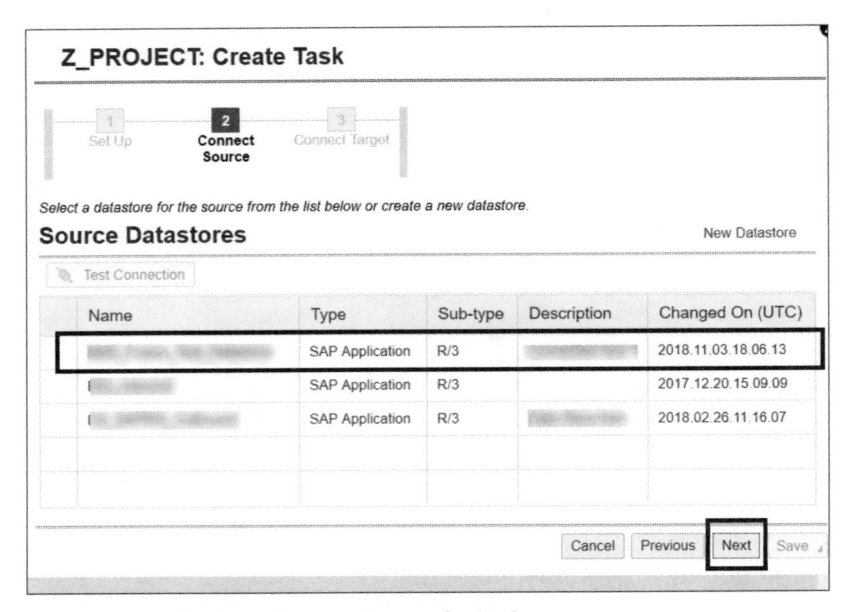

Figure 10.13 Selection of Source System for Task

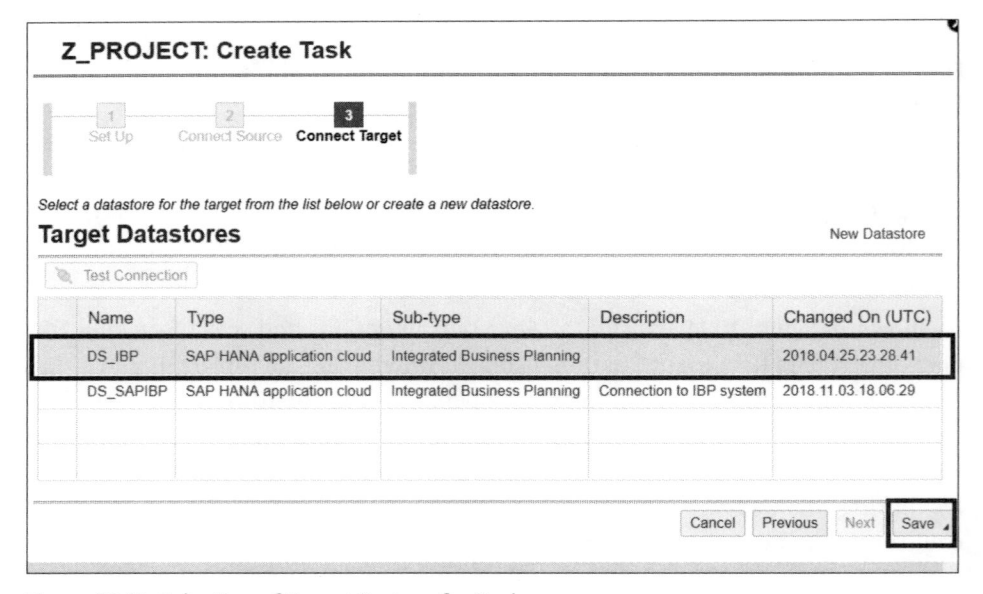

Figure 10.14 Selection of Target System for Task

10.3 Integration using SAP Cloud Platform Integration for Data Services

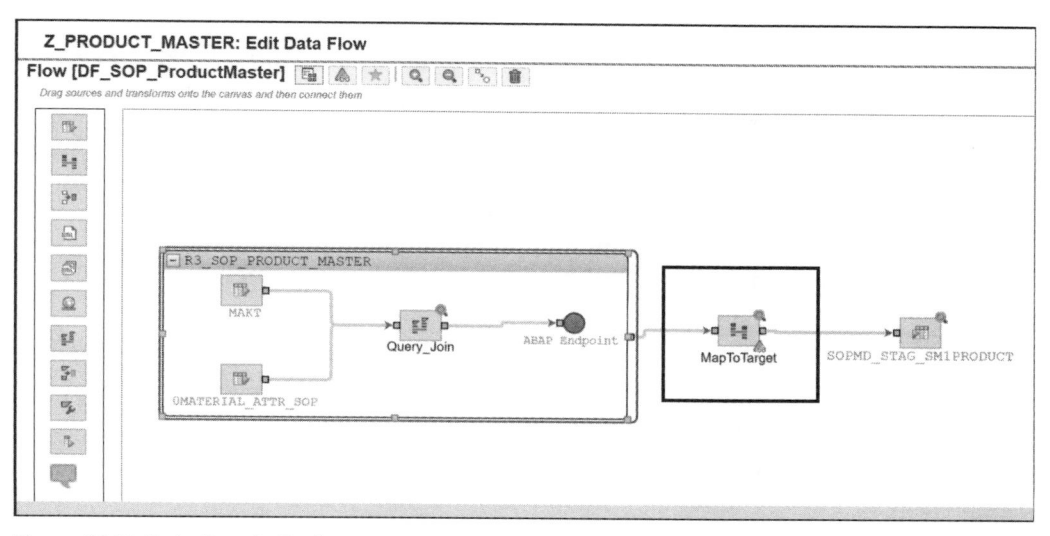

Figure 10.15 Data Flow in Task

Figure 10.16 shows the mapping and available data conversion functions in the data flow. The blue cross-link shows that a mapping exists for the target field from the source system. You can use any of the data conversion functions to transform the data from the source system before sending it to the target system.

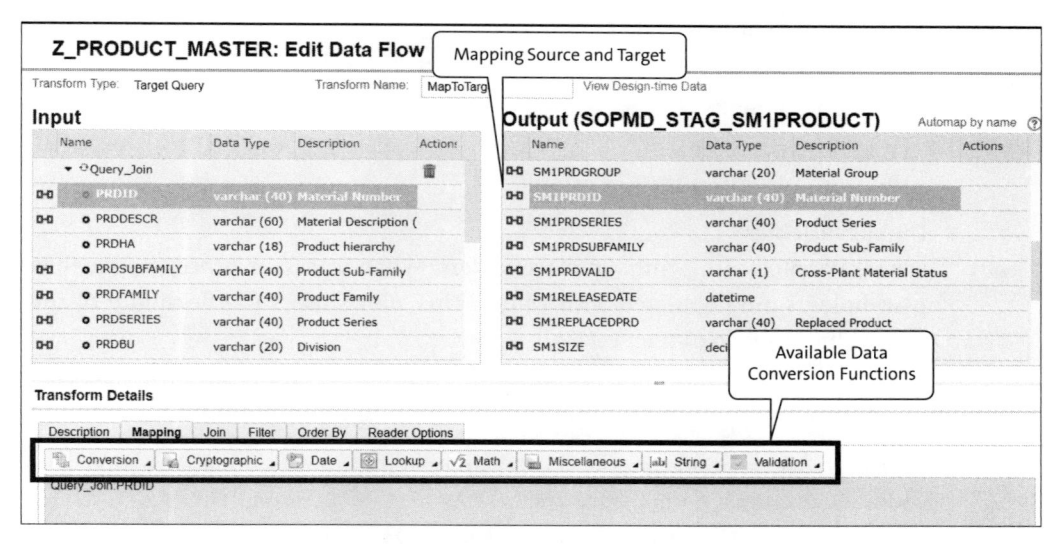

Figure 10.16 Mapping and Available Data Conversion Functions in Data Flow

10 Integrating SAP IBP for Inventory

After creating the data flow, you can edit, view, or schedule the task to execute the data flow. Figure 10.17 shows the control buttons to view, edit, schedule, or execute the task. Once the task is executed, you can view the history to check the status of previous runs of the task.

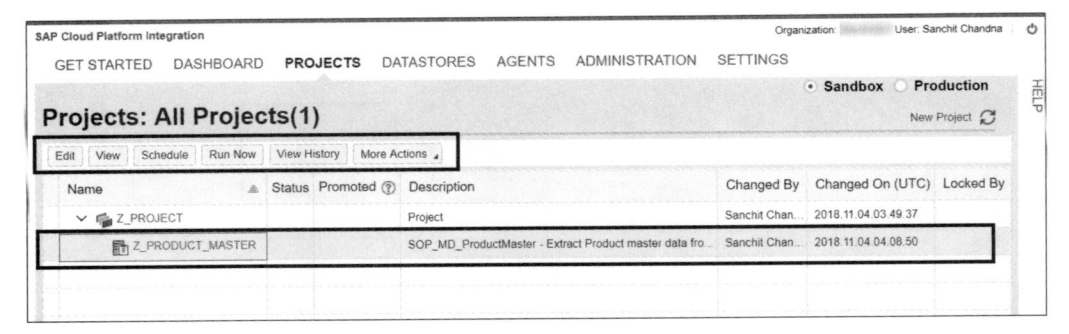

Figure 10.17 Edit or Schedule Task

Scripts, global variables, and functions can be used in tasks and processes in SAP Cloud Platform Integration for data services as follows:

- **Scripts**
  Scripts are single-use objects used to call functions and assign values to variables in a task or a process. A script can contain the following statements:
  – Function calls
  – If statements
  – While statements
  – Assignment statements
  – Operators

- **Global variables**
  Global variables are symbolic placeholders. When a task or process runs, these placeholders are populated with values. This allows users the flexibility of runtime values used in extractions.

> **Note**
> Certain global variables are used by the application to process the data after it's loaded. For example, SAP IBP requires $G_PLAN_AREA, $G_SCENARIO, $G_TIME_PROFILE, and $G_BATCH_COMMAND. If the global variables aren't included in the task or process, an error is returned.

- **Functions**
  Functions in SAP Cloud Platform Integration for data services take input values and produce a return value if necessary. Input values can be parameters passed into a data flow, values from a column of data, or variables defined inside a script.

10.4 With SAP IBP Applications in the Unified Planning Area

SAP IBP uses one data model for all tactical planning processes, and a lot of master data is common among different applications within SAP IBP. This is one of the greatest strengths of SAP IBP. For example, if you've implemented a full S&OP process, you already have all the master data types required to run inventory optimization, though you would need to populate some additional master data attributes to have a successful inventory optimization run. For example, in location-product master data you would need to populate attributes such as stocking indicator, periods between review, and so on.

Inventory optimization also requires certain transaction data as an input to calculate the recommended safety stock. These inputs, such as demand forecast and actual sales, can be copied into the inventory optimization key figures using the Copy operator or Copy and Disaggregate operator. Figure 10.18 shows the parameters of a Copy and Disaggregate operator by which we're copying the demand forecast from SAP IBP for demand to the IOFORECAST key figure.

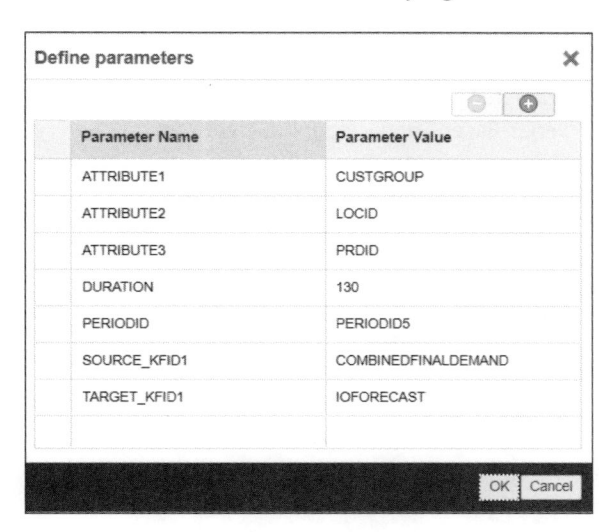

Parameter Name	Parameter Value
ATTRIBUTE1	CUSTGROUP
ATTRIBUTE2	LOCID
ATTRIBUTE3	PRDID
DURATION	130
PERIODID	PERIODID5
SOURCE_KFID1	COMBINEDFINALDEMAND
TARGET_KFID1	IOFORECAST

Figure 10.18 Copy and Disaggregate Parameters to Copy Forecast from Demand Planning to Inventory Optimization

Similarly, to use the results of inventory optimization in the supply planning algorithm, you can copy the final recommended safety stock to the safety stock key figure, which is an input for the supply planning algorithm. Figure 10.19 shows the parameters of a Copy and Disaggregate operator in which we're copying the final recommended safety stock from inventory optimization to the safety stock key figure used in the time-series-based supply planning algorithm.

Parameter Name	Parameter Value
ATTRIBUTE1	LOCID
ATTRIBUTE2	PRDID
DURATION	130
PERIODID	PERIODID5
SOURCE_KFID1	FINALIOSAFETYSTOCK
TARGET_KFID1	SOPSAFETYSTOCK

Figure 10.19 Copy and Disaggregate Parameters to Copy Recommended Safety Stock from Inventory Optimization to Time-Series-Based Supply Planning Algorithm

10.5 With SAP ERP and SAP S/4HANA

As explained earlier, for inventory optimization, the preferred source of integration is SAP Cloud Platform Integration for data services. SAP Cloud Platform Integration for data services offers predelivered content to help you get started with integration. With this content, you can connect SAP ERP or SAP S/4HANA (on-premise) with SAP IBP. The templates shown in Table 10.3 are those that are relevant for inventory optimization and available to integrate SAP ERP and SAP S/4HANA.

10.5 With SAP ERP and SAP S/4HANA

Object	Template Delivered with SAP Cloud Platform Integration for Data Services	SAP Application Source	Source of Data
Master Data			
Location	SOP_MD_LocationMaster	SAP S/4HANA, SAP ERP	Extractor OPLANT_ATTR_SOP, table T001W
Product	SOP_MD_ProductMaster	SAP S/4HANA, SAP ERP	Extractor 0MATERIAL_ATTR, Table MAKT
Location product	SOP_MD_LocationProd	SAP S/4HANA, SAP ERP	Tables MARA, MARC, MBEW
Customer master	SOP_MD_CustomerMaster	SAP S/4HANA, SAP ERP	Extractor 0CUSTOMER_ATTR, Tables KNVP, KNVH
Sales orders (initial load)	IBP_MD_SalesOrder_InitialLoad	SAP S/4HANA, SAP ERP	Extractor 2LIS_11_VASCL
Sales order (delta loads)	IBP_MD_SalesOrder_DeltaLoad	SAP S/4HANA, SAP ERP	Extractor 2LIS_11_VASCL
Deliveries (initial load)	IBP_MD_Deliveries_InitialLoad	SAP S/4HANA, SAP ERP	Extractor 2LIS_12_VCITM
Deliveries (delta loads)	IBP_MD_Deliveries_DeltaLoad	SAP S/4HANA, SAP ERP	Extractor 2LIS_12_VCITM
Key Figures			
Actuals/shipment history	SOP_KF_Actuals	SAP S/4HANA, SAP ERP	Extractor 2LIS_12_VCITM, Tables VBRK, VBRP
Initial on-hand inventory	SOP_KF_Inventory	SAP S/4HANA, SAP ERP	Tables MARA, MARC, MARD

Table 10.3 Standard Templaes Available to Integrate with SAP ERP or SAP S/4HANA

10   Integrating SAP IBP for Inventory

Object	Template Delivered with SAP Cloud Platform Integration for Data Services	SAP Application Source	Source of Data
Open orders	SOP_KF_OpenOrders	SAP S/4HANA, SAP ERP	Extractors 2LIS_11_VAHDR, 2LIS_11_VAITM, 2LIS_11_VAST
Sales forecast price	SOP_KF_SalesForecastPrice	SAP S/4HANA, SAP ERP	Extractor 2LIS_13_VDITM
Key Figures with Target as Unified Planning Area in SAP IBP			
Actual delivered quantity	IBP_KF_Actuals	SAP S/4HANA, SAP ERP	Tables LIPS, LIKP, WB2V, VBKR, and VBRP2
Initial inventory on hand	IBP_KF_InitialInventory	SAP S/4HANA	Tables MARD, MARA
Safety stock value in SAP S/4HANA	IBP_KF_SafetyStock	SAP S/4HANA	Tables MARC, MARA
Open orders from SAP S/4HANA	IBP_KF_OpenOrders_S4	SAP S/4HANA	Tables VBAP, VBAK, MARA
Open orders from SAP ERP	IBP_KF_OpenOrders_ERP	SAP ERP	Tables VBAP, VBAK, MARA, VBUP
Planned price	IBP_KF_PlannedPrice	SAP S/4HANA	Tables TCURR, MARA, WB2V, VBRK, and VBRP2
General Tasks			
General SAP ERP Task	SOP_ECC_Task	SAP ERP	–

Table 10.3 Standard Templaes Available to Integrate with SAP ERP or SAP S/4HANA (Cont.)

As noted in Table 10.3 there are some critical data objects that are very organization-specific that are not delivered with the standard objects, such as location source, production source header, production source item, and so on. You will have to create these extractions manually. You can use the other templates as a reference to create your data extractions for these data objects. You will also need some enhancements to the standard-delivered content to include the inventory optimization–specific master data attributes, such as stocking versus nonstocking node, periods between review, and so on.

10.6 With SAP APO

SAP Cloud Platform Integration for data services also provides templates to connect to SAP APO. To connect SAP Cloud Platform Integration for data services with SAP IBP, you'll have to create a data source for your planning area in SAP APO. The objects in Table 10.4 are delivered with SAP Cloud Platform Integration for data services and are relevant for inventory optimization.

Object	Template	Data Flow	Source of Data
Master Data			
Planning area	IBP_MD_PlanningArea	DF_IBP_ProductMaster	Extractor 9ADP_CUSTOM_PRODUCT, tables /BIO/9ATMATNR, /SAPAPO/MATKEY, T006A
		DF_IBP_UnitsOfMeasure	Extractor 9ADP_CUSTOM_PRODUCT, tables /SAPAPO/MATKEY, /SAPAPO/MARM, T006A
		DF_IBP_UnitsOfMeasure_Conversion	Extractor 9ADP_CUSTOM_PRODUCT, tables /SAPAPO/MATKEY, /SAPAPO/MARM
		DF_IBP_LocationMaster	Extractor 9ADP_CUSTOM_LOCATION, table /BIO/9ATLOCNO
		DF_IBP_CustomerMaster	Extractor 9ADP_CUSTOM_CUSTOMER, table /BIO/ /BIO/OIAPO_CUSTOM

Table 10.4 Standard Templates Available to Integrate with SAP APO

10 Integrating SAP IBP for Inventory

Object	Template	Data Flow	Source of Data
Key Figures			
Demand plan	IBP_KF_DemandPlannig	IBP_KF_DemandPlanning	Extractor 9ADP_CUSTOM_TOTAL_DEMAND_PLAN
General Tasks			
General SAP APO task	SOP_APO_Task	-	-

Table 10.4 Standard Templates Available to Integrate with SAP APO (Cont.)

During the implementation, replace the source master data table (9ADP_CUSTOM_PRODUCT, 9ADP_CUSTOM_LOCATION, or 9ADP_CUSTOM_CUSTOMER) with your data source of the same master data type.

10.7 With Non-SAP Systems

Using SAP Cloud Platform Integration for data services, you can connect SAP IBP with any other system of record, including the following databases:

- IBM DB2 for Linux, Unix, Windows, and IBM DB2 on iSeries
- Microsoft SQL Server
- Oracle
- MySQL
- Teradata

With SAP Cloud Platform Integration for data services, you can also connect with the following data sources:

- Delimited files
- XML files
- SOAP web services
- RESTful web services
- OData

10.8 Exporting Data Using OData Services

SAP IBP provides the capability to extract key figure and master data via an OData service. The extracted data can be used externally. For example, you can extract key figure data and integrate this data into external systems, such as a legacy system, or use it for external reporting tools. You can extract master data if you want to validate key information for your organization—for example, if you need a list of all the products for which you are recommending safety stock.

This service is not recommended when there are a lot of records. If the volume of the data to be extracted is high, it's best to use SAP Cloud Platform Integration for data services to extract the information and pass it to recipient systems.

To extract the data, you need to provide the level of the attributes, key figures, and the selection filters for the data you want to extract. The OData service returns the requested data in JSON format. The data can be extracted from any planning area, version, or scenario.

Before extracting the data using OData services, you need to perform certain steps to access the SAP IBP system from outside the cloud. You'll have to create one or more communication users in the Maintain Communication Users app and associate them with the SAP_COM_0143 communication scenario. The communication users are authorized to access the API. The system can be accessed using basic authentication or OAuth 2.0.

10.9 Summary

In this chapter, we covered the integration technologies available for inbound and outbound data from SAP Integrated Business Planning for inventory. The data elements included the master data and transactional data from source systems such as SAP ERP, SAP S/4HANA, or any other external systems. We also covered data integration using the Data Integration Jobs app, which allows manual upload of data into SAP IBP, and the data extraction services (OData) available in SAP IBP.

In the next chapter, we'll cover how to plan your implementation of SAP IBP for inventory. We'll also cover various project management methodologies for the implementation project.

Chapter 11
Planning Your Implementation

SAP IBP for inventory is a cloud application, which means its implementation follows a slightly different path than traditional software implementations. This chapter coaches you through several key decisions related to an inventory optimization project.

Now that we've provided recommendations to design your new inventory planning and optimization process, this chapter will guide you through the implementation considerations for the SAP IBP for inventory solution. We will start this chapter by focusing on the general considerations for cloud software implementations (Section 11.1). We'll make suggestions about what parts of the process and workflow can be automated (Section 11.2) and what the advantages are of an agile implementation methodology to implement SAP IBP versus the more traditional waterfall methodology (Section 11.3). We'll close the chapter in Section 11.4 by reviewing considerations for the roles and responsibilities of inventory planners in the supply chain organization.

11.1 Cloud Software Considerations

SAP IBP is enabled as a software-as-a-service or cloud system, which means the solution is hosted by SAP in its data center, and access is provided to your organization on signing a license agreement. In this section, we'll cover the provisioning, implementation implications, and upgrade approach for the SAP IBP solution. We'll close the section by zooming into the quarterly upgrade approach that SAP offers.

11.1.1 Provisioning

Because SAP IBP is a provisioned as a cloud-based solution, the system is hosted by SAP. Therefore, upon signing the licensing agreement, SAP will provide system access by sharing a web link and administration user access. With the administration user access, you can provision your own users to start the configuration of the solution.

11   Planning Your Implementation

To ensure the right memory size of the solution is provisioned, SAP will work with your organization during the contracting phase to assess the planning parameters. The combination of the number of modules licensed and the complexity of the supply network, as expressed by number of products, locations, customers, and their combinations, will help SAP determine the right system size for optimal performance.

After you sign the SAP IBP licensing agreement, SAP will provide access to three distinct environments:

- **SAP IBP**
  This will provide access to the SAP IBP environment itself, allowing you to create your own roles and users.
- **SAP Cloud Identity Access Governance**
  This is used to configure the identity provider that will be used to authenticate users.
- **SAP Cloud Platform Integration**
  The SAP Cloud Platform Integration for data services environment is used to establish data integration with the SAP IBP environment.

A typical SAP IBP implementation will be provisioned with two SAP IBP tenants, one for configuration and testing and another for production. SAP Cloud Identity Access Governance and SAP Cloud Platform Integration both have a single tenant, which caters to both the SAP IBP tenants.

SAP supports single sign-on, allowing you to leverage your corporate identity provider for authentication. This way, your users will be able to log in using their Windows credentials without the SAP IBP solution requiring additional user IDs and passwords. The system administrator should configure the authentication provider and create the configuration users that will take care of configuring the system to align with the business requirements that have been specified. At that point, the actual implementation work can start.

11.1.2   Implementation

When the configuration users receive access to the environments, typically the SAP IBP environment and the SAP Cloud Platform Integration environment, the actual implementation of the solution can start. Access to the cloud identity provider is typically reserved for the system administrator and is only accessed in the initial setup or when authentication services change in the organization.

11.1 Cloud Software Considerations

As the SAP IBP environment typically comes with two tenants—one for configuration and testing and one for production—all configuration and testing will be performed in the test tenant.

SAP caters for accelerating your implementation by providing sample planning areas. These planning areas act as a working example of a specific scope of planning. For example, the SAPIBP1 sample planning area provides a working example of all time series-based planning modules integrated into one complete planning area, enabling most of the algorithms that SAP delivers for time-series-based planning. Figure 11.1 gives an overview of all sample planning areas SAP IBP delivers out of the box. For inventory optimization, the focus of this book, the SAP3 planning area can be leveraged. It provides the complete configuration for a baseline inventory optimization model, from master data types and attributes to planning levels and key figures required by the algorithms to planning operators.

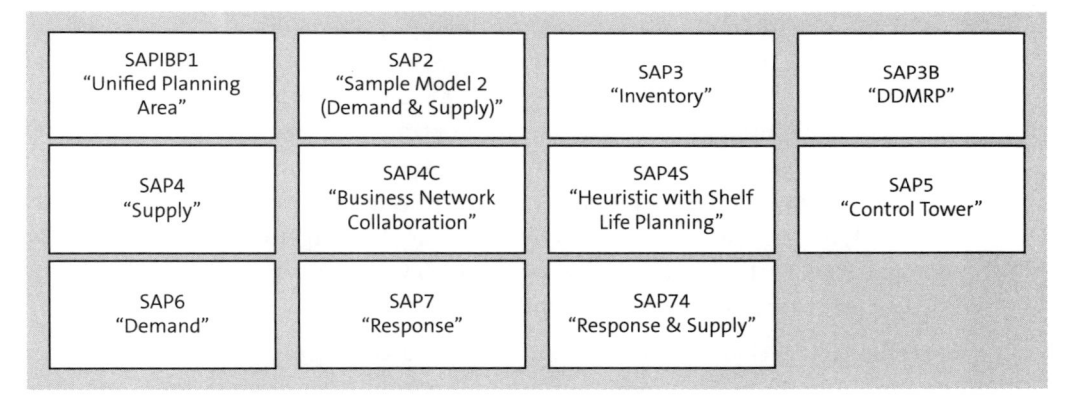

SAPIBP1 "Unified Planning Area"	SAP2 "Sample Model 2 (Demand & Supply)"	SAP3 "Inventory"	SAP3B "DDMRP"
SAP4 "Supply"	SAP4C "Business Network Collaboration"	SAP4S "Heuristic with Shelf Life Planning"	SAP5 "Control Tower"
SAP6 "Demand"	SAP7 "Response"	SAP74 "Response & Supply"	

Figure 11.1 SAP IBP Sample Planning Areas

We recommend starting from this sample planning area and making adjustments aligned with the business requirements. Adjustments typically start with adding the required master data attributes for users to easily identify, filter, and sort their products. These can be maintained in the configuration applications, added to the master data types, selected in the planning area, and added to the planning levels. Extra key figures can be added to provide an integrated planning flow between inputs, planning requirements, and key performance indicators. The planning operators can be tweaked per the settings described in Chapter 5, allowing a working planning area that meets the requirements of the business users.

Finally, with user self-service capabilities, dashboards, alerts, and planning views can be created either by the implementation team establishing the initial solution or by the business users as they work in SAP IBP.

All these activities can be performed initially in the test tenant. Upon completing the required testing, it's possible to transport the planning area to the production tenant, where it's recommended not to perform any direct configuration. All changes should be performed in the test tenant and tested carefully before they're transported to the production environment. This helps to ensure the planning area in the production environment enjoys maximum stability.

11.1.3 Integration

Before the solution can be deemed ready for productive use, typically you'll integrate the system with the execution backend systems in your corporate IT system landscape. Inventory optimization can be deployed standalone, as an advanced calculation engine for the inventory components, or as part of an integrated business planning process, completely enabled by SAP IBP. We described the integration approach in depth in Chapter 10. Inventory optimization requires inbound master data like product, location, and customer groups, as well as transactional operational inputs like sales order history and its variability, lead times and their variability, and the like. From an outbound perspective, typically the target safety stock would be provided back to the operational systems, which will take it into account during the detailed procurement, distribution, and production planning activities.

To connect the cloud-based SAP IBP system to on-premise IT solutions, you're required to install a data provisioning agent inside the firewall where the on-premise solutions are hosted. This agent acts as a gateway from the IT environment of your organization to the cloud-hosted SAP IBP solution. Exact instructions for the installation and the download package can be found on the SAP support website. This activity tends to be performed by a system administrator.

The integration implementation continues with identifying the backend systems required for integration. Typically inventory optimization in SAP IBP connects to an ERP system for its master data and elements of transactional data like actual sales order history. SAP Cloud Platform Integration for data services allows you to connect to any relational databases and recognize tables or view structures. When the ERP system of record is created as a data store in the SAP Cloud Platform Integration environment, it's possible to import the tables or views from that ERP system. From those views, integration tasks can be created, either inbound or outbound.

11.1 Cloud Software Considerations

Although it's possible to connect to all table structures that are available in the connected datastore, we don't advise performing complex data transformations in the SAP Cloud Platform Integration for data services layer because doing so may severely hamper the performance of the integration layer. For complex data objects, we recommend performing the transformation prior to exposing the data to the SAP Cloud Platform Integration for data services layer—for example, as an extraction structure in an SAP ERP system.

Once the integration tasks have been created to perform the data transfer from the on-premise backend systems, like the ERP system, the tasks can be executed to populate in the SAP IBP planning area in the test tenant for integration testing. If the test results are satisfactory, the tasks can be promoted to production, at which point they will connect to the production tenant of SAP IBP and the productive backend landscape—for example, the ERP environment.

11.1.4 Upgrades

As a cloud-hosted solution, SAP IBP is continuously kept up to date by SAP. There is a weekly maintenance window to perform patching, as specified in the licensing agreement with SAP, but there also is a major quarterly upgrade that SAP will apply to the solution. The upgrades are named per the year and month in which they occur and happen in February (e.g., 1902 for the February 2019 release), May, September, and November. At the time of publishing this book, SAP IBP was on the 1902 release.

The upgrade happens typically over a weekend, is announced in advance, and is performed on the test tenant one or two weeks before the production tenant. This allows you to perform the necessary regression testing and possible minor adjustments and ensure the upgrade is nondisruptive for your planning organization.

SAP will provide the release notes prior to the upgrade, and it's strongly recommended that you read through these notes to assess if the upgrade will have any direct implications for your implementation. Although it's not often the case, it might happen that SAP implements new checks on configuration or changes minor configuration procedures. In such a case, corrective action might be required in your planning area. Typically, SAP will communicate this clearly prior to the upgrade. Often there's a two-step procedure for these changes. The first upgrade will identify the configuration changes in the activation log as warnings, providing clear visibility. During the next upgrade, the same changes might be provided as errors. This gives you the opportunity to take up to a full quarter to resolve the configuration changes required.

Although SAP upgrades are typically packed with great new features, it's not mandatory to immediately adopt these changes. For some changes—for example, complete new algorithms—you need to perform additional setup steps in the system. These features consequently will not be available for users without making the configuration changes as specified. Some changes, however, are immediately available to planners merely by performing the upgrade, such as changes to Excel functions.

Finally, with every upgrade of the SAP system, there's typically a new release of SAP Integrated Business Planning, add-in for Microsoft Excel. This add-in is often required to make use of new functionalities, especially those that are really embedded in Excel. Although it's recommended to upgrade the add-in quarterly with a new SAP IBP release, it's not mandatory. All versions of SAP IBP, add-in for Microsoft Excel are backward compatible, allowing you to use the 1811 add-in, for example, with a 1902 version of SAP IBP. However, to leverage the new capabilities in Excel that are made available in the 1902 release, you must upgrade the add-in.

11.2 Manual versus Automated Workflow

Once your solution has made it through the initial implementation phase and is available in the production environment, new choices become apparent. The solution can be automated to a large extent if that aligns with your business reality. Jobs can be scheduled manually by the planners, or scheduling can be automated. In the middle, there's the opportunity to leverage the process management capabilities, which allows a structured supply chain planning process.

11.2.1 Job Scheduling

In the early days of a release of a planning system, it's very common for planners to keep very close control over when the planning service will be executed. This allows clear follow-up and allows planners to validate the parameters going into planning jobs prior to executing them. This very controlled environment typically is not sustainable in the long-run, however, because it generates a substantial dependency on the planner to actively operate the solution. In the longer run, high efficiencies can be achieved by moving toward a management-by-exception approach in which the planning jobs are executed automatically and planners focus their time and attention on areas in which they can have the biggest impact: the exceptions.

11.2 Manual versus Automated Workflow

SAP IBP allows various ways of automating job schedules. First, jobs can be scheduled by planners from Excel based on a simple calendar with recurrence. This allows jobs to be executed every day, week, or month at the same time, ensuring, for example, that target inventories are recalculated at an agreed-upon time during the week. To do this, you'd click on **Schedule** in the **IBP** tab in Excel, as shown in Figure 11.2.

Figure 11.2 Schedule Jobs

Selecting **Inventory Optimization** to start the inventory optimization planning jobs will open a dialog that allows you to select the planning job to be performed, as shown in Figure 11.3.

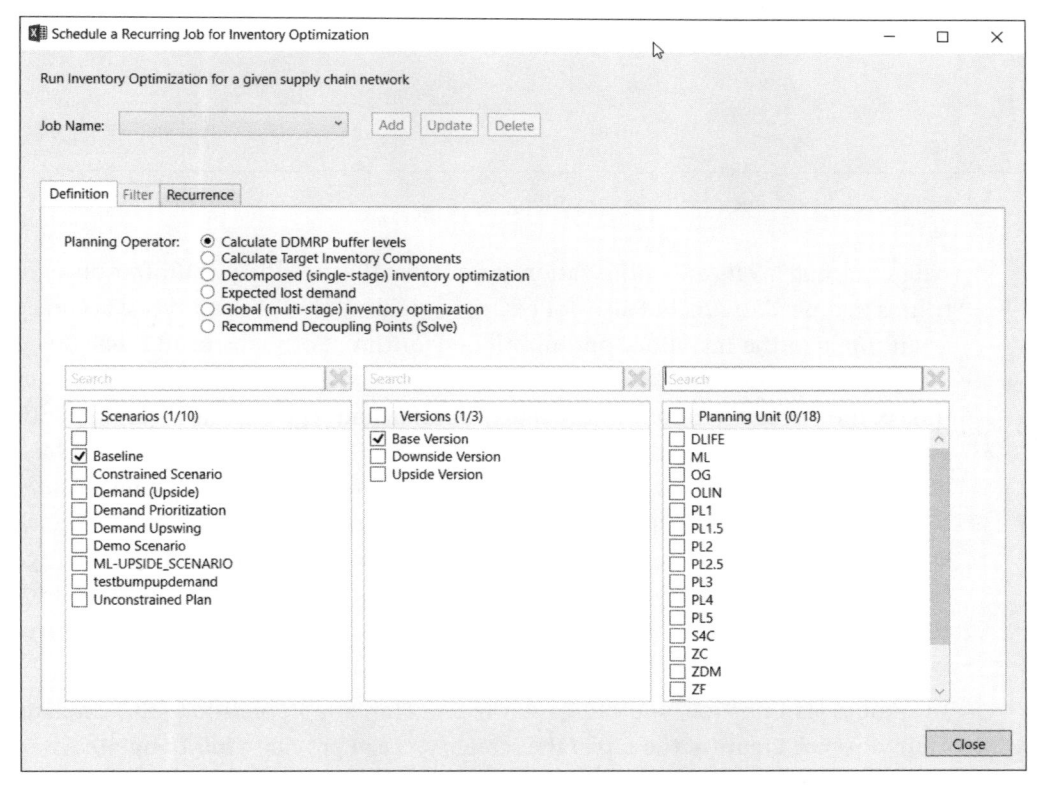

Figure 11.3 Schedule Recurring Inventory Optimization Job

375

11 Planning Your Implementation

Finally, by navigating to the **Recurrence** tab shown in Figure 11.3, you can schedule a job based on a cadence: daily, weekly, monthly, or yearly. Daily scheduling is achieved by selecting all the days after selecting the **Weekly** radio button, as shown in Figure 11.4.

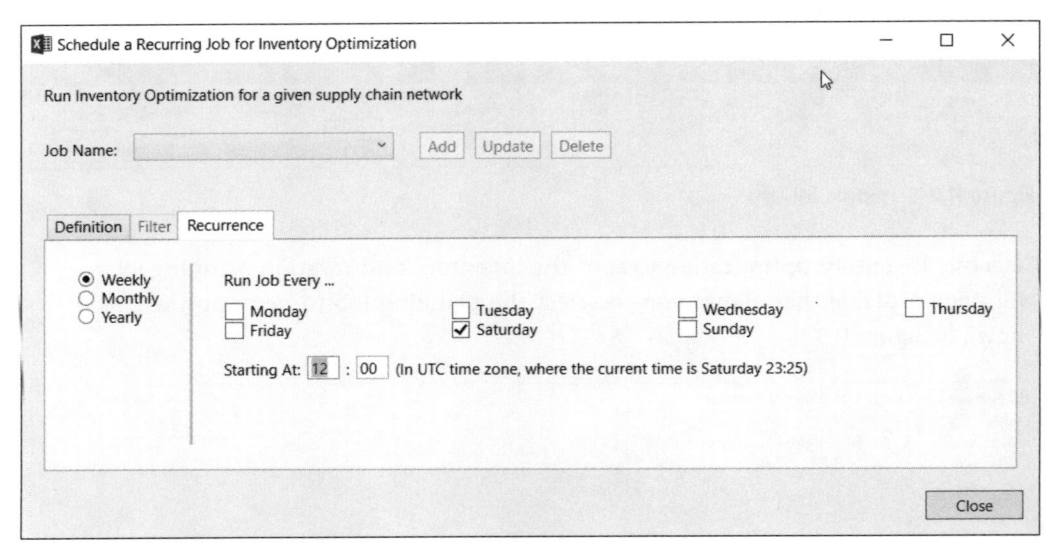

Figure 11.4 Select Recurrence in Scheduling

When running inventory optimization, it's not just the inventory optimization algorithms that need to run, but also, for example, recalculation of the forecast accuracy as an input to the inventory optimization algorithm. Both jobs can be scheduled independently, but that would leave the planner to guess the duration of the run time of the forecast accuracy task, build in a buffer, and schedule the inventory optimization algorithms slightly later. Of course, there's a better way, which is embedded in setting up planning tasks in the Application Job Template app. A planning job template can have multiple planning operators run in parallel. Here it's possible to combine integration jobs (e.g., load actual sales), for example, with planning jobs (e.g., calculate forecast accuracy and run inventory optimization). This allows an end-to-end planning job to run. These planning job templates can be made available in Excel for a planner to run or can be scheduled in the same time-based fashion.

To setup a planning job, you can go to the SAP Fiori app Application Job Template. After you click **Create** at the top of the screen, you can provide a **Job Template** name and define a **Recurrence Pattern**, as shown in Figure 11.5.

11.2 Manual versus Automated Workflow

Figure 11.5 Create Job Template

After you click the **Maintain Steps** button, you can add various steps to the application job template, as shown in Figure 11.6.

Figure 11.6 Add Steps to Job Template

11   Planning Your Implementation

Saving the application job template results in the application job template providing all the parameterization options, allowing you to specify the planning area, version, filters, and specific parameters pertaining to the jobs you selected as part of the template. In our case, we selected ABC segmentation, which asks for a segmentation ID, and the inventory planning job, which allows you to select the exact algorithm—consistent with the algorithms covered in this book—that should be executed, as shown in Figure 11.7.

Operator	Description
10002	Decomposed (single-stage) inventory optimization
10003	Global (multi-stage) inventory optimization
10004	Expected lost demand
10006	Calculate Target Inventory Components

Figure 11.7 Select Inventory Operator to Run

After saving, the job can be executed per the recurrence pattern specified.

Finally, the next level of complexity would be delivered via cross-system job schedulers. Imagine that a bit of processing is required prior to loading the actual sales into the SAP IBP system, such as making sure all actual sales are in the data store SAP IBP pulls them from. In this case, it would be valuable to leverage specific applications known as cross-system schedulers, which can interpret dependencies between systems to release planning jobs. SAP IBP allows you to leverage cross-system schedulers over web services. The schedule can call a web service in SAP IBP to trigger the start of

11.2 Manual versus Automated Workflow

a job and can then use a web service to learn if the job is completed. Upon completion, the next job can be started.

The more automated jobs run, the more important capabilities like management by exception become. When the jobs are running automatically, it's important to identify when something goes wrong. A good practice for doing this identification as a business user is to leverage custom alerts, as provided by SAP Supply Chain Control Tower, which allows for listing all the cases in which planning results are not aligned with the expectations of the planners.

For example, it's possible to create a key figure that contains the previous version of the target safety stock. When executing an inventory optimization run, it's possible to first copy the current results of the inventory optimization—say, the target safety stock key figure—to the previous version target safety stock using a copy operator. Both operators—the copy operator to perform the copy and the inventory optimization operator—can be grouped in a planning job template. Consequently, a custom alert can be created that compares the previous version target safety stock with the newly calculated one and raises an alert if the difference is more than 20%. An example is shown in Figure 11.8.

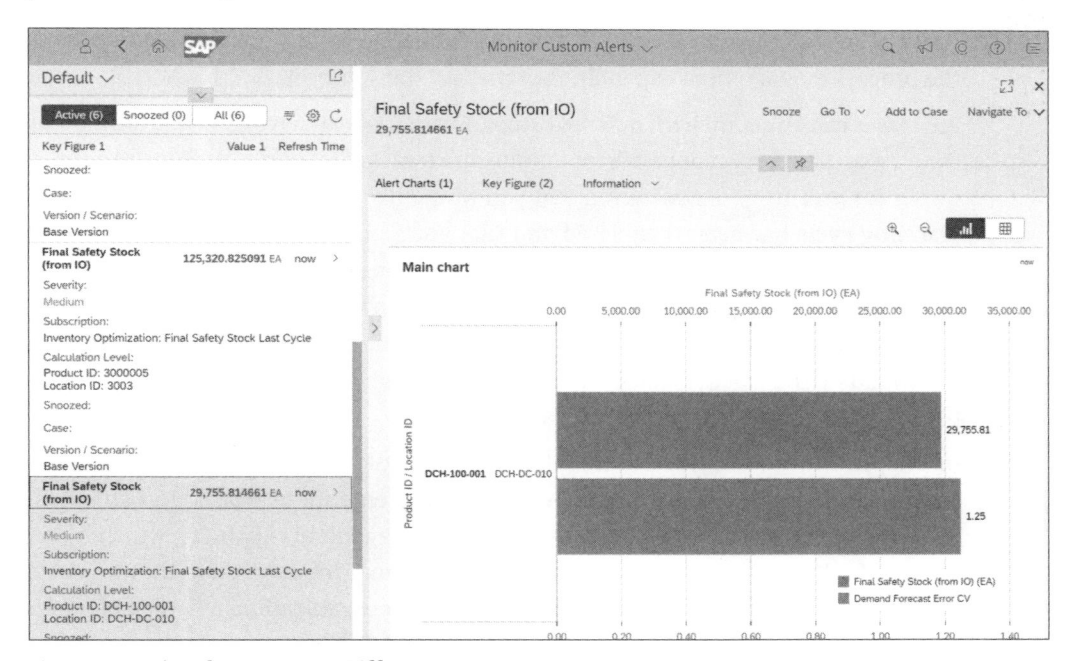

Figure 11.8 Alert for Inventory Differences

379

11 Planning Your Implementation

Different levels of alerts can be created, such as a medium-priority alert if the difference is more than 20% and a high-priority alert if the difference is more than 50%. This allows a planner not to spend too much time reviewing all the calculated results but focus on those cases in which there's a big shift. A big shift could occur, for example, because the forecast error suddenly becomes much higher. In such a case, the planner can create a case to leveraging SAP Supply Chain Control Tower and ask the demand planner what happened to cause this big decrease in forecast accuracy. Based on the information from the demand planner, the inventory planner can take action, either accepting the higher safety stock, tweaking the parameters or historical numbers (e.g., due to the sales history not being correctly recorded), or overwriting the results of the optimization if he believes it's warranted.

11.2.2 Process Management

The approach discussed in the previous section enables scheduling workflow in a technical sense; however, it fails to take into consideration process dependencies that require planners to complete specific tasks before moving on. For example, it could be considered important for the demand planning cycle to complete prior to running inventory optimization. These dependencies can be enabled by leveraging the process management capabilities of the SAP IBP solution.

Processes can be set up with different steps. Every step can have one or multiple step owners, or planners responsible for executing a task. For example, imagine as a global owner for inventory optimization that you would like to make sure that the demand planning cycle has been completed and that your local inventory planners in their regions have validated the key inputs they're responsible for (such as lead time and lead time variability). You could establish a process in which those steps are prerequisites to the inventory optimization run. You then have to run inventory optimization, validate the global results, and provide the go-ahead to your regional inventory planners to validate the next level of detail.

In Chapter 10, we provided a complete overview of establishing your process for inventory optimization. SAP IBP allows you to implement the process in SAP IBP for sales and operations by leveraging the process management capability, which is part of the SAP IBP for sales and operations application. This capability allows you to enable a truly integrated workflow throughout your organization, in which planners will act based on tasks generated by the process workflow. An example process can be generated as shown in Figure 11.9, in which we used a simple inventory optimization

11.2 Manual versus Automated Workflow

process, starting with demand review and preparing data, running inventory optimization, and validating inventory components.

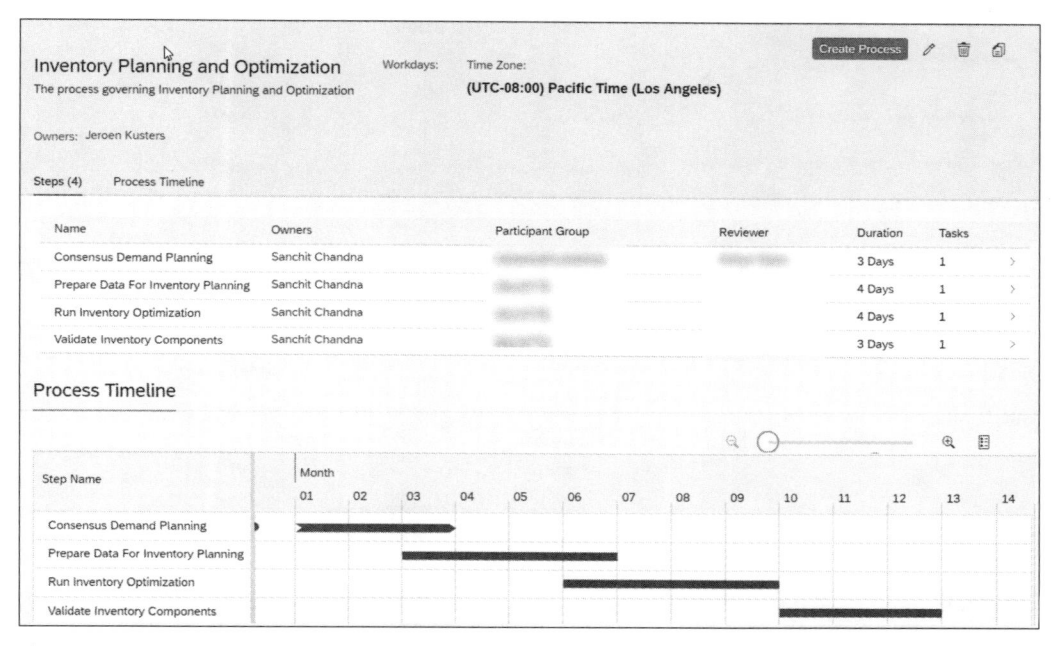

Figure 11.9 Process Management in SAP IBP

If you use the process management capabilities in SAP IBP, it's possible to leverage the process flow capability to trigger tasks. The process can be established in such a way that it can trigger application jobs at the start or end of each process step. Figure 11.10 shows the creation of a process template in which it's possible for every process step to define what jobs need to be triggered at the start and end of the process step. In the example shown, we can consider the demand review process a prerequisite to inventory optimization. The process of demand review starts with taking the demand history and running the statistical forecast. When the step is completed – which happens when all planners have completed the tasks that have been generated by the process management—the application job to copy the demand to inventory optimization is started automatically.

This approach allows you to enable a true workflow that will ensure the user-triggered dependencies in the organization are considered, promoting smooth process management.

381

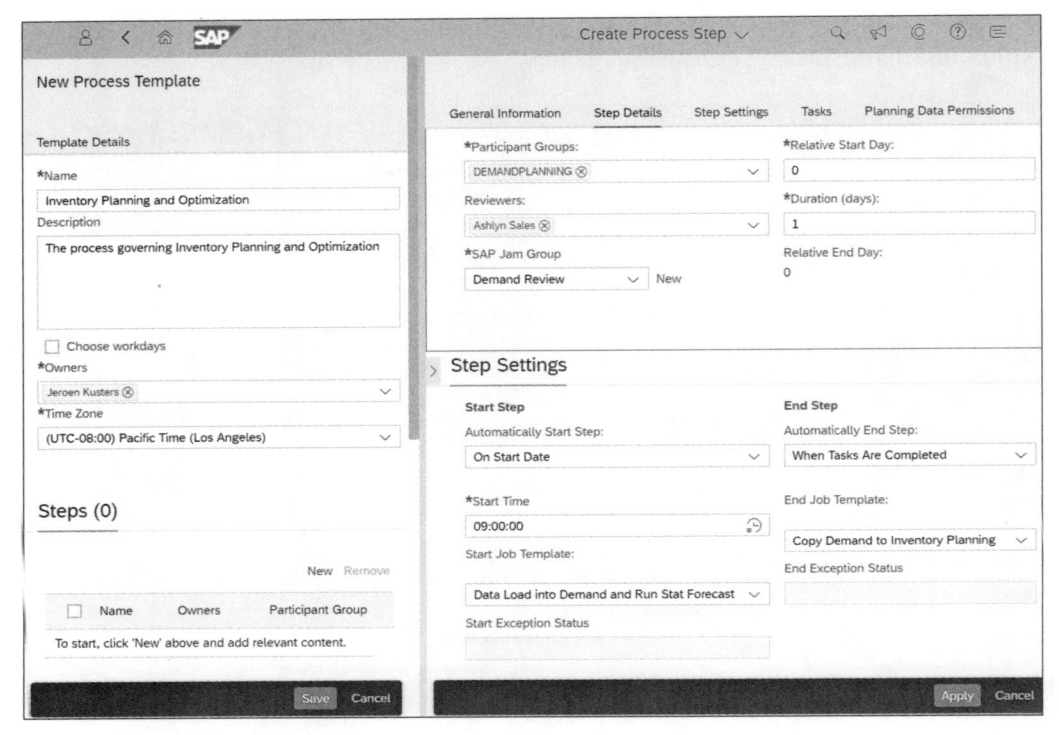

Figure 11.10 Create Process Template

11.3 Agile versus Waterfall Implementation Methodology

So far in this chapter, we've focused on the activities that need to be performed to create an inventory planning solution. To organize these activities into a project methodology, the agile implementation approach has gained a lot of momentum. Without trying to explain the full agile methodology in detail, in this section we'll give an overview of some key agile principles and describe how the SAP IBP solution is uniquely positioned to leverages these principles.

11.3.1 Agile Principles

Agile implementation principles change the foundation of an implementation approach compared to traditional implementation methodologies, typically referred to as *waterfall methodologies*. Figure 11.11 shows the three key considerations that are inherently part of every implementation: timeline, budget, and scope. In a traditional waterfall approach, mostly scope is considered the fixed constraint, with budget and timeline ending up de facto as estimates. This causes a lot of projects to run over time and over budget to deliver a predefined scope. Agile implementation approaches aim to turn this around and consider timeline and budget fixed, allowing the scope to vary. This ensures timely, on-budget delivery of a solution, but scope becomes more negotiable. To understand this better, we need to introduce a couple more agile concepts to recognize why this is a good idea.

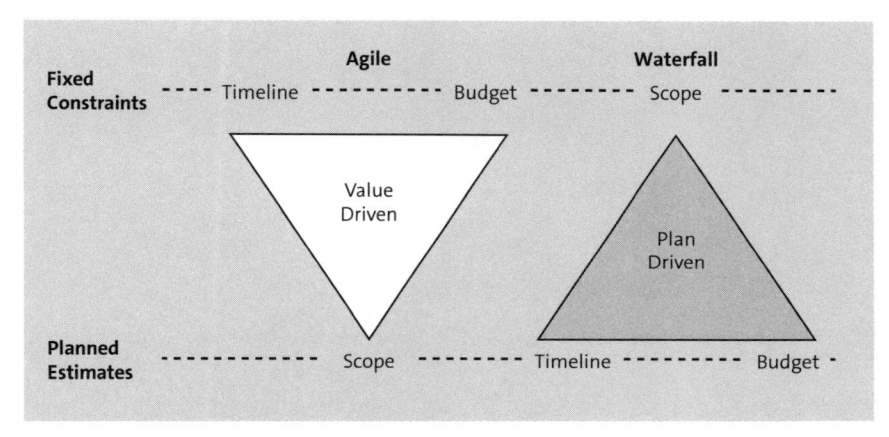

Figure 11.11 Agile versus Waterfall

The essence of why agile methodologies work is embedded in the realization that scope is never accurately defined at the start of a project. The scope is typically defined by asking planners what they need to realize the business objectives set forward for the program. Given that new solutions often provide disruptive capabilities, this question is almost impossible for planners to answer accurately prior to project engagements; it requires a certain understanding of the future solution to know what you need.

11.3.2 User Stories

In agile projects, typically requirements are broken down from conceptual objectives (themes) of the project to the lowest level of execution activities (tasks). Yet it's not required to have the lowest level of detail available at the start of the project; the mission statement can be articulated in themes and epics to start agile projects.

11　Planning Your Implementation

Figure 11.12 and Table 11.1 give an example of how requirements for an agile implementation can be decomposed.

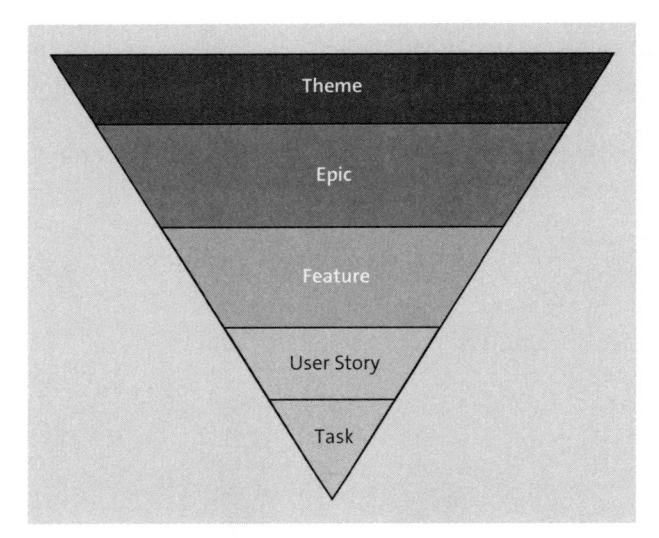

Figure 11.12 Levels of Decomposition of Levels in Requirements in Agile Implementation

	Definition	Agile Example
Theme	Themes are strategic objectives for the business.	Reduce the total available inventory while preserving customer service as status quo.
Epic	Epics are large scopes of work for a system or initiative.	Drive true multiechelon inventory optimization.
Feature	Features represent product benefits that are too large or too complex to complete in a single sprint.	Perform a multiechelon target safety stock calculation for products stocked in warehouses.
User story	User stories are descriptions of desired functionality, told from the user's perspective, that the team commits to deliver within a sprint.	As an inventory planner, I want to be able to execute a full multiechelon inventory optimization run for all products in division X so that inventory can be reduced while maintaining a 90% customer service level.

Table 11.1 Levels of Decomposition of Requirements in Agile Projects

	Definition	Agile Example
Task	Tasks are further decomposition of user stories. They're individual steps or activities that are required to consider a user story complete.	I should be able to execute the run from Excel.

Table 11.1 Levels of Decomposition of Requirements in Agile Projects (Cont.)

At the highest level of the requirements hierarchy in agile projects, typically the theme or epic level, the project objectives are stated. These set out the high-level direction the program is intended to pursue. The more detailed exact requirements—often referred to as *user stories*—provide the more specific requirements for users, including the role of the user ("As an inventory planner"), the user's requirements ("I want to…"), and the value statement ("so that…"), ensuring that a clear value is associated with the task. This value statement will help the project prioritize requirements per their value to ensure that within the fixed timeline and budget, the most important features are being enabled. Typically, those most important features, as expressed in the user stories, will make up a *minimum viable product*, which is used to ensure that the scope leveraged to go live is acceptable.

User stories don't have to be completely articulated at the start of the project and typically exhibit six key attributes, which are important to check as they will contribute to the success of the agile implementation. User stories are said to follow the *INVEST principle*:

- **Independent**
  There should be no dependencies between user stories, which means they should be able to be realized on their own.
- **Negotiable**
  They should allow further refinement with stakeholders to provide options for the value, time, and costs.
- **Valuable**
  Ensure there's a value associated with every requirement. If there's no value to realizing the user story, why should time and effort be invested in it?
- **Estimable**
  They should be specific enough to assess the workload associated with the user story to allow efficient prioritization and planning.

- **Small**
  They should be small enough be realized in one sprint (we'll introduce the concept of sprints shortly).

- **Testable**
  Clear acceptance criteria should be specified. What would it take for the user to accept the user story as done?

11.3.3 Agile Teams and Roles

To organize work efficiently, various roles are defined in agile projects, each with specific responsibilities:

- **Product owner**
  This individual is responsible for developing the product backlog, which is the list of all user stories to be considered during the project.

- **Scrum team**
  This team will be tasked will performing the activities defined in the product backlog. There might be one or multiple scrum teams—for example, one for demand planning, one for supply planning, and one for inventory planning.

- **Scrum master**
  The leader of the scrum team tracks progress, manages impediments, and facilitates the agile ceremonies we'll introduce in the next section.

- **Scrum of scrums**
  A meeting of the scrum masters of several scrum teams to ensure the full program is coordinated and aligned.

- **Users**
  These are the planners who will leverage the SAP IBP solution as their system for supply chain planning.

- **Stakeholders**
  The rest of the project and business organization members are all stakeholders.

This agile organization is responsible primarily for delivering upon the project objectives. This delivery is governed in different phases.

11.3.4 Agile Phases

The last difference we want to touch upon in comparing agile to waterfall in terms of implementation implications is the way project phases are organized in an agile implementation. The project phases are organized in such a way that they ensure the tuning and realization of user stories can be executed in the most effective way.

Agile projects typically start with a discovery phase, in which the high-level objectives the project sets out to realize are broken down from themes and epics to features and user stories. This is typically done hand in hand with establishing a baseline SAP IBP solution that will be demonstrated to the users. As we mentioned in Section 11.1, SAP IBP implementations should start from a sample planning area. That sample planning area makes a good baseline solution that can be demonstrated to users while working through the discovery phase. This allows users to understand what they're specifying when describing the required functionality, thereby avoiding the pitfall of trying to specify the requirements of a system they've never seen before.

In the discovery phase, key users will work closely with configuration experts to discuss the best approach to realize the business objectives. Different capabilities in SAP IBP will be shown, and the information gleaned will be translated to user stories, which will govern the next phase. Typically, the discovery phase can be closed with a series of conference room pilots, in which core capabilities are demonstrated to a broader set of users so that everyone understands the integrated capabilities. This ensures that, for example, demand and supply planners see the inventory planning capabilities, making sure that when they specify requirements for their business objectives, they keep track of the broader integrated solution objectives.

These conference room pilots become a recurring pattern when moving through the next phase of the project, which is typically referred to as the *agile build* phase. This phase is typically broken down into *sprints*, mostly ranging from one to four weeks, in which a set of user stories or features are selected to be realized. Preparing for a sprint and executing it is done via ceremonies, or events, which are typically as follows:

- **Sprint planning**
  The scrum team meets with the product owner, estimating and committing to which user stories will be delivered when, based on capacity for and priorities of user stories.

- **Daily standup meetings**
  These are very short daily touchpoints, in which the team is supposed to "stand up" to ensure the meeting doesn't drag into a detailed design discussion. The focus is on what activities were performed yesterday, what will be performed today, and what might be blocking team members from moving forward. If roadblocks are

identified, the approach to resolve them can be discussed, but not the solution itself.

- **Sprint review**
  The team will demo the completed user stories in the system for the users, obtaining agreement from the users that the capability of the tool as demonstrated will meet their acceptance criteria.

- **Sprint retrospective**
  This scrum team internal meeting asks what went well and what could be done better in future sprints.

Sprints can be organized in releases, which make up a consistent set of user stories—minimally the minimum viable product as defined—which are moved to a productive environment. Testing is performed during the sprints by the scrum team, but often there's also a phase of testing between the completion of the sprint and the release of the functionality to production. This testing can take different forms, from integration testing ensuring the connections to all systems work, to user acceptance testing ensuring users can use the solution to drive business value, to regression testing ensuring previously deployed releases still work. Upon completion of the required testing, the solution can be deployed to production. In SAP IBP, the full planning area is redeployed and activated every time it's moved to production.

It's unlikely that all user stories can be addressed in one release because users will continue to generate user stories throughout the project. Although a definite issue for waterfall approach projects, in which scope is the fixed constraint, this behavior is welcomed in agile projects. It ensures that the solution has a healthy backlog, ensuring it can grow with the business organization, maturing as the inventory planning capability matures. On the flip side, this might imply that the project is never over because there always will be improvements to make. Combine that with the idea of the SAP IBP solution itself—with its quarterly releases providing new capabilities—and you can see the paradigm shift away from implementations every decade and toward continuous improvements.

If this is well understood, it becomes a real asset in implementing integrated business planning solutions. Projects typically have a disruptive impact on companies because they take time away from business users who have a full-time job—for example, running inventory planning operations. Understanding that the solution is never complete allows companies to commission short, aggressive projects, which are disruptive but stay within an estimated timeline and budget. In these projects, a minimum viable product that meets the core business objectives should be established.

As soon as is realistically feasible, the business should revert back to business as usual, operating the newly implemented system. In that operation, however, continuous improvement needs to be embedded thoroughly. The users—who now know how to ask for improvements in terms of user stories with clear value statements—can continue to ask for smaller changes, which can be handled by lightweight scrum teams that remain active throughout the operation of the new solution. This ensures optimal usage of SAP IBP as a solution, supporting an ever-improving integrated business planning capability.

In this section, we introduced the key principles of agile implementation methodologies and showed how the SAP IBP solution, with sample planning areas and quarterly releases, is uniquely positioned to realize their best value.

11.4 Roles and Responsibilities

Before closing this chapter, let's take a minute to describe the key roles and responsibilities required to implement and maintain your SAP IBP solution, as follows:

- **Inventory planners**

    Inventory planners are the key users for your inventory planning and optimization solution, as enabled by SAP IBP. They're responsible for analyzing the inputs to inventory optimization, such as forecast accuracy, lead time and its variability, and service levels. They'll validate the results in terms of inventory targets, safety stocks, and inventory components.

    Typically, the user population is split into normal users and key users, depending on the depth of involvement in the inventory planning and optimization processes. Key users are more apt to understand the detailed calculations in the inventory optimization capability, but not every planner needs to have the same depth of understanding. Yet in many cases the sheer magnitude of products will require a bigger workforce to analyze the results, such as for a big retail organization with hundreds of thousands or even millions of location-product combinations. Most normal users will understand the drivers of inventory, such as higher service level driving higher inventories or why better forecast accuracy drives lower safety stock. Inf the results for specific observations don't make sense to the planners, they can work with their power users, who tend to have a deeper understanding, asking questions or making tweaks to the parameters to ensure the results are aligned with the business objectives.

In many cases, it makes sense to designate one of the power users as the product owner, as defined in the previous section. We noted that the product owner is a key role in the project, but the improvements of the SAP IBP solution should grow with the maturity of the inventory planning and optimization capability, so this role should continue beyond the project phase.

- **Configuration experts**
Configuration experts are typically found in the IT organization but can reside in the business organization as well—for example, as power users. They are responsible for performing the configuration required to make sure the SAP IBP solution meets the business requirements set forward by the planners in their user stories. Configuration in SAP IBP is much more accessible than in more traditional advanced planning solutions, so it's more apt to have functionality-inclined experts oversee it.

- **Integration experts**
Integration experts make sure that the data is integrated with the other applications in the organization, from the ERP system to possible planning execution systems on the production floor. Data integration work tends to be more technical in nature and thus resides mostly in the IT organization. It includes setting up the data extraction structures in the backend system and performing the SAP Cloud Platform Integration configuration to connect the data sources to the SAP IBP target tables and vice versa.

- **System administrators**
The system administrators are key IT employees who are responsible for connecting the authentication providers and making sure the system is accessible for all users. Typically, role creation and user creation is performed by system administrators aligned with the IT security approach of the organization. System administrators also carry a responsibility to communicate upgrades to the system, to SAP IBP, to SAP Cloud Platform Integration, and to the data provisioning agent, because they're the first ones to receive this information from SAP.

- **SAP cloud operations team**
Given that SAP IBP is deployed as a software-as-a-service application hosted by SAP, there's a lot of technical administrative work performed by SAP. The SAP cloud operations team is the key team responsible for hosting and uptime of the solution, aligned with the service level agreement specified in the licensing agreement.

The team is the first point of contact if stability issues arise and will respond to tickets related to the stability of the solution. It also communicates known service disruptions and upgrades.

- **SAP IBP product support team**
  Finally, the SAP IBP product support team is responsible for the SAP IBP product, its direction, and its future development. This team develops the solution and tends to be the second level of support in case of true functionality issues identified by clients with respect to the solution.

Aligned with the evolution toward more agile implementation methodologies, the SAP IBP product team itself is organized in a more agile way. This allows the team members to be more responsive to clients' business requirements, ensuring the SAP IBP solution continues to cater to the business imperatives it's meant to support. It is possible for clients to provide feedback and suggest improvements or new functionality via the customer influence portal. There, the improvement or functionality suggestions can be posted for other clients to assess and vote on. The improvement or functionality suggestions with the highest votes and aligned with the product direction will make it into the SAP IBP product backlog. This way, SAP tries to ensure the solution continues to evolve with direction from and in line with the priorities of its clients.

Every quarter—with the new release announcement—SAP publishes a roadmap that offers an outlook for the features planned for the next three releases. This allows you to plan your implementation accordingly, factoring in functionality planned for release in the future.

11.5 Summary

In this chapter, we provided an overview of the key aspects that are important when planning your implementation of SAP IBP for inventory. We covered some key considerations to keep in mind with respect to deploying cloud software. We talked about workflow, which can be automated to the extent applicable in your environment. We explained the difference between an agile implementation approach and more traditional ones and how the SAP IBP solution uniquely fits with more agile principles. We closed the chapter by covering some key roles and their responsibilities in an organization running SAP IBP.

Now that we've covered how to plan your implementation, we'll move into some examples of companies that have performed inventory planning and optimization implementations. In the next chapter, we'll introduce various examples and describe their backgrounds, cases for action, scopes and approaches, and finally their value drivers.

Chapter 12
Case Studies

In this final chapter, we'll try to bring inventory planning to life with the help of a series of case studies. These case studies will demonstrate how companies have implemented inventory planning and optimization enabled by SAP IBP for inventory.

This chapter will cover four different case studies, which allows us to demonstrate a variety of different applications of inventory planning and optimization enabled by SAP IBP for inventory. For every case study, we'll start with a short introduction of the company, followed by the case for action, explaining why the company embarked on its inventory journey. We'll then cover some details of the implementation, closing each section with the value the project has brought to this client and what we learned based on the implementation.

12.1 Case Study 1: Manufacturing Industry

In our first case study, we'll cover a company implementing SAP IBP in combination with execution in SAP APO. This is a very common scenario for the earlier releases of SAP IBP. We'll first introduce the company background, the case for action to engage in this SAP IBP implementation, the scope and approach, and the value drivers. We end by covering points that we hope are useful as gotchas to avoid in your own implementation.

12.1.1 Company Background

Our first case study takes us to a leading manufacturer of engineering, wood, and building products, listed on the New York Stock Exchange. The company's annual sales turnover is in the range of $2.5 billion. The company is headquartered in Tennessee and it has manufacturing plants in the United States and Canada. It has a considerable market share in the United States, with leading home improvement giants like Home Depot and Lowe's as its main customers.

12 Case Studies

12.1.2 Case for Action

With a complex supply chain network consisting of manufacturing plants, regional hubs, and warehouses, this company's primary focus was to ensure the right inventory in the right place. The company wanted to discard the traditional practice of safety stocks using the rule of thumb and instead generate inventory targets using scientific data. Because 80% of demand was forecast, it was important to balance the forecast accuracy with the right amount of inventory. The inventory targets would be one of the inputs to supply planning, to address storage capacity and transportation as the main constraints.

12.1.3 Implementation Scope and Approach

This implementation comprised a deployment of various key SAP applications: SAP Advanced Planning and Optimization (SAP APO) for planning execution, SAP IBP for more strategic planning, and SAP ERP for execution.

In SAP IBP, the following elements were implemented:

- **SAP IBP for sales and operations**
  This was a monthly process to generate forecast collaborations using statistical forecasting and consensus overrides.

- **SAP IBP for response and** supply
  The objective of SAP IBP for response and supply was to generate a high-level monthly constrained supply plan to be used for mid-term planning.

- **SAP IBP for inventory**
  This was mainly used for three purposes:
  - Generate time-phased safety stock targets in the multiechelon supply chain based on demand and supply variabilities for critical products
  - Offer key supply planning indicators for monitoring supply chain health
  - Provide insights to supply planners about which products need more attention

The implementation of SAP IBP was complemented with SAP APO to generate a tactical, more granular constrained supply plan based on inputs from SAP IBP. The main motivation to use SAP APO was to meet operational requirements like transportation constraint planning, quotas, deployment, and Transport Load Builder (TLB), which are missing in SAP IBP.

Finally, SAP ERP was the system of record and source for transactions. SAP ERP was integrated with SAP APO for execution of data such as purchase requisitions and planned production orders. SAP ERP was also connected to SAP IBP for stock on hand and firm supplies necessary for netting off of demands.

Zooming more into SAP IBP for inventory, ABC and XYZ segmentation was used. Due to a large number of products, it was important to identify which products to focus attention on. ABC classification was based on the volume of the past six months of shipment history and future six-month forecast, while XYZ was based on the past twelve-month forecast error CV. Based on this, statistical forecasting was monitored for A-Y and B-Y classes, while manual forecasting and inventory target adjustments were used for A-Z class.

The Forecast Error Calculation application was used to calculate the forecast error. Based on product maturity level, the forecast and shipments were aggregated at either the customer group-product level or customer group-plant-product level. Two distinct forecast error calculation profiles were configured for this. Various iterations and lead times in the supply chain were used to conclude that a lag of three periods gave better results. Error CV was based on MAPE calculation.

The multilevel inventory operator was used as a standard operator to perform inventory optimization. There was no planning unit used to create a product selection. Because MEIO was run weekly, periods between review of one was used. The default target service level was determined by ABC classification, with higher weight given to service levels maintained in the demand stream table. Because supply was planned at a monthly level, the production lead time was replicated as four weeks.

Target inventory components calculation was used, with the main output of this operator being the target inventory position. For supply planning, the target inventory position was used as the inventory target. The other outputs from this operator, like pipeline stock, cycle stock, and reorder point, were used for reporting.

The multilevel inventory optimization served as the input into supply planning in SAP IBP and SAP APO. A monthly target inventory position—using last period aggregation—was used by SAP IBP for response and supply as the inventory target for monthly supply planning. Weekly recommended safety stock was sent to SAP APO for tactical planning.

With this model, the company succeeded in bringing all applications together, from SAP IBP through SAP APO to SAP ERP, building a complete planning capability inclusive of inventory planning and optimization in an end-to-end integrated SAP environment.

12.1.4 Value Drivers

The value driven by this implementation can be summarized as follows:

- Inventory targets were based on more reliable data than the rule of thumb. The multiechelon calculation ensured inventory targets were based on global parameters instead of silos at the plant level.
- Homogeneous data in SAP IBP with other processes brought uniformity and reduced data latency.
- Fluctuations in demand were better responded to by time-phased inventory target calculations.
- Output metrics from MEIO were used to monitor the execution of stock transfers.
- Forecast error metrics were used for monitoring accuracy in the forecasting process.
- ABC/XYZ classification helped determine areas of focus based on the run rates of the products.

12.1.5 Lessons Learned

Out of this implementation, there are a couple of key takeaways:

- Because supply and MEIO were planned for in the same SAP IBP planning version, the inventory holding cost rate key figure impacted both inventory target calculations and the supply calculations.
- Lead time adjustments are required when MEIO and S&OP/supply are not planned in the same lowest buckets.
- Storage capacity was one of the main constraints for this company and it would have improved the solution (this is a standard constraint in MEIO now).

12.2 Case Study 2: Consumer Goods

In the second case study, we'll move to an industry in which inventory planning and optimization has been at the core for a long time. In the consumer goods industry, the number of stock-keeping units and locations and the lost sales paradigm drive a key focus on having the right products available at the right time.

12.2.1 Company Background

The second case study takes us to implementation of SAP IBP for inventory at a leading consumer goods company focused on beauty retail. A market leader in various American markets, this company was built up out of five business units working various retail channels. The company brings close to 500 product lines to its clients, generating close to 4 billion in sales.

12.2.2 Case for Action

The case for action for this big consumer products company to move toward implementation of inventory planning and optimization was based on the following core needs of the business:

- Multiple business units selling the same products without any visibility into the inventory situation across the units
- Unable to attain a high customer service level due to inefficient inventory planning
- Irregularity in maintaining stocks across the supply chain
- Unreliable inventory plans during peak periods of product phase

12.2.3 Implementation Scope and Approach

The implementation was focused on SAP IBP for inventory and deployed the following capabilities:

- Single-stage inventory optimization
- Multistage inventory optimization
- Lost sales inventory optimization
- Forecast error
- Inventory optimization

The IT team members at this organization were mainly managing and analyzing the results of multistage and single-stage inventory optimization, along with forecast error CV. For them, lost sales inventory optimization and inventory optimization deterministic were good options for analysis, but their existing supply infrastructure wasn't mature enough to fully utilize the results of those algorithms. As a result, they wanted to ensure the business could incrementally understand the results of a multistage inventory optimization run and evaluate the forecast error CV ranges for their different business units.

Single-stage inventory optimization was used frequently to determine the effect of local changes on any given product-location after the multistage inventory optimization was run in a simulation mode. They used it predominantly for their top products, for which the demand pattern was fluid in nature and more working capital was involved due to a high inventory carrying cost.

Forecast error CV was another crucial algorithm from the whole inventory optimization perspective; we observed a value out of range (generally CV greater than 0.35) used to have an exponential effect on the safety stock numbers. Again, there were various business reasons for it, but the IT team was more focused on affecting the results of the multistage inventory optimization run via operator inputs than on improving the demand quality, which was a known issue at this organization.

Before the MEIO implementation at this organization, inventory optimization was done by running the single-stage algorithm, which planned inadequately between the different links in the supply chain network (link-to-link), with isolated results generating overestimated inventory scaling. Implementing multilevel inventory optimization showed the coordinated planning results among all links of the supply chain network, thus eliminating redundant stocks along the chain.

Building strong demand and a network of supply propagation is the key to multilink inventory planning, and at this organization demand was an issue because it was implemented in a non-SAP system with high-level consensus demand plans for customer groups that were incorrectly reflective of the real scenarios.

In the outcome of phase 1 (sell-in) implementation from the process point of view, the team realized the following value:

- A better definition of security stock policies
- The best answer for inventory fluctuation within its supply chain, with more consistent numbers
- Facilitated the day-to-day work of its people, reducing the volume of information in worksheets
- Supported achieving the long-term goal of inventory turnover
- Improved inventory visibility
- Better predictability
- Strategic vision
- The possibility of execution of simulation scenarios

Some of the key elements that the team set up as a cadence were as follows:

- Individualized policies, respecting the characteristics of each business unit
- Review of inventory policies every 45 days
- The flexibility of security inventory in promotional campaigns and launches

12.2.4 Value Drivers

The implementation of SAP IBP for inventory had a clear, measurable impact, which can be summarized as follows:

- A 30% reduction in the inventory policy of the 90 SKUs of class C items
- Cost savings around $13M for 25% of the SKUs in SAP IBP for the first half of FY18
- Scenario inventory planning to help consider potential market expansion in other geographies
- Optimal inventory planning for products in the launch stage

12.2.5 Lessons Learned

We learned the following lessons from the project:

- For an SAP IBP for inventory implementation project, it's key that the input parameters be accurate and clearly defined (e.g., target service levels definitions may sound different to different organizations, but they greatly impact the final safety stock numbers).
- Following an agile implementation methodology was a new approach for most project stakeholders, in an organization historically accustomed to the waterfall project implementation methodology.
- Master data (especially for production source headers and items) should be set up correctly for a pull from source systems into SAP IBP with correct component coefficients.
- In order for SAP IBP for inventory to deliver value, companies need to keep relentless focus on understanding and tuning the parameters, making business decisions regarding services levels, and analyzing these choices in a closed loop cycle.

12.3 Case Study 3: High-Tech Company

Now we'll move toward a completely different segment, focused on highly complex configurable products. This shows the other side of the spectrum, in which customer service doesn't equal off-the-shelf availability.

12.3.1 Company Background

Our third case study brings us to a division of a global semiconductor company, in which SAP IBP was selected to enable a concurrent planning capability. This company was built up out of mostly external manufacturing capabilities, building both data center applications and consumer goods products in a highly competitive market.

12.3.2 Case for Action

The case for action was coming from pressure on inventory levels in the organization. The implementation of SAP IBP for inventory was part of a broader approach toward implementing a concurrent planning capability, which was aimed at bringing together previously independent master production scheduling processes over the different stages in the supply chain. The division has grown into a model in which different stages in the supply chain—four major ones—were solved for independently by a separate planning organization. The concurrent planning project was aimed at bringing all these solutions together into one integrated solution, dramatically improving the response times of planning. Originally it would take two weeks sequentially for every planning process to operate, delaying the demand signal by about eight weeks upstream. This led to a very push-like supply chain planning paradigm given the data latency. Bringing all optimization models into one integrated activity allowed the company to transform toward a more demand-driven planning organization.

The biggest effect of the data latency and the current model was a very clear example of bimodal inventory distribution, as we explained in Chapter 1. Given that it could take weeks, or even months, for the signal from the customers to find its way upstream and knowing the point of differentiation is early in the production cycle (at an early stage, manufacturing decisions will specify which product this raw material will turn into), this was the single biggest driver to engage in this implementation of SAP IBP.

Supporting that integrated planning model, the SAP IBP for inventory application was being implemented. The organization had experience with advanced inventory optimization modules, but its original focus was on finished products. The implementation of SAP IBP, combining the various stages into one model, focused on deploying the complete multiechelon inventory optimization capability, from finished goods to raw materials and every level in between.

12.3.3 Implementation Scope and Approach

In this project, as mentioned, the implementation of SAP IBP for inventory was part of the broader SAP IBP supply planning capability, in which supply network optimization was performed out of the period-based optimizer in SAP IBP for response and supply. Combining supply network optimization and inventory optimization requires a neatly thought-out approach.

The approach of replacing the various sequential supply chain solvers started upstream, at the customer replenishment and finished good assembly stage, and worked its way downstream toward the fabrication process. At every stage, a supply network optimization model was implemented, together with the inventory optimization capability. In order to connect the inventory optimization model from SAP IBP for inventory to the supply network optimization engine available in SAP IBP for response and supply, the calculation of sourcing ratios was leveraged as part of the integrated optimization capability.

We used a periodic inventory review on a monthly basis to calculate the inventory targets based on the network flows while leveraging the period-based supply optimizer weekly for the full network recalculation and daily for the distribution network fulfillment and for triggering requirements for configure-to-order products.

12.3.4 Value Drivers

While we're writing this book, this organization is about to go live with SAP IBP for inventory, so it's too early to quote the exact value delivered from the project. However, it's clear that by combining the sequential optimization runs into one concurrent plan, the following value drivers will be realized:

- Bimodal inventory distribution resolution: build the "right products" based on less data latency with a concurrent planning
- High service and reliability of the planning process via leveraging the advanced multiechelon inventory optimization capability at all levels of the supply network
- Reduced inventory via keeping the right amounts of inventory throughout the supply chain

12.3.5 Lessons Learned

Implementing SAP IBP in complex global organizations with an advanced supply chain always teaches us lessons. In this case, the biggest complexity—and a recurring complexity in most organizations—was the data model. The supply network for complex, high-tech companies exhibits a set of complexities that requires innovative modeling approaches in SAP IBP—for example, the existence of alternate components in bills of materials, alternate resources with different characteristics in supply planning, and the time dependencies of lead times. As the product matures, the manufacturing lead time tends to go down. To model all of this in SAP IBP, close collaboration with SAP was required to address some core challenges, and a flexible data integration model was required.

The next lesson we learned was related to the organizational change impact of implementing the complex, package technology optimizers required. In SAP IBP, tuning the period-based supply network optimization technology, in conjunction with the multiechelon inventory optimizer, exposes a vast list of parameters for planners to tune. These parameters are split over various stages in the supply chain and various functional domains, from capacity planning to inventory planning to master production scheduling. This led to complexity in managing the parameterization, which was identified late in the game. It takes time to move from a technically working solution that makes sense for a limited set of products planned to a globally scalable model that drives numbers that are understandable.

Finally, also on the organizational side, in companies coming from a bimodal inventory model, there are conflicting interests between customer-facing sales and internally focused supply chain groups. Bimodal inventory means having too much of the wrong product and not enough of the right one. Not enough of the right product makes sales personnel nervous because they can't sell what the clients are asking for. On top of that, too much of the wrong product makes supply chain personnel think inventory reduction is the answer. Telling sales to reduce inventories when they can't fulfill customer demand is not a popular message. The solution needs to be explained and considered holistically as a combination of reducing the inventories of the wrong products while increasing the inventories of the right products, thus driving better service at a lower total inventory cost.

12.4 Case Study 4: Consumer Products

Finally we'll look at a leading consumer products company that has recently implemented SAP IBP for inventory. We'll cover the process improvements that come with modeling and analytical advances from SAP IBP. In addition, we'll explain how the project-delivery strategy addresses the unique and evolving inventory optimization solution capabilities that have been codeveloped between the project team of the company and the SAP IBP for inventory product team.

12.4　Case Study 4: Consumer Products

12.4.1　Company Background

The consumer products company in question has more than $63 billion net revenue in 2017. The company's products are sold in more than 200 countries and territories around the world. The company's product portfolio includes a wide range of enjoyable foods and beverages, including 22 brands that each generate $1 billion or more in estimated annual retail sales. The company has more than 260,000 employees. SAP IBP for inventory was deployed across five North America business units focused on nutrition and beverages.

12.4.2　Case for Action

The implementation of SAP IBP for inventory was based on the following focal points from the business:

- **Automated inventory optimization solution**
  The business wanted to optimize safety stock by product-location to identify future inventory reduction opportunities and replace its legacy inventory optimization system.
- **Multiple inventory strategies**
  As shown in Figure 12.1, the business required one inventory module to handle multiple and complex scenarios from all business units.

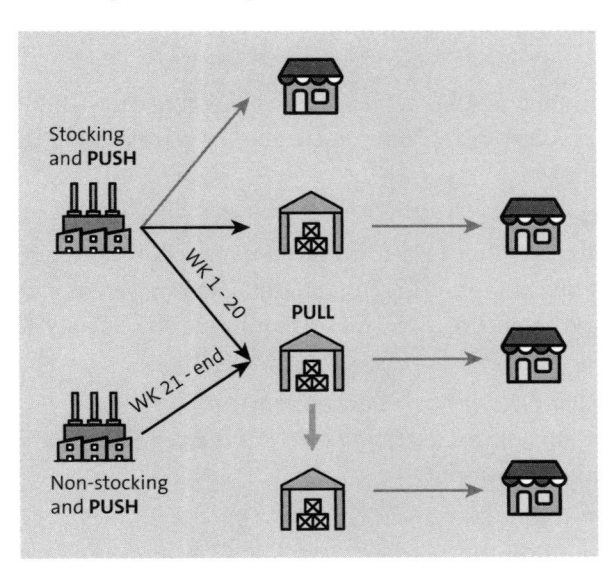

Figure 12.1 Supply Chain with Mixed Inventory Push versus Pull Strategies

12　Case Studies

For example, the solution must model inventory push to address warehouse capacity constraints, model inventory pull to minimize network inventory without warehouse capacity constraints, support effective date sourcing changes, and be able to display components with retail demand, incubation, and product interchangeability.

- **Seamless integration**
  The safety stock and cycle stock integration to supply planning need to be streamlined.

- **User experience**
  The business users required the inventory optimization solution to support exception management, allow aggregation/disaggregation at any desired level, and offer dashboards and charts for KPIs and analytics.

12.4.3　Implementation Scope and Approach

The implementation of SAP IBP for inventory was executed in the following steps:

- **Proof of concept/process design**
  This step involved testing initial inventory optimization model capabilities and inventory simulations, getting familiar with user flexibility and control with the SAP IBP UI and working with the business to define business processes. The goal of this step was to secure business harmony capital expenditure (CAPEX) approval.

- **Prototype**
  This was the initial design and modeling step. With the engagement of the SAP IBP for inventory product development team, 15 different scenarios were created to represent all business requirements.

- **Master data integration and security**
  The master data integration via SAP Cloud Platform was completed in this step. Single sign-on was enabled for business and IT access. SAP IBP planning areas and planning views were configured to ensure all business requirements were satisfied.

- **Transactional data integration and exception management**
  This was the detailed solution modeling and tuning step. All the key figure data integrations were also completed in this step.

- **Output integration and network simulation**
  Outputs from SAP IBP for inventory, such as safety stock and cycle stock, were integrated with the company's supply planning and the distribution requirements

planning system. The quality of solution team also performed model tuning to finalize the final inventory targets.

- **Business go-live and deployments**
A final user acceptance workshop was conducted successfully, and SAP IBP for inventory went live across five business units.

12.4.4 Value Drivers

There are clear benefits for both business and IT from the project, as follows:

- **Inventory reduction**
  - Optimal solution per inventory strategy
- **Scenario planning**
  - Be able to evaluate the impact of multiple scenarios on storage and invested capital
- **Time efficiency**
  - The end-to-end optimization time, including inbound/outbound data integration and optimization, is reduced from 14 hours (legacy solution) to 3 hours (SAP IBP for inventory)
- **Synchronized inventory strategies**
  - Push/pull strategy integrated with supply planning
  - Accurate safety stock and cycle stock at various planning levels across multiple planning systems

12.4.5 Lessons Learned

Key learnings and takeaways from the implementation are as follows:

- **Business engagement**
Business users were fully involved in the implementation project from the beginning and in an agile-like way. This enabled early process definition and effective user training.

- **Prototype**
Proving out the solution design and modeling approach early in the project by doing proofs of concept on small sets of data allows the business to see the potential value early on and creates momentum towards a broader implementation of the inventory optimization capability.

- **Cloud architecture**
  It's very important to schedule enough time for the project team to adjust to the SAP IBP cloud-based architecture and learn the SAP IBP platform (vs. SAP APO on-premise), security strategy (e.g., single sign-on), and plan for ABAP development for complicated business logic.

- **Data readiness and quality of solution validation**
  Using SAP IBP templates, having a well-defined quality of solution validation approach, and leveraging dashboards and alerts are very important to achieve a high solution acceptance rate from the business.

12.5 Summary

In this chapter, we covered four widely different case studies in different industries, covering companies with different drivers to engage in an inventory planning and optimization transformation. Every company had a different approach, a different scope, and a different technological footprint, but you can see there are quite a few similarities between the lessons learned. Data was a recurring source of complexity, which you should be sure to account for, and having the right people involved at the right moment is a key driver for success.

The Authors

Lei Wang is the director of product management, supply chain, at SAP and the product owner for the underlying supply chain algorithm library beneath SAP Integrated Business Planning for inventory and SAP Integrated Business Planning for demand. He has more than a decade of experience in the research and development of enterprise inventory and service optimization solutions. He has also worked with expert users, planners, supply chain analysts, and consultants on various SAP Integrated Business Planning for inventory implementations. Lei Wang has a PhD in industrial and systems engineering from the University of Minnesota.

Sanchit Chandna is a senior lead in the SAP supply chain practice at Deloitte Consulting Canada. He has more than 10 years of experience in the design and implementation of SAP supply chain solutions. He has worked extensively across different industries in the areas of demand management, master production scheduling, rough-cut capacity planning, inventory planning and optimization, and sales and operations planning. He specializes in supply chain planning processes and is an expert in SAP IBP and SAP APO. He has worked with multiple SAP IBP customers as a subject matter expert.

Jeroen Kusters is a leader in the supply chain management practice at Deloitte Consulting LLC. His focus is on helping clients increase revenue and improve margins by building a digital supply chain capability, enabled by cloud-based planning technology. As a thought leader in supply chain management, Jeroen focuses on bringing innovative digital solutions to clients that address complex business challenges. Jeroen started working on SAP Integrated Business Planning in the early days of the solution, led over a dozen of implementations, and advised on many more while leading Deloitte's SAP IBP practice in the United States. Jeroen started his career at Deloitte Belgium, focusing on complex global manufacturing companies. Today he serves as a senior manager at the San Francisco branch of Deloitte Consulting LLC, driving value for clients in the technology sector.

Atul Bhandari is the senior director of predictive supply chain analytics at SAP and product owner for SAP Integrated Business Planning for inventory. He has more than a decade of experience in helping companies adopt inventory optimization and demand-sensing capabilities. Atul acts as the SAP liaison for the SAP user group for inventory and service optimization.

Index

A

ABC analysis 46
ABC classification 96, 144, 320, 324
ABC segmentation 46, 271, 378, 395
Aggregation mode 127
Agile build phase 387
Agile implementation 382
    methodology 399
    phases 386
    requirements 384
    teams and roles 386
Alert key figure 124, 129
Analytics – Advanced app 153
Analytics app 322
Anticipation inventory 24
APICS classification 22
Application job template 378
Application Job Template app 376
Application tables 344
Architecture 105
Attribute app 109
Attributes 108
    as key figures 124
    checks 115
    creating 109
    master data 111
    transformation 124
    types 109
Automated inventory 403
Automatic periodic transfer 341
Average 80
Average demand interval (ADI) 213
Average expedites 317

B

Backlog 221
    calculating 223
    distribution 221
    downstream stocking nodes 224
    drivers 223
    lead-time variability 224

Base level 117
Base version 139
Bias 63
Bias adjustment methods 211
Bill of material (BOM) 58, 99, 177, 185, 247, 276
    many-to-many 100
    many-to-one 99
    one-to-many 99
Bimodal inventory distribution 36, 401
Buffer inventory 25
Bullwhip effect 163, 217
Business engagement 405
Business partners 166
Buyback 98

C

Capital costs 103
Case Management app 47
Case study
    consumer goods 396
    consumer products 402
    high-tech 399
    manufacturing 393
Centralized planning teams 254
Change history 46, 146
Change History app 299
Change History report 298
Characters 109
Charts
    creating 154
    dual axis line chart 323
    scenario comparison 322
Check network algorithm 263
Coefficient of variation 80, 82
Component coefficient 248
Compound master data 113
Conference room pilots 387
Configuration 105
    entities 107
Configuration app 145
Configuration experts 390

409

Index

Constrained, priority-driven heuristic 50
Continuous replenishment 94
Continuous review 187
Copacking 275
Copy options 136
Cost of inventory 71
Cost of lost sales 72
Cost optimization engine 260
Cross-system job schedulers 378
CSV file 344
Custom Alert app 299
Custom alerts 258, 264, 267, 379
   create 299
   input values 305
   levels 380
   metrics 308
   rules 307
Custom Alerts Overview app 304, 308
Customer 168
   attributes 169
   group attributes 170
   grouping 169
Customer lead time 66
Customer service level input 171
Customer service levels 34, 229, 336
Cycle inventory
   input parameter change 334
Cycle service level 70, 93
Cycle stock 23, 233–234, 249
   inventory drivers 189

D

Dashboard – Advanced app 153
Dashboard app 43
Dashboards 153, 267
   creating 154
   data integration 355
   demand 283
   filters 286
   forecast error analytics 285
   inventory plans 289
   navigating 282
   safety stock cost 287
   supply parameters 285
   uncertainty index 282

Data exporting 367
Data extraction 367
Data flow 355, 357
   executing 360
Data importing sequence 345
Data Integration Jobs app 342, 345
   features 344
   time periods 346
   uploading key figures 349
   uploading master data 348
Data latency 400
Data load reports 344
Data provisioning agent 372
Data readiness 406
Data stores 357
Datastores 106, 352
DDMRP Buffer Analysis app 54
DDMRP buffer levels 55
Decentralized planning teams 254
Decimals 109
Decision making levels 334
Decomposed inventory optimization 51
Decoupling points 55
Define and Subscribe to Custom Alert
   app 304
Delivery frequency 98
Demand
   calculating 216
   data cleansing 62
   distribution 78, 84
   forecasting 59
   historical forecast accuracy 204
   history 62
   intermittant 212–213
   propagation 218–219
   seasonality 86
   segmenting 271
   time-varying 200
   uncertainty 75
   variability 75, 216
   versions 312
Demand amplification 163
Demand distribution
   Gamma 193
   normal 192

Index

Demand forecast 57, 217–218
   net requirements 218
   uncertainty 219
Demand review 258, 381
Demand sensing 50
Demand variability 75, 87
   distribution 78
   example 77
   measuring 76
   single stage 237
Demand-driven MRP 53–54
Dependent demand 58
Dependent distribution demand 58
Disaggregation expression 128
Disaggregation mode 127
Discovery phase 387
Distribution 159
   centers 185
   channel 29
   lot size 326
   network 159
Document-based supply networks 157
Drop-shipping 160
Dynamic complexity 163

E

Economic order quantities (EOQ) 102
Empirical rule 83
Excel planning view
   settings 294–295
Excel templates 290
   comments 297
   days coverage alert 294
   days coverage alert indicator 294
   finalize plan 295, 298
   key figures 291
   settings 291
Excel workbook lists 264
Exceptions 263, 304
   managing 264
Executive review 259
Expected loss demand calculation 265
Expected lost demand 52
Extended supply chain network 29
External master data 115

F

Fill rate 70, 93, 196
   evaluating 197
Finished goods 27, 232
Fixed order quantity 102, 187
Fixed quantity 94
Fixed time 94
Forecast accuracy 214
Forecast bias 63, 208
   correcting 210
   correction settings 208
   estimating 210
   negative 63, 210
   positive 63, 210
Forecast error 61, 145, 204
   calculation settings 206
   CV 216, 398
   intermittant demand 213
   measure calculation settings 215
   measures 214
   outlier detection 207
   safety stocks 87
   variability 205
Forecastability analysis 60
Forecasts
   accountability 64
   baseline 59
   demand 217
   evolution 204
   future demand 216
   historical 205
   lag 204
   levels 64
   maintenance 60
   project lifecycle 60
   quantitative 61
Freight cost 98
Functions 361

G

Gamma distribution 193
   advantages 194
Gating factor analysis 50
Global demand plan 277

411

Index

Global inventory optimization 51
Global variables 360

H

Hedging inventory 25
Helper key figure 124
Hierarchy 116
Historical demand variability 205
Holding costs 103
Hybrid teams 255

I

Implementation 369–370
   agile 382
   waterfall 382
Independent demand 58
In-process stock 250
Input quality review 281
Integers 109
Integrated reconciliation 259
Integration 339, 372
   cloud to on-premise 372
   data 148
   data loading 344
   experts 390
   manual data integration 342
   non-SAP systems 366
   SAP Advanced Planning and Optimization (SAP APO) 365
   SAP Cloud Platform Integration for data services 350
   technologies 339
Intermittent demand 212
   calculation settings 212
Internal service level (ISL) 92, 186, 227
   customer service level 229
   optimizing 227
Intuition 333
Intuition building 311, 332
Inventory 22–23
   analysis 266, 268
   calculation 187
   cost 22, 71
   drivers 189, 282, 289

Inventory (Cont.)
   factors 92
   finished goods 27
   holding 28, 103
   holding cost 71
   holding cost ratio 228
   KPIs 279
   levels 400
   locations 28
   maintenance, repair, and overhaul (MRO) 27
   ownership 98
   performance 275, 277
   policies 96, 245
   service parts 27
   structuring 231
   targets 189, 396
   types 231
   variables 57
   work in progress 26
Inventory components calculation 241, 327
   inputs 243
   operator 241
   outputs 248
Inventory control systems 30
   periodic 30
   perpetual 30
   technology 36
Inventory management 31
   building an approach 29
   hybrid systems 32
   pull systems 32
   push systems 31
   technology 37
Inventory optimization 185, 259–260, 332
   algorithm 311
   analyzing results 266
   constraints 186
   data objects 341
   deploying 372
   global (multistage) 265
   network 185
   operator 311
   running 264–265
   validate inputs 262

Index

Inventory planning
    collaboration 276
    cycle frequency 255
    dashboard 261
    example supply chain 275
    finalizing 269, 294
    parameters 263
    process 253, 261
    review 287
    S&OP 258
Inventory planning and optimization 21
    integration 39
    objectives 34
    scenario planning 39
    technology 38
Inventory position 250
INVEST principle 385

J

Job scheduling 374
    automated 375
Just in time (JIT) strategy 66

K

Key Figure Calculation app 132
Key figures 121, 123, 182, 291, 302
    across time 315
    calculating 129–131
    calculation graph 132
    configuring 126
    creating 125
    delete 350
    editing 129
    fields 126
    insert/update 349
    integration 349
    inventory alerts 299
    replace 350
    safety stock 130
    types 124
Key performance indicator (KPI) 279
    recommendations 281
Key users 389

L

Late deliveries 177
Late orders 179
Lead time variability 25, 88
    input 198
    production 88
    safety stocks 89
    supplier 88
Lead times 64, 74, 175, 246
    customer 66
    manufacturing 64
    pipeline stock 66
    reducing 58, 66
    stocking policy 96
    supplier 65
    variability 224
Licensing agreement 370
Linkages 161
Local teams 254
Location 165
    attributes 165
    receiving 174
    supplying 174
Location product 171
    attributes 172
Location sourcing 175
    ratio 175
    rules 175
Lost sales 72
Lot for lot 101
Lot size 101, 246, 328
    impact 199

M

Maintain Communication Users app 367
Maintenance, repair and operational supplies
    (MROs) 232
Make to order 57
Manage Forecast Error Calculations – Inventory
    Optimization app 206
Manage Forecast Error Calculations app 315
Manual data integration 148, 340, 342
    architecture 343
    process 343

413

Index

Manufacturing facilities 28
Manufacturing lead time 64
Manufacturing plants 97
Market competition 74
Master data 111, 342, 399, 404
   cascading 348
   component 180
   customer 168, 170
   delete 348
   insert/update 348
   integration 347
   location 165
   location product 172
   product 167
   production source item 180
   production sourcing item 178
   replace 349
   ship-from location 174
   ship-to location 174
   source customer group 171
   source location 176
   version 139
Master data type 111
   adding attributes 115
   compound 113
   configuring 111
   creating 115
   external 115
   reference 113
   simple 111
   virtual 114
Material requirements planning (MRP) 37, 217, 241
Mean 80
Mean absolute deviation (MAD) 214
Mean absolute percentage error (MAPE) 46, 214
Mean absolute scaled error (MASE) 215
Mean percentage error (MPE) 215
Mean squared error (MSE) 215
MEIO implementation 398
Merchandizing stock 233, 236, 249
Merge facilities 336
Methodology 382
Microsoft Excel 107, 148
Minimum viable product 385

Minimum volume considerations 270
Monitor Custom Alerts app 304, 309
Multi-echelon inventory optimization (MEIO) 173
Multiechelon inventory optimizer 402
Multiechelon network
   calculating 201
   master data inputs 202
   service levels 92
   upstream and downstream 221
Multilevel inventory operator 395
Multilevel supply planning time-series-based heuristic 49
Multiple inventory strategies 403
Multistage network 158

N

Net inventory requirement 245
Network chart 181
Network inventory planning 51
Network propagation 260
Network topology 202
   building blocks 202
New facilities 336
Nodes 158, 161, 171
   stocking vs. non-stocking 337
Non-capital costs 103
Non-root attributes 121
Normal distributions 80, 192
Normal users 389

O

Obsolescence costs 71
Obsolete inventory 25
OData services 148, 340, 367
On-hand stock 249–250
On-time performance 97
Operation types 348–349
Operational planning 341
   integration technologies 341
   order-based 341
Operational review 259
Operators
   copy and disaggregate 361

414

Index

Operators (Cont.)
   mathematical 132
   multiple scenarios 321
Order crossover 198
   frequency 198
   impact 199
Order cycle 68, 172
Order fill rate 70
Order size 98
Order up-to level 187
Ordering costs 71
Outlier detection 207
Outliers 207
Over-forecasting 208, 210

P

Parallel interactions 163
Parameters 143
Partial copy 138
Period order 102
Period recalculation 256
Period weight factor 128
Periodic extraction 341
Periodic replenishment 94
Periodic review 187–188
Periods between review (PBR) 189, 234, 246, 328
   changing 329
   comparison 329
Physical supply networks 157
Pipeline stock 23, 66, 233, 235, 249
   input parameter change 334
   inventory drivers 190
Planning area 118
   activating 138
   copying 136
   creating 119
   sample 371
   setting up 134
Planning Area app 119
Planning data sets 118
Planning horizon 242
Planning level 120, 303
   average key figure 316
   base 121
   creating 122

Planning level (Cont.)
   sample 121
Planning model 105, 107
   constructing 107
   entities 107
Planning operators 143–144
   creating 145
   structuring 265
Planning tasks sequence 260
Planning views 148, 266
   comparison 321
   creating 150
   from template 151
   scenario comparison 324
Policy considerations 270
Postponement strategy 33
Power users 389
Proactive tasks 257
Process management 261, 380–381
   steps 380
Process modeling 261
Product 111, 167
   attributes 167
   network chart 182
Product allocations 50
Product lifecycle 63
   forecasting 60
Product owner 386
Product review 258
Production flow 158
Production shipment frequency 246
Production source header 178
Production sourcing 177
   attributes 178
   item 180
Project 355
   creating 356
Propagated demand mean 249
Provisioning 369
Pull systems 32
Push systems 31

R

Radio-frequency identification (RFID) 31
Raw materials 26, 232

415

Index

Reactive tasks 257
Reason codes 146
   creating 146
   default 146
Rebates 98
Recommended safety stock 329
Recurrence 376
Reference master data 114
Regional distribution center (RDC) 201
Regression techniques 59
Rejection 344
Release notes 373
Reorder point (ROP) planning 250
Replenishment 187
   cycle 69
   lead time 97
   strategies 94
Request level calculation 130
Risk pooling 332
Roles and responsibilities 389
Root mean squared error (RMSE) 215
Root-cause analysis 289, 293

S

Safety inventory 69
Safety stock 25, 69, 78, 233, 235
   allocation policy 172
   average view 317
   calculating 84
   dashboard 287
   days of supply 251
   decomposition 237
   demand variability 237
   distribution 289
   forecast lag 205
   forecasts 87
   generating 317
   input parameter change 334
   inventory drivers 190
   key figures 130
   lead-time variability 197
   lot sizes 200
   minimum 300
   push scenario 227
   service levels 86

Safety stock (Cont.)
   service variability 91, 239
   supply variability 238
Safety stocks
   calculating allocation 226
   exposure period 192
   lead time variability 89
   probability distributions for demand 192
   variability 222
Sales and operations 49
Sales and operations planning (S&OP) 258
Sample Model Entities app 135
Sample planning areas 115, 134
   accessing 135
SAP Advanced Planning and Optimization
   (SAP APO) 41, 394
   integration 365
SAP cloud operations team 390
SAP Cloud Platform Integration 340, 370
SAP Cloud Platform Integration for data
   services 148, 341, 350, 372
   architecture 351
   creating a project 356
   creating an integration 355
   dashboard 355
   key features 351
   mapping content 353
   non-SAP systems 366
   predefined content 354
   prepackaged content 353
   setting up 353
   uploading key figures 349
   uploading master data 348
SAP Data Services agent 351–352
SAP ERP integration 362
SAP Fiori applications 107
SAP Fiori launchpad 43, 305
SAP HANA smart data integration 148, 340–341
SAP IBP
   Excel ribbon 290
   history 40
   introduction 40
   Microsoft Excel planning 43
   platform capabilities 45
   user experience 42

Index

SAP IBP Excel add-in
   connecting 149
SAP IBP for demand 49
SAP IBP for inventory 40
   case studies 393
SAP IBP for response and supply 50, 260, 394, 401
   integration 341
SAP IBP for sales and operations ... 49, 261, 394
SAP IBP product team 391
SAP Jam 45, 106
SAP S/4HANA 353
   integration 362
SAP Sales and Operations Planning powered by SAP HANA 41
SAP Supply Chain Control Tower 47, 258, 264, 304
SAP3 .... 134, 371
SAP3B 134
SAP4 134
SAP4C 134
SAP4S 134
SAP5 134
SAP6 134
SAP7 135
SAP74 135
SAPIBP1 .... 135, 371
Scenario planning 266
Scenarios 45, 139, 142, 312
   ad hoc 337
   comparison 321
   creating 143, 320
   distribution lot size 326
   Excel comparison 321
   inventory components 328
   multiple 321
   PBR 328
   service level 320
   simulating 319
   versus versions 140
Scripts 360
Scrum master 386
Scrum team 386
Seasonal inventory 25
Segmentation 270
Selling, general and administrative expenses (SG&A) 23

Service factor 83
Service level metrics 195
   fill rate to non-stockout probability 196
Service level target 69
   cost of servicing 71
Service level type 92, 337
   fill rate 196
Service levels 69, 319
   cost to serve 74
   current 70
   lead times 74
Service parts 27
Service type 195
Service variability 91, 220, 222, 239
Shelf life 97
Shelf life period 97
Shut down facilities 336
Simple master data 111
Simulations 45, 333
   backlog distribution 222
   saving as a scenario 143
   strategic 336
   tactical 337
Single sign-on 370
Single-stage network 158
Six Sigma 66
Snapshot 145
Snapshot key figure 125, 128
Social collaboration 106
Source customer group 171
   attributes 171
Source type 248
Sourcing decisions 97
Sourcing managers 97
Sourcing rations 260
Sprints 388
Staging table 344
Stakeholders 105
Standard deviation 80
Static complexity 160
Statistical forecasting 49, 144
Statistical modeling 62
Stocking node type 246
Stocking policy 95
   factors 96
   raw material 97

417

Index

Stockouts 72, 257
Storage facilities 28
Strategic inventory positioning 35
Strategic planning 336
Subnetwork ID 172
Supplier lead time 65
   reducing 68
Suppliers 166
Supply Chain Network app 153, 315
Supply chain networks 28, 185
Supply chain operations reference (SCOR) ... 47
Supply network 157, 313
   customization 162
   dashboards 262
   elements 164
   modeling 157–158
   multiechelon 333
   network complexity 161
   nodes 158
   optimization 260, 401
   process complexity 163
   product complexity 162
   single stage 332
   visualizing 181
Supply Network Visualization app 181
Supply review 259
Supply uncertainty 88
Supply variability 238
System administrators 390

T

Tactical planning 340
   integration technologies 341
   time series-based 341
Target inventory 395
Target inventory components 53
Target inventory positions (TIPs) 188
Task 355
   creating 356
Templates 354
   analysis view 290–291, 296
   downloading 345
   Excel 290
   general purpose 354
   key figure 349, 354
   master data 347, 354

Templates (Cont.)
   planning job 376
   planning views 151
   process 381
   SAP ERP and SAP S/4HANA 362
Test tenant 371–372
Testing phase 388
Time buckets 331
Time periods 346
Time profile 116, 346
   accessing 116
Time Profiles app 116
Time series indicator 247
Time series techniques 59
Timestamp 109
Total absolute error (TAE) 215
Total error (TE) 215
Transactional data 342
Transit inventory 23
Transport Load Builder (TLB) 394
Transportation route 158
Transportation shipment frequency 246

U

Uncertain quantity 69
Uncertain time 69
Uncertainty index 282
Under-forecasting 208, 210
Unified planning area 119, 134
   copying 138
   integration 361
Upgrades 373
User interface 105
User stories 383, 388

V

Value statement 385
Variability 69
   drivers 75
Variance 80
Vendor transit stock 250
Version planning 45
Versions 139, 312
   baseline 315

Versions (Cont.)
  creating 141
  versus scenarios 140
Virtual master data 114
Volume discounts 98

W

Weighted average cost of capital (WACC) ... 103
Weighted MAPE (wMAPE) 215
What-if analysis 311
  performing 313
  strategic 334, 336
  tactical 337
  versions and scenarios 312
What-if planning 140, 142

Working capital 35
Work-in-process (WIP) 232

X

XYZ classification 96
XYZ segmentation 46

Y

Yearly buckets 318

Z

Zero quantity 206
Z-Score 83–84

419

- Configure and use the S&OP, demand, response and supply, and inventory planning applications
- Measure your progress with the SAP Supply Chain Control Tower
- Deploy SAP IBP and set it up in your landscape

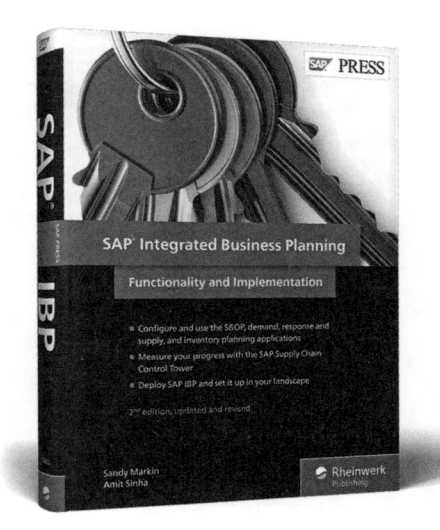

Sandy Markin, Amit Sinha

SAP Integrated Business Planning

Functionality and Implementation

What does it mean to move your supply chain to the cloud? With this guide to SAP Integrated Business Planning, get the complete S&OP, demand, response and supply, and inventory planning picture—and then learn to monitor and control these processes. You'll understand how to set up and use your SAP IBP system, from planning models to user roles. Using industry case studies, see what it takes to ensure a successful adoption of SAP IBP.

504 pages, 2nd edition, pub. 05/2018
E-Book: $69.99 | **Print:** $79.95 | **Bundle:** $89.99

www.sap-press.com/4615

Rheinwerk Publishing

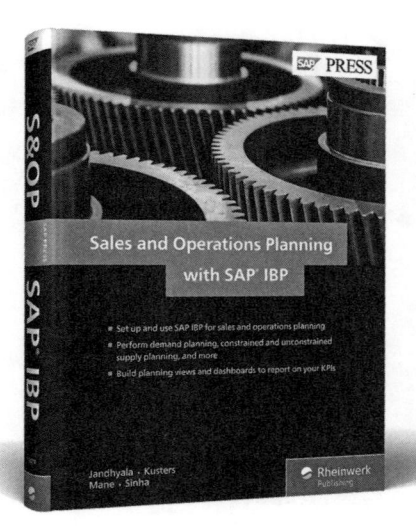

- Set up and use SAP IBP for sales and operations planning
- Perform demand planning, constrained and unconstrained supply planning, and more
- Build planning views and dashboards to report on your KPIs

Jandhyala, Kusters, Mane, Sinha

Sales and Operations Planning with SAP IBP

Ready to get S&OP working for you? See how to configure SAP Integrated Business Planning to fit your organization, from master data types to planning levels. Then execute demand planning, perform unconstrained or constrained supply planning, and consolidate the results into views with step-by-step instructions. Get more out of your new SAP IBP implementation with what-if scenarios, KPIs, dashboards, and built-in integrations.

499 pages, pub. 05/2018
E-Book: $79.99 | **Print:** $89.95 | **Bundle:** $99.99

www.sap-press.com/4589

- Learn what SAP S/4HANA offers for manufacturing, warehousing, procurement, and beyond
- Explore key SAP Fiori applications for reporting and analytics
- Discover SAP Leonardo technologies for the supply chain

Bhattacharjee, Narasimhamurti, Desai, Vazquez, Walsh

Logistics with SAP S/4HANA

An Introduction

What story does your data tell? See what SAP Lumira can do and how to identify trends and find hidden insights in your business data. Get the details on progressing from data acquisitions to data manipulation to data visualization so you can add some color to your data. See how SAP Lumira fits into existing BI landscapes and which administration options are best for each setup. This introduction to SAP Lumira will help make each picture—or chart—worth a thousand words.

589 pages, 2nd edition, pub. 01/2019
E-Book: $69.99 | **Print:** $79.95 | **Bundle:** $89.99

www.sap-press.com/4785

Rheinwerk Publishing

- Configure SAP S/4HANA for your materials management requirements
- Maintain critical material and business partner records
- Walk through MRP, inventory management, purchasing, and quotation management

Jawad Akhtar, Martin Murray

Materials Management with SAP S/4HANA

Business Processes and Configuration

Materials management has transitioned to SAP S/4HANA—let us help you do the same! Whether your focus is on materials planning, procurement, or inventory, this guide will teach you to configure and manage your critical processes in SAP S/4HANA. Start by creating your organizational structure and defining business partners and material master data. Then get step-by-step instructions for defining the processes you need, from creating purchase orders and receiving goods to running MRP and using batch management. The new MM is here!

946 pages, pub. 10/2018
E-Book: $79.99 | **Print:** $89.95 | **Bundle:** $99.99

www.sap-press.com/4711

Interested in reading more?

Please visit our website for all new book
and e-book releases from SAP PRESS.

www.sap-press.com